introduction to BUSINESS

Ranked by Assets, 1909-1983

1948

1. Standard Oil Co. (New Jersey)
2. General Motors Corp.
3. United States Steel Corp.
4. Standard Oil Co. (Indiana)
5. Socony Mobil Oil Co., Inc.
6. Texaco Inc.
7. E.I. duPont de Nemours & Co.
8. Gulf Oil Corp.
9. General Electric Co.
10. Ford Motor Co.
11. Standard Oil Co. of California
12. Bethlehem Steel Corp.
13. Sears, Roebuck & Co.
14. Union Carbide Corp.
15. Sinclair Oil Corp.
16. Westinghouse Electric Corp.
17. American Tobacco Co.
18. International Harvester Co.
19. Anaconda Co.
20. Western Electric Co.
21. Shell Oil Co.
22. Chrysler Corp.
23. Phillips Petroleum Co., Inc.
24. Montgomery Ward & Co., Inc.
25. Kennecott Copper Corp.

1970

1. Standard Oil Co. (New Jersey)
2. General Motors Corp.
3. Texaco Inc.
4. Ford Motor Co.
5. Gulf Oil Corp.
6. International Business Machines Corp.
7. Mobil Oil Co.
8. General Telephone & Electronics
9. International Telephone & Telegraph
10. Standard Oil Co. of California
11. United States Steel Corp.
12. General Electric Co.
13. Standard Oil Co. (Indiana)
14. Chrysler Corp.
15. Shell Oil Co.
16. Atlantic Richfield
17. Tenneco
18. Western Electric Co.
19. E.I. duPont de Nemours & Co.
20. Union Carbide Corp.
21. Westinghouse Electric Corp.
22. Bethlehem Steel Corp.
23. Phillips Petroleum Co., Inc.
24. Eastman Kodak
25. Continental Oil Co.

1960

1. Standard Oil Co. (New Jersey)
2. General Motors Corp.
3. United States Steel Corp.
4. Ford Motor Co.
5. Gulf Oil Corp.
6. Texaco Inc.
7. Socony Mobil Oil Co., Inc.
8. E.I. duPont de Nemours & Co.
9. Standard Oil Co. (Indiana)
10. Standard Oil Co. of California
11. General Electric Co.
12. Bethlehem Steel Corp.
13. General Telephone & Electronics
14. Sears, Roebuck & Co.
15. Shell Oil Co.
16. Union Carbide Corp.
17. Western Electric Co.
18. Phillips Petroleum Co., Inc.
19. International Business Machines Corp.
20. Westinghouse Electric Corp.
21. Sinclair Oil Corp.
22. International Harvester Co.
23. Aluminum Co. of America
24. Chrysler Corp.
25. Cities Service Co.

1983

1. Exxon
2. General Motors Corp.
3. International Business Machines Corp.
4. Mobil Oil Co.
5. Texaco Inc.
6. Standard Oil Co. (Indiana)
7. E.I. duPont de Nemours & Co.
8. Standard Oil Co. of California
9. Ford Motor Co.
10. General Electric Co.
11. Atlantic Richfield
12. Shell Oil Co.
13. Gulf Oil Corp.
14. United States Steel Corp.
15. Tenneco
16. Standard Oil Co. (Ohio)
17. International Telephone & Telegraph
18. Phillips Petroleum Co., Inc.
19. Sun
20. Dow Chemical
21. Occidental Petroleum
22. Eastman Kodak
23. Getty Oil Co.
24. Union Carbide Corp.
25. Union Pacific

introduction to
BUSINESS

James A. F. Stoner
Fordham University

Edwin G. Dolan
George Mason University

Scott, Foresman and Company
Glenview, Illinois / London, England

Developed and produced by Textbook Development Incorporated and Scott, Foresman and Company

Library of Congress Cataloging in Publication Data

Stoner, James Arthur Finch
  Introduction to Business.

  Bibliography
  Includes index.
  1. Management. 2. Business. I. Dolan, Edwin G.
II. Title.
HD31.S69625 1984   658   84-14124
ISBN 0-673-15975-2

CONTENTS

PART V   FINANCE   431

PART VI   BUSINESS AND THE WORLD   565

PREFACE

Peter Drucker says that management must be both efficient and effective. Efficiency means doing a thing well; effectiveness means doing the right thing. We think Drucker's admonition applies to textbooks, too. In the case of a textbook, efficiency means good pedagogy and effectiveness means properly focused content. Accordingly, we have built this book around a number of major content themes and teaching methods that we think will make the world of business come alive for today's students.

MAJOR THEMES

The diversity of American business.   Before starting the course, some students will tend to think of "business" as synonymous with large industrial firms like GM, IBM, and Exxon. Starting with the cover, this book broadens the field of vision to include small businesses as well as large ones, service firms as well as industrial firms, and the not-for-profit and government sectors as well as business. This emphasis on diversity is carried throughout the book. Examples include discussions of planning for small businesses, production and operations problems of service firms, marketing for not-for-profit organizations, and sources and uses of funds for government agencies.

Doing well by doing good.   Some students may start the course with the preconception that *profit* is a dirty word—that it means money gained at the expense of consumers, workers, and society as a whole. To balance this one-sided view of business, this book stresses the theme of "doing well by doing good." In one section after another the reader is shown that firms that care about people and practice corporate good citizenship are more, not less, profitable as a result. Social irresponsibility, discrimination, and dishonesty are portrayed as losing strategies. Examples of this theme in action include the following:

- Effective marketing is portrayed as a process of learning about customer needs and meeting them with high-quality products.
- Firms that understand that people are the key to productivity and make their employees feel like winners are themselves winners in the pursuit of profit.
- Topics like pollution, discrimination, and business ethics are treated extensively. Cutting corners in these areas is shown to be a shortsighted and self-defeating strategy.
- The duty of government is portrayed as that of creating a legal and regulatory environment in which doing good is the only way to do well.

The economic environment of business.   Business does not operate in a vacuum. It is part of a larger economic environment. Chapter 2 of this book provides an introduction to the economic environment of business. Later chapters explain how money, interest rates, inflation, unemployment, and other economic factors affect the decisions of large and small businesses. Numerous examples show how marketing, production, human resources, finance, and international business are affected by the economic environment.

Information and computers. A well-managed business is an informed one. Throughout the book the information needs of management are kept constantly in focus. Marketing information systems, human resources information systems, and financial information systems are all discussed. An entire chapter (7) is devoted to the use of computers in managing the information needs of business. This chapter frankly discusses the limitations of computers and the negative impacts poorly managed computer systems can have on people and organizations. From marketing research to CAD/CAM, however, computers are shown as a powerful management tool when properly applied.

Preparation for further study in business. This book is addressed to students who will have contact with businesses and other organizations throughout their lives, and who, in the short run, are likely to go on to other courses in business. With this in mind, it stresses the building of a basic business vocabulary. It uses dozens of real-world case studies and hundreds of shorter real-world examples to generate interest. And it develops the theme of careers in business and other organizations through a series of career sections at the ends of each of the six parts of the book.

TEACHING METHODS

We think the five focal points just listed make this book an effective one. To make your teaching efficient, we have also given careful attention to the following points of pedagogy.

Selection and use of cases. We think case studies and examples are the single most efficient way of teaching business subjects at the introductory level. Accordingly, the case studies in this book are designed into the text from the ground up. They are not added as window-dressing at a late stage of editing. This real-world material appears in four basic forms.

1. Each chapter opens with what we call a zinger—a short case, based on real-world experience, that whets the reader's appetite for the topics to be covered in the chapter. The zingers are not stories to be told and forgotten; in every case, the following chapter refers back to them to underline or illustrate a key point. They also often serve as a source of questions for review and discussion.
2. Boxed materials—additional cases, charts, photographs, and the like—are used frequently throughout each chapter. Each box is referenced in the text and intended to drive home an important point.
3. In addition to the numbered and boxed cases, hundreds of "one-liner" illustrations are used. Wherever possible these are drawn from the real-world experience of large and small businesses, not-for-profit firms, and units of government.
4. One or more review cases can be found at the end of each chapter. Like all the others, these are based on examples drawn from the business press or interviews conducted by the authors. The questions to follow these cases reinforce major points made in the chapter. Answers to the questions can be found in the instructor's manual.

Continuity. The chapters in this book are designed to flow from one to the next. Concepts developed early are reinforced by later applications. Earlier cases are brought back to illustrate later points. The classic pedagogic technique of telling the reader "Here's what's coming," "Here it is," and "Here's what we just did" is used at all levels—chapters, sections within a chapter, parts of the book, and the book as a whole.

Controversial issues. Controversial issues such as pollution, product hazards, affirmative action, equal pay for jobs of comparable worth, and business ethics, are integrated into the chapters of this book. We feel that these topics are too important to be set aside in boxes that a hurried reader might skip. We discuss these issues honestly and in depth, with no ideological ax to grind. Ethical lapses of business management and policy errors of government are presented not as "horror stories" but as mistakes from which something can be learned.

Design in service of content. We think this book looks good, and we hope you do too. But this is a textbook, not a coffee table book. It looks the way it does for more than just artistic reasons.

Take, for example, the single-column layout of the pages. The wide margins play a key role in our four-level system of vocabulary reinforcement. Each new term is printed in boldface type the first time it is used in the text. Opposite this point, a formal definition is given in the margin. New terms are listed for review at the end of each chapter, in the order in which they appear. Finally, all of the marginal definitions are gathered in an alphabetical glossary at the end of the book.

The single-column design is useful in another way, too. It gives added flexibility in the placement of photographs and boxes, permitting them in almost every case to appear on the same page spread where the topic is discussed in the text. This flexibility has made it possible to select photos, cartoons, and line art that best illustrate key points in the text—not just to fill up space on the page.

ANCILLARIES

This text is accompanied by a complete set of ancillary materials to aid the instructor in teaching the course and to help the student learn the material.

The basic aid to the instructor is a comprehensive instructor's manual. This contains learning objectives, chapter outlines, lecture notes, supplementary illustrations, answers to questions for review and discussion, and short chapter quizzes. In addition, there is a complete test bank with some 1,900 multiple-choice and true/false questions. The test bank is available in both booklet and computerized forms. Finally, there is an extensive package of acetates for overhead projection.

Students are supplied with two major learning aids. The first is a study guide that contains learning objectives, chapter outlines, programmed learning material, and self-test items. The second student learning aid is a computerized small-business game designed by the authors of this book for use with it. The game is available for use on the more popular minicomputers.

Your Scott, Foresman representative can supply details and samples of all the ancillaries.

ACKNOWLEDGMENTS

Finally, we would like to acknowledge the help of a great many people without whom this book could never have appeared. An enthusiastic and cooperative group of reviewers looked over the manuscript and commented on it in the light of their teaching experience. As a result of their efforts, a raw manuscript was turned into classroom-ready form. Those reviewers were:

Anita Bednar
Central State University

Rita Davis
Eastern Kentucky University

Les Dlabay
Lake Forest College

Glen Gelderloos
Grand Rapids Junior College

Kenneth Graham
Rochester Institute of Technology

Raymond Hannan
State University of New York at Alfred

Robert Higgins
Middlesex County College

Marie Hodge
Bowling Green University

Linda Jackson
Austin Community College

John Kaelber
St. Petersburg Junior College

Frederick Kiesner
Loyola Marymount University

Thomas Kinnear
University of Michigan

Tom Leonard
Tidewater Community College—Frederick Campus

John Lloyd
Monroe Community College

Ted Mah
Diablo Valley College

Jimmy McKenzie
Tarrant County Community College

Robert Nixon
Pima Community College

Neil Palomba
University of Maryland

Joseph Platts
Miami Dade Community College—South Campus

Lyman Porter
University of California at Irvine

Richard Randall
Nassau Community College

Richard M. Steers
University of Oregon

Jana Vice
Eastern Kentucky University

Charles Womer
DeAnza College

In addition to those who contributed formal written reviews, a number of people shared their views with us and helped shape this book. We would particularly like to thank Harlan Huston and Cheryl Johnson of the Community College of Denver, Red Rock Campus; Eleanor Iddings and Charles Howell of Broward Community College; and Arthur Rochlin of Miami-Dade Junior College.

We are especially indebted to Charles Wankel, a colleague of Jim's at Fordham, for numerous ideas and research strategies that are reflected throughout the book. Miland Rao was also very helpful in the early stages of research. In addition, many other people helped us track down the details we needed for a case here or a box there. These included Leo Troy, Richard Stroup, Stefan Halper, Hester Nettles, Joseph Heyman, Albert Sargent, Mark Levin, Thomas Ochsenschlager, Wendy Blazer, Marjorie Odle, and Cathy Abbott.

Finally, we want to thank all of the people who worked hard to turn our manuscript into a finished book. Editorial duties were performed by James Sitlington, John Nolan, and Patricia Nealon of Scott, Foresman and Company, and Jere Calmes, Robert Cobb, Carolyn Smith, and Maureen Conway of Textbook Development Incorporated. The interior design for the book was done by Marsha Cohen. Linda Benveniste designed the cover, and Freda Leinwand did photo research.

Having said all this, we accept full responsibility for any remaining errors and omissions.

James A. F. Stoner, New York City
Edwin G. Dolan, Great Falls, Virginia

Part I

THE WORLD OF BUSINESS

Businesses are private organizations that supply goods and services, seek profits, and compete with one another. The food we eat, the beds we sleep in, and the books we read are all provided by businesses. Businesses also supply most of the jobs in the United States. The importance of business as a source of jobs and careers is one of the main reasons for studying the subject.

American business has been widely praised and widely cursed. It provides citizens of the United States, on the average, with one of the highest living standards in the world—but it leaves pockets of poverty and unemployment. It provides consumers with a great variety of goods to choose among—some cheap and durable, but some shoddy or hazardous. Business makes homes, health care products, and tools for learning that make the world a better place to live in—but it also consumes resources and generates wastes. This book will look at all sides of business, the creative and the destructive, the excellent and the substandard. It will show that American business is doing a good job, but that there is room to do better still.

To many people the word *business* brings to mind the giants of American industry, such as General Motors, IBM, and Exxon. This book will look closely at how those giants work, but they are only part of the story. Nearly half of all goods and services are supplied by businesses with fewer than 500 workers. A third of all jobs and a much higher share of all new jobs are provided by firms with fewer than 100 workers. In every part of this book we will give small business the share of attention that it deserves.

Finally, although this is primarily a book about business, we will show that many of the same principles apply to other organizations. Units of government and not-for-profit organizations have as much need for management, marketing, and financial skills as business firms do. If these other organizations are not well managed, the American free-enterprise system cannot function as a balanced whole.

Chapter 1
BUSINESS AND SOCIETY

When you have completed this chapter, you should be able to

- Define *business* and list three things that all businesses do.

- Explain the input-transformation-output sequence and identify the role of *factors of production*.

- Define *profit* and *loss*, and explain where profits come from.

- Explain the social functions of profit in terms of signaling, providing incentives, and screening out mistakes.

- Understand the importance of *entrepreneurship*.

- Discuss the responsibilities of business managers toward owners, consumers, employees, and the environment.

- Discuss the responsibilities of government toward business and society.

Hester Nettles has learned that running a small business is hard, time-consuming work but that it can also be highly rewarding. Courtesy of Hester Nettles, The Scribe

THE SCRIBE

We are a friendly, efficient secretarial service using the latest in word processing and copier equipment. Each job — from a single-page letter to hand addressing invitations to legal briefs or large manuscripts — is handled with old-fashioned professionalism and confidentiality. We also offer a full line of stationery, business cards and invitations featuring the "The Flower Wedding Line." Let us know how we may help you!

759-5599

In December of 1982, Hester Nettles thought the end of the world had come. She had just liquidated a business in which she had invested two and a half years of ninety-hour weeks and thousands of dollars of her savings. The creditors had received eighty-seven cents on the dollar, considered quite good for a small-business liquidation, but Nettles was left with $10,000 of debt that she owed personally. Worst of all, she felt that she had been betrayed by the partner she had trusted and worked with. Looking back, she says it was the most traumatic event of her life.

The Great Falls Scribe, as the business was called, had started in the Nettles' basement eight years before, printing church bulletins on a small offset press. In 1980 the business outgrew the basement. Nettles and her partner formed a corporation and moved into a $2000-a-month suite in a commercial building. Their initial capital consisted of $15,000 plus the $30,000 worth of printing equipment they already owned.

In the new offices Nettles provided a line of custom secretarial services while her partner ran the printing operation. But although they always had plenty of work—too much to keep up with, in fact—the money seemed to go out as fast as it came in. Expenses for the printing business were high, but if they charged higher prices, they would be undersold by the competition. Also, the office work required by the printing side of the business took up to 60 percent of Nettles' time—time that took her away from her more profitable secretarial services. The partners never quite got to the point at which they could pay themselves regular salaries.

In the fall of 1982 a dispute developed between Nettles and her partner. Nettles discovered that the business was much worse off financially than she had realized. Believing that her partner had misused funds and materials belonging to the business, she insisted on liquidation.

At that point the last thing Nettles wanted to do was start a new business. Formerly she had worked as a secretary, so she started answering ads and going to job interviews. But when she scored 120 words per minute on typing tests, prospective employers laughed at her. "Our office morale would go to pieces in one day if we hired someone like you as an entry-level secretary," they said, "and upper-level positions are filled from inside."

Discouraged, Nettles sat down to do some hard thinking about the business she had just liquidated. The printing line had been marginal, the walk-in typing and copying business had lost money, and the $2000-a-month suite had been a drain on cash flow. But the medium- to large-scale secretarial jobs—legal documents, reports, book manuscripts—had been profitable. Perhaps a new business that limited itself to the profitable parts of the old one would make it.

Nettles' one remaining asset was the goodwill of former satisfied customers, including local lawyers, consultants, publishers, and others. A much smaller second-floor office suite would cost $385 a month. IBM was willing to set her up with a word processor on a lease-purchase plan, and Xerox provided a copier on the same basis. The firm's name was shortened to The Scribe, and Nettles was back in business.

In six months the new Scribe was doing better than the old one had ever done. Secretarial services alone were bringing in more than half the revenue of the old operation, and costs had been cut by far more than half. Best of all, 80 percent of Nettles' time could now be devoted to income-producing work. The ninety-hour weeks could be cut to sixty hours, leaving a little time for home and family concerns. Now Nettles takes pride in every aspect of the business—even down to the logo, which she designed herself. "If you try hard enough," she says, "you get rewarded. It just takes a little longer some days."

Business: A competitive, profit-seeking organization that produces and sells goods or services.

The Scribe is a **business**: a competitive, profit-seeking organization that produces and sells goods or services. It is typical in many ways of the tens of thousands of private firms that populate the U.S. economy. It is small—most businesses are small. It is always profit-seeking but not always profit-making—that goes for big businesses and small ones too.

Businesses come in all shapes and sizes, ranging from the sidewalk vendor to giants like the Boeing Commercial Airplane Company. Hot dog vendor—Marc P. Anderson; Cookies—Marc P. Anderson; Citibank—Marc P. Anderson; Wall St. Journal—© Sepp Seitz, Woodfin Camp; Boeing—Courtesy of Boeing Commercial Airplane Company

And it is part of a business system that includes suppliers, customers, and, always, competitors. Hester Nettles works hard at her business because business is hard work. She works hard and she gets things done. Getting things done is what business is all about.

Businesses are familiar; you deal with them every day. But how much do you really know about them? Why do they come in so many different sizes and shapes? What do they all have in common? How do they work, and how can you make them work for you? This book will set you on the road to answering these questions.

In today's world of inflation, unemployment, pollution, and high interest rates, many people are worried that the American business system is not working well. Layoffs, bankruptcies, and near-bankruptcies grab the headlines. Yet many companies—IBM, Procter & Gamble, McDonald's, and dozens of others—seem to know how to do things right. One major focus of this book will be on what two well-known business writers, Thomas J. Peters and Robert H. Waterman, have called the search for excellence.[1] Throughout the book we will look at examples of well-managed companies, large and small, as models of the way things should be done.

A second major focus of this book will be on how business principles can be applied to other organizations. Many of the organizations we deal with in daily life are not private, profit-seeking suppliers of goods and services. Schools and colleges, churches and clubs, park and police departments do not fit the definition of business given earlier in the chapter. But not-for-profit organizations and units of government do have much in common with businesses. They, too, can be well or badly managed, and they can serve their clients well or poorly. A healthy not-for-profit sector and a well-run government are as much needed as a strong business system.

A third major focus of this book will be on careers. Businesses supply careers as well as goods and services. They supply them at all levels, from workers on the shop floor to executives in the boardroom. This book will look at careers in business and other organizations from top to bottom.

WHAT BUSINESSES DO

In defining business, we noted three things that businesses do: supply goods and services, seek profits, and compete with one another. To get a better feeling for the world of business, let's look more closely at each of these.

Supplying Goods and Services

In 1983 U.S. businesses produced some $3310 billion worth of goods and services. Box 1–1 shows that goods—the products of farming, mining, construction, and manufacturing—made up a little under 40 percent of the total. The rest was accounted for by services. The major categories of transportation, wholesale and retail trade, and financial services are

---

[1]Thomas J. Peters and Robert H. Waterman, Jr., *In Search of Excellence* (New York: Harper & Row, 1982).

Box 1–1 Goods and Services Output of the Private Business Sector, 1983

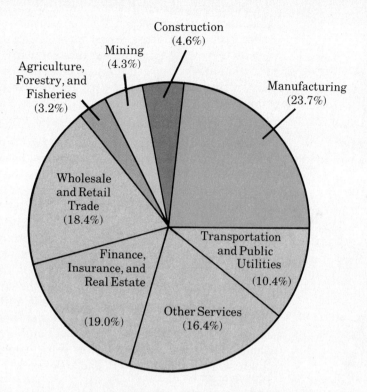

In 1983 U.S. business produced some $3310 billion worth of goods and services. Services dominated the economy, accounting for more than 60 percent of the total. Manufacturing, which provided a third of total business output in 1950, now provides only a quarter. Construction, mining, agriculture, forestry, and fisheries make up the rest.

Source: *Economic Report of the President* (Washington, D.C.: Government Printing Office, 1984), Table B-10.

labeled in the box. "Other services" include entertainment, communications, health care, auto repair, lawn care—the list goes on and on.

If the box gives you the idea that we live in a service economy and not a smokestack economy, you're right. In fact, *service* has become a key word even in industries whose main purpose is to produce goods. Caterpillar Tractor boasts that it can deliver parts anywhere in the world in forty-eight hours—that's one kind of service. Frito-Lay salespeople slog through rain and snow to visit 99.5 percent of their retail outlets every day—that's service too.

Businesses create the goods and services they sell by transforming inputs into outputs. The input-transformation-output sequence represents a constant flow through every business firm.

Inputs.   Inputs to the production process come in many forms. The three most basic inputs are labor, capital, and natural resources. These three basic inputs are called **factors of production**. The first, **labor**, includes the direct contributions to production made by people working with their minds and their hands. **Capital** includes all durable productive inputs that are made by people, such as machines, buildings, and office equip-

Factors of production: The basic inputs used in all production processes: labor, capital, and natural resources.

Labor: The direct contributions to production made by people working with their minds and their hands.

Capital: Durable productive inputs that are made by people, such as machines, structures, and office equipment.

Natural resources: Things that are useful as productive inputs in their natural state, such as farmland and mineral deposits.

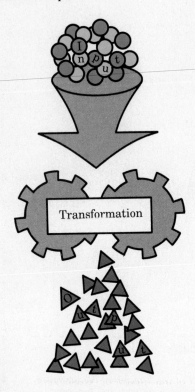

ment. **Natural resources** include everything that is useful as a productive input in its natural state, such as farm land, mineral deposits, and the like.

Normally, of course, firms don't make things from scratch out of the basic factors of production. Any one firm's inputs include the outputs of other firms. A furniture maker buys screws to put its chairs together and fabrics to cover them. An insurance company buys printed forms, pencils, and computers. Suppose you took a simple product like a radio and traced all the firms that make the inputs used in producing it, the firms that make the inputs of those inputs, and so on. You would discover a complex web of relationships that ties the whole economy together.

Transformation and outputs. A firm's outputs are all the things, whether goods or services, that a firm produces to serve its customers. The transformation process means everything the firm does to turn inputs into outputs. A manufacturing firm like a paper mill provides a familiar example. Inputs of pulpwood and chemicals come into the plant by the carload. There they pass through giant rollers and are transformed into long streams of paper. Finally, the rolls and cartons of freshly made paper go to the shipping dock to be sent to customers.

Businesses that produce services also fit the input-transformation-output pattern. In such firms, though, the emphasis is not on the flow of materials. Follow a box of paper from the mill's loading dock and it might end up at a bank. But the physical flow of the paper through the bank is a minor part of its business. What the bank is really doing is transforming paper and other inputs (clerical work, computer time, and so on) into financial services for savers and borrowers. Those services are the bank's real output.

Seeking Profits

Businesses don't serve their customers just for the fun of it. They are there to make a profit. As Box 1–2 shows, the total profits of U.S. businesses are small in relation to total production, but profits are more important than their size alone indicates.

A firm's **profit** is calculated by subtracting its costs from its revenues.

Profit: Revenues minus costs.

Ford Motor Company's Edsel was such a dramatic flop that the word *Edsel* has been associated with product failures ever since. Courtesy of Ford Motor Company

Box 1–2 Profits in the U.S. Economy

NATIONAL INCOME

| Corporate Profit (8.5%) | Proprietors' Income (4.8%) | Wages, Salaries, and Supplements (75.2%) | Other Income (11.5%) |

The profits of private businesses account for a smaller share of total national income than many people realize. These figures for the U.S. economy in 1983 show corporate profits making up just 8.5 percent of national income. Proprietors' income—which means, roughly speaking, the profits of unincorporated small businesses—accounts for another 4.8

percent. Wages and salaries bulk far larger, totaling more than three quarters of national income. "Other Income" includes consumer interest income and rental income of individuals.

Source: *Economic Report of the President* (Washington, D.C.: Government Printing Office, 1984), Table B-21.

Loss: Revenues minus costs in cases in which costs exceed revenues.

(Revenues are all the money it brings in from sales.) If costs are greater than revenues, the firm suffers a **loss** instead of earning a profit.

It follows that the key to earning a profit lies in the input-transformation-output sequence. To earn a profit, a business must transform the inputs it buys into goods or services that are worth more to customers than the inputs were to begin with. To put it another way, a firm can earn a profit only if it adds value to the inputs it uses.

Customers can be harsh judges of the value of a firm's product. A good or service isn't always worth what it cost to make it. In the late 1950s the Ford Motor Company found this out when it produced a new car, the Edsel, at a cost of millions of dollars. Consumers ignored it. Ford never earned back the investment, and the phrase "It's an Edsel" became synonymous with product failure.

Successful businesses stay close to their customers, constantly learning what they want and how much they are willing to pay for it. If they can't keep their costs within the value customers place on the product, they stay out of that market.

The Social Functions of Profits

The eighteenth-century economist Adam Smith called profits an "invisible hand" that helped channel production in socially useful directions. (See Box 1–3.) Modern economists, speaking in less fanciful terms, say that

Box 1–3   Adam Smith, Founder of Modern Economics

Adam Smith, born in 1723, is known as the founder of modern economics. For most of his life he was a professor of philosophy in Glasgow, Scotland. His first and only economics book, *The Wealth of Nations*, was not published until 1776, when he was 53.

Smith's purpose was to explain why some nations become wealthier than others. He was fascinated by the rise of industrialism in the England and Scotland of his time. In one of the book's most famous passages he describes a pin factory. There workers specialized in cutting wire for the pins, sharpening the points, attaching the heads, and so on. Smith saw that by working together, half a dozen workers with a well-organized division of labor could produce many times more pins than one person working alone. He commented that an extensive market system allowed workers and firms to become specialized, trading their products for everything they didn't make themselves. This specialization and trading allowed total national wealth to increase far above the level that would be possible in a more primitive economy in which each family or village had to produce everything it needed.

Smith saw that the market system and the division of labor greatly benefited society, but he also saw that these social benefits were actually by-products of individual, self-seeking actions.

> *It is not from the benevolence of the butcher, the brewer, or the baker that we expect our dinner, but from their regard to their own interest. . . . Every individual is continually exerting himself to find out the most advantageous employment for whatever capital he can command. . . . By directing that industry in such a manner as its produce may be of the greatest value, he intends only his own gain, and he is in this, as in many other cases, led by an invisible hand to promote an end which was no part of his intention.[2]*

Smith argued that competitive business was not just a possible way but the best way to increase the wealth of a nation. He thought government restraints on competition did more harm than good. He objected to government actions that shielded monopolies from open competition, and to restraints on international trade. Many of the controversies of Smith's time continue to the present day, and his proposed solutions are still often recommended.

[2]Adam Smith, *The Wealth of Nations*, 1776, book 1, chap. 2.

---

profits serve a number of useful functions: they send signals, provide incentives to bear risks, and screen out mistakes.

Signals and incentives. Profits are earned when businesses succeed in turning inputs into goods and services that are worth more than the inputs were worth to start with. Since productive inputs are scarce, it makes sense to use them wherever the step-up from the value of the inputs to the value of the outputs is greatest. In the business world, profits act as signals showing where the greatest increases in value are likely to occur.

Consider a well-known example. In the 1970s world oil consumption was outstripping the rate at which new reserves of oil were being discovered. The Organization of Petroleum Exporting Countries (OPEC) took advantage of this situation to increase the price of oil more than tenfold before the end of the decade. The price increase made oil exploration very profitable. Signals went out through the business world. The value of oil company stock soared. Resources flowed into oil exploration; new reserves of oil were found in the North Sea, Mexico, Wyoming, and elsewhere. By the 1980s these new reserves, plus efforts by users to conserve energy, had taken the pressure off oil prices. The profit signals flashed less brightly, and the pace of exploration slowed. Scarce resources that were no longer needed for oil exploration were shifted to other uses.

At the same time that profits act as signals telling where the best business opportunities are, they provide an incentive to invest in those opportunities. Investors who read about the profits of high-tech firms don't just say, "Oh, that's interesting." Instead, they pick up their phones and call their brokers. "Get me out of U.S. Steel and into Texas Instruments," they might say. What they are saying, in effect, is, "I want to put the resources I control to work producing something that's needed, not something that's in oversupply."

Some countries have tried to get along without the profit motive. They have devised other signaling and incentive systems. In the Soviet Union, for example, a central planning committee decides how resources should be used. Signals are sent to managers in the form of plans; incentives are provided in the form of bonuses for carrying out the plans. This system works after a fashion, but it is clumsy. Twenty-five years ago Soviet leader Nikita Khrushchev proclaimed that the Soviet economic system would bury the West by the 1980s. Today, while Soviet consumers still stand in line for meat and sugar, it is more common to find Americans wondering if they will bury themselves under mountains of video games and fast food.

Screening out mistakes. What we call the profit system should really be called the profit-and-loss system. Losses, the flip side of profits, perform a useful function too: they screen out mistakes. It is a mistake to put resources to work producing goods or services that are worth less than the inputs were worth to begin with. That's not production, it's destruction. Fortunately, firms that run top-grade sirloin steak into their meat grinders and get second-rate hash at the other end are screened out.

Even excellently managed companies make mistakes and lose money sometimes. The important thing for the health of the economy is not to avoid all mistakes but to avoid ongoing mistakes. When a firm loses money steadily, several explanations are possible. First, the problem may be diagnosed as a case of bad management. In such cases someone—a group of investors or another firm—may buy the loser, replace its management, and try to turn the business around. Second, the firm may be diagnosed as hopeless. Maybe someone just had a bad idea to begin with (such as a carry-out quiche stand across the street from a steel mill). Finally, maybe the firm makes a product for which there is less demand than there once was (this could be true of the steel mill itself). Hopeless losers simply disappear. Sometimes their owners wind them up gracefully, pay their bills, and go on to something else. If they don't, sooner or later they will be wound up by a bankruptcy court.

Competing

All businesses produce goods or services and seek profits. And they all compete with other businesses in doing so. Competition is so universal in business life that we have included it in our definition of business.

Kinds of competition and competitors. When you think of competition, you probably think first of the head-to-head rivalry of well-known firms and brands: Avis competing with Hertz, Tylenol with Anacin, United Airlines with American. A lot of competition is less direct than this,

The rapid increase in petroleum prices during the 1970s acted as a flashing signal to attract resources to oil exploration. In the 1980s oil exploration became less profitable and resources became available for other uses. Courtesy of Exxon Corp.

however. In many markets the number of sellers is so large that any one firm knows only a few of its competitors by name. Markets for farm products like wheat or soybeans are examples. In such markets competitors are not likely to have a sense of personal rivalry. A marketing success by Avis is a direct threat to Hertz; not so with Farmer Jenkins and his neighbor Nielsen. The wheat market is so huge that one farmer's sales are not seen as taking customers away from the other. As a result, Jenkins and Nielsen, unlike the auto rental rivals, are likely to wish each other well when they meet.

Businesses do not compete only in selling things. They also compete for inputs. Sometimes this competition can be as intensely personal as competition among sellers—think of two studios bidding for the services of a film star, or two developers bidding for a prime piece of real estate. But often the competition for inputs is indirect and impersonal. In hiring clerical workers, for example, law firms compete with mail order houses and retail stores. This competition would rarely take the form of rivalry over a single worker. Likewise, firms of all types compete indirectly in buying electricity, but what one firm buys usually doesn't have much effect on competing buyers.

Monopoly: A firm that has no competitors in the market where it sells its output.

There is a word for a business that has no competitors in the market where it sells its output. Such a business is called a **monopoly**. In the real world pure monopolies are hard to find. The U.S. Postal Service used to be the textbook writer's favorite example of a monopoly. Now, although it still has a monopoly in ordinary first-class mail, it competes with UPS in carrying parcels, with Federal Express in carrying overnight mail, and with satellites and telephones in carrying other kinds of messages. Even the rare firm that has a monopoly or a near monopoly in the market where it sells its products has to compete with other firms for the inputs it uses to produce them.

The U.S. Postal Service used to have a monopoly over the carrying of mail and parcels, but today it faces strong competition from UPS, Federal Express, and other courier services.

Competition, then, is universal in the world of business. In fact, as the example of the postal service suggests, government agencies and not-for-profit organizations also compete. They compete with businesses for inputs of labor, capital, and natural resources. Very often they compete with one another and even with private businesses in providing services. State governments, for example, compete with one another in providing services that will attract industries to their state. Schools and colleges compete with one another for students. Even environmental and consumer groups, while they like to think of one another as allies, compete for members and for political attention.

Entrepreneurship, the art of competition.   What is needed to stay afloat in the competitive world of business? More than just skill at repeating whatever worked in the past. If a business is going to survive in the face of competition, it needs a constant flow of new ideas. It needs managers who are good at developing new products, finding new ways to reduce costs, and thinking of new ways to make products attractive to consumers. These skills together are known as **entrepreneurship**. Entrepreneurship, in short, is the art of competition.

We usually think of entrepreneurship in connection with the founding of new businesses. Henry Ford and the Ford Motor Company, Mary Kay Ash and Mary Kay cosmetics are familiar examples. But creativity and innovation are needed in the day-to-day operation of a business too. Even the manager of a well-established business like a supermarket must be alert to new products, changing consumer tastes, and new technologies, such as automated checkout equipment.

In the world of business there is no rest for the weary. The bigger a firm's profits, the harder its rivals will go after them. Xerox is an example. For a while in the 1960s, this company had a series of patents that gave it a virtual monopoly on copying machines. Rivals like Kodak, Canon, and 3M poured huge amounts of money into finding ways to get around the Xerox patents. They succeeded, and now Xerox is just one among many competitors in the copier market.

Entrepreneurship: The ability to compete successfully by developing new products, finding new ways to reduce costs, and thinking of new ways to make products attractive to consumers.

THE RESPONSIBILITIES OF BUSINESS

Up to this point, we have reviewed what businesses do: they supply goods and services, seek profits, and compete with one another. In this section we turn to the topic of what businesses *should* do. What are the duties of managers toward the firms they work for? When, if ever, do businesses have a responsibility to be more than goods-producing, profit-seeking competitors? Questions like these are controversial. We will not be able to resolve the controversies here, but we can at least raise the questions.

Legal Responsibilities

When we talk about the responsibilities of business, we are really talking about those of business managers. Businesses—and government and not-for-profit firms—do not think, feel, or make choices. They only provide a framework within which people do these things. The focus of our discussion, then, must be on managers as individuals—who they are responsible to, what they should do when faced with choices that have social consequences? We will begin by looking at the legal duties of managers; then we will turn to duties that go beyond the dictates of law.

The duty to obey the law. To begin with, business managers are responsible for acting in ways that do not violate the Constitution of the United States or the laws laid down by federal, state, and local governments. A person in a management position has the same duty to obey the law that he or she has as a private citizen. In fact, the duty is even greater: business managers must obey not only laws like those against shoplifting or running red lights, which apply to all citizens, but also a host of other laws that apply specifically to businesses.

Business managers, to be sure, are not saints. Some of them break the law sometimes, and a few make a habit of it. But, as in the case of shoplifting or running red lights, the fact that a few break the law and get away with it does not mean that everyone else should act that way. As we move through this book, we will refer many times to laws that define the duties of managers in matters ranging from corporate mergers to labor relations.

The duty to fulfill contracts. Federal, state, and local laws impose many requirements on business managers, but that is only the beginning of the story. Managers also take on certain duties by contract. These duties are many and varied.

Managers are, first of all, responsible to the people they work for, that is, the owners of their firms. This is clearest in the case of a corporation whose managers and owners are two separate sets of people. As we will see in Chapter 3, the legal owners of a corporation are its shareholders. The shareholders invest the capital needed to start the firm and sustain its operations. In return, they benefit from whatever profit the firm earns. Shareholders elect a board of directors, who, in turn, appoint managers to conduct the firm's day-to-day operations. Corporate managers, then, are directly responsible to the board of directors and indirectly responsible to the shareholders.

The managers of a corporation have been hired to do a job for its owners. Earning a profit is a key part of that job. The managers are not supposed to seek personal power and prestige at the expense of profits. They are not supposed to take undue risks with the owners' capital, but neither should they avoid taking prudent risks just to make their jobs more secure. In order for the firm to survive and earn a profit, managers must maintain good relations with workers, customers, and the local community. In dealing with these groups, however, the manager is the legal representative of the owners, not a neutral mediator between the firm and other groups. If managers do not respect their duties, they can be removed by the board of directors acting in the name of the shareholders.

The responsibilities of the owner-managers of small businesses are not so strict with regard to profits. Most small-business owners run their

The managers of a corporation are responsible to its owners, that is, the people who own stock in the company. Corporations are required to hold periodic meetings at which they report to shareholders. Courtesy of International Paper Company

firms with the hope of making a profit, but they may have other goals as well. If owner-managers choose to give up some potential profit in exchange for the satisfaction of working for themselves, or the freedom of a flexible schedule, that is their right.

Second only to managers' duties toward owners are their duties toward customers. In practice, good customer relations are so basic to a firm's profits that it is hard to distinguish between the two. Many managers list customers as their first responsibility. In doing so, they do not mean to be disloyal to the owners who have hired them; it is simply that, as they see it, profits are out of the question without satisfied customers.

A firm's main duty toward its customers is to supply them with goods and services that are suitable for the purpose for which they are sold. Knowingly selling a good or service that won't do what the seller says it will is known as **fraud**. Selling a loaf of bread that is made of wood pulp instead of wheat flour is fraud. So is selling a headache cure that the firm's own laboratory tests have shown to have no effect on pain. So is selling insurance with the intent of pocketing the funds and disappearing before the claims come in. Flagrant cases of fraud are not just irresponsible—they are criminal offenses.

Besides the general duty not to defraud, firms often have specific contractual agreements with their customers. These may include guarantees, service contracts, agreed-upon delivery schedules, or any number of other things.

The third group toward whom business managers have contractual duties are employees. Formal contracts may cover pay, benefits, pensions, tenure, seniority, and the like. In smaller firms, such contracts may be made by a simple handshake, but the responsibility is there just the same. In addition to meeting the terms of the firm's contracts with its workers, managers must comply with state and federal laws regarding hours, safety, discrimination, and so on.

This is only a partial list of the responsibilities that business managers take on by contract. We could go on to discuss contracts with suppliers; voluntary agreements with federal, state, and local governments, and formal or informal agreements with organizations in the local community. In all of these, the principle is the same: once an agreement has been made, the manager's responsibility is to live up to it.

Social Responsibilities

The legal duties of managers are to obey the law, to honor contracts, and to try to make profits for the firm's owners. But are they all? Are there other duties, not defined by law or contract, that should guide the actions of managers? From the early years of the industrial revolution two centuries ago, critics of business have insisted that there are. In nineteenth-century England, Charles Dickens wrote about the terrible living conditions in urban slums. In the United States in the early twentieth century, Upton Sinclair and other "muckrakers" attacked what they saw as irresponsible practices on the part of business. Today environmentalists, consumerists, and minority group leaders all urge business to become more socially responsible.

In this section we will look at three forms of social responsibility: responsibility toward the environment, toward women and minority employees, and toward consumers. We will then discuss the problem of

Fraud: Knowingly selling a good or service that is not suitable for the purpose for which the seller claims it is suitable.

balancing these responsibilities against the legal duties of managers, especially the duty to seek profits.

Pollution and the environment. The natural environment—clean air, pure water, outdoor recreation areas—is one of our greatest assets. The environment is fragile, however, and is constantly under attack. Air and water are polluted, trees cut down, fields paved over. And the blame for polluting, cutting, and paving is often laid on the doorstep of business.

Business gets the blame for two reasons. First, businesses themselves do a lot of polluting and destroying. Smokestacks belch sulfur that may come down hundreds of miles away as acid rain. Farmers use fertilizers and pesticides that end up in steams and rivers. Developers fill in wetlands to build row upon row of new houses.

Second, although much polluting is done by households rather than by business, business often gets the blame because of the products it makes. If brewers didn't sell beer in throwaway cans, there would be fewer cans along the roadside. If Detroit made cleaner cars, our air would be cleaner.

To behave responsibly, the critics say, businesses must become more aware of the impact of their actions on the environment. Although everything businesses do has some effect on the environment, there are better and worse ways of doing things. Social responsibility consists in doing things the better way.

Women and minority employees. As we pointed out earlier, businesses are sources of careers as well as of goods and services. They have not, however, supplied careers for everyone equally. As Box 1–4 shows, white men have fared better in the job market than women or members of minority groups. The difference can be seen both in earnings and in unemployment rates.

Because private business supplies more than 85 percent of the jobs in the U.S. economy, many critics say that business is the cause of this unequal situation. They say that black/white and male/female wage differences are a result of discrimination, as are differences in unemployment rates.

Responsibilities toward consumers. Business could also do better, its critics say, in meeting its responsibilities toward consumers. Consumer complaints about low-quality or dangerous products are not new. What is new is a vocal, politically active consumer movement. Today many con-

To behave responsibly, businesses must take the environmental impacts of their actions into account. Often it turns out that environmental responsibility is also profitable. © Eric Kroll, Taurus Photos

Box 1–4   The Job Market Success of Men, Women, and Minorities

A.   Median weekly earnings by selected worker characteristics, 1981

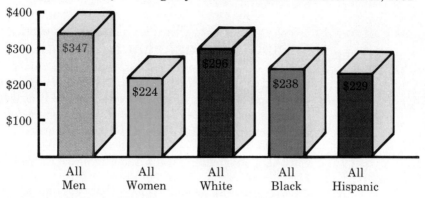

B.   Unemployment rates by selected characteristics, 1982

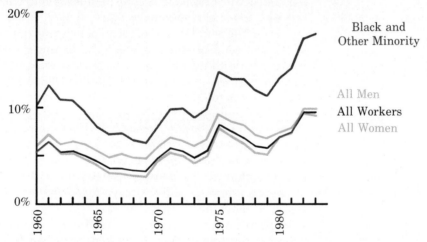

Private business is a source of careers, but not for everyone equally. As these diagrams show, women and minority group members have not been as successful in the job market as white men, whether success is measured in terms of earnings or in terms of unemployment rates. The role of private firms in creating this situation in the first place, and in changing it, is a major question in any discussion of the social responsibility of business.

Source: For median weekly earnings, U.S. Department of Commerce, *Statistical Abstract of the United States*, 103rd ed. (Washington, D.C.: Government Printing Office, 1983), Table 671; for unemployment rates, *Economic Report of the President* (Washington, D.C.: Government Printing Office, 1984), Table B-33.

sumer groups keep pressure on business through the media, through lobbies, and sometimes through direct actions.

Poor product quality is one major complaint of consumer activists. Imported products are often held up as examples of quality standards that

U.S businesses should, but don't, match. Health and safety are even more serious concerns. Businesses have been accused of selling everything from unsafe cars to oversalted and overly fatty foods. Service industries are not immune to criticism either. Insurance companies, for example, are often accused of practices that are unfair to certain groups and raise costs for everyone.

Social Responsibility and Profit

It would be hard to find a business manager who actively favors pollution, discrimination, or poor product quality. But that is hardly the point. Even the most vocal critics don't claim that businesspeople behave irresponsibly just because they like to. More often, they claim that social responsibilities are neglected for the sake of profits. Let's give some thought, therefore, to the question of when profits and social responsibility do or do not conflict.

Profits and the environment. The possibility of harming the environment is a built-in part of the input-transformation-output sequence on which production is based. Some damage is done when inputs are mined or harvested. More damage is done because, along with outputs of goods and services, firms also produce wastes.

From the point of view of social policy, any damage that might be done in the course of production should be balanced against the value of the product in deciding what to make, how to make it, and where to make it. But do business managers have any incentive to take environmental effects into account?

Sometimes, fortunately, they do. Box 1–5 shows how International Paper has made a profit by responsibly managing its vast holdings of forest land. Examples of environmental responsibility that is also profitable can sometimes be found in urban settings, too. Many companies realize, for example, that it is hard to attract workers to filthy, blighted areas. Paying workers a premium to live in a polluted area can be costly. It can also be costly to move away from the problem, and in any case it may not be possible to move away if the firm itself causes the problem. Cleaning up the urban environment thus can often be worthwhile, either for a single firm or for several firms working together.

However, for every case in which profits and environmental responsibility go hand in hand, there are many others in which the two pull in opposite directions. The problems come when the costs of environmental damage fall not on the firm itself but on others. Economists call costs of production that are imposed on others **external costs**.

External costs: Costs of production that a firm imposes on other firms or on the public at large.

Internal costs: Costs of production that are borne by the producing firm itself.

In the example just given, harm to wildlife on International Paper's land would be an **internal cost** because it would show up on the firm's profit-and-loss statement as reduced income from hunting leases. A plant that pollutes the neighborhoods where its workers live will bear an internal cost to the extent that, in the long run, it has to pay more to get workers to live in a polluted area. But often pollution results in external rather than internal costs. A plant that pollutes a river can cause a lot of damage downstream but only a little in the local area. Smoke from a plant in an urban neighborhood may have only a small effect on the plant's own workers but a large effect on the public in general.

Profitability and discrimination. All firms "discriminate" among potential employees on the basis of skills, training, motivation, and other

Box 1–5 International Paper: Conservation and Profit

International Paper invests heavily in wildlife management on its extensive land holdings. Its fishing and hunting leases are not only a technique of game management but a major source of revenue for the company. Courtesy of International Paper Company

International Paper (IP) is a major forest products company and the nation's largest private landholder, with some 7 million acres of land in the Southeast, Maine, and the Pacific Northwest. The company manages its resources with an eye to profits. Hunting leases are sold on most of its lands, and user fees are collected on some of those lands for other activities such as cross-country skiing and fishing. Campsite rentals for hunting and fishing lodges provide "fairly sizable" revenues in Maine, Vermont, New Hampshire, and New York.

Leasing patterns vary from one state to another. IP's leasing program is most extensive on its lands in the southeastern states. IP has 1.65 million acres under lease to hunting clubs at an average annual rate of $0.83 per acre. Individual permits on nonclub land average $0.62 per acre. Turkey, pheasant, quail, duck, and deer are the main animals hunted, and the clubs have exclusive hunting privileges. Squirrels and rabbits are not managed as game animals, although they are often hunted informally on IP lands. Fishing rights are leased only in a few places where IP has complete control of an entire lake. Two hundred thousand acres are leased at nominal fees to state game commissions. Hiking is permitted without charge on IP lands, except during the hunting season in areas leased by hunting clubs.

IP takes game management seriously. It has viewed leased hunting as an important source of revenue since the 1950s. Indeed, hunting leases are among the firm's best products in terms of the ratio of revenue to investment. IP employs three full-time biologists to conduct research on game management, controlled burning, the effect of human activi-

ties on wildlife, the effect of tree farming on wildlife, and the like. In addition, there are five or six biologists engaged in full-time wildlife management for the company's regional organizations. IP believes public acceptance of its programs has been high, and the company plans to expand its program of fee-based recreation.

IP writes of its wildlife management practices:

In recent years income from outdoor recreation has become significant. Improved public relations have been gained from wildlife/recreation programs, management of endangered species, and other aspects of multiple use. As forest management intensifies, provisions for wildlife must be better planned in all stages of management if we are to maintain our programs, realize their full benefits, and further increase returns from investments in wildlife resources. Professional judgment is required by foresters on the ground, for they are the wildlife managers of our forests.

International Paper today practices intensive wildlife management on much of its land, committing more acreage to managed wildlife production than any other private landowner or any state game agency in the United States. Application of IP's research is doubling and, in some cases, tripling game populations on these lands.

Source: Courtesy of William C. Dennis, Dennison University.

traits related to the jobs those workers will be asked to do. When choosing between two applicants who are similar in other respects, firms select the one who is more skilled. Likewise, more productive workers are usually paid more than less productive ones. Discrimination becomes a social problem only when it is based on traits that are not related to productivity, such as race or sex.

Race or sex discrimination is rarely profitable. A firm that passed over, say, a more qualified black computer programmer for a less qualified white candidate would give away a competitive advantage. Computers at rival firms would be better programmed. Or suppose it happened that women were paid less than equally qualified men for doing a certain job. Wouldn't employers who wanted to keep costs down hire only women, leaving men unemployed, until there were no more qualified women? And before hiring the high-priced men, wouldn't the same employers bid against one another, driving up women's wages until they were equal to men's?

The profit motive acts to reduce discrimination in the job markets, but this does not mean that discrimination disappears in an economy based on private business. This is true for at least two reasons.

First, business managers sometimes discriminate even when it is unprofitable. Imagine a corporation president who is convinced that women should be allowed into the executive suite only to take notes and serve coffee. Acting on his prejudices, he fails to promote qualified women to executive positions. He ends up surrounded by a group of male colleagues who are not quite the best people for their jobs. As a result, his firm does a little less well than it might have against competitors who promote on the basis of talent rather than sex.

A manager like the one just described clearly is acting irresponsibly. Among other things, he is failing to earn the greatest possible profits for the firm's owners. But if the decline in profits is slight, or the manager is able to cover his poor promotion policies with good performance in other respects, he may get away with his irresponsible behavior for a long time.

There is a second reason that discrimination does not disappear in the profit-oriented world of business. This is that discrimination persists elsewhere in society. Education is one example. In the past, and in some places still today, public schools have not educated minority students as well as white children. This is one reason that members of minority groups have done less well in the job market. A truly profit-oriented employer will be color-blind, but not blind to test scores and educational background. Patterns of employment in business may also reflect prejudice and discrimination in housing, labor union practices, or immigration law. The profit motive, by itself, cannot be counted on to offset discrimination in these and other areas.

Profits and the consumer. The duty of business toward consumers is to provide them with efficient service and products that work and last. Business writers widely agree that efficient service and good products are also the surest route to profits. (Part III of this book will develop this theme in detail.) But if profits and consumer satisfaction are so closely linked, why are businesses constantly being criticized by consumer activists? And why are cases of poor service and shoddy quality so often blamed on the profit system? There seem to be at least three problems here.

First, although well-managed companies serve their customers well, not all companies are well managed. Some businesses are managed downright stupidly. They fail to figure out what consumers really want or, if they know, fail to provide it. They have poor relations with their workers, who, in turn, develop a "don't care" attitude toward quality. They are slow to make changes that would reduce costs, and then they wonder why consumers complain that their products are overpriced. Pretty soon such companies are left wondering why imports are grabbing more and more of their markets. Finally they go down with a crash, taking consumers, profits, workers, and shareholders down with them.

Next comes the second problem. Although profits and consumer satisfaction go hand in hand when the business game is played by the rules, there are always a few people in business, as in all walks of life, who won't play by the rules and who persist in committing fraud. Consumers are not completely defenseless against fraud. Their main defense is the fact that frauds usually have a hard time getting the repeat sales on which most businesses depend. Also, there are strict laws against fraud. But sad to say, like laws against mugging or drunk driving, they don't deter everyone.

In addition to stupidity and fraud, criticism of business by consumer activists sometimes has a third cause. Profit-seeking businesses may be selling consumers exactly what they want instead of what the activists think they *should* want. Airbags for automobiles are an example. In the few cases in which automakers have offered airbags as an option, very few have been sold. People are not convinced that the added safety is worth the added cost. Perhaps this is not surprising in a country where 90 percent of drivers do not even buckle their seatbelts.

Responsibilities of Government

We have seen that business managers have many responsibilities urged upon them. They have duties to obey the law, to honor contracts with customers and workers, and to earn profits for the owners who employ them. And they have responsibilities toward the environment, toward employees, and toward consumers. To complete the picture, we need to say a few words about the responsibilities of government toward business and society.

The basic duty of government toward business and society is to define and enforce the rules of the game. Not just any set of rules will do, though. If a society wants to rely on private business to supply it with goods and services, and at the same time wants to remain free and prosperous, its government must establish a set of rules under which *business can do well only by doing good.*

How does the government of the United States in the mid-1980s rate by this standard? Not badly at all, compared with much of the rest of the world. But not perfectly, by any means. Let's look one more time at the three areas of responsibility discussed earlier.

All business activity uses some resources and produces some waste. A responsible business should bear the costs of the burdens it places on the environment. But if businesses are allowed to deplete public resources such as timber or range land without paying for them, or to pollute the environment without bearing the cost, profits and concern for the environment will pull in opposite directions. In such contests, the environment is usually the loser.

Government is responsible for making sure this does not happen. Where resources are privately owned, its chief duty is to help owners

The Environmental Protection Agency monitors the extent of air and water pollution and attempts to limit such pollution through regulation. Courtesy of U.S. Environmental Protection Agency

enforce their property rights. The most serious environmental problems, however, involve public resources—the air, water, and public lands. Business should not be allowed to treat these as free goods. Many ways to manage public resources have been suggested. One is to limit pollution through regulation, as Congress has done in the Clean Air and Clean Water acts. Another is to charge private users for access to public property, as in the case of cattle grazing on public lands. In still other cases, public resources could be transferred to private users by auction or some other means, and the new owners could take on the responsibility for their protection. Public policy toward the environment is still in an early stage, however. Both businesspeople and environmentalists agree that much remains to be done.

In the area of job discrimination, too, we have not yet reached the point at which business can do well only by doing good. In some cases, business practices are changing in step with changing social attitudes. In others the changes do not seem rapid enough.

Consider, for example, the fact that two decades of civil rights legislation have done little to raise the incomes of black households relative to those of white households. Is simply making discrimination illegal not enough? What else can government do? Should it force private firms to meet racial quotas regardless of seniority or talent? Should the main focus be on education and training, in the hope that business will find it profitable to hire more minority workers and to pay them more if they are better educated? Or should government focus on promoting growth by the economy as a whole, in the hope that a rising tide will raise all boats? These are among the central civil rights issues of the 1980s.

Finally, what about consumers? The high standard of living in the United States suggests that business is already serving consumers well, but some major controversies remain. International competition raises one set of issues. Should a firm like, say, Harley-Davidson be protected against foreign competition at the cost of higher prices and fewer choices for motorcycle users? Health and safety present another set of issues. For example, should a greater effort be made to protect consumers against hazardous drugs? Or, as others claim, are patients dying needlessly while strict regulations prevent them from getting the medicines they need? The consumer movement will continue to be heard from on these and other issues.

The social responsibilities of business and the responsibilities of government toward business and society are topics to which we will return throughout this book. Many questions will be raised, questions to which there are no easy answers. By the end of the course, however, we hope you will have a set of tools that will at least help you think about these problems.

SUMMARY

1. A *business* is a competitive, profit-seeking organization that produces and sells goods or services.

2. Goods and services are produced by transforming inputs into outputs. The most basic inputs are the factors of production: labor, capital, and natural resources.

3. Profits are calculated by subtracting a firm's costs from the revenues it brings in by selling the goods or services it produces. In order to earn a profit, a firm must turn inputs into outputs that are worth more than the inputs were worth to begin with. Profits serve a number of useful functions: they signal the best places to put resources to work; they provide incentives to use resources wisely; and they screen out mistakes.

4. All firms compete both in selling outputs and in buying inputs. A firm that faced no competitors in the markets where it sells its outputs would be called a *monopoly*. In the real world, pure cases of monopoly are rare, if they exist at all.

5. Successful competition requires a constant search for product improvements and better production techniques. The art of competition is known as *entrepreneurship*. Competition is not limited to business firms. Not-for-profit firms and government agencies also compete, both in buying inputs and in serving their clients.

6. Business managers have a duty to obey the law and to fulfill the terms of contracts they enter into. They have a duty to earn as much profit as they reasonably can for the owners of their firms. Businesses also have responsibilities toward the environment, employees, and consumers.

7. The major responsibility of government toward business and society is to establish a set of rules that minimize conflicts between profits and social responsibility. Ideally, a business would be able to do well only by doing good.

KEY TERMS

You should be familiar with the following terms and concepts. Check their meanings by referring to the marginal definitions in the chapter or to the glossary at the end of the book.

Business	Natural resources	Entrepreneurship
Factors of production	Profit	External costs
Labor	Loss	Internal costs
Capital	Monopoly	Fraud

QUESTIONS FOR REVIEW AND DISCUSSION

1. Write a profile of a large or small business of your choice, covering the following points:
   a. What goods or services does the firm sell? Describe the input-transformation-output sequence as it applies to this firm.
   b. Who are the firm's direct competitors in the market where it sells its output? Point out any indirect competitors (for example, a supermarket is an indirect competitor of a restaurant, in that eating at home is a substitute for eating out). Who are the firm's competitors in the markets where it buys its inputs?
   c. Does the firm earn a profit? Who receives the profit, if any? (For large corporations, you can find this out by asking for a copy of the firm's annual report. For small businesses, you may have to ask the owners or managers.)

2. Write a similar profile for a nonbusiness organization, either a private not-for-profit organization or a unit of government. Cover the following points:
   a. What goods or services does the organization provide? Are they sold, or are they provided free of charge? Describe the input-transformation-output sequence as it applies to this organization.
   b. What competitors, direct or indirect, does the organization face in providing goods or services? What competitors does it face in obtaining the inputs it needs?
   c. What are the organization's sources of funds—sales, voluntary contributions, or taxes? Do the funds it takes in exceed or fall short of its expenses? If it takes in more than its spends, what happens to the surplus? If it takes in less, how is the deficit covered?

3. Can you think of any way for a firm to earn a profit without transforming its inputs into goods or services that are worth more to its customers than the inputs were worth in the first place? If such opportunities exist, what actions, if any, should be taken by government?

4. Scan the business pages of a major newspaper until you find a story about a company that is very profitable. (The *Wall Street Journal* is one good source of business news. Other sources include *Fortune*, *Forbes*, and *Business Week*.) Do you see any sign that the profits earned by this firm are serving as a signal to attract resources to its line of business? Do you think it is socially useful for more resources to be attracted to this line of business? Why or why not?

5. As you scan the business news, look also for a news item about a firm that is losing money. Why is it losing money? Do you see any sign that the losses are acting to screen out mistakes? Do you think it is socially useful for resources to be moved away from this line of business? Or is this a case of a single firm that is badly managed? Discuss.

6. Finally, while reading the business news, see if you can find examples of entrepreneurship in action. Look for items about the development of new products, the discovery of new ways of reducing costs, and the discovery of new ways to make products attractive to consumers.

7. Investigate a case of pollution in your community. Is the pollution caused directly by a business? Is it caused by consumers' use of a product that could be designed to be less polluting? If you think a business is responsible for the pollution, do you think it would be profitable for the firm to take action to solve the problem? Why or why not? Do you think the example you have chosen should be viewed as a failure of business to meet its social responsibility or as a failure of government to establish the proper rules of the game? Discuss.

8. Think about a consumer product that has not satisfied you. What, in your opinion, was the origin of the problem? Do you think the firm would make more money if it corrected the problem? Do you think the product was not described accurately when it was sold to you? Did you bring your complaint to the attention of the seller? If so, what was the response?

Case 1–1: Beverly Enterprises

The nursing home industry, three quarters of which is owned by profit-seeking corporations and proprietors, may seem an unpromising place to mine gold. But that's exactly what Robert Van Tuyle, the tireless 70-year-old chief executive of the largest U.S. nursing home chain, Beverly Enterprises, has been doing. Since 1976 Beverly has increased its revenues twelve times over. In 1982 its sales rose by 68 percent, to $816 million, and its profits climbed by 62 percent, to $26 million.

Beverly has taken off so fast that it now represents 7 percent of the investor-owned nursing home industry—more than twice as many beds as its nearest competitor, National Medical Enterprises' Hillhaven Corp. Michael LeConey, a Merrill Lynch health care analyst, thinks the company could grab as much as one third of the nursing home business by 1990.

Unlike gold prospecting, Van Tuyle's industry has little to do with chance. More people are getting older no matter what happens to the economy, and government-backed Medicaid and Medicare programs pay about half the national nursing home bill.

The advent of Medicare and Medicaid in the mid-1960s unlocked new sources of revenue for the nursing home industry. The biggest of these was Medicaid for the poor, which now supplies nearly 50 percent of nursing home income. Medicaid pays for long-term "custodial" care of any oldster who is merely infirm—by far the majority of nursing home residents.

The new government programs unleashed an entrepreneurial gold rush into a field hitherto dominated by not-for-profit organizations. Tales of fraud and inhuman treatment of patients soon filled the media, and the profit-seeking part of the business acquired an unsavory image.

Although Beverly itself was untouched by scandal, the shakeout nearly brought the company down. When Van Tuyle took over, Beverly was almost bankrupt. Van Tuyle, who routinely arrives at his office at 5:30 A.M., set a new tone of hard work. On the medical side, he built up a centralized staff of trained nurses, now numbering 75, whose job is to monitor and control compliance with medical standards and regulations around the country. The company also initiated a nurse's aide training program, writing a manual that has become widely used in the industry and producing an imaginative training film in the form of a mini–soap opera telling how a patient feels upon being sent to a nursing home (not very good). Another Beverly innovation is an 800 hot-line to company headquarters that allows residents and others to phone in complaints. And upon discovering a popular "adopt a grandparent" program at a home in Florida, where local schoolchildren volunteer to make weekly visits to individual patients, Van Tuyle applied the idea to other homes in the Beverly chain.

Source: Thomas Moore, "Way Out Front in Nursing Homes," *FORTUNE*, June 13, 1983, pp. 142–150. Reprinted by permission from FORTUNE Magazine.

Questions:

1. Describe the input-transformation-output sequence as it applies to Beverly.

2. What competition does Beverly face in providing health care? What entrepreneurial measures has Van Tuyle taken to stay ahead of the competition?

3. Are Beverly in particular and the nursing home industry in general profitable? What evidence does this case offer to support the claim that profits serve a useful function by attracting resources to industries where they are needed?

4. Comment on the link between profit seeking and responsibility toward customers in the light of this case.

5. Comment on the Medicaid program as an effort by government to establish a system in which private businesses can "do well by doing good." The government could have built and run nursing homes of its own. What do you think the advantages or disadvantages of such a system would be?

Chapter 2

THE ECONOMIC ENVIRONMENT

When you have completed this chapter, you should be able to

- Explain the meaning of the terms *capitalism*, *free enterprise*, and *market economy*, and compare capitalism with *socialism* and *feudalism*.

- Explain how, according to the *law of supply and demand*, prices tend to change in response to surpluses and shortages.

- Review the recent experience with inflation in the U.S. economy, and explain the challenges that inflation poses for business.

- Distinguish among three types of unemployment, and explain what happens to the unemployment rate during a recession.

- Discuss trends in *productivity* in the U.S. economy during the 1970s and possible trends during the later 1980s.

- Compare alternative ways in which U.S. industry can react to foreign competition, and discuss the advantages and disadvantages of each.

- Discuss the importance of *fiscal* and *monetary* policy as factors in the economic environment.

The steel industry, once the muscle of the U.S. economy, ran smack into trouble in the 1980s. In 1982 it hit rock bottom. The combined losses of all firms in the industry came to a whopping $3.5 billion. Steel mills ran at less than 50 percent of capacity for the first time since the depression of the 1930s. "If anybody had told me this was going to happen," said Bethlehem Steel's president, Walter F. Williams, "I would have told him that he must be kidding."

But steel's problems were no joke. They amounted, in fact, to a triple whammy.

First, 1982 was a poor year for the U.S. economy as a whole. Output was down, unemployment up. Unemployed workers were not buying steel washing machines and refrigerators. Builders were not buying steel construction materials. The steelmakers cut their output, but not fast enough. Overcapacity and heavy inventories led to a price war that no one really wanted. Discounts ranging from 8 to 20 percent off list price became the only way to do business.

Second, in the 1980s the steel industry was feeling the effects of the oil price crunch of the 1970s. The auto industry had long been steel's best customer, but as gasoline prices rose, consumers bought smaller, more fuel-efficient cars. Cars for the 1983 model year were an average of one thousand pounds lighter than cars made just five years before. Wherever possible, strong, light aluminum and plastics were used instead of steel.

Third, the U.S. steel industry was hurt by trends in the world economy. Developing countries from Brazil to Korea had turned from customers into competitors. Other industrial countries, such as Japan and Great Britain, were trying hard to boost exports.

The cure for steel's ills was painful and uncertain. Cost cutting headed the list of remedies. A new contract was signed with the United Steel Workers that called for a $1.25-an-hour wage cut. (Before the cut, wages in the industry, at $20 per hour for many workers, were among the highest anywhere.) At Bethlehem, even the top managers took a 10 percent pay cut. Jobs were lost by the tens of thousands. Total employment in the industry dropped from 454,000 workers in 1976 to just 289,000 in 1982.

An upturn in the economy in 1983 provided a little hope. Output headed upward from its low point. But the steel industry was bound to end up a much smaller, leaner version of its former muscular self.[1]

[1]"Fading Muscle," *Washington Post*, April 24, 1983, p. F-1. © The Washington Post.

As the case of the steel industry shows, business does not operate in a vacuum. Every firm, from giants like Bethlehem Steel to the corner store, is part of a complex economic system. Every part of this system depends on every other part. Jobs gained or lost in one place affect demand for the output of firms halfway across the country. Price changes for one product set off chain reactions that affect prices and profits far away. And these effects don't stop at the water's edge. American business is part of a global economy.

The news is full of economics: price changes for goods and services like gasoline or hospital care; inflation in the average prices of all goods and services; trends in employment and unemployment; government policies that affect taxes and interest rates. The study of these events can, of course, be a specialty in itself—businesses employ thousands of economists. But every worker and manager can benefit from knowing enough economics to understand the news in the daily papers. This chapter's outline of the economic environment of business will give you a start.

CAPITALISM, FREE ENTERPRISE, AND THE MARKET ECONOMY

The American economic system goes by a number of names. Sometimes it is referred to as *capitalism*, sometimes as a *free enterprise system*, and sometimes as a *market economy*. For most purposes, these three terms can be used interchangeably. However, each of them throws light on a different aspect of the same complex system.

Capitalism

Capitalism: An economic system in which production decisions are controlled by those who invest capital in private businesses.

In Chapter 1 we learned that three factors of production are needed to make goods and services: labor, capital, and natural resources. The term **capitalism** refers to an economic system in which production decisions are controlled by those who invest capital in private businesses. Corporations raise capital by selling shares of stock to the public. The shareholders control the firm by electing its top managers. In small businesses, especially those that are not incorporated, the owners who put up capital to start the business usually serve as its managers.

This system, under which the owners of capital control business decisions, seems natural. It is by no means the only possible system, however.

Under feudalism, economic power rested with those who owned land; farming and light manufacturing took place on great estates under the direction of the lord of the manor. The Granger Collection

Under communism, economic decisions are made by a central government. This oil storage facility in Siberia must follow directives issued by officials in Moscow. © Howard Sochurek, Woodfin Camp

Feudalism: An economic system in which production decisions are controlled by landowners.

Socialism: An economic system in which production decisions are made by workers or their representatives.

Communism: A type of socialism in which key economic decisions are made by a central government acting in the name of the workers.

Mixed economy: An economic system in which private businesses exist side by side with industries owned and run by the government.

Free enterprise: An economic system in which businesses are free to choose whom to buy from and sell to and on what terms, and free to choose whom to compete with.

In western Europe in the Middle Ages, economic power rested with those who owned land, not those who owned capital. Building, weaving, and light manufacturing, as well as farming, took place on great estates under the direction of the lord of the manor. That system, which was replaced by capitalism, was known as **feudalism**.

Many economies in the world today operate under a different system, socialism. Under **socialism** the workers, not the owners of land or capital, are supposed to control production decisions. In a few countries, notably Yugoslavia, workers in each firm elect their own managers. Under **communism**, a type of socialism practiced in the Soviet Union, eastern Europe, and several Asian countries, a central government, which represents the workers only in name, makes most of the economic decisions. Many western European countries, including Sweden, Great Britain, and France, have **mixed economies**. In these countries, private ownership and control of some industries (capitalism) is found side by side with government ownership and control of others (socialism).

Free Enterprise

The U.S. economy is also referred to as a system of **free enterprise**. (Sometimes the French words *laissez faire*, which mean roughly the same thing, are used instead.) Freedom of enterprise means freedom to choose whom to buy from and sell to and on what terms, and freedom to choose whom to compete with. It also means freedom to choose for whom to work—or to work for oneself.

Freedom of enterprise is not total in the U.S. economy. Businesses are subject to laws and regulations governing everything from health and safety to minimum wages to forms of financial statements. Not all lines of business can be entered freely. Many, like hairstyling, taxi driving, and TV broadcasting, require licenses or permits. Government restrictions are an important part of the environment of business in the United States, as we will see at many points in this book. Even so, the important thing is that people who want to enter a line of business are free to apply for a license or permit, and they can expect their applications to be treated impartially. And once in business, although they must heed many regulations, there is always a wide range within which they are free to decide what and how to produce, what to sell, and how much to sell it for.

In these respects, too, our system is not the only possible one. In the Middle Ages there was little scope for free enterprise. Many businesses were given royal grants of monopoly that protected them from competition. Crafts like metalworking and weaving were ruled by guilds that controlled every detail of pricing and production. This rigid system of monopolies and guilds was breaking down in Europe at about the time that the American colonies were breaking away from European rule. Thus, the U.S. economy was a free enterprise system from the beginning.

Free enterprise also is largely absent in socialist and communist countries. The founders of socialism saw competition as wasteful and inefficient. They wanted to replace individual decisions with centralized planning. In most communist countries, and especially in the Soviet Union, almost all business decisions are subject to the dictates of central planners. In a few, such as Hungary, small-scale businesses have a little more freedom.

In some markets, such as this produce market, buyers and sellers actually meet to do business. In others they do business without meeting face to face. Marc P. Anderson

The Market Economy

In every economy the work of different firms has to be coordinated. Coal producers have to mine just the amount of fuel needed by steel mills and electric utilities. The hundreds of firms that make clothing must supply just the right mix of sizes and styles needed by consumers. Producers of lumber, paint, nails, wallboard, and a thousand other items must produce enough so that all the houses people want can be built. In our economy, this coordination is achieved by means of markets. Ours is, therefore, a **market economy**.

A **market**, as we use the term, means any set of arrangements through which buyers and sellers make contact and do business. In a few markets, buyers and sellers all get together in one place. The New York Stock Exchange (see Chapter 20) and the wholesale produce markets in big cities are examples. But most markets have no single meeting place. If we talk about the market for baby-sitting, for example, we mean all the arrangements though which parents find sitters for their children.

Not all economies depend on markets to coordinate their activities. In socialist economies the work of different firms is coordinated by means of a central plan. The plan tells the manager of each firm how much to produce and how much of each input to use. Plans also give details of how much each firm should spend on wages, where it must deliver its output, and what it must do with any profits it earns. To people who live in such a system, it seems surprising that something as complex as an economy can be coordinated *without* a central plan.

Market economy: An economic system in which coordination is achieved by means of markets.

Market: Any set of arrangements through which buyers and sellers make contact and do business.

The Price System and the Law of Supply and Demand

Every economy must solve the problems of what, how, and for whom to produce. In a market economy, where there is no central plan, how are

Law of supply and demand: The principle that prices tend to rise when there is a shortage and fall when there is a surplus.

these decisions made? A simple answer is that they are made by business managers, who produce whatever, however, and for whomever it is most profitable. But this answer only raises another question: Can we be sure that private firms, guided by the profit motive, will produce the right things, the right way, and for the right people?

To a great extent we can, thanks to the law of **supply and demand**. This "law" states that imbalances in the market between the quantity of goods that buyers want to purchase and the quantity that producers want to sell tend to be corrected by changes in prices.

The demand side of the law is concerned with the way buyers respond to price changes. Other things being equal, people tend to increase their purchases of a good or service when its price goes down, and to cut back on purchases of one whose price goes up. Changes in the price of gasoline are a case in point. When the price of gasoline soared at the end of the 1970s, people reacted by buying smaller cars, taking vacations closer to home, and joining car pools. When gasoline prices fell again in the early 1980s, some people went back to buying larger cars, taking longer trips, and driving to work in their own cars. In short, the demand for gasoline, like the demand for other goods, is elastic—it increases or decreases as the price changes.

The supply side of the law of supply and demand is concerned with the way producers respond to changes in the price of a good. Other things being equal, producers tend to respond to a rise in price by increasing their output (if it is possible to do so). Thus, the rise in oil prices at the end of the 1970s touched off efforts by oil companies to find new sources of supply. More wells were drilled, deeper offshore waters were explored, and crews looked for oil farther north in the Arctic. When oil prices fell again in the early 1980s, the pace of exploration slowed. What is true of oil is true of other goods and services as well—higher prices call forth efforts by producers to increase the supply.

Together, changes in supply and demand act to correct temporary shortages or surpluses. Suppose, for example, that a cold winter increases the demand for antifreeze. Retailers and wholesalers sell all the antifreeze they have on hand, with the result that there is a temporary shortage. The shortage puts upward pressure on the price of antifreeze, and producers see a chance to make an extra profit. They rush new supplies to market, and, although the price is higher, consumers soon have all of the product they need.

The story is much the same in the case of a temporary surplus. Suppose, say, that a slump in the building industry reduces the demand for lumber. Wholesalers and retailers are left with larger stocks of lumber than they can sell. They react partly by cutting prices and partly by cutting back on orders they place with sawmills. Seeing that prices are falling, producers reduce the number of trees they cut and the number of logs they saw into boards. Soon the amount of lumber supplied is brought into line once again with the amount that is demanded.

Box 2–1 shows the law of supply and demand at work in the case of a strategic metal, cobalt. The rapid rise and fall of the price of cobalt during the 1970s was a dramatic example of supply and demand in action, but the principles at work are the same as those that cause changes in the price of many more familiar goods and services, from eggs to hospital care. In this book we will see many examples of how businesses are affected by supply and demand in the markets where they buy and sell the goods and services that they produce.

Box 2–1 Supply, Demand, and the Price of Cobalt

Cobalt is a metal used in making turbine blades for aircraft engines, high-power magnets, cutting tools, and paints. Because several of its uses are defense-related, it is one of the "strategic" metals. The United States imports most of its cobalt from Zaire, the world's leading producer of the metal.

In 1978 some strange things happened in the market for cobalt. For years the metal had sold for less than $5 a pound. But by the end of 1978 the price had shot up to more than $40 per pound. What happened? The explanation lies in the law of supply and demand.

Demand for cobalt had been growing since the early 1970s. Aircraft output was up, use of cobalt in paints had increased, and new uses had been found for cobalt-based magnets. Other things being equal, an increase in demand like this tends to push prices

up, and that is what happened to the price of cobalt. By May 1978, the price had risen to $10 a pound.

Normally, producers react to an increase in price by trying to increase output. But in mid-1978 the supply of cobalt was interrupted. There was a strike in the mines in Zaire, followed by fighting between rebel troops and government forces. Coming on top of rising demand, this pushed the price of cobalt to record levels.

By the end of the year the strike and the threat of war were over. As supplies returned to normal, the price fell back to about $20 a pound, where it hovered for a year. Then a recession began in the United States, the biggest user of cobalt, and demand fell. This sent cobalt prices plunging downward. By 1982 cobalt was trading in the range of $4 to $5 a pound.

ECONOMIC CHALLENGES TO BUSINESS IN THE 1980s

Gross national product (GNP): The economy's total output of goods and services.

Business cycle: A cycle in which periods of economic expansion, often accompanied by rising prices, alternate with periods of falling output, accompanied by high unemployment.

Recession: A period of six months or more during which the total output of the economy declines.

The American economy supplies a standard of living that is the envy of much of the world. The economy's total output of goods and services each year is known as the **gross national product (GNP)**. The GNP of $3310 billion in 1983 amounted to more than $14,000 per person.

This highly productive economic machine does not always run smoothly, however. It is subject to a **business cycle** that alternates between periods of rapid expansion, often with rapidly rising prices, and periods of **recession** in which output falls and unemployment rises. If they are to perform well in the remaining years of the twentieth century, businesses must deal with many economic challenges. Here we discuss four of those challenges: inflation, unemployment, productivity, and foreign competition.

Inflation

Inflation: A sustained increase in the average price of all goods and services.

Inflation means a sustained increase in the average price of all goods and services. Although *inflation* is a familiar word today, for much of the nation's history it was something Americans read about only in foreign news columns. The inflation that developed in Germany in the 1920s helped bring Hitler to power. More recently, inflation has disrupted the economies of Brazil, Argentina, Israel, Italy, and many other countries. But the United States was spared such problems for nearly a century: from the end of the Civil War to the mid-1960s prices increased at an average rate of only 2 percent per year.

Box 2–2 Inflation in the United States

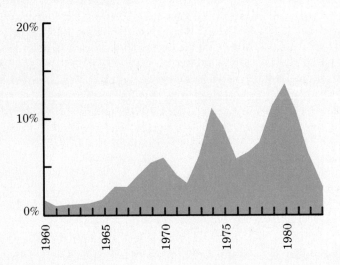

This chart shows trends in inflation in the United States since 1960. Inflation is measured as the annual rate of increase in the consumer price index, a broadly based average of prices paid by typical households. The trend was upward throughout most of the 1970s.

Source: President's Council of Economic Advisers, *Economic Report of the President* (Washington, D.C.: Government Printing Office, 1984), Table B-55.

Consumer price index (CPI): A weighted average of the prices of goods and services bought by a typical household.

As a result of the inflation that developed in Germany after World War I, money became almost worthless. It was cheaper to light a stove with it than to use it to buy kindling. UPI

Then things changed. In 1968 the inflation rate started a climb that carried it above 10 percent per year by the end of the decade. Box 2-2 shows the record of inflation in the United States as measured by changes in the **consumer price index (CPI)**. This index is an average of the prices of goods and services bought by the typical American family. As the box shows, the spiral of inflation was not brought under control until the long recession of 1981–82.

The years of high inflation were difficult ones for U.S. business. Inflation disrupts business in several ways. First, it makes long-range planning very hard. When costs cannot be forecast accurately, it is impossible to predict the profit potential of new products and investment projects. Second, inflation makes it difficult to raise capital. The stock market stagnated during the 1970s, making it hard for corporations to raise funds by selling new shares of stock. As we will see shortly, inflation also helped drive interest rates to record levels, making it expensive to raise funds by borrowing.

Inflation is bad for business in another way, too: when prices go up, business gets the blame. This happens, unfortunately, even when the blame is misplaced. Economists differ as to the exact causes of the inflation of the 1970s, but the pricing decisions of individual firms do not rank high on anyone's list of causes. Many economists believe the inflation should be labeled "made in Washington"—we will explain why when we discuss monetary policy in Chapter 19. Other economists blame much of the inflation on the increased price of imported oil. In short, when they raised their prices, U.S. firms were, to a large extent, reacting to forces beyond their control.

There is not much that businesses can do to prevent a return of inflation in the later 1980s if government policies and world events again turn inflationary. But although businesses cannot by themselves prevent inflation, during the 1970s they learned some skills that make living with inflation a little easier. For example, long-term contracts now are often written with clauses that allow a firm to raise the price of the goods or services it sells if inflation pushes up costs. This gives some protection to profit margins. Accountants have also developed ways to adjust financial reports to account for the distorting effects of inflation on the prices of inventory and long-lived equipment. With better financial information at hand, long-term planning is easier in an inflationary world. But nothing can make inflation completely painless.

Unemployment

Unemployment rate: The percentage of the labor force who cannot find jobs.

Unemployment is a second major challenge facing business in the 1980s. People are said to be unemployed if they are looking for work but cannot find it. The **unemployment rate**, as officially reported by the Department of Labor, measures the percentage of the labor force who cannot find jobs.[*] Box 2–3 shows the course of unemployment in the U.S. economy in recent years. Several features of the graph are worth noting.

Box 2–3 Unemployment in the United States

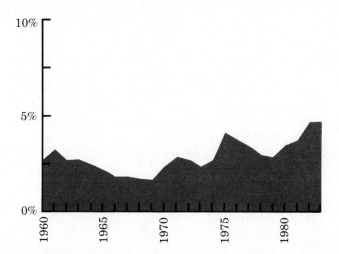

This chart shows trends in unemployment in the United States since 1960. Unemployment is measured as the percentage of members of the labor force who are actively looking for jobs but cannot find them. As the chart shows clearly, the trend has been upward.

Source: President's Council of Economic Advisers, *Economic Report of the President* (Washington, D.C.: Government Printing Office, 1984), Table B-33.

---

[*]At any given time, only about half the members of the adult population are working or looking for work. These people constitute the economy's *labor force*. People who are out of the labor force by choice (retired people, full-time students, and so on) are not *unemployed* in the official sense even though they are not working.

There are always people who are out of work for short periods. Unemployment becomes a serious problem when a recession puts a large number of people out of work or when there is a mismatch between the skills of available workers and the requirements of available jobs. © Alex Webb, Magnum

Cyclical unemployment: The extra unemployment, in excess of the normal level, that occurs during a recession.

Frictional unemployment: The part of total unemployment accounted for by people who are out of work for short periods, either between jobs or looking for their first job.

Structural unemployment: The part of total unemployment resulting from a mismatch between the skills of workers and the types of jobs available.

First, it is clear that the unemployment rate varies a lot from year to year in response to the business cycle. When output falls during a recession, businesses need fewer workers, and the unemployment rate tends to rise. Periods of recession are shaded in Box 2–3; the extra unemployment that occurs in these periods is known as **cyclical unemployment**.

Second, it can be seen that the unemployment rate never falls to zero. There are always many people who are out of work for short periods, either between jobs or while looking for their first job. Unemployment that lasts six weeks or less normally accounts for about half of all unemployment. This kind of joblessness, which is known as **frictional unemployment**, is normal in an economy in which people are free to change jobs whenever they want to.

Third, there is some unemployment that fits neither the frictional nor the cyclical pattern. It results instead from a mismatch between the skills of workers and the types of jobs available. This kind of unemployment is known as **structural unemployment**. Structural unemployment is hard to measure, but it is likely that at least some of the increase in the average unemployment rate during the 1970s and early 1980s was due to increased structural unemployment.

Structural unemployment poses a special challenge to business. Business already spends some $30 billion to $50 billion a year training workers in new skills. Much of that money goes to train workers who are entering the labor force for the first time. However, the number of sixteen- to twenty-four-year-olds entering the labor force will fall in the coming decade. Employers will have to look elsewhere to fill some jobs, and they will have to reshape their training programs. As jobs are lost in industries like steel, workers in those industries enter the pool of structurally unemployed workers. These people often are eager to be retrained and are productive in their new jobs. (See Box 2–4 for an example.) They are a resource that business should not neglect.

Productivity

Productivity: The quantity of output produced per worker.

Productivity means the quantity of output produced per worker. Higher productivity lowers costs, making possible lower prices to consumers.

Box 2–4 Surviving the Switch from Blue Collar to White Collar

When Frank LaRosa was laid off in 1981, he knew the layoff would never end.

He had grown up in the shadow of National Steel's giant Weirton works in Weirton, West Virginia, and had witnessed downturns before. But this time mills like Weirton were threatened with permanent closings. "There isn't a future here," LaRosa concluded. [Since LaRosa left, the Weirton plant has been sold to its workers in a bid to keep it open.]

Today the 23-year-old former steelworker has traded his work shirt and heavy boots for a dress shirt and tie—and a new role as a white-collar worker. He has retrained himself and found a new job as a computer programmer at a Pittsburgh management and personnel consulting firm. He is, he says, as skilled at writing programs in half a dozen computer languages as he used to be at working in a rolling mill.

But some days he feels like a refugee trying to adjust to a new country. "In the mill you put in your eight hours, said whatever you felt like saying, and then went out with your buddies for a beer," he says. "But if you're white collar and trying to get ahead, you've got to present yourself just so. And your work is always on your mind even after work."

Many blue-collar workers who have been displaced are trying to fit into the white-collar job market. In the process, they often suffer a sort of culture shock. Sales, office, and technical jobs may offer more prestige than blue-collar jobs, but often the pay is a lot lower, at least at first. Usually there aren't any unions to spell out job duties, and seniority doesn't count for much. Relations with co-workers and supervisors are different too.

LaRosa made the break by getting a $5,000 student loan, adding $2,000 of his own money, and taking a 14-month course at the Computer Systems Institute in Pittsburgh. Since he was only four years out of high school, he says he "hadn't forgotten how to study like some of the older guys who were trying to retrain." He graduated last winter with a straight-A average and a degree in computer programming.

The transition began when he obtained a three-month internship at Development Dimensions International, the company where he still works. On his first day at work his boss told him that he would have preferred to hire a college graduate and that LaRosa would have to prove himself. "I felt lower than most everybody else here," LaRosa says. When he was assigned his first programming project, he couldn't sleep for three nights. He pushed himself to finish the project a week ahead of schedule.

In February the company offered LaRosa a permanent job—which created another adjustment problem. The job pays only $13,000 a year, two-thirds the amount he earned as a steelworker.

Sometimes he also misses the satisfaction of making a product as basic and essential as steel. "Lots of times I've questioned what is actually being produced here," he says. He is glad, though, to have found a "job with a future."

Source: Carol Hymowitz, "Culture Shock Affects Steelworker Who Switched to White-Collar Job," *Wall Street Journal*, June 1, 1983, p. 33. Reprinted by permission of the Wall Street Journal. © Dow Jones & Company, Inc., 1983. All Rights Reserved.

More output per worker means higher pay, too. In the long run, increases in productivity are the source of all increases in our standard of living.

For the first twenty years after World War II, the productivity of U.S. workers grew at an average annual rate of 3.1 percent. After that, the rate of increase slowed abruptly. Between 1973 and 1980 output per worker rose by only 0.8 percent per year. In some years it actually fell.

Many economists found these figures alarming. Looking ahead, they saw many unmet needs. Later in the century there would be more older people to be supported by each person of working age. Many people were calling for a shift of resources from producing goods to improving the environment. These and other unmet needs called for a reversal of the poor productivity trends of the 1970s.

As is usual near the end of a recession, output per worker made some

"They say it's not an earthquake, just the economy beginning to move again."

From the Wall Street Journal. Reprinted by permission of Cartoon Feature Syndicate.

gains in 1982 and 1983. But U.S. business faces a major challenge in maintaining the gains for the rest of the decade and beyond. What are the prospects?

Fortunately, there are some hopeful signs. For one thing, the number of workers sixteen to twentyfour years old will drop as the "baby boom" workers born soon after World War II move into their most productive midcareer years. Also, the millions of women who entered the labor force for the first time during the 1970s have had time to gain experience and improve their skills. Finally, U.S. business has vastly more energy-efficient plant and equipment than it did a decade ago. These factors alone can be expected to improve output per worker.

The potential is much greater than these factors suggest, however. Well-managed firms came out of the 1981–82 recession with a renewed commitment to productivity. The much-discussed advances in technology, such as computers and robots, have an important role to play. But by 1990 U.S. industry is unlikely to have more than 150,000 robots at work, compared with a human labor force of well over 100 million.

The plain fact is that people remain the key to productivity. The real success stories are not assembly lines without people, but plants where workers and managers sit down at lunch together and talk over how, as a team, they can do a better job. Box 2–5 gives one example of this approach. The theme of productivity through people is one to which we will return many times in this book.

Foreign Competition

Still another challenge faced by U.S. business in the 1980s is foreign competition. Trade between the United States and other nations has more than tripled in the last twenty years. Some industries—computers, aircraft, medical products, and electrical machinery among them—have been winners in world markets. (See Box 2–6.) But many others, notably autos and steel, have been losers. How well can U.S. business cope with changing patterns of world trade?

Many companies have reacted to foreign competition by simply panicking. They have run to Washington to seek the government's protection in the form of restrictions on imports. Steel, automobile, and motorcycle manufacturers, to name just a few, have sought—and won—such restrictions. But import restrictions are very costly to the economy. Consumers are hurt by higher prices. And when one industry receives protection, others are hurt. Higher prices come back to industry as demands for higher wages. Import restrictions on a widely used industrial good like steel mean higher costs for all steel-using industries. (The auto industry's problems in the 1970s can be traced at least in part to import restrictions granted earlier to the steel industry.) And there is always the danger that other countries will retaliate by slapping restrictions of their own on goods that we export.

A better course for the economy would be to learn to live with and profit from foreign trade. It is possible to adjust. The textile industry is a case in point. In recent decades many thousands of jobs in the textile and clothing industries have been lost as a result of imports from low-wage countries. But that does not mean that the textile industry has disappeared from North America. Far from it. Companies like North Carolina's Burlington have found products that compete well on the world market in terms of both price and quality. Their ultramodern mills are

Box 2–5   A Plant Where Teamwork Is More Than Just Talk

Life inside a Cadillac engine plant in Livonia, Michigan, is worlds apart from the atmosphere of a typical auto factory. Hourly workers and supervisors dress much the same and cooperate closely on "business teams" that organize the work and make other decisions normally left to management. "It makes you feel like a part of what's going on," says Gary L. Andrews, an hourly worker and assistant team coordinator (ATC). A 14-year Cadillac veteran, Andrews says he would return to a traditinal auto plant "only if it was a choice between that and hitting the streets."

Livonia is one of nine General Motors plants that use the "pay-for-knowledge" team concept to make factory work less boring and more productive. This approach differs radically from the practice in most union shops, where workers perform narrow functions. At Livonia, production workers can learn all of the jobs in one section, giving management flexibility in assigning work and filling in for absent workers. Workers are paid according to the skills they acquire, giving them an incentive to learn new ones.

The system was introduced in July 1981, when GM's Cadillac Motor Car Division closed its engine works in Detroit and moved to the western suburb of Livonia. About 95 percent of the Detroit workers transferred with Cadillac. Local 22 of the United Auto Workers was involved in planning the change from the start and even had a voice in choosing salaried employees who would function as the team coordinators. (ATCs, such as Andrews, 32, are elected from the ranks.)

Livonia uses less manpower per engine than the Detroit plant while producing higher-quality products. It hit the breakeven point after one year, instead of the anticipated two years. The scrap rate has fallen by 50 percent. And in 1982 worker suggestions saved Cadillac more than $1.2 million.

The plant, which cranks out 1,200 engines a day, is divided into 15 departments that are in turn subdivided into business teams of 10 to 20 workers each, consisting of production workers who assemble the engines and perform nonskilled maintenance duties. The engines are still produced on an assembly line, but the employees have varied routines and participate in decison making. Moreover, dress codes are passé: Almost no one wears a tie, and some supervisors wear jeans. Managers and workers share the same cafeteria and compete for parking spots.

The teams meet weekly on company time to discuss issues such as safety and housekeeping. They decide when to award raises and rotate jobs, and they may even suggest redesigning the work flow. In the fall of 1981 Andrews took it on himself to analyze every job on two teams that attach components to already-assembled engines. "I sat with pencil and paper and figured out how to make it easier," he recalls. His teammates accepted his idea of spreading the work more evenly along the lines. Within 15 minutes, Andrews says, the changes were made without any downtime or loss of production. His reward: election as ATC.

The 23 members of Andrews' team rotate among 12 or 13 jobs on the line, 6 engine repair jobs, and 4 or 5 housekeeping and inspection jobs. As ATC, Andrews does a little of everything and helps the team coordinator plan work schedules.

In the old Detroit plant, there were 45 job classifications, each with its own wage rate. In Livonia, there are four wage levels for experienced workers, ranging from $9.63 an hour to a maximum of $10.08 for a "job setter"—a worker who sets up and changes tooling on the line. A worker reaches the top rating after learning all the skills on two business teams.

"In a traditional plant, you might have 90 to 100 job setters," says Peter J. Ulbrich, until recently Livonias's personnel administrator. "Here, you have the opportunity for 1,200 to 1,300 people to get there." This system can produce an expensive work force. "It is a neat way to get short-term productivity results," says one teamwork expert, "but you wonder what they will do when everybody reaches the top rate."

Source: "A Plant Where Teamwork Is More Than Just Talk," *Business Week*, May 16, 1983, p. 108.

Box 2–6   U.S. Export Winners

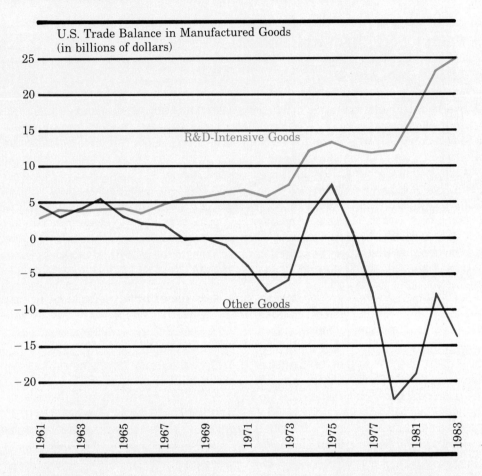

U.S. Trade Balance in Manufactured Goods
(in billions of dollars)

R&D-Intensive Goods

Other Goods

The good news for U.S. exports comes from products that require a lot of research and development (R&D). The leaders include telecommunications; office machinery, including computers; aircraft; medical products; and electrical machinery. The export surplus in these goods more than offsets net imports of other manufactured goods, leaving the United States still a net exporter of manufactured goods.

among the most productive in the world, and the synthetic fibers and fabrics they produce are big export items.

Instead of seeking import restrictions, U.S. firms should be planning, with or without government aid, to make the transition to a more competitive world economy. How can productivity and quality be improved? If jobs will be lost, how can workers be retrained? If the challenge of imports spurs U.S. companies to improve their management and U.S. workers to become more productive, that will be one of the biggest benefits to be gained from a policy of free trade.

Aircraft are a major American export. This Japan Air Lines cargo plane was made in the United States by Boeing. Courtesy of Japan Air Lines

ECONOMIC CHALLENGES TO GOVERNMENT

Government as well as business faces major economic challenges in the 1980s. The conditions that business needs if it is to prosper—economic growth, low inflation, and moderate interest rates—do not just happen. They require certain actions by policymakers in the federal government. In this section we will look at two major branches of economic policy.

Fiscal Policy

Fiscal policy: The branch of economic policy that is concerned with taxes and government spending.

The first major branch is **fiscal policy**. Fiscal policy is concerned with taxes and government spending. Box 2–7 gives a picture of the kinds of

Box 2–7 Outlays and Sources of Funds for the Federal Government

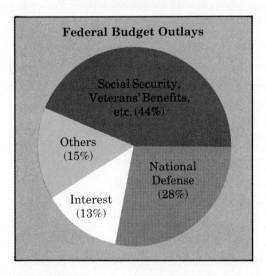

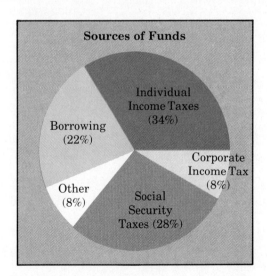

Fiscal policy is concerned with the tax and spending activities of the federal government. These charts show the main categories of federal spending for the 1984 budget year, and where the government got the funds to pay for that spending. Notice that total outlays were $854 billion compared with tax revenues of just $670 billion. The difference, called the federal budget deficit, had to be made up by borrowing.

Source: President's Council of Economic Advisers, *Economic Report of the President* (Washington, D.C.: Government Printing Office, 1984), Table B–72.

taxes that the federal government collects and the things those tax revenues are spent on. Fiscal policy is important to business in three ways.

First, government spending is a major source of demand. The federal government's outlays of $854 billion in 1984 were equal to about 25 percent of GNP. Some of that total was spent directly by government—to buy military hardware, pay the salaries of government employees, and so on. The rest was distributed to households under Social Security, welfare, and other programs. By boosting household income, that part of government spending also added to the demand for goods and services produced by businesses. Government is the main customer of many firms, and when the indirect impact of government spending is taken into account, it is a major source of demand for almost all firms.

Second, fiscal policy has an impact on business through taxes. Taxes on individuals, such as the personal income tax, affect firms indirectly by lowering the after-tax income that people have available for buying consumer goods. Taxes on business, such as the corporate income tax, affect business directly. By taxing away part of a firm's profits, the corporate tax leaves less for reinvestment.

Federal budget deficit: The difference between what the federal government spends and what it takes in as taxes.

Third, fiscal policy affects business via the government's need to borrow. The difference between what the federal government spends and what it takes in as taxes—$184 billion in 1984—is known as the **federal budget deficit**. The government must cover this deficit by borrowing from private sources. When the government borrows, it competes with businesses and consumers. A larger budget deficit, other things being equal, means fewer funds available for business and consumer loans.

The proper balance in fiscal policy has always been a source of controversy, but perhaps never more so than in the early 1980s. The Reagan administration came into office promising to cut taxes, cut government spending, and eliminate the federal budget deficit. A major tax cut was passed by Congress in 1981, but the rest of the program did not work out as planned. A limited number of cuts were made in government spending, but these were more than offset by increases in spending for defense. The result was that the deficit, instead of shrinking, grew to record size.

How best to reduce the federal deficit will continue to be a focus of debate in coming years. Some call for higher taxes; some would prefer cuts in spending, including defense spending. Many business leaders fear that continued large federal deficits will crowd out business and consumer borrowers, limiting investment and economic growth in the long run.

Monetary Policy

Federal Reserve System (Fed): The federal government agency that is charged with the conduct of monetary policy and with regulation of the banking system.

Two main forms of money are used in the U.S. economy—currency, which includes both paper money and coins, and checking account balances. As Chapter 19 will explain in detail, both forms of money are used by households and firms to pay for goods and services. A government agency known as the **Federal Reserve System**, or **Fed**, is charged with controlling the amount of money in circulation, that is, the money supply. The actions the Fed takes to increase or decrease the supply of money are known as **monetary policy**. Monetary policy is important because of its impact on inflation and on interest rates.

Monetary policy: The branch of economic policy that is concerned with controlling the supply of money and credit.

Suppose that the Fed pursues an "easy" monetary policy. This means that it allows the amount of money in circulation to rise and lets banks increase the volume of loans they make to businesses and consumers. More money and easy access to loans cause businesses and consumers to in-

Currency is printed by the U.S. Treasury, but the total amount of money in circulation, which includes checking accounts as well as currency, is controlled by the Federal Reserve System. © Alon Reininger, Woodfin Camp

crease their demand for goods and services of all kinds. Following the law of supply and demand, the prices of those goods and services begin to rise. The result is inflation. The old saying that inflation means "too much money chasing too few goods" is a good description of this process.

Instead, the Fed might pursue a "tight" monetary policy, restricting the amount of money in circulation and reducing the funds available to banks for making loans. Such a policy forces businesses and consumers to cut back their spending plans. Demand for goods and services drops. As demand falls, there is less upward pressure on prices, and prices of some goods may actually decrease. As a result, the rate of inflation falls.

The Fed's monetary policies have major effects on interest rates as well as on inflation. In the short run at least, a monetary policy that makes more money available to banks for making loans tends to cause interest rates to fall. In the long run, however, the Fed's control over interest rates is less than perfect. At best, it can control only the supply of funds available for banks to lend—it controls, that is, only one of the two forces that determine interest rates. Whatever the Fed does with regard to the *supply* of loans, a strong *demand* for loans can cause interest rates to rise.

The private sector—households and business firms—is one major source of demand for loans. If businesses decide to borrow heavily to buy new equipment or to build up inventories, upward pressure is placed on interest rates. The same is true if consumers borrow heavily for new cars and houses. The demand of firms and households for loans depends, in part, on changes in attitude that are hard to predict. This fact makes interest rates themselves hard to predict.

Governments—federal, state, and local—are another major source of demand for loans. Budget deficits at all levels of government must be made up by borrowing. When deficits are big, government demand for loans keeps interest rates high.

As we will see in Part V of this book, the level of interest rates is a matter of great importance to business. Firms constantly need to borrow. They need long-term loans to buy buildings and equipment. They need short-term loans to pay for raw materials until they are made into goods

The level of interest rates on both loans and deposits is a matter of great importance to business. Marc P. Anderson

that can be sold, and to pay for inventories of finished goods between the time they are made and the time they are sold. Interest paid on loans is, in short, a major cost for business.

The high interest rates of the late 1970s and early 1980s dealt business—especially small firms in housing and auto-related industries—a double blow. First, high interest rates pushed up their costs. At the same time, consumers were scared away by the high interest rates on consumer loans. Although by 1983 interest rates had fallen from their record highs of a few years earlier, business leaders continued to list high interest rates as one of their major worries for the later 1980s.

Unfortunately, there is no magic formula that can guarantee low and stable interest rates. The Fed does have some short-run power to nudge them downward with an easy monetary policy or upward with a tight monetary policy. This power is less than complete, however. If monetary policy is too easy for too long, it can cause inflation, which will push interest rates up in the long run. If private demand for loans is strong, interest rates will also rise. Above all, if budget deficits are large, government demand for loans can keep interest rates high no matter what the Fed does. For all of these reasons, the outlook for interest rates remains uncertain.

SUMMARY

1. The terms *capitalism*, *free enterprise*, and *market economy* are all used to describe the economic system of the United States. *Capitalism* refers to the fact that owners of capital control business decisions. *Free enterprise* refers to the fact that people are free to choose whom to buy from, whom to sell to and on what terms, and whom to compete with. A *market economy* is one in which decisions about what, how, and for whom to produce are a result of interactions between buyers and sellers in the marketplace.

2. According to the law of supply and demand, prices tend to rise when there is a shortage and to fall when there is a surplus. Other things being equal, an increase in the demand for a product causes its price to rise, while a decrease in demand causes its price to fall. Likewise, an increase in the supply of a product tends to cause its price to fall, while a decrease in supply tends to cause its price to rise.

3. Other economic systems include *feudalism* and *socialism*. Under feudalism, economic decisions are made by landowners. Under socialism, either the workers or central governments acting in the name of the workers make key economic decisions. The Soviet Union and many countries of eastern Europe and Asia have an economic system known as *communism*, which is a type of socialism. Many countries of western Europe have *mixed economies* that combine capitalist and socialist aspects.

4. Throughout the 1970s business decisions in the United States were affected by *inflation*. Although some other countries have seen higher rates of inflation, rates of more than 10 percent per year have been rare in the United States. Avoiding high rates of inflation remains a major challenge to American business in the 1980s.

5. *Unemployment* is another challenge faced by business in the 1980s. The main types of unemployment are *cyclical*, *frictional*, and *structural unemployment*.

6. *Productivity* is output per worker. In the long run, increases in our standard of living depend on higher productivity. During the 1970s productivity increases in the U.S. economy slowed to a crawl. Raising productivity is a major challenge for business in the 1980s.

7. Trade between the United States and other nations has more than tripled in the past twenty years. Many more industries are facing foreign competition than in the past. Business needs to find positive ways of reacting to foreign competition, rather than simply seeking import restrictions.

8. The federal government's economic policies are a major factor in the business environment. *Fiscal policy*, which has to do with taxation and government spending, is one major branch of economic policy. The *monetary policy* of the *Federal Reserve System* is the other major branch.

KEY TERMS

You should be familiar with the following terms and concepts. Check their meanings by referring to the marginal definitions in the chapter or to the glossary at the end of the book.

Capitalism

Feudalism

Socialism

Communism

Mixed economy

Free enterprise

Market economy

Market

Law of supply and demand

Gross national product (GNP)

Business cycle

Recession

Inflation

Consumer price index (CPI)

Cyclical unemployment

Frictional unemployment

Structural unemployment

Productivity

Fiscal policy

Federal budget deficit

Federal Reserve System (Fed)

Monetary policy

QUESTIONS FOR REVIEW AND DISCUSSION

1. The United States is not a pure capitalist, free enterprise, or market economy. Give examples of the following:
   a. A business firm that is controlled by workers, consumers, or someone else, rather than by owners or shareholders.
   b. Limits on a firm's freedom to charge whatever prices it wants to, compete with whomever it wants to, and sell whatever or to whomever it wants to.
   c. Cases in which actions by government attempt to override the law of supply and demand by directly controlling prices.

2. The United States has a capitalist economy, but not everyone is happy about this fact. Are any socialist or other anticapitalist groups active on your campus or in your community? If so, make it a project to find out why they are opposed to the capitalist system.

3. Go to your library and try to find the latest figures for the rate of inflation, the unemployment rate, interest rates, and the rate of productivity growth for the U.S. economy. Some of these figures can be found in newspapers. You can find all of them in the tables in the back of the latest edition of the *Economic Report of the President*, which is published early each year by the President's Council of Economic Advisers. The *Survey of Current Business*, *Federal Reserve Bulletin*, and *Monthly Labor Review* are other government publications from which you can get these figures.

4. Working from the data given in Boxes 2–2 and 2–3, make a graph showing the connection between the unemployment rate (horizontal axis) and the rate of inflation (vertical axis). For each year, locate the points representing the inflation and unemployment rates. Connect the points in order. Do you notice any sort of pattern?

5. Different interest rates are charged for different types of loans. Look in the financial pages of a major newspaper (the *Wall Street Journal* is best) and list all the different kinds of interest rates you can find. Don't forget to look at the ads to find the rates paid by banks, mutual funds, and so on, and the rates charged for mortgage and auto loans. Can you see any regular relationships between some kinds of interest rates and others?

6. If you have, or have had, a full- or part-time job, spend some time thinking about the concept of productivity as applied to your workplace. Is there an easy way to measure output per worker for your job? If not, what is the problem? Can you think of any way in

which output per worker could be increased? If so, discuss your idea with your employer and think about his or her reactions.

7. Scan the newspapers or the TV news for a story about an industry that is threatened by foreign competition. Is the industry asking the government for protection? If it were granted that protection, who would be helped? Who, if anyone, would be hurt?

Case 2–1: Challenges to the Soviet Economy in the 1980s

The short reign of Yuri Andropov as head of the Soviet government and the Communist party was marked by efforts to deal with chronic economic problems such as absenteeism, lack of discipline, and low productivity. Agriculture also suffered from mismanagement and lack of innovation. Andropov saw the extent of these problems, but his desire to make changes ran up against bureaucracies full of planners who were unwilling to experiment.

Andropov realized that more than speeches would be needed. He offered higher wages to workers who increased their output per hour. Unfortunately, he found that higher wages have only limited value as an incentive in the Soviet system. There is such a severe shortage of consumer goods that workers have little to buy with their pay. For a major consumer purchase like a car, people have to pay thousands of rubles just to buy a place on a waiting list. The list may be ten years long in some cases. Under these conditions, higher pay may not give workers a strong reason to put out more effort.

In 1983, good weather brought Soviet agriculture relief from a string of bad harvests, but the underlying weaknesses remained. The Central Committee of the Communist party pledged to reduce imports of farm goods and to raise the amount of meat, fruit, and vegetables in the average citizen's diet. To this end, one third of all investment funds were to be assigned to agriculture. These funds alone would not solve the problem of incentives, however.

One of Andropov's major achievements was to begin a campaign against corruption in the bureaucracy. Under the previous Soviet leader, Leonid Brezhnev, bribe taking, black-market sales of industrial goods, and use of industrial labor for building vacation homes and for other private purposes had become widespread. As long as the corrupt officials remained loyal to party leaders in Moscow, their misdeeds were overlooked. Andropov struck fear into those officials and fired many of them. This was seen as a first step toward carrying out lasting reforms.

The campaign against corruption was cut short when Andropov died of a kidney ailment in February 1984. The Central Committee selected Konstantin Chernenko, a close ally of Brezhnev's, as the new leader. No doubt many of the officials who had been threatened by Andropov breathed a sigh of relief. For the time being, at least, the cause of reform seemed to suffer a setback.

Questions:

1. From this case, do you see any similarities between the economic problems facing the Soviet Union in the 1980s and those facing the United States? What are they? What problems that are important for the U.S. economy are not mentioned in the article? What major problems for the Soviet economy are not problems in the United States?

2. What kinds of incentives appear to be needed to raise the productivity of Soviet industrial and agricultural workers? How do the proposed Soviet incentives compare with those available to workers in the United States?

3. Can a country that relies on individual incentives to increase productivity remain a socialist country?

Case 2–2: The RV Industry Bounces Back

Recreational vehicles, once written off as gas-guzzling relics of a bygone era, are coming back.

Falling interest rates and gasoline prices have turned RVs around. For the 7 million Americans who own RVs, it's a chance to hit the road again; for dealers and manufacturers, it's a chance to attract new business at last. And while the industry still is at the mercy of energy supplies and general economic trends, any upturn is welcome news for those who have endured several years of hard times.

"The market seems red hot," says David Humphreys, president of the Recreational Vehicle Industry Association. He notes that manufacturers shipped 48,000 RVs to dealers in January and February, nearly 54 percent more than they shipped in January and February of 1982. And analysts forecast total shipments of about 330,000 units in 1983, compared with 181,000 in 1980.

That projected level is still far below the 1972 peak of 583,000 units. But a double battering—in 1973–1974 and 1979–1980—left the industry nearly dead. Hit by scarce and expensive gasoline, high interest rates, tight credit, and recession, nearly half of the 200 RV makers that were in existence in 1973 have either folded or merged, while two-thirds of the dealers have left the business. In 1980 as many as 75 percent of the industry's factory workers were laid off.

But today fears of gas shortages have all but vanished, gas prices have dropped, interest rates are slipping, and the economy looks a bit better. Even though shipments are well below peak levels, RV makers expect some shortages because their capacity has been greatly reduced. Coachmen Industries of Middlebury, Indiana, says that 17 percent of its total work hours are overtime hours. And Fleetwood Enterprises of Riverside, California, says it may have to reopen some plants.

Manufacturers also hope that even if gas prices rise, RV sales won't suffer as much as they did in the past. That's because the manufacturers have come up with lighter models and are putting out diesel-powered motor homes. Today, as as result, motor homes get about 15 miles per gallon, about double their mileage a few years ago.

Source: Harlan S. Byrne, "Recreation Vehicles Start Selling Better, Sparked by Falling Rates, Gasoline Prices," *Wall Street Journal*, April 14, 1983, p. 31. Reprinted by permission of the Wall Street Journal. © Dow Jones & Company, Inc., 1983. All Rights Reserved.

Questions:

1. The chapter discusses a number of economic challenges that have faced and continue to face U.S. businesses. Which of these have been major problems for the RV industry in recent years? What changes are making things look better?

2. The chapter begins by making the point that no firm operates in isolation. Events in what other industries have had powerful effects on the RV industry?

3. If, as expected, shortages of RVs develop, what would you expect to happen to RV prices? Why?

4. What actions have entrepreneurs in the RV industry taken to try to protect themselves in the event of renewed fuel price increases?

Chapter 3
FORMS OF BUSINESS ORGANIZATION

When you have completed this chapter, you should be able to

- Define the three basic forms of business organization: the *sole proprietorship*, the *partnership*, and the *corporation*.

- List the advantages and disadvantages of each form under the headings of simplicity, ability to raise capital, liability, control, continuity, and taxation.

- Explain the special advantages of these hybrid forms: the *franchise*, the *joint venture*, the *limited partnership*, and the *cooperative*.

- Explain the relationships among stockholders, directors, and top management of a corporation.

- Discuss the process of corporate growth, including internal growth, growth by merger, and expansion abroad.

- Explain what a *not-for-profit firm* is, what purposes such firms serve, and how they are financed, organized, and controlled.

In 1983 two Washington, D.C., lawyers, whom we will call Sandra Ford and Leo Marx, decided to start an airline in their spare time. An airline, you might think, sounds like a big business—not a hobby for two lawyers. But Ford and Marx knew what they were doing. They had worked in the transportation industry and in the federal agencies that regulate that industry. In the business plan they issued to potential investors, their proposed Diplomat Airways was projected to be small but profitable.

Since the airline industry was deregulated in 1979, competition had driven down the fares on many U.S. routes to unprofitably low levels. The first key part of Diplomat's plan was to avoid those routes. Instead, the airline would seek authority to operate on the Detroit-London and Pittsburgh-London routes. Under an international agreement, no more than one U.S.-based airline would be allowed to serve each of these markets. (At the time Diplomat's business plan was issued, no one was offering nonstop service on these routes. Ford and Marx estimated that 100,000 passengers per year would use nonstop service on these routes if it were offered.)

A second key part of Diplomat's business plan was to keep costs low so that it could operate profitably at fares below those charged by the established airlines. Ford and Marx planned to lease a single DC-8-71 to fly 558 round trips per year, at a cost of $3 million per year. (A second plane would be leased for backup service when the first plane was scheduled for maintenance.) Five flight crews and five cabin crews would be hired at a cost of $1.7 million per year. The crew costs were based on nonunion pay rates that were below those of existing large airlines but somewhat higher than those paid by other nonunion carriers. Fuel costs were projected at $6.4 million per year, sales and marketing costs at $3.9 million per year, maintenance costs at $2.1 million per year, and so on, for a total projected operating cost of $22.9 million in the first year.

To get the airline off the ground, Ford and Marx would need to raise $3.5 million. Some of this they would put in themselves, and some they would seek from other investors. This start-up capital would be needed to cover expenses up to the time flights began. It would also provide working capital in the first year of operation. If all went according to plan, revenue for the first year of operations would be $23,500. The profit of $600,000 per year, and more in future years, would be a good return on the $3.5 invested in the airline.[1]

---

[1] Based on an actual business plan provided courtesy of Mark Levin.

The business plan of Diplomat Airways projects sales, revenues, costs, profits, and capital requirements. It describes the airline's operations in detail and all of the steps needed to start it up. One detail has not been mentioned, however. This is the *form of organization* the airline should take.

Firms can take a number of organizational forms, including proprietorship, partnership, corporation, and hybrid forms. In this chapter, we will look at the advantages and drawbacks of each.

In part, we will look at matters from the point of view of the firm itself. Should Diplomat organize as a sole proprietorship, a partnership, or a corporation? What form of organization would be best from the point of view of taxes? What form would be best from the standpoint of liability if (heaven forbid) passengers are injured or property is damaged in the course of the airline's operations?

In part, too, we will look at the advantages and drawbacks of various forms of organization from the point of view of public policy. Should our laws favor one form over another? Should different forms be taxed differently?

Our discussion of organizational forms will also include the not-for-profit sector. Why do some suppliers of goods and services choose not-for-profit or cooperative forms of organization? What is the proper balance between private profit-seeking, private not-for-profit, and government organizations? And in what ways do not-for-profit firms resemble profit-making businesses? An understanding of the legal structure of organizations will be useful at every stage of this book.

FORMS OF BUSINESS ORGANIZATION: AN OVERVIEW

In this section we will define three basic forms of business organization and review the pros and cons of each. Choosing the right form is crucial to anyone who is starting a business. But even if you spend your career as an employee of an existing business, it will be useful to know why that business takes the form it does.

The Basic Organizational Forms

All businesses take one of three basic forms: the sole proprietorship, the partnership, and the corporation.

A **sole proprietorship** is a business that is owned, and often run, by one person, who receives all the profits and bears all the liabilities of the business. Proprietorships are the most common form of business. In the United States there are more than 12 million of them. On the average, however, proprietorships are small. Although they account for more than 76 percent of all firms by number, they bring in only about 9 percent of all business receipts. (See Box 3–1.)

A **partnership** is a voluntary legal association of two or more people for the purpose of running a business. The partners, in effect, become co-owners of a joint proprietorship. Partnerships account for just 8 percent of all businesses and 4 percent of all business receipts in the United States. They are most common in the professions, where doctors, lawyers, accountants, and architects often form partnerships.

A **corporation** is a firm that exists as an independent legal entity, with ownership divided into shares. The owners of the shares are known as **stockholders** or **shareholders**. A key feature of the corporation is that the liability of the stockholders for debts of the firm, legal judgments against it, and the like is limited to the amount of money they paid to buy shares in the first place. Corporations account for only 16 percent of all firms in the United States. However, almost all large firms are corporations. The result is that this form of organization accounts for some 87 percent of all business receipts.

Sole proprietorship: A business that is owned, and often run, by one person, who receives all the profits and bears all the liabilities of the business.

Partnership: A voluntary legal association of two or more people for the purpose of running a business.

Corporation: A firm that exists as an independent legal entity, with ownership divided into shares.

Stockholder (shareholder): The owner of one or more shares of common stock in a corporation.

Box 3–1 Distribution of Basic Forms of Organization in American Business

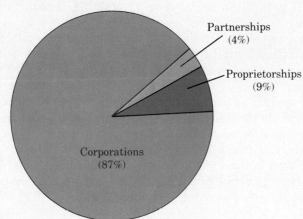

Total Business Receipts

Partnerships (4%)

Proprietorships (9%)

Corporations (87%)

Number of Firms

Corporations (16%)

Partnerships (8%)

Proprietorships (76%)

The two charts shown here show the distribution of the three basic forms of business organization in the United States. Proprietorships, the simplest form, account for about 76 percent of all firms. Since most proprietorships are small, however, all of these firms together bring in only about 9 percent of all business receipts. Corporations are in the opposite situation.

Only about 16 percent of all businesses are corporations, but since almost all really large firms take this form, they bring in about 87 percent of all business receipts. Partnerships are the least common form of organization; they account for 8 percent of all businesses and 4 percent of all receipts.

Source: U.S. Department of Commerce, *Statistical Abstract of the United States*, 103rd ed. (Washington, D.C.: Government Printing Office, 1983), Table 878. Data are for 1979.

Drawing by S. Gross; © 1983 The New Yorker Magazine, Inc.

"If that's Grandpa, tell him I've already left."

Advantages and Disadvantages of the Basic Forms

Proprietorships, partnerships, and corporations all have certain strengths and weaknesses. These can be discussed under six headings: simplicity, ability to raise capital, liability, control, continuity, and taxation. Let's look at each of these in turn.

Simplicity. In business, as in many areas of life, there is much to be said for the KISS principle: Keep It Simple, Stupid! Running a business is hard enough as it is. There is no point in taking on more paperwork and legal fees than you have to.

Of the three basic forms, the proprietorship is the simplest. The legal procedures for starting a proprietorship usually are limited to registering the company's name so as to avoid duplicate names. (Of course, many formalities, ranging from health department permits to zoning rules, may have to be seen to before the firm can open its doors. But these apply equally to all three forms of organization.) Once the propretorship is in business, accounting is simplified by the fact that income to the firm is counted as income to the owner. And a proprietorship can go out of business as easily as it goes in. Again, no legal procedures are required. The owner simply locks the door and disconnects the phone.

Starting a corporation is a little more complex. Papers must be filed to obtain a state charter. Certain reports that are not required for proprietorships may have to be filed. A separate set of books must be kept to segregate business transactions from the owners' personal dealings. In principle, a person who is starting a corporation can do all the paperwork without the help of a lawyer or accountant, but most writers on small business advise getting professional help.

Starting a partnership is less complex than starting a corporation, but somewhat more so than starting a proprietorship. Written articles of partnership are not required, but they are recommended. And because of the need to establish a clear division of authority, avoid disputes, and provide continuity, setting up a partnership may turn out to be no easier than starting a corporation.

Simplicity has its virtues, as we have said, and it may be why proprietorships are so popular. It is not the only thing to consider, however. Dan Steinhoff, an expert in small business, writes that "if the new firm owners choose a legal form of organization only because of its simplicity, they are probably demonstrating that they lack overall business competence and a thorough knowledge of legal forms, and that they are the type of owners who always look for the easiest way to make decisions."[2] Too many small businesses, he thinks, pass up the advantages of the corporate form.

Ability to raise capital. If simplicity is the proprietorship's main advantage, lack of ability to raise capital is its main weakness. The sources of capital for a proprietorship usually are limited to the owner's own savings plus loans from banks, relatives, or other sources. If not enough capital can be raised from savings or loans, another form of organization may be necessary. For example, neither Ford nor Marx considered organiz-

[2]Dan Steinhoff, *Small Business Management Fundamentals*, 3rd ed. (New York: McGraw-Hill, 1982), pp. 84–85.

Millions of Americans own stock in corporations. In this stockbroker's office, up-to-the-minute stock prices are flashed on an electronic display. © Gilles Peress, Magnum

ing Diplomat Airways as a proprietorship because neither of them had $3.5 million to invest in the firm.

One way to raise capital is to bring in one or more partners. Two or more people pooling their savings often have more funds than one person operating alone. They may also be able to get loans on better terms.

A much more powerful way to raise capital, however, is to incorporate. Incorporation, like forming a partnership, brings in new capital by bringing in new co-owners, but it is much more flexible. Ford and Marx chose this approach for raising capital for Diplomat Airways. In their business proposal, they planned to issue a total of 600,000 shares to themselves, partly in return for cash and partly in return for services. Another 1,400,000 shares would be sold to outside investors to raise $2,780,000 of the $3.5 million needed to start the airline. Another 500,000 shares were reserved for employees.

Venture capital market: A market in which specialists put entrepreneurs in touch with people who are willing to take risks by buying stock in new firms.

An important source of capital for new corporations is the so-called **venture capital market**. Specialists in venture capital put entrepreneurs in touch with people who are willing to take big risks in the hope of big gains by buying stock in new companies. According to Jane Koloski Morris, managing editor of *Venture Capital Journal*, more than $3 billion was raised in this way by new businesses in 1981 and 1982.[3]

Liability. A major difference among organizational forms is the degree to which owners are personally liable for debts of the business and legal judgments against it.

In a sole proprietorship, the owner is personally responsible for all liabilities. That means that if the business fails, creditors can claim the owner's property to pay off the debts of the business. It also means that the owner is liable for any legal judgments against the firm that may result from negligence or misdeeds, not only those of the owner but those of employees as well. This is commonly viewed as a major drawback of proprietorships. Owners of such firms can protect themselves against

[3]Reported in *Business Week*, April 18, 1983, p. 78.

many kinds of liabilities with insurance. But not all risks are insurable, and insurance is expensive.

For a partnership, business liabilities can be even more of a problem. Each partner is fully liable not only for any debts or wrongdoing of his or her own but for those of all the other partners too. (The situation is a little different for the so-called limited partnership, to be described shortly.) This can be a very serious matter in partnerships of doctors, lawyers, or other professionals, who may be sued for malpractice. For such partnerships, insurance is essential and is a major business expense.

Under the corporate form of ownership, on the other hand, stockholders are not exposed to the liabilities of the business. Creditors of the corporation, or parties bringing lawsuits against it, can at most make claims against the assets of the firm; the property of the owners is immune. Even in the worst case, in which debt or a legal judgment drives the corporation into bankruptcy, the owners at most lose only the capital that they put into the firm when they first bought their shares of stock.

Limited liability: A legal arrangement under which part-owners who contribute capital to a business are responsible for the liabilities of the business only to the extent of the capital they contributed.

This **limited liability** feature of the corporation is its biggest advantage. Without limited liability, it is almost impossible to raise capital by selling shares (that is, very small ownership stakes) to thousands or even tens of thousands of stockholders, as many corporations do. With limited liability, one person can own a few shares in each of a dozen corporations and still sleep easily at night. Without limited liability, failure by any one of those companies could result in claims against each owner's property.

Yet, advantageous as limited liability is, it is not quite enough to persuade all business owners to form corporations. There are a number of reasons for this.

First, there are cases in which a business owner can gain the trust and confidence of customers by standing fully behind the firm rather than "hiding behind a corporate veil." This is often true for partnerships in such professions as medicine, law, and accounting. (See Box 3–2.) This policy

Box 3–2 Partnerships in the Professions

Given the disadvantages of partnerships, the surprising thing is that there are very many of them. In the professions of law, medicine, and accounting, however, partnerships have long been the main form of business organization. Some of these partnerships are huge. At Peat Marwick Mitchell, one of the nation's largest accounting firms, the list of partners numbers in the thousands. Many of the partners have never even met. What explains the existence of these brontosauruses of the partnership world?

The answer, surprisingly, is that these organizations have avoided incorporation in order to avoid limited liability. The theory is that, for a doctor, lawyer, or accountant, taking full responsibility for one's judgments is a token of good faith. The client may be exposed to great loss if a judgment goes wrong. The professional, so the theory goes, should

take the same risk and, furthermore, should not take on partners in whom he or she has less than complete faith.

All this is not empty theory, either. Until quite recently these principles were strongly defended by ethics boards with the power to enforce their views.

One way or another, superpartnerships like the big accounting and law firms have developed ways to minimize disputes, ensure continuity, and cope with liability problems. But things are changing. Recently ethics boards (and sometimes state laws) have dropped their strict opposition to the corporate form of organization. As medical, legal, and other professional partnerships incorporate, the partnership share of total business activity can be expected to decrease.

may also aid very small businesses in getting bank loans. It is not uncommon for the owners of a small corporation to put up their own houses or other assets as collateral for business loans. But if they do so and the business fails, they are not much better off than they would have been if the business had been a proprietorship.

Second, for many types of business the risks of unlimited liability are not great. Consider a small office supply store. There is the risk that a customer could trip on the carpet, break a leg, and sue for damages, but even a corporation would carry insurance for that kind of thing. The owner may need to borrow to finance inventories, but in case the business fails, the creditors could repossess the inventories themselves. If the business never earns a profit, the owner will end up losing any money he or she put up to pay rent, utility bills, and so forth, but that money would be lost even if the business were incorporated. In short, the advantages of limited liability are worth thinking about, but they are not always decisive.

Control. People who start a business usually have strong ideas about how the business should be run. That, after all, is one reason they don't work for someone else in the first place. It is important to them to retain control over business decisions.

In a sole proprietorship, control is no problem. Neither ownership nor control is shared; the proprietor is the boss. But although this is often seen as an advantage, it is not limited to proprietorships. The owner of a corporation who owns all or nearly all of the stock has just as much control as a sole proprietor.

As a corporation sells more and more stock to raise capital, however, control can be eroded. How serious this problem is depends very much on such matters as who the other stockholders are. We will return to this question later in the chapter.

Partnerships have their own problems of control. In partnerships, two or more people are co-owners, and each of them may have strong ideas about how things ought to be run. There are no simple rules of the one-share, one-vote sort for settling disputes. Many partnerships break up simply because the partners don't get along. For example, the Washington law firm of Califano, Ross and Heineman broke up for just this reason. As one observer put it, "Lawyers are prima donnas. They all want to run the firm their own way."[4]

Continuity. Legally, proprietorships cease to exist when the proprietor dies. A partnership is dissolved when one partner dies. This lack of continuity is a disadvantage of these two forms of organization. A corporation, on the other hand, has an unlimited legal life apart from the mortal life of any one stockholder. For ventures that are expected to outlive their founders, this is a clear advantage.

But again, this advantage of the corporation is not decisive. For example, although a proprietorship ceases to exist when the owner dies, the assets are still there. An heir or a buyer can take over the business and run it under new ownership. Sometimes continuity may be threatened by the need to sell part or all of the firm's assets to pay estate taxes. (Many family farms have come to grief this way.) But life insurance and estate planning can overcome this problem. Certain large partnerships like those discussed in Box 3–2 have devised ways to maintain continuity as partners come and go.

---

[4]Seth Hufstadler, quoted in *Wall Street Journal,* June 8, 1983, p. 1.

The profits and losses of a proprietorship are taxed as personal income of the owner. Marc P. Anderson

Subchapter S corporation: A corporation that meets certain standards, such as a limit on the number of stockholders, and chooses to be taxed as a proprietorship or partnership.

Taxation. We come last to taxation—a topic that is complex enough to fill several books. The various forms of business organization are not taxed equally. Cutting down the tax burden is a very important factor in choosing a form for a new business or in choosing when to change the form of an existing one. Unfortunately, there are no simple rules for deciding what type of organization is best from the point of view of taxes; therefore, we will only touch on some general considerations here.

The tax situation is simplest for a proprietorship. All business income or loss goes right on the owner's personal tax forms, and federal and state taxes are paid by the owner.

Most partnerships are almost as simple. Profits and losses of the partnership are passed through to the owners as personal income according to a formula contained in the partnership agreement.

Corporations are treated differently. The profits of a corporation are subject to federal, and sometimes state, corporate income taxes. This often imposes a double tax burden. The income of the corporation is taxed at rates of up to 46 percent when the corporation earns it. When the after-tax income is paid out to stockholders as dividends, it is then taxed again as personal income at rates of up to 50 percent. It can be seen, thus, that of every $100 in profits earned by a corporation, as little as $27 may be left in stockholders' pockets by the time both corporate and personal income taxes have been paid.

Fortunately, the tax disadvantages of the corporation are not always as crushing as they appear at first glance. Since double taxation could be punitive to small businesses, Congress has provided some relief. If it meets certain standards, a small firm (and in some cases a large one) can choose to be a **subchapter S corporation**. Such corporations are taxed as if they were proprietorships or partnerships.

Striking a balance. It is clear by now, as stated at the outset, that no one form of organization is best for all businesses. Proprietorships have the virtue of simplicity. Partnerships permit the funds and talents of more than one person to be pooled. Corporations offer limited liability and unlimited corporate life. Any one of the three may, depending on the situation, reduce the total tax burden. A summary of the advantages and disadvantages of each form is given in Box 3–3.

Hybrid Business Forms

Since no one form of business organization is perfect from all points of view, crossbreeds and hybrids have been devised to suit special circumstances. Four of these are common enough to deserve mention here.

Franchise: An arrangement in which the owner of a trademark, trade name, or copyright (the franchisor) allows another firm (the franchisee) to use it, subject to certain agreed-upon conditions.

Franchises. Large corporations can raise capital, market their products nationwide, and spend heavily on research and development. Small local firms have the advantage of close control by their owners and often have tax advantages as well. One device that tries to have the best of both worlds is the franchise. A **franchise** is an arrangement in which the owner of a trademark, trade name, or copyright allows another firm to use it subject to certain agreed-upon conditions, including payment of a fee. The franchisor (who grants the franchise) and the franchisee (who buys it) are separate businesses. The franchisor is normally a corporation, while the franchisee may be a proprietorship, a partnership, or another corporation.

Box 3–3 Features of the Basic Forms of Business Organization

The Sole Proprietorship

Simplicity	Simplest to form and dissolve; free from some paperwork and regulations
Raising capital	Sources of capital largely limited to owner's savings plus loans
Liability	Owner responsible for all business liabilities
Control	Owner has full control over the business
Continuity	The firm ceases to exist upon the death of the owner
Taxation	Income to the firm is taxed as income of the owner; not subject to federal corporate income tax and certain state taxes

The Partnership

Simplicity	Nearly as simple to set up as a proprietorship, but written agreement is advised
Raising capital	Increases access to capital by permitting partners to pool their savings and borrowing power
Liability	Each partner is responsible for all business liabilities incurred by any partner; in limited partnerships, only the general partners have full liability
Control	Disputes over control can be a source of trouble; authority of partners should be spelled out in partnership agreement
Continuity	Partnerships normally cease to exist upon the death of any one partner; however, certain large partnerships achieve continuity despite this drawback
Taxation	Income is taxed as income to partners whether distributed or not (in some cases, but not always, this can be a tax advantage); earnings are not subject to corporate income taxes

The Corporation

Simplicity	Requires a state charter to begin operation; may be subject to more paperwork and regulations than proprietorships
Raising capital	Able to raise large sums of capital from many investors
Liability	Liability of owners limited to amount paid to acquire stock
Control	Entrepreneurs can retain control by retaining most of the common stock; managers of corporations with widely dispersed ownership may be subject to unfriendly tender offers and proxy contests
Continuity	Has limited lifespan
Taxation	Corporate income tax subjects earnings to double taxation; however, subchapter S corporations can elect to be taxed as proprietorships or partnerships

Franchises are very common in real estate, auto dealerships, fast-food restaurants, and small service businesses. The franchisor typically provides advertising and sells the franchisee the goods or materials needed to run the business. A contract between the two parties sets forth the standards the franchisee must meet. Franchise agreements usually also spell out the conditions under which the franchise can be ended, and provide ways of settling disputes. Because franchises are an attractive form of small business, we will say more about them in the next chapter.

A franchise like Kwik-Kopy combines some of the advantages of a large corporation with those of a small local firm. Courtesy of Kwik-Kopy Corp.

Joint venture: An association of two or more firms for a specific, limited purpose.

Syndicate: An association of two or more people or firms for a limited purpose, usually more limited than a joint venture.

Limited partnership: A partnership that includes one or more general partners who bear full liability and run the business, plus one or more limited partners who bear limited liability and do not have a voice in the firm's day-to-day management.

Cooperative: A business that is owned and controlled by its members, usually its customers or suppliers, but sometimes its employees.

Joint ventures and syndicates. Sometimes one firm does not have the resources to carry out a certain project. In such cases two or more firms may form a **joint venture** to do the job. A joint venture is an association of two or more firms for a specific, limited purpose. The firms may be proprietorships, partnerships, or corporations. For example, two or more oil companies might combine to share the expense and risk of exploring an offshore oil field. Another well-known example is the joint venture of General Motors and Toyota to make a small car designed by Toyota in an idle General Motors plant in California.

A **syndicate** is another type of association of firms, usually for more limited purpose than a joint venture. For example, a group of banks might form a syndicate to make a very large loan that none of them could make by itself.

Limited partnerships. For certain types of business ventures, partnerships have distinct tax advantages over corporations. In order to capture these advantages while avoiding the problem of unlimited liability, a special form of organization known as the **limited partnership** is used. A limited partnership has one or more general partners who put up some capital, run the business, and bear the liabilities of the business. In addition, there are one or more limited partners who put up capital but have no voice in the firm's day-to-day management and do not share its liabilities. The limited partners are in much the same position as stockholders in a corporation, except for tax purposes.

Real estate ventures such as construction of apartments and office buildings are often organized as limited partnerships. Ford and Marx gave some thought to organizing Diplomat Airways as a limited partnership. They would have used this form if it had suited the tax needs of their investors.

Cooperatives. A **cooperative** (or co-op) is a business that is owned and controlled by its members, usually its customers or suppliers but sometimes its employees. Cooperatives are like corporations in terms of limited liability and continuity. The two forms differ, however, both in terms of control (usually each member of a co-op has only one vote) and in how income is distributed. The net income of a cooperative is distributed to its members in proportion to the amount each member has purchased from or supplied to the co-op during the year.

The largest cooperatives are farmer co-ops. Some, like Agway and Southern States, provide a way for farmers to buy supplies at low prices. Others, like Associated Milk Producers and Sunkist, are outlets through which the farmers' produce can be sold. Cooperatives enjoy important tax and regulatory advantages that are not available to corporations.

Consumer co-ops are less common than farmer co-ops, but they are not unknown. There are many cooperative supermarkets, such as the ones in Berkeley, California, and the Hyde Park neighborhood of Chicago. In addition, housing co-ops are found in many cities; some campuses have co-op bookstores; and parents around the country have set up cooperative day-care centers.

FORMING AND RUNNING A CORPORATION

Corporations, as we pointed out earlier, account for some 87 percent of the revenues of all private businesses. They are also more complex in structure than proprietorships or partnerships. For both these reasons, they deserve a closer look. In this section we will explain how corporations come into being, how they are structured, and how they are controlled.

Forming a Corporation

To form a corporation, one must get a charter from a state government. (National banks and a few other organizations are chartered by the federal government.) The charter is a grant of authority that allows the corporation to operate within certain guidelines, which are usually quite broad.

One of the choices to be made is that of which state to get a charter from. For a small business that will operate in a limited area, it is almost always a good idea to incorporate in the state where the firm is located. A firm can be chartered in any state, however, and states compete with one another in offering corporate charters. State laws differ in terms of taxes, regulations, limits on corporate debt, and so on. Delaware and Florida have long been favorite homes for national firms because of their favorable laws.

The application for the charter explains how the corporation will operate, how much stock it plans to issue, and other details. A modest fee may be required.

The Stockholders

After the charter has been obtained, the shares of stock are distributed to the stockholders. Some states require a corporation to have at least three stockholders, but in recent years many states have begun to charter corporations with only one stockholder. In any case, if the founder of the firm wants full control, he or she can retain, say, 98 of 100 shares of stock while distributing one each to two friends or relatives. If the purpose of

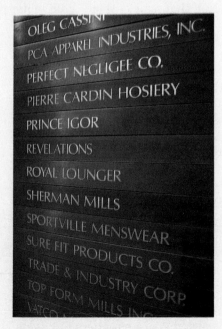

Marc P. Anderson

Closely held corporation: A corporation in which one stockholder or a close-knit group, such as a family, controls the firm by electing themselves or their allies to the board of directors.

Tender offer: An offer to buy shares of a corporation from its stockholders.

Proxy: A device by which stockholders can pledge the votes of their shares to a slate of candidates for the board of directors in a corporate election; in a proxy contest, backers of opposing slates try to collect pledges that represent a majority of the voting shares.

Common stock: Stock in a corporation that entitles the owner to a vote in the election of management and a share of the firm's profits when they are paid out as dividends.

Preferred stock: Nonvoting stock in a corporation that puts its holders first in line for dividends, ahead of holders of common stock.

choosing the corporate form of business is to bring in capital from co-owners, the shares are distributed in proportion to the amounts they contributed.

When the stock has been distributed, the stockholders must meet to elect the board of directors. Legally, the stockholders have the power to elect directors, and thus control the corporation, throughout its life. In practice, however, only stockholders who own large blocks of stock can exercise this power. Corporations in which one stockholder or a close-knit group such as a family controls the firm by electing themselves or their allies to the board of directors are called **closely held corporations**.

If there is no dominant group—for example, when the stock is widely dispersed among many stockholders—the board of directors may be quite independent. Usually in such cases stockholders are presented with a single slate of candidates for the board, and they must vote for those candidates if they bother to vote at all. Even so, the stockholders retain a latent power that can sometimes be mobilized to effect a change of management. Sometimes another company or group of individuals will make a **tender offer** for a corporation's stock, that is, they will offer to buy enough of its shares to elect its own candidates to the board of directors. In other cases the parties trying to gain control will solicit **proxies** from a firm's stockholders. Proxies are pledges to vote for a certain slate of directors. In these cases the willingness of stockholders to sell to the party making the tender offer, or to oppose the existing management in a proxy fight, determines whether the attempt to oust the existing board of directors succeeds or fails. (Case 3–1 describes a takeover battle.)

Some firms issue two kinds of stock, common and preferred. **Common stock** is the name for the ordinary shares we have discussed. These entitle the stockholder to a vote in the election of management and a share of the firm's profits when they are paid out as dividends. **Preferred stock** puts its owner first in line for dividends—nothing can be paid out to holders of common stock until holders of preferred stock have received a specified dividend. Preferred stock does not carry voting rights, however.

The Board of Directors

The board of directors approves the corporation's bylaws (its internal rules) and appoints its president and a few other top officials. The board also sets policy for the firm and makes sure top management obeys the law in running the company.

Three kinds of people sit on boards of directors. First, major stockholders often elect themselves to the board. Second, it is common for the top managers of a firm to serve as directors. And third, many corporations elect "outside" directors. These are people with special expertise or people (such as retired politicians) whose prestige and connections may be useful.

Managers appointed by the board direct the day-to-day work of the firm. The degree to which the board itself is active in management varies from one firm to another.

Corporate Growth

Most businesses that are big today started small. Many firms that are small today hope to grow large. Belief in the value of growth is ingrained in American business. Hence, it is worth looking at the various ways in which firms grow.

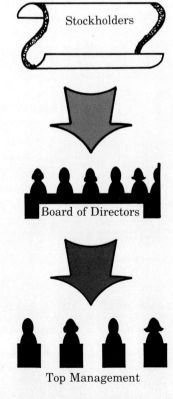

Stockholders

Board of Directors

Top Management

Retained earnings: After-tax profits that are held by a corporation for reinvestment rather than being paid out as dividends.

Internal growth.   One way to grow is to reinvest profits in new products, new plant, and new marketing efforts. Profits that are kept for this purpose, rather than being paid out as dividends, are called **retained earnings**.

Under U.S. tax laws it is often an advantage to stockholders to have the firm's earnings retained rather than paid out as dividends. If earnings are distributed, stockholders must pay personal income tax on them—even though, as explained earlier, the firm has already paid a corporate income tax. On the other hand, if retained earnings are invested in a way that increases the size and profits of the firm, the value of each share of stock rises. Stockholders can then sell their stock at a price higher than the amount they paid for it, thereby reaping a **capital gain**. Under current tax law the maximum tax rate on capital gains is only 20 percent, compared with 50 percent on dividends.

Capital gain: The profit made when a share of stock or any other asset is sold for a price higher than the amount paid for it.

Some economists have criticized the bias toward internal growth that results from the different tax rates on dividends and capital gains. They point out that internal investments may not be the best investments available. The economy as a whole would grow faster, they say, if all profits were paid out as dividends and individuals were free to reinvest them any way they chose. Whatever the merit of this argument from the point of view of the economy as a whole, the bias toward internal growth suits most corporate managers. Aside from the prestige of running a larger firm, it has been shown that the salaries of top managers are closely related to the size of the firms they run.

Growth by merger and acquisition.   The other common way for firms to grow is by buying other firms. One firm can acquire a controlling interest in another by mutual agreement, or by means of a tender offer or proxy contest. Sometimes two companies merge and become a single corporate entity. In other cases the acquired firm remains separate and becomes a **subsidiary** of the firm that acquired it. Top managers of the subsidiary are appointed by the board of directors of the parent company.

Subsidiary: A corporation that is controlled by a parent corporation that owns enough stock to enable it to appoint the subsidiary's top managers.

Mergers are a common way for firms to grow. The Norfolk Southern railway system was formed by the merger of Southern Railway and Norfolk & Western. Courtesy of Norfolk Southern Corp.

Horizontal merger: A merger between firms that compete in the same market.

Vertical merger: A merger between firms with a seller-customer relationship.

Conglomerate merger: A merger between firms in unrelated lines of business.

Antitrust laws: A set of laws that prohibit attempts to achieve a monopoly through mergers of competing firms or by other means.

One way of extending operations abroad is to establish a foreign branch like this New York office of Israel's Bank Leumi. Courtesy of Bank Leumi Trust Co. of New York

Mergers may be classified according to the relationship between the two firms. **Horizontal mergers** take place between firms that compete in the same market—two supermarket chains, for example. **Vertical mergers** take place between firms with a customer-supplier relationship, such as a supermarket chain and a meat packer. Mergers between firms in unrelated lines of business, such as a supermarket chain and an aircraft manufacturer, are known as **conglomerate mergers**.

Growth versus bigness. Although Americans have a strong tendency to think of growth as good, they also have a tendency to think of bigness as bad. Bigness is feared because it could result in monopolies in some markets, to the detriment of consumers and competitors. Bigness is also feared because economic power can often be translated into political power. In any case, a special set of laws, known as **antitrust laws**, puts limits on the ability of firms to grow.

Horizontal mergers are the most severely limited. Mergers between two competing firms that both have large market shares are rarely permitted. (If a firm is failing, however, merger with a competitor may sometimes be allowed.) Limits on vertical and conglomerate mergers are less strict, but they, too, have sometimes been challenged under antitrust law. Internal growth is the most acceptable form of growth under antitrust law. Firms have rarely been penalized for purely internal growth.

Expansion overseas. Business growth often extends across national boundaries. In 1981, total foreign investment by U.S. businesses came to $228 billion. In the same year, foreign firms had direct investments in the United States of almost $90 billion. U.S. business spent $45.5 billion on new capital investments abroad in 1981 alone. That was the equivalent of almost 10 percent of total private investment within the United States that year.

There are a number of ways for a firm to extend its operations abroad. The simplest way is to export goods made at home. Alternatively, the firm can grant a license to a foreign firm to produce its products abroad. If it wants to go beyond exporting or licensing, and carry out actual business operations abroad, it has still more choices. One is a joint venture with a foreign company. Another is to set up a foreign branch. Finally, the firm can form a foreign subsidiary, a separate corporation that operates under the laws of the host country and has its own board of directors. The parent company is able to appoint the board and control the subsidiary because it owns all or most of its stock. Chapter 23 will explore the world of international business in detail.

THE NOT-FOR-PROFIT SECTOR

Businesses, by definition, are private profit-seeking organizations. However, not all private organizations that produce goods and services are profit-seeking. There is a large not-for-profit sector that is made up of charities, churches, opera companies, universities, country clubs, and a host of other kinds of organizations. Together, according to one recent estimate, the revenues of the not-for-profit sector are about a twentieth as large as those of the business sector, and about a fifth as large as those of government.[5] Not-for-profit firms provide careers for many people. They also offer a way of getting some things done that neither government nor business can do as well.

Definition and Purpose

Not-for-profit firm: A private organization that is barred by its charter from distributing any earnings to outside ownership interests.

Not-for-profit firms are private organizations that are barred by their charters from distributing any earnings to outside owners. As such, they are different from business firms that happen not to make a profit, as well as from firms that earn profits but choose to retain them for internal growth. A not-for-profit firm is also distinct from a cooperative, which distributes its net earnings, if any, to its members.

Why do not-for-profit firms exist? In almost all cases the main purpose for which they are founded is to supply some good or service that the founders believe to be of value in itself and that is not provided, or not provided as well, by business or government. Sometimes the purpose may be lofty, as with a church or an art museum. Sometimes it may be simply to have fun, as with a fraternity or a country club.

Not-for-profit organizations like museums, colleges, and dance companies are formed to supply some good or service that is thought to be of value in itself and is not provided by business or government. Museum—Marc P. Anderson; College—© Freda Leinwand; Dance—© Falk, Monkmeyer

[5]Michelle J. White, "Introduction to the Nonprofit Sector," in Michelle J. White, ed., *Nonprofit Firms in a Three Sector Economy* (Washington, D.C.: Urban Institute, 1981), p. 1.

There is a another purpose of not-for-profit firms that helps explain why there are so many of them. That purpose is to provide jobs for the people who run them. In most not-for-profit firms the public purpose and the private interests of employees do not conflict. If a new ballet company is founded as much to give dancers a chance to dance as to entertain the public, no one sees anything wrong. Abuses sometimes come to light, of course. Sham charities, for example, have been known to devote almost all the funds they collect to paying the salaries of their officers and advertising to solicit more donations. Within reason, though, it is acceptable for people in the not-for-profit sector to do well by doing good, just as it is in the world of business.

Sources of Funds

Not-for-profit firms formed for many religious, educational, charitable, or cultural purposes have a special tax advantage that helps them raise funds. Donations to the organization can be deducted from the donors' personal income taxes. Suppose, for example, that a wealthy graduate of Linfield College, whose income is in the 40 percent tax bracket, gives $100 to the school's alumni fund. After taking the tax deduction, the donor will be out of pocket only $60. The other $40 is, in effect, a grant from the U.S. Treasury. Some organizations, such as churches, manage to collect quite a bit of money from people with low and moderate incomes who do not benefit so much from this tax break. But not-for-profits that cater mainly to the rich, such as New York's Metropolitan Opera (where seats can cost more than $50), would quickly find themselves in deep trouble if the federal tax laws were changed. In addition, not-for-profits often are exempt from local property taxes, state sales taxes, and other kinds of taxes.

It would be wrong to think of not-for-profit firms as relying solely or even primarily on donations as a source of revenue, however. No exact figures are kept, but it has been estimated that 70 percent of the total revenue of not-for-profit organizations comes from sales of goods and services.[6] In the health field, not-for-profit hospitals and nursing homes get less than 10 percent of their revenue from donations. Private schools and colleges rely on donations for only a fifth of their revenues. Nonprofit publications, such as *National Geographic* and *Consumer Reports*, bring in revenue from subscriptions and, in the former case, advertising.

Organization and Control

Almost all not-for-profit firms today are corporations. As such, they enjoy the same benefits of limited liability and legal continuity that business corporations do. There is one major difference, however: not-for-profit corporations have no stockholders. No outside owners have a claim on their net revenues or a voice in their management.

When it comes to control, not-for-profit firms fall into two classes. Some are run by independent boards of trustees or directors subject to no outside control at all. Members of these boards are free to act pretty much as they please as long as they stay within the broad purposes of the organization. Upon retirement, they choose their own successors. The

[6]Ibid., p. 2.

March of Dimes, the Educational Testing Service, the Catholic church, and many not-for-profit hospitals are of this type.

At other not-for-profit firms, day-to-day management is vested in a board of directors, but the directors are selected by members or contributors. The National Audubon Society, the American Automobile Association, country clubs, and some churches operate on this principle.[7]

Management

Despite the support they get from donations and tax advantages, not-for-profit firms cannot afford sloppy management. As Philip Kotler puts it in his book *Marketing for Nonprofit Organizations*, "To survive and succeed, organizations must know their markets, attract sufficient resources, convert these resources into appropriate products, services, and ideas, and effectively distribute them to various consuming publics."[8] Exactly the same could be said for profit-seeking business.

Case 3–2 illustrates the need for good management in not-for-profit firms. As we go though the various parts of this book—management, marketing, finance, and so on—we will make a point of emphasizing how each topic applies to not-for-profit firms.

Any study of the not-for-profit sector of the economy leads, in the end, to the question of the proper balance among business, private not-for-profit, and government organizations. In Chapter 2 we saw that socialist thinkers would prefer a shift away from private business. Supporters of free enterprise, on the other hand, call for cutbacks in the government sector. Given this clash of views, it is easy to look to the not-for-profit sector as a middle ground that should please everyone. But the not-for-profit sector has its critics too. In such fields as nursing homes, publishing, and some branches of education, profit-seeking firms tend to see not-for-profit competitors as enjoying unfair advantages. People who think income and wealth are distributed too unequally view tax-exempt museums, opera companies, and elite schools as subsidies to the rich. And some economists think not-for-profit firms are wasteful and laxly managed because they do not have to make profits. It seems that you can't please everyone.

SUMMARY

1. A *sole proprietorship* is a business that is owned, and often operated, by one person. Partly because of its simplicity, it is the most common form of business organization. Its disadvantages include unlimited liability, limited ability to raise capital, and lack of continuity upon the death of the owner.

2. A *partnership* is a voluntary legal association of two or more people for the purpose of conducting a business. Partnerships are common in the professions

of law, medicine, and accounting. Partners can pool their resources, but the partnership shares with the proprietorship the drawbacks of unlimited liability and lack of continuity. In the *limited partnership*, general partners bear full liability but limited partners do not.

3. A *corporation* is a firm that exists as an independent legal entity, with ownership divided into shares. A key advantage of the corporation is that the liability

[7]See Henry B. Hansmann, "The Role of Nonprofit Enterprise," *Yale Law Journal* 89, 5 (April 1980), pp. 835–99 for more about this classification of not-for-profit organizations.

[8]Philip Kotler, *Marketing for Nonprofit Organizations*, 2nd ed. (Englewood Cliffs, N.J.: Prentice-Hall, 1982), p. 6.

of stockholders is limited. The corporation has great power to raise capital and enjoys unlimited continuity. However, corporations are burdened with certain taxes and regulations from which proprietorships and partnerships are exempt. The subchapter S corporation, which is taxed as a partnership or proprietorship, is a popular organizational form for small businesses.

4. A number of hybrid forms of organization are tailored to specific situations. Important hybrid forms include *franchises*, *joint ventures*, *syndicates*, *limited partnerships*, and *cooperatives*.

5. The first step in forming a corporation is to get a charter. Shares of stock are then distributed to stockholders, who appoint a board of directors. The board of directors oversees the general policies of the corporation and makes sure it complies with the law. The board appoints the firm's top managers, who direct its day-to-day operations.

6. American business is strongly committed to growth. One path to growth is internal, using *retained earnings* or other sources of capital. Merger or acquisition of *subsidiaries* is another route to growth. Mergers may be *horizontal* (between firms that compete in the same market), *vertical* (between firms that have a supplier-customer relationship), or *conglomerate* (between firms in unrelated markets). Businesses can also expand abroad.

7. A *not-for-profit firm* is one that is barred by its charter from distributing net earnings to outside owners. Not-for-profit firms are usually formed to supply some good or service that the founders believe is not being provided, or not being provided well enough, by government or private business. Almost all not-for-profit firms are corporations. Some are controlled by members or donors, others by independent boards of trustees.

KEY TERMS

You should be familiar with the following terms and concepts. Check their meanings by referring to the marginal definitions in the chapter or to the glossary at the end of the book.

Sole proprietorship	Syndicate	Retained earnings
Partnership	Limited partnership	Capital gain
Corporation	Cooperative	Subsidiary
Stockholder	Closely held corporations	Horizontal merger
Venture capital market	Tender offer	Vertical merger
Limited liability	Proxy	Conglomerate merger
Subchapter S corporation	Common stock	Antitrust laws
Franchise	Preferred stock	Not-for-profit firm
Joint venture		

QUESTIONS FOR REVIEW AND DISCUSSION

1. Reread the story of Hester Nettles' business, The Scribe, which opened Chapter 1. Note that the firm was incorporated when it was moved from the Nettles' basement, but after the December 1982 liquidation it returned to the proprietorship form. On the basis of the information provided, comment on The Scribe's form at each stage of its existence.

2. Look around your community for one example each of a proprietorship, a partnership, and a corporation. Do you think the chosen form of organization is the best one for each of these businesses? Why or why not?

3. A friend who is a very good cook says to you, "Say, you've studied business, let's get together and start a restaurant. I can borrow some money from my family, I can run the kitchen, and you can handle the business end of things." You think it sounds like a great idea. What form of organization do you think you would choose for the business? Why?

4. During the summer you visit a relative who runs a good-sized apple orchard. You find out, somewhat to your surprise, that the business is not incorporated. "Why not incorporate?" you say. "You would limit your liability, have less trouble raising capital, and remove a limit on the continuity of your business." Your relative replies, "I've given it some thought, but in my situation it just isn't worth the trouble." Complete the dialogue, with you arguing for incorporation and your relative arguing against it.

5. Visit the office of a broker or investment adviser in your community (look in the Yellow Pages under "Investment" or "Stockbroker"). Explain that for a class project you would like to look at a prospectus for an investment opportunity in the form of a limited partnership. Describe the venture the firm will engage in. How will it raise money? What risks are borne by the general and limited partners? What tax advantages are offered to the limited partners? Why was the limited partnership form chosen for this venture?

6. Are there any cooperative businesses in your community? What about supermarkets, day-care centers, housing, or agricultural supply co-ops? If you can find such a business, learn what you can about it. How does one become a member? How are net earnings distributed? Who controls the co-op?

7. How would you classify each of these mergers or acquisitions: That of DuPont, a maker of petroleum-based chemicals, and Conoco, an oil company? That of Mobil Corporation and Montgomery Ward? That of Peugeot, the French automaker, and American Motors?

8. Examine the structure and operation of at least one not-for-profit firm in your community. You might choose your own school (if it is private and not-for-profit), a church, a social club, a charity, or whatever you want. Where does the organization get its money? Who controls it? Whom does it serve? What sorts of goods or services does it provide? What tax advantages, if any, does it enjoy? Does it face any competition from profit-seeking firms or from government agencies? If so, what advantages, if any, does it have over them?

Case 3–1: Supermerger

Mergers are often friendly affairs in which managers of the two companies see benefits to be gained from joining forces. Not all mergers are friendly, however. Hostile takeovers are also common. When DuPont, fifteenth on the *Fortune* list of the 500 largest industrial companies, bought Conoco, number fourteen on the *Fortune* list, it was the biggest merger battle in U.S. business history. It was also one of the most fiercely fought—at one point three corporations were bidding for Conoco.

The contest started in the spring of 1981. At that time Conoco stock was trading at about $50 per share, even though analysts believed the firm's oil and coal reserves to be worth up to $150 per share. It looked like a bargain.

First to go after the bait was Seagram, a comparative pigmy at 220 on the *Fortune* 500 list. Seagram made a tender offer for Conoco at $73 a share. But Conoco's managers couldn't get Seagram to guarantee that the offer was "friendly"; that is, it couldn't get Seagram to promise not to kick out Conoco's management as soon as it gained control.

So Conoco's managers went hunting for a "white knight." In merger parlance, a white knight is a friendly firm that comes in to outbid a firm that has made a hostile tender offer, thus saving the jobs of the target firm's managers. DuPont was persuaded to make an offer, seeing Conoco's oil and coal as useful raw materials for its chemical products.

DuPont offered $87.50 a share. Seagram countered, and the bidding soon reached $98 per share. At that point Mobil (number two on the *Fortune* list) made a surprise bid of $105 per share, which it soon upped to $120. That was a handsome

$22 per share better than DuPont's best offer. Could Conoco's stockholders resist?

They could and did. The U.S. Justice Department's antitrust division announced that it would have to take a close look at a merger between the two large oil companies. Conoco's stockholders decided that $22 per share wasn't worth the risk that the Justice Department would forbid the merger. In the end the white knight rode off with the lady.

Questions:

1. What does this case tell you about the relative power of Conoco's managers and its shareholders to control the fate of the company?

2. Classify the Mobil, DuPont, and Seagram offers as horizontal, vertical, or conglomerate.

Case 3–2: Dreams Depend on Money

The 1980s are perilous times for opera in America. The troubled New York City Opera is more than $2 million in the hole. Atlanta's Civic Opera canceled its 1982–83 season, and Colorado's Central City Opera couldn't scare up the money to perform in 1982, the opera's fiftieth-anniversary season.

In 1980 Chicago's Lyric Opera seemed to be on its last legs too. Its founder, Carol Fox, was dying and the company was deep in debt. The opera's patrons were distressed, its props warehouse mortgaged.

By 1983, however, the Lyric was thriving once more, setting an example, perhaps, for other companies around the country. The opera's 1982 season was 98 percent sold out. The Lyric had $1.1 million in the bank. Patrons were pleased, and critics were too. The Lyric owes it all to cost cutting, computers, and Ardis Krainik, its new general manager.

Krainik, who once sang mezzo in the chorus and occasional solo parts, cares about art but also about money. "Every decision has a financial repercussion as well as an artistic one. This is a business," she says.

What Krainik does with her computer printouts has everything to do with opera, because without them the Lyric would probably be defunct. By pushing everyone's nose into those printouts and challenging people to come in under budget, she has them searching for bargains for the first time. No longer are all wigs and costumes imported from Italy, regardless of cost. And by doing its own proofreading and scouting for low bids, the Lyric cut $32,000 from its printing budget.

Asked about the future she sees for the Lyric, Krainik waxes passionate. She speaks of baroque operas, new American composers, world premieres, discovering great young singing talent, and a longer season. But she stops herself to say, "For now, this is dreaming. Dreams depend on money."

Source: Based on Meg Cox, "Scaling Back," *Wall Street Journal*, June 3, 1983, p. 1. Reprinted by permission of the Wall Street Journal. © Dow Jones & Company, Inc., 1983. All Rights Reserved.

Questions:

1. What does this case tell you about the differences and similarities between business and not-for-profit organizations?

2. What are the Lyric's major sources of income? If it takes in more than it spends during a season, what happens to the money?

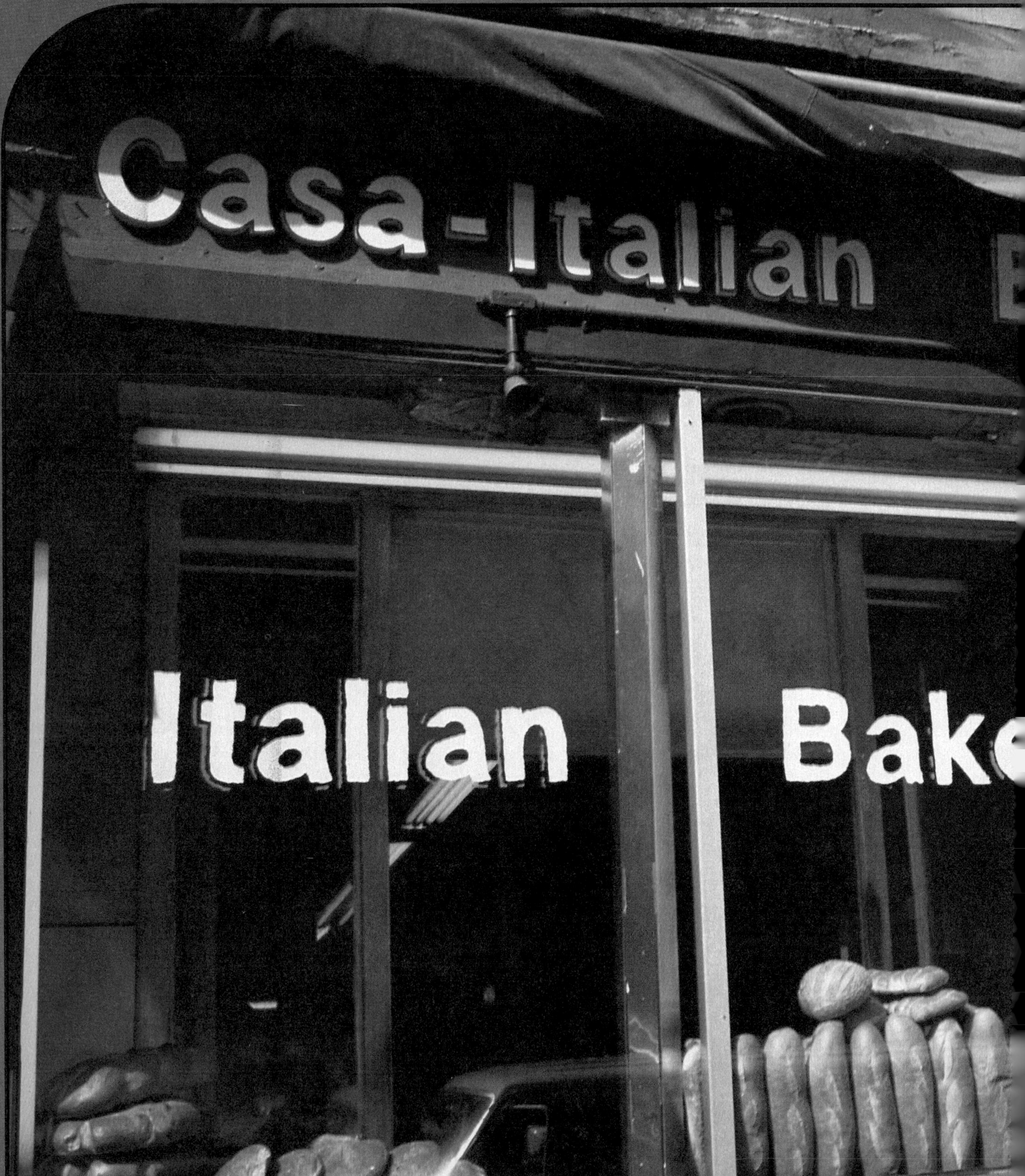
Casa-Italian
Italian
Bak

Chapter 4

SMALL BUSINESS IN THE U.S. ECONOMY

When you have completed this chapter, you should be able to

- Define small business and discuss its importance in terms of jobs, sales, and innovation.

- Discuss the advantages and disadvantages of small business compared with large business.

- Explain some of the reasons for failure of small businesses.

- Give some guidelines for starting and managing a small business.

- Explain the advantages and disadvantages of franchising from the points of view of both the franchisor and the franchisee, and give some guidelines for successful franchising.

In 1983 Louis and Frederick Ruiz were named small businessmen of the year. Their advice to entrepreneurs is to work hard and concentrate on quality. Courtesy of Ruiz Food Products, Inc.

In 1964 Louis Ruiz' son Frederick had just graduated from high school. The two of them decided to start a small business. They had noticed that the frozen-food sections of the supermarkets in Tulare, California, where they lived, were not well stocked with Mexican food, despite the growing popularity of frozen food in general and Mexican food in particular. It looked like a good opportunity. There were a few minor problems to be faced, to be sure. For one thing, Ruiz "didn't have a cent." In addition, he didn't know how to cook. "I had never even fried an egg before," he admits.

Even so, the father-son team plunged ahead. For a few hundred dollars they bought an old stove, a refrigerator, and a freezer. Adding the mixer from the family kitchen, they opened shop in a small warehouse. Their first products were frozen bean and cheese enchiladas, which they marketed under the trade name "Rosita-Si."

People seemed to like their enchiladas. The business started to grow and kept on growing. Soon it moved to a roomier 1400-square-foot building and then, in 1977, to an 11,500-square-foot location. In 1983 the two entrepreneurs began construction of still more offices and storage facilities. By this time the company also had warehouses in Oregon, Texas, and Canada.

Employment and sales grew, too. In 1982 the company logged sales of $9.6 million and was providing jobs for 200 people. *Inc. Magazine* listed Ruiz Foods as number 172 on its list of the fastest-growing privately held companies in the country. In 1983 Louis and Frederick Ruiz were named small-businessmen of the year by the Small Business Administration. They went to Washington to receive the award from President Reagan.

Father and son are active in community affairs. They make a special point of hiring the disadvantaged, offer their workers a management training course, and maintain a full-service day-care center. Employees also benefit from a stock ownership plan. "Our employees are our biggest asset," says Ruiz.

What is Ruiz' advice to entrepreneurs who are just starting out? Work hard and focus on quality. "Don't throw in the towel," he says. "People start a business thinking they'll get a pile of money rapidly, but that isn't true. It's a struggle."[1]

[1]Based on materials provided by the Small Business Administration.

X **Small business**: A business that is independently owned and operated and is not dominant in its field.

X Ruiz Foods is a small business—one of millions in the American economy. According to one widely used definition, a **small business** is one that has at least two of the following features.

1. Independent management
2. Owner-supplied capital
3. A local area of operation
4. Small size relative to its industry.[*]

[*]Researchers and government agencies also sometimes use numerical definitions. Often, for example, firms with fewer than 100 employees (fewer than 500 for manufacturing firms) are classified as "small." In applying numerical definitions, it is important to distinguish be-

However one defines it, small business is important to the U.S. economy. Box 4–1 shows, for example, that firms with fewer than 500 employees accounted for 45.3 percent of sales by all businesses in 1980. Measured in this way, the importance of small business varied from one sector of the economy to another. Agriculture, construction, wholesale and retail trade, and services are dominated by small businesses. In manufacturing, however, more than half of total sales are by firms with more than 10,000 workers.

Box 4–1 Small Business in the U.S. Economy

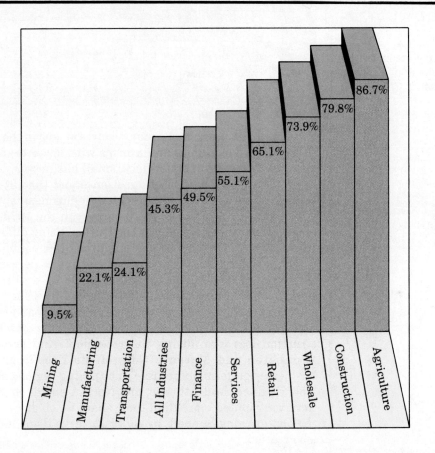

In 1980, small firms, here defined as firms with fewer than 500 employees, accounted for 45.3 percent of total sales of U.S. businesses. The role of small business is not the same in all parts of the economy. The sectors of agriculture, construction, wholesale and retail trade, and services are dominated by small firms. Mining, manufacturing, and transportation are dominated by large firms. Still, many small firms succeed in these industries by doing certain things that big firms can't do as well.

Source: Executive Office of the President, *State of Small Business*, (Washington, D.C.: Government Printing Office, 1983), p. 53.

tween independent small firms, on the one hand, and business establishments that are small but not independent, on the other. The latter include branches of banks, retail stores, and other large businesses. These establishments resemble small businesses on the surface and are lumped with independent small businesses in some government statistics.

Small businesses have accounted for more than their share of new jobs in recent years. © Jonathan Selig, Peter Arnold

Small businesses are a major source of jobs in the American economy. About a third of all jobs are in firms with fewer than 100 employees.[2] In terms of the creation of new jobs, small businesses seem to be even more important. One study of job creation found that from 1976 to 1980, 56 percent of all new jobs were created by businesses with fewer than 100 workers.[3] This figure rose to 70 percent in the 1978–80 period.[4] A more recent study by the Brookings Institution, using different methods, found the small business share of new jobs to be 51 percent for 1976–80.[5] Interestingly, all these jobs were created by about 15 percent of all small firms.

Small-business employment also held up well in the 1981–82 recession. Of the 2,649,000 jobs lost between July 1981 and December 1982, more than 90 percent were lost in sectors that are dominated by big business. Of the sectors that are dominated by small business, only construction lost jobs during the recession. And according to Catherine Armington and Marjorie Odle of the Brookings Institution, small businesses perform a vital role in declining regions of the country. In the New England, Mid-Atlantic, and North Central states, small businesses have contributed more than their share to job growth in recent years. In the fast-growing Sunbelt, by contrast, large firms have taken the lead in job creation.[6]

[2]Executive Office of the President, *The State of Small Business* (Washington, D.C.: Government Printing Office, 1983), p. 35.

[3]David L. Birch, "The Job Generation Process" (Cambridge, Mass.: MIT Program on Neighborhood and Regional Change, 1979).

[4]David L. Birch and Susan MacCracken, "The Small Business Share of Job Creation," report on research prepared for the Office of Advocacy, SBA, under contract no. SBA-5654-OA081 (Washington, D.C., November 1982).

[5]Unpublished research by Catherine Armington and Marjorie Odle, cited in *The State of Small Business*, p. 87.

[6]Catherine Armington and Marjorie Odle, "Sources of Job Growth," *Economic Development Commentary*, Fall 1982, pp. 3–7.

Finally, small businesses are an important source of innovation. This has been true ever since the Wright brothers, working in their bicycle shop, invented the airplane. It remains true today in the electronics industry. Box 4–2 lists sixty-five major innovations that have come from small businesses in the twentieth century. Not only do small businesses contribute at least their share of innovations; they also get them to market faster. In a small firm there are fewer people with the power to say no to a new idea. As a result, according to one recent study, small firms bring innovations to market almost a year sooner, on the average, than large firms.[7]

In this chapter we will take a close look at the dynamic world of small business. We will discuss the reasons that small firms succeed and fail, and give some guidelines for starting one. We will devote a special section to franchising, one of the most popular forms of small business. Then, throughout the book, we will return to the theme of small business in our discussions of management, marketing, operations, and finance.

HOW SMALL BUSINESSES SUCCEED AND FAIL

It is clear from what we have said so far that small business has been successful in carving out a place for itself in the U.S. economy. How does it manage in the face of the sometimes awesome power of the giants and supergiants? As we will see in this section, small business succeeds both by competing with large business and by complementing it. Small firms compete with large ones by being faster on their feet, by staying closer to customers, and sometimes by keeping costs lower. They complement big business by supplying parts and special services and by providing them with distribution channels. In this section we will discuss the factors that determine why and where small business succeeds.

First, however, we should note that although small business as a whole is successful, not all small businesses are. In fact, fewer than half of them live to see their fifth birthday. Readers who have any desire to start businesses of their own will want to pay attention to our discussion of the factors leading to the success or failure of a small firm. We will see, not surprisingly, that the key factor is management.

Advantages of Small Business

Small businesses cannot compete well in all markets. The first rule for success in small business, then, is to find a market in which being small is an advantage rather than a handicap. Situations in which smallness is an advantage include the following.

Size of market. Some markets are limited in size. Some goods, such as fresh flowers, can't be transported very far because they don't last long enough. Some, like bricks, are too heavy to ship far at a reasonable cost.

[7]Gellman Research Associates, Inc., "The Relationship Between Concentration, Firm Size, and Technical Innovation," prepared for the Office of Advocacy, U.S. Small Business Administration under award no. SBA-2633-OA-79 (Jenkintown, Pa.: May 1982), cited in *The State of Small Business*, pp. 122–23.

Box 4–2 Sixty-five Major Innovations by Small Firms

Acoustic suspension speakers	Link trainer
Aerosol can	Nuclear magnetic resonance scanner
Air conditioning	Nuclear magnetic resonance spectrometer
Airplane	Optical scanner
Articulated tractor chassis	Oral contraceptives
Artificial skin	Outboard engine
Assembly line	Overnight national delivery
Automatic fabric cutting	Pacemaker
Automatic transfer equipment	Personal computer
Bakelite	Photo typesetting
Biosynthetic insulin	Piezo electrical devices
Catalytic petroleum cracking	Polaroid camera
Computerized blood pressure controller	Precast concrete
Continuous casting	Prefabricated housing
Cotton picker	Pressure-sensitive cellophane tape
Defibrillator	Programmable computer
Double-knit fabric	Quick-frozen food
Dry chemical fire extinguisher	Reading machine
Electrical wire nuts	Rotary oil drilling bit
Fiber optic examination equipment	Safety razor
Fluid flow meter	Six-axis robot arm
Foam fire extinguisher	Soft contact lenses
Front-end loader	Sonar fish monitoring
Gas chromatograph	Spectrographic grid
Geodesic dome	Stereoscopic map scanner
Gyrocompass	Strain gauge
Hand-held fluoroscope	Strobe lights
Heart valve	Vacuum tube
Heat sensor	Variable output transformer
Helicopter	Winchester disk drive
Hetrodyne radio	Xerography
Hydraulic brake	Zipper
Large-capacity computer	

Courtesy of Talon, Inc.

Courtesy of Sikorsky Aircraft

Small firms are a major source of innovation in the U.S. economy. They also, on the average, bring innovations to market faster than large firms. For this list, a small business is defined as one with fewer than 500 employees. The innovation is assigned to the firm that first made a sale based on it.

Source: *State of Small Business*, p. 127.

And when the customer must come to the business, as in the case of hairstyling, restaurants, retail trade, and many other businesses, being small is a big advantage. All of these advantages are related to geographic limits, but some small firms do well by selling very specialized products to a few customers throughout the nation. You wouldn't think automobile manufacturing would be a good bet for a small business. Yet the maker of the Avanti has carved out a tiny niche for itself in the massive auto industry.

For some kinds of businesses, small size is essential. © Freda Leinwand

Innovation and change. Small firms have the advantage of being fast on their feet. In industries where styles or technologies change quickly, small firms can outmaneuver large ones. In the clothing industry, for example, there are many small firms not only in retailing but also in design and manufacturing. Small firms in high-tech industries also can sometimes beat out large ones. The giant IBM was a latecomer to the booming personal computer market. New firms like Apple got there first. When IBM finally did enter the field, its product proved very popular—so popular that the company couldn't meet the demand for it. The time it took IBM to get its assembly lines up to speed gave several small competitors a chance to sell to those unwilling to wait for IBM.

The personal touch. In some kinds of business small firms gain an advantage by offering a personal touch. In the case of a restaurant owner, time spent talking to customers can make them feel noticed and reveal a lot about their likes and dislikes. In many retail and service firms, social contacts at clubs and churches grow into business contacts. A personal relationship with employees can be an advantage too. Workers who are on a first-name basis with the boss often perform better than the employees of large, unionized companies. Finally, in firms where the owner's skills are central—a dental practice or auto repair shop—customers may like dealing with the top person rather than with a hired assistant.

Disadvantages of Small Business

Although small firms have some major advantages, they have some serious drawbacks, too. Some markets are tough ones for small firms. This is true for several reasons.

Unequal access to resources.   Small firms do not always compete with large ones on a level playing field. This is nowhere more true than in capital markets. Banks and other sources of loans view small businesses as greater risks than large ones, on the average. Thus, a small building contractor may have to pay a higher interest rate than a big developer. Also, small businesses often cannot take advantage of the volume discounts offered by suppliers. Sometimes they complain that they can hardly get the suppliers to notice them at all. (In some cases, small firms have formed buying cooperatives to overcome this disadvantage.) Local retailers complain that shopping mall owners prefer branches of big chains as tenants. Bankers and suppliers often have sound business reasons for acting as they do. But that does not lessen the frustration of the small-business owner.

Economies of scale: A situation in which the average cost per unit of output falls as the rate of output rises.

Lack of economies of scale.   A business is said to achieve **economies of scale** if its average cost per unit of output falls as its rate of output rises. Lack of economies of scale is one of the chief reasons for the low proportion of small businesses in manufacturing. Small firms can survive in an industry with major economies of scale only if this disadvantage can be offset by one of the advantages listed earlier. (See Case 4–1 for an example.)

Lack of internal specialization.   Specialization can be an advantage for a small firm when it means zeroing in on a small market segment that has been ignored by the biggies. But small businesses suffer a disadvantage when they lack *internal* specialization. A small-business owner has to wear many hats. If you were a top-notch writer of ad copy, for example, you could spend all your time doing just that if you worked for a big agency. But if you started an agency of your own, much of your time would be spent seeking clients, keeping the firm's books, settling problems with your landlord, and so on. You might not be very good at those other things, and the time they took away from your writing would hurt your business.

Government regulations.   The burden of government regulation on businesses of all sizes has increased greatly in the last twenty years. Many studies have shown that the burden on small firms is especially heavy.[8] Regulations often impose fixed costs that are about the same for businesses of all sizes. These costs may take the form of reports to file, safety equipment to install, and inspections to prepare for. Large businesses can spread these costs over many more units of output than small ones can. Large firms can also hire legal specialists and accountants to take care of these matters. The small-business owner is likely to have to do the job after the shop is closed, and not do it as well as a trained specialist would.

Small-business owner Jimmy Carter made reducing the burden of regulation on small business a key policy of his presidency. Free-enterpriser Ronald Reagan made the same pledge. Despite these good intentions, however, progress has been slow.

None of the disadvantages or advantages of small business is total. Some industries, as we have seen, are dominated by small firms because one or more advantages of small business apply throughout the market. Other industries are dominated by large firms. But even in those industries one can almost always find a few pigmies scrambling around among the feet of the giants.

[8]Several such studies are cited in *The State of Small Business*, chap. 7.

✗Survival and Failure Among Small Businesses

The failure rate among small businesses is very high. The smaller the business, the higher the rate. A new business in the smallest size class, zero to nine employees, has little more than a 75 percent chance of surviving for a year, and only about one chance in three of lasting four years or more. Firms that are only slightly larger, with at least twenty employees, have a first-year survival rate of over 95 percent and a four-year survival rate of over 50 percent.[9]

Business failures.   Thousands of firms go out of business every year. Most of them do so voluntarily, often at the death of a proprietor or partner. Other firms are dissolved because their owners see better opportunities in another line of business or choose to go to work for someone else.

When a business closes voluntarily, whatever the firm owns is sold and its debts are paid. Whatever is left over belongs to the owner or owners. If the firm was doing well, the owners may end up with many times the sum they invested in it. If the business was a marginal one, they

The smallest businesses have a very low survival rate; many fold in less than a year. © Freda Leinwand

[9]These approximations are based on the data given on pp. 70 and 71 of *The State of Small Business.*

Business failure: A firm that goes out of business without paying all its debts.

Bankruptcy: Legal recognition of a business failure through the filing of a petition with a federal bankruptcy court.

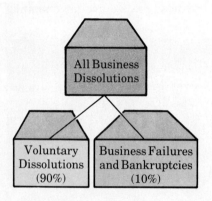

All Business Dissolutions

Voluntary Dissolutions (90%)

Business Failures and Bankruptcies (10%)

may end up with less than they put into it. In any event, the firm's creditors get back everything they were owed, and the owners get back at least part of what they invested.

If a firm that is going out of business cannot raise the money to pay its debts, it is classified as a **business failure**. In such a case the firm's creditors, who have first claim on everything the firm owns, lose at least part of what is owed to them, and the owners lose their entire investment. (In the case of partnerships or proprietorships, whose owners do not have limited liability, creditors may make claims against the personal property of the owners.) Sometimes a failed business is dissolved by mutual agreement, with the creditors accepting the best percentage they can get of what is owed to them. In other cases either the owners or the creditors may file a petition of **bankruptcy** with a federal court. Then the court decides how to dispose of the failed firm's assets.[*]

Why businesses fail.   Most businesses fail because of bad management. In many cases the mistake was to start a business that had no chance of success. Other new enterprises are viable in themselves, but they fail because the people in charge of them lack experience or skill. In still other cases an entrepreneur may do almost everything right, only to be done in by one fatal mistake in the first year of business, when the margin for error is paper-thin. There are so many ways in which bad management can ruin a new business, in fact, that it is almost a truism to call this the chief cause of business failure. Almost any cause of failure, short of a flood or tornado, could be linked to bad management.

Bad management is, we should say, the story one gets from professional observers of the small-business scene. If you ask the failed managers themselves, you get a different story. Many say they could not raise enough capital. Others blame competition, bad-debt losses, recession, poor location, or a dozen other causes. When one takes a closer look, however, these explanations do not always hold up. If the manager had made a realistic assessment of the amount of capital needed or the strength of the competition, perhaps the business would not have been started. A shortage of capital could also mean that capital was wasted on fancy office furniture and poorly chosen inventory. Excessive competition could mean inadequate sales efforts. Bad debts could mean lack of caution in granting credit. In short, the many apparent causes of small-business failures may be nothing more than symptoms of weak management.

Somehow, though, stories of business failures fail to scare off would-be entrepreneurs. For every two small firms that go out of business, three are started. It's a good thing, too, since we have seen that the economy needs small business. Let's turn, then, from the topic of failure to that of how to start a small business and how to run it right.

STARTING AND MANAGING A SMALL BUSINESS

In Chapter 3 we covered some of the mechanics of starting a new business. These include choosing a form of organization, raising capital, and ap-

[*] As Chapter 22 will explain, bankrupt firms are not always forced out of business. In a so-called Chapter 11 bankruptcy, the court can order that the business be *reorganized*. In such cases, creditors receive part of what is owed to them and the firm, with a reduced debt burden, continues to operate.

plying for a corporate charter, if necessary. In this section we want to look at some more concrete questions. The first is whether you are the kind of person who should start a business at all. The second is what kind of business to start. The third is whether to start from scratch or buy an existing firm. Once these start-up questions have been answered, we will say a little about managing a small business and about sources of help for managers of small businesses.

Are You the Type?

If you are like many people, you will think about starting a business of your own at one time or another. The freedom of working for yourself instead of for a boss is one major attraction. The desire to create something that is really your own, and to see your own name over the door, is another. The belief that you can do a job better, more cheaply, or more cleverly is still another. And even though you may know that successful small firms often earn no more than a decent living for their owners, you know that the sky is the limit.

Realistically, though, you will have to consider the drawbacks too.

1. *Long hours.* You will have to put in long hours, especially in the first year. You won't be able to come home and leave your troubles at the office. You may not have a boss anymore, but you will have traded your boss for a set of suppliers and customers who will have you at their beck and call; they will be people whom you simply cannot afford to ignore or offend.

2. *Responsibility.* You will be fully responsible for everything that goes on in your business. You will have to make decisions yourself. You will have to live with your mistakes, and you will have to get used to the fact that there is no one to give you a gold star when you do something right. You will not have the moral support of co-workers.

3. *Being a generalist.* You will have to become a generalist. There will be many hours each day when your special skills as a designer, engineer, salesperson, or whatever will go to waste as you interview job seekers, balance the books, or wheedle credit from suppliers. You will have to do some things you don't like to do and don't do well, and sometimes you will have to do business with people you would just as soon never see again.

4. *Financial problems.* You will have a whole new set of financial problems. You will put a big part of your savings at risk and you may lose it all. You may not be able to pay yourself a regular salary for some time. And you and your family will have to adjust to the constant thought that every dollar you spend on yourself is money that might have been reinvested in the business.

If you read through that list and say, "No problem, I can handle that," you are ready for the next step.

What Line of Business?

The next thing you need to decide is what line of business to go into. The key questions to be answered are these.

- What do you want to do?
- What are you able to do?
- What will customers buy at a price that will yield a profit?

Many, if not most, businesses that fail do so because the owner plunged in without a satisfactory answer to one or more of these questions. For example, if you are shy and work best alone, you could be miserable in a business that depends on daily, face-to-face selling. And many small retail shops are doomed the day they open because no serious thought was given to whether customers in the area wanted to buy their goods at a price that would cover costs.

Another common mistake is not to choose clearly among a number of lines of business. Perhaps you have seen little shops that display, say, saddles and bridles in the front of the store (but not as good a selection as that offered by the specialty shop down the street); an assortment of interesting but slow-moving antiques in the back; and a collection of homemade breads and jellies on the counter beside the cash register. Then, when you go in to buy a jar of jelly (on which the store will make a profit of a dime), you can't get waited on because the owner is on the phone selling real estate to someone. Such a shop may be useful as a way to keep the owner busy, but as a way of making money it doesn't have a chance.

Buy or Start from Scratch?

Going into business doesn't have to mean starting from scratch. Once you have decided what line of business to enter, you may be able to buy an existing firm. Box 4–3 shows some of the businesses advertised in one issue of the *Washington Post*. One of the firms was as old as twenty-five years, one as young as three months. Some were for sale by their owners, others by brokers. If you read the ads in your area and contact some of the brokers listed, you will uncover quite a variety of business opportunities.

Advantages of buying.   Buying a business, rather than starting from scratch, can have several advantages.

One major advantage is that less planning is required. You can start with what the old owner sells you and make improvements as you go along.

A second advantage may be a faster return on your investment. With a new business, it is often a year or two before the owner can take out any steady income. But with an existing business there may already be a flow of profits to draw upon.

A third advantage is reduced risk. As noted earlier, the rate of business failure is high in the first year. If the business has been around awhile, you at least know that it is not in the "hopeless from the start" category. But as we will see, buying a business has risks of its own.

Disadvantages of buying.   Buying a business can have drawbacks as well as advantages. First, you may not be able to find a business that exactly fits your plans. This may more than offset the advantage of not having to do all the planning yourself. Sometimes you can change a business so as to make it work for you. But it's better to start your own firm and get what you want than to buy one that is not right for you.

Box 4–3 Business Opportunities—A Sampler

FAST FOOD IN VA
PIZZA—Alex. $15K/mo. receipts.
MEXICAN—52 seats, $28K dn.
CHILI—So. of Beltway, $20k dn.
ICE CREAM/FAST FD—$25K dn.
SUBS—Franchise, $20K/mo.
DELI/GROC—Arl. $175K, 3 seats.
LOUDON CO—60 seat $140K rcpts
DELI/C'OUT—23 seat $15K dn
WINE/CHEESE—Alex. $116K Gr.
VR BUSINESS BROKERS

Many people prefer to enter the world of small business by buying an existing firm rather than starting from scratch. This box shows the businesses advertised for sale in one day's issue of the *Washington Post*. Which would you call first if you were thinking of going into business?

Source: *Washington Post*, June 15, 1983, p. C-24.

Second—and this is the biggest risk—the firm you buy may have some hidden defects. Why is the owner selling it? Suppose a restaurant has been profitable for twenty years and the owners say they want to sell it and retire to Florida. That sounds reasonable. But maybe they know, and you

The advantages of buying a business, rather than starting from scratch, include simplified planning, a faster return on investment, and reduction of risk. © Freda Leinwand

don't, that many of the people who have eaten there for the past twenty years are retiring and moving away too. It is impossible to imagine all the hidden problems in a business that is for sale. And don't count on the firm's books to reveal them to you. Just be cautious, and if you are in doubt, seek professional advice.

Third, when you buy an existing business you have to buy the bad along with the good. You hope to buy the goodwill of customers and suppliers—but you may also buy the bad will of those whom the previous owner has offended. You hope to buy access to a skilled labor force—but you may have to take some duds that are hard to get rid of. You should be especially careful about plant and equipment. It may all be in working order, but it may also be obsolete. Maybe the owner knew this before deciding to sell. Maybe a new business, with state-of-the-art equipment, will be a better buy.

How much to pay? Suppose the business looks sound and the owner's reasons for selling make sense. You still have the problem of deciding how much to pay. The best business in the world won't make money for you if you pay too much for it.

Figuring out the value of a business is a specialty, one that is far beyond the scope of this chapter. The basic concepts are simple, however. In valuing a business you look at three things: its **assets**, its **liabilities**, and its profit potential.

Asset: Anything of value that a firm owns.

Assets are all the things of value the firm owns. In valuing a firm's assets you add together the value of any real estate it owns, its equipment, its inventories, and so on. Make sure the values placed on old equipment and old inventories are realistic. The price these assets would bring if they were sold piecemeal gives you a rock-bottom value for the business.

Liability: Anything a firm owes to anyone.

The firm's liabilities are everything it owes to anyone. These include long-term debts such as mortgages, and short-term debts such as wages owed to workers and sums owed to suppliers.

Usually you will have to pay more for a firm than the value of its assets minus the value of its liabilities. The assets plus the skills of employees, the goodwill of customers, the network of supplier contacts, and so on add up to profit potential. Suppose you determine that the firm you want to buy will, if you run it at least as well as its former owner did, make a profit of $30,000 per year. The owner is asking $100,000. Is the business worth it?

Opportunity cost: The value of the best alternative way of using the time and capital put into a firm by its owner or owners.

To answer this question you have to compare the profit potential of the firm with the **opportunity cost** of buying and running it. The opportunity cost of going into business is the value of the best alternative way of putting your time and money to work. In your case, suppose the best alternative use for your time is keeping your present job, which pays $25,000 a year. The best alternative use for your equity capital (that is, the savings you would use to buy the business) is, let's say, a $100,000 certificate of deposit paying 10 percent interest, or $10,000 per year. Thus the total opportunity cost of buying the business is $25,000 in salary plus $10,000 in interest.

Is it worth it to give up $35,000 a year in salary and interest earnings in order to buy a $30,000-a-year profit potential? You be the judge. It might be if you place at least a $5,000-a-year value on the pleasures of working for yourself. Lots of people do. It might be if you really think you could make the firm more profitable by managing it better than its previous owner did. But on the face of it $100,000 is too high a price for the business we have just described. In fact, you would only barely break even if you got it for $50,000.*

Getting Started

When you have decided what business to enter and whether to buy or start from scratch, the next set of tasks must be faced. Many handbooks will guide you through such details as picking a location, getting permits, and hiring workers.

A location, equipment, and employees are obvious needs of a new business. Three others may be less obvious but are no less important. They are a banker, an accountant, and a lawyer. These specialists are needed by almost any business, no matter how much the owner knows. They are also hard to shop for and easy to misuse.

The first rule in shopping for these resources is to look for people who are willing to deal with small firms. Find out who their other clients are. Make certain they really want your business. Don't pick your banker, lawyer, or accountant just because they are close to your store—gas is cheap compared with what the wrong lawyer or accountant can cost you.

The second rule is to treat your banker, lawyer, and accountant as tools—don't expect them to make decisions for you. Expect them to help you solve financial, tax, and legal problems, but don't expect them to save you from having to think about them at all. Your accountant, for example, can offer advice in setting up bookkeeping and payroll systems, but you should run those systems yourself.

The third rule is to avoid conflicts with any of these key friends and their aids. You are going to have enough adversaries without adding three more! If you find yourself at war with one of these experts, it may be simply that you have forgotten that they are running businesses too. Don't expect them to help you in ways that will not make profits for both of you. It may also be that you have simply picked the wrong people—they don't under-

> Tuesday, June 19, 1979, 2:00 P.M.
> *I have just fired my accountant. I am disappointed in him for letting me down, with disastrous results for the business. I am angry with myself for my incompetence. I didn't know enough about what he should have been doing to know that he wasn't doing the job right. I feel betrayed—I trusted the man absolutely. I feel stupid—I not only trusted him, I relinquished to him responsibility that, as the owner and manager of my business, is essentially mine, and mine alone. Unfortunately, I cannot rationalize my way out of it—I am responsible for the mess.*
>
> —Irene Smith, *Diary of a Small Business*

Source: Irene Smith, *Diary of a Small Business* (New York: Charles Scribner's Sons, 1982), p. 83.

In choosing a lawyer, accountant, or banker, a small-business owner should look for someone who feels comfortable about dealing with small firms. © Freda Leinwand

*Note that the idea of comparing expected profits with opportunity cost is just as important when starting a new business as when buying an old one.

stand your business, or you have a personality conflict. If so, close the account and move on. Your customers feel free to leave you when you don't meet their needs. Feel free to do the same.[10]

Managing the Business

Once your business in under way, you must manage it. Concentrate on the basics. Small businesses should not imitate big-business methods. Many of the advantages that small firms have over large ones depend on doing things differently, not on imitating the giants on a small scale. For example, one key advantage of small business is being quick to react to opportunities. If you hire consultants, or insist on holding long meetings before you make decisions, that advantage is lost. You will have much more success if you stay close to your customers and find out what they want and need. If you do make mistakes, you can correct them faster than your big rivals can.

Government Aid

Although government does not always treat small business kindly (see our earlier comments on regulation), small business does have a friend in Washington. That friend is the Small Business Administration (SBA). The SBA was created by Congress in 1953 to help entrepreneurs get into business and to help those already in business to stay there. The SBA works to make the concerns of small firms known to other government agencies through its Office of Small Business Advocacy. It also helps businesses directly in a variety of ways. Some SBA programs are targeted toward firms that are owned by women and members of minority groups.

√*Financial assistance.* The SBA was not set up to replace private sources of capital. By law, any firm that applies to the SBA for financial aid must first apply to a bank or other private lending source. If private financing cannot be arranged, the SBA can help in several ways.

Sometimes the SBA makes loans directly to small businesses. More often, it arranges to guarantee up to 90 percent of a loan from another lending source. The guarantee means that if the borrower is unable to repay the loan, the SBA will repay the lender up to 90 percent of the amount. The SBA also sponsors special private venture capital companies called **small business investment corporations** (SBICs). SBICs can make loans only to small businesses using funds raised from private investors. In 1982, according to *Venture Capital Journal*, SBICs accounted for 18 percent of the entire pool of venture capital in the United States.[11]

√ *Management assistance.* The SBA provides several kinds of management assistance to small firms. Some aid is provided by SBA field offices located throughout the United States. The SBA also sponsors, without

---

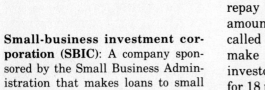

Small-business investment corporation (SBIC): A company sponsored by the Small Business Administration that makes loans to small businesses.

---

[10]For an excellent discussion of small-business relations with bankers, accountants, and lawyers, see Irene Smith, *Diary of a Small Business* (New York: Scribner's, 1982), chap. 10, on which these paragraphs draw.

[11]See *State of Small Business*, p. 111.

Through its SCORE and ACE programs, the Small Business Administration offers management assistance to small firms. Marc P. Anderson

charge, two programs that offer assistance by people with management experience. One of these is SCORE, the Service Corps of Retired Executives; the other is ACE, the Active Corps of Executives. Through these programs managers with small-business experience are put in touch with small-business owners to help them solve their management problems. Finally, the SBA sponsors the Small Business Institute, in which small firms get advice from faculty and graduate students of business schools.

Procurement assistance. Among its other services, the SBA helps small businesses bid for government contracts. It provides information about contracts that are open for bids and advice on bidding procedures. Many government agencies are required to set aside some contracts on which only small firms may bid. In 1981 some $19.7 billion out of a total of $126 billion in federal procurement contracts was awarded to small businesses.[12]

Assistance to women and minority group members. Finally, the SBA provides special aid to small firms that are owned by women or minority group members. In 1977, when the last census of minority-owned businesses was made, there were some 561,400 such firms in the United States, about 5 percent of all firms. Most of them were small. Minority-owned firms have special priority in bidding on some government contracts. They received about 2 percent of all federal contracts in 1981. The SBA also sponsors special **minority enterprise small-business investment corporations (MESBICs)** that provide venture capital for such businesses.

More than 2.5 million U.S. businesses are owned by women. This number is growing fast, especially in such areas as mining, manufacturing, and finance. Most of the businesses owned by women, like those owned by minority group members, are small. The SBA makes special efforts to encourage businesses owned by women through its Office of Women's Business Ownership.

Minority enterprise small-business investment corporation (MESBIC): A company sponsored by the Small Business Administration that provides venture capital for small businesses owned by members of minority groups.

[12]*State of Small Business*, p. 325.

FRANCHISING

Business format franchising: A form of franchising in which the franchisor supplies the franchisee with a complete business plan and the help needed to put it into operation.

Franchising is a very popular form of business ownership. Car rental agents, soft-drink bottlers, service stations, and fast-food chains are among the many kinds of businesses that use this approach.

In Chapter 3 we defined a franchise as an arrangement in which the owner of a trademark, trade name, or copyright (the franchisor) allows another firm (the franchisee) to use it, subject to certain agreed-upon conditions. The total sales of franchised businesses were close to $450 billion in 1983. In the same year the number of people employed in franchising, including part-time workers, was over 5 million.

The popularity of franchising stems largely from the fact that it combines the advantages of small and large businesses. In the traditional form of franchising, a manufacturer relies on franchisees to distribute its product. This form still accounts for three quarters of all franchising. Auto dealers, service stations, and soft-drink bottlers are prominent examples.

Recently another type of franchise arrangement, known as **business format franchising**, has become popular. In this kind of franchise, the franchisor supplies not only the product and trademark but a complete business plan, including a marketing strategy, operating manuals, quality control, and two-way contact. Restaurants, convenience stores, auto parts stores, real estate agencies, and exercise studios are just a few of the areas in which business format franchising is found.

Box 4–4 gives more details on the extent of franchising in the United States. In the rest of this section we will review the advantages and drawbacks of franchising from the points of view of the franchisor and the franchisee. We will conclude with some guidelines for successful franchising.

Courtesy of Hertz Corp.

Courtesy of Atlanta Coca Cola Bottling Co.

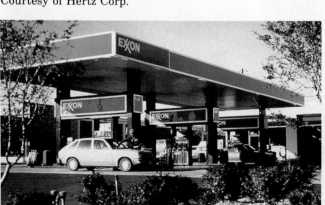
Courtesy of Exxon Corp.

Courtesy of Burger King Corp.

Box 4–4 Franchising in U.S. Retail Trade

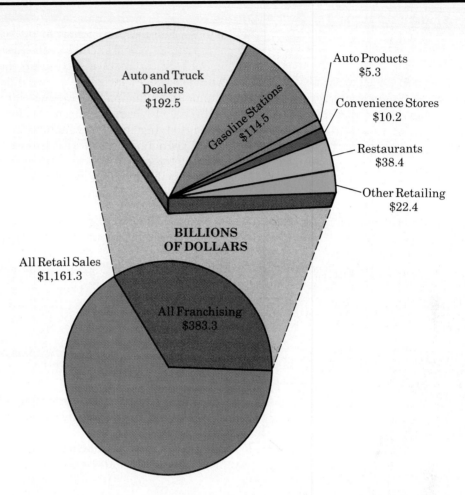

Auto Products
$5.3

Convenience Stores
$10.2

Restaurants
$38.4

Other Retailing
$22.4

Auto and Truck
Dealers
$192.5

Gasoline Stations
$114.5

BILLIONS
OF DOLLARS

All Retail Sales
$1,161.3

All Franchising
$383.3

According to the Department of Commerce, franchising accounted for a third of total U.S. retail sales in 1983. Auto and truck dealers and gas stations represent the traditional form of franchising. In these businesses, the franchisor contributes the trade name, national marketing, and the product itself. Convenience stores, restaurants, and many other kinds of retailing are examples of *business format* franchising. In these cases, the franchisor supplies the franchisee with a complete business plan and management training as well as the services supplied by a traditional franchisor.

Source: U.S. Department of Commerce, Bureau of Industrial Economics, "Franchising in the Economy, 1981–83" (Washington, D.C., January 1983), p. 12.

The Franchisor's Perspective

Although well-known franchisors like Hertz, Holiday Inn, and McDonald's are hardly small businesses, most of them started small. Kentucky Fried Chicken, for example, started when Harlan Sanders cashed his first Social Security check, got into his car, and drove off to sell his special method of making fried chicken to restaurant owners around the country. Because franchising is one way for a small company to grow, the franchisor's as well as the franchisee's point of view deserves discussion.

From the franchisor's point of view, the advantages of this way of doing business include the following.

- *Raising capital.* Franchising is a way of raising capital to expand the business. Some capital comes to the parent company through fees paid to acquire the franchise in the first place. More important, franchisees bear the costs of setting up their operations.
- *Economies of scale.* Franchising makes it possible to achieve economies of scale in producing the supplies that the franchisor provides to franchisees. The franchisor can also get discounts from its own suppliers by buying in large volumes.
- *Motivation.* Owners of local franchises often work harder and are more highly motivated than managers of branch outlets.
- *Responsiveness.* Franchisees may be more responsive to local conditions and may be able to bring in business through contacts with people in the local area.
- *Labor relations.* Because franchisees are not employees of the franchisor, problems of labor relations are avoided.

Franchising also has some drawbacks. These have caused some franchise operations to fail and have prevented franchising from gaining a place in some lines of business. Among the disadvantages, from the franchisor's point of view, are these.

- *Credit demands.* The franchisor often has to provide credit to franchisees. This cuts into the power of this business form as a means of raising capital.
- *Costs of control.* Quality standards cannot be maintained without the high cost of training franchisees and a staff of traveling supervisors.
- *Disputes.* Disputes with franchisees can arise over purchasing requirements, franchise terminations, exclusive territories, and so on.

The Franchisee's Perspective

Franchising has many attractions from the point of view of the person who wants to buy a business. Above all, the success rate for franchises is far higher than the average rate for all small businesses. The International Franchising Association claims that 90 percent of all franchises are successful. That compares very well with the high failure rates of independent firms reported earlier in this chapter.

The major advantages to the franchisee of this form of business include the following.

- *Management aid.* Weak management is by far the most common reason for small-business failure. Franchisees of a strong parent firm get help with all phases of management. First, they buy a pretested business concept—all they have to do is turn the key. Second, they often get special training at institutions like McDonald's famous "Hamburger U." Third, they get detailed instructions and support in every aspect of day-to-day operation, from menu planning to local advertising.

- *National marketing.* The marketing efforts of franchisors include not only advertising but also market research, development of new products, and so on. The advertising efforts of automakers, fast-food franchisors, and others are familiar to every television viewer.
- *Financial help.* Many franchisors finance part of the start-up costs of a franchise. Others provide short-term credit on purchased supplies. In many cases, training for franchisees includes tips on dealing with local banks and other financial institutions.

Franchises are not a sure road to instant wealth, however. Even when they are successful, they require the same hard work as other small businesses. And although franchisors often go to great lengths to protect their franchisees from outright failure, the profits may still be low. Among the other drawbacks, from the franchisee's point of view, are the following.

- *Sharing of profits.* The franchisees, unlike an independent proprietor, must share profits with the parent firm. The payments to the franchisor may take the form of a purchase price or a percentage of sales. In addition, the franchisor often builds a generous profit into the price of supplies sold to local outlets. (Some types of franchisors make all their profits in this way.)
- *Reduced independence.* The franchisee has nowhere near the independence of other proprietors. The parent company often insists on very detailed standards. This can be especially frustrating when it keeps the franchisee from cutting costs or adding to the product line in ways that would improve the operation.
- *Disputes with the franchisor.* Many franchisees have gotten into serious disputes with their franchisors. Nonrenewal of the franchise agreement for reasons that the franchisee considers unfair is one major source of dispute.

Guidelines for a Successful Franchise

When the pros and cons of franchising are weighed, it is easy to see why this business form has become so popular. Most of the drawbacks can be minimized with proper foresight. Above all, it should be kept in mind that a franchise reduces, but does not eliminate, the risks and responsibilities of owning a small business. Whether a franchise experience is successful will often depend on whether the following dos and don'ts have been heeded.

- *Don't* expect the franchisor to do all your planning for you. Just as if you were starting an independent firm, you must decide whether the franchise fits what you want to do and what you are able to do. You must also decide whether the product is one that can be sold for a profit in your area. Does your local "franchise strip" really need one more pizza parlor?
- *Do* pay attention to the quality of the training offered by the franchisor. Remember, this is the biggest single benefit of the franchise relationship. Is there a real training program, or just some printed material in a looseleaf binder?
- *Do* look closely at the franchisor's track record. Is the product a proven one or is it a gimmick? How long has the franchisor been in

business? How profitable have its franchisees been? Does the franchisor have a reputation for honesty and fairness?

✓● *Do* study the purchase price carefully. Just as when you buy an existing business, you should balance the potential profits against the opportunity costs in terms of time and equity capital.

✓● *Do* review the franchise agreement with a lawyer who is an expert in such matters. Is it full of restrictions and requirements that seem to benefit only the franchisor? Are the terms for canceling the franchise fair? If the franchisor buys back your franchise, will you be compensated for your work, or only for the money you put in?

LOOKING AHEAD

In a book that covers business in general, this chapter is the only one set aside for small business. But in the chapters that follow—those on management, finance, marketing, and the rest—you will find many mentions of small businesses. There are three reasons for this.

First, as we have already seen, small business accounts for almost half of the economy. It is too important to neglect.

Second, the small-business sector is the source of big businesses. The fact that most small firms never grow big, and may never intend to, should not obscure the fact that most big firms started out small.

Third, we think big businesses have a lot to learn from small ones. Many of the problems that plague American business today—slow reactions, losing touch with the customer, doing too many things and none of them well—are problems that small firms often avoid. When we want to give an example of how something looks when it is done right, a small-business example may be the most instructive one.

As you read through this book you will perhaps ask yourself whether there is a career for you in small business. What kind of people have

Drawing by Ed Fisher; © 1982 The New Yorker Magazine, Inc.

successful careers in small business? They seem to share certain traits. They are willing to take reasonable risks. They are self-confident. They are hard workers. They set goals and get satisfaction from working to achieve them, not from looking back on what they have achieved. They enjoy being accountable, both for what they do well and for the mistakes they make. Above all they are innovative; they are entrepreneurs.[13]

Do these traits describe you?

SUMMARY

1. A *small business* can be defined as one that is independently owned and operated and is not dominant in its field. Businesses with fewer than 500 employees accounted for 45.3 percent of sales of all U.S. businesses in 1980. Such firms account for more than their share of job creation.

2. Small firms have certain advantages that allow them to dominate some markets. They are especially well suited to limited markets and markets where innovation and a personal touch are important. Small businesses have drawbacks too. They do not always have equal access to resources, especially financial resources. As long as they remain small, they cannot achieve economies of scale. And because of the lack of internal specialization in a small firm, the owner must learn to wear several hats.

3. The failure rate among small firms is high. A new firm with twenty or fewer employees has only about one chance in three of lasting more than four years. Of the firms that go out of business each year, 90 percent do so voluntarily. The remaining 10 percent are *business failures*. The great majority of small-business failures are caused by poor management.

4. If you are thinking about starting a small business, you can increase your chances of success by following certain guidelines. First, you should ask yourself whether you really want the long hours, the responsibilities, and the financial problems that are typical of small businesses. Second, you must choose a line of business, asking yourself what you want to do, what you are able to do, and what customers will buy at a price that will yield a profit. You next need to decide whether to start from scratch or buy an existing business. Finally, you need to find a lawyer and an accountant who are willing to deal with a small firm. You may find it worthwhile to take advantage of the management, financial, and procurement assistance offered by the Small Business Administration.

5. Franchising combines the advantages of small businesses with those of large ones. It also offers a middle road between starting a business from scratch and buying an existing one. Largely because of the management aid provided by the franchisor, a franchise has a much higher chance of success than independent small businesses. However, franchising has its drawbacks, including lack of independence and the necessity of sharing profits with the parent company.

KEY TERMS

You should be familiar with the following terms and concepts. Check their meanings by referring to the marginal definitions in the chapter or to the glossary at the end of the book.

Small business	Business failure	Asset
Economies of scale	Bankruptcy	Liability

[13] This list of traits comes from Nicholas C. Siropolis, *Small Business Management: A Guide to Entrepreneurship* (Boston: Houghton Mifflin, 1982), pp. 32–36.

Opportunity cost

Small-business investment corporation (SBIC)

Minority enterprise small-business investment corporation (MESBIC)

Business format franchising

QUESTIONS FOR REVIEW AND DISCUSSION

1. What are four types of markets in which small firms have an advantage over large ones? Illustrate each with an example drawn from a small business in your community.
2. Given the advantages and disadvantages of small business as discussed in this chapter, can you think of any changes in public policy that would improve the survival rate of small firms? Do you think such changes would be good for the health of the economy as a whole? Explain.
3. In what ways are the guidelines for starting a business illustrated by the story of Ruiz Foods? What, if anything, did Ruiz do that would appear *not* to have increased the firm's chances of success?
4. After answering question 3 for Ruiz Foods, turn back to the story of The Scribe at the beginning of Chapter 1 and answer the same questions.
5. Explain the meaning of dissolution, business failure, and bankruptcy. Give examples (real or imaginary) of firms that are
   a. Successful, but undergoing dissolution
   b. Business failures, but not bankrupt
   c. Bankrupt, but not forced to dissolve
6. In 1982 Harold Williams lost his job as a mechanic in a filling station that had decided to convert to self-serve gasoline sales. Williams was a good mechanic and liked working on cars, but no one was hiring auto mechanics. His employer offered to keep him on to

pump gas at $5 an hour, but that didn't interest Williams. He found a service station for sale for $40,000, took all of his savings out of the bank, got a second mortgage on his house, and went into business. After two years of working eighty hours a week he was still in business, but try as he would he could barely earn enough to pay the second mortgage on his house. He blamed his troubles on a poor location, the recession, high-handed treatment by banks and big oil companies, and the failure of many of his customers to pay their bills.
   What do you think of the reasons Williams gave for his troubles? Why do you think he was in trouble?
7. Are you the type of person who should start a small business? Explain why or why not.
8. Look in your telephone directory and find out if there is a field office of the Small Business Administration in your area. If there is, visit the office and ask for information about the SBA's programs for helping small firms.
9. List the advantages and disadvantages of franchising from the points of view of both the franchisor and the franchisee. Next, identify at least three different kinds of franchise businesses in your community. (If you are not sure whether the business is a franchise, ask.) What features of those businesses make them suitable for franchising? Or are they perhaps not suitable?

Case 4–1: American Solar Heat

In 1976 Joseph Heyman, a contractor in Ridgefield, Connecticut, was asked to build a house to be heated by solar collectors installed on the roof. The available solar collectors didn't meet Heyman's standards, and he thought he could improve their design.
   Heyman took his collector design to a few small manufacturing firms, but the prices they

gave seemed far too high. He could not only design a better solar collector, he concluded—he could build it for less too. That is how American Solar Heat, Inc. (AMSOLHEAT) was born.
   Heyman quickly learned about the market for solar collectors. First, he found that it was highly fragmented. Each part of the country had a few small firms; no one in Illinois wanted to order

collectors from Connecticut, nor was anyone in Connecticut likely to buy from a competing firm in Illinois.

Second, he found that what customers really wanted was not just solar collectors but complete heating or hot-water systems. This was a natural for Heyman, with his experience as a contractor. He began to offer a package that included the collector, the controls, a storage tank, the plumbing and electrical work, and a guarantee on the whole system.

During the Carter administration solar energy received a lot of publicity and some tax breaks. Tax credits to homeowners greatly boosted AMSOLHEAT's sales. But the government help came with streamers of red tape attached.

At one point a government agency objected to a term in the AMSOLHEAT warranty. Heyman wrote back saying he would write it any way they wanted. What exactly did they want? The government replied that Heyman's legal staff would know what to do. "What legal staff?" replied Heyman. By the time the problem was straightened out—only a few words in the warranty had to be

changed—hundreds of hours of Heyman's time had been consumed writing letters and making phone calls.

With lower fuel prices and less publicity during the Reagan administration, AMSOLHEAT went into low gear. Still, it is one of the few survivors in the solar heat field. "I tell prospective customers," Heyman says, "to call all the solar heat firms listed in last Year's Yellow pages. None of the numbers are in service."

It is not just AMSOLHEAT's small competitors that failed to make it. Between 1976 and 1983 a number of large firms entered the business. Among them were Grumman, Corning Glass, Exxon, and Libby-Owens-Ford. None of them stuck it out. Heyman thinks they failed because they didn't sell complete systems. The big firms did a good job of manufacturing, though. Currently Heyman is installing surplus Libby-Owens-Ford collectors that he bought at a low price when that firm went out of the business. He will start making his own collectors again when those run out.

Source: Telephone interview with Joseph Heyman.

Questions:

1. How well did Heyman follow the guidelines for starting a new business? What strengths helped him avoid the danger of early failure?

2. Small business is less common in manufacturing than in any other major sector of the economy. How, then, has AMSOLHEAT, which has never had more than seven employees, survived while large competitors have come and gone?

3. How has government policy affected AMSOLHEAT? In what ways are Heyman's relations with government typical?

Case 4–2: Raymond Albert Kroc

"We take the hamburger business more seriously than they do," said Ray Kroc, explaining how his McDonald's Corporation overwhelmed its competitors to become the world's largest restaurant chain, with annual revenues of $2.8 billion. "We treat it as a regular business—and it is a regular business." One of the great marketers of modern times, Kroc served up an unbeatable combination—quality, speed, low prices, and cleanliness.

Leaving nothing to chance, he imposed assembly-line techniques on his operations, automating every cooking function, so that a handful of low-paid teenage employees can efficiently serve many hundreds of customers a day. He insisted on the strictest standards at each outlet. "The French fry would become almost sacrosanct for me," he declared, "its preparation a ritual to be followed religiously."

Case 4–2: Raymond Albert Kroc (Continued)

In his pursuit of excellence, one of Kroc's weapons was an explosive temper. He once chastised his San Diego Padres baseball team over the public address system. And he goes berserk at the sight of a litter-strewn McDonald's parking lot. McDonald's raised the expectations of customers everywhere and became the model against which other chains are judged. Kroc's methods prompted a Harvard Business School professor to describe him as "the service sector's equivalent of Henry Ford."

Throughout his youth and well into his middle years, Kroc seemed doomed to eternal obscurity. Born in a Chicago suburb, the son of a Western Union executive, he left school during World War I to become an ambulance driver, but the war ended before he got overseas. He resumed his schooling at his father's urging, but dropped out again when he found that "algebra had not improved in my absence." He sold ribbon novelties, worked as a board marker for a Chicago brokerage firm, and at the dawn of the Jazz Age became a professional pianist, playing for various bands and even doing a one-night stand at a brothel. He went to Florida to sell real estate during the great land boom there, and when the boom went bust he returned to Chicago, where he sold paper cups for a Lily-Tulip distributor, rising to sales manager for the Midwest region. Then he became the exclusive distributor for a company that produced milkshake mixers.

Not until 1954, as an ailing 52-year-old—arthritic, diabetic, missing his gallbladder and part of his thyroid gland—did Kroc hit upon the scheme that was to ensure him a place among the business immortals. He visited a couple of brothers named McDonald, who used his milkshake mixers at their small chain of hamburger stands based in San Bernadino, California. Greatly impressed by the efficiency and popularity of their operation, he became their agent in recruiting new franchisees. By 1961, feeling that the brothers had pointlessly obstructed his efforts to expand the chain, he bought them out for $2.7 million, which he borrowed at exorbitant interest rates—the ultimate cost topping $14 million. In retrospect, it was an incredible bargain. By the time of his death in 1984, Kroc's personal stake in McDonald's Corp. had grown to some $500 million.

Source: *FORTUNE*, April 4, 1983, p. 147. © 1983 Time Inc. All rights reserved.

Questions:

1. What features of the restaurant industry make it suitable for small business? Why was franchising a good way for Kroc to build an empire in an industry where economies of scale were thought to be unimportant?
2. What features of McDonald's have made it a model franchise from the franchisee's point of view?
3. Judging both from the information given in the case and from your own experience, if any, as a McDonald's customer, what advantages does this operation have compared with an independent fast-food restaurant? What disadvantages, if any?

SUGGESTED READINGS, PART I

Peters, Thomas J., and Robert H. Waterman, Jr. *In Search of Excellence: Lessons from America's Best-Run Companies*. New York: Harper & Row, 1982.

Hayes, Robert H., and William J. Abernathy. "Managing Our Way to Economic Decline." *Harvard Business Review*, July–August 1980, pp. 67–77.

Dolan, Edwin G. *Basic Economics*, 3rd ed. Chicago: Dryden Press, 1983. Chapter 3 covers supply and demand; Chapters 6–18 cover fiscal policy, monetary policy, and inflation.

President's Council of Economic Advisers. *Economic Report of the President*. Washington, D.C.: Government Printing Office, annual.

Pickle, Hal B., and Royce L. Abrahamson. *Small Business Management*, 3rd ed. New York: Wiley, 1984.

Brown, Deaver. *The Entrepreneur's Guide*. New York: Macmillan, 1980.

Newman, William H., and Harvey W. Wallender III. "Managing Not-for-Profit Enterprise." *Academy of Management Review*, January 1978.

Ritti, R. Richard, and G. Ray Funkhouser. *The Ropes to Skip and the Ropes to Know: Studies in Organizational Behavior*, 2nd ed. Columbus, Ohio: Grid, 1982.

Useful periodicals:

    Business Week
    Forbes
    Fortune
    The Wall Street Journal
    INC
    Ventures

CAREERS IN BUSINESS: AN OVERVIEW

What Is a Career?

"I work for a living" is something almost all of us will be able to say during many years of our lives. And as we have noted, businesses, large and small, provide the majority of jobs. What you learn about business in this book, then, has a direct bearing on your own future. This is true whether you are getting ready to enter the job market for the first time or sharpening your skills for a step forward in a career that is already under way.

C. Brooklyn Derr has defined a *career* as a sequence of work-related experiences that form a work history and reflect a chosen work-related life theme.[1] This definition says two things about careers. First, it says that a career is more than just a job. It is something that extends over a good part of a person's life and may include many separate jobs. The second thing the definition says is that a career involves choices. Choices of occupation (sales manager, plumber, beautician, and so on) are not the only ones. There are also choices between security and variety; between seeking promotion and staying at a level where you are content; and between work-related goals and other life goals. Even a person who just drifts through life can be thought of as choosing to do so, and therefore as having a career.

Notice that Derr's definition of a career does not contain built-in standards of success or failure. It does not say "up is good, down is bad." Neither does it limit the concept of a career to a narrow group of professions like manager, lawyer, or engineer. One can have a career as a taxi driver, a secretary, or a hospital orderly too. If there is any standard of judgment in the definition at all, it is that your career is a success if it blends work and nonwork activities into a "life theme" that satisfies you.

There is work that we enjoy and feel good about, and there is work that we don't enjoy. Every career includes some work of both kinds. How much of each kind there is in your career depends

[1]C. Brooklyn Derr, "Career Switching and Organizational Politics: The Case of Naval Officers," in Ralph Katz, ed., *Career Issues in Human Resource Management* (Englewood Cliffs, N.J.: Prentice-Hall, 1982), p. 65.

very much on decisions that you yourself make. Seeking work that is rewarding requires risks and effort, but risks and effort that for most of us are very worthwhile. If you enjoy your work, you will almost certainly do it better. If you do your work better, you will almost certainly be paid more for it. This appendix on careers and those at the ends of the other parts of the book are intended to help you make career choices.

Job and Career Alternatives

The variety of jobs and careers among which to choose is enormous. From astronaut, bookkeeper, and child psychologist to X-ray technician, yoga instructor, and zoologist, careers span the alphabet. The following are a few of the many possible dimensions of a career.

- *Sector.* Most jobs in the United States are supplied by private business, but you could also make a career in government or in the not-for-profit sector.
- *Location.* Your career could be in any state or country, and in a city, small town, or rural area. As we will see in later chapters, changes are taking place in where jobs are located.
- *Size of organization.* You could work for the federal government, with millions of employees; for a large corporation, with hundreds of thousands; or for a small firm, with just a few. As we saw in Chapter 4, small businesses have been key suppliers of new jobs in recent years.
- *Employment status.* Your career, like most, will very likely make you an employee of some organization. However, you may also be an entrepreneur for whom other people work, or you may work entirely on your own.
- *Type of industry.* Within any broad sector of the economy, your career could be in any of a number of industries—paper goods, trucking, education, and so on.
- *Activity within the organization.* Whether you work in business, government, or the not-for-profit sector, you may

specialize in one aspect of the organization's work, such as general management, marketing, production, or finance. If you start a small business, you will need to master all of these areas. Each of them will be covered in the chapters that follow.

These career dimensions can be put together in endless ways. You could be a technician at the Jefferson City, Tennessee, Magnavox plant. You could be a professor at Lewis and Clark College in Portland, Oregon. Or you could be a lawyer for Common Cause in Washington, D.C. But even the six dimensions just listed don't capture all the things that make one career different from another. The following dimensions cut across all of them.

- *Organizational style.* You could work for an organization in which lines of authority and job assignments are rigid, or for one in which everyone talks to everyone else. Your organization may be fired with company spirit from top to bottom, or filled with backbiting and office politics.
- *Occupational personalities.* Your choice of a career will make a difference in the kind of people you work with. If you work in sales, your co-workers are likely to be outgoing people. If you work in research, they are likely to be creative and independent-minded.
- *Kind of responsibility.* All jobs involve responsibility, but there are differences in the types of responsibilities attached to different kinds of jobs. A basic distinction is between a career in *management* and a career as an *individual contributor.* Managers practice the art of getting things done through people. They plan, lead, organize, and direct the work of others. Individual contributors are those who do the primary work of an organization—workers in a factory, doctors in a hospital, and so on.
- *Generalist versus specialist.* This is another distinction that contributes to the "personality" of a career. In part, the generalist-versus-specialist distinction is a

matter of formal training: a specialist, as the word implies, has received advanced training in a particular area, such as systems analysis or insurance underwriting, while a generalist has broad training in a general area such as business or economics. But it also has a lot to do with how you view yourself and your role in the organization you work for.

We have described nine career dimensions, and we could add more. You may find this list a bit frightening. With so many choices to make, what if you make a mistake? Don't worry too much about this. Your early career decisions are important and are worth careful thought. But within a career it is easy to change one of those dimensions, or a few at a time, as you move from job to job. If you love being a nurse but wish you were in Iowa rather than California, you can move. If you are happy being an accountant but would rather work for a smaller firm, you can look around.

Looking Ahead

This is the first in a series of sections on careers in business. It has given an overview of the concept of a career. The next four sections will fill in some details. The section at the end of Part II will discuss careers in general management and computers. The section at the end of Part III will look at careers in marketing—the area of business devoted to fitting the firm's product to its customers' needs. Part IV will include a section on careers in management of production, operations, and human resources. The section at the end of Part V will cover careers in finance, accounting, and insurance.

The final section on careers, found in Appendix A, will have a different focus. It will provide some guidelines for planning a career and taking the first steps in starting a career. The topics covered there will include assessing your interests and abilities, looking for career opportunities, writing resumes, succeeding in interviews, and getting settled in a new job.

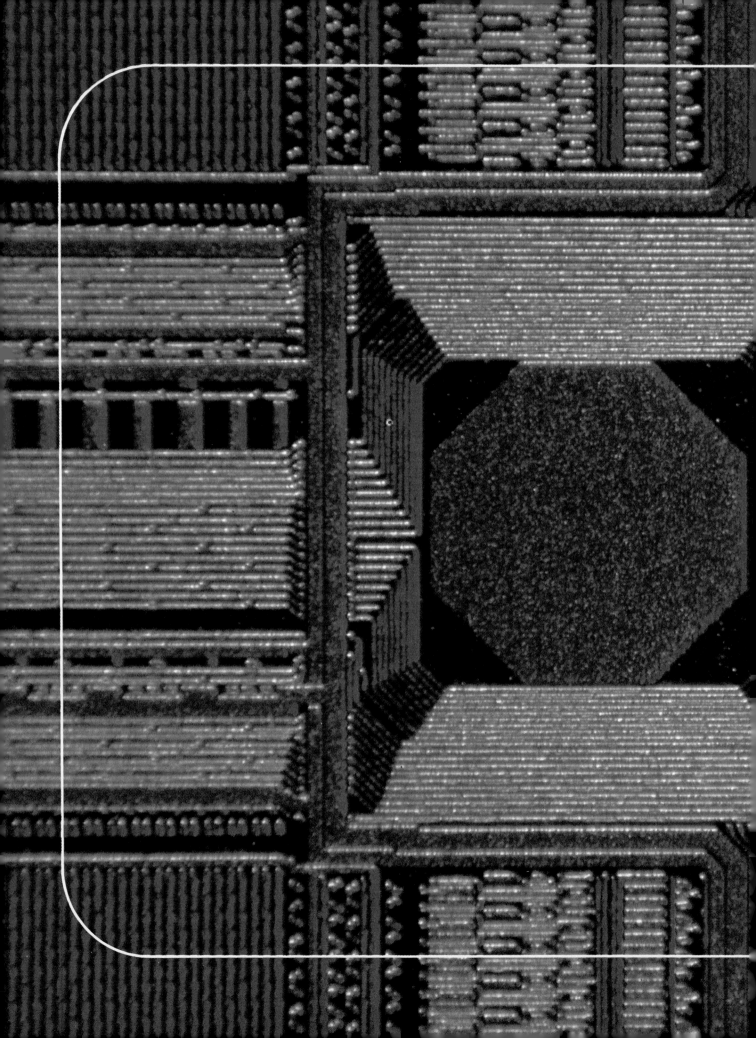

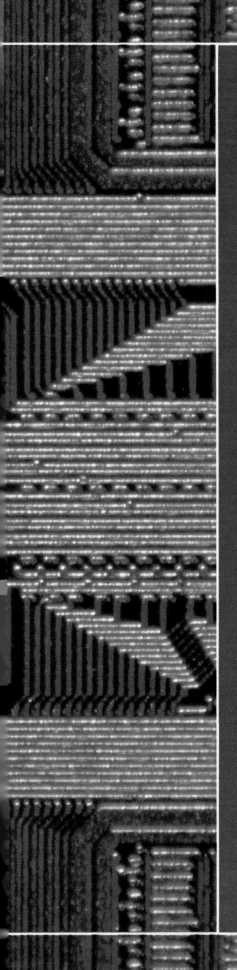

Part II

MANAGEMENT, ORGANIZATION, AND INFORMATION

Management is the art of getting things done through people. Managers plan, organize, lead, and control the work of others. They find opportunities and solve problems. Chapter 5 will give an overview of the manager's job, looking at the skills a manager needs and the ways in which those skills can be acquired. Later parts of the book will show how mangement skills are applied in specific areas, such as marketing, production, human resources management, and finance.

One of the manager's tasks, organizing, will be the subject of Chapter 6. Organizing means dividing up work among individuals and groups and coordinating their activities. As the chapter will show, a firm's structure must fit its goals. Large firms with many-layered structures are good for carrying out some tasks. For other tasks, small units do the job better. An effective manager must be flexible in forming departments, delegating tasks to subordinates, and making sure that each unit within the organization does its job.

In Chapter 7 we will turn our attention to a powerful new management tool, the computer. A computer is an electronic device for collecting, processing, and communicating information. Good information has always been a key to effective management. Properly used, computers can provide information that is more accurate, timely, and complete than has ever been possible before. As we will see, though, computers do not change the basic task of management—getting things done through people. If the human element is neglected, computers can do more harm than good.

Chapter 5

INTRODUCTION TO MANAGEMENT

When you have completed this chapter, you should be able to

- Define the term *management*, describe the *management hierarchy*, and explain the role of the player-manager.

- Distinguish between *efficient* and *effective* management.

- Discuss the process of management in terms of four aspects: *planning*, *organizing*, *leading*, and *controlling*.

- Explain *strategic planning* and its importance for small firms as well as large ones.

- Outline procedures for problem finding, problem solving, and opportunity finding.

- List ten roles of managers, under the general headings of *interpersonal*, *informational*, and *decisional*.

- Discuss the *human*, *technical*, and *conceptual* skills required at each level of the management hierarchy.

- List eight features of excellently managed firms.

John, a $65,000-a-year manager for a big New England firm, had a nasty little secret. He drank heavily, often at lunch. As he drank more and more, his job performance went steadily downhill. But for a long time his secretary and assistants helped him cover up. Some things that he did, he was still able to do well, but as time went by, he was able to do less and less.

One day his secret came out into the open. Returning from lunch, he was told that the company would have to recall one of its major products. John's job would be to plan how to explain the recall to the public. Upon hearing this news he flew into a drunken rage, shouting that it was always his job to clean up other people's mistakes. At this point it became plain to John's superiors and co-workers that he had a problem, and that it had become a problem for the company too.

How could the problem be managed?

John's boss, working closely with the firm's medical director, used a bold new tactic. A surprise meeting was called in which John's co-workers described the ways in which his performance had slipped. When John tried to play down the problem, the medical director said brutally, "Shut up and listen. Alcoholics are liars, so we don't want to hear what you have to say."

John was given just one choice: seek treatment or be fired.

This true story has a happy ending. After treatment, John is back on the job and is once again an effective manager.[1]

[1] Robert S. Greenberger, "Firms Are Confronting Alcoholic Executives with Threat of Firing," *Wall Street Journal*, January 13, 1983, p. 1.

WHAT IS MANAGEMENT?

Management: The art of getting things done through people.

The story of John's crisis is a clear example of what management is. In the words of Mary Parker Follett (see Box 5–1), **management** is "the art of getting things done through people."

John was a member of a team. The job of his boss, as manager, was to get the work of the company done through the skills and talents of John and his co-workers. Suppose John's boss had thrown John out and handled the product recall himself. That might have gotten the job done in the short run, but it wouldn't have been *management*. We will see that good managers often do things themselves, but the distinctive mark of the manager's job is getting people to work together to perform some task.

This chapter will provide an overview of the role of managers in business and other organizations. It will explain why management is necessary and what managers do. It will discusss the skills that managers must use and will explore the question of what makes management effective or ineffective. In doing all of this, it will build on the central concept of management as the art of getting things done through people.

The Need for Management

The term *executive* is often used as a synonym for manager. Looking at where this word comes from tells us a lot about the reason that managers

Box 5–1 Mary Parker Follett 1868–1963

Mary Parker Follett was born in Boston in 1868. She studied philosophy, law, and political science at Radcliffe College and then at Newham College in England and in Paris.

Her view of management was based on the principle that a person at work is motivated by the same factors that govern life away from the job. An effective manager should study and understand these factors. In order to get things done through people, a manager should harmonize people's efforts—not simply force people and drive them.

Some of Follett's ideas seem prophetic today. She was very interested in what she called the "group concept," which stressed a harmonious work environment in which each person could make the greatest contribution. In some respects this concept foreshadows the "Japanese" management techniques that are of such interest to managers around the world today.

Source: Claude S. George, Jr., *The History of Management Thought*, 2nd ed. (Englewood Cliffs, N.J.: Prentice-Hall, 1972), pp. 138–39 and 152–53.

are needed in every organization. The word *executive* comes from Latin roots meaning "to follow something to the end," that is, *to see that things get done*.

Managers are people who make things happen. They think in advance about the organization's goals and ways of doing things. They coordinate the resources needed to carry out plans. They work to get the best out of the people in their organization. They check to make sure progress is being made, and they take corrective action when it is not.

A good example of a manager is the conductor of an orchestra. The musicians bring a wealth of talent to the performance. The score embodies the brilliance of a Mozart or a Beethoven. But without the conductor, the symphony just couldn't happen. There would only be a roomful of musicians, each trying to make his or her version of the piece prevail and as a result making noise rather than music.

The Management Hierarchy

Management hierarchy: A ranking of members of an organization according to authority and, usually, status.

All but the smallest firms have a clear **management hierarchy** within which their members are ranked. At the bottom of the hierarchy are the people who do the actual work of the organization. These are the workers in a factory, the clerks in a government agency, the privates in an army. They do not supervise other workers. We will refer to people at this level as **individual contributors**.*

Individual contributors: The people who do the actual work of an organization and do not supervise other workers.

Above the individual contributors stands management. Whether management consists of a single proprietor or a many-layered pyramid, one trait sets managers apart: they spend at least part of their time supervising others. The distinction is not that managers make no individual contributions. They do, from the hammer-swinging construction

*The examples given imply that individual contributors have low status as well as a low position in terms of authority over others. This is not always so, however. The doctors in a hospital and the professors in a college are individual contributors with limited authority over others. However, they may have high social status and may count more than administrators in the eyes of outsiders.

A foreman in a manufacturing plant is a supervisor or first-line manager. © Dick Durrance, Woodfin Camp

Top managers like Olive Ann Beech, who helped develop Beech Aircraft into a highly successful company, are responsible for defining the broad goals and values of the organization. Courtesy of Beech Aircraft Corp.

Supervisory managers: Managers who direct the work of individual contributors but not that of other managers.

Middle managers: Managers in intermediate positions who spend at least some of their time directing the work of other managers.

Top managers: Managers who are responsible for defining broad goals and strategies and directing the work of middle managers.

The Organizational Hierarchy

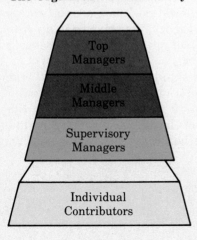

Top Managers

Middle Managers

Supervisory Managers

Individual Contributors

foreman to the corporate president making a key sales call. The distinction instead is that individual contributors do not supervise the work of others.

Within management there are three levels. **Supervisory** or **first-line managers** direct individual contributors only; they do not supervise other managers. Examples would be a foreman supervising workers in a manufacturing plant or an office manager supervising clerks and secretaries in a government bureau. **Middle managers** span a broad range of authority. Unlike supervisory managers, they spend at least some of their time directing the work of other managers. The main job of middle management is to make sure that essential tasks get done. The higher levels of middle management also help make plans and set goals for their own departments, and sometimes for the organization as a whole.

Top managers are responsible for defining broad goals, translating them into strategies, and shaping the organization's values. Top managers direct the work of middle managers. Typical titles of top managers are "president," "chief executive officer," or "senior vice-president." Depending on the size of the organization, of course, the same people who make plans at the top level may also take part in carrying out plans and directing workers. Top managers are responsible to the board of directors (in a corporation), voters or elected officials (in government), or trustees or members (in not-for-profit firms).

The Player-Manager

The essence of management, as we have said, is getting things done through people. But this concept falls short of describing the work of actual managers in one respect. Although they are skilled at getting other people to do things, effective managers make individual contributions as well. They act, in a word, as *player-managers*.

In small firms, the role of the player-manager can hardly be avoided. As we saw in Chapter 4, a small company cannot hire specialists for every job. For example, if you are the owner-manager of a small janitorial-

Gordon Moore, chairman of Intel, is a player-manager. While serving as the firm's chief executive officer, he also remains active as an engineer. Courtesy of Intel Corp.

Efficiency: Achieving goals with a minimum of expense, waste, or effort.

Effectiveness: Choosing the right goals on which to focus the energies of the organization.

service firm with a half-dozen employees, you can expect to push a mop in the afternoon and balance your own books in the evening. Even in much larger companies the absence of a single employee may require a manager to fill in.

A second common type of player-manager is the entrepreneur who builds a firm on the basis of skill. Many such people continue to act as individual contributors even after their companies have grown quite large. An example is Gordon Moore, a founder and now chairman of Intel, an electronics firm with $900 million annual sales. Moore, a chemist and physicist, remains in many ways the firm's chief engineer as well as its chief executive officer.

Still another reason that many managers do certain tasks themselves is to stay close to the marketplace. Top managers at large companies like Digital Equipment make a point of spending many days a year with key customers. The idea is not just to flatter the customer with lunch in the president's private dining room, although that can be useful too. More important, these managers find that by making key sales calls in person they find out what lies behind the marketing plans and sales reports that their subordinates send up to them through the hierarchy.

Effective Management

Managers differ in many ways. As we will see in the following pages, some are good at dealing with technical problems, others at handling human relations. Some are long-range strategic thinkers, while others react to events as they happen. As we look at the different ways of managing, however, we will be trying to answer one basic question: Why are some managers recognized as good at what they do and others as not good?

Management writer Peter Drucker has provided one of the more useful insights into what makes a manager good or bad. Management, he says, can be measured in terms of two standards, efficiency and effectiveness.

Efficiency means achieving goals with a minimum of expense, waste, or effort. The efficient manager takes human and material resources and gets the most out of them. Can more kilowatt hours be squeezed out of that mountain of coal behind the power station? An efficient utility executive will find a way. Can an unpromising group of recruits be made into a crack military unit? A sergeant who is an efficient manager of people will do the job.

But efficiency is not all there is to being a good manager. Even more important, one must be able to choose the right goals on which to focus the energies of the organization. Choosing the right goals is what Drucker calls **effectiveness**. Efficient managers, he says, do things right; effective managers do the right things.

Without effectiveness, efficiency is nothing. Many a firm has gone to its grave doing the wrong thing well. For example, early in the century Britain's Conway-Stevens Company became known for making the best fountain pens money could buy. But after World War II it made a fatal mistake when it decided that the ballpoint pen was a flash in the pan that would never catch on. The firm stuck to fountain pens and went bankrupt. As Drucker said in a seminar for federal executives, "The greatest temptation is to work at doing better and better what should not be done at all."

THE PROCESS OF MANAGEMENT

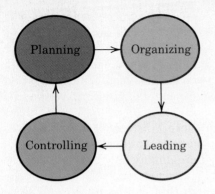

Planning: Setting goals and deciding how to achieve them.

We now have a general idea of what management is and why it is needed. The next step is to sketch in some details by looking at just what it is that managers do. Perhaps the oldest accepted way of looking at the manager's job is to break the process of management down into the aspects of planning, organizing, leading, and controlling. This approach can be traced to the writings of the French industrialist Henri Fayol. (See Box 5–2.) For many decades, Fayol's categories, or variations on them, have served as a guide for teachers and students of management.

Planning

Planning means setting goals and deciding how to achieve them. Planning can take place at many levels in an organization. It can cover time horizons ranging from very long to very short.

Box 5–2 Henri Fayol 1841–1925

Henri Fayol was born in France in 1841 into a middle-class family. At the age of 19 he became chief engineer of the mining company Conambault. By 1888 he was the firm's managing director. In this position he rescued the company from the verge of bankruptcy, leaving it in excellent financial health when he retired in 1918.

Fayol attributed his success not to his own talents but to a set of management concepts that he believed could be taught and learned. Fayol observed that management is not just a business activity but something that is needed for all human undertakings.

One of Fayol's ideas was that the process of management could be broken down into a number of aspects. He listed five of these, calling them planning, organizing, commanding, coordinating, and controlling. (Modern writers often group his "commanding" and "coordinating" functions together under the heading of "leading.") He subdivided these aspects of management into more specific ones, most of which still find a place, in one form or another, in management texts today.

Fayol first published his ideas in French in 1914. It was not until the 1950s, however, that his ideas became widely known in the United States. Today he is seen as one of the great management philosophers of the twentieth century.

Source: Claude S. George, Jr., *The History of Management Thought,* 2nd ed. (Englewood Cliffs, N.J.: Prentice-Hall, 1972), pp. 110–15.

Strategic planning: The systematic long-range planning process used to define and achieve organizational goals.

Strategic planning. Many big companies, units of government, and not-for-profit organizations have long-term plans that are formally drawn up, written down, and followed as far as possible. Such plans set out goals and the means for achieving them. For example, a trucking company might lay out a five-year plan for becoming a national carrier by expanding its fleet and merging with other carriers. The systematic long-range planning used to define and achieve organizational goals is often known as **strategic planning**.[2]

[2]James A. F. Stoner, *Management,* 2nd ed. (Englewood Cliffs, N.J.: Prentice-Hall, 1982), p. 101.

THE LOCKHORNS

"I **AM** GOING TO CLEAN OUT THE ATTIC....
I'M IN THE PLANNING STAGE."

Writers on strategic planning do not agree on a "best" way to put a plan together. They agree on certain points, however, including the following.

1. Strategic planning involves asking and answering very fundamental questions: What line of business are we in? What customers should we be trying to serve? What kinds of things do we do better than our competitors, and what kinds of things are we not very good at? It is less concerned with intermediate goals, such as bringing sales in the Mid-Atlantic region up to the national average by the end of the year.
2. Strategic planning must actively involve top management. Only top management has the authority to define and modify the firm's broad goals. Also, it is often the only level of management that can see the whole picture.
3. Strategic planning requires a conscious effort to stretch the organization's time horizon. It should pay special attention to long-term changes in the business environment. For example, many chemical companies are planning to adjust their operations to a society that has become more pollution-conscious. The faster the business environment changes, the more strategic planning is needed.

Short-term planning. Short-term planning is no less important than strategic planning. Short-term plans take a wide variety of forms. One form consists simply of breaking down long-term plans into shorter, more detailed segments. In the case of the trucking company, for the first year of its five-year expansion the equipment manager would have to plan how many new trucks to buy; the financial manager would have to plan how to raise the needed money; and the marketing manager would have to plan how to attract the new customers needed to keep the new trucks full. If all of these subplans are based on a well-thought-out long-term plan, the parts will fit together into a successful whole.

Strategic planning is as important for small businesses as it is for large corporations. Marc P. Anderson

Another kind of short-term planning consists of setting up procedures and policies for dealing with possible future events. What should the company's policy be in case of a strike? Should it shut down, or should the managers themselves try to keep it going? *Budgeting* is a third kind of short-term planning. Suppose a university has a long-term plan to improve its engineering school. Does it commit part of its annual budget to buying new equipment and hiring new faculty? If the long-term plan is not reflected in the budget, it will be nothing but empty words.

Planning for small businesses. Planning, especially strategic planning, is as important for small companies as for large ones. This fact tends to be obscured by some writers who focus on the formal planning process and on written strategic plans. Plans do not always have to be in written form, however. For example, if you are the manager of a small lumberyard, you may spend some time thinking about trends in the market you serve. If you think the construction of new houses in your area is likely to slow down in the coming years, you might plan to shift from serving contractors to meeting the needs of do-it-yourself homeowners.

Most important, a small firm, just like a big one, must decide what line of business it is in and what it can do well. Even when customers are hard to come by, taking on a job that doesn't fit the firm's key goals can be as much of a mistake for a midget as for a giant. Yet getting "top management" involved in planning may be harder in a small firm than in a large one. If the same person is president, supervisor, and an individual contributor as well, he or she may forget to find the time to do some strategic planning.

Finally, the environment changes just as fast for small firms as for large ones. Consider service stations. Price rises for oil products have been as traumatic for service station owners as they have been for any big corporation. Some stations have survived by turning themselves into cost-cutting self-service outlets. Others have built up their services so that they depend less on gasoline sales. In either case, the stations that have survived are those that saw what was going on and planned some kind of response.

The spread of self-service gas stations in the 1970s was a response to a major change in the business environment: a rapid increase in oil prices. Marc P. Anderson

Organizing

Organizing: Dividing work among individuals and groups and coordinating their actions.

Carrying out plans requires **organizing**, the second part of the process of management. Organizing means dividing work up among individuals and groups and coordinating their actions. A business, whether it is large or small, is well organized if everyone has a clear idea of what his or her job is and if all of its parts fit together to carry out the work of the firm as a whole. It is poorly organized if its units work at cross-purposes; if rival departments are constantly fighting over turf; or if some jobs fail to get done because they were never clearly assigned to anyone.

Well-managed firms tend to have lean, simple structures. It is easy, though, for an organization to grow fat and tangled. Urgent tasks get assigned to committees. Key managers, distracted by their committee work, plead for larger staffs. Meanwhile little work gets done. The U.S. Congress, with its huge staffs and its maze of overlapping committees and subcommittees, is a prime example of overly complex structure. Some private companies nearly equal it, however.

Managers must guard against rigid as well as complex structures. Good managers give their subordinates enough autonomy to make the most of their skills and talents. Autonomy does not mean anarchy if it is accompanied by suitable control. We will have more to say about organizing in Chapter 6.

Leading

Leading: Getting people to work together willingly to achieve the organization's goals.

A good manager must not only plan and organize so that subordinates know what they ought to be doing; he or she must also **lead** them so that they do their best.

Focusing the motivations of members on the goals of a company is one part of good leadership. You may have seen pictures of Japanese factory workers standing in uniform and singing company songs. Such activities can help workers identify with the company. They are one style of motivat-

Mentor: A supervisor or experienced worker from whom an employee obtains advice and support.

Staffing: The selection and training of specific people to fill positions in an organization.

Controlling: Checking to see that an organization is progressing toward its goals, and taking corrective action if it is not.

The Cycle of Control

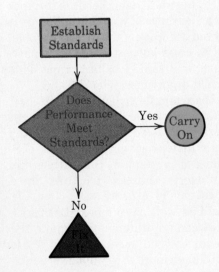

ing, one that may not be suited to all cultures. Pins, badges, and company bowling teams are less dramatic examples of this approach to motivation.

An important aspect of leading is taking note of good work by individuals and groups at all levels of an organization. People are much more likely to work as members of a team when they know that a job well done will be rewarded, whether formally or informally. We will have more to say about leading and motivating in Chapter 14.

As leaders, managers must also be concerned with the careers of subordinates who will be leaders in the future. Successful managers in both the private and public sectors often credit their success to **mentors**—superiors who set examples, dispensed advice, and provided challenges. **Staffing**, the choice of specific individuals to fill positions within the organization, is part of leadership and career development. We will take up these topics in Chapter 16.

Controlling

Controlling, as the term is used in the business world, means checking to see that an organization is progressing toward its goals, and taking corrective action if it is not. Formally, controlling can be broken down into a three-part cycle:

- Establish clear standards of performance.
- Find out if the actual performance meets those standards
- Fix the problem if the performance does not meet the standards.

The standards set for control purposes must be consistent with the organization's goals. Let's go back once more to the example of the trucking company whose goal is to expand nationwide. Suppose that while it was a regional carrier it used a control standard that set a fixed minimum profit on each load carried. Maintaining this standard, which was useful in the past, might prevent the firm from expanding. Instead, while the company is going after customers in new territories, the profit per load might have to be reduced for a while to allow for quantity discounts, special rates for long hauls, and the like.

A good information system is basic to effective control. Today firms of all sizes use computers to keep top management up to date. Computers can't solve all problems, though. Sometimes they become a way of hiding bad news from people higher up in the organization. Consider the case of Alden's, Inc., the now-defunct Chicago-based catalog sales company. Alden's reported 1981 profits of $2 million to executives of Wickes, its parent company. At the same time, it projected a 1982 profit of $14 million. But these figures reflected only about half of Alden's borrowing costs and no overhead expenses. Belatedly, Wickes' management found out that Alden had actually lost $25 million in 1981 and $32 million in the first nine months of 1982. It was too late to save Alden at that point. Wickes, which was in trouble itself partly because of this lapse of control, had to shut Alden down.[3]

Fayol and others viewed planning, organizing, leading, and controlling not as separate topics but, rather, as aspects of a unified process. We

[3]This account of Alden's troubles is based on Stephen J. Sansweet, "Management Mistakes Plus Old Problems Led to Collapse of Alden's," *Wall Street Journal*, January 6, 1983, p. 1.

will see again and again that managers must be skilled at all four aspects of the process of management.

PROBLEMS AND OPPORTUNITIES

Fayol's four mangement functions are one way to look at what managers do. Another approach, focuses on solving problems and finding opportunities. Anything that could keep the firm from achieving its goals is a problem; any chance to exceed those goals is an opportunity.

The activities of problem solving and opportunity finding cut across the functions of planning, organizing, leading, and controlling. Managers constantly encounter problems and discover opportunities while carrying out each of these functions.

Finding Problems

Before problems can be solved, they must be found. A rule of good management is to find problems before they find you. As a manager, how do you go about looking for problems? Some of the most fruitful ways are the following.

- *Compare present performance with past performance.* Have sales dropped? Have costs jumped suddenly? Have many employees left the firm in recent weeks? Any of these may indicate problems. Sometimes even something that seems good at first may signal a problem: Has output per worker increased suddenly? Before celebrating, check to see that your quality control staff isn't asleep on the job.
- *Compare actual performance with planned performance.* This is part of the control function. If you don't compare planned and actual performance, you are wasting your time making plans in the first place.
- *Look and listen outside your organization.* If you are in business, there is no better way of finding problems than listening to customer complaints. This is a major reason that top executives of well-managed companies spend much of their time with customers. Another reason to maintain contacts with people outside the firm is that your subordinates may not always pass bad news along to you. Within reason, take even gossip seriously.
- *Watch your competitors.* Your own business may be running smoothly when suddenly your competitor comes out with a better mousetrap. Now you have a problem. All good business managers keep a close eye on the competition.

Solving Problems

Not much has been written about the process of finding problems, but a huge amount has been written about solving them. Without going into detail, let's consider a few general guidelines drawn from a number of sources. They are as follows.

1. *Screen all problems.* When a problem comes to your attention, screen it to see if you are the one who should solve it. If it is simple or routine, it may be better to ask a subordinate to take care of it. (In problem finding, you have to guard against subordinates who don't bring you problems that they should bring to you. Here you have to guard against those who bring you problems that they should solve themselves.) Much less often, you may want to pass the problem up the ladder to a superior. (A problem that will affect other departments besides your own might fall into this category.)
2. *Analyze the problem.* The next step is to determine how the problem relates to your organization's goals. Might there be a cost overrun? Are quality standards falling? Has your division failed to reach its sales goals? If you can, get numbers showing the size of the problem.
3. *List the alternatives.* Proceed carefully here. Jumping at the first idea that comes to mind does not always give the best solution. Be creative; ask for suggestions. And consider doing nothing and letting the problem work itself out. Doing nothing is usually not the best way to solve a problem, but at this stage it should be on your list of alternatives.
4. *Check and test constraints.* Some of the alternatives, even if they are workable, may violate constraints imposed from outside. Is a competitor invading one of your territories? Cutting your price for only some of your customers may be illegal; antitrust laws are a constraint. Are you having trouble keeping unit costs down? Your union contract may limit your ability to assign workers to different jobs. But don't accept such constraints blindly. Test them to see if they are appropriate. If they are not, the solution may take the form of loosening the constraint. For example, suppose you think the only way to meet a strong competitive threat is to bring out a new product of your own, but your research and development budget isn't big enough. If the threat is really major, perhaps you should appeal to top management for a larger budget.
5. *Evaluate the remaining alternatives.* Make certain that your standards are consistent with your goals. For example, suppose your strategic plan aims at growth of market share. It may be a mistake to choose the lowest-cost solution to a manufacturing problem if a higher-cost solution will make your product more marketable.
6. *Decide, implement, and follow up.* Once you have decided, act. Then follow through with control. If the approach you have chosen doesn't solve the problem, go back and try another one.

Box 5–3 presents a summary of this problem-solving process.

Finding Opportunities

In the long run, opportunity finding is even more important than problem solving. Skill at finding opportunties makes the difference between management that is effective and management that is merely efficient.

It is hard to give a step-by-step guide to opportunity finding, but much of what we have said about problem finding and problem solving clearly applies. All of the ways of finding problems can also be ways of finding

Box 5–3 The Problem-Solving Process

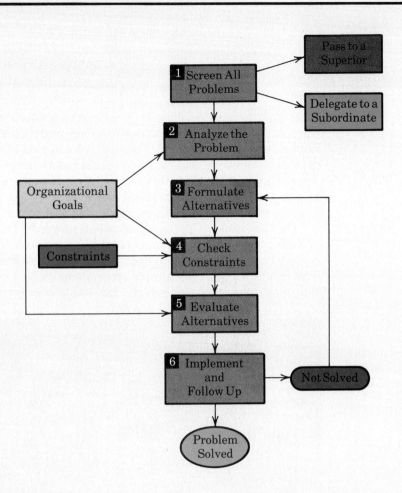

There are six steps in the problem-solving process: (1) Screen the problem to see if you should solve it yourself or send it to a superior or a subordinate. (2) Analyze the problem, making sure you understand how it relates to the goals of your firm. (3) List alternative solutions; don't just jump at the first one that suggests itself. (4) Check proposed solutions against outside constraints, testing the constraints to see if they are appropriate. (5) Evaluate the remaining alternatives in light of your company's goals. (6) Decide, implement, and follow up. If the solution doesn't work, try another one.

opportunities. Close contact with customers is the most important of these. Once an opportunity has been found, many of the steps for solving problems can be applied: Don't just jump at the opportunity—think about different ways of taking advantage of it. Be wary of constraints that might turn the opportunity into a problem. And evaluate the opportunity in terms of your strategic plan. An opportunity that looks good might lead you into a line of business that isn't really suited to your company.

One last comment: Don't forget your opportunity-hunting hat when you go out problem solving. What looks like a problem may reveal an opportunity if you look at it from another angle. (It is said that penicillin was discovered by observing a bothersome mold that kept growing on lab dishes.) In fact, it may sometimes be hard to tell a problem and an opportunity apart.

THE ROLES OF MANAGERS

From what we have said so far, it is clear that managers do many things. They plan, organize, lead, and control. They find problems, solve problems, and find opportunities. In this section, we will look at managers from still another perspective, that of the roles they play in their organizations. In order to find out what roles managers play, researchers have asked them to keep journals, have interviewed them about what they do, and have sometimes even followed them around as observers.

On the basis of his own and other research, Henry Mintzberg has classified the doings of managers according to three groups of roles: *interpersonal*, *informational*, and *decisional*. Mintzberg finds evidence of these roles in studies of presidents and street gang leaders, corporate executives and small-time entrepreneurs. He notes that managers shift quickly from

Ribbon-cutting ceremonies, television interviews, and conferences with employees are examples of the interpersonal, informational, and decisional roles of managers. Mayor—© Freda Leinwand; Interview—© Julian Calder, Woodfin Camp; Conference—© Freda Leinwand

one role to another. A study he made of five top managers showed that half of the activities they engaged in lasted less than nine minutes, and only 10 percent lasted more than one hour.[4]

Interpersonal Roles

Since getting things done through people is the essence of management, it is not surprising that managers spend much of their time on interpersonal roles. Managers have both the authority and the responsibility for getting people to work well either alone or together. Mintzberg lists three major types of interpersonal roles: the figurehead role, the leadership role, and the liaison role.

1. *Figurehead.* Every manager must sometimes act as a figurehead. Mayors cut ribbons, corporate presidents greet important visitors, and college presidents sit with wealthy alumni at football games. At a lower level in the hierarchy, a supervisor going to the wedding of a lathe operator would be playing a figurehead role.
2. *Leader.* Mintzberg includes in the leadership role such activities as motivating, setting examples, hiring and firing, and expressing approval or disapproval of the actions of subordinates.
3. *Liaison.* The liaison role involves contacts with colleagues at the same level in the firm and with people outside it. The informal, horizontal contacts that result from this role supplement the manager's formal, vertical contacts with subordinates and superiors.

Informational Roles

Because of their network of contacts, both formal and informal, managers are the best-informed people in their firm or agency. They serve as information centers. According to Mintzberg, informational roles, like interpersonal roles, fall into three categories.

1. *Monitor.* As monitors, managers scan the business environment for information of all types. Subordinates collect and feed them "hard" information, such as weekly sales figures. But because of their status, the managers themselves often are the only people with access to vital "soft" information. For example, by meeting with the head of a labor union, a corporate president may get a feel for areas of concern in upcoming contract negotiations.
2. *Disseminator of information.* A comment made over lunch by a key customer may be passed along to the marketing department for quick action. Managers also often pass information from one subordinate to another.
3. *Spokesperson.* Speeches, press releases, and interviews on radio and television are formal examples of the spokesperson role. Hints dropped over cocktails and the famous "trial balloons" floated by "high officials" in Washington are less formal examples.

[4]Henry Mintzberg, "The Manager's Job: Folklore and Fact," *Harvard Business Review,* July-August 1975, pp. 49–61.

Decisional Roles

Finally, Mintzberg found that managers spend a large amount of their time making decisions. He lists four decisional roles:

1. *Entrepreneur.* In this role, the manager acts as opportunity finder.
2. *Disturbance handler.* This is another name for problem solving.
3. *Resource allocator.* In this role, the manager decides how the company's resources are to be divided among its various parts.
4. *Negotiator.* Managers must engage in many kinds of negotiations. These include, of course, formal contract negotiations with workers, customers, and suppliers. They also include negotiations with other managers on such matters as size of budget and division of responsibility. Managers are well suited to the role of negotiator because of their status and authority, their central position in the firm's channels of communication, and the skill at getting things done through people that made them managers in the first place.

A final word about these roles: Because of the nature of their position, managers spend much or even all of their time in one or another of Mintzberg's ten roles. But nonmanagers do many of these things too. Wherever you are in an organization, you spend some of your time picking up or passing along information, some of it serving as leader or liaison, and some of it making decisions.

The Roles of Managers

Interpersonal
- Figurehead
- Leader
- Liaison

Informational
- Monitor
- Disseminator
- Spokesperson

Decisional
- Entrepreneur
- Disturbance Handler
- Resource Allocator
- Negotiator

THE SKILLS OF MANAGERS

By now it is clear that effective management requires not one skill but many. In this section we will make a few remarks about the skills managers need and how they can be acquired.

Human, Technical, and Conceptual Skills

In a classic article in the *Harvard Business Review,* Robert L. Katz described three basic management skills: *human, technical,* and *conceptual.*[5]

Human skills. Human skills are those required to get people to do their best as individuals and to work well with others. They lie at the very heart of the manager's job, which we have defined as getting things done through people. Human skills are vital to management at all levels. Katz argued that they are most important for supervisory managers, who are in constant contact with individual contributors. However, other studies have shown that even top managers spend as much as 75 or 80 percent of their time in direct contact with other people. Well-managed firms recognize that people, not machines or technology, are the key to productivity.

[5]Robert L. Katz, "Skills of an Effective Administrator," *Harvard Business Review,* February 1955 (reprinted September-October 1974). Katz's classification is quite similar to one proposed decades earlier by Fayol. Fayol's writings, however, were not widely known at the time in the English-speaking world.

Like all managers, an orchestra conductor must combine human, technical, and conceptual skills. Marc P. Anderson

Skills of Management

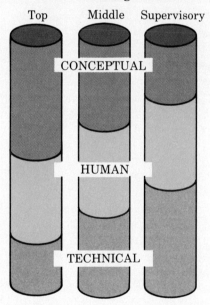

Technical skills. Technical skills are those required for turning out the actual products or services of the firm. Managers of a tax service must know something about accounting; managers of a forest products company must know something about trees; and so on. Katz felt that technical skills, too, are most important at the supervisory level. They are basic to the leadership function of supervisors (showing individual contributors how to do things) and to the control function (finding and correcting problems while they are still small). Middle management is less involved in production and operations, and hence relies somewhat less on technical skills. Top managers need technical skills the least, but even they must often rely on them in dealing with key customers or new product ideas.

Conceptual skills. Conceptual skills are those required to relate parts of the company's work to the whole. Strong conceptual skills are most important at the top level of management. Clearly, good conceptual skills are needed in planning and organizing. They are no less important in finding opportunities and solving the nonroutine problems that land on top managers' desks. Conceptual skills are least important for supervisors.

Although the work of managers differs from one level of management to another, all levels require at least some skill of each type.

Learning to Be a Manager

Learning to be a manager is not something that can be done once and for all. It is an ongoing process.

People who learn to be effective managers draw on a number of sources. By far the most important of these is experience. People learn to manage by doing it: by organizing a church fair, running a student association, or supervising a lawn-cutting crew on a summer job. The key is to experiment, to try things out and see how they work, and then to try something new.

The second major way of learning management skills is to watch good managers. Watching people who are good at something and imitating

Many television viewers have improved their cooking techniques by watching Julia Child's famous demonstrations. Courtesy of PBS

them is much more useful than watching people who are bad at it and trying to learn from their mistakes. There are all too few ways to do things right, and all too many ways to do them wrong. If you want to learn how to make pastry, watch Julia Child making it on TV. Don't watch a cafeteria cook warming up breakfast rolls and then try to figure out how to do it better.

Beyond good role models, there are more formal sources of management skills. There are books, tapes, and movies. There are college courses, from the level of this course on up through the MBA and beyond. And there are courses provided by companies for their employees.

There is one more way to learn management skills. Managing, as we have said many times, is largely a matter of managing human relationships. When you get your first or next job, one human relationship is sure to be important to you: your relationship with your boss. As Box 5–4 explains, learning to manage that relationship not only will get you ahead but will help you learn what management is all about.

Box 5–4 Managing Your Boss

What if you do not plan to become a manager? What if you do hope to become one someday, but are now in a junior position? That is no reason not to learn as much about management skills as you can. Manager or not, you will have to work with and within organizations all your life. To do so effectively, even at the individual-contributor level, you have to learn how to *manage your boss*.

Managing your boss doesn't mean manipulating or apple polishing. Instead, it means understanding the job of a manager, the pressures and responsibilities of a management position, and the strengths and weaknesses of your boss. If you know why your boss asks and does certain things, you will respond better. And if you can diagnose and accept your boss's weaknesses, you can adjust in ways that will help your boss and advance your own career.

Begin by recognizing that your relationship with your boss is one of *mutual dependence* between two *less than perfect* people. One common mistake is to fail to see how dependent your boss is on you. Your boss, and the company you both work for, can be severely hurt if you withhold information or cooperation. Your less than perfect boss may not always ask for needed help or information. Your boss may not

even be aware of what you know or can do. Be forthcoming!

The mirror image of this mistake is to fail to see how much you depend on your boss for help and information. Don't assume that your boss will magically know just what kind of help, information, and support you need. You will have to seek it, sometimes directly, always tactfully, in a way that suits the boss's style and your own.

And speaking of styles, you and your boss each have your own, but both of you must be willing to be flexible. As just one example, Peter Drucker divides bosses into "listeners" and "readers." A reader may respond better to your ideas if you put them in writing, sending in a short memo before a face-to-face meeting. A listener, on the other hand, may want you to walk right in and start talking, and may ask for a memo for the file only after a decision has been reached.

No doubt some employees will resent that on top of all their other duties they must also manage their relationship with their boss. But look at the positive side. Good management, from the bottom up as well as from the top down, means getting things done through people. And you and your boss are both people.

Source: Adapted from John J. Gabarro and John P. Kotter, "Managing Your Boss," *Harvard Business Review*, January-February 1980, pp. 92–100.

PUTTING EXCELLENCE INTO MANAGEMENT

We have seen what management is, what managers do, and what skills managers need. To pull these things together, we will ask a final question: What distinguishes good management from bad, and excellent management from the merely good?

To focus the discussion, we will turn again to the work of Thomas Peters and Robert Waterman, which we first referred to in Chapter 1. Peters and Waterman studied sixty-two companies that were known for excellent management. They found eight attributes that those companies shared. All of them have been mentioned in this and previous chapters. They are as follows.

1. *A bias toward action.* In excellently managed companies, the emphasis is on doing things. These companies plan, but they do not plan themselves to death. At 3M, for example, new-product plans are limited to five pages; at Procter & Gamble, one page is the limit. Well-managed companies also stress action in solving problems. For example, when DuPont became worried about its $800-million-a-year bill for transportation, it appointed a "czar" with the power to take action on a company-wide scale.
2. *Simple form and lean staff.* Although all the companies in the Peters and Waterman study were big, their units were organized along "Small is beautiful" lines. For example, fewer than one hundred people at the headquarters office run Dana Corporation, a firm with some $3 billion in annual sales.
3. *Closeness to the customer.* The excellently managed companies were customer-driven. At many of them, top managers make numerous sales calls. At some, customer service borders on the fanatic.
4. *Productivity through people.* The companies recognized that people, not equipment or technology, are the key to productivity. This value is stressed right on the shop floor. In some cases, small production teams help set their own output targets. Almost all the firms used "corny" but effective methods of motivation such as badges, pins, and medals.
5. *Autonomy to encourage entrepreneurship.* Well-managed companies are aware that opportunity finding should not be limited to top management. Plant and division managers are not just encouraged to look for opportunities; they are given the freedom to develop them. Many of the firms form "start-up" divisions to bring out new products.
6. *Stress on a key business value.* The strategy of each company stresses a key value that is appropriate to its line of business: customer service at IBM, ideas at Hewlett-Packard, productivity at Dana. The key value pervades the company at all levels.
7. *Doing what they know best.* The words of a former chairman of Johnson & Johnson say it all: "Never acquire a business you don't know how to run." As we saw in Chapter 4, sticking to a clearly defined line of business is a good rule for small firms too.
8. *Simultaneous loose and tight controls.* Well-managed firms choose

a few key variables and control them tightly, while allowing flexibility elsewhere. The variables that are closely controlled must be suited to the company's strategy. Trying to control too many variables at once only leads to confusion. Soviet planners are known for burdening managers with dozens of detailed goals. The result, often, is that none of the goals are met. A well-managed firm in a competitive market cannot afford this mistake.

Although Peters and Waterman focused on large companies, a little thought suggests that these eight points apply to small firms as well as large ones, and to government and not-for-profit organizations too. Don't overplan—do it. Keep it simple. Keep in touch with the people your organization serves. Remember that people are the key to getting things done. Give subordinates room to be creative. Stress a few key values. Stick to doing what you do best. Control, but don't constrain. These guidelines will serve the leader of a Cub Scout den as well as the president of IBM, Dana, or Procter and Gamble.

The attributes of excellent management listed by Peters and Waterman apply to small firms as well as large ones. © David Burnett, Woodfin Camp

SUMMARY

1. *Management* is the art of getting things done through people. Good managers should be *efficient*; that is, they should achieve the firm's goals with a minimum of effort and expense. They should also be *effective*, meaning that they should focus their efforts on the right goals.

2. All but the smallest organizations have a hierarchy in which members are ranked by status and authority. The lowest level consists of *individual contrib-* *utors*, who do the actual work of the organization and supervise no one. Above them are three levels of management. At the lowest level are *supervisory managers*, who direct the work of individual contributors. Next come *middle managers*, who spend at least some of their time directing the work of other managers. Finally, *top managers* are responsible for planning and for defining the goals of the organization.

3. The process of management is often broken down into the functions of *planning*, *organizing*, *leading*, and *controlling*. Planning means setting goals and deciding how to achieve them. Organizing means dividing work among groups and individuals, and coordinating their actions. Leading means getting the organization's members to work together willingly to achieve its goals. And controlling means checking to make sure the organization is progressing toward its goals, and taking corrective action if it is not.

4. While carrying out their other functions, managers must be on the lookout for problems and opportunities. Being able to find both problems and opportunities is as important as being able to solve problems.

5. Studies of managers on the job suggest that there are three sets of managerial roles. One set consists of interpersonal roles, those that directly involve getting things done through people. The second set consists of roles in which managers gather and disseminate information. The roles in the third set are decisional and include problem finding and problem solving.

6. Peters and Waterman found that excellently managed companies share eight attributes: a bias toward action; simple form and lean staff; closeness to the customers; productivity through people; autonomy to encourage entrepreneurship; stress on a key business value; doing what they know best; and simultaneous loose and tight controls.

KEY TERMS

You should be familiar with the following terms and concepts. Check their meanings by referring to the marginal definitions in the chapter or to the glossary at the end of the book.

Management	Top managers	Organizing
Management hierarchy	Efficiency	Leading
Individual contributors	Effectiveness	Controlling
Supervisory or first-line managers	Planning	Mentor
Middle managers	Strategic planning	Staffing

QUESTIONS FOR REVIEW AND DISCUSSION

1. The chapter begins with the story of John, the alcoholic manager. Think about what this story shows about John and his superiors in terms of (a) the functions of managers, (b) the roles of managers, and (c) the skills of managers.

2. A high school principal is a manager of a nonbusiness organization. Give examples of the functions of planning, organizing, leading, and controlling as they apply to the job of high school principal.

3. Identify people at your school who are individual contributors, supervisory managers, middle managers, and top managers. Sketch the duties of each. Are there any "player-managers" at your school?

4. The text stresses that a manager can be efficient without being effective. Can a manager also be effective without being efficient? If so, give an example, real or made up. If not, explain why not.

5. Turn back one more time to the story of The Scribe at the beginning of Chapter 1. Did Nettles' first attempt to set up a business illustrate good strategic planning? Was her second attempt any better in this regard? Explain.

6. Turn back to Cases 4–1 (American Solar Heat) and 4–2 (McDonald's). Which, if any, of Peters and Waterman's eight attributes of excellent management are brought out in each case?

Case 5–1: Reshaping Woolworth

In 1982 F. W. Woolworth, the nation's largest variety store chain, announced that it would close all of its 336 Woolco discount stores. In doing so, it would cut $2 billion from its total sales, thereby shrinking by 30 percent. Woolworth had failed at discounting because, unlike such competitors as K mart, it had not committed itself fully to the discounting concept.

Woolworth retained its variety stores, although these seem old-fashioned to many shoppers. And as it was shutting down Woolco, it was starting up a new type of store. These stores, called "J. Brannam" (short for "just brand names"), offer name brands at discount prices.

The decision to close Woolco threw some 25,000 people out of work. Wall Street applauded the move, however: the price of Woolworth's stock rose 27 percent after the shutdown of Woolco.

Source: Eleanor Johnson Tracy, "Ed Gibbons's Legacy to Woolworth," *FORTUNE*, November 29, 1982, p. 128.

Questions:

1. What does this case show about the need for strategic planning? Does good strategic planning always focus on growth? Why or why not?
2. What special problems of short-term planning, organizing, leading, and controlling will Woolworth's managers face as a result of the Woolco decision and the decision to start up J. Brannam?
3. Does this case touch directly on any of the eight attributes of excellent management listed by Peters and Waterman? Which one or ones?

Case 5–2: Corning Glass Shapes Up

Many companies have gone under because managers have failed to keep their goals and strategies under constant review. Many others have shaped up just in time. Such was the case with Corning Glass, a billion-dollar corporation that is still run by descendants of the man who founded it more than a century ago. Corning has never been in doubt about its chief line of business: it is a glass company. But what kind of glass in a changing world?

In the late 1970s and early 1980s, Corning's profits were slipping badly. By 1982, 20 percent of its workers had been laid off. Some of its major product lines were hard hit. Take light-bulb glass, for example. Corning made the glass for Edison's first bulb, and it had been in the business ever since. As recently as 1972, light-bulb glass had accounted for a third of Corning's sales. Then longer-lived bulbs and the energy crisis came along. The market shrank, and most of it went to General Electric, GTE, and North American Phillips. In TV picture-tube glass, another big line, Corning was battered just as badly, this time by imports.

Wall Street analysts blamed Corning's problems on slow reactions to new opportunities and a failure to shed declining product lines. Finally, though, Corning's management made some basic decisions:

- Dump unprofitable product lines. (Corning sold its light-bulb glass plants to GTE.)
- Play down lines that are vulnerable in recessions, such as glass for car headlights and the ceramic linings of industrial furnaces.
- Plunge headfirst into high-profit, high-growth products, taking advantage of the firm's excellent research and development facilities.

Optical wave guides were the hottest of Corning's hot new products. These are hair-thin glass fibers that allow telephone cables to carry as many as 300,000 conversations at once. Corning expects sales of wave guides to soar by 50 percent a year, reaching $1.7 billion a year by the end of the decade.

Corning's research labs have also produced other high-tech spinoffs from the company's traditional product lines. For example, complex biotechnology products have evolved from the simple business of making test tubes and lab dishes.

Finally, Corning found a new way to exploit its mature, low-tech lines such as TV picture-tube glass. A new division, Corning Engineering, sells whole TV-glass factories, instead of just the glass itself, to developing countries like China and India.

Sources: Myron Magnet, "Corning Glass Shapes Up," *FORTUNE*, December 13, 1982, pp. 90–109, and Ann Hughey, "With New Chairman, Corning Tries to Get Tough and Revive Earnings," *Wall Street Journal*, April 22, 1983, p. 31.

Questions:

1. In what ways are the decisions described in this case examples of strategic planning?

2. How does this case illustrate the processes of problem finding and problem solving?

3. Which of Peters and Waterman's eight traits of excellent management are illustrated by this case, in a positive or negative way?

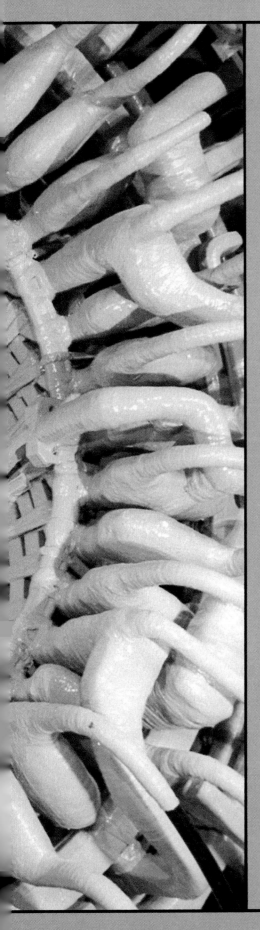

Chapter 6
ORGANIZING

When you have completed this chapter, you should be able to

- List the three steps in organizing and explain how they relate to planning, leading, and controlling.

- Read an organization chart and distinguish among *line organization*, *line and staff organization*, and *matrix organization*.

- Discuss the advantages of specialization, the dangers of overspecialization, and the concepts of job enlargement and job enrichment.

- Illustrate several forms of *departmentalization*.

- Explain what is involved in managerial coordination and what is meant by *span of management*.

- Discuss mutual adjustment, *task forces*, and markets as mechanisms of horizontal coordination.

- Explain the meaning of *delegation* and the proper balance among *responsibility*, *authority*, and *accountability*.

One day in 1982 Matt Sanders was told to leave his office at Convergent Technologies, a California computer maker. After a few days he found a new office—in a dumpy one-story building that used to house a credit union. Not a single colleague from Convergent came with him. He was on his own. "I felt bad for him," his boss, Allen Michels, told a *Wall Street Journal* reporter. "It was awful."

Another hardship story from the 1982 recession? It might sound like one, but it is not. Instead, Sanders' uprooting was the first step in one of the hot new organizing techniques of the computer industry—forming small, entrepreneurial "companies within companies."

Sanders' task was to design and build a portable computer in less than a year. Convergent gave him the task, a budget, and almost nothing else. Instead of letting him take Convergent employees with him, it encouraged him to raid companies like Texas Instruments and Motorola. Sanders' group, code-named "Ultra," was a typical start-up company in every way except the degree of financial risk involved.

Computer firms have turned to the company-within-a-company technique as a way of keeping up with the fast pace of change in their industry. Many of the most successful products in this field have lives of only a year or eighteen months before competition makes them obsolete. Small groups, it is felt, are faster on their feet. They also tend to have high morale. Apple Computer, Timex, and even the giant IBM have used this technique in one form or another.

By keeping things small, says Michels, "you inject a harmonious attitude. You give them the right amount of freedom so there is no sense of futility."

In 1983, after just nine months of work, Ultra's baby appeared on the market in the form of a tablet-sized machine called the Workslate.[1]

[1] Based on Erik Larson and Carrie Dolan, "Large Computer Firms Sprout Little Divisions for Good, Fast Work," *Wall Street Journal*, August 19, 1983, p. 1.

In business, the form of an organization must fit its purpose. That's the moral of the story of Convergent Technologies and the Ultra project. The same holds true for not-for-profit organizations—the Catholic church and small fundamentalist churches are organized in vastly different ways that suit their different strategies for spreading the Christian message. Government agencies may look the same from the outside, but anyone who has worked in more than one of them knows that even they have different missions, and hence differences in organizational form. Fitting form to purpose will be the theme of this chapter.

THE PROCESS OF ORGANIZING

Chapter 5 listed planning, organizing, leading, and controlling as key aspects of the management process. This chapter will focus on the second of these aspects, *organizing*, or putting resources to work in a coordinated fashion.

Work will progress more smoothly if people whose work is related are gathered into departments or divisions. Courtesy of the Maytag Company

Planning comes first because organizing must have a purpose. A clear business plan gives a manager a detailed picture of all the work that needs to be done to achieve the firm's goals. The next task, that of organizing the work set out in the plan, can then be broken down into three steps.

1. *Dividing up the work.* Organizations are formed to handle tasks that are too big for one person. Part of the manager's job is to break down those tasks into pieces that are small enough to be done by one person. In doing so, he or she must take the skills of each person into account and arrange things so that no one has too much or too little to do.

2. *Grouping tasks into logical units.* In most companies there are groups of two or more people whose work is related. Work will be done more smoothly if such people are gathered into departments or divisions. This part of organizing is called **departmentalization**.

3. *Coordinating the work.* Finally, the work of the various departments must be coordinated. This requires more than just settling conflicts as they arise. To prevent conflicts, coordination should be built into the structure of the firm. Well-designed coordinating mechanisms make leadership and control, the last two management functions, much easier.

Departmentalization: Grouping people who do related work into logical units or departments.

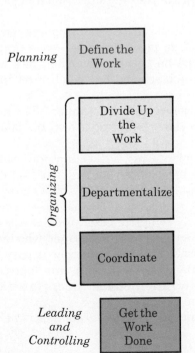

After the task of organizing is complete, the manager turns to leading and controlling, that is, to making sure the work gets done.

Understanding the Organization

In looking at organizing as an aspect of management, we will focus on creation and change. This is not the only reason to study the process of organizing, however. Another reason is to understand the structure of organizations that already exist.

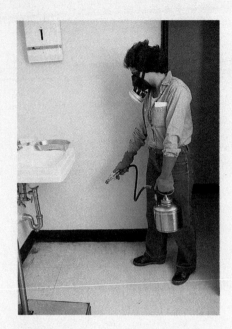

Once we are in an organization, we need to know what procedures must be followed to carry out certain tasks. © Freda Leinwand

Organization chart: A chart showing the division of work, the chain of command, and the departmentalization of an organization.

It is rare, after all, to have a chance to create a new organization from scratch. Sometimes a manager has to restructure one that already exists. But most often all the members of an organization—managers as well as individual contributors—view the structure they work in as given. Their main need is to learn how to work well within the organization as it is.

Once we are in an organization, we need to know how its work gets done and what part we play in it. We need to know who has the authority to make decisions. We need to know the procedures that must be followed to carry out certain tasks. What payoffs and prohibitions govern work within the organization? In short, whether we are managers or not, we view the organization as a set of constraints and guidelines.

The Organization Chart

Suppose you have found a summer job at Apex Exterminators. When you show up for work, everyone in the company has just arrived. The only person you have met so far is Amy, the person who interviewed and hired you. She walks you around the office and introduces you to the other employees.

"Brenda," she says, "this is Bill, our summer help. He's going to work on your team. We're going to start him off with some of the easier jobs so he can learn the basics.

"Here, Bill, I want you to meet Andy, too. Andy's the other team leader for household accounts. You'll meet his assistants, Al and Agnes, later—they're out loading the truck now. The three of them are going to take the harder jobs until we can get Brenda another assistant."

"Amy's our boss," explains Andy. "She does all the paperwork and keeps the customers happy. We just kill the bugs."

"This is Richard," Amy says, introducing an older man. "He does the same thing I do, except he works with commercial customers. This is Rachel, his team leader. Ralph, over there in the blue shirt, and Ron, next to him, are her assistants."

Amy then leads you from the shop into the office and introduces you to Carol, the office manager. "I'd like you to meet Carmine," says Carol. "She's the bookkeeper. And that's Carl on the phone. When he's not answering the phone he does invoices and scheduling. You'll meet him later."

Just then a friendly-looking man comes out of the inner office and says, "Hey, they always forget me. I'm Harry—all I do is own the place. You must be Bill. Glad to have you on board."

A few minutes later you have put on an Apex Exterminators T-shirt and are sitting in a truck with Brenda, headed for your first job. "I'm not sure I got all those names or what everyone does," you say. "Can we go over it again?"

In fact, you have been given a fairly complete description of Apex's organization. You were told who everyone is, what they do, and who they work for. But you didn't get this information in a form that is easy to understand or remember. Even for this small firm, with only fourteen people, it would help to have an **organization chart**. An organization chart for Apex Exterminators is shown in Box 6–1.

This simple chart, like the more complex charts for larger firms, shows five things about the company.

Box 6–1 Organization Chart for Apex Exterminators

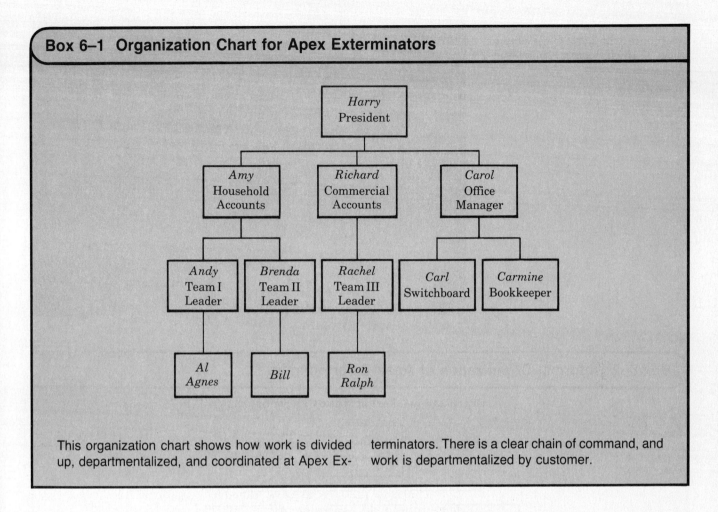

This organization chart shows how work is divided up, departmentalized, and coordinated at Apex Exterminators. There is a clear chain of command, and work is departmentalized by customer.

---

1. *The division of work.* As in all organizations, the work is broken up in a logical way so that everything gets done and no one is left with too much or too little to do.
2. *The type of work.* Labels in each box of the chart name the work done by each person.
3. *The chain of command.* The solid lines in the chart show who gives directions to whom and who reports to whom. This set of relationships is known as the **chain of command**.
4. *The management hierarchy.* The positions of the boxes show which members of the company are top managers (Harry), middle managers (Amy, Richard, and Carol), supervisors (Andy, Brenda, and Rachel), and individual contributors (Al, Agnes, Bill, Ron, Ralph, Carl, and Carmine).
5. *Departmentalization.* The chart shows the way related jobs are grouped into departments. At Apex, there are separate departments for household and commercial customers, plus an office staff.

Chain of command: The set of authority relationships, or who reports to whom, in an organization.

A great many business firms and other organizations use formal charts like the one shown in Box 6–1. Such charts tell a lot. They are not complete descriptions of how organizations work, however. And they don't provide all the information a person needs to work effectively in the organization.

An organization's chain of command determines who gives directions to whom. © Hugh Rogers, Monkmeyer

Box 6–2 Informal Organization of Apex Exterminators

Organization Chart of Apex Exterminators

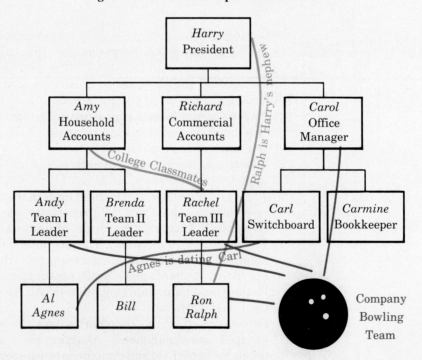

This box shows informal links among the employees of Apex Exterminators. These links cut across the formal chain of command. Most of the informal links help the company do its work better by improving morale and mutual adjustment. However, when Carl assigns all the best jobs to the team on which his friend Agnes works, other workers could become resentful.

The Informal Organization

Whatever organization you join, it won't take you long to find out that it has an informal as well as a formal structure. Understanding the informal structure is often crucial to getting things done. Box 6–2 shows the informal structure of Apex Exterminators. The company has four informal channels of communication.

1. *Ralph is Harry's nephew.* Harry gave him a job as a favor to his sister, Ralph's mother. The families are often together. At such times Ralph gives Harry a more candid, personal view of his employees than he can get at the office.
2. *Carol, Andy, Rachel, and Ralph have formed a bowling team.* Their friendship makes for relaxed working relationships. Last year, the team won the league championship and was a source of pride for the whole company.
3. *Amy and Rachel both took courses in entomology and toxicology at the state univeristy.* They are concerned about the possible health and environmental hazards of the chemicals the company uses. Rachel feels that her boss, Richard, is not sensitive to these issues. She knows, though, that she can talk to Amy about them. Amy will use her influence with Harry to change the company's procedures if necessary.
4. *Agnes and Carl are dating.* Carl takes orders from customers and assigns them to the teams. Since he started dating Agnes he has been giving the hardest jobs to Brenda's team.

The informal structure of Apex is typical in a number of ways. First, the informal links cut across the formal structure shown in the organization chart and skip some levels within it. Second, many of the relationships within it do not arise out of the job, although they affect the work of the company. And third, the informal structure has an important impact on how work gets done at Apex.

The informal structure of Apex is typical in another way as well: for the most part, it helps the company work better. For this reason, writers on management tend to have a positive view of informal structure. There are

Shared pursuits outside of the office can improve working relationships. © Gilles Peress, Magnum

dangers, however. If Brenda figures out that Carl is throwing the bad jobs her way, she will be resentful. And when and if Ralph is promoted, regardless of how much he deserves it, other employees may think it is just because he is Harry's nephew.

Although most of the rest of this chapter will be devoted to formal structure, the informal structure should be kept in mind too.

DIVIDING UP THE WORK

As we have pointed out, in any organization the work must be divided up; there is too much for one person to do alone. Clearly, work can be divided up in more than one way. To take a classic example, think of an automobile plant. It would be possible, given a full range of tools and parts, to have each worker build cars from start to finish, one at a time. That is not how auto plants work, however. Instead, each worker is given a small task—weld a certain seam or attach a certain part. This is done to each car as it comes along an assembly line. The result is vastly higher productivity.

Advantages of specialization. A major goal in dividing up work is to maximize the gains that can be made by specializing. Specializing permits employees to spend all their time doing what they do best, and to become experts in what they do. It reduces the amount of time spent moving from one task to another, getting new tools, or shifting mental gears. Finally, it makes training easier, since each task is simple and well defined.

Dangers of overspecialization. Despite the potential gains, specialization can be carried too far. One of the dangers is that overspecialized jobs will become dull and repetitive. When this happens, worker morale falls. As a result, workers may not stay with the firm for long, may frequently be absent, and may do poor-quality work.

Today, managers who are in charge of dividing up work must watch out for the pitfalls of overspecialization. Two ways of avoiding those pitfalls are job enlargement and job enrichment.

Charlie Chaplin's movie *Modern Times* made fun of the effects of mindless division of labor. The Granger Collection

Job enlargement: Making a job more interesting by giving the worker a broader range of tasks.

Job enlargement means giving each worker a broader range of tasks. Job enlargement can sometimes be achieved by combining two or more jobs into one. Or workers can be rotated among jobs to give them more exposure to the whole range of work being done in a firm. In one experiment with job enlargement, Volvo, the Swedish automaker, set up a system in which teams of workers were given the job of assembling automobile engines from start to finish. The idea was that the teams would be large enough to benefit from specialization within the team. At the same time, they would be small enough to permit job rotation and to allow each worker to get a feeling for the whole task.

Job enrichment: Making a job more interesting by giving the worker more decision-making power and more control over his or her work.

A different way to counter the effects of too much specialization is **job enrichment**. This involves giving workers a larger *vertical* slice of the work by giving them more control over their own jobs. In a typical job enrichment program, workers are allowed to make more decisions about their work—decisions that are commonly made by supervisors. In exchange, they become more accountable for their work.

COMBINING THE WORK INTO UNITS

In any but the smallest of organizations, people who do similar work are grouped together. This sounds simple until we think about how many ways there are in which work can be similar. In some companies, work may be grouped into departments by function. In others, departments may be formed on the basis of customer, product, or geographic area. Larger organizations, as we will see, may combine work into units in more than one way.

Departmentalization by Function

One of the most common bases for departmentalization is function. Managers and other employees who make the product form one department. Those whose job is to sell the product form another department. Those who look after the financial health of the firm form a third, and so on. The heads of all of these departments report to the firm's president.

Box 6–3 shows how this approach is used by the Kansas, Pacific, and Eastern Railroad. This is an imaginary medium-sized railroad centered in the lower Midwest. Three vice-presidents report to the president. The vice-president for transportation is in charge of actually moving goods from place to place. The vice-presidents for finance and for sales and marketing keep the company financially healthy and keep customers coming to it. Within the Transportation Division, the operations and maintenance sections represent a further level of departmentalization.

Other Bases for Departmentalization

Functional departmentalization is suited to firms that operate in a limited area and make a limited range of products. For larger firms, this approach may not work as well. For example, if the company makes both baby food and ball bearings, the people who sell the two products may have little in

Box 6–3 Functional Departmentalization of the Kansas, Pacific, and Eastern Railroad

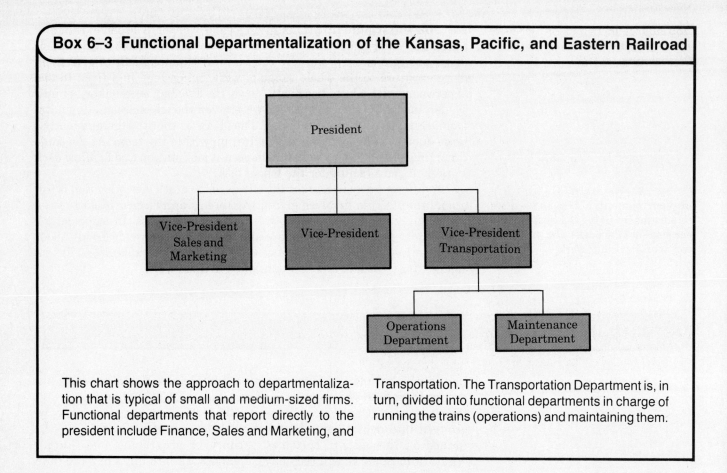

This chart shows the approach to departmentalization that is typical of small and medium-sized firms. Functional departments that report directly to the president include Finance, Sales and Marketing, and Transportation. The Transportation Department is, in turn, divided into functional departments in charge of running the trains (operations) and maintaining them.

common. Departmentalization by product would be a better approach. If a firm makes something like cement for local markets in plants located around the country, it would make sense to treat each plant as a separate unit. For a textbook publisher, departments might be based on types of customers—schools, colleges, or general bookstores.

Clearly, two or more types of departmentalization can be combined. Look at Box 6–4. It shows an organization chart for the company that was shown in Box 6–3, after a decade of growth. The company, now called KPCorp, has added two new lines of business. One is a subsidiary that sells long-distance private-line telephone services to businesses and government agencies. The other division has been formed to exploit oil, gas, and other mineral deposits on land lying along the railroad's right of way. In addition, the firm's business has been expanded through a merger with another railroad, this one based in the South.

Four types of departmentalization can be seen in Box 6–4. At the level below the president, there are three divisions that represent the company's three main products. The Transportation Division is now divided along geographic rather than functional lines. The Midwestern Division is based on the old Kansas, Pacific, and Eastern Railroad, whereas the Southern Division is based on the newly acquired railroad. These divisions cooperate but are independent; they exchange freight at Memphis, where their tracks meet. Each railroad, in turn, has functional departments such as operations and maintenance.

Over in the Communications Division, work is grouped by type of customer served—business or government. Both kinds of customers use

The Chessie and Seaboard Systems are separate divisions of CSX Corp., but they cooperate in a variety of ways. Courtesy of Chessie Systems

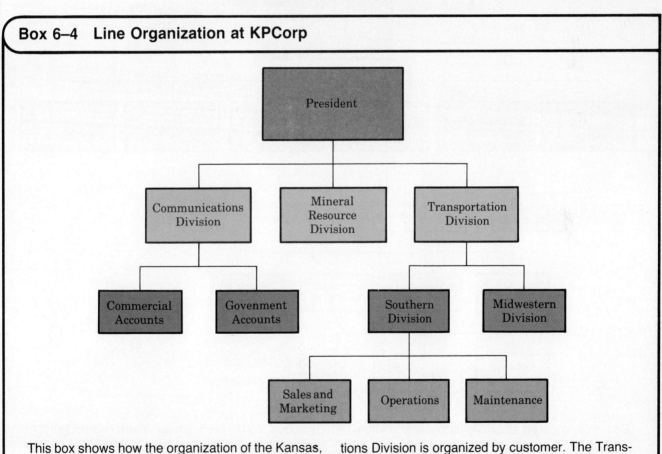

Box 6–4   Line Organization at KPCorp

President

Communications Division

Mineral Resource Division

Transportation Division

Commercial Accounts

Govenment Accounts

Southern Division

Midwestern Division

Sales and Marketing

Operations

Maintenance

This box shows how the organization of the Kansas, Pacific, and Eastern Railroad might change as the company grows. Here the firm has acquired two new divisions, one for communications and one for mineral resources. Thus, at the vice-presidential level departments are based on product. The Communica-tions Division is organized by customer. The Transportation Division, which has been expanded by a merger with a second small railroad, is organized by territory. Within each railroad, departments are based on function.

the same equipment, but it makes sense to have different divisions because they require different sales and marketing techniques.

Line and Staff Organization

Line organization: An organizational structure in which all units are linked to those above and below them by a clear chain of command.

The organization charts for Apex exterminators and KPCorp both show a clear chain of command. Except at the highest level, each person works under the direction of one supervisor. Except at the lowest level, each person supervises the work of employees at the next lower level. An organization of this type is called a **line organization**.

Box 6–5   Line and Staff Organization at KPCorp

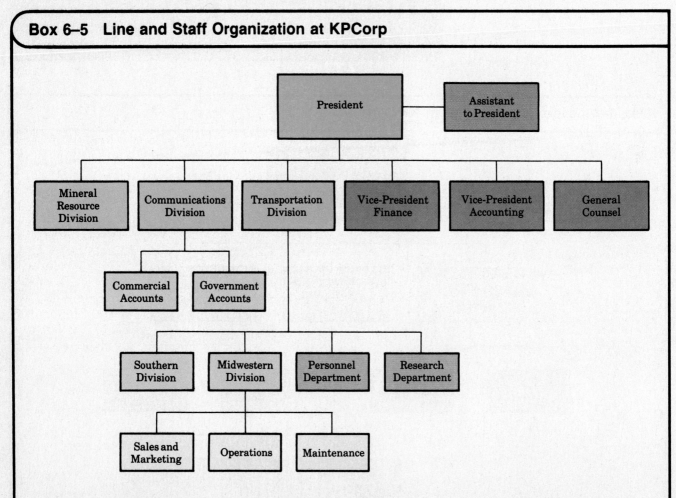

Box 6–4 showed only the line organization of KPCorp. A company of this size would also have many staff positions. At the top level, the president has a group of staff assistants to help with planning and other top management functions. Two staff vice-presidents and a general counsel report to the president and advise the vice-presidents of the product divisions. Within the Transportation Division, personnel and research staffs assist the managers of the two railroad divisions. Note that the staff departments are not linked directly to departments at lower levels of the firm. Their job is to give advice, not to give orders.

Staff positions: Positions that lie outside the chain of command and offer advice or support services to line managers.

Line and staff organization: An organization that includes both line and staff positions.

BEES

WORKER QUEEN

DRONE CONSULTANT

mcrawford

Drawing by M. Crawford; © 1983 The New Yorker Magazine, Inc.

The line organization works well for small firms, but it is rarely found in large ones. Large firms need people like lawyers, financial experts, and printers to provide advice and services. Such people are not part of the chain of command, in the sense that they do not give orders to employees working at lower levels. Instead, they give advice and provide services to other employees. Their jobs are known as **staff positions**. An organization that includes staff positions as well as line positions is known as a **line and staff organization**.

An organization as large as KPCorp would need a line and staff organization in order to function effectively. Box 6–5 shows how staff departments would relate to the line organization shown in Box 6–4. Three groups of staff positions are shown. First, the president has a small staff of assistants to help with planning and other functions of top management. Second, there are three staff officers who report directly to the president. These are the financial vice-president, the accounting vice-president, and the general counsel (the company's chief legal adviser). Third, under the vice-president for transportation two other staff departments are shown, one for personnel and one for research.

Notice that the staff departments in Box 6–5 are not directly connected to departments at lower levels of the company. Their job is to give advice—not to give orders. For example the general counsel offers legal advice to the vice-presidents in charge of the communications, mineral resource, and transportation groups. Legal problems that arise at lower levels within these groups are channeled to the general counsel via the vice-presidents' offices.

Line and staff organization has some major advantages. It is more flexible than simple line organization, and it allows line managers to back up their decisions with expert advice. It has some drawbacks, though. One is a blurring of lines of authority. For example, the transportation and communications divisions of KPCorp might make conflicting demands on the general counsel's office. These would have to be resolved by the president. Another danger is excessive growth by staff departments. This may occur because line managers demand too much of staff departments; because they hide behind experts instead of making their own decisions; or because the directors of staff departments are empire builders. As we noted in Chapter 5, well-managed companies get by, on the whole, with lean staffs.

COORDINATING THE WORK OF THE UNITS

The final stage in organizing, after dividing up the work and grouping it into units, is coordinating the work of the units. In this section, we will look at two methods of coordination, vertical and horizontal.

Vertical Coordination

The basic technique of coordination in any firm is the chain of command. Managers coordinate the work of the subordinates who report to them. At the same time, they depend on their own superiors to coordinate their work with that of other departments. In a furniture plant, for example, a super-

Vertical coordination: A technique of coordinating the work of departments that depends on instructions passed along the chain of command.

Span of management: The number of subordinates reporting to each manager.

visor makes sure the paint applied by one worker to each dining room chair matches the upholstery that the next worker will add. The supervisor, in turn, depends on middle managers to make sure that the chairs match the tables that are being made elsewhere in the plant. Each higher level of management sees a broader picture, leaving details to managers at the next-lower level. Top managers pull together the work of the whole organization.

Use of the chain of command to make the parts of the organization work together can be called **vertical coordination**, because it depends on directives passed to departments at each level by managers on the next higher level. Vertical coordination is simple enough to describe, but trying to make it work raises some practical questions. Two of these are how many layers of management there should be and how many subordinates should report to each manager. The number of subordinates reporting to each manager is called the **span of management**.

Box 6–6 illustrates a basic trade-off related to the span of management. It shows organization charts for two firms, each of which has twenty-four workers at the individual-contributor level. In firm A, four middle managers report to a president, and each of these managers directs six individual contributors. Firm B uses a narrower span of management. At the top and middle levels, each manager has only two subordinates. Each first-line manager directs only three individual contributors, rather than six as in firm A.

A broad span of management like that in firm A has two advantages. First, it requires fewer managers—just five, including the president, compared with fifteen for firm B. Second, the channels of communication between the top and bottom of the organization are short. For example, if a worker on the plant floor has a major problem or a bright idea, it has to pass through only one level of management to get to the president's desk.

The tall, narrow hierarchy of firm B has an advantage of its own, however: employees at each level are more closely supervised. The president of firm A may spend too much time in meetings with subordinates and may get too involved in shop floor problems. The president of firm B, who has the help of more middle managers, may have more time for strategic planning.

How large a span of management is best, if one weighs the advantages against the disadvantages? There is no one answer that fits all organizations. The proper span of management depends on the nature of the manager's job and the work done by the company. Among the factors that affect the proper span for a given managerial job are the following.

- A broader span can be used if the jobs that are supervised are similar and are located close to one another. An example would be supervision of a large team of lettuce pickers by a field boss.
- A narrower span should be used if the jobs supervised are complex. An example would be supervision of a group of engineers designing the parts of a new airplane.
- A broader span can be used if subordinates are capable of working independently, given general guidelines, and do not need detailed instructions for each task. An example would be supervision of professors by the chairman of a college math department.
- The more highly skilled the manager and the subordinates, the broader the span of control. The college math department would serve as an example here too.

Box 6–6 Broad versus Narrow Spans of Management

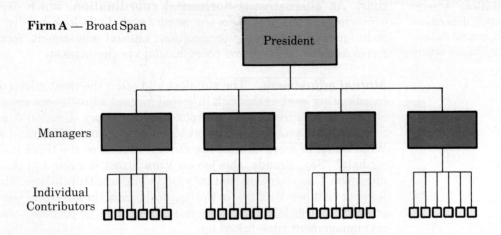

Firm A — Broad Span

President

Managers

Individual
Contributors

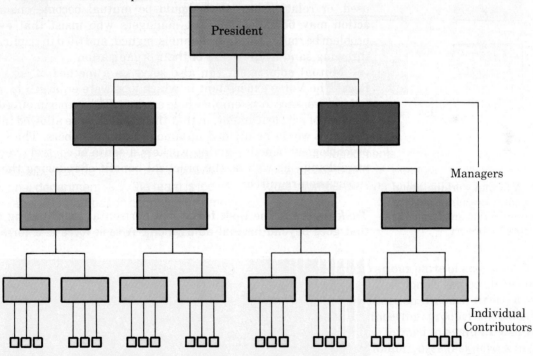

Firm B — Narrow Span

President

Managers

Individual
Contributors

These charts show the structures of two firms, each of which has twenty-four individual contributors. Firm A uses a broad span of management. This scheme requires just five managers, but direct supervision of each subordinate is limited. Firm B uses a narrow span of management that produces a "tall" hierarchy with fifteen managers. Although more managers are needed, each one can supervise his or her subordinates more closely and still have time left over for things like planning.

QUESTIONS FOR REVIEW AND DISCUSSION

1. Look at the way your school is organized. How is the work divided up? How is it departmentalized? Are there line and staff departments? How is the work of different departments coordinated? Are both vertical and horizontal coordinating mechanisms used? Give examples of each if possible.

2. Draw organization charts for at least two organizations of which you are a member. (Your school can serve as one of these; the other could be a business, a club, a church, or anything.) What is your own position on the chart? That of a manager, a staffer, or an individual contributor? Bonus project: for at least one of the organizations, sketch in as much of the informal structure as you can. Discuss the effects of the informal structure on the organization's ability to perform its mission.

3. Look at the following list of problems. Comment on the features of the organization that might tend to create such problems.

    a. A whole day's production by a furniture factory has to be scrapped because a worker mixed a batch of varnish wrong and no one caught the problem in time.

    b. Ada complains that she cannot do her work effectively because her boss keeps popping into her office to ask for progress reports, make suggestions, and meddle in other ways.

    c. Amber Company's Phylox project is six months behind schedule. It got started late because of a dispute between the finance and marketing departments that had to be resolved by the president. Then, when the research department finally had the design ready, it was found that the production department had not installed the equipment needed to make the thing.

    d. Why is this boss saying these things to his subordinate?

        "I told you to get the problem in the generator section straightened out—I didn't say you could spend ten thousand dollars on it without asking me. And who said you could get rid of Richardson and put White in his place? Who do you think's in charge here, anyway?"

4. Comment on Convergent Technolgies' Ultra project in terms of delegation, responsibility, authority, accountability, and autonomy.

Case 6–1: Organization of the Federal Government

The federal government of the United States has a rather unusual structure. At the top are the president (elected), Congress (elected), and the Supreme Court (appointed by the president and confirmed by Congress, but independent of both because the justices hold office for life). Each of these agencies has large staffs. There are personal staffs, such as Supreme Court clerks, and appointed agencies, such as the Council of Economic Advisers.

At the second level of government one finds a wide variety of agencies, including

- The lower federal courts, whose judges are appointed by the president, confirmed by the Senate, and subordinate to the Supreme Court in matters of law
- Independent agencies like the Interstate Commerce Commision, whose members are appointed by the president and confirmed by the Senate, and report to Congress on policy matters
- Cabinet departments, such as the Department of Defense, whose heads are appointed by the president, and confirmed by the Senate, and report to the president on policy matters

At the third level of government one finds different agencies using different forms of organization. The lower courts are organized by territory. The Interstate Commerce Commission has separate departments for trucking regulation and railroad regulation. The Defense Department is divided into Army, Navy, Air Force, and Marine Services.

Questions:

1. Draw an organization chart for the federal government. Include all the units mentioned in this case. You may need a few different kinds of dotted and dashed lines to show the relationships among agencies, such as "appointed by" and "reports to."

2. Does the federal government follow the princi- ple of unity of command? If so, explain how. If not, explain how it gets along without it.

3. Do you think private firms would be more efficient and effective if they adopted a structure more like that of the federal government? Are there any features of that structure that would not work for business yet are suited to the conduct of government? If so, explain.

Case 6–2: Problems of Delegation in Small Business

A *Wall Street Journal* column zeros in on the delegation problems of small firms with the following examples.

- The president and owner of an East Coast manufacturing firm that has only recently grown past the one-man-band stage comments, "When I was involved in the day-to-day stuff, I could see immediate results. I knew I had helped get that done or that straightened out." He says he is still tempted to jump in and solve problems even when this might bother a subordinate. "I still have to remind myself not to get involved in day-to-day details."

- "There's no way the company can grow if you're doing it all yourself," says Sandy Brown, president of Rhode Island Welding Supply Company. But since the company has only twenty-nine employees, he has to pitch in sometimes. "I'm available; all my people know that," he says. However, after

he has helped load a truck or solve a technical problem, he goes back to his own work.

- The founder of a California company is the firm's chief salesman, bringing in most of its $2.5 million in annual sales. The time he spends selling leaves little for planning. Still, he feels that no one else does the selling job as well. "If I leave it to other people and they fail, we wouldn't have any sales," he says. Yet the firm clearly needs planning for orderly growth. "I drive people crazy because I do things in an unplanned way," says the owner. "But if I quit doing things in an unplanned way, nothing will happen."

Source: Sanford L. Jacobs, "Owners See Need to Delegate Authority as Concerns Grow," *Wall Street Journal*, July 18, 1983, p. 21. Reprinted by permission of the Wall Street Journal. © Dow Jones & Company, Inc., 1983. All Rights Reserved.

Questions:

1. The first two stories illustrate managers who have learned to delegate. What temptations have they avoided? What lessons can you draw from these examples?

2. The third story illustrates a manager who is not yet willing to delegate. To what extent should he continue to be a player-manager? What other solutions could you suggest?

Chapter 7

INFORMATION AND THE ROLE OF COMPUTERS

When you have completed this chapter, you should be able to

- Describe the flow of *data* and *information* through a company and list five characteristics of high-quality information.

- Define *data processing systems*, *management information systems*, and *decision support systems*, and explain how each is used.

- List the basic operations that *computers* can perform, and discuss the limitations of computers.

- Give examples of each of the main groups of computer *hardware*: *input devices*, *output devices*, *central processing units*, and *storage devices*.

- Explain the role of *software*.

- List five steps in effective use of computers and explain the management skills needed at each step.

- Discuss the possible negative impacts of computers on people and organizations, and explain how these can be minimized by good management.

In the beginning Ellen Wessel knew nothing about designing or sewing clothes, but she did know that her running shorts fit poorly. Like just about every other pair on the market then, they were cut for the male physique. They were "too tight in the rear," she says, and the fabric "bunched up in the crotch." Worst of all, they chafed.

Wessel believed that other woman runners would willingly pay as much as $15 for shorts that showed more respect for the female anatomy. Her resulting business, Moving Comfort Inc., blossomed as women's running gained popularity. In 1982, sales of the Alexandria, Virginia, company were $2.5 million; sales of $3.5 million to $4 million were expected for 1983.

She declines to disclose earnings, but the company's gross profit margin is a respectable 45 percent to 48 percent of sales.

Moving Comfort's experience shows how far a neophyte can go with a worthy idea, optimism, and a little luck. But it also suggests that those factors aren't enough once a business starts growing.

In May 1977 Wessel, then twenty-six, quit her job with the Department of Housing and Urban Development to sell shorts that her running partner, Valerie Nye, made from a modified men's pattern. The profit was meager, and Nye bailed out after three months. Wessel, who doesn't sew, began parceling out fifty precut shorts kits a week to four home sewers. For a year she lived off savings.

It was a year marked by blunders. At first Wessel couldn't place her small orders with fabric wholesalers, so she paid retail prices. The first time she ordered in quantity, she was shocked when a semitrailer arrived and dumped 1000 yards of cloth at the apartment where she worked.

Her network of running friends helped. One was married to a vice-president of Washington's Riggs National Bank, where Wessel got her first loan, for $7,000. Another was a buyer for a store in Bethesda, Maryland, where she got her first account. She wrote an article for a friend's magazine, *Running Times*, and got a free ad as payment. It lured five accounts.

Perhaps the biggest break came when an apprentice tailor named Elizabeth Goeke got a pair of Moving Comfort shorts for her birthday. She promptly exchanged them. They were "very unflattering," she says. "They had stiff, terrible elastic and just sat on my hips."

Goeke volunteered to redesign them. In March 1978 she became senior vice-president and a 50 percent partner. The company sold 5800 pairs of shorts that year, for revenue of $73,000. In 1979, sales soared to $450,000.

But as the company started to flourish, the lack of fiscal know-how began to show. Rapid growth swamped the company's primitive invoicing and warehouse system. Moving Comfort kept two full-time and four temporary typists busy and still couldn't get invoices out on time. That hurt cash flow.

In the warehouse, chaos reigned. Shipping clerks scurried among bins of clothing with long, cumbersome lists in hand, never sure what was in stock. Unsold clothing languished in the bins. Inventory turned over a sluggish two and one-half times a year, and the company was paying a commercial finance company an interest rate six percentage

Ellen Wessel (rt.) and Elizabeth Goeke discovered the value of computers in solving problems of invoicing and inventory management. Courtesy of Moving Comfort Inc.

points above prime, then about 20 percent, to finance the unwanted goods.

Wessel considered selling the business, but instead she found salvation in software. She hired an accountant, Andy Novins, who installed $26,000 of computer equipment and $6000 of programming for it. He says it saves at least $75,000 a year in interest. The company doesn't use temporary typists any more but gets invoices into the mail the day after shipment.

The warehouse operation is more efficient. A year ago, five shipping clerks would scramble from 6:00 A.M. until 5:00 P.M. to get $10,000 worth of clothes out the door. Now two clerks can start at 8:00 A.M. and finish the same job by noon. Inventory turns over five times a year.[1]

[1]Mary Williams, "Fresh Idea, Optimism, Luck Helped Running-Wear Maker," *Wall Street Journal*, June 27, 1983, p. 31. Reprinted by permission of the Wall Street Journal. © Dow Jones & Company, Inc., 1983. All Rights Reserved.

Information and the ability to use it are crucial to good management. We have already mentioned this many times. In Chapter 5 we listed the informational roles of managers. In Chapter 6 we showed how organizations must set up good channels of communication to achieve effective coordination. The story of Moving Comfort is just one illustration of the kinds of problems companies face when their ability to handle information does not keep up with their needs.

The flow of information through a company can be compared to the production process discussed in Chapter 1. In that process, inputs of raw materials are transformed into the goods and services that are the company's outputs. In much the same way, the flow of information begins with the collection of **data**, the raw material of information. Data are unorganized facts—names, numbers, quantities, and so on.* Data must be processed to become useful. When raw data are sorted, organized, or listed so that they can be used in making decisions, they become **information**.

As we will show in this chapter, managers need high-quality information to make the best decisions. The quality of information depends on five factors:

- *Accuracy.* Information should be free from errors. (Note, however, that there may be a point beyond which the costs of increasing accuracy may exceed the benefits.)
- *Timeliness.* Information should be based on recent data.
- *Completeness.* Decisions are improved when the number of gaps that have to be filled by guesswork is kept to a minimum.
- *Conciseness.* Balancing the need for completeness is the need to state information concisely so that decision makers can grasp it quickly and easily.
- *Relevance.* Completeness also must be balanced against the need for relevance. Top priority should be given to information that is actually needed for making decisions.

Today, **computers** can greatly improve the quality of information reaching managers' desks. Computers are electronic machines that pro-

Data: Unorganized facts such as numbers, names, and quantities.

Information: Data that have been processed so that they can be used in making decisions.

Computer: An electronic machine that processes, stores, and communicates information.

Data is a plural word of Latin origin. The rarely used singular form *datum* means a single item such as a number, name, or quantity.

Computers can enhance the accuracy, timeliness, completeness, conciseness, and relevance of information. Courtesy of Sperry Corp.

cess, store, and communicate information. As the cost of processing information goes down, accuracy, timeliness, and completeness can be raised to standards that would have been far too costly a few years ago.

Most of this chapter focuses on computers, but it should be kept in mind that computers are not the whole answer to managers' information needs. In well-managed companies, executives take a hands-on approach to gathering information. At companies like United Airlines and Hewlett-Packard, this is called "management by wandering around." By visiting branches and talking to middle managers, individual contributors, and customers, the top managers of such companies learn things that they would never learn from formal reports and printouts.

COMPUTERS AND MANAGEMENT

Computers are everywhere. Sometimes out in front, sometimes behind the scenes, they are helping all kinds of organizations do their jobs. Our paychecks are made out by computer. When we spend our pay, the groceries we buy are likely to be checked out through a computerized system that updates the store's inventory records at the same time that it totals our bill. If we get a parking ticket while we are in the store, a police department computer will, alas, make sure we pay the fine.

Word processor: A specialized computer used to prepare written material such as letters and reports.

Computers are busy in the workplace, too. They monitor the flow of materials in steel mills and oil refineries. Computerized robots take over dangerous jobs in factories. **Word processors**—specialized computers used to prepare written material—help secretaries get letters and contracts typed accurately and on time. At present fully half of all investment in plant and equipment by U.S. business goes for computers, instruments, and electronic and communications systems.[2]

[2]Edward E. David, Jr., "By 1990 All Industries Must Be High Tech," *High Technology*, April 1983, pp. 65–68.

General Motors uses computer-controlled robots to perform dangerous tasks on the assembly line. Courtesy of General Motors

Computers do so many things, in fact, that we do not have room to talk about all of them in this chapter. We will have a chance to discuss the use of computers in operations and production in Chapter 13, and in accounting in Chapter 18. In this chapter we will focus on the use of computers by managers in business, government, and not-for-profit firms. We will begin with a survey of three levels at which these uses occur: processing data, supplying information to management, and aiding in making decisions.

Data-Processing Systems

Data-processing system (DPS): A system that captures data, processes them, and communicates the information it produces.

The most common way of using computers is in **data-processing systems (DPS)**. A data-processing system is any system that captures data, processes them, and communicates the information produced in this way.

Steps in Data Processing

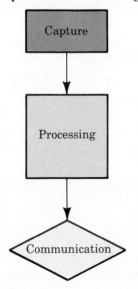

Capturing data. Data, we recall, are simply facts. At every moment of the day we are bombarded by facts. Consider the case of Myra Fenton, a worker who assembles audio cassettes for MTD Corporation. Between 11:35 and 11:38 one Friday morning, the following facts might come to her attention.

- The cassette she is working on is her 435th of the morning.
- The box of screws she is using is almost empty.
- Her tooth hurts; she should see a dentist.
- For the fifteenth time that morning she has had to throw away a cassette because the screw holes were not lined up.
- Freddy Booth, her supervisor, has a gravy stain on his tie.
- Looking out the window, she can see that it is about to rain.

It doesn't take an expert to see that some of these data are relevant to MTD's business and some are not. If the business is to be run well, the data that are relevant must somehow be captured by writing them down, punching them into a computer terminal, or recording them in some other way. One of Booth's jobs will be to turn in daily reports on each worker's output. He should also be required to make a daily or weekly report on the number of rejected cassettes. And when a new box of screws is brought to Fenton's workstation, someone in the stockroom should make a note of the fact. Data on toothaches, weather, and gravy stains need not be captured.

Processing data. MTD's system will next process the data it has captured. Processing means such things as sorting the data into categories, making summaries, and multiplying quantities sold by unit prices to get total dollar values. For example, Fenton's output for Friday will be added to her output from other days to get her weekly total. The number of boxes of screws used will be subtracted from the number in stock at the beginning of the week to get an updated inventory figure. The number of rejected cassettes will be divided by the total number produced to get the percentage of rejects. These operations convert raw data into useful information.

Communicating information. The third step in data processing is to communicate the information produced to the people who need to use it. Information may be put out as reports or placed in computer files so that it can be retrieved from a terminal.

In the case of MTD, the data we have been tracking will appear as parts of weekly inventory, production, and quality control reports. Information on Fenton's weekly output will be combined with data from the personnel file to produce her paycheck.

The capture, processing, and communication of information is illustrated by the work of a weather forecaster. Temperature, barometric pressure, and other weather conditions are recorded (capture), analyzed with the help of a computer (processing), and converted into useful information (communication). © Freda Leinwand

Box 7–1 A Typical Data-Processing System

A Typical Data Processing System

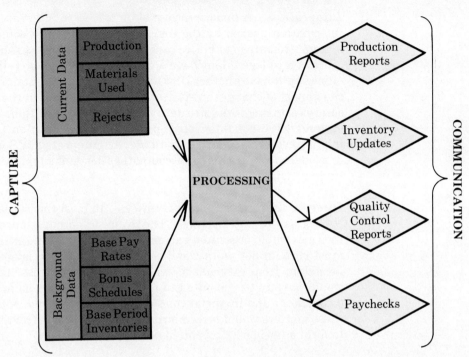

A data-processing system must capture data, process them, and produce useful information. This diagram shows the MTD Corporation's DPS. In this system, data on each worker's output, materials used, and defective parts are captured during assembly line operations. Background data on base pay rates, bonus schedules, base-period inventor- ies, and so on have been stored in the computer's memory. Data from the two sources are processed by the computer and communicated in the form of reports on production, inventory, and quality control. The system also produces weekly paychecks, another form of communication.

A diagram of the DPS just described is shown in Box 7–1. Note that the operations shown here do not have to be done by computer. They could be handled by clerks, with pencil, paper, and card files. However, when data processing tasks are routine, they are ideal for computers.

Management Information Systems

Data processing systems are the most common use of computers in business today. For many firms, however, a DPS is only a first step. The next logical step is to set up a **management information system (MIS)**. An MIS is a data processing system designed to supply all levels of management with internal and external information needed to make decisions.

Management information system (MIS): A data-processing system designed to supply all levels of management with internal and external information needed to make decisions.

Data processing in an MIS. As the definition implies, an MIS is an extended DPS. Like every DPS, an MIS captures data, processes them, and communicates the information produced. An MIS differs from a simple DPS in the range of data captured, the types of processing done, and the extent of communication.

Integration. A major purpose of an MIS is to integrate all the types of information needed by the firm. Various parts of a company may have systems that are not able to "talk" to one another. For example, the payroll office of a college might have a DPS to handle the payroll and the dean's office might have another DPS to keep track of students' grades. A study of the impact of changes in students' choice of majors on the college's future salary costs might require data from both offices. If their data processing systems were not integrated, printouts of information from each office might have to be compared by hand. An integrated MIS would be able to draw data from both sets of computer files and supply concise, relevant information.

Internal and external information. In most firms, the use of computers begins with internal data. The inventory, production, and payroll data in the example presented earlier (MTD Corp.) are internal data. An MIS must cast its net more widely, however. Many decisions depend on information from external as well as internal sources. External sources would have to be consulted to find out such things as prices charged by competitors and financial conditions in the economy. Information about these matters would be combined with information from internal sources to form a basis for decision making.

Levels of management. Simple data processing systems are designed to automate clerical work and to help in routine decison making. Issuing paychecks and restocking inventories are typical functions at this level. Management information systems, in contrast, are designed to provide all levels of management with information needed for planning, organizing, leading, and controlling. For example, the planning functions of top managers require a lot of external information. The leading and controlling functions that take up more of the time of middle and first-line managers rely more on internal information. Also, the planning and organizing functions of top managers require general information, whereas the leading and controlling functions require more detailed information. A fully developed MIS should be able to serve all levels of management.

Decision Support Systems

Decision support system (DSS): A system that puts high-quality information at the fingertips of managers and aids them in the analysis of complex problems.

A few companies are moving beyond the MIS to what are known as **decision support systems (DSS)**. A DSS puts high-quality information at the fingertips of managers and aids them in the analysis of complex problems.

Information versus analysis. The driving idea of the DSS is that computers can do more than just supply information. DSS designers think computer analysis can actually help managers make decisions. It is still true that no computer this side of pure science fiction can replace human management. Supporters of DSS think, however, that computer analysis can help with some highly structured aspects of decision making, leaving managers free to focus on aspects that require judgment and intuition.

As an example, consider Brandaid, a DSS developed by J. D. C. Little.[3] Brandaid is designed to help marketing managers who are trying to find the right mix of pricing, advertising, and sales effort to promote a new product. Such a decision can be broken down into two steps.

First, the manager needs to estimate how sales of the product will respond to changes in price, advertising, and sales effort, taken one at a time. No scientific way of making such estimates is known. They depend on the manager's judgment and intuition as applied to each product and type of customer.

Second, after the impacts of price, advertising, and sales effort have been estimated, the best mix of the three has to be found. In the past, this was a time-consuming trial-and-error process. A change in price, for example, is likely to affect consumers' response to advertising and sales effort. Many combinations of these variables need to be tried, and it is hard for the human brain to juggle all of them at once.

The use of a computer can make this trial-and-error phase much easier. That is where the Brandaid DSS comes in. Once the manager has made some initial judgments about the way consumers will respond to price, advertising, and sales effort, the DSS makes it easy to explore many combinations and find the best one.

Involvement of management. The Brandaid DSS is typical in the way it combines the manager's judgments with computer analysis. It is typical as well in stressing hands-on use by managers. In fact, some decision support systems are custom-designed for one person. In contrast, the emphasis of an ordinary MIS is on the production of reports. True, managers may request quick, custom-tailored reports from such a system. But unless they enjoy punching computer keys, actual operation of an MIS can be left to lower-level employees.

HARDWARE AND SOFTWARE

In describing how computers are used in business, we have treated them as "black boxes" into which one puts data and from which one gets information. In this section we will, very briefly, take the lid off and look at what lies inside.

What Computers Can and Cannot Do

People have long used machines to help process data in a way that is accurate, timely, and complete. The abacus, which uses beads that slide on a frame to add and subtract, has been around for centuries. The slide rule, a mechanical device for multiplying and dividing, was invented more than a hundred years ago. Adding machines and typewriters were familiar to our parents and grandparents.

Computers belong to the same family of devices as the abacus and the slide rule. To many people, one of the surprising things about computers is

[3]This account of the Brandaid DSS is based on Peter G. W. Keen, "Decision Support Systems: Translating Analytic Techniques into Useful Tools," *Sloan Management Review*, Spring 1980, pp. 33–44.

how little they can do. Basically, they can do only three things: they can do arithmetic (add, subtract, multiply, and divide); they can compare two numbers and decide which one is larger; and they can store and retrieve information.

In a sense, then, computers can do nothing that cannot be done with pencil and paper. The power of computers comes not from the things they can do but from how well they do them.

First of all, computers do their work very fast. Even the smallest computers are able to perform hundreds of thousands of additions, subtractions, and comparisons per second. The really fast ones can perform millions of operations per second.

Second, computers are very accurate. They almost never make mistakes. What we call "computer errors" are errors made by computer operators.

Finally, computers have vast storage capacity. Large modern computers have room in their memories for millions of bits of data. And as we will explain shortly, external storage devices like magnetic tapes can expand storage capacity almost without limit.

All of the amazing things that computers can do stem from their speed, accuracy, and storage capacity. In fact, we are so used to the things computers can do, from playing video games to making airline reservations, that we are more likely to overestimate their powers than to underestimate them. Still, there are some things that computers still do not do well. Some of these limitations are being overcome by research and development, but others remain.

First of all, some jobs that are very simple for humans strain the abilities of even the largest computers. In tasks that require pattern recognition, such as finding a familiar face in a crowd or picking out a tank in an aerial photo, humans easily do better than computers. Speech is even harder for computers to handle. Computers that understand conversational speech are still many years away.

Second, although computers do what they are told to do quickly and accurately, they do *only* and *exactly* what they are told. As we will see when we discuss software, writing instructions for computers requires special skills. If the instructions are wrong, the computer will give the wrong answers—or no answers at all.

Above all, the accuracy of computers is limited by the accuracy of the data fed to them. In computer jargon, this is called the **GIGO principle**. GIGO stands for "garbage in, garbage out." Consider the poor record of computerized economic forecasting. The moment at which an economy turns from recession to prosperity depends on such things as changes in consumer confidence, the investment plans of business firms, and the money supply plans of the Federal Reserve. Forecasters do not have good data on these things. Therefore, when they want to obtain forecasts from their computer models, they supplement the data with educated guesses. No matter how complex the models are, if people put wrong guesses into them, they get wrong forecasts out.

> I hate this darned computer,
> I wish that they would sell it!
> It won't do what I want it to,
> It just does what I tell it!
> —Graffiti found on the wall at a
> computer center.

GIGO principle ("garbage in—garbage out"): Computer jargon for the principle that useful information cannot be derived from inaccurate data.

Hardware

Hardware: In a computer system, the physical equipment that performs input, output, processing, and storage functions.

In computer jargon, **hardware** means the physical equipment that performs input, output, processing, and storage functions.

Input device: Any device, such as a keyboard, through which data and instructions can be fed into a computer.

Output device: Any device, such as a printer, by means of which a computer supplies information to users.

Central processing unit (CPU): The part of a computer in which arithmetic, comparison, and other operations are performed.

Primary storage: Storage space contained within the CPU, used to store instructions and data that are currently in use.

Secondary storage: A storage device outside the CPU, such as magnetic tapes or disks, used to store information that is not currently in use.

Input devices are the means by which data and instructions are fed into the computer. Keyboards are the most commonly used input device. At one time, punched-card readers and paper-tape readers were popular input devices, but in many places these have been replaced by devices that read data stored magnetically on tapes or disks. Optical character scanners, which can read information printed on ordinary paper, are an increasingly common way of putting data into a computer.

Output devices are the means by which computers supply information to users. Video display terminals (VDTs), which look like television screens, are one of the most common output devices. They are usually linked to a keyboard to form an integrated input/output unit. Printers are used when a permanent record of the output is desired. They come in all sizes, ranging from simple typewriter-like devices to high-speed machines that use ink jets or laser beams. Computer output in graphic form can be displayed on a VDT or drawn with mechanical devices called plotters. Speech synthesizers that allow computers to "talk" to users are a fairly recent output device that has already been used in teaching machines and in telephone information services.

In order to turn inputs of data into outputs of useful information, computers must be able to process them. This part of the computer's job takes place in its **central processing unit (CPU)**. The CPU controls the flow of operations and performs arithmetic, comparison, sorting, and other tasks.

Finally, every computer system needs one or more storage devices. The CPU itself has capacity for **primary storage**, that is, storage of instructions and data that are currently in use. Most computer systems also include devices for **secondary storage** in which information that is not currently in use can be placed. The magnetic tapes and disks mentioned earlier are the most common secondary storage media at present, although paper cards and tapes are still used in some systems. Other storage media, such as laser disks, will probably become more widely used in the future.

Some common types of computer hardware are shown in Box 7–2.

The most common output devices are video display terminals. These are used in a wide variety of ways, including editing newspaper articles and checking research results. Left—Courtesy of International Business Machines Corporation, Right—Courtesy of AT&T Bell Laboratories

Box 7–2 Computer Hardware

In this photograph of the Professional 350 mini-computer by Digital Equipment Corp., the operator is using a keyboard, attached to a VDT, as an input device. The VDT also serves as an output device. A permanent copy can be made with the printer at the operator's left. This machine uses floppy disks for secondary storage. The unit built into the desk at the operator's right contains the disk drive, which reads and stores information on the floppy disks and the central processing unit.

Courtesy of Digital Equipment Corp.

Courtesy of Control Data Corp.

Magnetic media such as the ones shown here are the most commonly used secondary storage devices. Flexible magnetic disks, often called floppy disks, are used by minicomputers. More powerful computers use hard disks and magnetic tape to store vast amounts of information.

Courtesy of Radio Shack, A Division of Tandy Corp.

Many kinds of printers can be attached to computers to produce written output. Other output devices can produce pictures. This Radio Shack plotter, produced by Tandy Corporation, uses colored pens to draw vivid graphs in response to instructions given by the computer operator.

Courtesy of Timex Sinclair

Computer systems come in all sizes. The Timex Sinclair unit shown here, although no larger than a notebook, can serve many practical household and small-business uses. The CRAY-1 supercomputer

Courtesy of Cray Research, Inc.

lies at the other end of the scale. These huge number crunchers are used for the most demanding tasks, such as weather forecasting, oil exploration, and national defense.

The Family of Computers

Computers come in a wide range of sizes and prices. New members are constantly being added to the computer family—tinier, cheaper babies at the low end of the line and awesome monsters at the upper end. The following terms are often used to classify computers by size.

Microcomputer: A small, inexpensive computer designed for home use or limited business uses.

Minicomputer: A computer that is somewhat larger and more expensive than a microcomputer and is designed for home use by professionals or small businesses.

Mainframe: A large, powerful computer that permits a full range of applications.

Supercomputer: A term reserved for the largest, most powerful class of computers.

- **Microcomputers** are the smallest. They range from "home computers" that can be bought in department stores or even toy stores for less than $100, to "personal computers" that can do many useful jobs for small firms.
- **Minicomputers** are the next-larger size. They include more powerful personal computers that cost several thousand dollars, and moderate-sized business computers. Some of them are as powerful as the biggest machines of a decade ago.
- **Mainframes** are still more powerful computers that can cost hundreds of thousands of dollars. Because mainframe computers are so expensive, they tend to be shared by many users and attended twenty-four hours a day by a professional staff.
- **Supercomputers**. This term is reserved for the largest, most powerful number crunchers available. They are used in national defense and major research institutions. This, too, is a shifting category, since tomorrow's mainframes always catch up with today's supercomputers.

The Role of Software

Computer hardware is nothing but a collection of expensive junk until it is told to do something useful. A detailed set of instructions that tells a computer to perform some useful task is known as a **program**. Together, programs and computer languages (to be discussed shortly) are known as **software**.

Hardware and software are equal partners in the world of computers. Advances in both areas have accounted for the explosion of computer uses in recent years.

Program: A detailed set of instructions that tells a computer to perform some useful task.

Software: A collective name for programs and computer languages.

A typical computer program. Computers, as we have said, can do nothing but arithmetic, comparison, and storage and retrieval of data. In order to program a computer to do any useful task, one must break the task down into a sequence of these basic operations. Box 7–3 gives a rough idea of how this might be done for the job of making out monthly invoices for the customers of a firm like Moving Comfort.

The program, written by a specialist, is stored in the computer's memory. To run it, an operator, who need not be a programmer, simply types the words "RUN INVOICES" on a keyboard attached to a VDT (step 1). The rest of the job is done automatically, following the instructions in the program.

The program begins with a set of instructions that tell the computer to retrieve the company's price list from storage (step 2) and then to retrieve the first customer's file from storage (step 3). Each day during the month, an operator has entered all of that day's shipments into the computer, where they have been sorted and stored under the customers' names. Each customer therefore has a separate file in the computer's memory.

Box 7–3 Flowchart of an Invoice Preparation Program

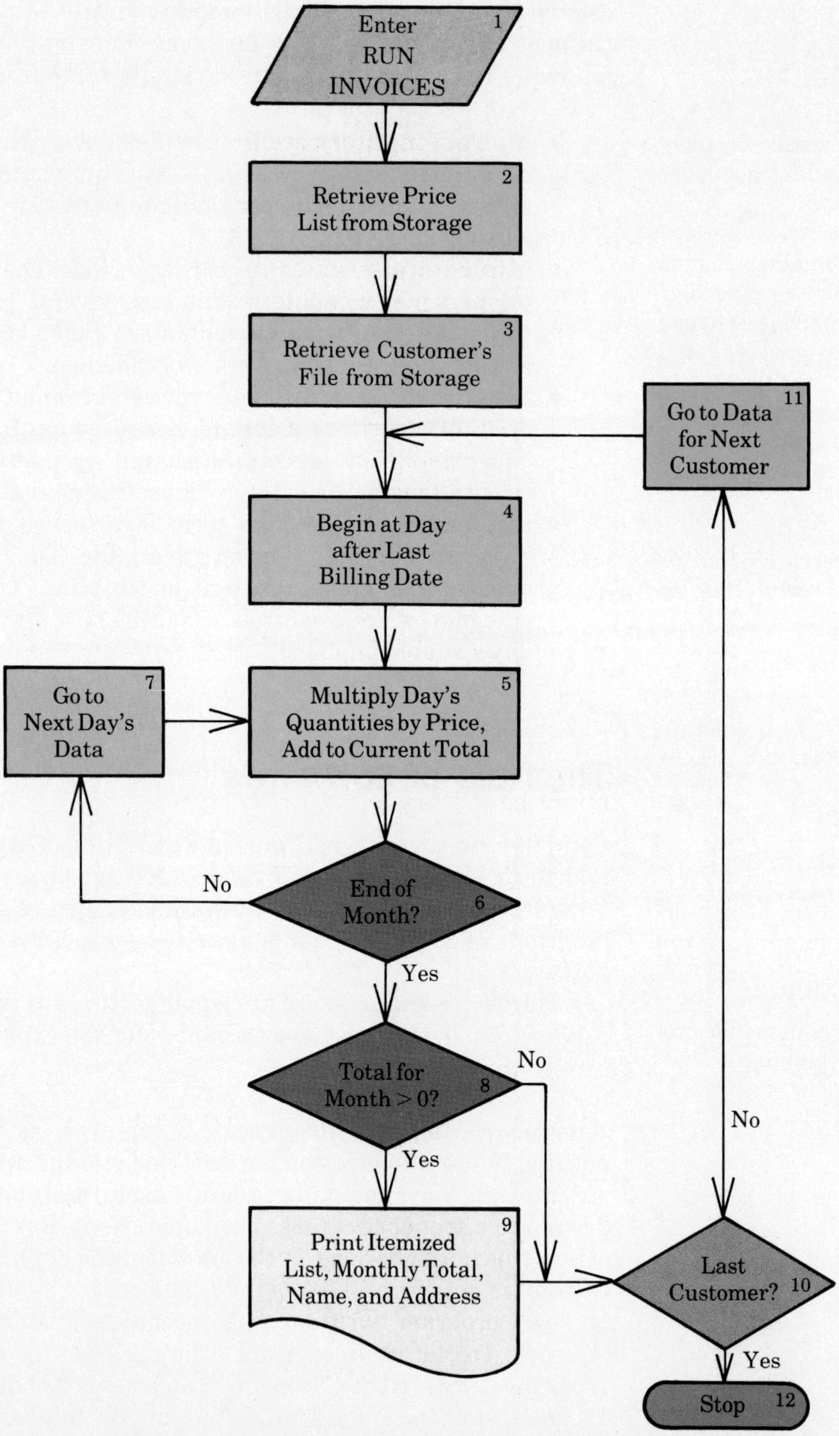

Enter
RUN
INVOICES *1*

Retrieve Price
List from Storage *2*

Retrieve Customer's
File from Storage *3*

Go to Data
for Next
Customer *11*

Begin at Day
after Last
Billing Date *4*

Go to
Next Day's
Data *7*

Multiply Day's
Quantities by Price,
Add to Current Total *5*

End of
Month? *6*

No

Yes

Total for
Month > 0? *8*

No

Yes

No

Print Itemized
List, Monthly Total,
Name, and Address *9*

Last
Customer? *10*

Yes

Stop *12*

A flowchart is a diagram that shows the main features of a computer program. This flowchart outlines twelve steps in a program that prepares monthly invoices for the regular customers of a small firm. The purpose of the program is to break the task down into arithmetic, comparison, storage, and retrieval operations. To be read and understood by a computer, this flowchart would have to be translated into a series of commands written in a programming language such as BASIC, COBOL, or FORTRAN.

Beginning on the first day after the last billing date (step 4), the computer multiplies the quantities of goods shipped to the customer that day by their prices (step 5). The total for the day is added to the total so far, which begins at zero and increases as the month goes on. The program next tells the computer to compare the date it has just processed with the number of days in the month (step 6). If the end of the month has not been reached, it moves on to the next day (step 7) and repeats step 5.

When the end of the month has been reached, the program asks for another comparison (step 8): is the month's total greater than zero? If so, the computer goes to step 9 and prints the invoice, retrieving details such as the customer's name and address from memory. One last comparison is then made (step 10) to see if the number of customers processed so far is equal to the total number on the list. (If a customer's total charges for the month are zero, no invoice need be sent, so a shortcut is taken from step 8 to step 10.) If the end of the list has not been reached, the program tells the machine to move on to the next customer (step 11). When all the customers have been processed, the program stops (step 12).

Flowchart: A diagram that shows the main features of a program in a form that is easy for a human to read and understand.

Programming language: A set of rules for writing the instructions that are fed into a computer.

Programming languages. Box 7–3 shows the invoice program in the form of a **flowchart**—a diagram that shows the main features of a program in a form that is easy for a human to read and understand. Computers are not able to read flowcharts, however. Instead, the program must be written in a **programming language** that the computer can understand. In a programming language, the twelve steps shown in Box 7–3 would be broken down into dozens of detailed instructions. For example, in a typical programming language the instruction in step 3 that tells the computer to retrieve the customer's name, address, and record of quantities purchased might be written

READ NAME, ADDRESS, QUANTITY

The instruction in step 5 that asks the computer to multiply the quantity of product n by the price of product n might be written

LET TOTAL = QUANTITY(N)*PRICE(N)

There are many programming languages. Most machines can be "taught" to understand any of them simply by changing the instructions stored in the CPU. The most widely used programming languages are the following.

- BASIC (Beginners All-purpose Symbolic Instruction Code). BASIC is the easiest language to learn and is flexible enough for most business tasks.
- FORTRAN (FORmula TRANslator). Work began on FORTRAN in 1954, making it one of the oldest computer languages. FORTRAN is not quite as easy to learn and use as BASIC, but it has its advantages. For one thing, programs written in FORTRAN are more compact, thus saving storage space in the computer. FORTRAN is also better suited to scientific uses.
- COBOL (COmmon Business Oriented Language). COBOL is widely used in business. In some ways, instructions written in COBOL resemble ordinary English more closely than instructions in other programming languages. This feature makes it easy for nonexperts

to follow the logic of a COBOL program. COBOL also is better suited than FORTRAN to the processing of alphabetic characters, a major advantage when names, addresses, and so forth must be processed.

It is not hard to learn any of these languages. A person can begin to write useful programs in BASIC after only a few hours of instruction. But it is not necessary to learn a programming language to use a computer. Large numbers of "canned" programs are available that require only simple instructions in ordinary English. For example, the program in Box 7–3 is activated simply by typing the words "RUN INVOICES." Only the person who wrote the program, not the user, would have to know BASIC, FORTRAN, or COBOL.

EFFECTIVE USE OF COMPUTERS

When properly programmed, computers can do many useful things for many kinds of organizations. But getting the most out of a computer requires more than just unpacking it and slipping in a software disk. Using computers *effectively*—getting them, that is, to *do the right things* and not just put on a show—requires the same planning, organizing, leading, and controlling skills as any other management task. Using Box 7–4 as our guide, let's look at the steps in effective use of computers.

Defining the Need

In any organization, the idea of using a computer begins with awareness of a problem or an opportunity. Moving Comfort's problem—a shortage of working capital in a time of high interest rates—is typical. The first step in using a computer to solve the problem is to define the need clearly. There is no computer solution to the vague problem of "a shortage of working capital." In Moving Comfort's case, no progress could be made toward a computer solution until the problem was defined as a failure to get invoices out on time and a failure to control inventory.

No two firms ever have quite the same problem. Even so, there is one hard-and-fast rule that applies to all cases: all the potential users of the system must help define the problem. "All" means everyone from top management to clerical help. Top managers are needed both to define the strategic goals of the system and to provide the leadership needed to get others involved. At the same time, hands-on workers, such as clerical help, may be the people who understand most clearly what is wrong with the current way of doing things.

"A small group of managers and secretaries make better decisions about office organization than office automation experts," says Richard Barry, administrative operations cooordinator at the World Bank. As an example, Barry cites the word-processing system that was developed for the bank's East Africa group. His first idea was a central office where all the group's word processing would be done. But a task force of professionals and secretaries pointed out some drawbacks. Professionals worried that they would be unable to get high-priority work done fast through such a

Box 7–4 Steps in Effective Use of Computers

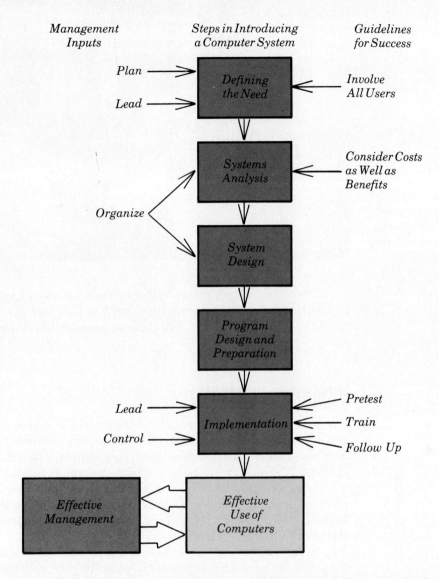

Effective use of a computer calls for more than buying the hardware and slipping in a canned program. The most crucial step is the first one—defining the need clearly. If there is no need, don't buy the hardware. Systems analysis and system design help match the computer system to the organization. After the system has been translated into a program, great care must be taken to implement it properly. Guidelines for success and needed skills are shown in the side columns.

center—they did not want a first-in, first-out system. Secretaries were afraid they would lose touch with professionals and not understand the work they were doing. The task force recommended a decentralized word processing system. Such a system was successfully put in place.[4]

[4]This example is taken from Jonathan Schlefer, "Office Automation and Bureaucracy," *Technology Review*, July 1983, pp. 38–39.

It is important to involve potential users of a new computer system in every phase of the design and implementation of that system. Courtesy of International Business Machines Corp.

There is no bigger waste of money than buying expensive hardware and hiring specialists to program it, only to find that the system doesn't meet the user's real needs. The time to prevent this error is right at the start.

Systems Analysis

The second step in effective use of computers is systems analysis. This begins with a careful look at how things are currently being done. If invoices are being made out by hand, for example, a flowchart like the one in Box 7–3 should be made to describe the way it is done.

Using the current way of doing things as a starting point, systems analysts look for ways of improving it. Can timeliness be improved? Accuracy? Outside consultants who know how computers are applied elsewhere are often brought in at this point.

As part of the analysis, the costs and benefits of different approaches should be explored. Computers may not be the most cost-effective solution. Perhaps something as simple as redesigning the forms on which invoicing is done would solve the problem.

System Design

Once a way of solving the problem has been chosen, system design begins. At this point a detailed flowchart of the new system is drawn up. This includes sources of data, location of users, and storage requirements. At this stage a choice of hardware is also made.

Although many aspects of system design are jobs for experts, line managers must also be involved. A computer system should not simply be imposed on the existing structure. Often, minor or even major changes in the management hierarchy, in departmentalization, or in staffing will be needed to make the new system work well.

Program Design and Preparation

After the system and the needs it will serve have been clearly stated in flowchart form, the system is translated into a programming language. The programs are then tested and debugged. This job may be done by the firm's own computer staff or by an independent software specialist.

Implementation

The job is not done when the programs are written. Great care must be taken in implementing the new system. The following are some guidelines for implementation.

- Pretest every part of the system with simulations and "dry runs" before any actual work is entrusted to it. Not only the program itself but procedures for entering data, for supervising the system's operators, and for coordinating the new system with other activities must be tested. There will always be bugs to be worked out before everything runs smoothly.
- Again, involve all users, especially in pretesting. Also needed is strong leadership by management. Employees may reject a new system if they do not understand why and how it is important.
- Provide thorough training. At all costs, avoid a situation in which highly paid systems analysts and programmers walk away, fee in hand, leaving no one who knows how to make the new system work.
- Follow up. Controlling is as important in making a computer system work as it is in making other parts of the organization work. Probably changes will have to be made after the system has been in use for a while. Unfortunately, the implementation phase is usually where mistakes in defining the problem are revealed. Better to fix them late than never.

THE IMPACT OF COMPUTERS

We have placed this chapter early in the book because of the tremendous impact computers have on the way people do their jobs. From a simple word processor on a secretary's desk to the most complex decision support system, computers have great potential for raising productivity. But if they are misused, they cause more problems than they solve. As Michael Hammer, an MIT office automation expert, puts it, "Automating a mess yields an automated mess."[5] Our discussion of computers would not be complete without some mention of the problems, as well as the opportunities, that they create.

Negative Impacts on Organizations

Disruptions of the chain of command. A computer system, especially an MIS or DSS, gives top managers direct access to information in all parts

[5]Ibid., p. 32.

of the organization. In the past, this information would have reached them only through subordinates, if at all. This greater access to information can cause trouble. For one thing, an MIS lets top managers look over the shoulders of middle managers in new ways. What the manager calls controlling or guiding, the subordinate may call meddling. Even worse, top managers may come to believe the picture of the organization that they see through their terminals is the whole picture. By neglecting walk-around management, they may end up with less information, not more.

Crime and security. As firms use computers in more and more ways, new risks are created. Horror stories in which bank tellers make deposits to their own accounts or payroll clerks have checks drawn for friends and relatives have become common. Some firms have lost millions of dollars through such schemes. And experts believe that only a tiny fraction of computer crime is reported.

Drawing by Stevenson; © 1983. The New Yorker Magazine, Inc.

"Here's the story, gentlemen. Sometime last night, an eleven-year-old kid in Akron, Ohio, got into our computer and transferred all our assets to a bank in Zurich."

Computers are being used to spy on competitors, too. New-product designs, pricing strategies, and market share data can all be stolen from a firm's computer files. A whole branch of the computer industry is concerned with protection against this sort of thing, but some experts fear that the computer crooks and spies have the edge.

Negative Impacts on People

Unemployment. Computers have created many jobs. Those of programmers and technicians are examples. Computerization creates jobs in other

The computer revolution has created many new kinds of jobs. At the same time, it has made other jobs obsolete. Workers who held those jobs must learn new skills or find employment elsewhere. Courtesy of International Business Machines Corp.

Computers make work easier in many ways, but in some situations they create dull, repetitive jobs. Job enlargement and job enrichment can help reduce boredom in such jobs. Courtesy of Metropolitan Life Insurance Co., New York

ways too: by making some products cheaper, it leaves consumers with more income to spend on other things. But there is a dark side to the job-creating potential of computers. The people who lose jobs to computers—welders who are replaced by robots, file clerks who are replaced by optical character scanners—often are not the ones who get the new jobs. Retraining is often proposed as a solution to this problem, but retraining is hard, especially for older workers. Look back for a moment to Box 2–4 (page 37), which describes Frank LaRosa's problems in making the switch from steelworker to computer programmer.

Reduction of job quality. Computer jobs are often portrayed as glamorous and interesting, and many are. Sometimes, however, computers create new forms of drudgery. A recent study by the U.S. Public Health Service looked at the jobs of clerical workers who perform such tasks as processing insurance claims. Those who use video display terminals were compared with those who do the same work by hand. The VDT users showed more physical and mental stress. They have to follow rigid procedures and have very little control over their work. And because the computer keeps track of their performance, down to the average number of rings taken to answer the telephone, they feel oppressed by overly close supervision. The response to studies like this has been a new interest in job enlargement and job enrichment in the automated office.

Invasions of privacy. Banks, insurance companies, police departments, tax bureaus, employers, and countless other companies and agencies have been collecting and storing data about people for years. In the past, however, these data sources were kept separate, and often it was hard for even the keeper of the file to recall the data in an orderly way. Today, the trend is toward integration of files and quick retrieval of data. This makes many people uncomfortable. How would you feel, for example, if your employer, your banker, or your local police department could quickly call up the following data.

- A list of all the people you have talked to on the phone in the last month
- A list, drawn from insurance files, of all the illnesses and injuries you have ever suffered, explaining how they occurred
- A list, drawn from airline computers, of every plane trip you have made in the last five years
- A complete financial statement showing your income, savings, loans outstanding, and loans in arrears
- A list, drawn from the records of your pay-TV outlet, of every TV movie you have watched in the last year, complete with its rating of PG, R, or X

Would you be angry? Embarrassed? Threatened? Of course you would. Yet the capacity to put together a list like this is already here. The keepers of many data files promise to respect privacy—but we know how good computer security systems are!

But Should We Blame Computers?

Should we blame computers for these negative impacts? Perhaps not. A close look at the list of problems suggests that every one can be seen as a failure of management, not of hardware or software.

Is the chain of command disrupted by a new computer system? Only because managers have failed to adjust the structure of the firm to fit the new system. Is security a problem? Only because control has not kept up with technology.

Are skilled workers who have been displaced by computers going to waste? Only if managers fail to view them as a valuable resource. Are workers unhappy with their new video display terminals? Time for a creative manager to try a dose of job enlargement or job enrichment. Is privacy being invaded? Only if systems are badly planned and controlled.

The truth of the matter is that computers can no more cause problems than they can solve them. Like every new device since the steam engine, they are only machines that can be used for better or worse by good managers or bad ones.

SUMMARY

1. The flow of information in a company can be compared to the input-transformation-output sequence discussed in Chapter 1. *Data* (raw facts) are collected and then processed (sorted, organized, listed, and so on) to turn them into *information*. To be useful for decision making, information should be accurate, timely, complete, concise, and relevant.

2. The most common way of using computers in business is in *data-processing systems* (DPS). Such systems capture data, process them, and communicate the information they produce. A *management information*

system (MIS) is a data-processing system that is designed to supply all levels of management with the internal and external information needed to make decisions. A *decision support system* (DSS) is an MIS with added analytic functions. Although computers cannot replace the judgment of managers, certain aspects of decision making may be structured so that computers can help.

3. Computers can perform three basic types of operations. They can do arithmetic; they can compare two numbers and decide which one is larger; and they can store and retrieve information. Their power comes from the fact that they can do these things very fast and accurately. However, the accuracy of computers is limited by the quality of the instructions and data that are fed into them. The *GIGO principle* warns computer users that if they put garbage into the computer, processed garbage is all they will get out of it.

4. *Hardware* is the physical equipment of a computer system. Every computer system includes four kinds of hardware: one or more *input devices*, one or more *output devices*, a *central processing unit*, and one or more *storage devices*, usually including both *primary* and *secondary storage*. Depending on the size and power of the hardware, computer systems are classified as *microcomputers*, *minicomputers*, *mainframes*, or *supercomputers*.

5. The instructions that tell computers to perform some useful task are known as a *program*. Together, programs and *computer languages* are known as *soft-*

ware. All programs must break a task down into a precise sequence of operations.

6. The steps in effective use of computers include defining a need, systems analysis, system design, program design and preparation, and implementation. Strong management skills are needed to use computers effectively; computers cannot serve as a crutch for weak management. It is important to involve all users of a system in every phase of the design and implementation of a new system.

7. Computers can have negative as well as positive impacts. They can disrupt the chain of command and pose problems of crime and security. For individuals, they can cause unemployment, reduced job quality, and invasion of privacy. However, these problems should not be blamed on computers themselves; rather, they are results of poorly managed computer systems.

KEY TERMS

You should be familiar with the following terms and concepts. Check their meanings by referring to the marginal definitions in the chapter or to the glossary at the end of the book.

Data	GIGO principle	Minicomputer
Information	Hardware	Mainframe
Computer	Input device	Supercomputer
Word processor	Output device	Program
Data-processing system (DPS)	Central processing unit	Software
Management information system (MIS)	Primary storage	Flowchart
Decision support system (DSS)	Secondary storage	Programming language
	Microcomputer	

QUESTIONS FOR REVIEW AND DISCUSSION

1. When Ellen Wessel of Moving Comfort ran into a cash flow problem that she thought might be solved through the use of a computer system, she hired Andy Novins as an adviser. On the basis of the information given about Moving Comfort's situation, and what you know about the effective use of computers, describe the first meeting between Novins and Wessel. At this meeting Novins goes over the steps that will have to be taken, gives some guidelines for each step, and stresses the actions that Wessel herself, as top manager, will have to take in order to make the new system work. Novins should also warn Wessel about possible negative impacts on the company and its members, and suggest what steps might be required to avoid them.

2. If you are to manage your college career effectively, your school must provide information about the courses being offered each term. Is the information you get about courses accurate, timely, complete, concise, and relevant? Could you suggest any improvements that would make it easier for you to choose your courses?

3. Make a list of all the computerized forms that you receive—subscription renewal forms, grade reports, phone bills, bank statements, and so on. Behind each of these forms is a data-processing system. Choose at least one item from the list and describe the data capture, processing, and communication steps that must take place to put the finished form in your hands.

4. Can you think of any ways in which the DPS you described in answering question 3 might be expanded into an MIS or even a DSS? Pretend you are the top manager. Think about the kinds of decisions you have to make and the information you need to make them.

5. If you are not already familiar with computer hardware, make a couple of field trips to look at, touch, and, if possible, even play around with some of the devices pictured in Box 7–2. One field trip should be to a computer store. There you will find small, inexpensive input and output devices, CPUs, and storage devices. With any luck, you will also find a friendly salesperson who will explain how all the boxes work. A second field trip, if you can arrange it, should be to a place where you can see a mainframe system at work. The computer center at your school is one possibility. A large bank or other business is another.

6. One thing people often find surprising about programming computers is the extreme detail required. A computer cannot do anything, even the simplest and most obvious thing, without being told. To get a feel for the amount of detail required, try writing a "program" that would get a robot to read this chapter and remember all the terms and definitions. (Your program need not be written in BASIC or COBOL—plain English or a flowchart will do.) Did you remember such details as telling your robot to retrieve the book? To turn the pages one by one? To check whether each page turned is the last one of the chapter? To identify new terms and store them in memory? Does it strike you as remarkable that a person can do all these things without being programmed, simply in response to the command "Read chapter 7 and remember the terms"?

7. Have you ever had any problems that were caused by computers? If so, describe one or more. How might they have been avoided if the computer system had been managed better?

Case 7–1: By Being Organized, One Man Builds a Business

Alan Cadan is the entrepreneurial equivalent of the one-man band. He is the owner, founder, and chief executive of Alynn Neckwear, Inc., as well as its head designer, bookkeeper, salesman, order taker, typist, shipping clerk, and telephone operator.

His four-year-old necktie business booked sales of $1 million. Cadan runs the business from his house in Stamford, Connecticut. He is the only full-time employee. He manages that because he is well organized. He's probably that way, he says, because he admired an uncle who was a compulsive organizer. The uncle wrote his own obituary and died on a weekend, his family says, so as not to inconvenience his loved ones.

"The only way you can run a business by yourself is to be organized," Cadan says. "You have to be on top of things." Working at home

saves him commuting time, but the trade-off, he says, is that the office is always present "to remind you of all the work there is to do. You forget to take time to play."

His wife, Lynn, and their four children, ages 11–15, help out. Mrs. Cadan does some bookkeeping and mailing chores and tones down some of her husband's ideas for tie designs, which tend to be clever. A rodent in a jogging outfit is the figure on the Rat Race tie; a design of thumb tacks is sold as the Tacky Tie.

Cadan's fabrics are made in U.S. and European mills; a New York City factory turns them into ties. But all of Alynn Neckwear's shipments are from the Cadans' home.

Packing and shipping are the most time-consuming tasks. Everyone in the family packs ties, a chore that extends into the late hours during the Christmas season, when the company ships 50 percent of its annual volume. Cadan's 79-year-old mother drove 40 miles a day to help out last year. "It's a one-man business," Cadan says, "with a lot of elves."

It's also a no-frills business. The shipping department is in the basement, where boxes of ties—there are 62 designs—sit on tables made of doors and sawhorses. It is equipped with an old, hand-operated tape machine and a worn bathroom scale.

Cadan's desk is a door covered with blotting paper that rests on two sawhorses. His office used to be the garage. A $10,000 computer system was acquired in 1982, but he prefers to use clipboards to keep track of things. The clipboards hang in neat rows on the wall behind the desk. One holds orders to be shipped; another has documents that show when fabric went from the mills to the New York tie makers. The computer could track the inventory, but it is simpler and quicker to subtract each day's shipments from what's on hand to keep a continuous inventory count, Cadan says.

The inventory data are on one of the clipboards on the wall. Cadan can reach it without putting down the phone. "You have to be able to save time if you're doing everything yourself," he says.

The computer is used mostly to make out invoices. Previously, with nearly 1,000 retail stores, 36 mail order houses, and 196 corporations buying his ties, Cadan sometimes had to spend entire days typing invoices. The computer also tabulates accounts receivable and prints monthly statements.

But Cadan uses a manual system to track accounts receivable. A file at his desk contains unpaid invoices grouped by customer. He says he can update the file faster than he could if the information were in the computer. He also can get current information about the account quicker by pulling the unpaid invoices than he could if he had to depend on the computer.

Source: Sanford L. Jacobs, "By Being Organized, One Man Builds a Thriving Tie Business," *Wall Street Journal*, February 14, 1983, p. 19. Reprinted by permission of the Wall Street Journal. © Dow Jones & Company, Inc., 1983. All Rights Reserved.

Questions:

1. Draw a flowchart of Cadan's DPS, showing capture, processing, and communication of inventory and invoice information.

2. When Cadan talks about "being organized," he isn't talking about departmentalization, line and staff offices, and so on. What he seems to mean is maintaining an orderly flow of information through his firm. Comment on his methods in terms of accuracy, timeliness, completeness, conciseness, and relevance.

3. Put yourself in the shoes of a systems analyst looking at Cadan's inventory control system. Do you think he should program his computer to keep track of inventory? Why or why not? (Assume that the hardware he already has would be adequate for this job.) How, if at all, does your opinion depend on the fact that Cadan is so "well organized"? What if he were the type of person who tends to write important things on odd slips of paper and misplace them in pockets, desk drawers, and shoeboxes?

4. Compare Alynn Neckwear with Moving Comfort. Both firms computerized their invoicing, but only Moving Comfort computerized inventory control. What differences between the two firms do you think account for the difference in their use of computers?

Case 7–2: Real Managers Don't Use Computers

Ray Moritz, vice-president of services for Computervisions, one of the highest of the high-tech companies—it is the world technological and market leader in CAD/CAM, or computer-assisted de-

Case 7–2: Real Managers Don't Use Computers (continued)

sign and computer-assisted manufacturing—says that even after twenty years in the computer business he wouldn't touch one of the things. He has no need for one. Many of Moritz's subordinates must use computers, but as a manager he must manage his complete function. He understands that even in the computer age, management skills are what produce results through others—not flashy displays.

Marty Anderson, formerly with IBM and a management information training specialist currently with Ryder Truck, says she doesn't own a personal computer because it can't do enough for her to justify its purchase. She can balance her checkbook and do her budget far faster and more cost effectively with a pencil and paper. When she needs detailed data for her work, she knows who can get it for her. No terminal is required.

Managers still must do fundamental things like manage the people who produce the results that pay the light bills. Sure, computers are useful. In some cases they are indispensable tools. But the key word is *tool*, i.e., something a laborer uses to produce results.

If you are the president of a company and you fly the corporate jet, it had better be a hobby. That task is best left to the corporate aviation service. If you are a production manager, you had better not be out running a machine no matter how sexy that new devil is. If you are a manager, keep your hands off those keys and printouts.

If you need information that a computer can supply, let someone with the time and talent filter it for you. Don't do it yourself except under extreme circumstances.

Top managers must learn to cultivate ignorance. The higher you go, the less you really should know about what is actually going on. Managers must rely on others to know. If they don't, they are not managers, they are meddlers. Subordinates will bounce the most trivial decisions up the ladder if that behavior is reinforced.

Managers don't have to be computer literate. And there's no reason to feel inadequate because 16-year-olds are supposedly writing computer programs in school that are more complex than Einstein's theory of relativity. Back in the automotive age, 16-year-olds discovered hot rods and spent countless hours in garages rebuilding rear ends and connecting dual carburetors. Did that mean you had to enroll in automotive engineering courses in order to understand spark plug firing order and thus become automotively literate? All you had to learn was how to drive.

If you as a manager want a hobby or a toy, then go to it, get that terminal fired up. But please don't impose those tools between yourself and actually managing people and enterprises.

Instant information in the hands of a manager is actually dangerous. Let those as far down in the organization as possible have the instant information. Let them react and do what must be done and then pass on the results. Give them a chance to use their lead time to take appropriate action.

Source: Jack Falvey, "Real Managers Don't Use Computer Terminals," *Wall Street Journal*, February 7, 1983, p. 22. Reprinted by permission of the Wall Street Journal. © Dow Jones & Company, Inc., 1983. All Rights Reserved.

Questions:

1. Jack Falvey, the author of this controversial editorial, compares learning to use a computer with learning to use a car: a manager needs to learn how to drive but does not need to learn about spark plug firing order. Would you agree that managers should keep their hands off computer terminals? Or could it be argued that learning to use a terminal *is* like learning to drive, and that not learning to use one is like depending on a chauffeur? Discuss.

2. Falvey is concerned that some kinds of computer use by managers could have negative impacts on their companies. What kinds of negative impacts? How do Falvey's concerns relate to the discussion in this chapter?

SUGGESTED READINGS, PART II

Drucker, Peter F. *Management: Tasks, Responsibilities, Practice.* New York: Harper & Row, 1974.

Mintzberg, Henry. "The Manager's Job: Folklore and Fact." *Harvard Business Review*, July-August 1975, pp. 49–61.

Stoner, James A. F. *Management,* 2nd ed. Englewood Cliffs, N.J.: Prentice-Hall, 1982.

McGregor, Douglas M. *The Human Side of Enterprise.* New York: McGraw-Hill, 1960.

George, Claude S., Jr. *The History of Management Thought,* 2nd ed. Englewood Cliffs, N.J.: Prentice-Hall, 1972.

Gabarro, John L., and John P. Kotter. "Managing Your Boss." *Harvard Business Review*, January-February 1980, pp. 92–100.

Katz, Robert L. "Skills of an Effective Administrator." *Harvard Business Review*, September-October 1974, pp. 90–102.

Sanders, Donald H. *Computers Today.* New York: McGraw-Hill, 1983.

Zmud, Robert W. *Information Systems in Organizations.* Glenview, Ill.: Scott, Foresman, 1983.

Kidder, Tracy. *The Soul of a New Machine.* Boston: Little, Brown, 1981.

McWilliams, Peter A. *The Personal Computer in Business Book.* Los Angeles: Prelude Press, 1983.

————. *The Word Processing Book: A Short Course in Computer Literacy,* 6th ed. Los Angeles: Prelude Press, 1982.

Useful periodicals:

Harvard Business Review
Computers and Electronics
Computerworld

CAREERS IN MANAGEMENT AND COMPUTERS

This section is the first in a series of four that give examples of career opportunities in business and other organizations. Two kinds of careers are covered. First we give some examples of careers in management. Because anyone whose duties include getting things done through people is a manager, we do not try to cover the whole field here. Many other management jobs—in marketing, sales, production, personnel, finance, and so on—will be discussed in the career sections at the ends of Parts III, IV, and V.

The other group of careers that we discuss here has to do with computers and their applications in business. Computer technology and its applications are changing rapidly, and career patterns are changing too. Still, the examples should give you an idea of the kinds of opportunities available.

This section and those that follow discuss a wide variety of jobs. In each case we will briefly describe the nature of the work, the training and qualifications required, the job outlook and opportunities for advancement, and earnings. The career information given here is based on that given in the *Occupational Outlook Handbook*, which is published each year by the U.S. Department of Labor. The latest edition of the handbook can be consulted for details.

Job Title: Supervisor

Description. Supervisors, also known as first-line managers, direct the work of the individual contributors in their organizations. In manufacturing firms, supervisors are often known as foremen. In other industries, they may have titles like straw boss, gang leader, and so on. Whatever the title, supervisors tell workers what work has to be done and then make sure the work is done right, whether it is loading a truck or building a washing machine. Supervisors play a key role in communications within the firm. They have formal reporting and record-keeping duties, and are often the first to spot problems and opportunities that require action by middle and top managers. Also, they are expected to tell employees about company policies. In unionized firms, supervisors serve as liaison between management and the union.

Qualifications. In most industries, supervisors are promoted from the shop floor. A talent for leadership and the ability to command respect and get along with people are crucial. In most firms, completion of high school is the minimum educational requirement, although one or two years of college are often useful. A growing number of firms, especially those in high-technology industries, are now hiring supervisors with a college or technical-school background.

Job outlook. About 1,300,000 people worked as supervisors of blue-collar workers in 1982. Half of them worked in manufacturing. Most of the rest worked in the construction industry, wholesale and retail trade, and transportation. Supervisory jobs are found in all parts of the country.

Employment of supervisors is expected to grow about as fast as the average for all jobs through the 1980s. Outstanding supervisors are often promoted to middle-management positions.

Earnings. In 1982, the average income of people supervising blue-collar workers was $22,100. It is common for the salaries of supervisors to be set 10 to 30 percent above those of the most highly paid production workers.

Job Title: Hotel Manager

Description: This is an example of a management position in a service industry. Hotel managers are responsible for operating the hotel profitably and satisfying hotel guests. Duties may include directing the food service operation; determining room rates; and managing housekeeping, accounting, and security. In a small hotel or motel, the manager may do many of these jobs without assistance.

Qualifications. Experience in the hotel industry is a key consideration in selecting managers, but college education is increasingly important. A bachelor's degree in hotel and restaurant administration provides strong preparation for work in this field. Part-time or summer work in hotels and restaurants is important for students in this field. Some large hotels and motel chains sponsor on-the-job training programs.

Job outlook. About 67,000 people worked as hotel or motel managers in 1982. The number of jobs in this field is expected to grow faster than the average for all occupations throughout the 1980s. Many seasonal and part-time jobs will also be available.

Earnings. Trainees who are graduates of hotel management programs can expect starting salaries of around $22,000 per year. For experienced managers, earnings vary greatly according to the size of the unit managed. In 1982, salaries of hotel managers ranged from $20,000 to $80,000, and those of hotel food and beverage managers ranged from $16,000 to $40,000.

Job Title: City Manager

Description. This is an example of a management position in the government sector. City managers administer the day-to-day operations of the city. They are responsible for tax collection and disbursement, law enforcement, and public works. They also hire department heads and prepare budgets. City managers are appointed by the community's elected officials and are responsible to them.

Long-range planning is also part of the city manager's job. Plans must be made for future growth and development, and for expansion of city services. In larger communities the city manager will have a number of management assistants.

Qualifications. A master's degree, preferably in public administration or business, is essential for those seeking a career in city management. Opportunities for candidates with only a bachelor's degree are limited. Many degree programs include an internship of six months to a year. Most managers begin as management assistants and work in such positions for several years while gaining experience. People seeking work as city managers or management assistants should like to work with details and to be part of a team, and should be able to work well under stress.

Job outlook. About 3,300 city managers, and several times that many management assistants, were employed in 1982. Most city managers work for cities that have the council–manager form of government, in which an elected city council appoints the manager. Some also work in cities that have the mayor–council form of government. In this case, the mayor appoints the manager as the chief administrative officer of the city. Employment in this field is expected to grow about as fast as the average for all jobs.

Earnings. In 1980, the average salary for all managers was more than $33,000. In cities with 5,000 to 10,000 inhabitants, the average was $28,000. In cities with 500,000 to 1 million inhabitants, the average was $70,000. Salaries of assistant managers ranged from $18,000 in small cities to $25,000 in larger ones.

Job Title: Health Service Administrator

Description. Health service administrators direct the activities that help make a health organization run smoothly. Duties include budgeting, setting rates for services, directing the hiring and training of personnel, and directing and coordinating medical and nursing services. Administrators may also help carry out fund-raising drives and promote public participation in health programs. Health service administrators are found in the not-for-profit, government, and private for-profit sectors of the health care industry.

Qualifications: A sound knowledge of general management skills is the main qualification.

CAREERS IN MANAGEMENT AND COMPUTERS (CONTINUED)

Bachelor's, master's, and doctoral degree programs at colleges and universities provide different levels of career preparation. The master's degree is the standard preparation for many positions. A degree in business or public administration may also be the route to a career as a health service administrator. To enter a graduate program in health administration, a bachelor's degree is required, with courses in natural sciences, psychology, sociology, statistics, accounting, and economics.

A few health departments require chief administrators to be physicians, but the trend is away from this. Directors of nursing are often chosen from among registered nurses with demonstrated administrative abilities.

Job outlook. Employment of health service administrators is expected to grow faster than average throughout the 1980s. However, graduate programs in health administration are growing rapidly, so competition for the available jobs is expected to be keen. Jobs for candidates without graduate degrees may continue to be available in nursing homes and other long-term care facilities.

Earnings. Chief administrators in medium-sized hospitals earned an average of $37,000 per year in 1982. Entry-level salaries for recent graduates with master's degrees averaged about $24,500 per year. Administrators of nursing and personal-care homes usually earn lower salaries than hospital administrators.

Job Title: Management Consultant

Description. Management consultants offer problem-solving skills, analysis, and practical recommendations to client organizations, which may be businesses, units of government, or not-for-profit firms. Although management consultants advise rather than manage, the work provides broad exposure to business problems. Many management consultants come from management backgrounds. Many others move into management jobs or start their own firms.

Qualifications. Most management consulting firms hire holders of the master of business administration (MBA) degree and holders of other ad-

vanced degrees. Preference is often given to candidates with work experience before or after the MBA. Specialization in finance, data processing, accounting, or industrial engineering is often useful.

Job outlook. Growth of employment in management consulting is expected to be about the same as the average for all occupations.

Earnings. According to the Association of MBA Executives, the median starting salary for management consultants in 1983 was $34,000.

Job Title: Programmer

Description. Computer programmers write detailed instructions called programs that list the steps a computer must follow in processing data. They usually work from descriptions prepared by systems analysts who have studied the task that the computer system is going to perform, for example, preparation of a payroll. The programmer translates the outline provided by the systems analyst into an appropriate programming language, such as BASIC or COBOL. There are many

specialties within the field of computer programming. Some programmers specialize in engineering or business applications. Others, called systems programmers, create and maintain the software that keeps a computer system running.

Qualifications. Most computer programmers are college graduates, but there are some openings for job seekers with courses in data processing but no college degree. In hiring programmers, employers look for people who can think logically and are capable of highly analytical work. The job calls for patience, persistence, and the ability to work accurately even under pressure. Because of rapidly changing technology, programmers must continue their training while on the job, often by taking courses offered by employers or by sellers of software.

Job outlook. About 66,000 people worked as computer programmers in 1982. The number of jobs in this area is expected to grow faster than the average for all occupations. Jobs for systems programmers will increase especially fast. The jobs of some applications programmers may be eliminated by software that allows computers to be oper-

ated by people with little specialized training.

The demand for college graduates in computer science and related fields is expected to exceed the supply. Graduates of two-year programs in data processing should also have good prospects, primarily in business applications. Opportunities for advancement to the position of systems analyst are good for programmers with demonstrated ability.

Earnings. Salaries of programmers ranged from $17,940 to $29,640 per year in 1982. Systems programmers earn somewhat more than applications programmers. In general, programmers earn about twice the average for all nonsupervisory workers in private industry.

Job Title: Systems Analyst

Description. The job of the systems analyst is to plan efficient methods of processing data, usually with the use of computers. If a new inventory system is required, for example, systems analysts determine what data need to be collected, what hardware is needed to carry out computations, and what steps need to be taken in processing the information. Once a system has been developed, the analyst describes the system in terms that managers or customers can understand, and also lays out detailed specifications for programmers to follow in translating the system into a computer language. Analysts also assist programmers in "debugging" the system, that is, getting it to operate smoothly.

Qualifications. There is no one best way of preparing for the work of a systems analyst, but college graduates are generally preferred. For the

more complex jobs, graduate degrees are required. Employers usually want analysts with a background in accounting, business management, or economics for business applications, and in physical sciences, mathematics, or engineering for scientific applications. Many employers also seek analysts with degrees in computer science or related fields. Many systems analysts have previous experience as computer programmers.

Job outlook. About 254,000 people worked as systems analysts in 1982. Employment in this field is expected to grow much faster than the average for all occupations through the 1980s.

Earnings. Entry-level salaries for systems analysts averaged about $23,192 per year in 1982. Experienced analysts earned up to $26,780.

Part III

MARKETING

Marketing is the process of finding out what customers need and channeling a flow of products to fit those needs. As such, marketing is important for every part of the economy. Business firms, units of government, and not-for-profit firms all must find out what their customers or clients need and find ways of satisfying them. The marketing efforts of all organizations taken together determine how the productive potential of the economy will be used to satisfy individual and social needs of all kinds.

The first chapter in this part provides an overview of marketing and looks at the job of the marketing manager. We will see that marketing managers not only need certain technical skills—they also need to understand the behavior of the customers with whom they deal.

The next four chapters discuss four aspects of the overall process of marketing. In Chapter 9 we look at the process by which a firm designs a product to serve customer needs and packages it in a way that customers find attractive. Chapter 10 deals with the distribution system—wholesaling, retailing, transportation, warehousing, and other functions needed to get the product from the producer to the customer. In Chapter 11 we turn to the topic of promotion—the process of telling customers about the product and persuading them to buy it. Advertising, personal selling, sales promotions, and public relations are covered. Finally, Chapter 12 covers pricing. No matter how well a firm meets customer needs, it cannot earn a profit unless it sets the right price for its product. Too high a price will drive too many customers away; too low a price will not cover the costs of production.

Throughout these chapters we will encounter many controversial issues. Are products safe enough? Do intermediaries earn too much profit on the goods they distribute? Is advertising wasteful or deceptive? Are prices too high? Dealing with these issues one by one will indicate both the strengths and the weaknesses of the American marketing system.

Chapter 8

THE MARKETING PROCESS

When you have completed this chapter, you should be able to

- Define *marketing*—both *micromarketing* and *macromarketing*.

- Compare and contrast the *production*, *sales*, and *total marketing orientations*.

- Define a *marketing information system* and list its components.

- Discuss the process of *marketing research*.

- Describe the buyer decision process and explain why knowledge of buyer behavior is important to good marketing management.

- Define *marketing strategy*, *target market*, and *marketing mix*. Explain the relationships among these concepts. List the "four Ps" of marketing.

It's about time someone realized that not every American derrière cottons to those snug and smug designer jeans.

Coming down the road is a new label aimed at a very seat-conscious market: "Long Haul Jeans for the professional truck driver. Quality made by Americans in the good old USA." Ads for the jeans, which are sold solely at truck stops, first appeared in *Overdrive* and *Owner Operator* trucking magazines last fall. Orders are, well, barreling right along.

"I hate to put up with these tight, regular blue jeans. I've got a pair on right now, and they're so inflexible I don't see how people can wear them," says Linwood Kennedy, a former trucker and retired mechanic who lives in Mechanicsville, Virginia. Kennedy needs loose-fitting jeans for the long drives he makes to attend regional automobile shows. He bought a pair of Long Hauls at Jarrell's Truck Stop in Doswell, Virginia. "You put them on the first time, and it seems like they're years old. They're excellent," he says.

Unlike the poured-into look that designer jeans offer, Long Hauls are made of stretch denim cut wider in the seat and thighs. The back pockets are wider, too, because truckers wanted them that way.

"These guys are not only mean and ugly—they're very large people," says Marshall Banks, vice-president of Jonbil, Inc., the Chase City, Virginia, company that makes the jeans. "They need the space."

"When you're up and down that big hike to the cab all day, you got a high stretch. These stretch with you. Drivers seem to really like that," says Billie Johnson, who runs a truck stop in Edinburg, Texas, where the jeans are selling well.

Jonbil predicts it will sell 100,000 pairs this first year, though Long Hauls are available only in 130 truck stops and through Sears and J. C. Penney catalogs. But Banks hopes the big jeans are heading to all 3,000 truck stops nationwide.[1]

[1] Dennis Kneale, "Now, the Latest in Truck-Stop Chic: Big, Stretchy 'Long Haul' Jeans," *Wall Street Journal*, January 3, 1983, p. 37. Reprinted by permission of the Wall Street Journal. © Dow Jones & Company, Inc., 1983. All Rights Reserved.

Long Haul jeans are marketed to a specific consumer group: professional truck drivers. Courtesy of Marshall Bank

Staying close to the customer, it seems, doesn't always mean staying right next to the customer's skin. But it does mean that successful business ventures are based on a clear knowledge of what customers want and need. This concept—that the whole enterprise is shaped around the customer's needs—is the key to understanding marketing, the subject of this chapter and the next four.

We have purposely placed the chapters on marketing before those on operations and production. One of the classic business mistakes is to start production of a good or service and then worry about whether anyone wants to buy it. We want you, the reader, to learn to see things from the point of view of customer needs before getting into the details of how goods and services are produced.

THE CONCEPT OF MARKETING

Marketing is a very big part of what organizations do—all of them, not just business firms. It affects all of us every day. Yet many people have an incomplete understanding of what marketing is.

Many people think marketing means advertising and selling. Such a definition is too narrow. Advertising and selling, as we will see, are parts of marketing but by no means all of it. We will begin this chapter with two very broad definitions of marketing. The first looks at marketing from the firm's point of view. The second looks at it from the point of view of society.

Marketing and the Firm

Marketing (micromarketing): The process of finding out the needs of customers or clients and channeling a flow of goods or services to meet those needs.

From the point of view of the firm, **marketing** can be defined as the process of finding out the needs of customers or clients and channeling a flow of goods or services to meet those needs. The term **micromarketing** is sometimes used to refer to marketing in this sense. This definition deserves a few comments.

Marketing includes many activities. The following are all parts of the marketing process.

1. *Finding out the customer's needs.* What kinds of goods are needed? What sizes and shapes? When and where will the goods or services be needed?
2. *Finding out what customers are willing to pay.* Are they willing to pay enough to cover the costs of production? If the price is changed, how will the quantity that can be sold change? If the good or service is to be supplied free of charge, how much will be demanded?
3. *Telling customers about the good or service and the terms on which it is available.* Should the product be advertised? If so, in what media? Should a sales staff be employed? Will news media carry stories about the product? Will word of mouth be enough?
4. *Getting the good or service from the point of production to the point of distribution.* What means of transportation should be used to deliver goods to customers? In the case of services, should customers come to the producer or should the producer make house calls?

What kinds of intermediaries (such as wholesalers or retailers), if any, should be included in the chain of distribution?

5. *Making sure customers are satisfied.* Is the good or service really filling the need it is intended to fill? Are ongoing repair or other services required? Do the experiences of customers suggest changes that should be made in the product?

This last activity—making sure customers are satisfied—completes the cycle and brings us back to the first one—finding out what customers need. The complete cycle is shown in Box 8–1. Each activity in the cycle will be discussed in detail in this chapter or one of the next four.

Box 8–1 The Cycle of Marketing Activities

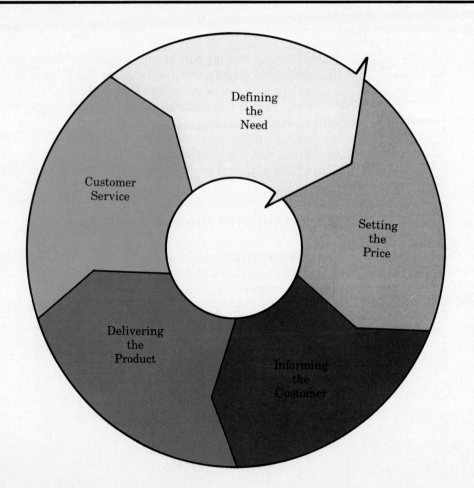

Marketing can be seen as a cycle of five activities. First the firm must find out what kind of product will best serve customers' needs. A price must then be set that will attract customers and at the same time permit a profit. Customers must then be told about the product through advertising, personal selling, or other means. The product must be delivered to the point of sale, perhaps by way of intermediaries such as wholesalers or retailers. Finally, follow-up services should be provided after the sale. This is important not only to get repeat business but also as a source of ideas for improving the product.

Marketing is not limited to business firms. When the full range of marketing activities is taken into account, it is clear that marketing is not limited to business firms. Every organization must market the goods or services it produces.

Take the not-for-profit Nature Conservancy, whose marketing program is described in Box 8–2. In a sense, its "clients" are the endangered

---

Box 8–2 Marketing the Idea of Conservation

The Nature Conservancy markets the idea of conservation in a way that many large corporations find attractive. Courtesy of the Nature Conservancy

In a time when conservation organizations go in for high visibility, the Nature Conservancy is different. It avoids political controversy, focusing instead on its mission: to preserve disappearing habitats for plants and wildlife. Typical of the Conservancy's efforts is an 8000-acre tract of virgin redwood and Douglas fir along the California coast. The Conservancy owns half of this land outright and manages the other half for the federal government.

The Coast Range Preserve is just a part of the 2-million-odd acres that the Conservancy owns and manages throughout the United States. The organization owes its success to astute marketing: identifying a group of clients whose needs it can serve, making itself known, and delivering the product.

Prominent among the Conservancy's clients are some of America's largest corporations, such as Standard Oil, Getty Oil, and BankAmerica Corporation. Corporations and corporate foundations have donated more than $10 million in cash and millions more in land to the Conservancy over the past three

years. Says Nathaniel Reed, a former under secretary of the Department of the Interior who has worked with the Conservancy, "They approach businesses with an opportunity other groups can't match: That is, you can make a major grant in cash or land; you can invest in conservation; you can help save unique, lovely lands worth saving. And unlike, say, a Sierra Club or Audubon Society, the Conservancy won't criticize or sue you for any of your past evil deeds."

The Conservancy has enlisted some high-powered executives as salespeople for its cause. Leland Prussia, chairman of BankAmerica Corporation, once wrote a letter to every bank in California pushing the Conservancy's cause. He was won over by the Conservancy's businesslike approach to explaining what land was critically needed and how it should be valued.

Source: Based on Ken Wells, "In Distinct Departure, Environmental Group Woos Big Business," *Wall Street Journal*, February 7, 1983, p. 1.

species of plants and animals that are sheltered on its lands. But its human clients—at whom its marketing efforts are aimed—are people who want to do something about the problem of disappearing natural habitats.

Micromarketing, as we have defined it, is important in government too. Each unit of government, from the local fire department to the Department of Labor, has a mission to serve some group of clients. To perform its mission well, the agency must learn its clients' needs, inform them, deliver the product, and see if they are satisfied with it. Some units of government do this job rather well. Most members of Congress, for example, are good marketers. The fact that they stay in office shows that they know how to appeal to voters at election time. Between elections they employ aides whose job is to keep in touch with voters and help them solve problems with other branches of the government. Government agencies that are described as "impersonal" and "bureaucratic" are usually those that neglect marketing.

Marketing is for small business too. Marketing is not just for big firms. It is crucial to the success of small ones, too. In firms that are too small to have a marketing department, the owner is head of marketing as well as head of production.

Many of the keys to success in small business that we discussed in Chapter 4 relate to marketing. For example, we stressed the importance of choosing a line of business. Is the good or service that the firm will offer something that customers really want and need? Will they pay a price high enough to cover costs? For a big business, as we will see in the next chapter, the success or failure of a new product depends on the answers to questions like these. For a small business, the survival of the firm depends on them.

We also pointed out in Chapter 4 that small firms have some advantages over big ones. Almost all of these relate to marketing. In markets that are limited by product life (flowers) or transportation costs (bricks), small companies often can deliver the goods better than their larger rivals. Small firms also have the advantage of being fast on their feet. They can often respond to changing customer needs faster and bring new products to market faster. Finally, small firms have an edge when it comes to the personal touch. Contacts made at the church or the club make for satisfied customers.

Marketing is not just for big businesses. It is crucial to the success of small firms, too. © Freda Leinwand

Marketing and Society

Let's turn to a second definition, which looks at marketing from the point of view of society as a whole. Looked at this way, **marketing** can be defined as the process by which the productive potential of the economy is used to satisfy individual and social needs of all kinds. Marketing in this sense is sometimes called **macromarketing**.

Macromarketing, like micromarketing, extends beyond private businesses. Not-for-profit firms and units of government at the federal, state, and local levels also play important roles. Taxes set by governments at all levels channel part of the economy's output away from uses that meet individual needs to uses that meet social needs. How tax revenues are spent—on defense, education, welfare, and so on—determines which social needs are satisfied.

Marketing (macromarketing): The process by which the productive potential of the economy is used to satisfy individual and social needs of all kinds.

Box 8–3 Marketing—Eye of the Needle

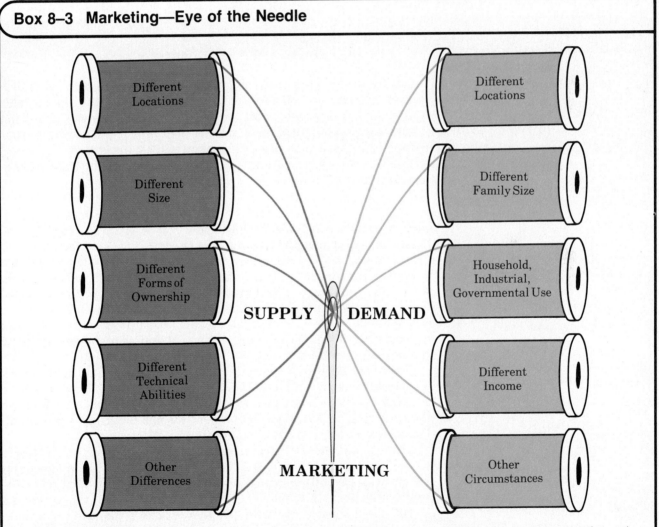

In a free enterprise system, economic activities are coordinated by supply and demand. Supply and demand are not blind forces like gravity and momentum, however. The work of millions of people is required to match all the different sources of supply with millions of sources of demand. Marketing is the eye of the needle through which the threads of supply and demand pass.

Marketing and the Economy

In Chapters 1 and 2 we explained how a market economy works. We saw that profits are a key incentive in the private sector, and we saw that the law of supply and demand helps profit-seeking firms put their resources to work where needs are greatest. But making supply and demand work in a complex modern economy is no easy job. As Box 8–3 shows, the sources of supply are many and varied. The businesses that supply goods and services differ in location, in size, in form of ownership, in technical ability, and in a hundred other ways. The households that demand goods and services vary no less widely. They, too, are scattered by location. They also differ in size, age, income, cultural background, and so on. Finding the best source of supply to satisfy each demand is what marketing is all about. Marketing is, in a sense, the eye of the needle through which all the threads of supply and demand must pass.

THE MARKETING CONCEPT AND ITS SIGNIFICANCE

Marketing, in the sense of micromarketing, is something that every firm must do. It must have some idea of what its customers want. It must have some way of letting people know that its product is there, and of delivering it. But saying that all firms must market their products is not the same as saying that they all put equal emphasis on marketing, or that they see all parts of it as equally important. There are at least three different orientations toward marketing.

The Production Orientation

Production orientation: An orientation toward marketing that focuses on producing a good-quality product at low cost.

A firm with a **production orientation** puts all its efforts into making a good-quality product at low cost. Such a firm asks, "What can we produce best?" It is taken for granted that people will need the product, provided that costs can be controlled so that the price is right. Advertising, if it is used at all, is simple and informative. The product is moved to market in the least costly manner. Little emphasis is placed on customer service, or on following up after the sale.

At one time the production orientation was the dominant point of view in business firms. When industry was in its early stages of growth, a need for simple goods such as food and clothing could be taken for granted. At that time, finding better production methods and lowering costs were all that was needed to expand the market.

Some production-oriented firms can still be found today. Farming is still largely production-oriented. This is especially true for commodities like grain or food oils, where the output of one farm is the same as the output of another. In consumer goods, too, some firms thrive by selling no-frills products at a low price and holding marketing costs to a minimum. In industrial goods, some firms single-mindedly pursue efficient production and cost cutting. For these firms, the production orientation may be the right one. Nonetheless, it tends to have a bad name. The reason is that a great many firms cling to the production orientation when it is not right for them. Some not-for-profit firms and units of government also are production oriented when they should not be. Universities sometimes structure their courses to suit the research projects of professors rather than the needs of students. And state motor vehicle departments have procedures for giving out license plates that suit their own convenience, not that of people who own cars.

The Sales Orientation

Sales orientation: An orientation toward marketing that stresses persuasive selling efforts.

A firm that has a **sales orientation** does not simply assume that there is a need for its product. It does almost the opposite—it assumes that its product will not be bought unless it is sold. Its sales and advertising efforts go far beyond just telling consumers about the goods that it produces. Instead, all the techniques of persuasion are brought into play. But once a sale is closed, it's good-bye. Customer service gets little attention.

The sales orientation belongs to a later stage of business development than the production orientation. In the depression of the 1930s, some production-oriented firms realized for the first time that customers wouldn't always buy everything the firm could make. They were forced to switch to the sales orientation.

Many firms remain sales-oriented to this day. But this orientation also tends to have a bad name. Too often, the sales orientation is a sign that other aspects of marketing are being neglected. Managers sense that customers are hesitant to buy their firms' products. But instead of changing the product to fit the customers' needs more closely, or improving customer service, they tell their sales forces to twist the customers' arms a little harder.

The Total Marketing Orientation

Total marketing orientation: An approach to marketing in which the firm plans all of its operations around customer needs and uses a balanced mix of marketing activities.

A firm with a **total marketing orientation** plans all of its operations around customer needs. It strikes a balance among the various marketing activities. It views marketing as a closed cycle in which customer service is the source of feedback—feedback that can be used to develop better products.

Peters and Waterman describe marketing-oriented firms very well when they say that "*whether their basic business is metal bending, high technology, or hamburgers, they have all defined themselves as service businesses.*"[2] In this sense, the total marketing orientation makes the distinction between goods and services obsolete.

The total marketing orientation is a stage of business development that follows the production and sales stages. That does not mean that production and sales can be neglected by a marketing-oriented firm, however. In coming chapters we will see that both product quality and control of production costs are vital parts of a balanced marketing program. In much the same way, careful attention must be given to selling, provided that attention is also given to finding out what the customer needs. The one thing that is obsolete in today's business world is the firm that doesn't take the time to think about its customers' needs at all.

Box 8–4 compares the production, sales, and marketing orientations.

[2]Thomas J. Peters and Robert H. Waterman, Jr., *In Search of Excellence* (New York: Harper & Row, 1982), p. 168. Emphasis in original.

Box 8–4 Three Possible Business Orientations

Three Possible Business Orientations

Activity	Production Orientation	Sales Orientation	Total Market Orientation
Defining the Need	Need is taken for granted	Product won't be bought unless it is sold	Constantly under review
Setting the Price	Control cost for a low price	Prices are seen as a sales tool	Important but not dominant
Informing the Customer	They'll find us if the price and quality are right	Whatever helps sales	Important but not dominant
Delivering the Product	Use the most cost-effective means	Whatever helps sales	Tailored to customer needs
Customer Service	Little emphasis	Little emphasis	Very important as a sales tool and a source of product ideas

Beyond the Total Marketing Orientation

Popular though the total marketing orientation is, there are some circles where it, too, has a bad name. The promise of this orientation is a society that meets consumer needs, but the result is not what everyone considers a good society. We discussed this issue in Chapter 1 under the heading "Social Responsibilities." Here we will look at some concerns that are directly related to marketing.

First there are the concerns of the consumer activists. They complain that many companies pay lip service to marketing but still deliver shoddy goods, overprice their products, and turn their backs when customers protest. It is hard to disagree with them. Clearly, more than lip service is needed. On the other hand, there is strong evidence that the most profitable firms are the ones that are most consumer-oriented. In time their competitors will either catch on or disappear.

Second, there are the concerns of the environmentalists. They complain that the very things firms do to serve their paying customers may be harmful from a broader social point of view. As examples, they point to firms that skimp on pollution control in order to please their customers with low prices, or that package their products in wasteful ways in order to give customers greater convenience.

Third, there are critics to whom the whole idea of giving consumers what they want is suspect. Consumers, they say, sometimes want things that aren't really good for them. The advertising of tobacco and alcohol is seen as one kind of abuse. Beyond these "sin goods," these critics are concerned that marketing creates "needs" for goods that people could get along without, such as infant formulas to replace mother's milk, highly processed foods with little nutritive value, and large, gas-guzzling cars.

The critics urge businesses to adopt an approach called social marketing. This approach is based on the concept that the wants and needs of consumers are shaped, at least in part, by the kind of society they live in. Efforts to serve consumers through marketing should not, in the critics' view, treat their needs as given. Businesses should try not to create needs for goods that are socially harmful. They should use their marketing talents to encourage healthful, environmentally sound life-styles.

THE MKIS, MARKETING RESEARCH, AND BUYER BEHAVIOR

Marketing is important. In a totally marketing-oriented firm, the marketing manager is a key decision maker and other top managers always keep marketing in mind. But managers in such a firm must be supplied with a constant flow of timely and accurate information. Systems for handling such information are the topic of this section.

The Marketing Information System

Marketing information system (MKIS): A set of procedures for collecting, processing, and presenting information on which marketing decisions can be based.

A set of procedures for collecting, processing, and presenting information on which marketing decisions can be based is a **marketing information system (MKIS)**. (The K is added to distinguish the marketing information system from management information systems [MIS] like those discussed in Chapter 7.)

In today's business world an MKIS is likely to be computerized. This is not required, however. In a small firm, many kinds of information can be kept more cheaply in simple card files than in computer memories. (See Case 7–1, page 174.) Even in large firms some kinds of marketing information are not handled by computers—judgments about consumer tastes or guesses about competitors' strategies are examples. The important thing about an MKIS is not whether it is computerized but whether it is well planned and gets results.

An MKIS can have up to four parts. The first two exist, even if only informally, in all firms, large and small. The second two are optional.

Internal accounting system: As part of a marketing information system, a set of procedures for keeping track of income, costs, and other financial information.

The internal accounting system. Every firm has some kind of **internal accounting system**. Managers must keep track of income, costs, sales, profits, losses, and many other flows and uses of funds. We will discuss accounting systems in Chapter 18. Here we simply note that some kinds of accounting information are important in marketing decisions.

At a bare minimum, the system must tell managers how well each of the firm's products is selling and whether each of them, at current prices, is bringing in profits. Other accounting data—on inventories, amounts owed by customers, and so on—may also be covered by the MKIS.

Marketing intelligence system: A set of procedures for collecting information about consumers and competitors in the market where the firm sells its product.

The marketing intelligence system. Every firm also has procedures of some sort for watching the markets it sells in. What are consumers buying? What are competitors selling? How large a share of the market does each seller have? The firm's procedures for getting this kind of information can be called its **marketing intelligence system**.

Some marketing intelligence systems are quite complex. Not all are, however. Good marketing intelligence can often be obtained simply by asking sales representatives to keep their ears to the ground and report back to the boss. However formal or informal, the marketing intelligence system gives managers information about the marketing environment to go with the data obtained through the accounting system.*

Marketing research: A systematic, objective way of getting information needed to solve specific marketing problems.

Marketing research. Together, the internal accounting system and the marketing intelligence system provide ongoing streams of information to marketing managers. Often, however, the flow of a firm's business is interrupted by specific marketing problems. Sales of a key product may begin slipping—why? A new product has been developed in the lab—how should it be put on the market? Solving problems like these is the job of **marketing research**. In contrast to the wide-angle lens of marketing intelligence, marketing research zooms in to get a close-up view of a specific situation. Marketing research is part of the MKIS, but it is also a major topic in itself. We will return to it shortly.

Marketing decision support system: A decision support system that has been set up to serve the needs of marketing decision makers.

The marketing decision support system. A fourth possible component of an MKIS is a **marketing decision support system**. As the name suggests, this is a decision support system that has been set up to serve the needs of marketing decision makers. The Brandaid DSS discussed in Chapter 7 is an example of a marketing decision support system. Such a system stresses mathematical and analytical techniques and calls for hands-on use of computers by managers. Such systems are not yet common, but as the use of computers spreads they will no doubt become more so.

Box 8–5 gives an overview of the marketing information system and its four components. As a whole, the system provides both a steady flow of internal and external information and the ability to solve problems as they arise.

Marketing Research

We mentioned marketing research as part of an MKIS. Marketing research is a systematic, objective way of getting the information needed to

*A marketing intelligence system, as the term is used here, means simply an information-gathering service for marketing management. It does not mean a system of illegal or unethical spying on competitors.

Box 8–5   The Structure of a Marketing Information System

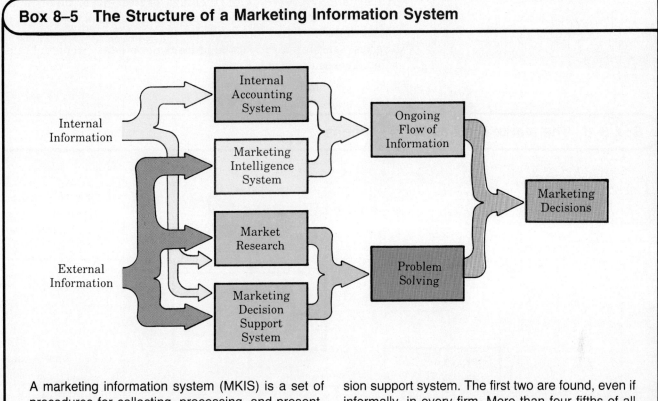

A marketing information system (MKIS) is a set of procedures for collecting, processing, and presenting information on which marketing decisions can be based. The four components of an MKIS are an internal accounting system, a marketing intelligence system, marketing research, and a marketing decision support system. The first two are found, even if informally, in every firm. More than four fifths of all large firms have marketing research departments, but marketing decision support systems are found in only a few firms.

solve specific marketing problems. Four fifths or more of all large firms now have marketing research departments. Because it has become so important, marketing research warrants a separate discussion here.

Uses of marketing research.   The uses of marketing research are as varied as the marketing concept is broad. The following are among the more common targets of marketing research.

- *Market or product potential.* Before deciding to put some new product on the market, a firm needs as good a forecast as possible of its product's sales potential. Marketing research can develop such a forecast. The same is true when a firm enters any market for the first time, even if the product is not a new one.
- *Special studies.* The MKIS is supposed to provide a steady flow of information to managers. Sometimes, though, special, in-depth studies on such subjects as market shares or attitudes toward rival products are needed. That sort of job goes to the marketing research department.

- *Advertising research.* This includes pretesting of advertising themes and follow-up studies of the effectiveness of ads.
- *Sales support studies.* Research may be needed to decide what are the best sales territories or the proper sales quotas. Studies of sales effectiveness are also common.

Box 8–6 The Marketing Research Process

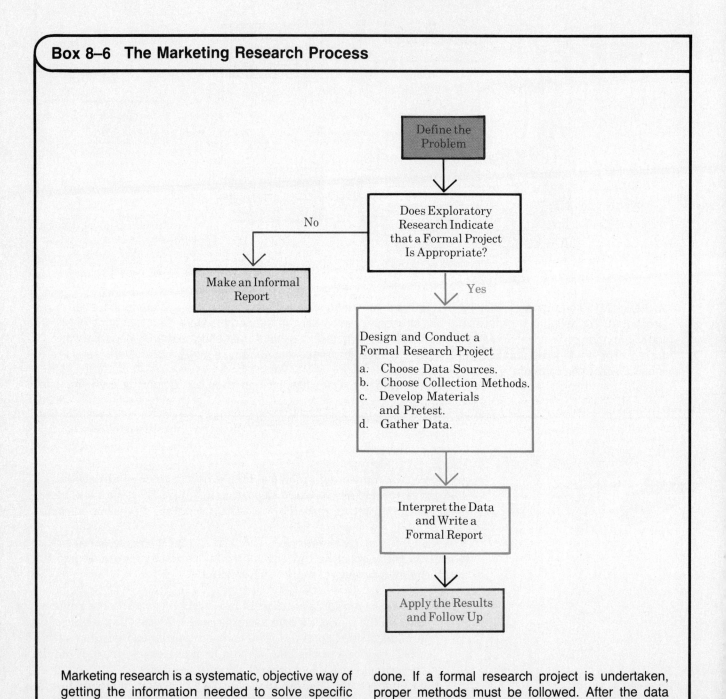

Marketing research is a systematic, objective way of getting the information needed to solve specific marketing problems. It begins with a clear definition of the problem. Before a formal research project is planned, informal exploratory research should be done. If a formal research project is undertaken, proper methods must be followed. After the data have been interpreted and a formal report has been written, the results of the study should be applied and followed up.

This is only a partial list of the projects that might come across a marketing researcher's desk. Clearly, flexibility and creativity are needed to handle such a wide range of tasks.

The marketing research process. *Systematic* and *objective* are key words in the definition of marketing research. Knowledge of sampling techniques, questionnaire design, and statistical analysis is required. Marketing research, like any other kind of research, should be clearly focused and should use scientific methods.

For an overview of the marketing research process, turn to Box 8–6. Let's go through the steps shown there.

First, the problem must be defined clearly (step 1). This is not always easy. The assignment may be something like "Hey, can you guys find out why we aren't doing so well on the West Coast?" Informal, exploratory research may be needed. Reviews of sales patterns by region or informal talks with salespeople in the field might provide starting points. Jumping right in with mass mailings of questionnaires could be a big waste of money if no one knows what questions need to be asked.

When the problem has been explored informally, one can ask whether a formal research project is worthwhile (step 2). Perhaps it is not. Perhaps talks with salespeople suggest that the problem on the West Coast lies in the nasty personality and sloppy work habits of the regional sales manager. If it does not seem useful to proceed, an informal report should be submitted in which the results of the exploratory research are explained (step 3).

Suppose the initial research suggests that weak sales on the West Cost have something to do with a regional difference in people's perception of the product. A formal research project to look into this problem is approved. Once the green light is given, many things must be done (step 4). Sources of data must be chosen. A method for gathering data must be selected—written questionnaires, telephone interviews, or whatever. Materials for data collection must be prepared and pretested. Meanwhile, a sample of respondents needs to be chosen that is suitable in terms of geography, consumer income, and whatever other traits are relevant. Finally, the actual process of data collection must be carried out.

When the data are in, they must be analyzed and interpreted (step 5). The end product of the research project will be a formal report. After this, one further step is shown in Box 8–6: use the information contained in the report and follow up to see if it helps (step 6). Strictly speaking, this is a job for the marketing manager, who is a line officer in the firm, and not a job for the marketing research staff. Even so, we have included it as part of the process of marketing research. A good report that is filed without being read is just as useless as one that is badly designed or carried out.

Buyer Behavior

In addition to an MKIS and good marketing research, an understanding of buyer behavior can be of value to a marketing manager. The term **buyer behavior** refers to the decision process that buyers go through in deciding what products to buy and from what sources.

The consumer decision process. We have stressed again and again that marketing means solving the problem of how best to meet customer

Buyer behavior: The decision process that buyers go through in deciding what products to buy and from what sources.

A marketing manager can benefit from an understanding of the process that buyers go through in deciding which products to buy and from what sources. © Freda Leinwand

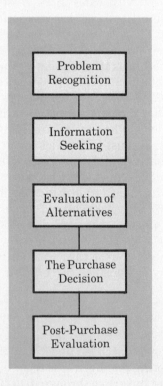

needs. The main thing to understand about buyer behavior is that customers are working to solve the same problem. They, too, want to find out how best to meet their needs.

Let's begin with a decision that you yourself might have to make as a buyer. You are driving through a city far from home when you hear an ominous noise under the hood of your car. You recognize that there is a problem to be solved. Seeking information, you stop at a phone booth. You look in the Yellow Pages. You call several garages, looking for one that is not too far away, charges a reasonable hourly rate, and can work on your car without delay. Evaluating the information you have gathered, you decide that Smedley's Garage is the best bet. You decide to go there, and soon your car is fixed. Driving on down the road, you are pleased with the smooth-running sound of your car. You decide that you made a good choice.

This thought process is typical of all consumer decisions. Stated formally, the process can be broken down into five steps, as follows.

1. *Problem recognition.* This is the point at which you become aware that you have a need. Sometimes problem recognition is triggered in a very direct way: your car starts making funny noises. At other times the cues are more subtle: spending every night in front of the TV is beginning to make you feel restless instead of relaxed. Maybe you need to sign up for a class at the local community college and learn something that will broaden your mind.
2. *Information seeking.* Whatever your problem is, chances are there is more than one way of dealing with it. Your first task is to find out what alternatives are open to you. You look in the Yellow Pages to find what garages are in the area. You write for the course catalogs of local colleges and universities. You talk with friends about their experiences. All of these are ways of seeking information.
3. *Evaluating alternatives.* Not all of the possible ways of dealing with your problem are equally suitable. When you call the garages, you want to know how far away they are and how soon they can work on your car. When you get the course catalogs, you want to know how closely the courses fit your interests, how convenient the class hours are, and how much the courses cost. You take all this information into account, weigh it, and decide which alternative will best meet your needs.
4. *The purchase decison.* At this point you have to decide whether to buy or not to buy. If you car has broken down, you have little choice but to go with the best alternative you can find. If your need is less direct, you may decide not to take any action. Maybe after you have looked at all the college catalogs from your area you decide that the courses aren't interesting enough, or are given at the wrong times, or cost too much. You may decide not to put out your money for any of them. Or you may decide that one of the alternatives is worthwhile. You stick the application form in the mail and commit yourself.
5. *Postpurchase evaluation.* After making the purchase you must evaluate your decision. Did the garage do a good job on your car? If so, you will stop there another time. Was the course interesting? If so, you might try another. If it was a bore, you may go back to TV.

Factors that influence consumer decisions. The consumer decision process does not take place in a vacuum. Studies show that purchase

Cultural factors have a lot to do with what people buy. Some firms produce entire product lines geared to specific ethnic groups. Grocery store—© Freda Leinwand; Swanson—Courtesy of Campbell Soup Company

decisions are influenced by many factors. Psychological, social, and cultural factors have a lot to do with what people buy. So do demographic factors like age, sex, and education. Marketing managers must understand all of these factors.

Marketing managers must also understand how factors that they can control affect consumer behavior. Product features, the distribution system, advertising, sales effort, and price are just a few of the things that can affect whether a consumer buys or does not buy a product. In the following chapters we will see that each of the five steps in consumer behavior creates chances to attract buyers to the product a firm is selling. The efforts of firms to sell their products and the efforts of consumers to satisfy their needs are two sides of the same coin.

Industrial and government buyers. Not all firms sell to consumers. Many also sell to industrial and government buyers. Marketing managers for these firms should learn as much as they can about how their customers make purchase decisions, just as sellers of consumer goods should learn how consumers make decisions.

Industrial and government buyers can be thought of as going through the same steps as consumers: problem recognition, information seeking, evaluation of alternatives, the purchase decision, and postpurchase evaluation. In practice, however, dealing with buyers in government and industry can be quite different from dealing with consumers. For one thing, the buyers are much more likely to be experts in their fields. Formal specifications and bidding procedures may have to be followed. Finally, it is important for sellers to understand the structure of the buyer's firm or agency, and its influence on the purchase decision.

The skills that enable a firm to sell its products to consumers do not always serve equally well in selling to industrial or government buyers. Consider the case of Apple Computer, which sells personal computers to individuals and small businesses through a well-developed dealer network. As personal computers became more advanced, it became clear that there was a market for them in big firms, too. Apple tried to crack the corporate market by using its own sales force, rather than selling through dealers, but it was steamrollered by IBM, which knew the corporate market inside and out. After a year of effort, Apple President John Sculley admitted that it was "difficult and unrealistic for Apple to sell to corporate America like IBM does." When it came time for a company like Traveler's

Insurance Company to buy 12,000 personal computers, IBM's knowledge of corporate buyer behavior carried the day.[3]

MARKETING STRATEGY AND THE MARKETING MIX

Marketing strategy: The choice of a target market and a marketing mix to serve that market.

Target market: The particular group of customers whose needs a firm aims to satisfy.

Marketing mix: The mix of product, distribution system, promotion, and price that a firm uses to serve customers in a target market.

With the help of a marketing information system, marketing research, and an understanding of buyer behavior, a firm plans its **marketing strategy**. In a truly marketing-oriented firm, the marketing strategy is a central part of the strategic plan, and all top managers, not just the marketing manager, should be involved in setting it up. Planning a marketing strategy means choosing a target market and a marketing mix to serve that market. The **target market** is the particular group of customers whose needs the firm aims to satisfy. The **marketing mix** is the mix of product, distribution system, promotion, and price that the firm uses to serve the target market.

Copyright © 1983 United Features Syndicate, Inc.

Choosing the Target Market

A production-oriented firm defines itself in terms of the goods or services it produces: "We are a soup maker. Anyone out there who wants soup, come and get it!" A marketing-oriented company starts by choosing a target market. It is not that marketing-oriented companies cannot do a good job of production. Instead, it is a matter of how they think about what they do: "What kinds of food do people need?" they ask. "What kind of people use soup to satisfy their food needs? How can we best serve those people?"

Market segmentation: The process of dividing a market into submarkets, each made up of groups of customers who are alike in some key way.

Market segmentation. A total marketing orientation leads to the recognition that not all buyers are alike and that there are submarkets within markets. The process of dividing a market into submarkets, each made up of groups of customers who are alike in some key way, is known as **market segmentation**.

Market segmentation can help a firm in several ways. First, it allows firms to tailor their products and promotional efforts to customer needs.

[3]See "Personal Computers: And the Winner Is IBM," *Business Week*, October 3, 1983, pp. 76–83.

BMW pursues a concentrated marketing approach, focusing on high-income, quality-oriented consumers. Courtesy of BMW of North America, Inc.

Second, it helps the firm find specific groups of customers whose needs are not being served well by competitors. Finally, it makes it possible to use resources more effectively; money can be saved, for example, by placing ads only in magazines that are likely to be read by people in the target market.

Concentrated marketing: An approach to marketing in which the firm chooses a single market segment as its target and tries to offer the ideal marketing mix for that segment.

Differentiated marketing: An approach to marketing in which the firm produces a range of related products or brands, each one tailored to the needs of a specific market segment.

Which segments to serve? After market segments have been identified, the next step is to decide which segment or segments to serve and how. Three approaches can be used.

A firm that takes a **concentrated marketing** approach chooses a single market segment as its target and tries to offer the ideal marketing mix for that segment. A good example of concentrated marketing is the German automaker BMW. BMW's product development, advertising, and sales efforts are directed toward people who want a high-performance sports sedan and have plenty of money to spend on a car.

A firm that takes a **differentiated marketing** approach produces a range of related products or brands, each one tailored to the needs of a specific market segment. An example would be Anheuser-Busch, the country's leading brewer. Besides its best-selling Budweiser brand, popular among college students and blue-collar workers, it produces Busch, a less expensive brand for price-sensitive buyers; Bud Light and Natural Light for calorie watchers; Michelob for those who prefer a premium beer; and Michelob Light for those who want a premium beer that is also low in calories.

Finally, some companies pursue an **undifferentiated marketing** approach, offering a single product to all consumers. An example is Scott Paper's Cut-Rite brand of waxed paper. The same waxed paper is sold all over the country to customers of all kinds.

As the examples show, any one of the three approaches can be successful, as long as it is suited to the market and to the abilities of the producer.

Planning the Marketing Mix

Once the target market has been chosen, the next step is to develop a marketing mix that is suited to the market. Earlier we defined the marketing mix as the mix of product, distribution system, promotion, and pricing that the firm uses to serve the customers in the target market. The distribution system is used to get the firm's output to the place where it is needed; thus, *Product*, *Place*, *Promotion*, and *Price* are often referred to as the "four *P*s" of marketing.

Product. As an element of the marketing mix, *product* refers to matching the nature of the product to the target market. Designing new products is part of that process. So is improving old products in response to feedback from users. Note that *product* can mean both goods and services, including follow-up services to users. The product element of the marketing mix will be the subject of Chapter 9.

Distribution. Distribution—place, in the four *P*s—is concerned with getting goods and services to the customer. Perhaps it is true that if you build a better mousetrap the world will beat a path to your door; but if so, mousetraps are unique. Typically, a firm must beat its way to the customer's door. Problems of transportation and warehousing come under the heading of distribution. So do decisions on how to use intermediaries, such as wholesalers or retailers. Chapter 10 will be devoted to distribution.

Promotion. Promotion means telling and selling. Consumers cannot buy your firm's product if they do not know about it. Advertising is the most obvious way to tell consumers about the product, but it is not the only way. News stories, reviews in consumer-oriented magazines, and plain old word of mouth are also important.

After the telling is done, selling is still needed to convince potential customers that your product, and not someone else's, is the one that will best serve their needs. Consumers may use products that are familiar to them even when you know that you have something new and better to offer. Selling is not always directed at the consumer. Active efforts may be needed to persuade retailers and other intermediaries to carry your product and display it so that consumers will notice it. Finally, follow-up service is a major promotional tool. We will discuss promotion in Chapter 11.

Undifferentiated marketing: An approach to marketing in which the firm offers a single product to all consumers.

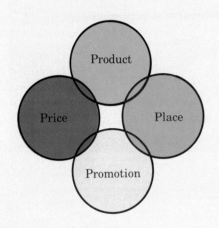

Transportation is part of the distribution or "place" element of the marketing mix. © Freda Leinwand

Price. Finding the right price for the product is crucial to a firm's success. There is a story about two brothers who bought hay for $1.00 a bale in Vermont, where hay was plentiful. They then trucked it to Massachusetts, where hay was scarce, and sold it for $0.90 a bale. After a couple of months they had a lot of satisfied customers, but they found out that they were losing money. "Maybe we need a bigger truck," said one to the other.

The moral of this story is that finding customers and filling their needs is not enough. To stay in business and meet consumer needs in the long run, a firm needs to set a price that is high enough to allow it to make a profit. Not just any price higher than the cost of making the product will do, though. Too high a price can drive too many customers away or draw in too many competitors. Problems of pricing are the subject of Chapter 12.

Box 8–7 summarizes the process of planning a marketing strategy.

Marketing is one of the most interesting aspects of business. Along with production and finance, it is one of the major tasks of managers in organizations of all kinds. There are many careers in marketing, but even

Box 8–7 Planning a Marketing Strategy

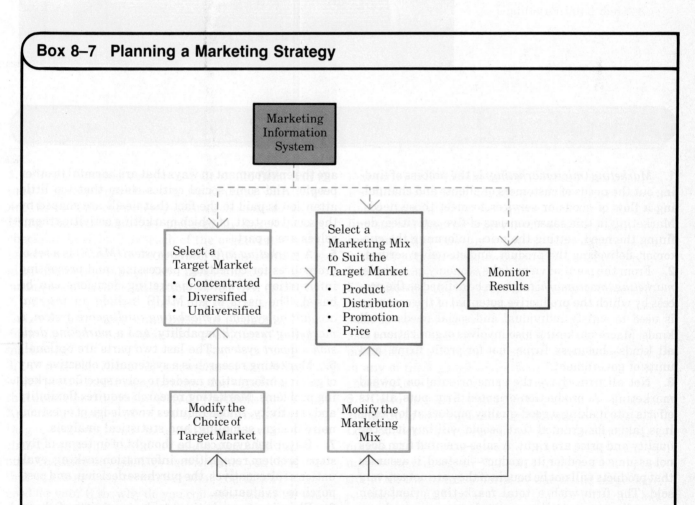

A marketing strategy is part of a firm's strategic plan. It consists of choosing a target market (a specific group of customers that the firm aims to serve) and then choosing a marketing mix (product, distribution system, promotion, and pricing) to serve that market.

Case 8–1: How to Please the Businesswoman-Traveler?

The hotel industry seems thoroughly confused over how to please female business travelers, who make up the fastest-growing segment of the hotel market.

About 30 percent of all business travelers are women, up from just 1 percent in 1970, according to a Cornell University study. And the number of traveling businesswomen is growing three times faster than the number of traveling businessmen.

Yet the nation's hotels can't agree on the best way to attract women customers. Some offer rooms and suites just for women that include special amenities. Some even have entire floors for them. But other hotels don't believe women want to be treated differently than men, and some have dropped the special services they once offered for female customers.

A Ramada Inns Inc. year-long research effort indicates that women don't want special rooms or special all-women's floors, says Ron Nykiel, an executive vice-president. So the chain has decided on a different way to try to appeal to women. It wants to make employees aware of any chauvinistic attitudes they might have. All employees at its 550 U.S. hotels have just taken a seminar about female travelers that emphasizes special security for women and offers tips on how to avoid typical slights.

But another big chain, Hyatt Corporation, thinks women do want special rooms. It says its 15 rooms for businesswomen at the Hyatt Regency O'Hare hotel in Chicago have been a hit. And Hyatt recently started offering rooms for women in five of its hotels in Indianapolis, Minneapolis, suburban Chicago, and Des Moines, Iowa. The rooms include things like special makeup mirrors, hair dryers, and makeup accessories.

Other hotel chains that have had special programs for traveling businesswomen are now retreating from that approach.

Westin Hotels, a United Airlines affiliate with 50 hotels, started a training program for employees on how to handle women business travelers in 1977 and discontinued it in 1980. "We did as much as we could," says a spokeswoman. "We found that all women want is to be treated like everybody else."

Hilton Hotels Corp. was a forerunner of the current attempts to woo the woman business traveler in the 1960s with its "Lady Hilton" program. The program featured special "Lady Hilton" rooms with light, female-oriented decor and amenities. There was a "Lady Hilton" representative in each Hilton lobby to serve women guests.

But Hilton discontinued the four-year-old program in 1968 "after women began telling us they didn't want to be isolated or segregated," says Lucille Skerston, Hilton's director of commercial sales.

Skerston is among the many hotel executives who admit to being frustrated by the issue. "I'd like to round up large panels of traveling businesswomen and female opinion leaders and find out once and for all what they want us to do," she says.

Source: Earl C. Gottschalk, Jr., "Hotel Industry Seems to Be Baffled on How to Please Businesswomen," *Wall Street Journal*, June 15, 1983, p. 37. Reprinted by permission of the Wall Street Journal. © Dow Jones & Company, Inc., 1983. All Rights Reserved.

Questions:

1. Do you think the hotels discussed in this article are product-oriented, sales-oriented, or marketing-oriented? How can you tell?

2. Of the five activities shown in Box 8–1, which one seems to be giving hotels the biggest problem? Why do you think this is the case?

3. Comment on this article in terms of the differentiated, undifferentiated, and concentrated approaches to defining a target market. Which approaches can you find examples of in the article? Does the article suggest that women business travelers are a meaningful market segment in the hotel business, that they are not a meaningful market segment, or that there are subsegments within that segment?

4. Put yourself in the position of a marketing researcher who has been asked to develop an approach to serving traveling businesswomen. What kinds of questions would you want to ask of a sample or panel of such women?

Case 8–2: Marketing Problems in Socialist Economies

Janos Kornai is one of the best-known economists of Eastern Europe. He is a celebrity in his native Hungary, where he has played a central role in economic reforms. He is equally respected as a creative theorist in the West. Recently, Forbes *Magazine discussed problems of socialist economies with Kornai. Here are some excerpts from the interview:*

Why doesn't socialism work very well? A fundamental reality of socialist economies, replies Kornai, is that they are characterized by shortage. As a result, they are sellers' markets with scant incentives for producers to innovate. Kornai offers the example of Eastern Europe's automobile industry, which he and two colleagues have recently investigated.

"Let's take a car like the Trabant, an East German car that is the most common in Hungary because it is the cheapest. Today in Hungary there is a five-year waiting list for Trabants. In East Germany the wait is eight to ten years. In Hungary you have to pay half the price when you join the waiting list. It is forced savings in effect.

"Now the Trabant is a car of the 1950s. Not just the body style, the whole car is 30 years old. Why should the Trabant company produce a modern car if the old one is sold out for a whole decade in advance?

"Now compare this with the buyers' market for cars you have in the West—the very cruel competition between Japanese, German, American, and so on, cars on the world market. To sell in this buyers' market, you have very strong incentives to develop new technologies in fuel savings and pollution controls—and the Trabant, by the way, is not a very fuel- or pollution-efficient car."

The same goes for the socialist countries' desperate housing shortage, "one of the most depressing social problems that arises from shortage," according to Kornai. Even in relatively prosperous Hungary, the wait for a subsidized, state-built apartment is five years. "So why should construction firms think about technological improvements to apartments—even simple things like windows and doors that close properly and reduce heat-loss—when the firm's output is sold out five years in advance?

"This is a central problem of socialism: namely, that without the competitive pressure of a buyers' market, there is not sufficient motivation for creative product innovation. As long as we don't have competitive buyers' markets to force producers to make creative improvements, we will have to rely on imitating Western innovation."

Source: Lawrence Minard, "The Problem with Socialist Economies," *Forbes*, August 1, 1983, pp. 64–66. Reprinted by permission of Forbes Magazine, August 1, 1983, pp. 64–66. © Forbes Inc., 1983.

Questions:

1. To what extent is macromarketing needed in a socialist economy? What about micromarketing? Comment in the light of this article.

2. How would socialist firms be classified in terms of the product, sales, and total marketing orientations discussed in the text? What evidence do you find in this case? Is the orientation of a firm like Trabant suited to its situation? In what sense yes? In what sense no?

3. Describe Trabant's marketing mix in terms of the four Ps. Do you think the mix is suited to the market? Why or why not? If not, what changes do you think should be made?

4. In Kornai's view, what changes are needed to improve the marketing efforts of Eastern European firms?

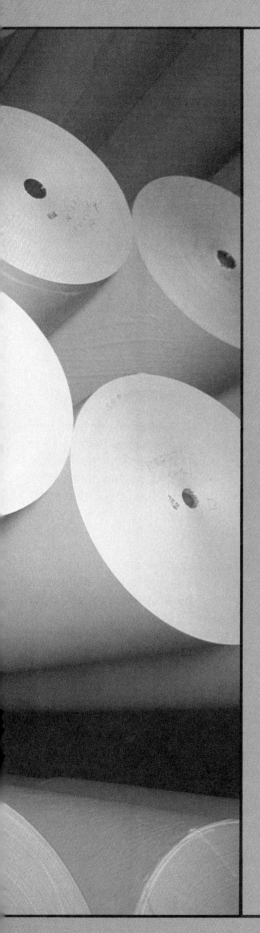

Chapter 9
THE PRODUCT

When you have completed this chapter, you should be able to

- Define *product* and list the main types of consumer and industrial products.

- Explain why firms sell many products, and discuss the concepts of *product line* and *product mix*.

- Describe the product life cycle and explain its uses and limitations.

- List the chief sources of new-product ideas and the stages of product development.

- Explain and illustrate product *positioning*.

- Discuss *branding* and *packaging* in terms of their benefits for producers and consumers.

- Discuss quality, service, and safety as sources of consumer discontent and as parts of a marketing strategy.

One of the more popular products in the emerging "office of the future" is something out of the past: notepaper. Not just any notepaper, but paper with a thin strip of adhesive on the back so it can be stuck on telephones, desks, walls, and office reports to get attention.

Hardly a revolutionary idea for the computer age, but Post-it notes are a big winner for Minnesota Mining & Manufacturing Company (3M), which introduced the product several years ago. Sales are about $40 million a year and increasing (3M won't say exactly how rapidly), and yellow Post-it notes have become fixtures in many offices. "I have them all over my desk," says Chester Kane, a new-product consultant in New York.

The success of 3M's Post-it notes shows that some of the best new products are obvious ones that marketers somehow have overlooked. "Many people think that the market is saturated with stuff, and unless you come up with a real new product you won't come up with anything big. There's nothing further from the truth," says Thomas D. Kuczmarski, a consultant who has studied new-product development for Booz, Allen & Hamilton, Inc.

Many big winners, in fact, are products that anyone could have invented by using readily available parts, ingredients, or technology. Disposable lighters and razors, hot-air popcorn poppers, home smoke detectors, and briefcase-sized umbrellas—all products that can be found in countless homes today—were ideas waiting to be hatched.

Some of these products succeed for the same reason they were overlooked: they are simple. "Post-it notes are a better piece of scratch paper," says Edward Tauber, chairman of the marketing department at the University of Southern California. "The product didn't force the consumer to make a big leap. Things where the consumer has to make a big change, those are hard to establish."

The idea for Post-it notes came from a 3M employee who belongs to a church choir. The slips of paper he used to mark songs in his hymn book frequently fell out, and he suggested an adhesive-backed note paper.

In its labs, 3M already had developed a light-tack adhesive that would stick firmly to a variety of surfaces—including paper—and release easily without damaging the surface. The adhesive was used on a couple of minor products, such as a bulletin board; the tacky front of the bulletin board holds objects but remains sticky after they are removed.

But office-supply vendors had doubts about the need for a sticky-back notepaper. "When we showed it to people, their attitude was, 'You're making a big deal out of a three-by-five-inch notepad,'" says Jack P. Wilkins, a 3M marketing director. Nonetheless, 3M test-marketed Post-it notes in 1977. Results were mixed until the company blitzed offices with samples, a strategy that proved important. Until secretaries actually use Post-it notes, they don't realize how convenient they are, Wilkins says.

So far, 3M has had the U.S. market for itself, partly because the light-tack adhesive isn't easy to imitate. "It appears to be a simple product, but it isn't a simple product in manufacturing," says Francis S.

Webster, Jr., vice-president of 3M's commercial tape division. Competition could develop, however, as companies in Germany and Japan recently introduced similar products.[1]

[1]Lawrence Ingrassia, "By Improving Scratch Paper, 3M Gets a New-Product Winner," *Wall Street Journal*, March 31, 1983, p. 31. Reprinted by permission of the Wall Street Journal. © Dow Jones & Company, Inc., 1983. All Rights Reserved.

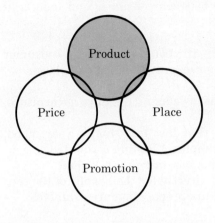

Post-it notes are just one of some 45,000 products that 3M, a superstar in product innovation, claims to make. They run the gamut from the well-known Scotch brand of cellophane tape to skin lotion and artificial hips. By the time this book is printed, 3M will no doubt have added a few dozen more to the millions of products turned out by the American economy. The development and management of these products—the first of the four Ps of marketing—will be the subject of this chapter.

WHAT IS A PRODUCT?

Product: Anything that can be supplied to a market in order to satisfy customer needs.

A **product** is anything that can be supplied to a market in order to satisfy customer needs. This is a broad concept. It includes both goods and services. It includes things that can be bought and carried away, like a ballpoint pen, and things that sit still while people come to look at them, like the exhibits at the Chicago Museum of Science and Industry. Not-for-profit firms and units of government have products too. A country club provides entertainment and recreation services. A town government provides roads, schools, and fire protection.

The Objective and Subjective Products

The definition suggests that there are two ways of looking at a product: It can be viewed as a thing that is supplied or as a way of satisfying a need. These two ways of looking at a product can be called the *objective* product and the *subjective* product.

Objective product: A good or service described in terms of its physical properties.

The **objective product** is the good or service described in terms of its physical properties. A roll of Scotch tape is a long strip of cellophane with an adhesive backing wound up on a spool. A performance of *La Traviata* by the Metropolitan Opera is a sequence of songs and stage actions based on a written score. The objective product, in short, is what the firm sells.

Subjective product: A good or service described in terms of the needs it will satisfy.

The **subjective product**, on the other hand, is what the customer buys—a way of satisfying a need. Consider a simple product like a bottle of deodorant made by Procter & Gamble. The fine print on the back label describes the objective product: zirconium-aluminum-glycine-hydroxychloride. But the brand name Sure on the front label tells us more about the subjective product. Buyers of Sure brand deodorant do not want a bottle of chemicals. What they want is enough self-confidence to ride a crowded bus on a hot day.

Product Types

Products are often classified according to types of buyer and ways of shopping. The most basic division is between consumer and industrial goods.

Consumer goods. Consumer goods are bought to satisfy consumer needs. In government statistics such goods are classified as follows.

- **Durable goods**, or those that last a year or more, such as furniture, appliances, and cars.
- **Nondurable goods**, or those that last less than a year. Food, gasoline, and medicines are examples. Clothing is counted as nondurable, even though some items last more than a year.
- **Services**, or actions performed directly for the benefit of the consumer. Haircuts, concerts, and tax preparation are examples.

Durable goods: Goods that last a year or more, such as furniture, appliances, and cars.

Nondurable goods: Goods that last less than a year, such as food, medicines, and fuel.

Services: Actions performed directly for the benefit of the consumer, such as haircuts, concerts, and tax preparation.

Chair—© Freda Leinwand; Clothes—Courtesy of Sears, Roebuck and Company; Restaurant—© Freda Leinwand

In recent years services have accounted for about half of all consumer purchases, nondurable goods for about 35 percent, and durable goods for about 15 percent. The proportion spent on services has been rising steadily.

A second way of classifying consumer goods is based on how people shop for them, rather than on the nature of the goods themselves. This results in the following categories.

- **Convenience goods**, which are bought often, routinely, and with little comparison shopping. Eggs, pencils, underwear, and cigarettes are examples.
- **Shopping goods**, which are bought only after an effort to gather information on the price, quality, and other features of competing brands. Most consumer durable goods are shopping goods.
- **Specialty goods**, which are bought without much comparison shopping because they are thought to offer unique features or brand images. A Rolex watch and a Porsche are products that, at least in the minds of some consumers, have no substitutes.

Convenience goods: Goods that are bought often, routinely, and with little comparison shopping.

Shopping goods: Goods that are bought only after an effort to gather information on the price, quality, and other features of competing brands.

Specialty goods: Goods that are bought without much comparison shopping because they are thought to offer unique features or brand images.

Pencil—Courtesy of Eberhard Faber; Washer—Courtesy of the Maytag Company; Rolex—Courtesy of Rolex Watch U.S.A. Inc.

Derived demand: Demand for a good that is derived from its usefulness in making consumer goods.

Capital goods: Industrial goods that are durable additions to the buyer's plant or equipment.

Expense goods: Goods that are used up in the course of producing the buyer's output, such as raw materials, component parts, and maintenance supplies.

Industrial goods.   Many firms, of course, sell to other firms rather than to consumers. Their products are called industrial goods. Effective marketing of those products requires some knowledge of why and how they are bought. Industrial goods are bought not for the direct benefits they provide but to be used in making other goods to satisfy consumer demand. For this reason, the demand for industrial goods is said to be a **derived demand**. For example, the demand for natural rubber is derived from the demand for tires; the demand for printing presses is derived from the demand for newspapers; and so on.

Industrial goods fall into two broad groups.

- **Capital goods**, which are durable additions to the buyer's plant or equipment. Examples are industrial boilers, assembly line robots, and office equipment.
- **Expense goods**, which are used up in the course of producing the buyer's output. Raw materials, component parts, and maintenance supplies are expense items.

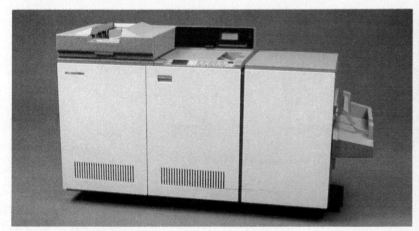

Courtesy of Xerox Corp.

Courtesy of Xerox Corp.

PLANNING A PRODUCT STRATEGY

Planning a product strategy is part of the job of planning a marketing strategy. It includes not only deciding which products to make but also deciding when to bring out new products and when to retire old ones. It means deciding how to help the consumer perceive the product relative to those of competitors in terms of quality, features, and image. Finally, it means working out the details of branding, packaging, warranty, and service. Of course, all of these plans must fit together smoothly. They must also mesh with distribution, promotion, and pricing plans. In this section we will briefly review the main aspects of planning a product strategy.

Product Line and Mix

Some firms make just one product. For example, the E. E. Dickinson Company of Essex, Connecticut, makes witch hazel and nothing else. But one-product firms are the exception. Most firms produce a variety of goods or services.

Product line A group of products that are closely related in the way they are used.

A group of products that are closely related in how they are used is known as a **product line**. The cream of tomato, chicken noodle, and other soups sold by the Campbell Soup Company are a product line. So are the 727s, 737s, 747s and other aircraft made by Boeing.

Product mix: The complete list of products offered by a firm, including all of its product lines.

Often firms have more than one product line. The complete list of products offered by a firm, including all of its product lines, is known as its **product mix**. A good example of a firm that includes many distinct product lines in its product mix is 3M. Box 9–1 shows the structure of 3M's very broad product mix.

Only a few firms offer just one product. An example is the E. E. Dickinson Co., which makes only witch hazel. Courtesy of the E. E. Dickinson Co.

These Chunky soups are one of several product lines offered by the Campbell Soup Company. Courtesy of Campbell Soup Co.

Box 9–1 Product Lines and Product Mix at 3M

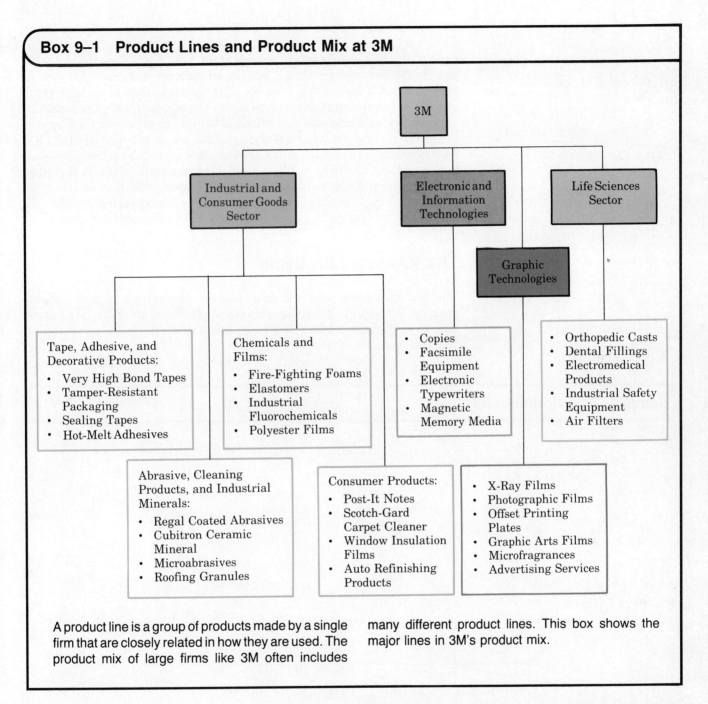

A product line is a group of products made by a single firm that are closely related in how they are used. The product mix of large firms like 3M often includes many different product lines. This box shows the major lines in 3M's product mix.

Why do some firms have extensive lines of closely related products? It has to do with the nature of the needs that those firms seek to satisfy. Campbell Soup makes a big effort to satisfy its customers' need for variety. Some people eat soup every day, but they don't want the same kind of soup every day. In other cases, broad product lines are a way of serving a diverse market. Each of Boeing's many airplanes is tailored to a specific market segment. The segments have different aircraft needs because they differ in the length of their routes and the number of people they serve.

There are also several reasons for a firm to carry more than one line within its product mix. Sometimes product lines are related in terms of production techniques. For example, about 95 percent of 3M's products are related in some way to various coating and bonding techniques. Other firms add product lines to their mix because opportunities for growth in their primary markets seem limited. For example, CSX, a railroad company in the East and Southeast, has begun work on an optical fiber system that will run parallel to its tracks. CSX believes that in coming years growth in communications will be faster than growth in railroading.

Finally, new products may be added to balance sales over the business cycle. The product strategy of Corning Glass, which was discussed in Case 5–2 (page 124), is a case in point. Corning was worried about the boom-and-bust problems of products like automobile headlight glass. It therefore added to its mix products that had more stable growth prospects. One product line that Corning expanded was its line of medical instruments, an offshoot of its original business of making test tubes and lab dishes.

The Product Life Cycle

The fact that firms add and drop products from time to time reflects changes in strategy. But it also reflects the fact that products, like people, tend to go through a life cycle. The classical product life cycle, pictured in Box 9–2, consists of four stages.

Box 9–2 The Product Life Cycle

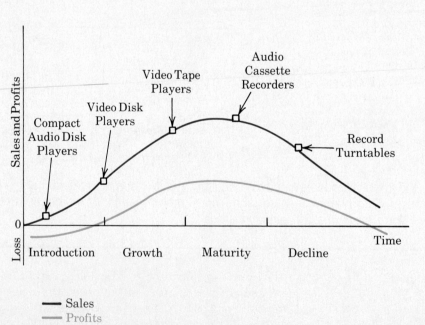

Many products have a life cycle that consists of four stages: introduction, growth, maturity, and decline. During the introduction stage, marketing efforts focus on telling consumers about the product. Profits are likely to be low because production and marketing costs are high. During the stage of rapid growth, production costs fall and profits rise. Competitors begin to enter the market. In the maturity stage, sales level off and competition becomes more intense. Decline begins when consumer tastes change or a new technology makes the product obsolete. Profits fall and producers drop out one by one. In this diagram the stages of the life cycle are illustrated with various home entertainment products.

1. *Introduction.* When a product is first brought out, people do not even know it exists. Promotional efforts are aimed toward informing consumers and getting a core of early users who will help build the product's reputation. Because production volume is low, costs are likely to be high in this stage. It is not unusual for products to lose money in this stage. However, the first firms to introduce a new type of product have few competitors.

2. *Growth.* In this stage sales grow quickly. With volume up and early production problems solved, costs fall. Profits may be high. During the growth phase, however, high profits begin to attract competitors. The firm's marketing strategy often is aimed toward getting a large share of the market. Product improvements based on suggestions by early users also help sales.

3. *Maturity.* Total sales of the product may continue to rise, but not as fast. The products of different firms are likely to become more similar as unsuccessful features are dropped and successful ones are imitated. Competition becomes more intense and prices fall. The greatest profits in this stage are likely to go to firms that improve their production systems and keep their costs low. A large market share gained in the growth phase makes this easier.

4. *Decline.* Demand for the product finally begins to fall. This may happen because of changing tastes or because new technologies make the product obsolete. Price competition becomes intense. It becomes hard to keep profits up, especially if falling production volume leads to higher costs. Some producers drop out. In some cases the product is withdrawn from the market entirely. In other cases it will continue to be produced in small volumes as a specialty item.

Box 9–2 shows the stages of the product life cycle occupied by five home entertainment products in the early 1980s. Compact disk stereo systems had just come onto the market. Video disk players were struggling to get into the growth phase, while video tape recorders were nearing maturity. Audio cassette players were a fully mature product. Conventional record turntables were in decline, under pressure from audio cassettes and compact disks.

In many cases the product life cycle can be a useful guide to planning a marketing strategy. In the introductory stage, the strategy is to inform. In the growth stage, it is to build market share. In the maturity stage, it is to cut costs. And in the decline stage the strategy is either to exit gracefully or to convert the product into a low-volume specialty item. But these guidelines should be used with caution. Many products go through this life cycle, but some do not.

For one thing, the usefulness of the life cycle concept depends on how the product is defined. In general, the narrower the definition of the product, the shorter its life cycle. Consider video tape recorders. The concept of a machine that can be plugged into a TV set to record and play back TV programs was nearing maturity by the mid-1980s. By that time the more narrowly defined Beta technology, with which Sony first developed the market for home video recorders, was already on the decline. But the broader concept of the home video system, in which the recorder is just one component along with cameras, tuners, monitors, and other devices, was poised for rapid growth.

Second, some products do not follow the classical life cycle. Often certain brands, such as Jell-O or Arm & Hammer baking soda, live on and on. Sometimes a product that has been mature for years can stage a sudden surge, the way roller skates did a few years ago. Sometimes a group of products, such as horse shoeing supplies and services, can stage a modest revival after decades of decline.

Because not all products follow the classical life cycle, marketing managers should be careful in using the concept. If their reaction to the first sign of falling sales is to slash the product's promotional budget, the life cycle may become a self-fulfilling prophecy. Products may be laid to rest, that with a little care would have had years of life left in them.

New Products

Careful marketing can prolong the life of many products, but at some point the firm will need new ones. At 3M, some 25 percent of revenues come from products that are under five years old. Where do all the ideas for these products come from? And how should they be brought to market?

Sources of new-product ideas.   The two most common sources of new product ideas are customer suggestions and internal research. A key to successful product innovation is getting these two sources to work together. The Post-it notes described at the beginning of this chapter are a case in point. Researchers at 3M had developed the light-tack adhesive but had not found any major uses for it. A potential user (who in this case was a 3M employee but need not have been) had a need that no existing product would satisfy. In the 3M climate, where new-product ideas are encouraged, the need and the means to satisfy it were matched.

There are other sources of product ideas as well. Suppliers sometimes make suggestions. Some ideas come from outside inventors or from published reports of the work of researchers. Finally, some product ideas come from studying competitors' products—and their mistakes.

Product development.   Getting an idea is only the first step in the process that brings new products to market. In all, there are six steps in the development of a new product.

1. *Idea generation.* At this stage, the more ideas the better.
2. *Screening.* Ideas are given a preliminary evaluation. Do they meet a major customer need? Do they fit into the firm's overall marketing strategy? Do they fit its technical abilities?
3. *Business analysis.* A more formal analysis is done on ideas that survive the preliminary screening. Estimates are made for such things as sales, market share, costs, and profit potential.
4. *Design.* Up to this point the product has been just an idea. Now it takes on a physical form. Prototypes are made. Machines to produce the product are designed. The product is given a name, packaging is designed, and so on.
5. *Test-marketing.* Samples of the product are put on the market in selected places. Getting user reactions to the product is a major goal at this stage. Other goals are to test reactions to the distibution, promotion, and pricing elements of the marketing mix.
6. *Commercialization.* Full-scale production is begun. The product is made available to anyone who might want to buy it.

Box 9–3 illustrates the product development process. At each stage of the process, some ideas fall by the wayside. A recent study by Booz, Allen &

Box 9–3   The Product Development Process

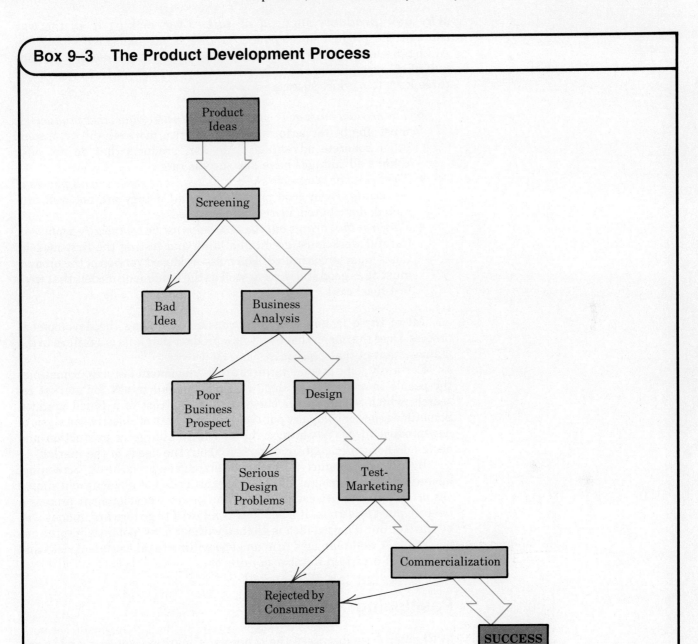

Product development begins with product ideas. Customer suggestions and research are the most common sources of ideas for new products. Ideas are screened to weed out those that are not worth further development. Business analysis involves looking at the product idea in terms of potential sales, profits, costs, and so on. In the design stage the product begins to take physical form. Decisions on positioning, branding, and packaging are also made at this stage. Next the product is tested in selected markets to get consumer reactions. If the test-marketing is successful, the product is commercialized. Products can be rejected at any stage, including the final one.

Hamilton estimated that only one out of seven product ideas leads to a successful new product.[2]

Why new products succeed or fail. Even making it all the way through the product development process is no guarantee of success. Although success rates vary from one class of products to another, perhaps half of all new products fail. In a recent study, Robert G. Cooper listed three keys to product success.[3]

- *The product must meet customer needs better than other products.* It must offer better performance, lower price, more reliability, or some other concrete advantage. "Me too" products that do not offer unique advantages have low success rates.
- *The firm that brings out the product must be skilled in all phases of marketing.* Even good products can fail if they are not well promoted, distributed, priced, and serviced.
- *The firm that brings out the product must be technically proficient.* Careful work must go into building and testing the first models. Costs must be controlled. The mass-produced version of the product must be as good and work as well as the handmade models that were test-marketed.

All of these factors should be considered during the development process. Does this mean that every new product that fails is a failure in the management of that process?

Certainly some product failures are management failures. Sometimes the people in charge of product development fail to ask for market research, which would be far cheaper than the cost of a failed product. Sometimes egos or company politics get in the way of objective analysis of new-product ideas. Sometimes the people in charge of production and design do not get enough information about the needs of the market.

But not all product failures are management failures. Screening, business analysis, design, and test-marketing do not always yield simple yes or no answers. At each stage in the product development process a balance must be struck. If a bad idea is allowed to go forward, money will be wasted. But if a good idea is ditched without a try, potential profits are passed up. A well-managed firm must be willing to take prudent risks and to shrug off a certain number of failures.

Positioning

In Chapter 8 we discussed the concepts of market segments and target markets. In order for a product to succeed, it must be designed and promoted in a way that will appeal to the target market. The process of fitting the product's image to the needs of its target market is known as **positioning**.

Positioning begins with the design of the product. The product must be able to meet the needs of its intended consumers. For example, the Mer-

Positioning: The process of fitting a product's image to the needs of its target market.

[2]Booz, Allen & Hamilton, Inc., "More New Products Die Aborning Than in 1968," *Marketing and Media Decisions*, May 1982, p. 48.

[3]Robert G. Cooper, "The Dimensions of Industrial New Product Success or Failure," *Journal of Marketing*, Summer 1979, pp. 93–103.

cedes car is aimed at quality-concious buyers. There is no way that the image of quality can be sustained if real quality is not built into the car. Likewise, the Corvette, which has a high-performance image, must really be able to perform. General Motors once tried putting smaller, more efficient engines in its Corvettes. The experiment was a market failure. By failing to perform as well as buyers expected it to, a Corvette with a small engine fought against its own image.

The design of the product is only the first step, however. Design is just the physical basis on which the product's image is built. The image itself exists in the mind of the consumer. Positioning the product in the consumer's mind demands that the firm pay attention to all parts of the marketing mix—product, distribution, promotion, and pricing.

Box 9–4 shows the interaction between design and subjective factors in the case of cigarettes. The cigarette market is shown as a map over which customers are spread. Men occupy the left half of the map and

Box 9–4   Positioning of Cigarette Brands

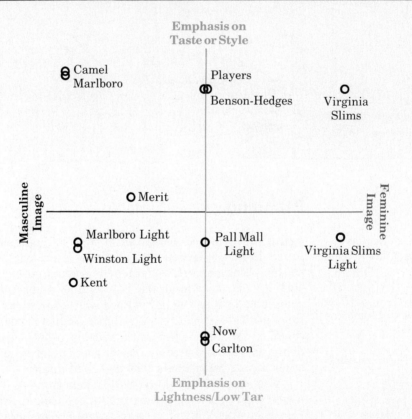

Positioning is vital to the success of a brand of cigarettes. In this diagram the positions of various brands are shown spread out over a map of the market. The Camel and Marlboro brands are aimed at smokers who are concerned about taste rather than health and respond to a masculine image. Now and Carlton brands emphasize low tar and nicotine content; no hint of a masculine or feminine image is given in the ads. Pall-Mall Lights, Players, and Benson-Hedges try to appeal to members of both sexes with ads that show men and women having fun in stylish settings.

women the right half. Toward the top we find smokers who are concerned mainly with taste and style. Toward the bottom we find those who want to reduce health risks by smoking lighter, lower-tar cigarettes.

The cigarette market is large and diverse. No one product can ever be just right for all smokers. Hence, all the major tobacco companies have many brands of cigarettes, each aimed at one of the zones shown on the map. The top-to-bottom positioning of a brand depends partly on the product's design—that is, its tar and nicotine content—and partly on how much emphasis is given to it in ads. The right-left positioning of a brand depends almost entirely on the way it is promoted.

In Chapter 11 we will return to the role of advertising in product positioning. But two aspects of positioning—branding and packaging—are viewed as part of the product element of the marketing mix, so we will discuss them here.

Reprinted by permission: Tribune Company Syndicate, Inc.

Branding

Branding: The use of a design, symbol, name, or some mix of these things to identify a product.

Brand name: The part of a brand that can be spoken—a name or a combination of letters and numbers.

Trademark: A symbol or brand name that is legally protected.

Branding is the use of a design, symbol, name, or some mix of these things to identify a product. A **brand name** is the part of a brand that can be spoken—a name, such as Perrier, or a combination of letters and numbers, such as V-8. A **trademark** is a symbol or brand name that is legally protected, such as the name Ford written in script inside an oval. All of these devices serve to distinguish the product from its competitors. In some cases, in fact, there is almost nothing besides the brand name that is distinctive about a product. Bayer aspirin, for example, would be like any other aspirin without its famous brand name.

Brands are everywhere. Surely something as widespread as branding must be doing someone some good. Let's look at the benefits of branding, first from the point of view of the producer and then from that of the consumer.

Benefits to producers.   Producers find branding useful for a number of reasons.

- Branding leads to repeat purchases and customer loyalty, as long as consumers are satisfied with the branded product.

- Branding aids in positioning. Cigarettes (see Box 9–4) illustrate how a firm can use brand names to go after different market segments: Players, Benson-Hedges, Marlboro, Merit, and Virginia Slims are all brands of cigarettes made by Phillip Morris, Inc. The company's name appears in its ads only in very small print.
- Other firms use branding in almost the opposite way: they use it to tie their products together rather than to set them apart. For example, the brand name Head is used for that company's line of skis as well as its line of tennis rackets.

An established brand name is a major asset. Firms go to great lengths to protect their brand names. Outright fakes are one threat to brand names—especially if they put low-quality goods on the market under a familiar label. Brand names can also be lost if they become so familiar that consumers confuse the brand with the type of product. *Nylon, cellophane,* and *kerosene* were once protected brand names that now name a type of product. Today the brand names Xerox, Coke, and Kleenex are used by some consumers to refer to a class of product, rather than just the brand.

Benefits to consumers. Not all the benefits of branding go to producers. If branding did not serve consumer needs in some way, it wouldn't be such a useful marketing tool. Among the benefits of branding to consumers are the following.

- Brands help consumers identify products with which they have had a good experience in the past. If you liked your Head skis, you might want to buy a tennis racket made by the same people.
- Brands often serve as an index of quality. Levi's jeans and Craftsman tools are known to be well-made products. K Mart, on the other hand, is known to provide adequate quality at a much lower price.
- Brands help consumers shape their own image in the eyes of friends and associates. If you drive into your school parking lot in a Pinto, a Datsun 280-Z, or a Buick, you are telling people, "This is the kind of person I am." Part of the image that the company has built for its product rubs off on you.

Of course, the benefits of branding do not come free to consumers. Advertising and other efforts to promote a brand tend to raise the product's price.* Since branded products sell well, it is clear that some consumers think the higher price is worth paying. But in our free enterprise economy it is no surprise to find that some firms find ways to make profits by serving customers who don't want to pay higher prices for brand names.

House brand: A brand given by a large retail chain to a line of products sold only in its own stores.

Generic product: A product whose label identifies it only by the type of product.

One choice for consumers who shop by price rather than by image is to buy the **house brands** of large retail chains. A&P's Ann Page line of foods is an example. Retailers order these products in large lots from producers that are willing to give them a discount. The discount—often as much as a third of the price—is passed along to the consumer.

Often consumers can save even more by buying **generic products**. The labels on generic products identify them only by the type of product— "dishwashing liquid," "bathroom tissue," and so on.

---

*There can be exceptions, for example, when branding increases sales enough to permit production in larger quantities that cut manufacturing costs.

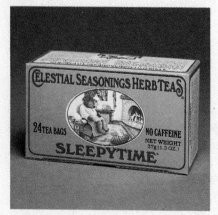

An attractive package can go a long way toward building brand recognition. Courtesy of Celestial Seasonings

Packaging

Packaging is also part of the product element of the marketing mix. Well-designed packaging can benefit both the producer and the consumer. Three major aspects of packaging are promotion, protection, and convenience.

Promotion. The box or can in which a product is sold is an important means of promoting the product. Here packaging is a substitute for advertising. When the purpose is to make a brand familiar to consumers, an attractive package can be more cost-effective than print or TV ads. When the purpose is to educate the consumer, the back of a box or package has room for a lot of print. In addition, packages are a good vehicle for such devices as coupons and factory rebates.

Protection. Life would be easy if every product came in its own perfect natural package the way a banana does, but such is not the case. Products must be packaged well enough so that they reach the consumer in good condition. And for many products, from grass seed to bacon, the package must be designed to protect the unused part of the product after it has been opened.

Protective packaging can be costly. For some items, the package costs more than the contents. It follows that reducing the cost of packaging can give producers a marketing advantage. Consider aseptic packaging. This technique puts a sterilized product, such as a fruit drink, in a sterilized pouch or box. The shelf life for such products is as long as it is for products that are canned or bottled. But aseptic packaging saves energy and shipping costs and results in a better-tasting product. Ocean Spray, a maker of cranberry juice and other drinks, has made the "drink in a box" a key part of its marketing strategy.

Ocean Spray's drink-in-a-box packaging is a key part of its marketing strategy. Courtesy of Ocean Spray Cranberries, Inc.

Convenience. Packaging does more than just promote and protect products. It provides convenience, too. Sometimes, in fact, convenience is the chief need that is met by a packaged product. Sugar in lumps costs more than sugar in a bag. Whipped cream in a can costs more than cream in a carton. Tea in tea bags costs more than tea in bulk. But in each case many consumers find the convenience worth the price.

What about consumers who do not think fancy packaging is worth the price? Marketers have responded to their needs too. For example, selling goods in large packages almost always reduces packaging costs per unit. Some products, such as dog food, are sold in quantities of up to fifty pounds. Selling in bulk from bins cuts costs even more. This technique is a favorite of consumer co-ops. And for all package sizes, generic products tend to be packaged as cheaply as possible.

QUALITY, SERVICE, AND SAFETY

Throughout this chapter we have drawn a picture of firms hard at work to meet consumer needs. With all this effort, shouldn't people be satisfied with the products they get? Most of the time they are, but sometimes they are not. Consumer advocates and people responding to surveys say that

Newly developed motor oils allow cars to run much longer between oil changes than was possible in the past. Courtesy of Mobil Oil Corp.

many products are not good enough. We will conclude this chapter with a brief look at three problem areas: quality, service, and safety.

Quality

Not long ago the American Society for Quality Control surveyed 7000 consumers. Some 49 percent of them said that the quality of U.S. products had declined in the last five years. And 59 percent said that they thought quality would stay low or drop in the next five years.[4] Yet both business leaders and independent studies say that the quality of many American-made goods, if not most of them, is high and rising. Radial tires last longer than the old bias plies. Cars run longer before they need service. Paints, fabrics, and plastics are stronger and last longer than they did just a few years ago. Even pole-vaulting poles are better, as the steady rise in the world's record shows. So why all the fuss about quality?

Understanding the paradox. The answer to this paradox lies in economics—inflation, competition, and the law of supply and demand.

During the 1970s inflation made people more aware of the need to get value for money. When things cost more, people expect them to last longer. At the same time competition, especially foreign competition, became more intense. The Japanese, widely viewed as the biggest competitive threat to U.S. business, made quality the cornerstone of their strategy for entering American markets. Fairly or unfairly, consumers tend to judge the quality of each product in comparison to its competitors. There is no doubt that the Ford Escort is a much better car than the Pinto it replaced. But consumers won't see it as a top-quality machine unless its performance and finishes match those of the Honda or Toyota down the street.

This brings us to supply and demand. U.S. firms may supply better-quality products than they did in the past, but the demand for quality seems to have grown even faster. The strongest evidence for this is the fact that quality-conscious firms make higher-than-average profits. This is true even when quality means a high price tag. Certainly there will always be a place in the market for many levels of quality. Not everyone wants or needs the top of the line. But the fact that makers of high-quality goods make high profits indicates there is still room for more firms to enter the high-quality end of the line.

How to meet the demand for quality. If American firms are to cope with this major shift in consumer demand, they need to change their attitude toward quality. Quality needs to become the focus of the whole company. Writing in the *Harvard Business Review*, Frank S. Leonard and W. Earl Sasser assert that managing quality means paying attention to it at every stage of product development—from design to sales.[5] In the past, they say, quality was seen as a concern of the quality control staff, the manufacturing department, or blue-collar workers. From now on, quality should be a responsibility of general managers, and it should be a factor in

[4]Results published in the *Boston Globe*, January 25, 1981, and cited in Hirotaka Takeuchi and John A. Quelch, "Quality Is More Than Making a Good Product," *Harvard Business Review*, July-August 1983, p. 139.

[5]Frank S. Leonard and W. Earl Sasser, "The Incline of Quality," *Harvard Business Review*, September-October 1982, pp. 163–71.

all performance reviews. In the past, also, defects were hidden, and if they were exposed, they led to blame and excuses. From now on, defects should be given the spotlight, and managers should cooperate in trying to correct them.

Achieving higher quality is not, after all, a hopeless task. First, there are those high-quality imports—somewhere over there, someone has already put these ideas into practice. And second, U.S. firms that have learned to manage quality are making money at it. We will return to the theme of quality in Part IV.

Service

Consumers expect more than a product that works when they take it out of the box. They expect the product to keep on working, and they expect the seller to fix it if it does not. For these reasons, warranties and follow-up service should be viewed as basic parts of the product. A firm's willingness to stand behind the products it sells is seen by consumers as a sign of quality.

A **warranty** is a statement of what the seller will do if a product is defective or fails to work the way it should within a specified period after the sale. Many products come with written warranties, which must conform to the provisions of the Magnuson-Moss Warranty Act of 1975. Also, the Uniform Commercial Code states that all products carry an *implied* warranty. This simply guarantees that the product is suitable for the purpose for which it is sold. Thus, whether it comes with a written warranty or not, a boat must float, a drill must be able to make holes, and a pen must write.

In addition to providing a warranty, makers of durable goods must consider the need for follow-up service. More and more, firms are finding that good service is a powerful marketing tool. Good service demonstrates a firm's confidence in the quality of its product, and this rubs off on the customer.

Warranty: A statement of what the seller will do if a product is defective or fails to work the way it should within a specified period after the sale.

© Freda Leinwand

Safety

Safety has been a watchword of the consumer movement since the publication of Ralph Nader's first book, *Unsafe at Any Speed*, which criticized the General Motors Corvair. In the minds of consumers, safety is more than just an aspect of quality—sometimes it is a matter of life and death. In recent years, product safety has become a concern of the law too.

The federal government has passed a number of laws that set safety standards for products. The Food and Drug Act of 1906 is the grandfather of them all. The National Traffic Safety Act of 1966 created safety standards for cars. The Child Protection Act, passed in the same year, banned hazardous toys and flammable children's clothing. And the Consumer Product Safety Act of 1972 created a special agency, the Consumer Product Safety Commission, to oversee the safety of all types of products.

Besides having to comply with laws like these, firms may be subject to product liability suits. In a product liability suit, an injured person sues the maker of the product that may have caused the injury. Courts have tended to side with the consumer in such suits. Manufacturers have been found liable even when defects in their products were not caused by negligence on their part. They have even been found liable in cases in which the consumer was negligent in using the product.

Safety regulations and strict product liability laws raise the cost of doing business in two ways. First, they cause firms to spend more on safety features. Second, they require firms to buy insurance or build up financial reserves to pay claims against them. One might wonder whether consumers are getting their money's worth from these efforts.

Consumer advocates say yes, and they press for even more stringent standards. Business managers often say no, and they sometimes exaggerate the costs of safety features. Outside observers tend to say sometimes yes, sometimes no.

The biggest criticism of current trends in safety laws is that they tend to treat all safety issues as problems of product design rather than use. But design changes are not always a cost-effective solution to product misuse. Beginning in 1983, for example, lawnmower makers were required to add a device that would shut off the engine as soon as the user let go of the handle. The purpose was to keep people from sticking their hands under the blades of a running mower to pull out sticks and jammed grass. Everyone who buys a mower has to pay for the device—even the vast number of users who would be smart enough to turn the mower off before reaching under it. What is more, the device will not protect everyone it is supposed to protect. A user can defeat it by simply wrapping a piece of tape around the release handle. In short, there is little that manufacturers can do to keep people from misusing their products if they want to do so. And the burden of trying to protect everyone falls on responsible users.

Quality, service, and safety are not the only concerns of the consumer movement. The movement's leaders have also raised questions about business practices in the areas of distribution, promotion, and pricing. We will return to these issues later.

SUMMARY

1. A *product* is anything that can be supplied to a market in order to satisfy customer needs. A product can be described in terms of its physical properties (the *objective* product) or in terms of how it is perceived by the buyer (the *subjective* product).
2. Some goods are sold directly to consumers, while others are sold to industrial users. Consumer goods can be classified as *durable goods*, *nondurable goods*, and *services* or as *convenience goods*, *shopping goods*, and *specialty goods*. The demand for industrial goods is derived from their usefulness in making consumer goods. Industrial goods can be classified as *capital goods* and *expense goods*.
3. A group of products that are closely related in terms of how they are used is known as a *product line*. The whole range of products made by a firm, including all of its product lines, is known as the firm's *product mix*.
4. Products tend to pass through a life cycle. When they are first brought out, both production volume and profits are low. As sales begin to grow, volume increases, costs drop, and profits rise. After the product has reached maturity, sales grow more slowly or level off. Competition becomes more intense, putting downward pressure on profits. When tastes change or a new technology comes along, the product enters a stage of decline and may be withdrawn from the market.
5. Product development begins with new-product ideas. The two major sources of those ideas are research and customer suggestions. New-product ideas pass through the following stages: screening, business analysis, design, test-marketing, and commercializa-

tion. Only about one idea in seven gives rise to a successful product.

6. *Positioning* is the process of fitting a product's image to the needs of its target market. It begins with the design of a product that is able to meet the needs of its intended consumers. However, good design is not all there is to positioning—branding, packaging, distribution, promotion, and pricing also play a part in building the right image.

7. *Branding* is the use of a design, symbol, name, or some mix of these things to identify a product. For producers, it is a way of building customer loyalty, an aid in positioning, and a way of tying their products together. For consumers, brands help identify products that have satisfied them in the past. They also serve as an index of quality and a means of shaping a personal image. Cost-conscious consumers can avoid the costs of branding by buying *house brands* or *generic products*.

8. Packaging is an important aspect of a product. A package serves first of all to protect the product during shipment and sometimes after purchase. Second, a package is a means of promoting the product. Third, packaging can be used to make the product more convenient. Large unit packages, sales in bulk, and cheap packaging of generic goods serve the needs of cost-conscious consumers.

9. The quality, service, and safety of the products made by U.S. firms has increased in recent years, but not as fast as the demand for these features. This demand creates profit opportunities for firms that make these concerns a central part of their marketing strategy.

KEY TERMS

You should be familiar with the following terms and concepts. Check their meanings by referring to the marginal definitions in the chapter or to the glossary at the end of the book.

Product	Shopping goods	Positioning
Objective product	Specialty goods	Branding
Subjective product	Derived demand	Brand name
Durable goods	Capital goods	Trademark
Nondurable goods	Expense goods	House brand
Services	Product line	Generic product
Convenience goods	Product mix	Warranty

QUESTIONS FOR REVIEW AND DISCUSSION

1. In each of the following cases, the objective product is the same. What is the subjective product?

a. A single woman stops by a small store on her way home from work to buy one can of cat food, paying $0.79.

b. A woman shopping for her family buys twelve cans of the supermarket's house brand of cat food, paying $0.38 per can.

c. For her own dinner, an elderly woman living on a small pension buys a can of tuna packed for cats, saving $0.10 compared with the price of tuna packed for humans.

2. Classify each of the following products as a durable good, a nondurable good, or a service, and also as a convenience good, a shopping good, or a specialty good. Would the categories be the same for all consumers?

a. A hair cutting/styling session
b. A refrigerator
c. A carton of ice cream
d. A bottle of perfume

3. Make a trip to a grocery, sporting goods, or clothing store. Find at least one producer that offers a product mix that contains more than a single product line. Describe the product mix and the lines within it. Do you think the items in the product mix fit together as part of a logical product strategy? Discuss.

4. Describe the product life cycle for (a) the automobile, (b) the V-8 powered automobile, (c) automobiles with tail fins. What differences are there among the three life cycles?

5. Going through your college catalog, you find that the business department at your school does not offer a course in environmental issues for business management. You decide to propose that this new product be added to the school's line of business courses. Describe the product development process for the new course from the time of your proposal to the time when it is "commercialized" as an offering in the catalog. What hurdles would the idea have to pass at each stage of development? What information would decision makers need at each stage?

6. The U.S. Treasury made two new-product efforts in the last decade: bringing back the two-dollar bill and introducing the Susan B. Anthony one-dollar coin. Both were flops. Why do you think they failed?

7. How brand-conscious are you as a shopper? Do you think you benefit from the advantages of branding listed in the text? Why or why not? For what products do you always buy a specific brand? For what products do you change from brand to brand? Why do you change? For what products do you seek out house brands or generics?

8. Have you bought any products that you thought were overpackaged? Have you bought any for which the packaging seemed to produce too much trash or waste? If so, describe how the package could have been changed to provide the same amount of satisfaction at a lower cost. Why do you think the producer chose the type of package that was used?

9. What product has been the greatest disappointment to you in terms of quality, service, and/or safety? Describe the problem. Does the quality, service, and/or safety of this product seem to differ from one producer to another? Do you think your disappointment is shared by other consumers? Is it caused by a management failure? Discuss.

Case 9–1: Frito-Lay Spares No Effort to Tantalize Munchers

Twenty managers at Frito-Lay Inc. sit at a conference table, nibbling thick, white tortilla chips. The chips taste good, but the managers aren't there for idle munching.

Small tortilla-chip makers in the West have been winning customers who like corn chips to eat with meals, rather than just as a snack. Their paler, blander chips are hurting sales of two Frito stars, Doritos and Tostitos. The chips the Frito managers are sampling, a proposed new offering called Sabritas, are supposed to put a stop to that.

But there are problems. The marketing people want Sabritas to be made only of white corn so they will be pale, but Frito-Lay plants now use yellow corn or a yellow-white mix. Will a new grain bin have to be built for the white corn?

Another thing: The competing chips have a twist tie around the top of the bag. Twist ties are expensive and are a bother to put on. But shoppers might not think of Sabritas the way they do the others if Sabritas' bag doesn't look the same.

Wayne Calloway, the company's president, gives the objectors a meaningful look. "Jerry, Jim, we need to get with this one," he says. "We're already late." A committee is formed to solve the problems so that test-marketing can begin. The product manager for Sabritas has scored a small victory.

This may seem like a rather elaborate approach to a commodity most people just crunch absent-mindedly. But Frito-Lay didn't get to where it is by taking tortillas for granted. The PepsiCo Inc. subsidiary takes in $2 billion on snack food a year, easily topping big rivals like Nabisco and Borden, not to mention the regional makers.

Coming up with new products is essential to keeping this lead, and Frito-Lay is good at it. Company managers consider hundreds of suggestions each year, but their screening process is so tough that only five or six get much past the idea stage. To go from being a gleam in the eye to a bag on the

Case 9–1: Frito-Lay Spares No Effort to Tantalize Munchers (continued)

shelf, a new chip has to make it through the test kitchen, consumer taste testing, naming, package design, ad planning, manufacturing, and test-marketing. A poor grade on one of the tests—or a poor decision about the name or ad theme—can kill a new product.

A successful one, though, can be worth $100 million or more a year in added revenue. So, although Frito-Lay develops certain products to meet specific competitive threats, its researchers are constantly trying to dream up new ideas simply in hopes of selling more snacks.

These days, Frito-Lay has several up-and-coming new chips, chief among them Ta-Tos and O'Gradys. These are both made of potatoes, but they are not to be confused. Around Frito-Lay, Ta-Tos are known as "super-crispy wavy." O'Grady's aren't like that. They are "extra-thick and crunchy."

In finding a name for O'Grady's, product managers set about finding one that would give the right impression. Mr. Todd explains the thinking: "This product was of the earth, it was thicker, a natural-tasting product." It also would have local competitors. So Frito began screening hearty names that would make the potato chips sound locally made.

Among the candidates was O'Gradys. Consumers were asked what a person named O'Grady might be like. They replied, variously, that O'Grady would be fun, jovial, male, happy-go-lucky, hearty, and big. It was just the image Frito wanted.

A wrong name can hold back a worthy chip. Tiffles "light corn chips" failed in two test markets, until a different product manager got hold of them and called them Sunchips, the "corn chips for potato chip lovers." They are in a third test market now, and are selling almost twice as well as before.

For Ta-Tos, Sunchips, Sabritas, and the rest, the final hurdle is the test market. To Frito-Lay, it doesn't matter how crunchy a chip is; if the thing can't sell $50 million to $100 million a year, forget it. And that had better not be money the shopper was going to spend on Lay's or Doritos. If a new chip is taking too many of its sales from another Frito product, it probably will never go national.

Source: Excerpted from Jane Guyon, "The Public Doesn't Get a Better Potato Chip Without a Bit of Pain," *Wall Street Journal*, March 25, 1983, p. 1. Reprinted by permission of the Wall Street Journal. © Dow Jones & Company, Inc., 1983. All Rights Reserved.

Questions:

1. Compare the product development process at Frito-Lay with the process outlined in Box 9–3. Can you find an example of each step in the process? What factors could lead to the rejection of a product at any step? Do you think Frito ever makes the mistake of killing a product that could be profitable? What makes you think so?
2. Does Frito seem to be concerned with product positioning? What evidence is there that it is or is not? Give specific examples if you can.
3. How important is branding to the success of a new chip? What role does it play in positioning a new product?
4. How important is packaging to the success of a new chip? What are the pros and cons of using twist ties for the new Sabrita bag? If the company decides to use twist ties, will there be any benefits to offset the increased cost to consumers?

Case 9–2: Tin Can in the Trash Can for Campbell Soup

Frank Terwilliger spends his days in his small office at Campbell Soup Co.'s headquarters puttering around with plastic containers of all shapes and sizes.

He fills some with soup, sends them down a chute, and watches them crash into a wall. He puts others on vigorously vibrating trays. And he drops others from a height of several feet.

Terwilliger, Campbell's packaging director, goes through these machinations because Campbell has decided to phase out the tin soup can. The famous can, with its red-and-white label and gold medallion, has been a cherished corporate symbol since Campbell's founding family introduced it in 1897. The company's annual canned-soup sales top 2 billion units, and Campbell is the nation's third largest can manufacturer, behind American Can Co. and Continental Group.

But Campbell has recently come to believe that the future of food packaging lies in snazzier and more convenient containers like the aseptic boxes and plastic, microwavable dishes that Terwilliger is testing. Gordon McGovern, Campbell's president and chairman, has pushed hard for the change. He has privately compared sticking with the can to the refusal of U.S. automobile makers to change their ways in the face of the Japanese challenge.

"The can isn't as user friendly as it used to be," says Anthony Adams, Campbell's director of marketing research. In consumer preference surveys, he says, "it's being battered and beaten."

Campbell's decision to develop a new package reflects the almost religious zeal about meeting consumer preferences that has dominated the company since McGovern took over three years ago. Campbell used to emphasize products compatible with existing production facilities, an approach that produced sluggish profits.

The company hopes the new packages will expand the soup market by luring people who have shunned canned soup, particularly convenience-minded singles. So far, "we're not even getting invited into the ballpark to compete with other foods," Adams says. But offering a dud as a substitute for the tin can could be disastrous. "Deep down, everybody feels good about the can," Terwilliger says. "We don't want to muck it all up by changing that good solid conservative image."

The major rap against the soup can is inconvenience. Consumers don't like having to use a can opener, mix the can's soup with water if the soup is condensed (which it usually is), heat the mixture, and then clean several utensils.

Many younger consumers also associate cans with preservatives and artificial ingredients. They believe that cans don't preserve nutrients effectively. Such attitudes are hard to dispel. Furthermore, what used to be the big advantage of the can—extended shelf life—has been eroded by technological advances that make plastics nearly impervious to oxygen.

Frustration with the soup can peaks in the growing segment of U.S. households that use microwave ovens, which aren't designed for metal containers. As a result, most of the alternatives that Campbell is testing are made of plastic shells that are compatible with microwaves.

So far the company hasn't settled on a specific alternative to the tin can. A 17-member task force headed by Terwilliger is still evaluating other containers in consumer surveys and various physical tests. A likely, if conventional, possibility is a plastic container shaped just like a metal can; it even includes a red-and-white label. Perhaps the funkiest alternative is a stand-up aluminum foil pouch, with a vaguely pyramidal shape that makes it resemble a deformed bag of coffee.

Other possibilities have included squat rectangular boxes, yogurt-style containers, and lanky cartons. The company has rejected dishes with peel-off aluminum tops (they don't always work in microwave ovens). And Terwilliger says it recently ruled out a plastic bowl that came with a small pouch containing a "silly little knife" designed to cut off the bowl's plastic cover. "It just kind of looked dumb," he says.

Source: Paul A. Engelmayer, "Campbell Plans to Drop Its Tin Soup Can, Reflecting New Emphasis on Convenience," *Wall Street Journal*, March 28, 1984, p. 35. Reprinted by permission of the Wall Street Journal. © Dow Jones & Company, Inc., 1983. All Rights Reserved.

Questions:

1. Is Campbell a production, sales, or totally marketing oriented company? Have there been any recent changes in this regard?

2. What changes in the marketplace prompted Campbell to look for new product packages? What will be the benefits to consumers? To the producer?

3. How will the new package affect soup as an objective product? As a subjective product?

4. How many product development stages can you identify in this article? What is the role of marketing research in introducing the new container?

Chapter 10
DISTRIBUTION

When you have completed this chapter, you should be able to

- Define and list the three main kinds of *intermediaries*.

- Explain the role of *coverage*, *control*, and *cost* in designing distribution systems.

- Illustrate the concept of a *distribution channel* and discuss the kinds of problems that arise in such channels.

- Define *wholesaling* and list the services offered by wholesalers to producers and retailers.

- Define *retailing* and discuss various types of retailers in terms of product lines offered and emphasis on service versus price.

- Discuss *physical distribution* in terms of five functions: order processing, inventory management, packaging and materials handling, warehousing, and transportation.

- Discuss how legal restrictions on distribution affect producers and consumers.

Two-year-old Jessie Vangrofsky races across the kelly green carpet and collides with an eight-foot stuffed giraffe. Then she heads for a bright yellow table filled with plastic toys.

This isn't a nursery school. Jessie is in a corner play area at Kids "R" Us, one of Toys "R" Us Inc.'s new children's apparel stores, and her mother is shopping for her just a few feet away.

Mrs. Vangrofsky is delighted with the $17 Osh Kosh brand overalls she has found here for $11.97. Kids "R" Us is "going to change my shopping habits for sure," she says. In the past, she has "shopped sales" at fancy department stores like Bloomingdale's, Macy's, and Saks Fifth Avenue. But, she says, if Kids "R" Us offers the same merchandise for less money, "why should I go to a department store?"

Comments like Mrs. Vangrofsky's are reverberating through the children's wear business these days. "This new chain has upset everyone in the market," says Tom Mendelson, president of the Youth Fashion Guild, a New York buying office that represents 285 specialty and department stores nationwide. Recently, Mendelson accompanied a Pittsburgh-area children's store owner to see the colorful Kids "R" Us outlet in Paramus.

"All I can tell you is his face turned white," says Mendelson. "You come up against a giant like this, with every major line discounted, and where do you go? If you're the average kiddy shop next door, do you take gas or cut your throat?"

For years, giant chains like J. C. Penney Company and Sears, Roebuck & Company have dominated the children's wear market, selling moderately priced apparel under their store labels. Big department stores and neighborhood specialty shops featured the more expensive labels.

In recent years, though, partly in response to the recession, consumers have begun turning to off-price retailers, seeking top brand-name goods at big discounts. Toys "R" Us is among the first big retailers to move into the booming off-price children's market. But it doesn't have the look of some discounters, which have a bargain basement or "pipe rack" appearance. And instead of selling end-of-season or irregular goods, like some off-price stores, Kids "R" Us promises a full assortment of first-quality, in-season apparel. It offers all the accessories, too, from Carter's crib sheets to Buster Brown shoes.

There are some naysayers. The chief executive of a competing chain suggests that Kids "R" Us will face tough competition in the days ahead because everybody else in the business will match its prices. Others speculate that Kids "R" Us will eventually have to raise prices to cover the costs of running its spacious, well-decorated stores.

But Toys "R" Us's chairman, Charles Lazarus, is convinced his stores will outperform the competition. "This is the store of tomorrow," he says. To suggestions that his new stores aren't producing the sales volume he expected because nearby stores have cut prices, Lazarus responds with a long, loud laugh. The crowds got so big in the store one recent weekend, he insists, that they caused traffic jams.[1]

[1]Claudia Ricci, "Children's Wear Retailers Brace for Competition from Toys 'R' Us," *Wall Street Journal*, August 25, 1983, p. 21. Reprinted by permission of the Wall Street Journal. © Dow Jones & Company, Inc., 1983. All Rights Reserved.

Intermediary: A firm that provides distribution services for firms that choose not to deal directly with users of their products.

Retailing: Selling directly to consumers.

Wholesaling: Selling to retailers, industrial customers, or other wholesalers.

Physical distribution: All the functions required to move goods from the producer to the consumer.

Middleman: An intermediary.

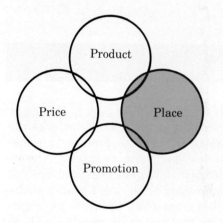

What does Kids "R" Us have to do with marketing? It does not make children's clothing. It does not consume children's clothing. Yet, clearly, its innovative methods have had a major impact on the marketing of children's clothing. What kind of enterprise is it?

The answer is that Kids "R" Us is an **intermediary**, a firm that provides distribution services for firms that choose not to deal directly with users of their products. The business of intermediaries is "place," the second of the four Ps of marketing. In this chapter we will look at three things that intermediaries do.

1. **Retailing**, or selling directly to consumers
2. **Wholesaling**, or selling to retailers, industrial customers, or other wholesalers
3. **Physical distribution**, or all the functions required to move goods from the producer to the consumer

Intermediaries are sometimes called **middlemen**, but this term is misleading. For one thing, not all intermediaries are men. Also a "middleman" is often thought of as an unproductive link in the chain from producer to user—one who skims off profits without doing anything worthwhile in return. Joe Doe in the city calls his cousin Jane on the farm. Joe complains about the high price of bacon and Jane gripes about the low price of hogs. Within a minute the two of them have joined in cursing the "middlemen" who seem to be the cause of all their troubles.

A major purpose of this chapter is to distinguish the real role of intermediaries in the marketing process from the image of "middlemen" as parasites. Intermediaries, as we will see, are producers too. They produce services—distribution services—just as barbers and singers produce services. Their services play a key role in meeting consumer needs. A crate of apples in a farmer's shed in Yakima, Washington, can't meet any needs besides those of the farmer's own family. The same apples in a pie on Sis Barker's Thanksgiving table in Goshen, Indiana, satisfy needs of time, place, and convenience. To be sure, the Barkers could get along without the intermediaries between them and the Yakima apples. They could plant an apple tree. They could wait for it to grow, spray the fruit for bugs, and enjoy apple pies each fall when the crop comes in. But is it any wonder that some families are willing to pay for the services of intermediaries?

While it is clear that consumers need intermediaries, some intermediaries serve their needs better than others. In this way they are just like other firms. In wholesaling, retailing, and physical distribution there is always room for new ideas. What consumers need is not fewer intermediaries but better ones. That is why air freight has replaced the mule train. It is why retailers like Kids "R" Us have full parking lots. It is why distribution poses a challenge to managers in any firm.

PLANNING A DISTRIBUTION STRATEGY

Products cannot serve customer needs until they reach the customer. That makes distribution a key part of marketing strategy. A firm's distribution strategy must fit with the decisions it makes about product, promotion, and price. The outside team of intermediaries that a firm sets up to distribute its product is as important as its inside teams of managers and workers.

Three factors shape a firm's distribution strategy: *coverage*, *control*, and *cost*. These are sometimes called the "three Cs" of distribution. The stress placed on each of them depends on the nature of the product and the target market.

Coverage deals with customers' access to the product. For convenience goods like soft drinks, coverage is vital. Vending machines are one way in which soft-drink makers achieve intensive coverage. With specialty goods, wide coverage is less important because customers will seek out the product. It is common for specialty goods to be sold through only one outlet in each area.

The importance of control also depends on the nature of the product. Control is very important when a marketing strategy emphasizes service. For example, in Case 4–2 (page 96) we saw that McDonald's makes control over quality and cleanliness a key part of its marketing strategy. When customer service is less important, control may be less important too.

The factor of cost may also depend on how much stress the firm puts on service as part of its marketing strategy. As we will see, some firms do not like to distribute their goods through low-cost discount retailers because they think they do not provide enough service. Other firms find that discounters serve their marketing strategy very well.

Throughout this chapter we will see how coverage, control, and cost affect all aspects of distribution strategy.

TYPES OF DISTRIBUTION CHANNELS

Distribution channel: A series of firms that take part in buying or selling a good as it moves from the producer to the user.

Merchant: An intermediary that takes title to a good and then resells it.

Agent: An intermediary that brings buyers and sellers together without taking title to the good or service.

A **distribution channel** is a series of firms that take part in buying or selling a good as it moves from the producer to the user. It includes the producer, the user, and any wholesalers or retailers used as intermediaries. The intermediaries may be either *merchants* or *agents*. A **merchant** takes title to a good and then resells it. An **agent** brings buyers and sellers together without taking title to the good or service. Agents are also often known as **brokers**. Intermediaries that provide physical-distribution services but do not act as merchants or agents—such as railroads—are not counted as part of a distribution channel.

Channels are often classified by how many levels of intermediaries they contain. Box 10–1 shows several cases.

In a zero-level channel, no intermediaries are used. This is the most common kind of channel for industrial goods, especially when the target market consists of a small number of large buyers. Firms that sell consumer goods through catalogs or door-to-door sales also use zero-level channels.

One-level channels contain one intermediary. Some consumer goods are sold that way. Automobile dealerships are a good example. Large retail chains, such as Kids "R" Us, that buy directly from manufacturers are another example. One-level channels are used for industrial goods when there are many customers, as in the case of maintenance supplies. Some manufacturers use agents to sell industrial goods in order to save the cost of having their own sales departments.

Box 10–1 Distribution Channels

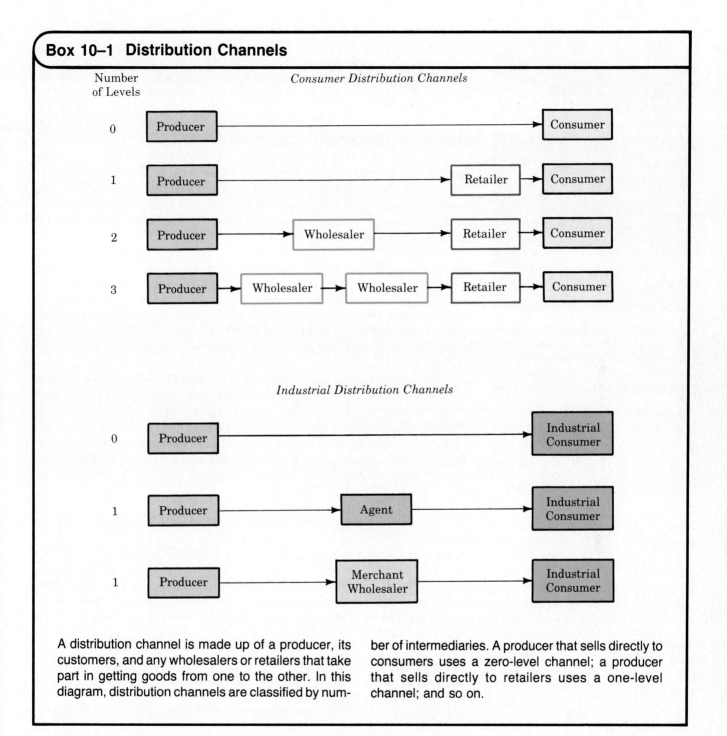

Number of Levels

Consumer Distribution Channels

0 Producer → Consumer

1 Producer → Retailer → Consumer

2 Producer → Wholesaler → Retailer → Consumer

3 Producer → Wholesaler → Wholesaler → Retailer → Consumer

Industrial Distribution Channels

0 Producer → Industrial Consumer

1 Producer → Agent → Industrial Consumer

1 Producer → Merchant Wholesaler → Industrial Consumer

A distribution channel is made up of a producer, its customers, and any wholesalers or retailers that take part in getting goods from one to the other. In this diagram, distribution channels are classified by number of intermediaries. A producer that sells directly to consumers uses a zero-level channel; a producer that sells directly to retailers uses a one-level channel; and so on.

Two-level channels with both a wholesaler and a retailer are the most common means of distributing consumer goods. Many convenience goods, hardware items, and groceries are distributed in this way. Two-level channels are not as common for industrial goods.

A few goods pass through three or more intermediaries on their way from the producer to the consumer. Some food products follow channels of this kind.

Automobile dealerships are an example of a one-level distribution channel: the dealer is the only intermediary between the producer and the consumer. Marc P. Anderson

Channel captain: A channel member that controls a distribution channel as a result of its size or economic power.

Vertically integrated marketing channel (VIMC): A distribution channel in which a producer and one or more intermediaries are bound together by ownership or contract.

For completeness, it should be added that a firm can use more than one channel of distribution. For example, a clothing firm may sell to large retail chains directly and to smaller retail stores through a wholesaler. Likewise, many publishers sell books by mail order and also through bookstores.

Cooperation and Conflict in Distribution

Ideally, the members of a distribution channel should work as a team. They should have a common strategy based on a shared idea of how best to meet customer needs. Each team member should focus on the jobs it does best and respect the abilities of the others. The result should be high-quality service at low cost.

Needless to say, this ideal is not always reached. It is hard enough to get all the departments of a single firm to work as a team. Small wonder that conflicts arise when the members of a distribution channel are separate firms. Channel members share the goal of serving their customers well, but each wants as large a share of the profits as possible. In addition to the tug-of-war over profits, conflicts can arise from different views of customer needs, different marketing strategies, or different management styles.

The best way to avoid conflicts is to have one member of the channel clearly in charge. When control of a channel evolves informally, as a result of one member's size or economic power, that member is called a **channel captain**. Producers are the natural captains for most channels. Firms like Coca-Cola, Polaroid, and Gillette are examples. Powerful retailers, such as Sears or J. C. Penney, can also be channel captains. Super Valu Stores, Inc., a wholesaler of goods sold in supermarkets, acts as a channel captain.

Vertically Integrated Marketing Channels

Some firms want more control over their distribution channels than they can have as informal channel captains. One way to get more control is to set up a **vertically integrated marketing channel (VIMC)**. A VIMC, sometimes called a vertical marketing system, is a channel in which all levels are formally brought under unified control. There are two main types of VIMCs.

- *Corporate VIMCs*, in which one firm owns all the levels of the channel. Firestone, which makes tires and sells them through its own chain of tire stores, is an example.
- *Contractual VIMCs*, in which a number of firms are bound together by contract into a unified channel. Franchising, which was discussed at length in Chapter 4, is the leading example.

WHOLESALING

We have defined wholesalers as intermediaries that sell to retailers, industrial customers, or other wholesalers. They include both merchant wholesalers, which take title to the goods they deal in, and wholesaling

Box 10–2 Wholesaling in the United States

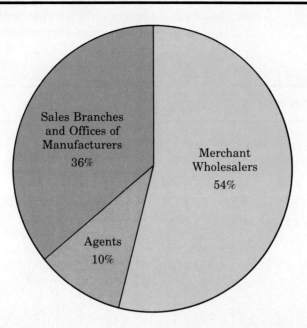

Merchant wholesalers take title to goods. Agent wholesalers or brokers bring buyers and sellers together but do not take title to the goods. Sales branches and sales offices of producers perform many of the same functions as wholesalers but are not independent firms. This chart shows how total wholesale trade in the United States is divided among merchant wholesalers, agent wholesalers, and sales branches and offices of producers.

Source: *Statistical Abstract of the United States*, 104th ed. (Washington, D.C.: Government Printing Office, 1983), Table 1440.

Sales branch: A branch of a producer, separate from the manufacturing plant, that maintains a sales force and stocks inventories of the product.

Sales office: A branch of a producer, separate from the manufacturing plant, that maintains a sales force but that does not stock inventories of the product.

agents, which arrange sales without taking title to the goods. **Sales branches** and **sales offices** of manufacturers are often grouped with wholesalers because they perform many of the same functions. Strictly speaking, though, they are not intermediaries, as we use the term, because they are not independent firms. Box 10–2 shows how much wholesale trade is accounted for by each type of wholesaler.

Services of Wholesalers

No one *has* to sell or buy through a wholesaler. Wholesalers have to prove their worth every day by providing services. The most important service they provide is that of centralizing transactions. This is crucial when many small retailers each carry the products of many small producers, as is true of drugstores or hardware stores. Box 10–3 shows how centralization works in the case of six retail stores, each of which deals with six producers. Without the wholesaler, thirty-six transactions would be needed. Each would require sales calls, placement of orders, billing, paying of bills, and so on. With a wholesaler, the total number of transactions is reduced to twelve.

Wholesalers provide a number of other services as well, both to producers and to retailers.

Services to producers. The services provided by wholesalers to producers may include some or all of the following.

Box 10–3 Centralization of Transactions

A. Without a Wholesaler

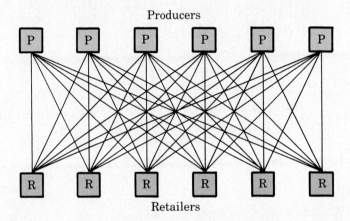

B. With a Wholesaler

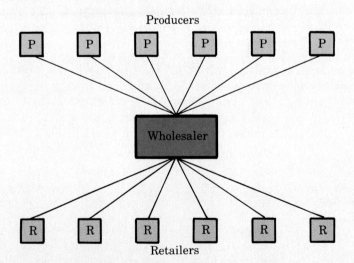

The main service performed by wholesalers is that of centralizing transactions in cases in which a number of small retailers each carry the products of a number of small producers. These diagrams show the importance of centralization in the case of six retailers, each of which deals with six producers. Without the wholesaler, thirty-six transactions would be needed. The wholesaler reduces the number to twelve.

The most important service of wholesalers is centralizing transactions, especially when many small retailers each carry the products of many small producers. © Freda Leinwand

- *Sales services.* Wholesalers reduce a producer's need for a sales staff. Some producers do all their selling through wholesalers. Others use their own sales staff to reach major customers, and use wholesalers where sales volume is smaller. Both merchant and agent wholesalers provide sales services.
- *Information services.* Both merchant and agent wholesalers serve as channels of communication between producers and their customers. They let producers know what customers need, and they let customers know what producers have to offer.
- *Physical-distribution services.* Most merchant wholesalers (but not agents) provide warehousing and transportation services.
- *Risk bearing.* Merchant wholesalers (but not agents) relieve producers of certain risks by taking title to the goods. Many large wholesalers are good credit risks even when the small retailers they deal with are not. Selling to a wholesaler also relieves producers of the risk that goods will fall in value before they can be sold to customers.

Services to retailers.   Wholesalers also make life easier for retailers by providing them with many services. These include the following.

- *Purchasing services.* Wholesalers offer retailers a number of sources of goods and help them choose among them.
- *Information services.* Wholesalers often are better informed than small retailers about trends in demand, the needs of certain market segments, and so on. They can help stores stock goods that will sell well and avoid slow-selling items.
- *Credit services.* Merchant wholesalers (but not agents) may be willing to sell to retailers on credit.
- *Physical-distribution services.* Merchant wholesalers (but not agents) provide physical-distribution services to retailers as well as producers. Warehousing and prompt local delivery reduce the inventories that retail stores need to carry. Wholesalers are also able to buy in bulk and resell in units that are more convenient for small retailers.

Costs of Wholesale Services

Wholesalers do not provide all these services for nothing. Costs plus profits for all wholesalers average about 9 percent of their total sales.[2] (Probably less than a third of that sum is profit.) Costs of merchant wholesalers tend to run a bit higher than the average; those of agents tend to be quite a bit lower.

It appears that people find wholesale services to be worth the cost. Wholesale trade is alive and well. In recent years there has been a slight trend away from wholesalers in consumer markets. But this has been more than offset by increased use of wholesalers in industrial markets.

[2]*Statistical Abstract of the United States*, 104th ed. (Washington, D.C.: Government Printing Office, 1983), Tables 1423 and 1440.

RETAILING

Retailers are intermediaries that sell directly to consumers. They include retail stores and nonstore retailers like mail order houses. As of the most recent census of retail trade, there were more than 1.5 million retail firms in the United States. If branches of retail firms are counted, that number climbs to 1,855,000. Retailers had more than 13 million paid employees that year, plus well over a million working proprietors.[3]

Box 10–4 lists various categories of retailers in terms of the percentage of retail sales accounted for by each category. As you can see, the largest category by far is supermarkets and other food stores, with 23

Box 10–4   Retailing in the United States

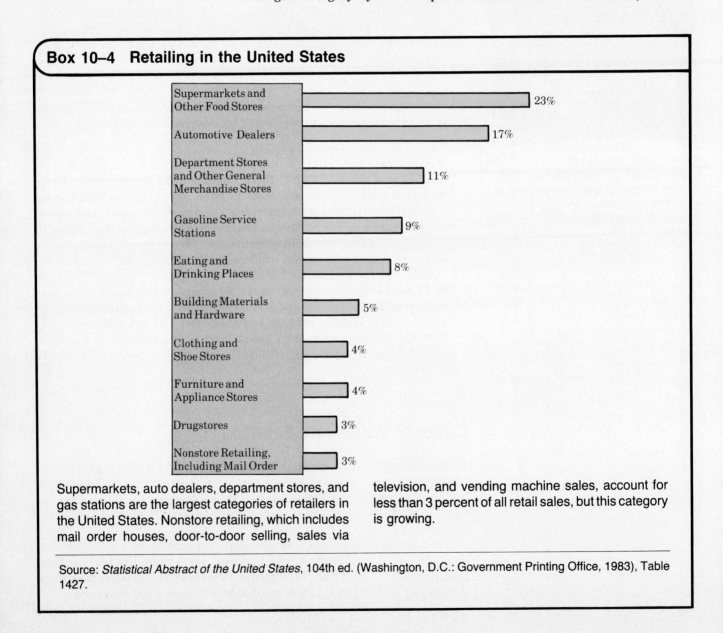

Category	Percent
Supermarkets and Other Food Stores	23%
Automotive Dealers	17%
Department Stores and Other General Merchandise Stores	11%
Gasoline Service Stations	9%
Eating and Drinking Places	8%
Building Materials and Hardware	5%
Clothing and Shoe Stores	4%
Furniture and Appliance Stores	4%
Drugstores	3%
Nonstore Retailing, Including Mail Order	3%

Supermarkets, auto dealers, department stores, and gas stations are the largest categories of retailers in the United States. Nonstore retailing, which includes mail order houses, door-to-door selling, sales via television, and vending machine sales, account for less than 3 percent of all retail sales, but this category is growing.

Source: *Statistical Abstract of the United States*, 104th ed. (Washington, D.C.: Government Printing Office, 1983), Table 1427.

[3]Data are from the 1977 census of retail trade, as cited in *Statistical Abstract of the United States*, 104th ed., Table 1425.

percent—almost one quarter—of total sales. The second-largest category is automotive dealers, with 17 percent, followed by department stores and other general merchandise stores, with 11 percent. These three categories together account for more than half of all retail sales.

The top twenty firms in retail trade are listed in Box 10–5. They include some familiar names: Sears, Safeway, K mart, J. C. Penney, A&P. These twenty firms together account for about 16 percent of total retail sales.

Box 10–5 *Fortune's* Twenty Largest Retailers

Rank 1982	Rank 1981	Company	Sales ($1000)	Net Income ($1000)	Rank
1	1	Sears Roebuck (Chicago)	30,019,800	861,200	1
2	2	Safeway Stores (Oakland, Calif.)	17,632,821	159,660	9
3	3	K mart (Troy, Mich.)	16,772,166	261,823	4
4	5	Kroger (Cincinnati)	11,901,892	143,758	10
5	4	J.C. Penney (New York)	11,413,806	391,687	2
6	7	Lucky Stores (Dublin, Calif.)	7,972,973	92,228	19
7		Household International (Prospect Heights, Ill.)	7,767,500	125,400	14
8	9	Federated Department Stores (Cincinnati)	7,698,944	232,776	5
9	8	American Stores (Salt Lake City)	7,507,772	90,371	21
10	11	Winn-Dixie Stores (Jacksonville, Fla.)	6,764,472	103,513	17
11	13	Southland (Dallas)	6,756,933	108,051	16
12	6	F.W. Woolworth (New York)	6,590,000	353,000	50
13	10	Great Atlantic & Pacific Tea (Montvale, N.J.)	6,226,755	101,633	48
14	16	Dayton Hudson (Minneapolis)	5,660,729	206,716	8
15	12	Montgomery Ward (Chicago)	5,583,861	74,611	47
16	14	Jewel Companies (Chicago)	5,571,721	88,109	22
17		BATUS (Louisville)	5,165,439	213,955	7
18	17	Grand Union (Elmwood Park, N.J.)	4,137,447	24,652	41
19	18	Albertson's (Boise)	3,940,117	58,375	28
20	19	May Department Stores (St. Louis)	3,670,371	141,656	12

This table lists the twenty largest retailers in the United States from *Fortune* Magazine's annual list of the fifty largest. The two most profitable retailers, in terms of the ratio of profits to sales, are not among the twenty largest. They are McDonald's (number 30 in sales) and Tandy, which runs the chain of Radio Shack stores (number 39 in sales).

Source: 20 Largest Retailers *FORTUNE*, June 13, 1983, pp. 168–69. Reprinted by permission from FORTUNE Magazine.

Types of Retailers

All retailers aim to please their customers, but their strategies for doing so vary. Box 10–6 spreads retailers out over a map on two dimensions: product lines stocked and service versus price. Retailers that carry a broad range of lines in order to meet many shopping needs at one location are placed toward the left-hand side of the map. Specialty stores are placed toward the right. At the top are stores that stress service and convenience. Stores that go for price-conscious consumers with a no-frills approach are at the bottom. Let's take a brief tour of this map of retailing, starting at the top and working toward the bottom.

Department store: A store that carries a broad range of product lines and offers a variety of services.

Full-service stores. We begin at the upper left-hand corner with **department stores**. Top-of-the-line stores like Bloomingdale's are full-service, full-line outlets for the latest styles and fashions. Sears, the

---

Box 10–6 Types of Retailers

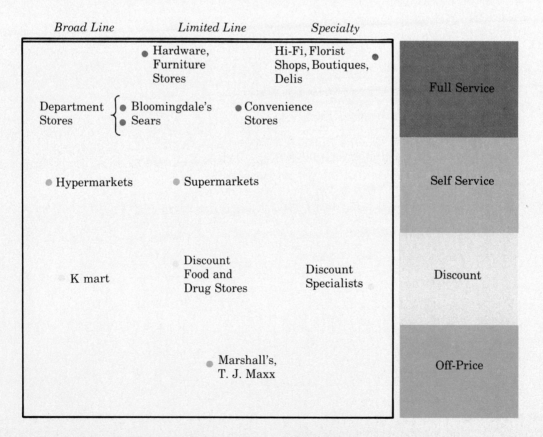

In this diagram retailers are classified by their position on a two-dimensional map. The horizontal dimension puts retailers with a broad range of product lines at the left and those with a narrow range at the right. The vertical dimension puts retailers that specialize in service or convenience at the top and those that specialize in low prices at the bottom. Thus, department stores are placed near the upper left-hand corner, off-price retailers near the center bottom, and so on.

biggest department store chain, is a bit less style-conscious. It offers a broader range of goods and services, however, including insurance, auto repair, and financial services. Department stores have accounted for nearly 10 percent of all retail sales, but they have had to work hard to defend that market share in recent years.

The top row includes many full-service stores that carry fewer lines of goods. Furniture, hardware, and office supply stores fall into this group. It also includes specialty shops that offer only one or a few lines. These include boutique-type clothing stores, electronics stores like Radio Shack, and gift shops, to name just a few. In all of these stores customers can get help from salespeople who are familiar with the product. Products are often demonstrated in the store. Sometimes they can even be tried out at home. Many specialty shops also provide follow-up services.

Convenience stores. Convenience stores are also found near the top of Box 10–6. These stores offer a different kind of service. Stores like 7-Eleven cut shopping time with convenient locations and no-wait checkout. They carry fewer lines of goods and charge higher prices than supermarkets. Neighborhood jewelers and clothing shops also compete largely on the basis of convenience.

HARDWARE RETAILING

"If it doesn't work, you can return it; and after a lot of unpleasant haggling, we'll return your money . . ."

Reprinted by permission, Hardware Retailing, Indianapolis, Indiana.

Courtesy of Radio Shack. A Division of Tandy Corp.

© Freda Leinwand

Courtesy of K mart Corp.

Courtesy of T. J. Maxx

Retailers can be classified according to their emphasis on full service versus low prices. Radio Shack is a full-service store; the supermarket is a self-service store; K mart is a discount store; and T. J. Maxx is an off-price retailer.

Self-service stores. Self-service stores cut costs by cutting out personal selling. Supermarkets are a well-known type of self-service store. This approach has spread to supermarket-type home improvement centers, drugstores, and auto parts stores.

Discount store: A store that carries complete product lines at low prices, which are made possible by aggressive cost cutting.

Discount stores. **Discount stores** make low prices the focus of their strategy. They offer complete selections and current styles in the product lines they carry. Often they pay the same wholesale prices as full-service stores. They maintain their edge on prices by aggressively cutting costs. They cut store personnel to a minimum and seek out less expensive locations. Their decor tends to be spartan.

Stores like K mart and Zayre's carry a broad range of goods. They are really discount department stores. Discount supermarkets like the Basics chain carry generic goods and may do without costly meat and produce departments. Toys "R" Us and its new Kids "R" Us offshoot are limited-line discount stores. There are specialty discount stores too, where consumers who know just what they want can buy such items as cameras or TV sets. New York's 47th Street Photo is a specialty discounter that does a large mail order business in addition to its in-store business.

Off-price retailer: A store that can offer even lower prices than discount stores because it carries incomplete product lines bought below normal wholesale prices, such as factory overruns and imperfect items.

Off-price retailing. **Off-price retailers** go one step further than discounters. They cut costs in their stores, but they also buy their goods at prices below normal wholesale prices. Off-price stores like Marshalls and T. J. Maxx are the home of the factory overrun, the imperfect, and the discontinued style. Shoppers at these stores cannot be sure that they will find every size or color. What they can find, though, is brand-name products, including designer labels, at half-price or less. Off-price stores are one of the fastest-growing types of retailing.

The Future of Retailing

Retailing must face challenges in the late twentieth century. Some 47 percent of personal income is still spent on retail goods, but this has slipped from 62 percent in 1948. Taxes, housing, medical services, and other expenses are taking an ever-larger share of the consumer dollar. As retailers fight for the rest, a number of trends can be seen.

One trend is toward what is sometimes called *scrambled merchandising*. In this type of retailing, stores expand their range of product lines—supermarkets sell motor oil, gas stations sell milk, and so on. Scrambled merchandising reaches its height in the so-called *hypermarket*. A hypermarket is a store with an extremely wide range of product lines—a supermarket and a self-service department store rolled into one.

These trends represent a movement away from the center of the retail map of Box 10–6 toward the left-hand edge. There are other movements away from the center, too. The supermarket sector seems to be splitting apart. The fastest-growing segments of this sector are gourmet supermarkets where shoppers can buy fresh pasta and five kinds of smoked salmon, and generic stores where shoppers buy low-priced basics direct from the carton. These changes represent a movement away from the center of the retail map toward both the top and bottom edges.

Also, specialty shops are doing well. They were helped during the 1960s and 1970s by the growth of enclosed shopping malls. These malls make wandering from one shop to another as convenient as wandering about in a department store. In the 1980s many cities rebuilt old factories and waterfront buildings. In these places smaller, more specialized shops flourish. These shops occupy the upper right-hand corner of the retail map.

Still another trend is toward nonstore retailing. This sector accounts for only 2.5 percent of retail sales today, but it is growing. The combination of a television ad, a toll-free telephone line, and a credit card number is already selling many goods. The spread of cable TV, the rise of electronic banking, and changes in the telephone system mean that more goods will be sold this way in the future.

Some writers view these changes as showing that forms of retailing, like products, have a life cycle. Electronic selling is just coming onto the scene. Off-price clothing stores are in a stage of rapid growth. Discount stores and supermarkets have reached maturity. Department stores seem to be in a stage of decline.

Malcolm P. McNair has suggested that the rise and fall of forms of retailing follows a cycle called the *wheel of retailing*.[4] According to this theory, new concepts like the department store win acceptance through low costs and low prices. As they mature, they add product lines, services, and features. This makes them more attractive, but it also raises their costs. At some point the stores face new, lower-cost competitors like the discount store.

Baltimore's Harborplace is a renovated waterfront building filled with a variety of small, specialized shops. Courtesy of the Rouse Company

The use of "800" phone numbers in television ads is part of a growing trend toward electronic retailing. © Freda Leinwand

However the trends in retailing are interpreted, the struggle between old and new forms will be intense. Innovations that boost productivity, such as electronic product code scanners and computerized inventory systems, will be key weapons. Whatever happens, consumers seem bound to benefit.

PHYSICAL DISTRIBUTION

Physical distribution includes all the activities required to move goods from the producer to the customer. Good physical distribution is a major

[4]See M. P. McNair, "Significant Trends and Developments in the Postwar Period," in A. B. Smith, ed., *Competitive Distribution in a Free, High-Level Economy and Its Implications for the University* (Pittsburgh: University of Pittsburgh Press, 1958), pp. 17–18.

part of meeting customer needs. If one firm's product isn't in stock in the right store at the right time, consumers will buy a competitor's product. And industrial buyers rank the quality of physical distribution second only to that of the product itself in choosing sources of supply.[5]

In physical distribution, quality means that

- Products are available when and where they are needed.
- Orders are filled correctly.
- Orders are filled and the product delivered fast.
- Performance is dependable and consistent.

The Functions of Physical Distribution

Physical distribution can be broken down into five functions: order processing, inventory management, packaging and materials handling, warehousing, and transportation. Each of these has a lot to do with both cost and service quality.

Order processing. Order processing consists of taking orders, checking them, and giving instructions for sending the product on its way. It is a type of information processing. Orders placed by customers are data that the system must be able to capture. Orders can be taken by mail, by telephone, or by salespeople who visit customers. Incoming orders must be checked to make sure they are accurate, and someone must check to see whether the items ordered are in stock. If goods are sold on credit, order processing may include credit checks. The output of order processing includes information needed to update inventory and financial records, as well as instructions for sending goods on their way to customers.

Order processing is a key to accurate distribution. Efficient order processing is also required for speed. Since the use of computers tends to increase both speed and accuracy, many order-processing systems have been computerized.

Inventory: A stock of finished goods on hand and ready for shipment.

Inventory management. Stocks of finished goods on hand and ready for shipment are termed **inventories**. Firms hold inventories for two reasons: so that they can ship goods when they are ordered and so that the timing of production does not have to match the timing of orders.

Look at the toy business. The heavy selling season is just before Christmas, but to use their equipment and workers efficiently, toymakers need to produce throughout the year. Toys that are produced early in the year remain in inventory until retailers begin stocking up for the Christmas season.

Other firms hold inventories because they cannot make all their products at the same time. For example, a maker of wallpaper may produce hundreds of patterns. Once the printing press has been set up for one pattern, it is efficient to run off thousands of rolls and not print that pattern again for months. Many rolls of each pattern are kept in stock and used to fill orders.

Inventory management is a tough job. It requires skill at forecasting the timing and volume of orders. Such forecasting has to take into account

---

[5]Based on a survey of 216 purchasing agents by William D. Perreault, Jr., and Frederick A. Russ, "Physical Distribution Service in Industrial Purchase Decisions," *Journal of Marketing*, April 1976, pp. 3–10.

past buying patterns, the state of the economy, and the expected effects of the firm's promotional efforts. Once the forecasting has been done, a production schedule must be set up to fill inventories to the desired level. For example, the wallpaper maker would have to decide how many rolls of each pattern to print and what order to produce them in so that just enough, but not too much, of each pattern could be kept in stock to meet the expected demand.

Carrying costs: The costs of keeping goods in stock, including interest expenses, inventory taxes, and storage costs.

Inventory managers must also keep an eye on costs, especially **carrying costs**, or the costs of keeping goods in stock. These include interest expenses, taxes on inventories (in some states), and storage costs. The higher the level of inventories, the higher the carrying costs. But if inventories are cut too far in an effort to save carrying costs, the firm may lose customers because goods are not in stock at the time that they are ordered.

Packaging and materials handling.   In Chapter 9 we discussed the use of packaging to make products more attractive to consumers. Packaging also plays a role in physical distribution. Goods must be packaged so that they reach customers without being damaged. The amount of heat, cold, or vibration encountered in transportation must be taken into account. The requirements of *materials handling*—movement of goods within the producer's plant or warehouse—must also be taken into account in package design.

Warehousing.   It is not always economical to ship goods straight from the plant to the customer. Using warehouses that are close to customers can often increase speed and lower distribution costs at the same time. Depending on the nature of the product and the demand for it, firms can either build their own warehouses or rent space in public warehouses. Warehousing is among the services provided by many wholesalers.

Transportation.   Transportation is the biggest single expense in the distribution of many goods. The United States has a complex transportation system that offers many choices. One of those is the mode of transportation to use for a given product. Each of the five major modes has its own set of advantages and disadvantages, as follows.

- *Rail.* Railroads carry more tons of freight than any other mode. Rail is the cheapest mode for bulky goods like grain or coal, except where the shipper has access to a waterway. The U.S. rail network still covers the nation fairly densely, although railroads have abandoned many branch lines in recent years. Better management and deregulation have tended to make rail service faster and more reliable.
- *Truck.* Motor carriers are the only transportation mode that can serve every shipper and every delivery point. Shipping by truck is usually more expensive than shipping by rail, but it is often faster. It also is very reliable. Truckers that specialize in partial loads handle small shipments that railroads will not take.
- *Air.* Air freight is usually the fastest mode for distances of 200 miles or more. (On shorter routes, trucks can beat airplanes because they deliver from door to door.) For small shipments, the advantage of speed can offset the high cost of air freight. The air freight network does not cover the country as densely as trucking, however.

- *Water*. Coastal shipping and inland barge lines are the cheapest mode for bulk goods like grain. They are slow, however, and their coverage is limited.
- *Pipeline*. Pipeline is the best mode for liquids and gases. For such products it is cheap and much safer than shipment by rail or truck. Coverage is fairly good.

The advantages and disadvantages of the five major modes of transportation are listed in Box 10–7.

Box 10–7 Comparison of Five Major Transportation Modes

	Speed	Availability	Reliability	Cost per Unit of Weight
Rail	Fair	Fair	Good	Low
Truck	Good	Excellent	Very Good	Moderate
Air	Fastest	Good	Good	Highest
Water	Slow	Limited	Fair	Lowest
Pipeline	Slow	Limited	Excellent	Lowest for Liquids and Gases

Recent years have seen a great increase in the range of choices open to transportation planners. This has occurred because of the following changes.

- *Regulatory changes*. Until recently, air freight, trucking, and railroad rates were all closely regulated by the government. In the late 1970s and early 1980s, these regulations were relaxed. Physical-distribution managers are now free to negotiate special contracts and rates that would not have been allowed in the past. The easing of regulation has also greatly increased competition within and between these modes, to the benefit of shippers.

Intermodal transportation: The use of more than one mode of transportation to move goods from one point to another.

● *Intermodal transportation.* **Intermodal transportation** refers to the use of more than one mode to move goods from one point to another. Changes in regulation and improved technology have led to the rapid spread of intermodal transportation. The "piggyback" mode, in which a truck trailer is shipped long distances on a railroad flatcar and then delivered locally over the road, is the most popular choice. It is cheaper and more fuel-efficient than long-haul trucking, and often faster. **Containerization** is another form of intermodal transportation. Goods are packed in truck-body-sized containers. These are hauled by road or rail to ports, where they are loaded onto oceangoing ships.

Containerization: A form of intermodal transportation in which goods are packed in truck-body-sized containers, which are hauled by road or rail to ports, where they are loaded onto oceangoing ships.

A popular form of intermodal transportation is the "piggy-back" mode, in which truck trailers are shipped long distances on railroad flatcars and then hauled locally by road. Santa Fe Industries Photo

● *Express companies.* Several firms provide excellent express service for small shipments and documents. Companies like Federal Express and Emery ship by air and guarantee twenty-four-hour delivery almost anywhere in the country. UPS, which ships by truck and piggyback, is almost as fast as the air express companies, and often cheaper. These private firms offer better service and better rates on most routes than the U.S. Postal Service, although the government carrier has improved its service in an effort to meet the competition.

Federal Express offers guaranteed 24-hour delivery of small shipments and documents. Courtesy of Federal Express

The Total-Cost Approach

The costs of physical distribution average some 20 percent of the price of consumer goods. Therefore, firms that manage physical distribution well have a big advantage over competitors. Physical-distribution costs are best controlled by means of the total-cost approach. In this approach managers consider all physical-distribution costs at the same time and look for ways to trade off one cost against another.

Box 10–8 gives just a few examples of ways in which spending more in one area can save in another. Money spent to computerize order processing might pay off in better inventory control. Modernizing warehouses might result in lower inventory handling costs. Faster order processing might make it possible to use a slower, cheaper transportation mode. On the other hand, the use of air freight might permit a firm to get rid of some of its warehouses. And paying extra for temperature-controlled transportation might reduce packaging costs.

Box 10–8 The Total-Cost Approach to Distribution

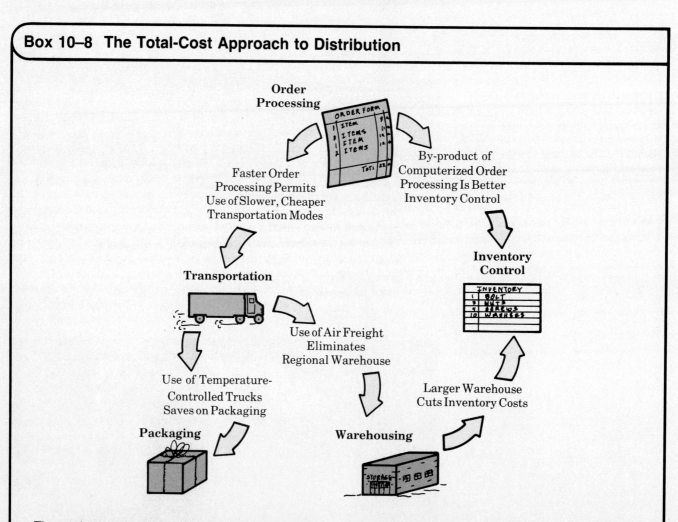

The total-cost approach to distribution looks for ways of saving on one aspect of distribution by spending more on another. Some examples are given in this diagram. Distribution costs must also be weighed against other marketing goals, such as customer service and price.

These are only a few of the possible trade-offs. Physical-distribution costs and service quality must also be traded off against other marketing goals. Caterpillar, for example, does not minimize its costs by guaranteeing forty-eight-hour delivery of parts anywhere in the world. Cost-conscious Dana Corporation, on the other hand, makes hard bargaining with railroads and truck lines a key part of its marketing strategy.

LEGAL ISSUES

Firms at all channel levels should be aware that there are legal constraints on the design and operation of distribution systems. These are part of the antitrust laws—the Sherman Act of 1890, the Clayton Act of 1914, and the Robinson-Patman Act of 1936. Some of these laws limit producers' control over distribution channels. Others place limits on firms' ability to increase efficiency and improve services. Let's look at some examples.

The Robinson-Patman Act

During the 1920s and early 1930s there was a revolution in American retailing. Its leaders were chain stores like A&P. These retail channel captains set up large, integrated buying systems that reduced distribution costs and allowed the chains to charge lower prices than smaller stores. The small stores fought back in Congress. In 1936 they won passage of the **Robinson-Patman Act**, also known as the chain store act.

Robinson-Patman Act: A 1936 law, also known as the "chain store act," that outlaws certain forms of price discrimination.

The Robinson-Patman Act tried to outlaw certain cost-cutting tactics used by the chains. First, it limited their ability to bargain with suppliers for discount prices. A producer had to sell to all stores or wholesalers at the same price unless different prices could be justified by differences in selling costs. The courts interpreted the law narrowly, making it difficult to justify price differences and, hence, difficult to pass along to consumers the benefits of the chains' greater bargaining power. Second, the act tried to protect wholesalers. In cases in which a chain like A&P bypassed the wholesaler and bought from the producer, the act made it illegal to pass along the cost savings to customers.

The Robinson-Patman Act failed to prevent the spread of chain stores. The advantages of chains over small stores were too great to resist. Even so, hundreds of cases were brought under the act, and some cost-saving ways of doing business had to be abandoned. In recent years federal officials have stopped prosecuting Robinson-Patman Act violations and have campaigned for repeal of the law. They, and most legal scholars, see it as doing more harm than good. Yet the law remains on the books, and lawsuits are sometimes brought under it by private firms.

Restraints on Control

Clayton Act: A 1914 antitrust law that prohibits certain techniques of control of distribution channels, when the effect is to limit competition.

Control over channels—one of the three Cs—tends to make distribution more efficient. However, the **Clayton Act** of 1914 outlaws certain kinds of control when their effect is to reduce competition. Among the tactics limited by the act are the following.

Dealer selection: A situation in which a producer selects its customers and will not sell to some intermediaries.

Exclusive dealing: A situation in which a producer does not allow intermediaries to carry its competitors' products.

Tying contract: A situation in which a producer sells one product on the condition that the customer also buy another product from the same producer.

Exclusive territories: A situation in which a producer requires intermediaries to sell only to customers in certain territories.

Sherman Act: An antitrust law passed in 1890 that outlaws price fixing and certain other monopolistic practices.

Price fixing: An agreement among competing firms to hold prices above some minimum level.

Vertical price fixing: An agreement between a producer and retailers of its products to hold prices above some minimum level.

Consumers' best protection is competition among producers and brands. © Freda Leinwand

- **Dealer selection**. A producer selects its customers and will not sell to some intermediaries. (The maker of Osh Kosh overalls might decide to sell only through department stores and not allow Kids "R" Us to carry its products.)
- **Exclusive dealing**. A producer does not allow intermediaries to carry its competitors' products. (Volkswagen of America might tell its dealers that they cannot sell Japanese cars.)
- **Tying contract**. A producer sells one product (for example, a computer) on the condition that the customer also buy another product (such as computer paper) from the same producer.
- **Exclusive territories**. A producer requires intermediaries to sell only to customers in certain territories. (RCA might tell its dealers in St. Paul that they cannot sell to customers from Minneapolis.)

None of these tactics is illegal in every case. For example, small firms that are trying to break into a certain market can sometimes get away with them when large, established firms could not. But none of these control tactics should be used without legal advice.

Vertical Price Fixing

Under the **Sherman Act** of 1890, competing firms may not agree to hold prices above some minimum level. Such agreements are known as **price fixing**. The ban on price fixing is viewed as the cornerstone of antitrust law and is strongly enforced.

Vertical price fixing—that is, price agreements between a producer and retailers of its products—also is illegal in many cases. Restraints on vertical price fixing make it hard for producers to prevent discount retailers from cutting their prices below the producer's recommended price. For many producers this is no problem. They see discount retailers as a successful way of getting their goods to consumers. Discounting does cause problems, however, for producers that favor a full-service distribution strategy.

Suppose that a maker of top-quality stereo speakers wants to sell through hi-fi showrooms where models are set up and salespeople demonstrate and explain them to customers. Such showrooms are costly. A store can afford them only if it charges high prices. But what if people can come into the full-service showroom, watch the demonstration, and then go down the street and buy the same brand of speaker off the shelf at a discount store? The full-service store might be forced out of business, and then the discounter would be the dealer's only outlet. Consumers would no longer be able to choose between sellers with different distribution strategies, and they would no longer have the choice of buying from a full-service store if they thought it was worth the price.

Recent Trends

The laws that we have just discussed have been subject to much criticism in recent years. Economists have concluded that in some cases they are not needed to protect consumers—for example, consumers are protected against being charged overly high prices by full-service retailers because not all producers want to be limited to full-service channels. In other cases, economists are concerned that the law has harmed consumers by banning cost-effective methods of distribution—for example, preventing chain stores from passing on the savings achieved by avoiding some kinds of intermediaries.[6] The best protection for consumers, they say, is competition between separate producers and brands. In markets where a number of producers compete, each of them should be allowed to distribute its products in whatever way it thinks will best serve the customer.

Over time, antitrust officials at the Federal Trade Commission and the antitrust division of the Department of Justice have come to agree with the critics. As mentioned earlier, the government has largely stopped enforcing the Robinson-Patman Act. Beginning in 1981, the Justice Department and the Federal Trade Commission have also backed away from enforcing restraints on vertical price fixing and channel control. Even so, all of these laws remain on the books. The government no longer brings cases under them, but private lawsuits can still arise. Managers of distribution systems must be aware of these laws.

SUMMARY

1. An *intermediary* is a firm that provides distribution services for firms that choose not to deal directly with users of their products. The three main types of intermediaries are *retailers*, *wholesalers*, and *physical distributors*.

2. *Coverage*, *cost*, and *control* are the "three Cs" of distribution strategy. The role of each of these factors in planning a distribution strategy depends on the nature of the product and the target market.

3. A *distribution channel* is a series of firms that take part in buying or selling a good as it moves from the producer to the user. Both *merchant* and *agent* intermediaries are included in the channel. Intermediaries that provide only physical-distribution services, such as truck lines, are not included. Distribution channels can be classified by the number of intermediaries they contain.

4. It is important for members of a distribution channel to work as a team. Conflicts can arise from a tug-of-war over profits, from different views of customer needs, or from different management styles. A strong *channel captain* can often control such conflicts. In some cases it is worthwhile to set up a *vertically integrated marketing channel*.

5. Wholesalers are intermediaries that sell to retailers, industrial customers, or other wholesalers. For producers, they provide sales services, information services, physical-distribution services, and risk bear-

ing. For retailers, they provide purchasing services, information services, credit services, and physical-distribution services.

6. Retailers are intermediaries that sell directly to consumers. They include both retail stores and nonstore retailing methods like vending machines and catalog sales. Retailers range from *department stores* that carry many lines of goods to specialty shops that carry only a few. They also range from high-price, full-service stores to *discounters* and *off-price retailers*.

7. Physical distribution includes all the activities required to move goods from the producer to the customer. The quality of physical distribution is measured in terms of availability of products, accuracy in filling orders, speed, and dependability. The functions of physical distribution include order processing, inventory management, packaging and materials handling, and transportation.

8. In the *total-cost approach* to distribution managers consider all costs at the same time and look for ways to trade off one against another. For example, the extra cost of air freight may be justified by a reduced need for warehouses. The costs of physical distribution must also be balanced against other marketing goals, such as price and service quality.

9. There are a number of legal constraints on the design and operation of distribution systems. The *Robinson-Patman Act* of 1936 tried to slow the growth

[6]For a discussion of these issues see Robert H. Bork, *The Antitrust Paradox* (New York: Basic Books, 1978), especially chaps. 14 and 15, and F. M. Scherer, *Industrial Market Structure and Economic Performance*, 2nd ed. (Chicago: Rand McNally, 1980), chap. 21.

of chain stores by outlawing price discrimination. The *Clayton Act* of 1914 outlaws certain channel control techniques, such as *dealer selection*, *exclusive dealing*, *tying contracts*, and *exclusive territories*, when those techniques are used to limit competition. The *Sher-man Act* of 1890 has been interpreted as banning *vertical price fixing*. Government antitrust authorities have begun to enforce some of these laws less strictly, but they remain on the books.

KEY TERMS

You should be familiar with the following terms and concepts. Check their meanings by referring to the marginal definitions in the chapter or to the glossary at the end of the book.

Intermediary

Retailing

Wholesaling

Physical distribution

Middleman

Distribution channel

Merchant

Agent

Broker

Channel captain

Vertically integrated marketing channel (VIMC)

Sales branch

Sales office

Department store

Discount store

Off-price retailer

Inventory

Carrying costs

Intermodal transportation

Containerization

Robinson-Patman Act

Clayton Act

Dealer selection

Exclusive dealing

Tying contract

Exclusive territories

Sherman Act

Price fixing

Vertical price fixing

QUESTIONS FOR REVIEW AND DISCUSSION

1. Has your feeling about "middlemen" changed as a result of reading this chapter? When are consumers justified in disliking intermediaries? When are they not?

2. List some goods that are sold using a strategy of intensive coverage. What are some that are sold through exclusive outlets? What outlets are used in each case? What aspects of the product or the target market make each strategy suitable? How does the choice of intensive versus exclusive coverage interact with issues of cost and control?

3. The text focuses mainly on distribution channels for goods. What about channels for services? Describe the channels for some consumer services that you use, such as haircuts, movies, and insurance.

4. Review the discussion of franchising in Chapter 4. In the light of what you have learned in this chapter, what are the advantages of franchising as a distribution strategy?

5. The text discusses wholesalers and retailers as distinct categories. In practice, however, many intermediaries do some wholesaling and some retailing. Look in the Yellow Pages for your city or a good-sized city near you. Can you find some firms that advertise both wholesale and retail sales? Try plumbing supplies, auto parts, and office equipment for a start. Can you find others?

6. Real estate brokers are a special type of intermediary. What services do they supply to buyers? To sellers? Are they agent or merchant intermediaries? What similarities and differences to you see between real estate brokers and other kinds of intermediaries? Do you think real estate brokers could be thought of as market captains?

7. Using the map in Box 10–6 as a framework, classify a dozen retailers in your area. Where do they belong on the map?

8. Discuss the problems of inventory management faced by your campus bookstore. How does it forecast demand? How does it process orders? Is it ever out of titles that you want? If so, why do you think it does not carry a large enough inventory to be sure it is never out of stock?

9. Comment on dealer selection, exclusive dealing, tying contracts, and exclusive territories in terms of fairness. When might wholesalers or retailers find these practices unfair? When might they be unfair to consumers? At present these practices are sometimes permitted but often banned. Do you think they should be more widely permitted? More strictly forbidden? Why or why not?

Case 10–1: Off-Price Retailing Means Tough Choices for Producers

The choices that off-price retailing offers consumers are welcome ones, but they are not always so welcome to producers of brand-name clothing. According to *Fortune* Magazine, the problem is that the department stores on which brand-name producers depend do not like to deal with those who sell to off-pricers. And the department stores have a powerful weapon. After all, says *Fortune*, the attraction of off-price retailing depends on the item's being sold *on*-price somewhere else. Brands that are found only off-price soon lose their appeal. As one department store manager put it, "We're not going to hold up price umbrellas for brands that are being discounted every day."

The producers, says *Fortune*, "clearly have some tough choices. They can sell only to department stores and thus maintain the long-term respectability of their brands, at the cost of profits and growth. Or they can do business with off-price establishments, risk the wrath of department stores, and reap sales and profit growth for the short term. Or they can try to develop different labels for different distribution channels. The problem with this last strategy is that most off-pricers are only interested in the labels they see in department stores."

Fortune cites Levi Strauss as a company facing this problem. A few years ago a falling share of department store sales led Levi to start selling to Sears and J. C. Penney. Fortune reports that "some department stores were furious and cut way back on their orders. But Levi doesn't regret moving to the mass merchandisers. 'We had to take action,' says [Levi vice-president James] McDermott. At the same time, he says, Levi is 'doing everything we can' to get that department store business back. That includes personal visits by corporate honchos and the extension of loans to help a department store pay for Levi's inventory. Of its 14 major accounts, all but Macy's have increased their orders."

The problem will be worse, *Fortune* thinks, for high-volume brand-name producers like Levi. Limited-line producers have all the business they can handle selling to department stores when one of their high-fashion items catches on. At the other end of the scale, "plain vanilla" labels like Arrow shirts, which don't have much fashion status in any case, have little to lose by selling to the off-pricers.

Source: Based on Ann M. Morrison, "The Upshot of Off-Price," *FORTUNE*, June 13, 1983, pp. 122–30. Reprinted by permission from FORTUNE Magazine.

Questions:

1. Off-price retailing, as discussed in this article, raises some questions of fairness. Is it fair for department stores to drop producers that sell to off-pricers? Who is hurt when this happens? Are the

Case 10–1: Off-Price Retailing Means Tough Choices for Producers

long- and short-run effects the same? Is it fair for off-price stores to take a "free ride" on brand names in which producers and department stores have invested large promotional budgets? Do you think this practice might be self-defeating in the long run?

2. The Justice Department favors legalization of vertical price fixing. Producers could then use minimum retail prices as a weapon to prevent discounting. Do you think this tactic would work? Do you think it would be fair to consumers? What protection would consumers have against abuse of this practice? Do you think all producers would use it, or just some? Which kinds of retailers would be most likely to use it? Do you think department stores could force producers to use minimum retail pricing?

3. Levi's conflict with department stores over sales to Sears and J. C. Penney raises some issues of cost and control. Describe the conflict. Judging from the information given in this case, do you think there is a clear captain in Levi's distribution channels? If so, who is it? Can conflicts between members of a channel be avoided if there is a clear channel captain? Even when there is not a clear captain?

Case 10–2: Super Valu Does Two Things Well

"We want to make people rich," says Michael Wright, and he seems to mean it. Wright, 44, is president and chairman of Super Valu Stores Inc., the nation's largest grocery wholesaler, headquartered in the Minneapolis suburb of Eden Prairie. The people he is referring to are supermarket operators. And in that glamourless business, some do get rich.

Super Valu does two things very well, and one of them is help people run supermarkets. If you're a Super Valu kind of person—some retail experience, entrepreneurial aggressiveness, a few bucks tucked away—the company can have you knocking heads with the chains in no time. Super Valu can find the site, design the store, finance the equipment, set the shelves, train the butchers and clerks, plan the promotions, write the advertising, count the money, and insure the whole works, bologna to bagboy.

Santa Claus in a grocer's apron Wright is not. The more food he can get Super Valu's 2300 affiliated stores to sell to the public, the more Super Valu can sell to them. Wholesale groceries account for more than 85 percent of the company's sales and earnings. For the fiscal year that ended in February, total sales came to around $5.2 billion and net earnings to $68 million.

The other thing Super Valu does very well is operate warehouses. It has 16 of them, and their efficiency gives the company a competitive edge. With both its special proficiencies going for it, Super Valu has been thriving. Since 1977 its wholesale food sales have doubled in real terms.

Super Valu's success comes partly from its ability to tip economies of scale in its retailers' favor without burdening them with the overhead of a large corporation. The retailers it serves have no national marketing plan, no single image, no vertical integration, and generally no problem making a living.

For its independent retailers, Super Valu is the great equalizer. It has made a religion of giving them advantages only chains are supposed to have: low prices, up-to-date stores, good locations, and sophisticated operations systems. Put independents on an equal footing with the chains, says Michael Wright, and usually they'll "do a superior job."

Intense competition has prompted integrated retailers to take a second look at their warehouse investments. Last October, Super Valu purchased a warehouse in Omaha from Cullum Companies, which operates the 40-outlet Hinky Dinky supermarkets in that city. Cullum still runs the stores, but Super Valu is now the supplier. Says Cullum controller James Stiles, "Super Valu, in effect, could lay product into our store as cheaply as we could, or even more cheaply."

Source: Bill Saporito, "Super Valu Does Two Things Well," *FORTUNE*, April 18, 1983, pp. 114–18. Reprinted by permission from FORTUNE Magazine.

Questions:

1. Comment on Super Valu's success in terms of the services provided by wholesalers to retailers.
2. What does it mean to call Super Valu a channel captain? What advantages does Super Valu have over the vertical distribution systems of retailers like Safeway or A&P? What disadvantages, if any?
3. In the early years of supermarkets, A&P sometimes gained big cost savings by bypassing wholesalers. According to this case, however, Cullum Companies decided to add an extra level to its distribution channel by bringing in Super Valu. Why?
4. What is the part played by physical distribution in Super Valu's success?
5. What are Super Valu's net earnings (profits) as a percentage of sales? What does this suggest to you about the role of "middlemen" in raising the retail cost of food?

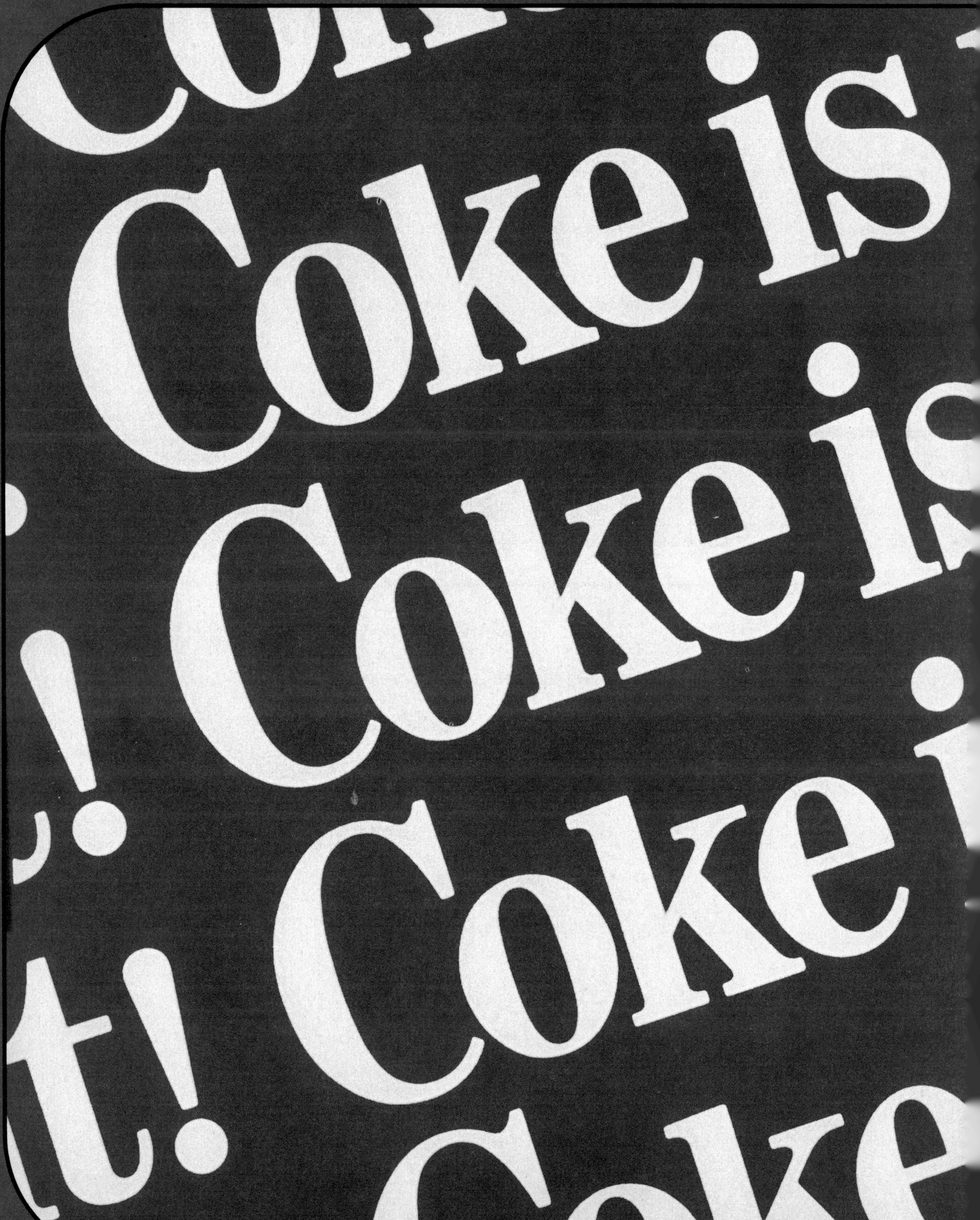
Coke is
Coke is
t! Coke
Coke

Chapter 11
PROMOTION

When you have completed this chapter, you should be able to

- Outline the planning of a *promotional strategy* in terms of what to say, how to say it, and whom to say it to.

- Explain how promotion affects each step of buyer behavior—problem recognition, information seeking, evaluation of alternatives, the purchase decision, and postpurchase evaluation.

- Define *push* and *pull* tactics and give examples of each.

- Discuss several kinds of *advertising messages* and *media*.

- List the four tasks in *personal selling*.

- Give examples of *sales promotions* and their uses.

- Explain how *public relations* is related to *publicity*.

- Discuss legal limits on promotional tactics and the ethics of advertising and other forms of promotion.

The sweetest direct mail campaign in years netted a phenomenal 100 percent response rate for American Telecom Inc. (ATI) of Anaheim, California.

The supplier of telecommunications equipment has been in business for years, but its low profile has not exactly made it a household word in the industry. So when ATI decided to set up a network of independent distributors for its new Elite Focus private access branch exchange (PABX), it needed a calling card that would make distributors sit up and take notice.

Enter Ralph Lenac, president, Lenac, Warford, Stone, Inc., advertising and public relations, of Newport Beach, California.

"Tons of garbage arrive every day on the desks of these dealers, so the question was how we could get them to notice our direct mail piece," Lenac recalled.

"I remembered reading about a retail outlet that specialized in producing chocolate forms of various types, and I thought it would be nice if they could produce a chocolate telephone for us so we could offer a sweet deal to these dealers."

The chocolate telephone was born. Although the mailing cost an average of $50 per piece, compared to an average cost of $3.50 each for telegrams and other traditional mail campaign pieces, the unheard-of response rate more than offset the additional cost.

The three-and-one-half-pound solid milk chocolate phone was crated in a wooden box with labeling reminiscent of a Hershey's chocolate bar. Inside the box was a sample of the distribution contract ATI was offering, introductory literature about ATI, and the business card of the regional sales manager.

"When our guy called, the reaction was, 'Oh, yes, you're the guy who sent us the chocolate telephone. Let's talk,'" Lenac said.

The chocolate phones were sent to 279 independent dealers of communications equipment, he said, and all of them expressed interest in handling the Focus Elite line. ATI was in the enviable position of being able to pick and choose which of the dealers would form its network of sixty distributors in six regions throughout the country.

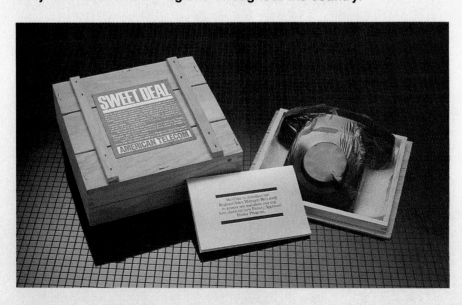

American Telecom Inc.'s chocolate telephone was a highly effective promotional device. Courtesy of American Telecom, Anaheim, Ca.

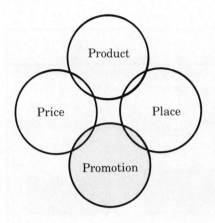

Promotion: The process of telling consumers about a product and getting them to buy it.

"**Fifty dollars is a lot to spend on a direct mail piece**," said Lenac, "**but in comparison to what ATI got out of it, they were very happy. In a sea of white golf balls, we were the red one.**"[1]

[1]"Sweet Sell Garners 100 Percent Response for Phone Equipment Manufacturer," *Marketing News*, April 1, 1983, p. 3. Reprinted by permission *Marketing News*, author or editor, March 5, 1983, p. 5, and the American Marketing Association.

ATI had a marketing problem—but what kind? As far as we know, its product was a good one. It seems that the company needed to improve its distribution system. But before it could do so it had to solve another problem: the name ATI was not well enough known. The company had a problem with *promotion*, the third of the four Ps.

Promotion means telling consumers about a product and getting them to buy it. It is a form of communication—of informing and persuading. We will begin this chapter by making some points about the goals and methods of promotion. Next we will look at four major promotional tools. The chapter will end with a short section on legal and ethical issues.

PLANNING A PROMOTIONAL STRATEGY

Promotional strategy: A plan that states what the content of a promotional message will be, how it will be delivered, and whom it will be delivered to.

Planning a **promotional strategy** means deciding what to say, how to say it, and whom to say it to. What you say depends on what kind of effect you want to have on buyer behavior. How you say it depends on the nature of the target market and on how customers can best be reached. And to whom promotion is directed—consumers or intermediaries—depends on the distribution channel. All three parts of the promotional strategy also depend on the nature of the product. Let's look at each of these decisions—what, how, and who—in turn.

What: Promotional Goals and Buyer Behavior

The goal of all forms of promotion is to affect buyer behavior. In Chapter 8 we broke buyer behavior down into five steps: problem recognition, information seeking, evaluation of alternatives, the purchase decision, and postpurchase evaluation. What you choose to say when you promote a product depends on which step of buyer behavior you want to affect. Each step is an opportunity for promotion, as shown in Box 11–1.

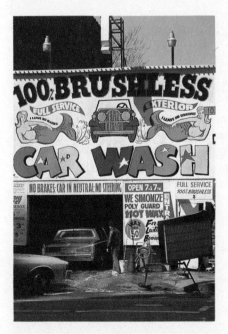

At the problem recognition stage of buyer behavior, the main goal of promotion is to get attention. Marc P. Anderson

- *Getting attention.* At the problem recognition stage, the goal is to get attention. The promoter wants to make buyers aware that they have a need and that a product exists that can meet that need. The message at this stage is, "Hey, look at us!"
- *Supplying information.* The goal at the information-seeking stage is to give buyers facts on price, place of sale, product features, and so on. Catalogs, sales representatives, and product reviews in magazines are examples of promotion with this goal. At this stage the message is, "Everything you ever wanted to know about X."
- *Creating a preference.* When the buyer is looking at alternatives, the seller's goal is to create a preference for the seller's product. The

Box 11–1 Promotion and Buyer Behavior

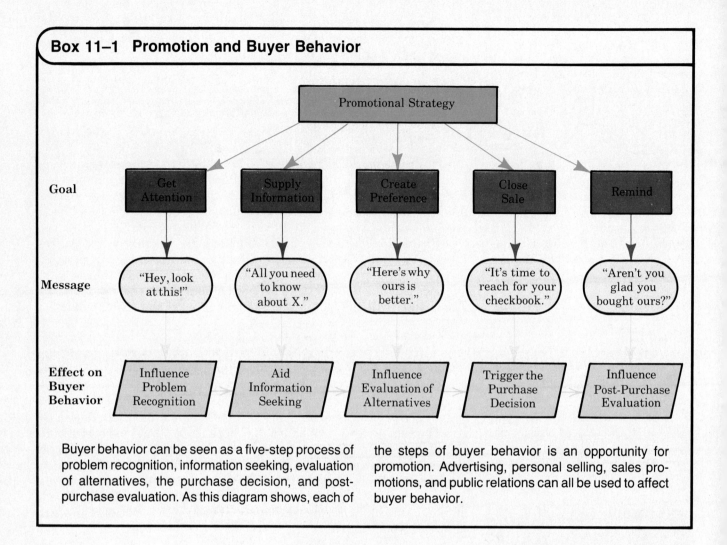

Buyer behavior can be seen as a five-step process of problem recognition, information seeking, evaluation of alternatives, the purchase decision, and post-purchase evaluation. As this diagram shows, each of the steps of buyer behavior is an opportunity for promotion. Advertising, personal selling, sales promotions, and public relations can all be used to affect buyer behavior.

promotion attempts to move the seller's product up to the top of the buyer's list of alternatives. The message is, "Here's why ours is better."

- *Closing the sale.* As the purchase decision draws near, the goal is to close the sale. This means turning preference into action. At this stage the message is, "It's time to reach for your checkbook."
- *Reminding.* During the postpurchase evaluation, the goal is to remind the buyer of the product's virtues. The message is, "Aren't you glad you bought ours?"

How: Communication Methods

Just as there are many choices of what to say, there are many choices of how to say it. A promotional strategy can make use of one or more ways of communicating with buyers.

- **Advertising** is the delivery of a paid promotional message to a large number of potential customers through a public communications medium such as television, magazines, or billboards. It is a

Advertising: The delivery of a paid promotional message to a large number of potential customers though a public communications medium such as television, magazines, or billboards.

Personal selling: A promotional presentation made directly to a potential customer, usually in a face-to-face meeting.

Sales promotion: The use of short-term incentives, such as store displays, special discounts, or coupons, to boost sales of a product.

Public relations: A planned effort to create a good image of a product or firm by some means other than paid advertising.

Promotional mix: The mix of advertising, personal selling, sales promotions, and public relations used to promote a product.

nonpersonal form of selling. It does not require face-to-face contact, and the message is not directed at any one customer.

- **Personal selling** is a promotional presentation made directly to a potential customer, usually in a face-to-face meeting.
- **Sales promotion** is the use of short-term incentives, such as store displays, special discounts, or coupons, to boost sales of a product.
- **Public relations** is a planned effort to create a good image of a product or firm by some means other than paid advertising. It includes getting the right kind of attention in news media, meeting with opinion leaders, making speeches, and the like.

The use of one of these methods does not preclude the use of any of the others. They are most effective when they are combined. For example, an advertising campaign can make consumers aware of a brand; this in turn makes personal selling easier. The blend of methods used to promote a product is known as the **promotional mix**.

Who: Push versus Pull

To whom should the message go? Each member of the distribution channel deserves some attention in a balanced promotional strategy. Depending on the member at which promotion is aimed, the strategy can be described as either "push" or "pull."

Pull: Any promotional effort aimed at consumers.

Pull.   In the **pull** approach, producers promote to consumers. If the campaign works, consumers will look for the product at their local retailer and ask for it if it is not in stock. The retailers will order the product from wholesalers, and wholesalers will demand it from producers. In this way the product will be "pulled" through the distribution channel.

Advertising is well suited to the pull approach. Through advertising, a producer can reach millions of consumers without knowing exactly who they are.

Push: Any promotional effort aimed at wholesalers or retailers in the distribution channel.

Push.   In the **push** approach, promotion is aimed at wholesalers or retailers in the distribution channel. They, in turn, promote the product to consumers. Personal selling is viewed as the best way of pushing a product. Ads in trade journals that are read by wholesalers and retailers can also be used. So can sales promotions such as dealer allowances.

Some producers use only the pull approach. Direct sales via TV ads are an example. Others use only push techniques. For example, a maker of paper goods sold as house brands would not promote to the public. But for most goods and services it is common to use pull and push tactics together. Box 11–2 shows how push and pull techniques can be combined in a two-level channel.

Balancing the Marketing Mix

No matter how well thought out it is, a promotional strategy cannot stand by itself. The message it sends to consumers must blend with those sent by other parts of the marketing mix. In Chapter 9 we saw how promotion interacts with product design, branding, and packaging to position a product in the minds of consumers. Choices of distribution channels—

Box 11–2 Push and Pull Techniques

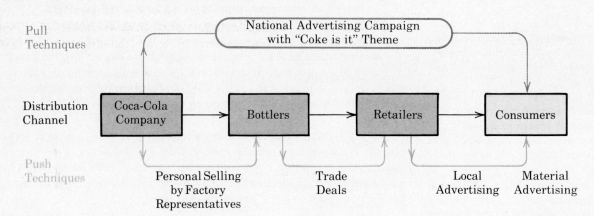

In 1982 and 1983 the Coca-Cola Company brought out some new products, including Diet Coke and caffeine-free versions of Coke, Diet Coke, and Tab. To promote these products the firm used a combination of pull and push strategies. The pull was supplied by a national advertising campaign based on the slogan "Coke is it." Factory salespeople coached bottlers, who are franchisees, on the advantages of the new products. The bottlers, in turn, blitzed retailers with "trade deals"—a mixture of limited-time discounts and reduced prices for volume purchases. Retailers followed up the national campaign with local ads of their own in which the discount-priced Coke products were featured.

boutiques versus discounters, exclusive coverage versus intensive coverage—also interact with the choice of a promotional strategy. And as we will see in Chapter 12, pricing and promotion affect each other too.

Box 11–3 gives an overview of promotional strategy in relation to other parts of the marketing mix. It should be kept in mind as we take a more detailed look at the major forms of promotion.

ADVERTISING

I don't know who you are.
I don't know your company.
I don't know your company's product.
I don't know what your company stands for.
I don't know your company's customers.
I don't know your company's record.
I don't know your company's reputation.
Now—what was it you wanted to sell me?

—Text of a McGraw-Hill ad soliciting advertising in business publications.

Advertising, the delivery of paid promotional messages to a broad public, is the most familiar of all marketing activities. Total spending on advertising is surprisingly small, however. As Box 11–4 shows, it amounts to only about 3 percent of all consumer spending. That compares with about 14 percent for freight transportation, 26 percent for costs and profits of wholesale and retail trade, and about 50 percent for all marketing costs combined.

Even for the largest advertisers, the amount spent on advertising is a small percentage of sales. Box 11–5 lists the ten leading advertisers in the United States. None of them spends more than 7 percent of sales on advertising. The average for these top ten is less than 2 percent of sales.

But even though advertising isn't the biggest item of marketing costs, it is an important one. For many producers, it is the only way of getting in touch with consumers. It also plays a big role in positioning products. And it is flexible. Creating a new product, building a distribution channel, and training a sales force are time-consuming and involve long-term commit-

Box 11–3 Promotion as Part of the Marketing Mix

What?	How?	To Whom?
Get Attention Supply Information Create Preference Close Sale Remind	Advertising Personal Selling Sales Promotions Public Relations	Consumers (pull) Intermediaries (push)

Product   Distribution   Promotion   Price

Marketing Mix

A promotional strategy is a plan that tells what message will be sent, how it will be sent, and to whom it will be sent. What message to send depends on the goal—to get attention, supply information, create a preference, close a sale, or remind. Methods for sending the message include advertising, personal selling, sales promotions, and public relations. The mix of methods chosen is known as the promotional mix. The message can be sent to consumers in order to "pull" the product through the distribution channel. Or it can be sent to intermediaries in order to "push" it through. The promotional strategy must fit well with the other parts of the marketing mix—product, distribution, and price.

ments. Advertising campaigns are much more flexible. They can be turned on and off, and they can be changed to fit changing conditions.

In the rest of this section we will look at three aspects of advertising. First, we will look at the kinds of messages that advertising carries. Second, we will discuss the strengths and weaknesses of television, radio, magazines, and other media for carrying ads. Finally, we will look briefly at the role of advertising agencies, which are intermediaries in the advertising market.

The Message

Product-specific advertising: Advertising that tells potential buyers about the virtues of a specific brand or product.

Product-specific advertising is the most common kind. As the name implies, it tells buyers about the virtues of a specific brand or product. Ads for RC Cola, Perdue chicken, or Zenith television sets are examples.

Box 11–4   Marketing Costs in Relation to Consumer Spending

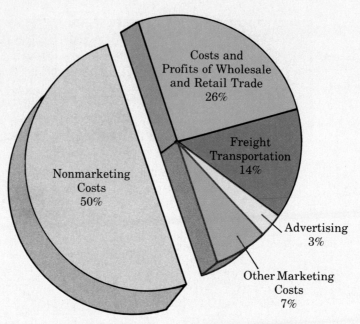

Costs and
Profits of Wholesale
and Retail Trade
26%

Freight
Transportation
14%

Nonmarketing
Costs
50%

Advertising
3%

Other Marketing
Costs
7%

This chart shows how marketing costs compare with total consumer spending in the United States. Marketing costs as a whole account for about half of all consumer spending. The costs and profits of wholesale and retail trade account for about half of this. Freight transportation takes another 14 percent. Total advertising costs equal only about 3 percent of consumer spending.

Box 11–5   The Top Ten U.S. Advertisers

Company	Advertising Expenditures (millions)	Advertising as Percent of Sales
1. Procter & Gamble	$726.1	5.8
2. Sears, Roebuck & Co.	631.2	2.1
3. General Motors Corp.	549.0	0.9
4. R. J. Reynolds Industries	530.3	4.1
5. Phillip Morris, Inc.	501.7	4.3
6. General Foods Corp.	429.1	5.2
7. AT&T Co.	373.6	0.6
8. K mart Corp.	365.3	2.2
9. Nabisco Brands	335.2	5.7
10. American Home Products	325.4	7.1

This table lists the top ten advertisers in the United States in 1981. None of them spends more than 7 percent of its sales on advertising. The average for the ten is less than 1.5 percent.

Source: *Advertising Age*, "100 Leaders Spend 14 Percent More," September 8, 1983, p. 1 and 167. Reprinted with permission from the September 1983 issue of Advertising Age. Copyright 1983 by Crain Communications, Inc.

Comparative advertising: Advertising that mentions competing brands by name.

Direct-action advertising: Advertising that aims to close a sale.

Institutional advertising: Advertising that promotes the virtues of a firm rather than any of its products.

Primary advertising Advertising, usually by a trade association, that promotes a certain type of product rather than a specific brand.

Public service advertising: Advertising that aims to change consumer behavior in a beneficial way, for example, by promoting the use of auto seatbelts.

A closer look at the message in product-specific ads would show that many of them aim to affect a certain aspect of buyer behavior. Some aim simply to get attention and build awareness. Others supply information. Many try to affect the buyer's evaluation of alternatives. **Comparative advertising**, in which competing brands are mentioned by name, falls into this category. So do ads that try to link a product with a certain image or life-style. Another kind of ad aims to close a sale with a coupon, an order form, or some other device. This is called **direct-action advertising**.

But not all ads are product specific. Some, known as **institutional advertising**, promote the virtues of the firm rather than any of its products. The idea is that people won't buy your product unless they know who you are. Often a firm tries to portray itself as a good citizen. Mobil Corporation has sponsored the *Masterpiece Theater* program on public television in order to show its interest in the arts.

Another kind of advertising promotes a certain type of product, such as milk or lemons, rather than a specific brand. This is known as **primary advertising**. Finally, **public service advertising** is used by government

The American Cancer Society's anti-smoking ads are an example of public-service advertising. Courtesy of the American Cancer Society

units and not-for-profit firms to change consumer behavior in a beneficial way. Examples are ads with the "Buckle up for safety" theme that promote the use of auto seatbelts, and antismoking ads with the theme "It's a matter of life and breath."

The Media

Advertising medium (plural **media**): Any means of bringing an advertising message to the public.

An **advertising medium** (the plural is *media*) is any means of bringing an advertising message to the public. Box 11–6 shows how much is spent on advertising in various media. Newspapers and television together account for almost half of all advertising in the United States. (Television is dominant in national advertising, newspapers in local advertising.) Direct mail, radio, and magazines follow, in that order. Outdoor advertising accounts for only 1 percent.

Intrusiveness: The degree to which consumers cannot avoid seeing or hearing an advertisement.

Each of these media has its strengths and weaknesses. Some offer the advantage of **intrusiveness**, meaning that consumers can't avoid seeing or hearing the ad. Others are flexible, making it possible to reach a target market defined in terms of income, region, or occupation. Some have the virtue of being cheap. Some are good at closing sales. But no one medium is perfect for all purposes.

Box 11–6 Spending on Advertising in Various Media

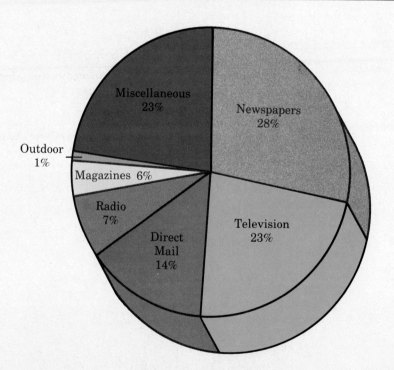

This chart shows the amounts spent on advertising in various media in the United States in 1982. Newspapers and television are the leaders. They carry about half of all advertising. TV dominates for national ads, newspapers for local advertising. Direct mail, radio, and magazines follow, in that order.

Source: *Statistical Abstract of the United States*, 104th ed. (Washington, D.C.: Government Printing Office, 1983), Table 968.

Newspapers.   More is spent on newspaper advertising than on any other form. The great virtue of newspaper advertising is flexibility. Stores can advertise products and sales promotions; national companies can use newspapers for test-marketing; small firms can reach their limited customer pool. Newspaper advertising also is not very expensive. Its cost per thousand people reached, or **CPM**, is moderate, and the ads do not cost much to prepare. Newspapers are also a good way of distributing coupons. But they are not very intrusive. Many ads go unseen or unread even by people who buy the paper. Other disadvantages include the inability to reach a national audience (at least until the advent of the national paper *USA Today*) and poor-quality color reproduction.

CPM: The cost of an advertisement per thousand people reached.

Television.   TV is a close second to newspapers in total ad spending and ranks first for national advertising. TV commercials are the most intrusive of all ads; it is hard to tune them out.[*] TV also is the best medium for product demonstrations, and it is very flexible. Ads can be run nationwide through the networks, or only on local stations. A wide range of programs, each of which appeals to its own target audience, further increases the flexibility of this medium. Coupons cannot be given out on TV, but the use of toll-free phone numbers works almost as well for direct-action ads. Although a thirty-second ad on *60 Minutes* or the Super Bowl may cost more than $100,000, the CPM of TV advertising is not high because so many people watch those programs. TV ads are expensive to prepare, however.

Direct mail.   Direct mail, the third most popular medium, is in some ways the most flexible of all. Mailing lists can be tailored to almost any occupation, age, or interest group. Mailings can be made to specific areas that are full of rich people, minorities, or apartment dwellers. When an organization like Greenpeace wants to get in touch with high-income whale lovers with liberal political views, nothing beats direct mail. The use of coupons and postage-paid envelopes makes this medium good for direct action. There are some limits to direct mail, though. Its CPM is

Direct mail is a popular advertising medium, but some people receive so much of this "junk mail" that they throw it away unopened. © Freda Leinwand

[*]Advertisers are very nervous about the practice of "zapping," in which the viewer uses a remote-control device or a video recorder to delete commercials when watching a program.

higher than that for any other medium, although the ability to fine-tune the target audience helps offset this. Direct mail also ranks low in intrusiveness. Many people treat it as "junk" to be thrown away unopened.

Radio. Radio is the fourth most popular advertising medium. It is nearly as intrusive as TV. It is among the cheapest forms of advertising in terms of both CPM and preparation costs. Like TV, it is flexible. Radio even reaches some people who never watch TV. Phone numbers included in radio ads draw good direct-action response. The greatest drawback of radio is that it cannot carry a picture. It can't imprint the image of a package on the listener's mind, and it does not work for most kinds of product demonstrations.

Magazines. Magazines are the fifth most popular medium. They are highly flexible. National magazines like *Newsweek* and *Time* are printed at a number of locations, so that both local and regional ads are possible. Regional magazines like *Sunset* and city magazines like *Washingtonian* have grown rapidly in recent years. And of course, magazines geared to special audiences—radio amateurs, dentists, joggers—offer unique opportunities for producers of specialty goods. Magazines offer the highest-quality color reproduction. They are also the favored medium for cigarette and liquor ads, which are banned from TV. Magazine advertising is fairly expensive, however, and not very intrusive. Buying cover pages or foldouts increases intrusiveness, but at a high cost.

City magazines have become very popular in recent years and are an attractive medium for some kinds of advertising. © Freda Leinwand

"It may be blight, but it's high-class blight."

Other media. Other media, including outdoor media, account for 24 percent of all ad spending. Billboards, posters, and transit ads present printed messages. Point-of-purchase posters and displays help get attention and close sales. Telephone calls direct to consumers rate high in intrusiveness (and consumer annoyance!). Display booths, street sampling, package inserts, and even blimps have their uses.

Advertising Agencies

Advertising agency: A firm that can be hired to create advertising messages and buy media services.

Some companies and not-for-profit firms prepare and buy all their own advertising, but many others use **advertising agencies**. These agencies create advertising messages and buy media services. Some can plan a firm's whole marketing strategy, not just the part of it devoted to advertising. Agencies can also pretest and evaluate an advertising campaign.

Many of the best-known advertising agencies are located along Madison Avenue in New York. "Madison Avenue" thus has become a synonym for the world of advertising. At least ten agencies handle a billion dollars or more of advertising a year.

PERSONAL SELLING

Personal selling is promotion that occurs in a face-to-face meeting with the customer. It far outweighs advertising in terms of total spending. For most firms, personal-selling costs tend to run three to five times the amount spent on ads. More than 6 million Americans hold sales jobs, compared with less than half a million in all advertising agencies combined.

Organizations of all kinds, not just businesses, engage in personal selling. Officials of the Nature Conservancy (see Box 8–2, page 189) change from hiking clothes to three-piece suits to sell the idea of conserva-

Saint Paul the Apostle could be considered one of the greatest salespeople in history. The Granger Collection

tion. Universities send recruiters to sell their schools to budding football players and scholastic achievers. Political candidates, even in the TV age, must "press the flesh." And Saint Paul the Apostle surely was one of history's greatest salespeople.

Personal selling is important for another reason too: it is a first-rate career opportunity. Openings are plentiful, and there are few better ways to get to know a company's product and its users. Firms that succeed in staying close to their customers see a personal-selling background as useful in almost any job, from receptionist to researcher.

The Salesperson's Job

When people are asked to describe the salesperson's job, they often respond with phrases like "high pressure," "arm twisting," or "fast-talking." This comic strip image—the man with a suitcase full of widgets ringing Dagwood Bumstead's doorbell—has little place in modern marketing. It is left over from the days when production was seen as the main job of management. The sales department's job was to push goods out the door in order to make room for the next batch coming off the assembly line.

In a marketing-oriented firm, the salesperson's job is much more complex. Although promotion is the salesperson's main job, he or she contributes to other marketing functions too. Salespeople, because of their close contact with customers, are a key source of new-product ideas. They are part of the distribution channel; they are as likely to work for intermediaries as for producers. Finally, especially for goods that are custom-made and deals that include trade-ins, salespeople often negotiate with customers over prices. The whole of the salesperson's job should be kept in mind as we take a closer look at the personal-selling process.

The Personal-Selling Process

The heart of personal selling is a face-to-face meeting with the customer. Personal selling begins before that meeting, though, and goes on after it. Whatever you are selling, you need to do four tasks.

Prospecting: The process of locating potential customers.

1. *Homework.* You must do your homework before you go out selling. The first step is to learn as much as you can about what you are selling. The second step is **prospecting**—getting the names, addresses, and phone numbers of potential customers. Once you have a list of customers, the third step is to learn as much as you can about them, their companies, and their needs before you meet them. You may also want to get their attention as ATI did with its chocolate telephone.

2. *The sales presentation.* As you get down to the real selling, your knowledge of buyer behavior comes into play. If you are lucky, you will already have the customer's attention. If your job is one of the few that involves **cold canvassing**—making walk-in presentations with no previous prospecting—you will have to get that attention fast. Your product knowledge will put you in a position to supply information and answer questions. After setting out the facts, you try to persuade the customer to prefer your product over your competitor's.

Cold canvassing: A sales technique in which potential customers are approached without any previous prospecting.

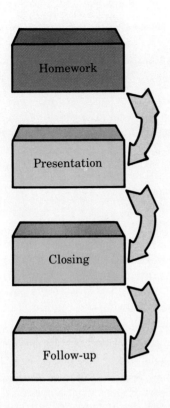

3. *The closing.* Personal selling is better for closing sales than any other promotional method. After making the presentation, you ask for the order. Be ready to answer any questions. If the person to whom you have made the presentation doesn't have the power to make the purchase decision alone, ask to see the other people involved before you go.

4. *Follow-up.* In order to close the sale you may have made some promises. If you have promised quick delivery, a discount, or start-up supplies, make sure you come through. (And make sure you have the authority to do so before you make the promise!) Call back to see how the customer is getting along. Many customers go through a period of doubt just after closing. Your product probably isn't quite as good as your competitor's in at least one way. Remind the customer of the features that led to the decision to buy. If the product is one that needs service, be available as a liaison between the customer and your firm's service staff.

Does it sound as easy as 1-2-3-4? Maybe you have a career in personal selling ahead of you.

Sales Management

Managing a sales force, like other kinds of management, is a matter of planning, organizing, leading, and controlling. We will discuss the management of human resources in detail in Chapters 14 through 16. Much of what we will say there applies to managing a sales force. Three aspects of sales management merit some comment here, however. They are recruitment and training, compensation, and control.

Recruitment and training. There is a long-running debate as to whether good salespeople are made or born, that is, whether training or the recruitment of "natural" salespeople is the key to success. There is evidence that some people are better suited to selling than others. Box 11–7 presents one version of what makes a good salesperson. A well-managed sales program should include some way of screening applicants along these lines.

Even the best natural salespeople cannot just be turned loose with a briefcase full of product samples. They must be trained, both in basic selling skills and in knowledge of the firm's product. Product knowledge is not acquired all at once, either. Products change all the time. Managers must set up channels through which product information can reach the sales force. They must also motivate salespeople to spend time updating their product knowledge.

Compensation. Salespeople are more likely than any other group of employees to have their pay tied to their productivity. According to a survey by Dartnell Corporation, about 21 percent of salespeople are paid solely by commissions, while another 57 percent get a combination of salary and commissions. Only about 22 percent of all salespeople work on straight salary.[2]

---

[2]These figures are cited in John A. Byrne, "Motivating Willy Loman," *Forbes*, January 30, 1984, p. 91.

Box 11–7   What Makes a Good Salesperson?

What makes a good salesperson? Usually not the pushy, loud-mouthed type of comic strip fame. Good salespeople are more likely to be polite and considerate. Height and good looks don't mean instant success either. Instead, according to David Mayer and Herbert M. Greenberg, the keys to success in selling are two traits that they call *empathy* and *ego drive*.

Empathy is the ability to feel what the customer feels. It is different from sympathy. Sympathy means agreeing with the other person's feelings. Empathy means understanding those feelings and taking them into account whether one agrees with them or not. Mayer and Greenberg say that using salespeople who lack empathy is like using the old-fashioned kind of point-and-shoot antiaircraft gun. If the target moves in a straight line, such a gun can score a hit, but if the target changes course, it will miss. A salesperson with empathy is like a modern heat-seeking missile. Such a missile picks up signals from the target that allow it to score a hit even if the target changes its course.

Ego drive is the feeling that the sale has meaning for the salesperson in a way that goes beyond the money to be gained. The salesperson with ego drive

feels that he or she *has* to make the sale; that the customer is there to help meet this personal need. Since any one sales presentation may be a failure, the salesperson's ego cannot be weak. Failure should act as a trigger toward greater effort, which will bring the success on which this personality type feeds.

Both empathy and ego drive are needed. A salesperson with good empathy but low ego drive will be liked by everyone—but all too often will stop one step short of closing the sale. A salesperson with ego drive and little empathy will bulldoze a way through to some sales but will offend many potential customers.

People who lack one or both of these traits may be able to do a good job elsewhere in the firm, but selling is not likely to be their strong point.

Source: David Mayer and Herbert M. Greenberg, "What Makes a Good Salesman," *Harvard Business Review*, July–August 1964, pp. 119–25. Reprinted by permission of the Harvard Business Review. Excerpt from "What makes a good salesman" by Herbert M. Greenberg and David Mayer (July–August 1964). Copyright © 1964 by the President and Fellows of Harvard College. All rights reserved.

Each of these systems has its virtues and its faults. The straight commission plan offers the strongest incentive to sell. It can work well when salespeople have few nonsales duties or are agents rather than employees. Straight commission may not be seen as fair, however, if the firm's sales territories are not all equally fruitful, or if the firm's sales are subject to strong downturns during recessions. The straight salary plan equalizes pay when sales territories are unequal. It may be suitable for trainees and for opening up new territories. Some firms use the straight salary plan when they think "hard-sell" tactics would not fit well with their overall marketing strategy. Digital Equipment Corporation pays its salespeople a straight salary. "That means they are interested in the customer and not in their paychecks," explains DEC's founder Kenneth Olsen.[3] But for most firms the straight salary plan offers too little incentive. That is why mixed compensation schemes are so popular. The salary offers fair compensation for time spent doing homework and nonsales tasks, while bonuses and sales quotas can be fine-tuned to take differences between territories into account.

Control.   Control is the process of comparing planned performance with actual performance, and taking corrective action if necessary. The failure rate in sales jobs is fairly high, although it can be reduced by good recruiting. When a salesperson is not performing up to standards, the sales manager must find out why. More training may be the answer, but not

[3]Ibid.

always. People who do not work out in sales should not just be sent packing. They may do quite well in other jobs. People who start their careers in sales often end up as superior performers elsewhere because their sales experience taught them to stay close to the customer.

SALES PROMOTION

Sales promotion is the use of short-term incentives, such as coupons, store displays, and dealer bonuses, to boost sales. Good data on total spending for sales promotion are hard to come by, but the amount is believed to equal or even exceed the total spent on advertising. What is more, sales promotion is one of the fastest-growing parts of the total promotional budget.

Coupons are a popular and effective form of pull-type sales promotion. © Freda Leinwand

Types of sales promotions. The variety of sales promotions is limited only by the ability of marketers to think up new ones. Like other types of promotion, they can be described as push or pull techniques, depending on their targets.

Pull-type sales promotions are aimed at consumers. *Coupons* offering cents off a product's list price are among the best known of these. They can be given out in stores, on packages, in print ads, or through the mail. *Premiums* are small gifts, such as a toy in a cereal box or dishes given in exchange for proof-of-purchase seals. *Rebates* are checks sent by firms to consumers who show proof of purchase. All of these techniques create a preference for the product and help close sales. Other pull-type sales promotions have the goal of drawing attention to a brand. *Contests* (games of skill), *sweepstakes* (games of chance), and *free samples* are examples. *Demonstrations* in stores serve both to get attention and to supply information.

Push-type sales promotions are aimed at intermediaries. *Sales incentives* are ways of getting the salespeople of agents, wholesalers, or retailers to favor the firm's product. They include sales contests with rewards such as trips to Hawaii, and direct payments to salespeople who work for the intermediary. *Dealer allowances* give retailers a chance to buy at a price below the normal wholesale price in return for setting up point-of-sale displays, window signs, or other sales aids. *Trade show displays* are used to get the attention of dealers and, in some cases, to tell them about the benefits of carrying the firm's product line.

Box 11–8 lists the most common types of sales promotions and shows the aspect of buyer behavior that each tries to influence.

Advantages of sales promotions. Sales promotions would not be so popular if they did not add something to the promotional strategy. They are often used along with advertising to boost brand awareness or counter a rival's move. Premiums to give away—pens, lighters, desk sets—help salespeople get a foot in the door. They also serve as a reminder after the salesperson has gone. Sales promotions can also be combined with pricing policy. In Chapter 12 we will compare the use of coupons, rebates, and allowances with the effects of simply changing the list price.

Drawbacks of sales promotions. Sales promotions have some drawbacks. One is their cost. On grocery items, where profit margins are very low, even a few cents off a box cuts deeply into profits. What is more, it is not always clear that sales promotions raise long-term sales. Suppose that

Box 11–8 Common Types of Sales Promotions and Their Effects on Buyer Behavior

"Pull" Techniques

	Get Attention	Supply Information	Create Preference	Close Sales	Remind—Get Repeat Sales
Coupons			X	X	
Premiums			X	X	
Rebates			X	X	
Contests and Sweepstakes	X				
Free Samples	X				X
Demonstrations	X	X			X

"Push" Techniques

	Get Attention	Supply Information	Create Preference	Close Sales	Remind—Get Repeat Sales
Sales Incentives				X	
Promotional Allowances				X	
Trade Show Displays	X	X			X

a dealer allowance program boosts sales of Ajax cleanser to 115 percent of normal for the three weeks in which it goes on. In the next three weeks sales fall to 85 percent of normal, and then they return to where they were before. What did the program do? It led consumers to fill their cupboards at a lower-than-normal price. As a way to raise long-term sales, it had no effect. Unless a sales promotion does more than shift the timing of sales, it is not worthwhile.

PUBLIC RELATIONS, PUBLICITY, AND WORD OF MOUTH

We have defined public relations as a planned effort to create a good image of a product or firm by some means other than paid advertising. The targets of a public relations campaign may be customers, but they are just as often workers, stockholders, members of the local community, or government officials. Not-for-profit firms and government agencies often have smaller budgets for advertising and personal selling than businesses do. For these organizations, public relations may be the most effective part of the promotional strategy.

In small firms, the owners usually handle public relations themselves. In larger firms, there is often a public relations department. Such a department is in charge of making press releases, unveiling new products, lining up speeches for company officers, and so on. The public relations office also monitors public opinion, conducts surveys, and collects news clippings.

Publicity: Any nonpaid public mention of a company or its product.

A major goal of public relations is to create good **publicity**. Publicity can be defined as any nonpaid public mention of a company or its product. Magazine articles, items on the TV news, use of the product by celebrities, and the like all count as publicity. Unfortunately, not all publicity is good. A great deal of it is bad.

During 1983, for example, a court case over alleged defects in the brakes of certain General Motors cars created a lot of bad publicity for the company. In a case like this it is the job of the public relations department to try to limit the damage. After the fact, however, there often is little that can be done. The best protection is to make a quality product and to fix it at the first sign of trouble.

Public relations and publicity both involve public media. Consumer attitudes and choices are also influenced by private communication, however. According to Trendex, a Westport, Connecticut, research firm, word of mouth accounts for three times as many sales as advertising.[4] Some small firms get almost all their business from referrals by customers. For example, Holiday Exterminators of Herndon, Virgina, has tried advertising in the Yellow Pages, newspaper advertising, and direct-mail coupons without success. "You don't plan ahead for pest problems," says one of the company's employees. "When you do get a problem, the first thing you do is ask your neighbors if they know anyone who can get rid of it for you."

Often one influential person can produce thousands of dollars in sales. For example, although Eric Fernsten didn't make much of a mark as a backup center for the Boston Celtics, his teammates thought of him as a guru when it came to buying clothes, TV sets, and even stocks. Someone like Fernsten can be found in almost every plant or office. (Fernsten himself went professional as a giver of advice, which seems to be his true talent. He is now a stockbroker.[5])

How can firms make use of this powerful selling tool? It is not easy. Sending samples and product information to sources like car or hi-fi magazines might help, since influential people get information from them. Sending samples to opinion leaders can help too. Paid endorsements by well-known figures are often used in advertising, but these are a weak substitute. People value the opinions of "experts" in their own workplaces largely because they do not have a stake in selling the product.

[4]Data cited in Stephen P. Morin, " 'Influentials' Advising Their Friends Sell Lots of High-Tech Gadgetry," *Wall Street Journal*, February 23, 1983, p. 23.

[5]Ibid.

LEGAL AND ETHICAL ISSUES

The aim of all promotion is to persuade. There are legal and ethical limits to the tactics that can be used for this purpose, however. When a criminal gang threatens to break the thumbs of restaurant owners who don't use the right garbage collection service, that is salesmanship carried too far. Free samples are sometimes frowned upon too. When the local drug pusher hands out samples to the kids on the playground, he may be creating customers but he isn't winning friends. And lying is out. When a firm takes your money on a promise to repave your driveway and then sprays it with used motor oil, the line between promotion and fraud has been crossed.

But it would be naive to think that illegal and unethical methods of promotion are confined to the underworld. Well-known companies like North American Phillips, Bristol-Myers, and Reader's Digest have ended up on the wrong side of the law in recent years. Laws against deceptive and unethical practices have to be taken seriously by every business. Let's run quickly through a few of those laws.

Deceptive Advertising

Corrective advertising: Advertising that corrects false or misleading claims made in previous ads.

The Federal Trade Commission has authority over advertising on a national level. It is backed up by state agencies. The FTC does more than just bar advertisers from saying things that can be shown to be false. It often requires evidence that statements in ads are true. The FTC has been especially hard on ads for over-the-counter drugs, such as painkillers and cold remedies. It has insisted that firms produce scientific studies to back up their claims. It can also order violators to pay for **corrective advertising**. Ads for Profile bread, for example, used to claim that each slice of Profile has fewer calories than a slice of ordinary bread. The FTC made the firm run ads stating that a slice of Profile has fewer calories only because it is cut thinner.

Just how strict the FTC should be is a matter of debate. In the past, the FTC often acted against ads if it thought that they tended to mislead, even if no actual damage could be shown. For example, it once brought a case against the maker of a "permanent hair dye" on the ground that a consumer might think that the dye would change hair color forever with just one treatment. The current FTC chairman, James C. Miller III, thinks the agency should take action only against ads that are likely to cause actual harm to a "reasonable" consumer. "An ad for Danish pastry shouldn't be considered deceptive just because someone might think it was made in Denmark," says a Miller aide.

Commercial puffery: Claims made in advertising that cannot be proved but do not really mislead the consumer.

It should be added that the law has always allowed a certain amount of **commercial puffery**. Puffery consists of claims that cannot be proved but do not really mislead the consumer. When Carlton Sales Company runs an ad claiming "you'll never forget" your first taste of St. Pauli Girl beer, it doesn't have to back up the ad with scientific memory tests. Everyone knows that this sort of claim is meant to be taken with a grain of salt. Still, exaggeration, even when it does not break the law, is not always good advertising. Consumers resent ads that go too far. One survey found that 70 percent of consumers thought advertisers had not "cleaned up their act" with regard to deceptive and exaggerated claims.[6] Perhaps that is why so many people ignore ads and depend on word of mouth instead.

Restraints on Personal Selling

Bait-and-switch: A sales tactic in which customers are drawn into a store by ads for a cheap model of a product and then pressured into buying a more expensive model.

The law also limits personal-selling tactics. One practice that is outlawed is **bait-and-switch**. In this tactic, a customer is drawn into a store by an ad for a cheap model of a product (say, a vacuum cleaner). Although the cheap model may really exist, the salesperson shows that it isn't worth buying, and pressures the customer into buying a more expensive model.

For many types of purchases a consumer can, by law, cancel an order or return a product within three days if he or she decides that the purchase was unwise. This is a further protection against high-pressure selling. Door-to-door as well as in-store selling is subject to this law.

Limits on Promotions

Some types of sales promotions are limited by law. Contests and sweepstakes are among the most strictly regulated. The chances of winning must be disclosed, and entry cannot be confined to people who buy the product.

The Robinson-Patman Act limits certain push-type sales promotions. Among other things, it requires that if promotional allowances are offered to any retailers, all sellers must get an allowance that is related to the amount of the product they sell.

Ethical Issues

Consumers object to many ads that are not false or illegal. They see them as offensive, too intrusive, or in poor taste. What protection do they have?

They have some protection in the fact that ads that offend often do not sell. For example, sex is often used in ads to get attention. Some ads of this kind are effective, but many backfire. The Gallup and Robinson research firm studied a series of sexy ads for Sergio Valente jeans. It found them high in "stopping power" but low on "favorable buying attitude" scores.[7]

A second line of defense is self-policing by business groups. The National Advertising Division of the Council of Better Business Bureaus acts as a clearinghouse for complaints by consumers and competitors. The following are typical of NAD investigations.[8]

- National Distillers and Chemical Corporation ran an ad for Windsor Canadian whiskey that claimed, "Windsor's taste beats V.O.! Nationwide tests prove it." The ad went on to cite opinions of more than 10,000 drinkers to support its claim. NAD objected that the

[6]Survey by Yankelovich, Skelly, and White, cited in Jennifer Alter, "Public Is Still Wary of Ads: Study," *Advertising Age*, June 23, 1980, p. 3.

[7]Study cited in B. G. Yovovich, "Sex in Advertising—The Power and the Perils," *Advertising Age*, May 2, 1983, p. M-4.

[8]*Advertising Age*, January 17, 1983, p. 12, and April 18, 1983, p. 10.

claims were based on a bar promotion and were not a scientific test. National Distillers changed the ads to make it clear that the claims were based on informal tests in selected bars.

- Six Flags Corporation, an amusement park operator, ran TV spots showing people on roller coasters waving their hands. The Children's Advertising Review Unit complained that this might be dangerous. Six Flags noted that its rides have safety bars that leave the hands free, but it agreed to withdraw the ads. It pledged to avoid showing ads that could encourage unsafe habits.
- Dayton-Hudson Corporation was challenged for in-house ads claiming 40 to 50 percent off on gold and diamond jewelry sales. It backed up the claim with detailed records showing prices at which the goods had formerly been sold. The proof was accepted by NAD.

Another ethical issue has to do with the promotion of products that are harmful or can be abused. Tobacco and alcohol are the most controversial of these. Ads for cigarettes and liquor are not allowed on TV, and some magazines and newspapers refuse to carry them. Ads that link alcohol and cigarettes with youth, health, and "with-it" life-styles are especially offensive to parents.

Advertising is not the only questionable method that is used to sell such products. Public relations material put out by tobacco companies in an attempt to dismiss the health risks of their product border on the irresponsible. Producers of liquor do a little better. Their ads sometimes advise moderation in the use of alcohol, and their trade association spends some money on ads warning about the dangers of alcoholism.

Other marketing activities besides advertising raise legal and ethical issues. We will return to these issues at the end of Chapter 12.

SUMMARY

1. Planning a *promotional strategy* means deciding what to say, how to say it, and whom to say it to. What you say depends on how you want to affect buyer behavior. How you say it depends on the target market and the *advertising media* that will best reach that market. Sometimes advertising is aimed at consumers in an effort to "pull" the product through the distribution channel. Other ads are aimed at intermediaries in an effort to "push" it through.

2. Each aspect of buyer behavior is an opportunity for promotion. At the problem recognition stage, the goal is to get attention. The buyer can then be supplied with information. Persuasion and comparison can be used to create a preference for the seller's product as the buyer evaluates alternatives. Sale-closing tactics can spur the buyer to make the purchase decision. Finally, reminder techniques can be used to influence postpurchase evaluation and bring in repeat sales.

3. *Advertising* is the delivery of a paid promotional message to a large number of potential customers through a public communications medium. Total spending on advertising is equal to about 3 percent of total consumer spending, or about 6 percent of all marketing costs. Newspapers and TV account for about half of all spending on advertising, followed by direct mail, radio, and magazines.

4. *Personal selling* is a promotional presentation made directly to a potential customer, usually in a face-to-face meeting. The personal-selling process can be broken down into four tasks: homework, the sales presentation, the closing, and follow-up.

5. *Sales promotion* is the use of short-term incentives to boost sales of a product. Pull-type promotions, such as coupons, premiums, rebates, contests, and demonstrations, are aimed at consumers. Push-type promotions, such as sales incentives and dealer allowances, are aimed at intermediaries.

6. *Public relations* is a planned effort to create a good image of a product or firm by some means other than paid advertising. Public relations efforts may be directed at consumers, workers, members of the community, or government leaders. The goal of public relations is to create good *publicity* and, when necessary, to limit the damage done by bad publicity.

7. A number of laws bar deceptive advertising, high-pressure sales tactics, and other unfair promotional techniques. Trade associations and advertising media also set standards regarding fair practices. Consumers are protected to some degree by the fact that offensive advertising often does not sell the product. Despite these safeguards, however, opinion polls show that public respect for advertising is quite low.

KEY TERMS

You should be familiar with the following terms and concepts. Check their meanings by referring to the marginal definitions in the chapter or to the glossary at the end of the book.

Promotion	Push	CPM
Promotional strategy	Product-specific advertising	Advertising agency
Advertising	Comparative advertising	Prospecting
Personal selling	Direct-action advertising	Cold canvassing
Sales promotion	Institutional advertising	Publicity
Public relations	Primary advertising	Corrective advertising
Promotional mix	Public service advertising	Commercial puffery
Pull	Advertising medium	Bait-and-switch
	Intrusiveness	

QUESTIONS FOR REVIEW AND DISCUSSION

1. Get some newspapers and magazines and a pair of scissors. Clip ads that illustrate getting attention, supplying information, creating a preference, closing the sale, and reminding. Discuss each ad in terms of its effects on buyer behavior.

2. Reread the example of Post-it notes at the beginning of Chapter 9. Discuss it in terms of push versus pull strategies.

3. Get copies of some business publications like the *Wall Street Journal*, *BusinessWeek*, and *Fortune*. Find examples of pull ads, push ads, product-specific advertising, comparative advertising, direct-action advertising, institutional advertising, primary advertising, public service advertising, public relations, and publicity.

4. Sit in front of your TV set for an hour during prime time. Take notes on each commercial shown during that time. What aspect of buyer behavior does it try to influence? Classify the ads as product-specific, institu-tional, public service, and so on. What other concepts discussed in this chapter are illustrated by the ads you see? Do you think any of them is deceptive, offensive, or unethical? If so, why? Do you think any of them has an impact on your own buying? Why or why not? Have you ever had so much fun watching TV?

5. Arrange a meeting with a salesperson in which you are the potential customer. Try an auto dealer, a hi-fi store, or some other full-service retail outlet. If you have a job, you might arrange to sit in on a meeting with a salesperson who is trying to sell something to your firm. Do not tell the salesperson that this is a homework assignment—at any rate, do not do so until the end of the session. Do you think your salesperson did his or her homework? How good was the sales presentation? Was the salesperson able to answer questions? Did the salesperson try to close the sale? If so, describe the technique used. Did the salesperson make any promises about delivery, service, or anything else that would need to be followed up? If you made the purchase, was the follow-up carried through? Do you think the salesperson had empathy and ego drive? Why or why not?

6. Make a trip to your local supermarket. Tour the store, looking for examples of sales promotion techniques. Pay special attention to the displays near the checkout counter. In what ways do they try to affect buyer behavior? Is there a display that puts candy within reach of children? If so, comment on the ethics and effectiveness of such a display. Look for push-type as well as pull-type promotions. You might ask about the push-type promotions suppliers use.

7. Scan the newspapers for a story that gives a company or product good publicity and one that does the opposite. Are there any references to efforts of the firm's public relations department? Are spokespeople for the company quoted?

8. Write a paragraph on each of the following: the most offensive ad you can find; an ad that you think might be illegal or close to it; an ad that you think is deceptive or unethical; an ad that contains harmless puffery; the most informative ad you can find; the funniest ad you can find; and the most effective ad you can find. If you prefer, you may use an example of personal selling, sales promotion, or public relations.

Case 11–1: Wrangler Strategy Features Sales Promotions

Sales of jeans peaked in the United States in the late 1970s and have fallen slightly since then. Designer jeans have been especially hard hit, but jeans makers like Wrangler, a division of Blue Bell, Inc., have been affected too. Unlike designer jeans, which are distributed through department stores and appeal to the status-conscious consumer, Wrangler's jeans are distributed through mass marketers and are aimed at rugged, "down to earth Americans."

Since 1981, Wrangler has relied heavily on sales promotions to reach these people. Among the events it sponsors are these.

- *Rodeos.* In the towns where they are held, these rank next to Christmas in terms of sales impact, a company spokesman says.
- *Motorcycle and stock car racing.* The "Wrangler Jeans Machine" race car was scheduled for thirty events in 1983.
- *A series of thirty tractor pull competitions* to be held in major farm market areas.
- *The "Wrangler Country Showdown,"* a country music talent contest carried by 400 radio stations.
- *The "Wrangler Horse Reward,"* a sweep-stakes that challenges consumers to identify the Wrangler horse logo.
- *A back-to-school rebate offer* aimed at families.

Local retailers are given a chance to tie into each of these events. Store displays and store advertising are made available. Wrangler's cooperative advertising program pays an allowance to merchants who run local ads that feature Wrangler products. Retailers are given tickets to sponsored events that can be given out as premiums. During the back-to-school promotion, Wrangler offers discount coupons and refunds. Retailers must order at least six dozen Wrangler items to take part.

Dave Allen, Wrangler's special-events director, says that each of the sponsored events has a distinct national impact that is important to the Wrangler brand.

Source: Based on "Wrangler Relying on Multiple Sales Promotions to Help It Combat Flat Bluejean Market," *Marketing News*, March 5, 1983, p. 5. Reprinted by permission *Marketing News*, author or editor, March 5, 1983, p. 5, and the American Marketing Association.

Questions:

1. How do Wrangler's sales promotions help position its product? Compare Wrangler's efforts with those of makers of designer jeans. Comment on the roles of product, distribution, and promotion in positioning blue jeans.

2. How are push and pull elements combined in Wrangler's promotional strategy? Draw a diagram like Box 11–2 for the Wrangler program.

Case 11–2: Selling the Palmer National Bank

In May 1983 Stefan Halper quit his job as deputy secretary of state to start a bank. The Palmer National Bank set up shop in the "new downtown" of Washington, D.C., on a corner where more than 120,000 people pass every day.

In the already crowded banking field, all hope for success rested on the strength of the new firm's marketing program. Halper and his partners saw two target markets that they felt were not well served by banks in the area. The first were the small, high-tech growth companies sprouting up around Washington's beltway. These firms were often forced to deal with junior loan officers at the area's leading banks. Palmer would offer them personal attention and custom-tailored services. Second, Halper felt that international business was not well served in the Washington area. International deal makers had to go to New York to do business. The Palmer National Bank would try to get some of this business to stay in Washington.

As the date for opening Palmer's doors drew near, Halper worked hard at public relations. He was rewarded with feature articles and shorter pieces in all the major local media. The articles explained the new bank's goal of getting high-tech and international business. They built an image of the bank as creative and willing to break with tradition when profits could be made by doing so.

By its first anniversary Palmer's deposits were far ahead of schedule. Where did these deposits come from? Not many came from the general public, which was no great surprise since the bank had not spent a penny on advertising. Instead, almost all the deposits had been brought in by the personal-selling efforts of the bank's officers. These had been carefully assembled so as to provide useful contacts for the bank. Halper himself had many high-level political and international contacts. The vice-chairman, Harvey McLean,

was a wealthy real estate developer with ties to the Republican party. Palmer's president, Webb C. Hayes IV, a descendant of President Rutherford B. Hayes, was a well-known banker. The fourteen-member board of directors included a former agriculture secretary; a former deputy secretary of transportation; the executive vice-president of Marriott Corporation, who was also a former White House personnel director; a former member of Congress with major restaurant and lumber interests; the president of Hazelton Labs, an international drug company; the former chairman of Washington's oldest bank; and the president of Miller & Long Construction Company, a large local firm. "This is not a bank of automobile dealers and funeral directors," says Halper.

To make it easier to attract deposits, Palmer pays interest rates that are somewhat above the average rate paid by competing banks. One promotion featured a ninety-day certificate of deposit with a $10,000 maximum and a 15 percent interest rate, some five percentage points more than other banks were paying. It was hoped that deposits attracted by this one-time offer would become regular accounts when the offer ended.

Halper finds the life of a banker very different from that of a high State Department official. "When you're in business," he says, "you have to be willing to talk to people. I go out of my way to meet with people who wouldn't even have gotten their phone calls returned from my office at the State Department." Personal selling is a big part of Halper's job as chairman. This requires some adjustment too. "No matter who you were in government or how important your title was, when you go out to make a sales call, you get treated like a salesman."

Source: Courtesy of Stefan Halper.

Questions:

1. Describe the Palmer National Bank's marketing strategy and marketing mix in terms of the concepts discussed in Chapters 8–11. How does each of the four Ps enter into Palmer's strategy?
2. Describe Palmer's positioning strategy. What promotional mix is used?
3. Outline Palmer's promotional strategy in terms of what, how, and who. What aspects of promotional strategy discussed in this chapter are illustrated by this case?
4. Discuss the role of personal selling in Palmer's promotional strategy. What is unusual about Palmer's sales force? Is the bank's approach to personal selling well suited to its market? Why?

Chapter 12
PRICING

When you have completed this chapter, you should be able to

- Define *price* and discuss the goals of pricing for business firms, units of government, and not-for-profit organizations.

- Discuss demand, cost, and competition as factors that affect pricing.

- Explain *markup pricing*, *target pricing*, and *break-even analysis*, and show how these methods serve as a starting point for applying judgment and experience to pricing.

- Discuss how price should be meshed with other elements of the marketing mix in the positioning of a product, promotional pricing, and the pricing of new products.

- List the major legal restraints on pricing and discuss their effects on competition.

- Evaluate the success of micromarketing and macromarketing in the American economy.

Buying a new car can be a miserable experience. Dickering with salespeople over a dizzying array of options and prices is apt to leave all but the most sophisticated customers confused and disgusted.

But in Lake City, Minnesota, a tiny town on the banks of the Mississippi, John Peterson is taking much of the pain out of purchasing a new car. For $49 over the factory invoice price a customer can buy any General Motors Corporation model, from the cheapest Chevette to the fanciest Cadillac. No pressure, no dickering. Buyers who choose to can even order the car by phone.

By offering a clearly established, rock-bottom price for a new car, Peterson has turned Lake City into a mecca for Minnesota car buyers. In the seven months since he began offering cars for $49 over invoice cost, he has gone from selling fewer than twenty cars a month to selling nearly two hundred. Many of his customers drive more than an hour from Minneapolis–St. Paul and Rochester to buy cars from him. Peterson says he also has gone from the verge of bankruptcy to solid profitability. It is all the result, he says, of eliminating the fear and loathing that many customers feel about buying a car.

Peterson is one of a dozen GM dealers who have become disciples of Howard Van Bortel, a former GM dealer who preaches—and sells—the idea that buying a car needn't be a contest of wits between a salesman and the customer.

Van Bortel says he originated the $49 over invoice idea in 1977 after twenty-four years of successfully selling Oldsmobiles and Chevrolets in Palmyra, New York. "I finally got tired of trying to rape and rob every customer who came in the door," he says. "I did some polls that showed me that 70 percent of the people don't like the way car dealers do business. When that many people don't like the way you do business, it's time to change."

Styling himself the "people's dealer," Van Bortel set about formulating a plan that would eliminate the bargaining that accompanies most car purchases. First, he pared his overhead costs by getting rid of his salesmen, who had been paid 25 percent of the dealership's profits on sales they made. Then he eliminated the inventory of new cars that most dealers carry. The lower overhead enabled him to make money selling cars at lower prices than other dealers did. Profits flowed from the sharply higher volume of sales as buyers were attracted by his prices. From an average of 800 or so cars a year before 1977, Van Bortel says, his sales increased to 8000 units by 1979.

Having to wait for the factory to deliver is an essential part of the scheme. When a customer answers one of Peterson's ads, he is given a firm price for a new car. If he telephones, one of Peterson's order takers will send the customer a factory price list that includes all the options that are available on the car in question. All the customer then must do is to fill out an order form that adds $49 to the factory base price, plus the price of each option ordered, and return it to Peterson with a deposit of $500. The usual wait, says Peterson, is six to eight weeks.[1]

---

[1]Douglas R. Sease, "You Can Buy a Car at $49 Over Invoice, but It'll Take Time," *Wall Street Journal*, September 21, 1983, p. 1. Reprinted by permission of the Wall Street Journal. © Dow Jones & Company, Inc., 1983. All Rights Reserved.

Price: The amount of money a customer must pay for a product.

The marketing strategy devised by Van Bortel and practiced by Peterson rests squarely on pricing, the fourth of the four Ps. The **price** of a product is the amount of money a customer must pay for it. But a lower price—$49 over invoice—is not the only difference between what customers get from Peterson and what they get elsewhere. As always, each part of the marketing mix depends on each of the others. Peterson gives customers a different product than they can get elsewhere—a car built to order, not one that happens to be on the dealer's lot. He offers less than other dealers in terms of place—his location in Lake City is not convenient for most people, and they have to wait six or eight weeks for a car. And his promotional mix uses advertising to attract business, but it cuts personal selling to mere order taking.

Most of this chapter will be devoted to pricing and its connection with product, distribution, and promotion. Goals of pricing, factors that affect prices, and pricing methods will be discussed. Then we will round out the series of chapters on marketing with an evaluation of marketing as a whole.

GOALS OF PRICING

Profit

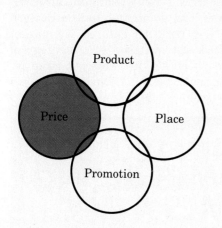

The most obvious goal of pricing is to earn a profit. To do so, the price must be high enough to cover all the costs of making the product and all the costs of other parts of the marketing mix.

As we explained in Chapter 1, managers of corporations have a duty to earn a profit. They are hired for that purpose by the firm's shareholders. In addition, managers of all firms, not just corporations, must earn profits if they want to stay in business. This need to survive dominates all business decisions. In Chapter 4 we stressed that no one should start a business unless he or she is sure customers can be found at a price high enough to cover all costs. And in Chapter 9 we included price as a key item in the business analysis stage of product development. A new-product proposal should not be allowed to go forward unless it can be priced in a way that will contribute to the firm's profits.[*]

Growth of Sales

Although no firm can ignore the need to make a profit, other goals often play a role in pricing. The second most common goal of pricing is growth of sales. This goal is sometimes expressed in terms of a percentage rate of growth, and sometimes in terms of growth of the firm's share of the market for the product. The price of the product is set low enough to achieve the target rate of growth.

Firms that make sales growth the focal point of pricing cannot set aside the goal of making a profit. If you sold dollar bills for ninety-nine

---

[*]Sometimes a product can be priced in a way that contributes to profits indirectly. For example, Polaroid keeps the prices of its cameras low as a way of promoting sales of Polaroid film. The film is priced to allow an ample margin of profit.

cents each, you could expect very rapid growth of sales, but what would be the point if you lost money on each unit sold? Sometimes, however, putting growth of sales or market share ahead of profits in the short run may be the best route to profits in the long run. For example, as we will see, firms often put a low price on a new product so as to build market share fast, in the hope of earning profits later once the product has a firmly established place in the market.

Status Quo Pricing

Firms that have profit or sales growth as their pricing goal tend to treat price as an active weapon in their marketing strategy. Not all firms do so, however. Some firms take a passive view of pricing. Their main goal is not to upset the stable price structure in their industry.

Some firms feel that they have no real control over price. In the case of commodities like wheat or copper, prices are set by the forces of supply and demand in a world market. No one firm can affect the price. In other cases, one large firm may act as a **price leader**, while others are content to follow in its footsteps.

Price leader: A firm whose price changes are followed by other firms in the same industry.

Some firms could use price as an active marketing weapon, but instead they focus on product development, distribution, or promotion as ways of bringing in customers. Often passive pricers with a full-service approach exist side by side with aggressive, no-frills price cutters. Each serves a different market segment. The New York–Washington air corridor is a case in point. This market was long dominated by the Eastern Airlines shuttle. In the early 1980s New York Air entered the market charging lower prices. Later New York Air switched to a strategy of matching Eastern's prices and beating it on service. This left room for no-frills PEOPLExpress to serve the price-conscious traveler.

PEOPLExpress has made a place for itself in a highly competitive market by cutting prices to a minimum. Marc P. Anderson

Pricing Goals for Other Organizations

Not-for-profit organizations and units of government must set prices too. As we saw in Chapter 3, about 70 percent of the income of not-for-profit firms comes from sales of goods and services. Sources of such income include the subscription fees charged by magazines like *Consumer Reports*, the fees that not-for-profit hospitals charge their patients, and the tuition charged by not-for-profit schools. Governments also charge for many goods and services. Postal service is the leading source of nontax revenue for the federal government, while university tuition brings in the most nontax revenue for state and local governments. Public hospital fees, park admission fees, sewage charges, and sales of liquor by state stores are other sources of nontax revenues. In all, some 18 percent of all government revenue comes from sales of goods and services.[2] All of them must be priced.

What replaces profit as the goal of pricing for nonbusiness organizations? In the not-for-profit sector, the goal is service—and, of course, survival. Organizations that are set up to do good have to get money from somewhere in order to continue doing good. Voluntary contributions are one source, but they are not always enough. Not-for-profit hospitals, for example, provide some services as charity, but they must charge most of their patients enough to cover costs. Not-for-profit firms often set the prices of some of their services above cost. In this way they obtain a surplus to offset the costs of the services that they provide free. Government officials, too, keep survival in mind when making pricing decisions. By charging for some services, they reduce the burden on taxpayers and, at the same time, increase their chances of reelection.

Fairness is a second pricing goal for many not-for-profit firms and units of government. Consider private colleges. They set high list prices for their product—tuition is over $10,000 at many private colleges. Then, in fairness to students who cannot pay that much, they give large discounts off the list price. The discounts are called scholarships. Government pricing decisions, too, often take fairness into account. For example, the Department of the Interior has proposed charging higher fees for admission to national parks. In support of this proposal, officials cite surveys showing that incomes of park users are about twice the national average.

FACTORS THAT AFFECT PRICE

Which pricing goal should a firm adopt—the highest possible profit, long-run profits through growth of sales, or status quo pricing that seeks profits through other parts of the marketing mix? Once a goal has been chosen, just what price level will serve it best? There are no simple answers to these questions. However, we can offer a list of factors to be kept in mind when making pricing decisions. In this section we will look at the factors of demand, cost, and competition. A later section will cover legal restraints on pricing. Those restraints form another set of factors to be kept in mind.

Demand

Demand: The amount of a product that customers are willing and able to buy at a given price.

The first factor affecting price is **demand**. The demand for a product means the amount customers are willing and able to buy at a given price.

[2]*Statistical Abstract of the United States*, 104th ed. (Washington, D.C.: Government Printing Office, 1983), Table 464.

Demand curve: A graph that shows the relationship between the demand for a product and its price.

The lower the price, other things being equal, the more units of a product will be bought.

The link between price and demand can be shown by a **demand curve** like the one in Box 12–1. The demand curve is a graph that shows how much of the product can be sold at each price in a range of prices. Movies offered by a campus film club are used as an example. The graph shows that if tickets are priced at $2.00 each, 100 will be sold. At $1.00 per ticket, 150 would be sold; at $3.00, only 50.

Box 12–1   A Demand Curve

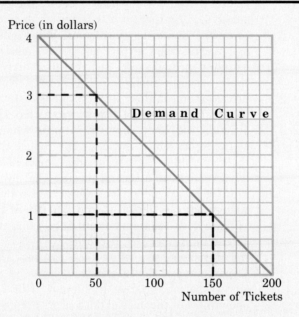

The demand curve for a product shows the amount customers are willing and able to buy at any given price. This curve represents the demand for tickets to movies shown by a campus film club. At a price of $3, 50 tickets would be sold for each showing; if the price were cut to $2, 100 would be sold; at a price of $1, 150 would be sold; and so on.

Clearly, it would be useful for a firm to know the demand curve it faces in deciding what price to charge for its product. What ticket price would bring in the most revenue for the film club? The revenue the club would earn can be found by multiplying the price times the number of tickets that can be sold at that price. Given the demand curve shown in Box 12–1, selling 100 tickets at $2.00 each would bring in $200, the maximum revenue.* What ticket price would just fill a 75-seat auditorium? The demand curve shows that a price of $2.50 would attract 75 people. If it costs $150 to rent a certain film, what is the lowest price the club could charge and still break even? The demand curve shows that no price below $1.00 would bring in enough revenue to cover the cost.

*Any price either higher or lower than $2.00 would bring in less total revenue. For example, selling 50 tickets at $3.00 each would bring in only $150; selling 140 tickets at $1.20 each would bring in just $168; and so on.

It is not easy for a firm to learn the shape of the demand curve for each of its products. Sometimes the curve can be estimated by statistical techniques, but doing so can be quite costly and the results cannot always be trusted. Sometimes test-marketing can provide useful information about the demand curve. In this approach, a product is introduced at different prices in several test markets, and careful records are kept of the results.

But all methods of learning about demand curves face one major problem: the curves do not stand still to be measured. For example, the number of tickets the film club can sell will be different for each film, and it will be lower as exam time approaches than earlier in the semester. In the same way, the number of cars Ford or Chrysler can sell at a given price varies with the ups and downs of interest rates and unemployment.

When demand is strong, more of a product can be sold at any given price, and the demand curve shifts to the right. Firms can take advantage of such a shift to sell more, to raise prices and increase profit per unit, or to do a little of both. When demand is weak, the curve shifts to the left. Under weak demand conditions a firm may have to cut prices and accept a lower profit per unit to keep total sales at the desired level.

In short, the demand curve is helpful as a framework for thinking about pricing decisions, but judgment, experience, and a feel for the market are needed to estimate just where the curve lies at any given time.

Cost

Demand is not the only thing that counts in setting a price. When the goal of pricing is to earn a profit, cost must also be kept in mind.

Here is an example. Suppose your campus snack bar could sell 100 ham sandwiches a day at $1.50 each and 200 a day at $1.00 each. Cutting the price from $1.50 to $1.00 would raise total revenue from $150 a day to $200. But suppose each sandwich costs $0.75 to make. Making the extra 100 sandwiches would add $75 a day to the snack bar's costs. That would more than offset the $50 in added revenue. Cutting the price of a ham sandwich from $1.50 to $1.00 would be a losing move.

Economics textbooks give the following rule for balancing revenues against costs when setting prices: cutting the price to increase the quantity sold will add to a firm's profit only as long as the added revenue is greater than the added cost of making the larger quantity. However, this rule is useful as a guide to pricing only when the firm has a fairly clear idea of the shape of its demand curve. As we have seen, firms often do not have this information.

Even when economic rules of pricing cannot be applied exactly, they do suggest some general rules. For example, the need to balance costs against demand means that a firm will usually be forced to raise its prices when its costs rise, even though doing so will reduce sales volume. Any reduction in unit costs, on the other hand, gives the firm a chance to lower prices, increase sales, and improve profits, all at the same time.

In setting prices, a business must take demand, cost, and competition into account. Marc P. Anderson

Competition

Competition is a third factor that affects pricing. This factor sets a limit on how much a firm can raise its profits by raising its prices. The more competitors a firm has, and the less difference there is between its products and those of its rivals, the greater the chance that customers will turn elsewhere if the firm raises its prices. In much the same way, a firm can be placed under great pressure to cut its prices when its rivals cut theirs.

The effect of competition is to push prices down toward costs. Prices can be held well above costs for a long time only when a firm is protected against competition (for example, by a patent). The tendency of competition to keep prices close to costs is, of course, a great benefit to consumers—one of the greatest benefits of a free enterprise system. For producers, however, competition means walking a fine line between profit and loss. Firms that fail to control their costs but cannot raise their prices because of competition are driven out of the market.

Competition fails to hold down prices only when all firms raise their prices by about the same amount at about the same time. It is illegal for firms to agree to raise prices in concert—we will return to that subject shortly. However, when all the firms in a market are affected the same way by, say, an increase in wage rates or an increase in demand, they will all tend to raise their prices at once even without an agreement to do so.

PRICING METHODS

Good pricing decisions must take into account demand, cost, and competition. There are no formulas that can take the place of judgment and experience in weighing these factors. However, there are a few simple methods that are often used as a starting point for pricing decisions. In this section we will discuss the methods known as markup pricing, target pricing, and break-even analysis.

Markup and Target Pricing

Markup pricing: Any method of pricing a product that begins by adding a certain percentage to its cost.

Markup pricing refers to any method of pricing that begins by adding a certain percentage to cost. Markup pricing is widely used in wholesale and retail trade. Wholesalers sell goods at prices 5 to 10 percent higher than the prices they pay for them, depending on the range of services they supply. Full-service retailers like department stores and boutiques often mark goods up by 100 percent. Discounters' markups are much lower.

Markup percentage: The amount by which the price of a product is raised above its cost, expressed either as a percentage of cost or as a percentage of the selling price.

The **markup percentage** can be expressed either in relation to the cost of the item or in relation to its selling price. For example, a grocery store might buy tuna at a wholesale price of $0.50 per can and sell it at a retail price of $0.75. The markup percentage could be expressed either as 33 percent of the selling price or as 50 percent of cost.

Factors affecting the markup percentage. A number of things affect the markup percentage. One, which we have already mentioned, is the level of service. The markup percentage of a retail store must cover the costs of the store building, the salaries of salespeople, and other expenses, and still leave room for profit. If a firm spends more on these things in an effort to improve its service, it must apply a higher markup.

Rate of turnover: The average number of times per year that goods in stock are sold and replaced.

A second factor affecting the markup percentage is the **rate of turnover** of the goods being sold. The rate of turnover means the average number of times per year that goods in stock are sold and replaced. The

Discount retailers stock fast-moving items in order to keep turnover high and prices low. Marc P. Anderson

rate of turnover can also be measured by the ratio of the total annual sales of a good to the quantity of the good held in stock. For example, a boat dealer who sells 150 boats a year and keeps an average of 30 boats in stock would have a turnover rate of five times per year.

We saw in Chapter 10 that the carrying costs of keeping goods in stock are a major cost in wholesale and retail trade. The faster the turnover, the lower these costs and, hence, the lower the markup needed to earn a profit. Stores with fast turnover, such as supermarkets, are able to operate with low markups compared with stores with slower turnover, such as clothing stores. Discount retailers often do not stock slow-moving items. Department stores and other full-service stores carry them, even though it is costly to do so, in order to offer a fuller selection.

Target pricing: A method of setting prices that is intended to yield a desired rate of return on the capital invested.

Target pricing. Markup pricing as it has just been described is used mostly in retailing and wholesaling. A closely related method, known as **target pricing**, is often used in other businesses. In this method prices are set in a way that will yield a desired rate of return on the capital invested. Suppose, for example, that you have invested $100,000 to buy a house, which you plan to rent out for income. You want to earn at least a 10 percent rate of return on your investment—otherwise you might as well have put your money in the bank. The desired 10 percent return on $100,000 comes to $10,000 per year, or $833 per month. Suppose that your monthly costs for taxes, insurance, and upkeep come to $700. Using target pricing, you would add the desired return of $833 to the $700 of costs and set a monthly rent for the house of $1533. The target pricing method can be applied to manufacturing, services, or almost any line of business.

Allowing for demand and competition. Neither markup pricing nor target pricing is a complete answer to the pricing problem, but either can be a good starting point. The markup percentage or target rate of return used in any given line of business will tend to be one that has been found, through trial and error, to reflect average market conditions. When conditions are not average, the price should be raised above or cut below the usual markup or target price. A few examples will show how judgment and experience can be combined with the methods just described.

- A retail store holds a January sale during which its usual markup is cut in half. This is done because demand is very slack in the post-Christmas season. The low prices help reduce inventories, thereby cutting carrying costs.
- A new airline begins service on the New York–Florida route. In the past, carriers have set fares so as to produce a desired target rate of return on the equipment used. When the new airline sets a low introductory fare, the established airlines cut their fares to meet the competitive threat.
- Hotels in Los Angeles normally set room rates to achieve a target rate of return. The Olympic Games are likely to boost demand for hotel rooms. To take advantage of this opportunity, the hotels raise their rates during the games.

Break-Even Analysis

Fixed costs: Costs that are the same regardless of the quantity of a good or service produced.

Markup pricing does not always take into account the quantity sold. It is sometimes useful to do so, however, especially when a firm has high fixed costs. **Fixed costs** are those that must be paid to introduce a new product or to stay in a market regardless of the quantity sold. Other costs, which change as the quantity produced changes, are known as **variable costs**.

Variable costs: Costs that change along with the quantity of a good or service produced.

As an example, think about the costs of publishing a book. The costs of editing the manuscript, setting it in type, making corrections, and producing illustrations are all fixed costs. They are the same regardless of the number of copies of the book that will be sold. Other costs, such as printing, paper, binding, and author's royalties, are variable costs. They increase with the number of copies sold.

Break-even analysis: A method of pricing that involves comparing fixed and variable costs with estimated revenues at several possible prices and levels of output.

The break-even chart. A technique known as **break-even analysis** is an aid to pricing in cases in which both fixed and variable costs are important. Box 12–2 uses a publishing example to explain how the method works. In this case an author approaches a publisher with a manuscript for a children's horse story. Is the book worth doing? The publisher, Carolyn Smith, estimates that setting the story in type, making corrections, and hiring an artist to draw the illustrations will cost $40,000. This fixed cost is marked on the vertical axis of the break-even chart as shown in the box. The variable costs of printing, paper, binding, and author's royalties will be $5 per book. When this is added to fixed costs, Smith can figure total costs for any number of books—$65,000 ($40,00 fixed and $25,000 variable) for 5000 copies; $90,000 ($40,000 fixed and $50,000 variable) for 10,000 copies; and so on. The relationship between total cost and the number of copies is shown by the total-cost line on the break-even chart.

Next, Smith has to estimate the revenue that the book will bring in. She knows that competitors are selling hardback children's books for about $10.00. If her press also charges $10.00 per copy, the new book will bring in $50,000 in total revenue if it sells 5000 copies, $100,000 if it sells 10,000 copies, and so on. The relationship between revenue and number of copies sold is shown by the total-revenue line in Box 12–2.

The break-even chart is now complete. It allows total costs to be compared with total revenue for any number of copies. If fewer than 8000 copies are sold, total costs will exceed revenue and there will be a loss, as shown on the chart. If more than 8000 copies are sold, there will be a profit.

Box 12–2 Break-Even Chart for Publishing a Book

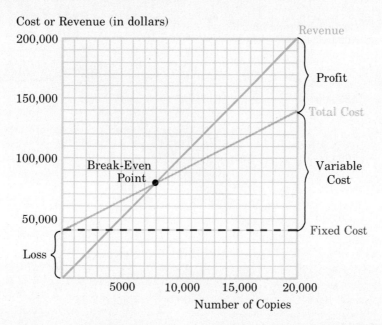

In deciding whether to publish a manuscript, a book publisher might use a break-even chart like the one shown here. Fixed costs for publishing the book (setting type, making corrections, and drawing illustrations) are estimated at $40,000. These costs are the same for any number of copies. Variable costs (printing, paper, binding, and author's royalties) are estimated at $5 per book. Adding fixed and total costs together gives the total-cost line. The total-revenue line in this chart assumes a price of $10 per copy. At that price, 8000 copies would have to be sold to break even.

The break-even point for this book, thus, is 8000 copies if it is priced at $10.00.

Applying break-even analysis. Notice that break-even analysis does not by itself say whether the book should be published. It is a "what if" tool—it shows what the profit or loss will be if a certain number of copies are sold at a certain price. To decide whether to publish the book, and how to price it if it is published, Smith must combine break-even analysis with her own judgment and experience concerning the market for children's books. The manuscript looks like a good one, in her judgment. Her experience is that a horse story will sell about 10,000 copies if it is priced at the same level as competing books. At 10,000 copies, the book would earn a profit of $10,000 (revenue of $100,000 minus variable costs of $50,000 and fixed costs of $40,000). It appears that the book is worth bringing out.

But maybe $10.00 is not the best price. To evaluate other possible prices, the break-even chart is modified as shown in Box 12–3. In that box, two new revenue lines have been added for the prices of $15.00 and $7.50. The $15.00 price lowers the break-even point to 4000 copies, but how many copies could be sold at that price? On the basis of her feeling for the market, Smith thinks that not even 4000 copies would be sold at a price so much higher than those of competing books. The $7.50 price raises the break-

Box 12–3 A Break-Even Chart with Alternate Prices

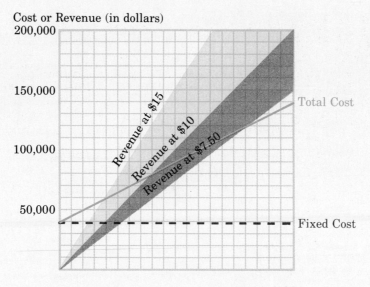

Cost or Revenue (in dollars)

Copies Sold

This box expands the break-even chart in Box 12–2 by adding total-revenue lines for two other prices— $15.00 and $7.50. At the higher price, the break-even point would be lowered to 4000 copies. At the lower price, it would be raised to 16,000 copies. To use this chart as the basis for a pricing decision, the publisher must estimate the number of copies that would be sold at each price.

even point to 16,000 copies, and 20,000 would have to be sold to make the same profit that 10,000 books at $10.00 would bring in. Smith's experience tells her that the lower price would sell more copies, but nowhere near twice as many as could be sold at $10.00. The break-even analysis confirms her guess that $10.00 is about the right price.

PRICE AS PART OF A MARKETING STRATEGY

No price is right or wrong in and of itself. A price is right only when it is part of a complete marketing strategy designed to serve a target market with a balanced marketing mix. The story at the beginning of this chapter illustrates this point perfectly. The $49-over-invoice offer is more than just a pricing strategy. It begins with the selection of a target market: buyers who know just what they want and are willing to go to a little trouble to get it at the lowest price. All the other parts of the marketing mix are adjusted to fit the $49 markup: the product is custom-ordered; dealer inventories are avoided; and personal selling is dropped from the promotional mix. In this section we will look at some ways in which pricing meshes with other parts of the marketing strategy.

Price and Product Positioning

In Chapter 9 we discussed *positioning*, the process by which a product's image is fitted to its target market. Price can be a key tool in positioning. In fact, as Box 12–4 shows, price has a strong effect on the way consumers perceive a product even when no other cues about the product are given.

One of the reasons price works as a positioning tool is that price is taken as a sign of quality. For many products this makes good sense. Using the best-quality inputs raises the cost of making a product, so it must be sold at a higher price. Keeping price low often requires cutting corners. But in the minds of consumers the link between price and quality carries over even to products for which there are few real differences in quality. This effect helps sell high-priced brands of goods like aspirin, even though there may be no difference between them and their low-priced competitors.

A high price can also be used to give a product "snob appeal." The target market in this case consists of people who want to use a product to make a statement about themselves: "Look at me, I've got it made and this proves it." Royal Doulton china, Rolex, and Rolls-Royce are examples of goods that are sold partly on the basis of snob appeal. A firm that wants to give its products snob appeal must be careful about how those products are distributed. As we saw in Chapter 10, makers of designer clothing often try hard to keep their goods away from discounters and off-price stores.

Low prices as well as high ones can be used to position a product. Low prices are a major part of the image of many retail outlets. Selling all cars at $49 over the invoice cost creates a stronger image for Peterson's dealership than would a policy of varying the markup from one model to another—even if the average markup was only $49.

Some products are priced to appeal to upper-income, quality-conscious consumers. Courtesy of Royal Doulton

---

Box 12–4 Price and Consumer Perceptions of Quality

In an experiment at Stanford University, a panel of students were offered a choice of three different brands of beer once a week for twelve weeks. The beers were labeled only as "M," a premium-priced beer, "L," a medium-priced beer, and "P," a budget-priced beer. The students did not have to pay for the beer, but to make the price difference seem realistic, "refunds" were taped to the bottles—a nickel on each bottle of brand P and two pennies on each bottle of brand L. The students kept the money if they chose one of these beers.

The students were told that the experiment was a taste test of a local brewery's new products. In fact, however, all three "brands" were the same beer, drawn from the same vat. Only the labels differed.

The prices of the three brands (the only information given to the panel members) had a clear effect on how they were perceived. In one part of the ex-

periment, students were asked about the beers. The brands were scored according to a list of favorable words such as *tangy*, *smooth*, and *full-bodied* and a list of unfavorable words such as *flat*, *watery*, and *bitter*. The high-priced brand M drew the most favorable comments. "M is a good strong malty beer," commented one student. "P would poison me—make me ill." In all, brand M scored 93, brand L, 73, and brand P, 57, in terms of favorable words. The scores for unfavorable words were reversed. The low-priced brand P drew 101 unfavorable words, compared with 82 for brand L and 71 for brand M.

Sources: J. Douglass McConnell, "The Development of Brand Loyalty: An Experimental Study," *Journal of Marketing Research*, February 1968, pp. 13–19, and "Effect of Pricing on Perception of Product Quality," *Journal of Applied Psychology*, August 1968, pp. 331–34.

Limited-time discounts are a commonly used promotional pricing technique. Marc P. Anderson

Skimming: A strategy in which a new product is brought out at a high price, which is then reduced a step at a time.

Penetration: A strategy in which a new product is brought out at a low price in order to build up a large market share quickly.

Promotional Pricing

Promotional pricing, as the term itself makes clear, is another area in which parts of the marketing mix interact. A firm that uses promotional pricing sets the list price for a product on the basis of average levels of demand, cost, and competition. When one of these factors changes, the list price is kept the same, but the price that the consumer must pay is cut by means of a cents-off coupon, a limited-time discount, or something of the sort.

Promotional pricing has some advantages over simple changes in the list price. First, it is useful when the conditions that trigger a price change are temporary. The seller must look ahead to the need to raise the price again when conditions return to normal. Ending a sale or stopping the distribution of coupons is less likely to offend consumers than an increase in list price.

Second, promotional pricing can be used as a focal point for other parts of the promotional mix, such as advertising and personal selling. Thus, coupons are a way of getting attention as well as a way of lowering the price. And a discount offered for a limited time is a strong aid to closing sales.

Finally, promotional pricing sometimes makes it possible to sell the same product at different prices to different segments of the same market. Shoppers who are highly aware of prices will make the effort to clip and use coupons, or will get to the store on the day of a sale. Shoppers who make their choices on some basis other than price often do not bother to use coupons or look for sales. They are willing to pay the normal price.

Pricing New Products

Perhaps in no other case must price be more carefully balanced with other parts of the marketing mix than when a new product is first brought out. There are two basic ways of pricing a new product. They are known as skimming and penetration.

In a **skimming** strategy, the product is brought out at a high price. Few people can afford to pay such a price, but good profits are made on sales to people who feel that they just have to have the latest thing. When most consumers in this group have bought the product, the price is dropped a step at a time in order to broaden the market. This part of the process is called "sliding down the demand curve." Compact disk stereo systems were brought out with a skimming strategy, no doubt in the hope that high initial profits could be earned from a limited number of high-income consumers.

A **penetration** strategy, in contrast, brings out a new product at a very low price—perhaps at or below cost. The goal of this strategy is to build up a large market share quickly before competitors enter the market. As the volume of production increases, it is hoped, costs per unit will drop, permitting a profit even at the low price.

The choice between skimming and penetration must take many factors into account. Skimming offers high early profits, but it may attract competition more quickly. A high initial price tends to give the product a high-class image that will persist in consumers' minds even after the price has been cut. Will this image help by creating a reputation for quality, or will it slow the growth of sales volume? Penetration allows the firm to get a jump on the competition, but how long will it have to wait for profits? A penetration strategy can backfire if strong competitors come in anyway and prices have to be cut again and again. Texas Instruments ran into this problem when it used penetration to introduce its digital watches and pocket calculators. The company was never able to make a profit from these product lines.

LEGAL RESTRAINTS ON PRICING

Throughout this chapter we have stressed that firms can be highly flexible in setting prices. Prices can be set with the goal of profit, sales growth, or just preserving the status quo. They can be changed to reflect changes in demand, costs, or competition. They can be used to project an image, to skim, or to penetrate. But our discussion of pricing would not be complete without a mention of the legal restaints on pricing, some of which are quite far-reaching. Managers of all firms, large and small, must be aware of these legal restraints. When in doubt, seek professional legal advice.

Types of Restraints on Pricing

Price fixing.   As we already mentioned in Chapter 10, price fixing is illegal under the Sherman Antitrust Act. The point is worth repeating. Price fixing, meaning any agreement with a competitor about the level of prices, is a felony. People are sent to jail for it. The courts define price fixing very broadly. Firms can be found guilty of price fixing even when they have not made a formal agreement to keep prices at a certain level. Often it is against the law even to discuss prices with a competitor. For example, any discussion of prices between firms that are bidding for a contract is likely to be viewed as price fixing. It is best not to bring up the subject of pricing when talking with competitors.

Price discrimination: Selling a product at different prices to different buyers.

Price discrimination.   Certain forms of **price discrimination**—sales of a product at different prices to different buyers—are illegal under the Robinson-Patman Act. The laws in this area are not quite so strict as those on price fixing. It is often legal to sell goods to different customers at different prices as long as certain conditions are met. For example, different grades or qualities of a product need not be sold at the same price. Different prices can also be justified by differences in costs, as in the case of discounts for volume purchases that reflect the lower costs of selling in larger lots. And price discrimination is sometimes allowed when it is a response to the actions of competitors.

Predatory pricing: Selling a product at a price below cost in order to drive competitors out of the market.

Predatory pricing.   Selling at a price below cost in order to drive competitors out of the market is called **predatory pricing**. This practice is illegal under the Sherman Act. Simply underselling competitors is not illegal, though. Fair competition becomes predatory only when sales are made below cost and when the intent is to get rid of rivals.

Dumping: Selling a product in a foreign country at a price less than that at which it is sold in the home market.

Dumping.   Firms that sell their goods abroad must comply with international agreements that prohibit dumping. **Dumping** means selling goods in a foreign country for a lower price than that charged in the home market. Nations that believe their industries are being hurt by dumping can impose tariffs in order to raise the prices at which the imported goods are sold.

Deceptive pricing. Certain deceptive pricing techniques have been declared illegal by the Federal Trade Commission. One of these, the bait-and-switch technique, was mentioned in Chapter 11. It is also illegal to claim that a good is being sold below list price, or below a competitor's price, unless the claim can be proved. Such devices as two-for-the-price-of-one promotions can be illegal if the price of the item is raised to cover the cost of giving one unit away with each one that is sold. State and local agencies as well as the Federal Trade Commission enforce the laws against deceptive pricing.

Copyright © King Features Syndicate, Inc. World rights reserved.

Price and rate regulation. The prices of some products are controlled by regulatory boards. Electric utilities are a well-known example. State utility commissions supervise pricing in detail, usually by setting a maximum allowable profit. Taxi fares are regulated in many cities. There has been a trend away from rate regulation in recent years, however. As

In many cities taxi fares are regulated and must be clearly displayed on or in the vehicle. Marc P. Anderson

mentioned in Chapter 10, since 1980 truck lines and railroads have been freed from some Interstate Commerce Commission regulations.

Price controls and anti-inflation guidelines. During World War II and a few times since, the federal government has imposed controls on prices and wages in an attempt to reduce inflation. The price controls in force during World War II were very strict and were accompanied by rationing of certain goods, such as tires and gasoline. President Nixon imposed binding wage and price controls between 1971 and 1974. Presidents Kennedy and Carter tried to control inflation with "voluntary" price guidelines, which in practice were not so voluntary, since they were enforced by withholding of government contracts and other threats. Economists who have studied the results of these policies have little that is good to say for them. The Nixon, Kennedy, and Carter policies failed to bring inflation under control.[3] The World War II controls succeeded only at the cost of severe shortages and black markets. The failure of recent price control programs makes it less likely they will be tried again, but a new round of inflation could bring them back.

Pricing Restraints and Competition

To the extent that they protect the competitive process, laws that regulate pricing decisions are good for the economy. Fair competitive bidding and honest retail pricing are worthwhile goals. Unfortunately, there is another side to pricing restraints that is less desirable. The point at which the laws go astray is when they are used not to protect the process of competition but to protect some firms against competition by others.

Case 12–2 shows how a firm can sometimes use the antitrust laws to shield itself from certain tactics of its competitors. The example given is not unique. The antitrust laws are so complex that it is easy for corporate lawyers to bring nuisance suits against rivals who threaten their markets with new products or lower prices.

AN EVALUATION OF MARKETING

In Chapter 8 we pointed out that the term *marketing* has two meanings. In the sense of micromarketing, it means the process by which a firm finds out what its customers need and channels a flow of products to meet those needs. In the sense of macromarketing, it means the broader process by which production is directed toward meeting needs of all kinds, social as well as individual.

Micromarketing can be judged to be successful if it serves the goals of the organization. For a private firm, the goal may be simply to maximize

[3]See, for example, Alan S. Blinder and William J. Newton, "The 1971–1974 Controls Program and the Price Level, an Econometric Postmortem," *National Bureau of Economic Research Working Paper No. 279* (New York, September 1978). Blinder and Newton conclude that the Nixon controls actually made inflation worse. The paper also discusses some earlier studies.

profits, to increase long-run profits through growth of sales, or, for the owner of a small firm, just to make a living. Not-for-profit firms and units of government have goals of their own. We have tried to give examples of micromarketing strategies that seem to work, as well as some guidelines for avoiding mistakes.

It is somewhat harder to evaluate the success of macromarketing. Private firms seem to do a pretty good job of meeting individual needs, as those needs are defined by people themselves. Private business does not meet all social needs, but that is largely because our economy is based on a division of labor in which private firms meet private needs while government and not-for-profit firms meet social needs. We also leave to government and not-for-profit organizations the job of protecting people from their own desires for things that are not good for them—to the extent that we try to offer such protection.

Just to say that marketing succeeds in meeting consumer needs is not enough, however. We should not give the system a passing grade unless we also think that it does its job at a reasonable cost. After all, marketing costs constitute about half of the total amount spent on consumer goods and services. How much waste is there in that figure?

If we look at the question from a micromarketing point of view, there is no doubt that there is a lot of waste. The fact is that not all companies are managed well, and that goes for marketing as much as for any other activity. Millions of dollars are spent bringing out products that fall flat on their faces, just because no one asked the right questions at the right time. Huge retailing empires like Woolco and W. T. Grant fail after spending fortunes on strategies that simply don't work. The media are full of expensive ads that insult the intelligence and, in doing so, fail to sell. And some worthy products bite the dust because someone puts the wrong price on them.

It is tempting to say that these micromarketing mistakes are just part of life—that the world is also full of stupid diplomats, careless soldiers, and ministers who can't preach a decent sermon. Yet there are many examples of companies that do things right. L. L. Bean's customers like its prompt service and liberal returns policy, so they come back to buy again and again. Ocean Spray takes the lead in packaging with its drink in a box. Toys "R" Us earns a place as the child's best friend with low prices and broad selections. These examples and countless others show that improvement is possible.

What about the macromarketing view of costs? Is too much spent on marketing? A strong case can be made that it is not. The case rests on the fact that most marketing costs are driven by demand. After all, businesses can't force consumers to pay marketing costs. Consumers have too many choices open to them.

If consumers don't want to pay the costs of transporting goods, they can buy goods that are produced closer to home. In the case of some goods, such as bricks, they do just that. But if they want the cost savings that come with large-scale production at a central location, the transportation costs have to be paid.

If consumers don't want to pay the costs of branding and advertising, they can buy generic goods. Many do. There are generic versions of almost every good. Even generic cigarettes survive in a market where image and positioning are the name of the game. But most people choose not to buy generic goods, even when they are displayed side by side with more costly branded products. What other reason can there be, except that the branded goods serve their needs better?

L. L. Bean has succeeded largely because of its excellent marketing strategy, which emphasizes prompt service and a liberal returns policy. Courtesy of L. L. Bean Inc.

And should consumers have to pay the markups of 50 percent, 100 percent, or more that many stores charge? They shouldn't have to and they don't. As we saw at the beginning of this chapter, the trend toward discount retailing has even reached car dealerships. But don't expect full-service stores to disappear. A lot of people like them, and pay the markups without complaint. In fact, fancy boutiques with ultrahigh markups are growing just as fast as discounters.

Marketing costs account for 50 percent of consumer spending because American business delivers such a huge variety of products through so many channels. As long as consumers are free to vote with their checkbooks, and as long as firms are free to enter the market with new products or new kinds of stores, we have the best protection we can get against excessive marketing costs.

SUMMARY

1. The *price* of a product is the amount of money customers must pay for it. For a business firm, the first goal of pricing is to earn a profit. To do so, the price must be high enough to cover both the costs of making the product and the costs of product development, distribution, and promotion. A second common goal of pricing is growth of sales or market share. Many firms see growth of sales as the key to profits in the long run. Some firms set prices that will not upset the status quo. Governments and not-for-profit firms balance the goals of survival and fairness in setting prices.

2. The *demand* for a product means the amount that customers are willing and able to buy at a given price. The lower the price, other things being equal, the more units of the product will be bought. This linkage between price and quantity sold is often shown in the form of a downward-sloping demand curve. An increase in demand (a rightward shift of the demand curve) gives firms a chance to sell more or increase prices, or both, thereby raising profits. A decrease in demand (a leftward shift of the curve) may force price cuts and reduce profits.

3. The demand for a product determines how much is earned by selling any given amount of that product, but revenue must be balanced against costs when setting the price. Cutting prices in order to increase the quantity sold adds to a firm's profits only as long as the added revenue more than offsets the added costs of producing the extra output. Firms react to rising costs partly by raising their prices and partly by reducing their output. They react to falling costs partly by cutting prices and partly by increasing output.

4. Competition is a third factor that affects prices. The more competitors a firm has, and the more similar their products are to its own, the greater the pressure to keep prices close to costs.

5. Good pricing decisions must take all three factors into account—demand, cost, and competition. This requires judgment, experience, and a feel for the market. Pricing methods such as markup pricing, target pricing, and break-even analysis often serve as useful starting points, however.

6. No price is right or wrong in and of itself. A price is right only when it is part of a complete marketing strategy. The price must be attractive to people in the target market, and it must mesh with product, distribution, and promotion. It is especially important to keep the whole marketing strategy in mind when using price as a positioning technique, when using promotional pricing, and when pricing new products.

7. Although firms can be very flexible in setting prices, a number of legal restraints must be kept in mind. The antitrust laws ban price fixing, price discrimination, and predatory pricing. International agreements limit dumping. The Federal Trade Commission and certain state and local agencies enforce laws against deceptive pricing. Some prices, such as the rates charged for gas and electricity, are regulated by special commissions. And from time to time the federal government has imposed general price controls and anti-inflation guidelines. These restraints are helpful when they protect the competitive process. However, they are sometimes abused to protect some firms against competition by others.

8. Not all firms do a good job of marketing, but American business as a whole does a good job of meeting consumer needs as those needs are defined by consumers themselves. Fifty percent of all consumer spending is a lot to pay for marketing, but marketing costs are driven by consumer demand. Consumers who want to save on those costs have many choices, such as discount stores and generic goods.

KEY TERMS

You should be familiar with the following terms and concepts. Check their meanings by referring to the marginal definitions in the chapter or to the glossary at the end of the book.

Price

Price leader

Demand

Demand curve

Markup pricing

Markup percentage

Rate of turnover

Target pricing

Fixed costs

Variable costs

Break-even analysis

Skimming

Penetration

Predatory pricing

Dumping

QUESTIONS FOR REVIEW AND DISCUSSION

1. What is the pricing policy of the school at which you are taking this course? Is tuition charged? If so, how much of the cost of the course is covered by tuition? What services, if any, are offered without charge? What services, if any, are provided at prices that cover or more than cover costs? How do the goals of survival and fairness enter into your school's pricing policy? Is growth also a goal of that policy?

2. Look at the demand curve in Box 12–1. Calculate the total revenue for each point along the curve at intervals of twenty tickets. On a piece of graph paper, plot a curve that shows the relationship between total revenue (vertical axis) and quantity sold (horizontal axis). What does this curve tell you about the effect on total revenue of an increase or decrease in price?

3. Gilbert Schmauder, an auto dealer in Runaway, Michigan, has been selling 500 cars a year at an average of $400 over the factory invoice cost. Howard Van Bortel convinces Schmauder that by cutting prices to $49 over invoice he can sell ten times as many cars. Schmauder figures that his selling costs per car, including carrying costs and commissions, have been about $200 per car. He estimates that his selling costs per car will drop to $30 under the Van Bortel system. Will the switch to the new system increase Schmauder's profits? Suppose that he has other sources of profit—dealer-installed options, a service department, and bonuses from the manufacturer based on sales volume. All of these increase along with sales. How much per car would Schmauder have to make from

these sources in order to make the Van Bortel system pay?

3. Martha White runs a small health food store in a town where there are several other stores like hers. When she opened the store she experimented with pricing. She found that whenever she cut her markup in order to advertise lower prices, her rivals matched her price cuts. But if she raised her markup above the average of other stores, her rivals did not match her prices. After a while she decided to stick with the standard markup used by the other health food stores, and to adopt a strategy that stressed the superior freshness and variety of the foods in her store. Does this status quo pricing policy seem sensible? Why or why not?

4. Using news stories, ads, or your own experience, list some products whose prices have changed recently. Include some increases and some decreases. What factors do you think lie behind each change—demand, cost, competition, or a combination of the three?

5. Ho Hoang does not like his job as a grocery clerk—the pay is bad and it keeps him indoors all day. He learns that a local quarry is paying $50 a load to dump truck owners to haul gravel to construction sites. He takes a careful look at this business opportunity. Payments, insurance, and depreciation on a truck will come to $2000 a month. Fuel, tires, and maintenance will cost $25 per load. Use a break-even chart to find out how many loads Ho will have to haul each month before he makes a profit. How many loads will he have to haul before he earns more than the $600 a month he makes as a clerk?

6. Visit a high-priced department store or clothing boutique. How well do product, place, and promotion mesh with the store's pricing policy? Give details. Also visit a discount or off-price clothing store and answer the same questions. If you want, choose a product other than clothing.

7. Question 6 at the end of Chapter 11 asked you to visit a supermarket and take notes on its sales promotions. Using those notes as a guide, discuss the store's use of promotional pricing. Base your discussion on what you have learned about pricing in this chapter.

8. Airlines practice a form of price discrimination in which different seats on the same plane are sold at different prices. (This is perfectly legal.) Why is the airline able to charge different prices for seats on the same plane? How does this benefit the airline? Do some or all of its passengers benefit? If so, which ones? Do you think this practice should be outlawed and replaced by a one-price policy? Why or why not?

9. At the end of this chapter we argued that consumers are protected against excessive marketing costs because if they choose they can turn to discount stores, generic goods, and so on. Do you agree? Why or why not? Can you give examples of products that this argument seems to fit and some that it does not? What about taxicabs? Postal services? Textbooks?

Case 12–1: J. P. Stevens Takes the Designer Route

In September 1983 *Business Week* ran a story on what it called "one of the boldest, riskiest—and most novel—concepts the retailing world has seen in quite a while." J. P. Stevens, a firm that is known as the leading conservative of the textile industry, was about to unveil a new collection of products designed by Ralph Lauren, a designer with a big name in high-fashion clothing. The collection would include sheets and towels, and also such items as crystal stemware and wood furniture.

"Not only is this one of the largest designer collections ever assembled," *Business Week* reported, "but it also will be among the most unusually displayed. Stevens is demanding that participating stores spend up to $250,000 constructing free-standing, wood-paneled boutiques that will span at least 1,000 square feet of floor space to house the merchandise. And the retail prices are steep: One of the least costly items is a $17 terry towel; terry-cloth robes cost $195, hand-blown wine goblets $35, and a five-piece, stainless-steel flatware place setting runs about $100."

According to *Business Week*, Stevens' vice-chairman David M. Tracy saw the Lauren project as a way both to earn profits and to perk up his firm's reputation. Stevens spent $5 million in eighteen months to develop the collection. Industry observers were surprised when Stevens announced that it would not allow the Lauren line to be marked down for white sales, a standard practice. "We're sending off some shock waves," said Tracy. A bold advertising strategy will also be used. Besides launching a $1 million advertising campaign in *Vogue* and other fashionable publications, Stevens will require stores to buy twenty-eight-page full-color catalogs. These catalogs will be mailed to selected customers but will contain no price or ordering information.

Source: "J. P. Stevens Takes the Designer Route," *Business Week*, September 19, 1983, pp. 118–22.

Questions:

1. What is the target market for Stevens' Ralph Lauren collection? How is the line of goods being positioned for that market?

2. Discuss the way Stevens has adjusted other parts of its marketing mix to fit the high price of goods in the Lauren collection.

3. What were the fixed and variable costs of bringing out the Lauren line? Do you think Stevens' managers might have used break-even analysis when they were thinking about this project? How could they have applied this method?

Case 12–2: Utah Pie versus Continental Baking

With the spread of home freezers in the late 1950s, sales of many kinds of frozen foods grew rapidly. In 1957 the Utah Pie Company, a small, family-owned firm in Salt Lake City, decided to take advantage of this situation by bringing out a line of frozen pies. The pies were a quick success. By the next year Utah Pie had captured two thirds of the city's frozen pie market.

Three large national food producers, Continental Baking Company, Pet Milk Company, and Carnation Company, had already been selling frozen pies in Salt Lake City. Utah Pie took business away from them by selling its pies at lower prices. The three big companies fought back with lower prices of their own. In fact, because the competition in Salt Lake City was more intense than that which they faced elsewhere, they sold their pies in Salt Lake City at lower prices there than those they charged in other cities. These tactics did not stop the growth of Utah Pie's sales, but they did cut the local firm's share of the fast-growing pie market to 45 percent by 1961.

Utah Pie's income grew from a loss of $6461 in 1957 to a modest profit of $9216 in 1961, but the firm saw that it could make much larger profits if it could end the price competition in the Salt Lake City market. It filed suit under the Robinson-Patman Act. It argued that its rivals' tactic of targeting Salt Lake City for promotional discounts was illegal price discrimination. The Supreme Court agreed. It found Continental, Pet, and Carnation guilty of having contributed to a "deteriorating price structure."

Source: *Utah Pie* versus *Continental Baking Co.*, 386 U.S. 685 (1967).

Questions:

1. What is the difference between protecting the competitive process and protecting one firm against competition by others? Which of these two results did the Supreme Court's ruling in *Utah Pie* have? Or did it have both? Discuss.

2. Do you think Salt Lake City consumers benefited from the *Utah Pie* decision? Why or why not? Do you think consumer interests should be taken into account in cases of this type? If so, how?

3. Price discrimination means charging different prices for the same good in different markets. Continental, Pet, and Carnation could have eliminated the price discrimination in one of two ways: by raising prices in Salt Lake City or by lowering prices in other markets. Which would have been better from the consumer's point of view? From the point of view of each of the companies?

© Freda Leinwand

SUGGESTED READINGS, PART III

Kinnear, Thomas C., and Kenneth L. Bernhardt. *Principles of Marketing*. Glenview, Ill.: Scott, Foresman, 1983.

Stanton, William J. *Fundamentals of Marketing*, 6th ed. New York: McGraw-Hill, 1981.

Kotler, Philip. *Marketing for Nonprofit Organizations*, 2nd ed. Englewood Cliffs, N.J.: Prentice-Hall, 1982.

Anderson, Ralph E., and Joseph F. Hair, Jr. *Sales Management: Text and Cases*. New York: Random House, 1983.

Hutt, Michael D., and Thomas H. Speh. *Individual Marketing Management*. Chicago: Dryden Press, 1981.

Levitt, Theodore. "Marketing Myopia." *Harvard Business Review*, July-August 1960, pp. 45–56. Also, "Retrospective Commentary" on that article. *Harvard Business Review*, September-October 1975.

Kotler, Philip, and Sidney J. Levy. "Broadening the Concept of Marketing." *Journal of Marketing*, January 1969, pp. 10–15.

Leavitt, Theodore. "Exploit the Product Life Cycle." *Harvard Business Review*, November-December 1965, pp. 81–94.

Pope, N. W. "Mickey Mouse Marketing." *American Banker*, July 27, 1979, and "More Mickey Mouse Marketing," *American Banker*, September 12, 1979.

Useful periodicals:

Advertising Age
Journal of Marketing
Industrial Marketing
Women's Wear Daily
Madison Avenue

CAREERS IN MARKETING

Marketing is the cutting edge of every business, the point of contact between the firm and its customers. Without a product that meets customers' needs at a price that they are willing to pay, and without the skill to bring the product to customers' attention and persuade them to buy it, no business can survive. The importance of marketing to the firm, plus the constant chance for contact with people, makes marketing an attractive career.

Marketing also has the advantage of being one of the best sources of entry-level jobs. This is especially true of sales, which offers the largest number of jobs within marketing. If one wants to make a career in an industry, whether it is computers, clothing, or asphalt paving, it is essential to get to know the industry's customers. The daily face-to-face contact of a selling job is the best way to do that.

Whether or not one wants a career in sales or marketing, such jobs are a chance to learn a wide range of skills. These include skills in communicating and making presentations, listening, managing time, persuading, and following up on commitments. These skills are valuable in any kind of work.

Several kinds of sales jobs will be discussed in this section, but sales jobs are not the only kind within marketing. There are others to suit a variety of skills and personal preferences. The jobs of purchasing agent, real estate broker, travel agent, public-relations worker, and marketing research analyst will also be covered. These jobs are found throughout the economy, in business, government, and the not-for-profit sector.

Job Title: Retail Trade Sales Worker

Description. The success of any retail business depends on courteous and efficient sales workers. Whether they are selling furniture, appliances, or clothing, their primary job is to interest customers in merchandise by explaining how it is made, showing how it works, and finding models and colors to suit the customer's taste. In selling standardized articles, the sales worker may do little more than take payments and wrap purchases. However, many retail sales jobs require special skills and knowledge related to the product. Most retail salespeople work in stores, but there are also positions in door-to-door, telephone, and direct-mail sales.

Qualifications. Many retail sales jobs are open to people with a high school education or even less. Opportunities for advancement from sales to other marketing and management jobs are much better, however, for people with an associate or bachelor's degree. Large retail businesses often hire college graduates as management trainees and start them in sales positions. In small stores where one person, usually the owner, does the management

work, opportunities for advancement are limited. However, a sales job in such a store can provide the experience needed to start a small business of one's own.

Job outlook. More than 3.3 million people were employed as retail sales workers in 1980. Such jobs exist in every part of the country. This group of jobs is expected to grow about as fast as the average for all occupations through the 1980s. Retail sales is an especially good source of part-time jobs.

Earnings. The starting wage in many retail sales positions is the minimum wage of $3.35 per hour, or about $6,700 per year for a standard 40-hour week. Median earnings, including bonuses and commissions, ranged from $8,300 to $14,200 in 1980. Earnings tend to be higher than the median for jobs that require technical knowledge of the merchandise, for example, automobile sales. In jobs where bonuses or commissions are paid, the earnings of people with exceptional selling skills can be many times the average.

Job Title: Wholesale Sales Worker

Description: Wholesale sales workers visit buyers for retail, industrial, and commercial firms, and also institutions like schools and hospitals. They show samples or catalogs of the items their company stocks. Often they are called upon to show how their products can save money or improve productivity for the buyer.

In addition to selling, wholesale sales workers provide many services to their customers. For example, wholesalers may check a retail store's stock and order items for replacement, advise the store on ordering and inventory systems, and help with advertising and sales promotions. Those who sell machinery may help with installation and maintenance. Wholesale sales workers often work out of their homes, have irregular hours, and do a great deal of traveling.

Qualifications. The background required for jobs in wholesale sales varies widely from one product line to another. Complex products require technical backgrounds. For example, drug wholesalers look for people with college degrees in chemistry, biology, or pharmacy. For nontechnical products like food, general sales ability is more important, and some openings may be available for high school graduates. Trainees often begin in "inside" jobs, such as the stockroom or shipping department, before being sent out to deal directly with customers. Many people transfer to wholesale sales jobs from retail sales jobs. Their familiarity with products and customer needs gives them an advantage.

Job outlook. About 1.1 million people were employed as wholesale sales workers in 1980. The number of jobs in this field is expected to grow about as fast as the average for all occupations. For those with good product knowledge and selling ability, opportunities for advancement to supervisor or sales manager are good.

Earnings. Compensation plans differ from one firm to another. Some workers earn salaries; others work for bonuses and commissions; and still others work for a mix of the two. Beginning workers in wholesale sales earned an average of $18,500 in 1980. Experienced workers earned considerably more. Including bonuses and commissions, the highest-paid sales workers earned from $33,000 (in food products) to $49,000 (in lumber and building materials).

Job Title: Manufacturer's Sales Worker

Description: Depending on the structure of the chain of distribution, manufacturers' sales workers may sell to wholesalers or to retail firms and institutions like hospitals and schools. Some jobs in this field closely resemble those of wholesale sales workers. Others are highly technical. For example, a sales worker for a maker of electronic equipment might be expected to suggest improvements in a customer's manufacturing or inventory procedures, to adapt products to the customer's special requirements, to negotiate a sale, and to help in training the buyer's employees to operate the new equipment. Manufacturers' sales workers often cover large territories and may work away from home for weeks at a time.

Qualifications. Most employers look for candidates with college degrees. For nontechnical products, they seek graduates with degrees in liberal arts or business. For technical products, graduates with degrees in science and engineering are preferred. Many firms have formal training programs for newly hired workers; these programs may last two years or longer. As in the case of all sales jobs, a pleasant personality and appearance, as well as the ability to get along with people, are assets.

Job prospects. Some 440,000 people were employed as manufacturers' sales workers in 1980. In addition, there were many self-employed people working as independent sales agents. The number

CAREERS IN MARKETING (CONTINUED)

of jobs in this field is expected to grow about as fast as the average for all jobs. Opportunities for advancement are good. Workers with good sales skills may advance to sales supervisor, branch manager, or district manager. Those with managerial skills can advance to jobs in general management. Frequent contact with other firms helps sales workers transfer to other jobs.

Earnings. As in other sales jobs, earnings depend on the type of compensation plan used. A combination of salary and commission is the most common plan. In 1980 starting salaries ranged from $13,900 to $15,400 per year. Experienced workers earned from $17,400 to $23,100. Sales supervisors earned from $32,400 to $37,400.

Job Title: Retail Buyer

Description. Buyers seek goods that will satisfy their store's customers and can be sold at a profit. They learn about available goods from trade shows, in manufacturers' showrooms, and from wholesale and manufacturers' sales workers. Some jobs in this field, such as that of buyer of high-fashion clothing, can be very glamorous. Other buyers deal with more mundane products like canned soups and automobile tires. Buyers must be skilled at assessing the retail price at which their store will be able to sell the goods they buy. They must know the needs of their customers and must be good judges of quality and style.

Qualifications. An associate or bachelor's degree is increasingly required. Courses in marketing or retailing may help in getting started, but they are not essential. Most stores will accept graduates in any field and will train them on the job. Previous experience in retail sales—for example, in part-time or summer jobs—is an asset. Workers in this field should have good communication skills and should be able to make decisions quickly and work under pressure.

Job outlook. Approximately 180,000 people worked as retail buyers in 1980. The growth in number of jobs is expected to be average. Competition for jobs is expected to be keen.

Earnings. The earnings of buyers depend on the quantity and type of goods purchased. Buyers for discount department stores, chain stores, and other mass merchandisers are among the most highly paid. Most buyers earned between $19,000 and $28,000 a year in 1980. Many stores have bonus and incentive plans in addition to salaries.

Job Title: Purchasing Agent (Industrial Buyer)

Description. The job of a purchasing agent, also known as an industrial buyer, is to obtain the materials, supplies, and equipment that a firm needs to carry on its business. Purchasing agents must judge the quality of the goods they buy and must seek the lowest price for the required quality. They are responsible for making sure that adequate supplies are always available. Some jobs—for example, purchasing custom-made machinery or electronic equipment—require advanced technical knowledge. Units of government and not-for-profit firms as well as businesses employ purchasing agents.

Qualifications. Smaller companies seek applicants with associate or bachelor's degrees. Larger companies may look for candidates with bachelor's degrees in technical fields, or MBA degrees. As in the case of sales jobs, the ability to communicate and to develop good working relationships is essential.

Job outlook. About 172,000 people worked as purchasing agents in 1980. Growth of employment in this field is expected to be average. Many opportunities will arise in service organizations like hospitals and schools. Graduates of two-year programs will continue to find good opportunities, especially in smaller firms. Qualified workers can advance to assistant purchasing manager or purchasing manager. However, continuing education is essential for advancement.

Earnings. College graduates hired as junior purchasing agents earned about $16,200 a year in 1980. Experienced agents buying standardized goods earned about $20,300. Those buying technical goods earned more, averaging about $25,200 per year.

Job Title: Public Relations Worker

Description: Public relations workers help businesses, units of government, and not-for-profit organizations build and maintain a positive public image. They may handle press, community, or consumer relations, political campaigning, interest-group representation, or fund raising. In addition to telling their employer's story, public relations workers must understand the attitudes and concerns of customers, employees, and various other "publics" with which their organization comes into contact. They also arrange and conduct programs in which company officials come into direct contact with the public, such as speeches and press interviews.

Qualifications. An associate or bachelor's degree is normally required. The field of study is most often journalism, communications, or public relations. However, some employers prefer a background in an area related to the firm's business, such as finance or engineering. Some employers seek candidates who have worked for the news media. Such extracurricular activities as writing for a school publication or part-time work in a radio or television station are an advantage.

Job outlook. About 87,000 people were employed as public relations workers in 1980. The rate of growth in the number of jobs in this area is expected to be about average. Competition for entry-level jobs is keen, as the glamour and excitement of public relations attract many applicants. Opportunities for advancement to supervisor or public-relations manager are good for workers with demonstrated ability and management skills. Some experienced workers start public relations firms of their own.

Earnings. Competition for jobs tends to hold starting salaries to a modest level. College graduates beginning as public-relations workers earned from $10,000 to $13,000 per year in 1980. Experienced workers in larger organizations earned from $30,000 to $50,000.

Job Title: Real Estate Agents and Brokers

Description. Real estate brokers are independent businesspeople who sell real estate owned by others, rent and manage properties, make appraisals, and assist in developing new housing projects. They often also help buyers arrange financing. Real estate agents are independent sales workers who contract their services with a licensed broker. In addition to selling, much of a broker's time is spent obtaining "listings," that is, agreements by owners to sell their properties through the firm.

Qualifications. Real estate agents and brokers must be licensed by the state in which they work. All states require a college diploma and passage of a written test. The test, which is more comprehensive for brokers than for agents, includes questions on basic property law. Many large firms seek college graduates to fill sales positions. However, personality traits are as important as educational background. A pleasant personality, honesty, tact, and enthusiasm are necessary.

CAREERS IN MARKETING (CONTINUED)

Job outlook. According to the Bureau of the Census, some 580,000 people sold real estate as their primary occupation in 1980. Many more sold on a part-time basis. Growth of employment in this field is expected to be faster than the average for all occupations. Competition for jobs in this field is keen. There are opportunities for advancement to management positions in large firms. Also, many people start their own businesses after working for a large firm.

Earnings. Commissions are the main source of earnings for real estate agents and brokers. The rate of commission depends on the type of property sold. In many firms, the agent selling the property gets half of the commission, with the other half going to the firm. In 1980, the median income of real estate agents who worked 30 hours a week or more was $14,700. The earnings of brokers averaged $29,000. As in all jobs that are paid on a commission basis, earnings in real estate sales vary widely. Brokers with exceptional skills may earn many times the average for their profession.

Job Title: Travel Agent

Description: Travel agents arrange transportation and lodging for travelers. They must be able to recommend vacation travel packages that suit their clients' needs. Travel agents do considerable promotional work and often visit hotels, resorts, and restaurants to assess their quality.

Travel agents serve both business and vacation travelers. These two kinds of clients require different approaches. Vacation travelers often plan long in advance. They must often be "sold" on the destination, as well as, the mode of travel. Business travelers, on the other hand, usually know where they want to go. They often require arrangements to be made on short notice. Economy and convenient schedules are more important for these travelers.

Qualifications. There are few formal qualifications for the job of travel agent. Experience as a traveler is an asset, as is a pleasant and patient personality. Many employers prefer applicants with an associate or bachelor's degree. Home study and vocational-school courses can also be helpful.

Job outlook. About 52,000 people worked as travel agents in 1980. The number of jobs in this field is expected to increase much faster than average throughout the 1980s. There will be good opportunities for starting new agencies as well as for working in existing firms.

Earnings. The earnings of people who own their own agencies come mainly from commissions from airlines, tour operators, and lodging places. Total earnings depend on experience, sales ability, and the size and location of the agency. Salaries of agency employees ranged from $9,500 to $18,000 per year. In order to familiarize travel agents with their services, airlines, hotels, and resorts often offer them transportation and lodging at greatly reduced rates. Many workers in the field consider this a major benefit of the job.

Job Title: Marketing Research Analyst

Description. Marketing research analysts study the wants and needs of the buying public. They plan, design, and implement surveys and test-marketing campaigns. They are called upon when problems arise, for example, when a firm's frozen foods are selling poorly in a certain city. After studying the situation, they might recommend more advertising, redesign of the product, or concentration on other markets where consumers are more inclined to buy the firm's product.

Qualifications. A bachelor's degree is usually sufficient for a trainee position, but a graduate degree is required for many specialized positions. College study should emphasize statistics, English composition, communications, psychology, sociology, and economics as well as general business and marketing courses. A strong background in computers is helpful.

Job prospects. About 29,000 people worked as marketing research analysts in 1980. Employment will grow at all levels, but opportunities will be best for people with strong computer backgrounds and graduate degrees. College graduates can expect to start as research assistants or junior analysts, positions that include clerical duties like coding questionnaires. After learning interviewing skills and gaining experience, these trainees will become analysts. The most able analysts may be promoted to the position of supervisor or director of marketing research.

Earnings. Starting salaries of marketing researchers with bachelor's degrees ranged from $12,000 to $17,000 per year in 1980. Holders of master's degrees started at salaries averaging $21,500. Senior analysts earned $27,000 on the average, and directors of marketing research earned from $40,000 to $50,000.

Job Title: Advertising Workers

Description. Advertising work covers a wide range of specific jobs. Advertising agencies are a major source of employment. Account executives are in charge of the advertising efforts of the agency's clients. They plan ad campaigns and maintain good relations with the client. Copywriters write the text of ads, called copy, and scripts for radio and TV ads. Art directors are responsible for the visual appearance of ads. Production managers arrange to have the ad printed, filmed, or recorded. Media buyers buy space or time for ads in newspapers and magazines, on radio or TV, and so on. Ad agencies also employ marketing research workers.

Not all advertising workers are employed by ad agencies. Companies that have marketing departments usually have a director of advertising and several assistants. These may conduct ad campaigns themselves or work with an agency in doing so. Finally, advertising media like newspapers, magazines, and radio and television stations employ advertising sales workers who persuade advertisers and agencies to buy services from their employers.

Qualifications. Given the wide range of advertising work, there is also a wide range of qualifications. A bachelor's degree is usually the minimum requirement. Courses in advertising are helpful, but a liberal-arts or journalism background can be just as useful for positions like copywriter or art director. For managerial and research jobs, employers often prefer holders of the MBA degree. Sales experience can also be helpful.

Job outlook. About 100,000 workers were employed in advertising agencies in 1980, and many more than this in other firms. Advertising agency jobs are concentrated in New York and a few other large cities. Nonagency jobs are found throughout the country. Employment growth in this field is expected to be about average. Advancement within the field can be quite rapid for those with outstanding talent.

Earnings. Earnings vary widely, depending on experience and ability. Beginning workers started at salaries ranging from $10,000 to $18,000 a year in 1980. Holders of the MBA degree received starting salaries in the range of $18,000–25,000 per year. Account executives with five to ten years of experience earned from $25,000 to $40,000. Top managers and people with exceptional talent often make much more than this.

Part IV

OPERATIONS, PRODUCTION, AND PEOPLE

As we explained in the chapters on marketing, no firm can succeed without understanding the needs of its customers and how they can be met. However, an idea for meeting customer needs is not enough. To survive, the firm must be able to turn that idea into a good or service at a cost that leaves room for a profit. This part of the book is devoted to the management skills needed to turn the product idea into reality.

Chapter 13 covers production and operations management—the task of managing the transformation of inputs into outputs. It will show how production systems are planned, how decisions are made about their location, and how production activities can be harmonized with the environment. Throughout the chapter, the linkages among productivity, quality, and flexibility will be stressed.

The next three chapters turn their attention from the management of physical production systems to the management of human resources. As we have said many times, people are the key to productivity and quality in every organization, whether it is a business, a unit of government, or a not-for-profit firm.

Chapter 14 addresses the task of leadership—focusing the motivations and energies of employees on the goals of the firm. Chapter 15 looks at labor unions and the special problems and advantages of managing human resources in a unionized firm. Chapter 16 covers personnel management. It shows how planning, organizing, leading, and controlling are needed to make sure the best available person fills each job in the organization.

Source: Jeremy Main, "Ford's Drive for Quality," *FORTUNE*, April 18, 1983, pp. 62–70. Reprinted by permission from *FORTUNE* © 1983 Time Inc. All rights reserved.

Questions:

1. Comment on Ford's experience in its Louisville plant in the light of the Model T example given at the beginning of the chapter. What was the relative importance of human relations and technology in each case?

2. Discuss the relationships among quality control, product design, and process design as shown in this case.

3. How does this case illustrate the principle that quality should be built in, not inspected in?

Chapter 14

MOTIVATION, LEADERSHIP, AND PRODUCTIVITY

When you have completed this chapter, you should be able to

- Define *motivation* and explain the link between motivation and performance.

- Discuss Maslow's *hierarchy of needs,* Herzberg's two-factor theory of motivation, and expectancy.

- Explain the importance and limitations of pay as a motivator.

- Compare three approaches to managing for productivity and quality: the *traditional approach*, the *human relations approach*, and the *human resources approach*.

- Discuss ways of creating clear expectations and providing feedback, including the technique of *management by objectives*.

- Explain the importance of organizing in managing for productivity and quality.

- Discuss techniques of leadership that can raise productivity and quality.

When Dennis E. Hacker moved out of the crowded room where he and other TRW Inc. software designers hammered out computer code, two things happened. He felt isolated and his productivity soared.

TRW put Hacker and thirty-four of his colleagues into private, windowless offices wired with state-of-the-art computer equipment: terminals that talk to the company's computer network, electronic mail, teleconferencing, and programs that help write programs. The company expected the programmers to become more productive, but it didn't expect an increase of as much as 39 percent in the first year. "The results were so good we were reluctant to believe them," says Robert Williams, vice-president of systems information and software development.

Hacker says he missed the friendly chaos of the bullpen during his first few days in his new office. "I didn't feel like part of the team any more," he recalls. But he soon came to like his new surroundings. "I'd close the door and grind away at my work, and the next thing I knew I was getting hungry. I realized it was six P.M. and I'd worked right through the day."

To find out how to raise productivity, TRW went to the programmers themselves. "Nobody knows what it takes to generate programs better than programmers," says Henry P. Conn, TRW's former vice-president for productivity and a consultant for the company.

The result was an office design that Hacker says he found "claustrophobic" at first but later learned to love: the beige, soundproof, windowless space contained only a chair built to fit the human body, a white board, a bookshelf, a work table, and a computer terminal. Instead of working on code in their three- or four-person offices and then running to the bullpen to feed a batch of work into the system, programmers stay in their offices, writing and testing their work as they produce it.

To avoid time-consuming filing and telephone calls, files are stored and messages exchanged by computer. Again, the programmer doesn't have to move from his chair.

But psychologists warn about the long-term effects of such changes in the quality of people's work lives. Optimistic goals like TRW's can be dashed in the long term if care isn't taken to measure human factors as well as product output, says Alexandra Saba, a Los Angeles industrial psychologist. Saba worked on a study of workplace changes for Verbatim Corporation, a supplier of magnetic storage media. She says the study found that depriving workers of face-to-face contact could be harmful.

"If you stick people into little cubicles, they start suffering psychological effects and physiological effects of worker alienation," she says. "In the long term, productivity can actually go down."

Hacker says that is not true in his case. He had to leave the new office when a code-writing project that he was working on ended. Back in the old offices, surrounded by other people, he says he felt "an immediate decrease" in his productivity. He says he has learned to prefer a conference call on a computer screen to a casual chat in the corridor.[1]

---

[1]Geraldine Brooks, "Faced with Changing Work Force, TRW Pushes to Raise White-Collar Productivity," *Wall Street Journal*, September 22, 1983, p. 33. Reprinted by permission of the *Wall Street Journal*. © Dow Jones & Company, Inc., 1983. All Rights Reserved.

The story of Dennis Hacker's new office is repeating itself in workplaces all over America. Managers have come to see productivity and quality as major goals. They do not neglect equipment and technology—Hacker's new office had the latest of both. But they recognize that the real key to productivity is people. Getting extraordinary performance out of ordinary people is one of the features that sets excellently managed companies apart from the crowd.

The experiment that gave Hacker his new office has some aspects that are widely accepted and some that are not. The idea that surroundings have a lot to do with productivity has been around for years. The idea that you find out how to raise productivity by asking the people who do the work is a little newer, but it is now widespread. The idea of making people more productive by sticking them into sterile little rooms is controversial. But controversy is commonplace in the field of productivity improvement. As we will see in this chapter, no one has a formula that works in all cases, and probably no one ever will.

This chapter continues the discussion of production and operations management that began in Chapter 13, but it changes the focus. It begins by reviewing some general concepts of motivation, performance, and satisfaction. Next it explains how theories of managing for productivity and quality have evolved. The last section stresses the need for leadership to achieve these goals.

The surroundings in which people work have a strong influence on their productivity. Courtesy of TRW Inc.

THEORIES OF MOTIVATION

Motivation: A psychological drive that gives a person's actions purpose and direction.

It is common to speak of effective leaders as people who are good at "motivating" their subordinates, but when we think about it, this is an odd use of the term. **Motivations** are the psychological drives that give people's actions purpose and direction.[2] Those drives come from within. We motivate ourselves. So when we talk about leaders "motivating" others, we

[2]This definition is based on one given by Robert Kreitner. See *Management*, 2nd ed. (Boston: Houghton Mifflin, 1983), p. 329.

Who is motivated, the schnauzer or the trainer? © Freda Leinwand

are really talking about the ways in which they focus and channel people's motivations in order to direct their actions toward the goals of the organization.

Frederick Herzberg tells a story about his pet schnauzer that makes much the same point. "I hold up a biscuit when I want the schnauzer to move. In this instance, who is motivated—I or the dog? The dog wants the biscuit, but it is I that want it to move."[3]

Needs, Motivation, and Satisfaction

Box 14–1 shows four factors on which performance depends. Skills and abilities are one; a clear understanding of the nature of one's job is a second; expectations about what will happen if the job is done well or poorly are a third, and motivation is a fourth. Motivation is the dynamic factor—the one that sets people in motion. (The word *motivation* comes from the Latin word *movere*, which means "to move.")

The diagram shows the link between motivation and performance as part of a closed loop: motivation arises from unsatisfied needs, and the action that it gives rise to, if successful, satisfies the needs. Satisfaction of needs does not put an end to motivation, however. Some needs, such as hunger, are never satisfied for more than a short time. Even if some needs—say, the need for friendship—are satisfied on a lasting basis, other needs remain to act as motivators.

The picture shown in Box 14–1 is a very general one. For it to be of practical use, many details need to be filled in. What specific needs give

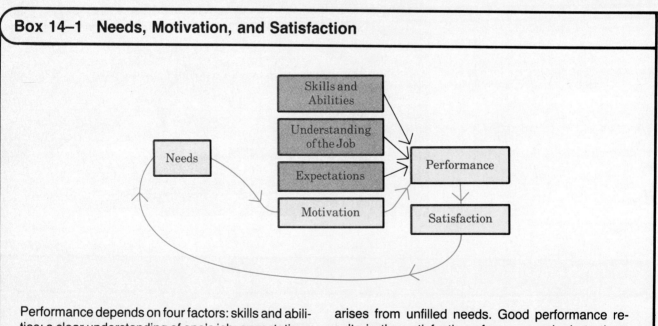

Box 14–1   Needs, Motivation, and Satisfaction

Performance depends on four factors: skills and abilities; a clear understanding of one's job; expectations about what will happen if the job is done well; and motivation. Motivation is part of a closed loop. It arises from unfilled needs. Good performance results in the satisfaction of some needs, but others emerge to take their place.

[3]Frederick Herzberg, "One More Time: How Do You Motivate Employees?" *Harvard Business Review*, January-February 1968, p. 54.

rise to motivation for a certain person at a certain time? In what kinds of environments does motivation lead to good performance? And what happens when a given need is satisfied? Let's look at some attempts to fill in the picture.

Maslow's hierarchy of needs.   In 1943 the psychologist Abraham Maslow suggested that people are motivated by five kinds of needs. The needs, he thought, form a hierarchy, in which any one need becomes a motivator only after lower-level needs have been met. Maslow's **hierarchy of needs**, from lowest to highest, is as follows.[4]

Hierarchy of needs: A ranking of five levels of needs originated by Abraham Maslow in which one need becomes an important motivator only after lower-level needs have been satisfied.

1. *Physiological needs.* These are needs for food, water, sleep, and other things needed to sustain life.
2. *Safety needs.* After enough of the physiological needs have been met, Maslow said, a new set of needs—safety needs—emerges. These include the needs for security, protection, order, and freedom from fear.
3. *Affection needs.* After safety needs have been met, a set of needs for love and belongingness come to the fore. People who are well fed and secure feel a need for friends and family, and a need to be a part of a group. These needs are also called social needs.
4. *Esteem needs.* The next level of the need hierarchy consists of the needs for self-respect and recognition. Status, prestige, fame, glory, attention, and dignity are all examples of what Maslow called esteem needs.
5. *The need for self-actualization.* The highest level of need, according to Maslow, is the need to fullfill one's potential—to become everything one can become. This need could find an outlet in many different ways—writing poetry, raising a family, inventing things, or almost anything else.

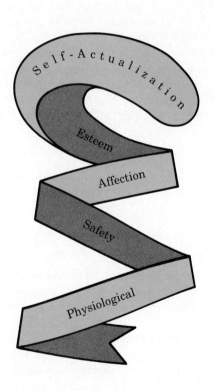

Maslow's theory came out of a study of neurotic patients. Maslow and his followers then went on to study successful, self-actualizing people. The need hierarchy has now been applied to many fields, including management. Here the lesson is that managers must understand the needs that motivate people if they are to succeed in getting them to do things.

Needs that are satisfied do not act as motivators. A prison camp guard may be able to get a burst of effort from a starving inmate with nothing more than the promise of an extra crust of bread. But a six-figure pay raise might not be as effective as a transfer to a challenging new assignment in motivating a top executive with a need for self-actualization. Between these two extremes, the needs for security, affection, and self-esteem are also recognized by effective leaders—and ignored by authoritarian ones, who end up getting less than the best from their hard-driven subordinates.

Herzberg's two-factor theory.   Another theory of motivation was put forward by Frederick Herzberg—the man with the schnauzer. Herzberg interviewed large numbers of employees to find out what factors caused them to be satisfied with their jobs and what factors led to dissatisfaction. He found that satisfaction did not result simply from the absence of factors that cause dissatisfaction. Instead, there were two sets of factors at work. Those that were mentioned most often as sources of dissatisfaction were

---

[4]This description of the need hierarchy is based on Abraham H. Maslow, *Motivation and Personality*, 2nd ed. (New York: Harper & Row, 1954), chap. 4.

company policies, supervision, work conditions, salary, relations with family and fellow workers, status, and job security. Those that were mentioned as sources of great satisfaction were achievement, recognition, work content, responsibility, advancement, and growth.[5]

Herzberg concluded that effective leaders need to pay attention to both sets of factors. They need to avoid conditions that lead to dissatisfaction, but this by itself is not enough to get the best from employees. They need also to give employees opportunities for recognition, advancement, growth, and so on.

Herzberg's theory does not contradict Maslow's. We can say that job dissatisfaction arises from factors that interfere with the satisfaction of lower-level needs (pay, job security, relations with fellow workers), whereas the greatest satisfaction comes when the job offers a chance for self-actualization.

Expectations and performance.   Some writers believe that motivation produces good performance only if certain expectancy conditions are met. Suppose, for example, that each year at graduation your school honors outstanding students in a special ceremony. Will you respond by working harder? Maslow or Herzberg would say that you will if esteem is a motivating need for you. Writers who emphasize expectations say that such an incentive will not lead to greater effort unless two other conditions are also present. First, you must expect greater effort to lead to better grades. And second, you must expect the better grades to lead to the recognition you want. What if you think your professors fail to recognize good performance when they assign grades? Or what if you think the outstanding students who are honored at graduation are chosen partly on the basis of favoritism? Negative expectations like these can break the link between incentives and performance.

The lesson for management is clear: besides understanding employees' needs, leaders must create strong expectations that hard work pays off and that good performance will be rewarded. We will come back to this theme later in the chapter.

Motivation and Pay

In the light of all these theories, what becomes of that good old motivator, the fat paycheck? The answer is that pay still plays a key role in drawing forth productivity and quality, provided that other motivators are present too.

Competition is the first reason that pay is important. If a company does not pay its workers and managers enough, they will go to work for someone else. Nothing Maslow, Herzberg, or anyone else has to say contradicts the fact that if they can choose between two equally satisfying jobs, people will tend to pick the one that pays more.

A second reason that pay is important is that money is a symbol of status and a means for satisfying many kinds of needs. Money does more than buy food and pay insurance premiums. A person's salary is a symbol of status within the firm, and the things the salary buys are symbols of status on the outside. And although money can't buy love, money problems have ruined many otherwise loving relationsips.

[5]Herzberg, p. 57.

But several things can make pay less effective as a motivator. First, it does not work as an incentive unless there is a clear expectation that greater efforts will get better results and that better results will be recognized. Second, good pay may not get good performance if the sources of job dissatisfaction listed earlier are present. And third, people have to believe that harder work and higher pay won't have negative side effects. Will the hard worker on the assembly line be hated by fellow workers as a "rate buster"? Will the hardworking district manager get a bonus this year, but a higher quota to meet next year? Effective leaders must take steps to avoid these dangers.

THREE APPROACHES TO MANAGING FOR PRODUCTIVITY AND QUALITY

Using the theories of motivation we have discussed as background, we will next look at three approaches to managing for productivity and quality. In part, these approaches reflect different assumptions about human nature and motivations. They also reflect the evolution of management practice. That evolution is not complete, however, since more recent ways of managing have not completely replaced the older ones.

The Traditional Approach

The traditional approach dates from the era of scientific management. Following the lead of Frederick Taylor, managers saw their job as one of improving supervision with the help of a scientific analysis of each task.

The traditional approach is based on three assumptions about human nature. The first is that most people dislike work. The second is that few people are willing or able to do work that requires responsibility, creativity, or self-direction. The third, which follows from the first two, is that the only reason most people are willing to work or accept responsibility is the pay, which allows them to meet the needs of their nonworking hours. Douglas McGregor has called this set of assumptions **theory X**.[6]

Theory X: A set of assumptions about people, including the assumptions that they dislike work, lack creativity, and are motivated mainly by pay.

These assumptions led to methods that were typical of the scientific-management era. Suppose that you are a manager who wants to raise the productivity of a crew that unloads crates of parts from freight cars. You assume that there must be one best way to do the job and that you are the person who is best equipped to find it. Stopwatch in hand, you go out to the loading dock to watch the work. Soon you see what the problems are. "O'Higgins," you say, "don't pick up the crate that way—lift with your knees, not your back. And Weiss, don't stack those things seven high—you'll get more work done and you won't get as tired if you start a new stack after five." When you have gotten the job down to a simple routine of steps that can be easily repeated, you train your foreman in the new method and he closely supervises each move from then on. Productivity rises, and you are happy to share part of the gain with the loaders in the form of a pay increase. Of course, in giving them the increase you explain that they are getting it because they have followed the new work method that you thought up.

Box 14–2 shows this approach in the form of a diagram. Productivity and quality rise as a result of scientific supervision and decent pay.

The Human Relations Approach

In the late 1920s a series of experiments was conducted at Western Electric's Hawthorne plant. In one of the experiments a group of employees was placed in a room where the brightness of the lighting could be varied. A control group was placed in an identical room in which the lighting was

---

[6]Douglas McGregor, *The Human Side of Enterprise* (New York: McGraw-Hill, 1960), pp. 33–35.

Box 14–2 The Traditional Approach

ASSUMPTIONS

- People dislike work.
- They lack creativity and avoid responsibility.
- They are motivated mainly by pay.

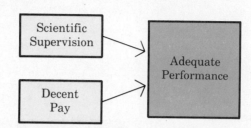

This box gives a graphic picture of the traditional approach to managing for quality and productivity. Performance is seen as a product of scientific super-vision and decent pay. The assumptions that under-lie this approach have come to be called theory X.

Hawthorne effect: The tendency of people to do a better job when they are made to feel useful and important.

Human relations approach: An approach to managing for productivity and quality based on the assumptions that people want to feel useful, are motivated by social rewards in the workplace, and are willing to take responsibility for routine matters.

held constant. The purpose was to discover the one best level of lighting, but the results were not as expected. When the lighting was increased, productivity went up. So far, so good. But when the lighting was decreased, productivity went up some more. Some workers maintained a normal level of output even when the light was made as dim as moonlight. At the same time, productivity went up in the control group too, even though the lighting in the room didn't change at all.

Western Electric called in a team of researchers led by Elton Mayo of Harvard to explain the puzzling results. After repeating some of the experiments, Mayo's team decided that the gains in productivity had nothing to do with lighting. Instead, the workers in both the experimental group and the control group were responding to the attention they were getting. The experiment made them feel useful and important, and that, in turn, made them do a better job. This result later became known as the **Hawthorne effect**.

A whole new approach to management arose out of Mayo's work—the **human relations approach**. It was based on some assumptions about human nature and motivation that were quite different from the tradition-al ones: First, people want to feel useful and important. Second, the social rewards that people get from their work, especially as members of informal groups, rank together with pay as a key motivating factor. Third, the way to make workers feel useful and to keep them productive is to show consideration. This means giving them some responsibility in routine matters, sharing information with them, and discussing decisions that affect their work.

As Raymond E. Miles has put it, participation is a lubricant that oils away resistance to formal authority. By discussing problems with sub-ordinates and taking account of their needs and desires, the manager hopes to build a team that is willing and eager to work to high standards.[7]

Box 14–3 summarizes the human relations approach. Participation improves worker satisfaction and morale. This, in turn, makes people more productive and willing to go along with the directives of managers.

[7]Raymond E. Miles, "Human Relations or Human Resources?" *Harvard Business Review*, July-August 1965, pp. 149–50.

Box 14–3 The Human Relations Approach

ASSUMPTIONS

- People want to feel useful and important.
- Social relations in the workplace are a major source of satisfaction.
- Information sharing and responsibility for routine matters will increase satisfaction.

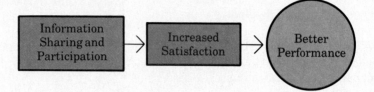

Information Sharing and Participation → Increased Satisfaction → Better Performance

This box illustrates the human relations approach to managing for productivity and quality. Participation is seen as a means of making workers more cooperative and willing to follow the directives of managers.

A famous series of experiments at Western Electric's Hawthorne plant led to the discovery of the "Hawthorne effect": participation in an experiment made workers feel useful and important, and this, in turn, increased their productivity. Courtesy of AT&T

The Human Resources Approach

Some parts of the human relations approach have stood the test of time. Informal work groups do affect productivity and quality. Social rewards on the job are a powerful motivator. And participation and information sharing are powerful management tools. But other assumptions of this approach have not held up as well. In particular, it was found that satisfied workers are not always productive. The "hard" methods of the scientific managers had often produced results at the expense of people. But the "soft" management methods of the human relations approach often made people happier without making them better workers.

By discussing problems with subordinates and taking account of their needs and desires, managers help them feel useful and important. © Sepp Seitz, Woodfin Camp

Theory Y: A set of assumptions about people, including the assumptions that people find satisfaction in their work, are creative, and are eager to participate in the whole range of management functions.

Human resources approach: An approach to managing for productivity and quality that is based on the assumptions that people find satisfaction in their work, are creative, and are eager to participate in the whole range of management functions.

Disappointment with "soft" management methods led to criticism of the human relations approach. The problem was that the human relations approach changed assumptions about people's needs but did not deal with their capabilities. This led to still another set of assumptions about human nature and motivation: First, workers find satisfaction not just in the social relations of the workplace but in the work itself; work is as natural and rewarding as play or rest. Second, imagination and creativity are common traits, but under industrial work conditions these traits are not fully used. Third, given the chance, workers are eager not just to accept responsibility for routine tasks but to participate in the full range of management functions. McGregor calls these assumptions **theory Y**. The view of management that is based on them has come to be known as the **human resources approach**.

The human resources approach, unlike human relations, challenges the traditional relationship between managers and workers. Getting workers to help solve problems of productivity is not seen as mere considerateness, a way of making them feel good. It is seen as a genuine source of ideas about how to do the job better. If you were to go back to the loading dock wearing your human resources hat, here is how the scene might go:

MANAGER: This job shouldn't be so hard. What can we do about it?

O'HIGGINS: I can tell you one problem—the freight cars aren't level with the loading dock. If you had a crew come in here and reballast the tracks with an extra four inches of gravel, we could run a forklift right into the car. Then we wouldn't have to carry them out and stack them by hand.

WEISS: And I'll tell you another thing. If we had just a little more room on this dock, we'd only have to pile the crates five high and the job would go twice as fast. Why don't we cover that old stairwell to make the extra space? We never use it. If we ever needed to go down under the dock, we could go around the back way.

MANAGER: Good thinking!

O'HIGGINS: And more money in the profit-sharing plan, right?

This little scene represents a real revolution in management thinking. In the human resources approach, managers see their job not just as one of giving directions and getting workers to cooperate, but as one of mobilizing the untapped abilities of everyone in the company. Box 14–4 shows how the human resources approach reverses the causal link be-

Box 14–4   The Human Resources Approach

ASSUMPTIONS

• People find satisfaction in work.
• Imagination and creativity are widespread
• People are eager to take responsibility and make decisions.

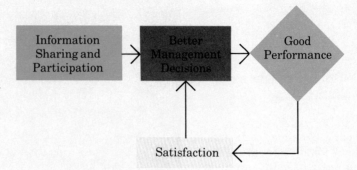

Information Sharing and Participation → Better Management Decisions → Good Performance

Satisfaction

The diagram shown here illustrates the human resources approach to managing for productivity and quality. Participation is seen as a way of improving decision making and performance. Better perform-ance, in turn, leads to more satisfaction. The assumptions underlying this approach are called theory Y.

Under the traditional approach to management, good pay and close supervision were thought to be enough to ensure quality and productivity. Under today's human resources approach, these workers would be expected to participate in decision making and take greater responsibility for their work. © Bruce Davidson, Magnum

tween participation and productivity. Participation leads directly to improved decision making. The better-run workplace, in turn, leads to improved satisfaction and morale.

As we said early in this section, the evolution from the traditional approach to the human resources approach is not complete. This is so for two reasons.

First, the traditional and human relations approaches have not been entirely abandoned because they are not entirely wrong. If Maslow's theory is taken as a guide, for example, we might expect the traditional approach to work well for workers who are motivated primarily by physiological and security needs. For them, a clearly defined task and a fair day's pay for a good day's work may be just the thing. Likewise, the human relations approach seems well suited to workers at the affection-need level of Maslow's hierarchy. It is not that these approaches are wrong for all workers; it is simply that they waste the potential of workers who are eager and able to be creative partners of management.

Second, the traditional and human relations approaches have not yet been abandoned because many managers have not yet accepted the theory Y view of the world. Case 14–1 shows a work situation in which theory X is fully in control. When workers are treated as lazy, ignorant, and incompetent, even those with the potential to do more tend to act the way they are expected to. In other kinds of work situations, managers use the human resources approach in dealing with their superiors and the human relations approach in dealing with subordinates. They think they are just as smart and capable as their bosses, and they want their ideas to be taken seriously. But they have little real faith in their subordinates. They listen to them and share information with them mainly as a way of getting them to take orders more willingly.

The evolutionary process continues, however. Successful applications of the human resources approach, as at Ford's Louisville plant (Case 13–1, page 346) and GM's Livonia plant (Box 2–5, page 39), are persuading more and more managers to change their views.

QUALITY AND PRODUCTIVITY THROUGH PEOPLE

Concern for the problems of American business is mirrored in the success of popular books on managing for quality and productivity. In the early 1980s a whole series of books on this subject made the best-seller lists. Among them were William Ouichi's *Theory Z*, Richard Pascale and Anthony Athos' *The Art of Japanese Management*, Kenneth Blanchard and Spencer Johnson's *The One Minute Manager*, and Peters and Waterman's *In Search of Excellence*.

Some of these writers focused on the management practices of successful Japanese firms, such as Sony, Matsushita, and Toyota. To be sure, these firms do a lot of things better than many American companies. But the studies of Japanese firms uncovered two facts. First, not all Japanese firms do things the same way. And second, while the "typical" Japanese firm may be different from the "typical" American firm, excellently managed companies everywhere are similar in many ways. In fact, when a Japanese translation of *In Search of Excellence* appeared, the first printing of 50,000 copies sold out in two days. After reading the book, Matsushita's president, Toshihiko Yamashita, remarked that "this business of 'Japanese management' is nonsense. . . . I find there is no difference between the West and the East." And Michihiro Nishida, a former Honda executive, said, "In listening to the eight attributes of excellent American companies, I thought I was hearing the history of my own company!"[8]

---

[8]Quoted in Kenichi Ohmae, "Japan's Admiration for U.S. Methods Is an Open Book," *Wall Street Journal*, October 10, 1983. Ohmae himself did the Japanese translation of *In Search of Excellence*.

One of the traits shared by well-managed companies everywhere is their emphasis on people. © Bonnie Freer, Peter Arnold Inc.

One of the traits shared by well-managed companies everywhere is their emphasis on people. They see people as their most important resource, as the key to productivity and quality. In almost all firms top managers pay lip service to the idea that people are important, but the most effective managers really live by the idea. Getting ordinary people to perform to high standards requires good leadership, of course, but it is not a matter of leadership alone. As we will see in this section, productivity and quality through people is a theme that should carry through all the functions of management—planning, organizing, and controlling as well as leading.

Planning and Controlling

We will discuss planning and controlling together because in terms of motivation they are closely linked. Planning means setting goals; controlling means monitoring performance and taking actions to make the performance conform with the goals. Clear goals and the expectation that performance will be monitored are, as we saw earlier, very important to motivating.

Creating clear expectations. In order to channel people's energies toward a set of goals, they must know what the goals are and what they are expected to do to achieve them. Top managers are responsible for setting the goals. They must have a clear strategic plan that defines the firm's line of business, who its customers are, and how the customers' needs are to be served. It does not matter whether the strategic plan is a formal document or not. What matters is whether it provides a framework within which each person's job can be clearly defined. The same goes for short-term plans. They, too, should be simple and clear. Recall the story of Matt Sanders of Convergent Technologies (page 128). When he left company headquarters for his dumpy new office over a credit union, he was given a clear goal: develop a portable computer and get it on the market in less than a year. Sanders succeeded in part because he knew exactly what he had to do.

Goals must not only be set, they must be clearly stated. There is more to this than just giving managers and individual contributors the numbers and dates contained in the plan. Actions often speak louder than words. What kinds of expectations are really being created by a manager who makes a speech about quality once a year and then pressures subordinates ten times a week to meet some short-term production target? Not the expectation that putting quality first is the way to get ahead.

Providing feedback. The clearest plans in the world are no good as motivators unless they are followed up with feedback. That is why control—monitoring performance and keeping it on track—is so closely linked to planning.

Peters and Waterman, as well as others who have studied the matter, stress the importance of keeping both formal and informal channels of communication open. One way of keeping informal channels open is the practice of "management by wandering around." A second way is staying in touch with customers in order to find out what they think of the product they are buying. A third, very simple technique is keeping the office door open—and making sure it isn't guarded by a fierce army of assistants. Contrast the out-of-the-office, open-door manager with the one who sits behind closed doors calling up data on a management information system. The manager may think of this as monitoring, but the people at the other end of the line are more likely to see it as snooping.

Positive reinforcement and punishment. When managers find out what is going on, they should, of course, act on what they learn. We tend to think of the control process as one of fixing things when they go wrong, and that is partly true. Managers should be available to handle unusual problems, but they should let their subordinates handle the routine ones. They should not be meddlers.

Positive reinforcement: Rewards given for desirable behavior.

But although meddling should be avoided, it is a mistake for managers to think they should stay out of sight except when things go wrong. A major part of controlling—and motivating—is providing **positive reinforcement** when things go right. Psychologists who apply their training to management argue that reprimands and punishment should be used sparingly and should be balanced with praise and rewards for good performance.

Punishment alone may change behavior in the wrong way. Suppose you are a sales clerk in a dress shop. Nervous about a date, you forget to thank a customer and give her a shopping bag in which to carry home her purchase. Your boss sees this happen. "I can believe you're an idiot," she says, "but I can't imagine how anyone could be so rude!" Five minutes of scolding follow. This changes your behavior all right. The next time you see a customer heading into the shop you duck into the stockroom. If your boss praised you when you did something nice for a customer, would you be hiding in the stockroom or forgetting shopping bags? Probably not, or not as often.

The connections among expectations, positive reinforcement, and punishment are the theme of Blanchard and Johnson's *One Minute Manager*. Box 14–5 presents three simple rules from that book that are well worth keeping in mind.

Box 14–5 The One Minute Manager

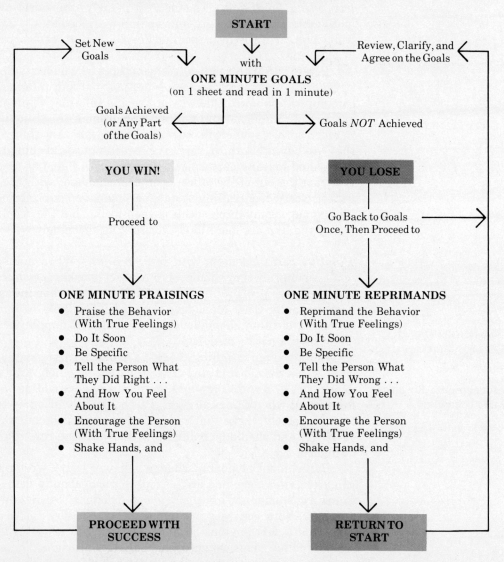

A very brief summary of
THE ONE MINUTE MANAGER'S "GAME PLAN"
How to give yourself and others "the gift" of getting
greater results in less time.
Set Goals; Praise and Reprimand Behaviors; Encourage
People; Speak the Truth; Laugh; Work; Enjoy . . .
and encourage the people you work with to do the same as you do.

START

Set New Goals

with

Review, Clarify, and Agree on the Goals

ONE MINUTE GOALS
(on 1 sheet and read in 1 minute)

Goals Achieved (or Any Part of the Goals)

Goals *NOT* Achieved

YOU WIN!

YOU LOSE

Proceed to

Go Back to Goals Once, Then Proceed to

ONE MINUTE PRAISINGS
- Praise the Behavior (With True Feelings)
- Do It Soon
- Be Specific
- Tell the Person What They Did Right . . .
- And How You Feel About It
- Encourage the Person (With True Feelings)
- Shake Hands, and

ONE MINUTE REPRIMANDS
- Reprimand the Behavior (With True Feelings)
- Do It Soon
- Be Specific
- Tell the Person What They Did Wrong . . .
- And How You Feel About It
- Encourage the Person (With True Feelings)
- Shake Hands, and

PROCEED WITH SUCCESS

RETURN TO START

Kenneth Blanchard and Spencer Johnson's best-selling book *The One Minute Manager* is based on simple principles of goal setting and reinforcement. The book gets its title from the fact that its hero reduces each step in managing people to a form that takes a minute or less. He insists that people set goals for themselves that take less than a page to write down and less than a minute to read. When he "catches someone doing something right," he gives them a "one-minute praising" to reinforce their behavior. When people have the skills and knowledge to reach their goals but fail to do so, the manager gives them a "one-minute reprimand." The reprimand is always followed by praise for the person's basic worth and ability. The chart itself can be read in one minute.

Participation. Planning and controlling are management tasks, but it would be wrong to think of them as things that managers do to their subordinates, or for them. Instead, good managers encourage employees to participate in both of these functions.

For example, one of the best ways to make sure that subordinates clearly understand what is expected of them is to let them set their own goals. "What! Let people set their own goals? They'll set their goals at zero!" says the horrified theory X manager. The theory Y manager knows better. If people are given a strategic plan that sets a few overall goals for the firm, they tend to set ambitious targets for themselves. Not only will they tend to set ambitious goals, but having set them, they will be committed to them.

Participation goes for control as well as planning. "You can always fool the boss," says Rene McPherson, former head of Dana Corporation, "but you can't hide from your peers. They know what's really going on."[9] With this in mind, Dana stages a twice-yearly "hell week" during which all of its managers meet to swap ideas.

Management by objectives (MBO): A formal system in which each manager, in cooperation with his or her superior, sets specific medium-term goals and is periodically reviewed for success in achieving them.

Management by objectives. In many companies, participation in planning and control takes the form of **management by objectives (MBO)**. MBO is a formal system of work planning and progress review in which each manager, in cooperation with his or her superior, sets specific medium-term goals (commonly for one year) and is periodically reviewed for success in achieving them.

Since Peter Drucker described the MBO concept some thirty years ago, as many as half of all major American corporations have adopted it.[10] MBO is often, but not always, effective. Certain conditions must be met for MBO to work.

1. *Top management must be fully committed.* It must be made clear to everyone that the firm's top managers take MBO seriously. They must take the time to participate in goal setting and review, and they must also take the time to train themselves in MBO techniques. If managers start an MBO program but subvert it by maintaining an authoritarian management style, the program will fail.
2. *Goals must be set clearly.* For MBO to work, people must be able to set clear goals for themselves. They cannot do this unless there are clear plans for the firm as a whole. MBO is most likely to succeed when goals are expressed in concrete terms—achieve a 10 percent growth of sales; get a new product out by June. It is better to set a few clear goals than to make a long, detailed list.
3. *Participation must be genuine.* Imposing goals on subordinates is contrary to the spirit of MBO. On the other hand, subordinates should not be left to set goals entirely on their own. Managers must be ready to offer help and guidance.
4. *Feedback must be honest and constructive.* Participants in an MBO program must have frequent feedback so that they know exactly where they stand in relation to the goals they have set. The relationship of goals to performance must be taken seriously in granting raises, bonuses, and promotions. Top managers must have the human skills needed to make such feedback constructive.

[9]Quoted in Peters and Waterman, p. 252.

[10]The MBO concept was first described by Drucker in *The Practice of Management* (New York: Harper & Row, 1954).

Organizing

Managers who want to get quality and productivity from the people who work for them must organize in a way that will help them do their best. Rosabeth Moss Kanter points out that people work best within a clearly defined structure. "It is imporant," she says, "to establish for people, from the beginning, the ground rules and boundary conditions under which they are working: what can they decide, what can't they decide?"[11] Without some ground rules, groups are likely to spend more time defining their task than doing it. In this section we will look at some guidelines for effective organizing.

Role clarity.   Every member of the organization must understand his or her role clearly. Box 14–5, which lists "one-minute" management rules, stresses that goal setting and feedback are needed for role clarity. The MBO technique is also based on goal setting and feedback. But neither informal techniques nor the formal MBO approach will succeed unless the work is divided up in a way that makes sense.

Chapter 6 covered several types of structures. It compared departmentalization by function, product, place, and customer. It also compared line organizations with line-and-staff and matrix structures. Each of these structures has its place, but none will work unless each box on the organization chart stands for a clearly defined job and the person assigned to that job understands what he or she is supposed to do.

Autonomy and small size.   In Chapter 4 we listed some advantages that small firms have over large ones—closer ties between managers and workers, quicker reaction time, and so on. Peters and Waterman found that big companies that are excellently managed try to retain some of these advantages by keeping their production units small. At Emerson Electric, most plants employ fewer than 600 workers. That, thinks Chairman Charles Knight, is the largest size at which managers can maintain personal contact with employees. Blue Bell, the number two-company in the apparel industry, limits its plants to 300 people. Its chairman, Kimsey Mann, says that the result is "a management that is quickly responsive to problems . . . a staff that serves workers." Motorola president John Mitchell says that "when a plant starts to edge toward fifteen hundred people, somehow, like magic, things start to go wrong."[12]

Job structure.   Productivity and quality can often be improved by changing the structure of people's jobs. Two ways of doing this, which were first discussed in Chapter 6, are job enlargement and job enrichment. Job enlargement broadens the range of tasks that a person does. For example, rather than dividing data entry, filing, and telephone answering among three people, the work might be divided by project, with one person taking care of all three aspects. Job enrichment means giving workers greater control over their jobs. Both the human relations and human resources approaches see job enrichment as a useful technique.

Flexible hours.   Some thought should be given to rearranging work schedules as a means of raising productivity. **Flexitime** is one way of doing

Flexitime: A system in which members of an organization set their own hours of work, usually with the requirement that they all be present during certain core hours.

[11]Rosabeth Moss Kanter, *The Changemasters* (New York: Simon & Schuster, 1983), p. 248.

[12]Thomas J. Peters and Robert H. Waterman, Jr., *In Search of Excellence* (New York: Harper & Row, 1982), pp. 274–75.

this. In a flexitime system, workers can choose when they come to work and when they leave, as long as they work an agreed-upon number of hours per day. Usually they must also be present during certain core hours so that meetings can be held with everyone there. A typical flexitime scheme is shown in Box 14–6.

Flexitime has a number of benefits. First, it makes it possible for some people to hold full-time jobs when they could not otherwise do so. (For example, one parent can leave for work after the children have left for

Box 14–6 A Typical Flexitime Plan

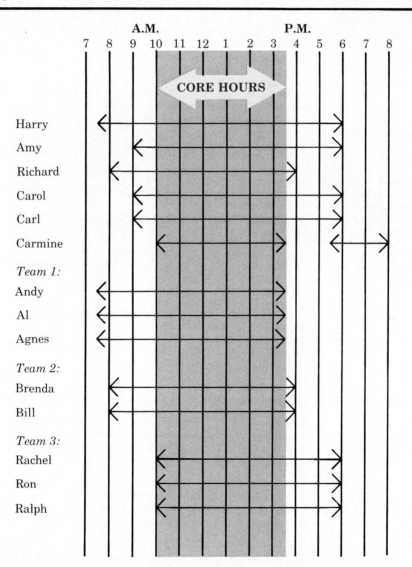

This chart shows a flexitime plan as it might be applied to Apex Exterminators, the company described in Chapter 6. During the core hours of 10:00 A.M. to 3:30 P.M. (which include a thirty-minute lunch break), everyone is required to be at work. During this time meetings can be held and everyone can get in touch with everyone else. Everyone has to work at least eight hours a day, including the core hours. The exterminating is done by teams that have to work together as a unit. Members of the teams agree among themselves on the hours during which the team will work.

In a quality circle, workers and managers meet on a regular basis to discuss ways of improving productivity and quality. Courtesy of General Electric

Quality circle: A group in which workers and managers meet on a regular basis to discuss ways of improving quality.

Scanlon plan: A plan for rewarding useful suggestions in which bonuses are shared by the worker who makes the suggestion and his or her work group.

school, and the other can come home from work by the time the children get out of school.) Second, it means that workers do not have to abuse sick leave or use up their vacation time in order to do personal chores or errands. Finally, in line with the Hawthorne effect, flexitime may raise productivity by giving people more control over their jobs. However, flexitime is not possible in every work situation. In jobs where everyone must work together as a team (assembly line workers, cooks and waiters in a restaurant), opportunities for flexitime are limited.

Bottom-up communication.   According to theory Y, people who actually do a job may know the most about how to raise quality and productivity. But putting this theory into practice requires managers to learn the art of bottom-up communication—how to get workers to share what they know with managers, and how to get managers to listen.

One technique is the **quality circle**. This is a group in which workers and managers meet on a regular basis to discuss ways of improving quality. The managers listen to ideas and explore ways of making them work. They also provide the workers with feedback on quality problems and ways of solving them. Quality circles, long popular in Japan, are becoming common in the United States.

The right incentives are needed to make bottom-up communication work. Sometimes quality circles and suggestion plans fail because workers with good ideas feel negative pressure from their peers. Giving one worker credit for a suggestion that might have come out of the group's experience can cause resentment.

On the other hand, companywide profit-sharing plans sometimes fail for the opposite reason. They spread rewards so thinly that no one worker has much incentive to put forth an idea. One attempt to avoid these two extremes is the **Scanlon plan**. In this plan, suggestions are submitted to joint committees of workers and managers. If an idea is adopted and raises quality or productivity, the person who put the idea forward and the group he or she works with share a bonus. The reward is immediate, and resentment is avoided.

Leading

Participation is often the key to quality and productivity, but it will not work without leadership. Kanter warns against treating worker participation schemes like refrigerators: the firm that buys a "quality circle package" from a consultant and expects to plug it in and watch it work is sure to be disappointed.[13] In fact, a good way for a hostile manager to "prove" that participation won't work is to throw such a package at workers and middle managers and then fail to provide leadership.

Treating people like adults.   For effective leadership nothing—absolutely nothing—is more important than treating people like adults. If a firm's policies are based on the assumption that people can be trusted, 95 percent of its employees will live up to the trust. If policies are based on the assumption that the average person will goof off or screw up if given the chance, adults will start behaving like preschoolers. In this sense, the assumptions that underlie theory X are self-fulfilling. Fortunately, those that underlie theory Y are self-fulfilling too.

[13]Kanter, p. 249.

Treating people like adults, by the way, doesn't mean that they should never have any fun. Peters and Waterman point out that well-managed companies know the value of hoopla and even just plain silliness. McDonald's holds a sort of Olympic Games to select the best hamburger flipper in the country. Maybe you think that's all right for a hamburger chain but not for a company that makes serious products. Then how about Caterpillar's picnics, at which bulldozers are dressed up in costumes and have mountain-eating contests?

Sharing information. A big part of treating people like adults is sharing information with them. Peters and Waterman are amazed at the secrecy with which many firms treat the most basic information. They ask workers to be productive, but they won't tell the first shift how the second shift is doing. They ask their salespeople to devote themselves to growth of market share, but they guard the results as if they were matters of national security. What is the excuse? Usually, the need to hide sensitive information from competitors. But in hiding information from their competitors such firms deprive their own workers and managers of vital feedback.

Well-managed firms, by contrast, share information. They like to share good news and reward small achievements because that is the way to unlock the power of positive reinforcement. Bad news should be shared too. What is the point of asking workers for loyalty and then shutting down a failing plant on twenty-four hours' notice? If the problems were revealed, someone might come up with a solution. Even if the problems were hopeless, a little honesty might salvage some scraps of goodwill.

In Search of the Corporate Culture

Corporate culture: A system of shared values, memories, priorities, and unwritten rules about how things are done in a corporation.

When all the elements of planning, organizing, leading, and controlling fit together and make a company work, it may develop a strong **corporate culture** that keeps it running smoothly. A corporate culture is a system of shared values, memories, priorities, and unwritten rules about how things are done. Management by objectives, bottom-up communication, information sharing, and many other management techniques come naturally to a firm with a strong culture, because everyone from the boardroom to the production line tends to see things the same way. But how does a company get such a culture?

In some firms a culture of excellence can be traced back to a strong founding figure like Thomas J. Watson at IBM. But other strong founders, such as Henry Ford, were not able to establish a positive culture that held up over time. Some companies even develop negative cultures of authoritarianism, secretiveness, and distrust that hamper their performance. According to some observers, firms with cultures of excellence often make an effort to instill the company's values in newly hired managers. But others think a culture is best maintained by hiring people who already share the values of the firm. Recent years have seen the rise of consulting firms that specialize in corporate cultures, but it is hard to find a successful "cultural transplant."

It may well be that the much-admired cultures of well-managed firms are not the cause of their success but, rather, a by-product. Strong corporate cultures may arise over time as a result of excellent management, especially good leadership. But regardless of how these cultures arise, they are successful in making everyone feel like a winner. And there seems to be little doubt that making people feel like winners is one key to getting extraordinary performance from ordinary people.

Making people feel like winners is a key to getting extraordinary performance from ordinary people. Courtesy of Sharp Electronics Corp.

SUMMARY

1. Motivations are the psychological drives that give people's actions purpose and direction. These drives come from within. When we talk about managers "motivating" the people who work for them, we are really talking about the way managers focus and channel people's motivations so as to direct their actions toward the firm's goals.

2. Motivation arises from unsatisfied needs. According to Abraham Maslow, needs form a hierarchy in which any one need becomes a motivator only after lower-level needs have been met. The five levels of needs are physiological, safety, affection, esteem, and self-actualization. Frederick Herzberg has proposed a two-factor theory of motivation. The factors leading to dissatisfaction seem to be related to lower-level needs, while those leading to satisfaction seem to be related to self-actualization. A third view holds that unsatisfied needs act as motivators only if certain expectancy conditions are met. The person must expect that greater effort will lead to better performance, and that better performance will be rewarded.

3. Good pay is an important motivator. In a competitive market, good pay is needed to attract workers and managers. Pay is also important for satisfying needs, including symbolic needs like status. But pay by itself

will not lead to productivity and quality unless other motivators are also present.

4. The traditional approach to managing for productivity and quality dates from the era of scientific management. It was based on the assumptions that people dislike work, avoid responsibility, and are motivated mainly by pay. These assumptions are now known as *theory X*. In the 1920s the *human relations* approach emerged. It was based on the assumptions that people want to feel useful and important, that social rewards in the workplace are important motivators, and that people are able to take some responsibility for routine matters. This approach stressed information sharing and participation as ways of making workers more willing to follow managers' orders.

5. Since the 1960s the *human resources approach* has begun to replace the human relations approach. It is based on the assumptions that workers find satisfaction in their work, that imagination and creativity are common traits, and that, given a chance, people are eager to participate in the full range of management functions. These assumptions are called *theory Y*. Theory Y managers encourage participation not just to make workers feel better about their jobs but as a means of finding better ways to do things.

6. In managing for quality and productivity, it is important to create clear expectations and provide frequent feedback. *Positive reinforcement* should be used frequently to reward large and small achievements. Punishment should be used sparingly. *Management by objectives* is one technique that is used to create clear expectations and provide feedback. It emphasizes joint goal setting by managers and those who work for them.

7. Organization is a key aspect of managing for productivity and quality. The role of each person and department should be defined clearly. Work units should be kept small and given autonomy. Job enlargement, job enrichment, and *flexitime* can often raise productivity. Bottom-up communication should be encouraged.

9. The key to good leadership is treating people like adults. Sharing information is especially important. Good leadership, when combined with good planning, organizing, and controlling, results in a *corporate culture* that helps get extraordinary performance from ordinary people.

KEY TERMS

You should be familiar with the following terms and concepts. Check their meanings by referring to the marginal definitions in the chapter or to the glossary at the end of the book.

Motivation

Hierarchy of needs

Theory X

Hawthorne effect

Human relations approach

Theory Y

Human resources approach

Positive reinforcement

Management by objectives (MBO)

Flexitime

Quality circle

Scanlon plan

Corporate culture

QUESTIONS FOR REVIEW AND DISCUSSION

1. What kind of environment do you choose for studying? Do you prefer a comfortable, quiet, isolated room like Dennis Hacker's? Or do you like to study where there are other people around? Do you think you could improve your productivity by changing the environment in which you study? Discuss.

2. Which of the needs in Maslow's hierarchy do you feel are most important for you? Do you know, or have your read about, people who seem to be at other levels of the hierarchy? Describe those people.

3. What jobs have you held? For each job, discuss your boss's approach to management. Was it the traditional, human relations, or human resources approach? Or was it a mix of these approaches?

4. An office manager wants to raise productivity by supplying clerical workers with word processors. This may require rearrangement of the workplace, changes in job responsibilities, training for some of the workers, and several other changes. Write brief dialogues to show how managers would address the problem under the traditional, human relations, and human resources approaches.

5. Find a current list of best-selling nonfiction books. The book review sections of the *New York Times* and other big-city newspapers carry such lists. Are any management books on the list? If so, visit a bookstore and glance through the book. (Better yet, buy it and read it!) What is the book's main theme?

6. Reread the story of Louis Ruiz's Mexican-food business (page 72). What is Ruiz' attitude toward the people in his firm? What has he done to make their jobs satisfying? Comment on how the management guidelines discussed in this chapter can be applied to small businesses.

7. Look back to Box 7–4 (page 167), which lists the steps in effective use of computers. Comment on those steps in the light of what you have learned in this chapter.

Case 14–1: Life in the Fields

In the summer of 1983, a Washington Post *reporter, Neil Henry, disguised himself as a drifter and caught a ride south to work in the fields. Here are some excerpts from the articles he wrote after he returned to Washington.*

With six other black men who had accompanied me from a Washington slum to the fields, I was picking plum tomatoes in a weather-damaged field for 30 cents a bucket, 9 and 10 hours a day under a merciless sun.

Our workday was not determined by the clock. It started about 6:30 A.M. and didn't end until the last flatbed truck was full.

I was an average worker. My first day I cleared 15 buckets. The second, 35. The third, 45. These totaled about 40,000 tomatoes weighing at least 2,350 pounds. For those 25 hours of work I was paid $28.50, minus $1.92 for Social Security and $15 for meals at the camp. It amounted to about a dollar an hour, and I had $11.58 to show for my work.

On top of all this, there were two aspects of migrant labor that exasperated me even more. One was the apparently ingrained passivity of the regular migrants, some of whom had been working the fields for as long as 20 years and seemed to have accepted exploitation as just another way of life.

The other was the word *nigger*.

"It ain't nothin' but an expression," Covey, a black Vietnam veteran who slept in a bed adjacent to mine, said one night in the bunkhouse when I complained about the slur. "*Niggah* just means an ignorant person."

Garland, in an upper bunk, had a quick reply. "That's the point, man," he said. "That's the point."

The migrants were a grab bag of contradictions. Many of them suffered from a number of ailments—emphysema, alcoholism, diarrhea, hypertension. Yet they remained disciplined, seemingly tireless laborers who saw the misery of the camps and the work not as a temporary state, but as a full-time profession and way of life.

One Friday, Pointer and I and a couple of others were designated to pull weeds in a 45-acre sweet potato field owned by a white man named Ted West, whose tobacco, potato, and dairy empire is one of the biggest in that part of the state. It was a special day for all of us, for it meant we were guaranteed to earn the minimum wage, replete with, as Pointer put it, "lunch breaks and everything."

The weeds didn't stand a chance against Pointer that day, for he figured the best way to impress West was to work like the devil.

When the day was finished, we returned to West's farm to hoist bundles of tobacco sacks into a barn. At one point West, a beefy middle-aged man in khaki pants and a baseball cap, asked me, "How ya liking it over at the camp?"

I told him I didn't and explained in a couple of curse-filled sentences why not.

"Well you know," he replied, "a lot of 'em over there just don't want it any better. That's the problem, I think."

But there were a select few, like Robert Pointer, who occasionally confessed that they still had dreams. As we rode back to camp that night I asked him if he had approached West about the possibility of a full-time job. He replied, "Nah. I never got up the nerve."

Source: Neil Henry, "A Wretched Reality of Life in the Fields," *The Washington Post*, October 12, 1983, p. 1. Copyright © *The Washington Post*.

Questions:

1. Discuss the approach to management taken by the employers in this case. What assumptions do you think they make about the workers? In what ways are those assumptions justified? In what ways are they not?

2. Do you think the management approach used by these employers is suited to the work at hand and the nature of the work force? Do you think a change in the approach would make growing crops like tomatoes and sweet potatoes more profitable? Why or why not?

Case 14–2: Factory Magic: A Japanese Plant in Memphis

When word spread that Sharp Corporation of Japan was planning to build an electronics factory here, a lot of people thought the Japanese were making a big mistake.

After all, RCA Corp. had built a TV plant in Memphis in 1966—and shut it down five years later. That facility had suffered just about every labor and management affliction imaginable: wildcat strikes, union-authorized strikes, apparent sabotage of the product, and a series of layoffs that took the payroll from a peak of 4200 workers down to 1600. At times, so many hundreds of defective TV sets clogged the assembly-line aisles that technicians had difficulty repairing them. Finally, RCA pulled the plug, shipped most of the machinery and work off to Taiwan, and left the Memphis labor force with a black eye.

Yet Sharp came here anyway. "People said it was labor problems that caused RCA to close," says Paul Hagusa, the president of Sharp Manufacturing Company of America, "but we didn't think so. We felt it was RCA's lack of quality in the product."

Sharp has not only proved the sceptics wrong but also vindicated the city's work force. Despite some problems with labor unions, its 500,000-square-foot plant has, in the past four years, rolled out a million color-television sets and a million microwave ovens. Best of all, Sharp products shipped from Memphis get high marks for quality and durability from consumer groups.

The assembly-line workers themselves credit the Japanese style of management. At its core, it demands very hard work and an obsession with quality, an obsession with making every seam weld and switch of the product perfect. A Sharp manager agrees, saying, "It's not what we do, but how well we do it. It's the constant striving for excellence."

"The important path to quality," says Hagusa, "is that employees feel that they are of one family, playing an important role in the company."

How is a familial feeling instilled? "There must be a change in the way that management in the U.S. treats its employees," he says. "Otherwise it is difficult for employees to respond."

On a recent day, one of Sharp's "quality circles" is meeting. Led by a trained leader, Sharp's quality circles "brainstorm" ideas, select a problem to be solved, and then collect data on the problem. Later, the problem and possibly a solution are presented to Hagusa and other members of management.

At one table, five microwave assembly workers are discussing one worker's innovation: a metal dowel that fits into the center hole of a five-hole microwave-oven bracket. "I saw that people were having trouble lining up the holes," says Randy Howle, "but if someone before them had put in the center screw, the person didn't have a problem." So Howle developed the metal dowel, which, when slipped into the middle hole, aligns the bracket while the other four holes are screwed down.

Source: L. Erik Calonius, "In a Plant in Memphis, Japanese Firm Shows How to Attain Quality," *Wall Street Journal*, April 29, 1983, p. 1. Reprinted by permission of the *Wall Street Journal*. © Dow Jones & Company, Inc., 1983. All Rights Reserved.

Questions:

1. Why was Sharp able to get productivity and quality out of a work force that RCA could not handle? Do you think the methods used are uniquely Japanese? Could RCA's problems have contributed to Sharp's success? Explain.

2. Discuss the case in terms of the human relations and human resources approaches to management. Which view of the world does Hagusa seem to take? What evidence supports your answer? Do you think the approach taken by Hagusa is the best one for the situation?

Labor uni
ers formed
ployer ove
conditions

Collective
by which a
proved wag
for its men

Box 15

Fifty yea
America
growth.

Source: [
Later dat

Chapter 15

MANAGEMENT AND LABOR UNIONS

When you have completed this chapter, you should be able to

● Review briefly the history of labor unions in the United States from the 1880s to the present.

● Explain the main provisions of the *Norris-La Guardia Act*, the *Wagner Act*, and the *Taft-Hartley Act*.

● Discuss the reasons why workers join unions.

● List the steps in the collective bargaining process and the main issues in collective bargaining.

● Explain what determines the relative bargaining power of unions and management, and list the main weapons used by each side.

● Explain the meaning of *mediation*, *arbitration*, and *grievances*.

● Discuss the prospects for achieving improved productivity, higher product quality, and better working conditions in a unionized environment.

The Taft-Hartley Act was unpopular with unions because it allowed the government to intervene in certain strikes. © Alex Webb, Magnum

WHY WORKERS JOIN UNIONS

Why do workers join unions? It is not costless to do so. At the very least, members have to pay dues. If the union calls a strike, the workers may lose many days of pay. If the union demands too much, the jobs of some workers may be lost. Clearly, workers expect to get something in return for the costs and risks they take on when they join a union.

Wages and Working Conditions

The Disney characters mentioned earlier joined the Teamsters for a simple reason: they were unhappy with hot costumes and low wages. Wages and working conditions have been major reasons for joining unions since the earliest days of the labor movement.

When we look back at the wages and working conditions of a century ago, we can hardly be surprised that workers wanted something better. To mention just one example, steelworkers worked a seven-day week, twelve hours a day. Their work was hard and dangerous. Every week the night and day workers traded shifts. When this happened, one shift got twenty-four hours off—but the other had to work twenty-four hours straight! If we add to this a pay scale that left workers below what we would consider a poverty level, it seems that no other reason would be needed.

But there is a curious thing about the pay-and-working-conditions explanation of why workers join unions. Unions did not begin among the workers who were most oppressed and most poorly paid. Instead, they began among skilled workers who, by the standards of the time, were well paid. To keep things in perspective, we should remember that in the nineteenth century farmers, sailors, and frontier housewives also worked long hours for low pay under dangerous conditions. The printers, machinists, teamsters, and railroad engineers who led the union movement were the elite workers of their day. As late as 1935, Teamster president Daniel Tobin described mass-production workers as "rubbish" unfit to be members of the AFL.[2] Even today, unions are weak among the lowest-paid workers.

[2]Quoted in Arthur A. Sloane and Fred Witney, *Labor Relations*, 4th ed. (Englewood Cliffs, N.J.: Prentice-Hall, 1981), p. 77.

Like man
the charac
a labor un
wages an
Tiers, Mo

Safety, Affection, and Esteem

Wages and working conditions alone do not seem to give a complete explanation of why workers join unions. For a fuller explanation, let's turn to Maslow's need hierarchy, which was discussed in Chapter 14.

Physiological needs, such as the needs for food and shelter, are the lowest level of needs in Maslow's scheme. It appears that workers for whom these needs are unfilled are not the ones who are most likely to join unions. But once people advance beyond this level, other needs emerge that they may seek to satisfy by joining unions. Unions can meet safety needs by guarding workers from arbitrary firing, and also by insisting on greater safety in the workplace. The need to belong to something can be gratified by taking part in the union's economic activities (including strikes) and in social functions sponsored by the unions. Union membership can also add to a worker's self-esteem; the union makes the worker feel needed and important even if the employer does not. Surveys confirm the importance of safety, affection, and esteem needs in motivating people to join unions.[3]

It seems that people at the very top of Maslow's hierarchy, like those at the very bottom, are less likely to join unions—except, perhaps, those who seek self-fulfillment by becoming union leaders. Workers who are concerned with achievement and self-expression may feel that unions will limit, rather than increase, their opportunities. At worst, a union may mean a whole set of work rules and seniority rules added to those imposed by management.

Unions as a Response to Management Failure

From what we have just said, it seems that at least some workers join unions in response to failures of management. As we saw in the last chapter, a job in a well-managed firm should give people more than a paycheck—it should also make them feel needed and important, and it should make the most of their creativity. Managers who fail to structure jobs in ways that meet human needs not only get workers who are less productive—they also get workers who are more likely to join unions. When those managers turn around and blame problems of quality and productivity on the unions, they are failing to see that many factors that cause workers to join unions are under the control of management. We will return to this theme in the last section of the chapter.

THE COLLECTIVE BARGAINING PROCESS

Workers have many reasons for joining unions, but once they join, they all become part of the process of collective bargaining. Like all bargaining, collective bargaining begins with the belief that there are mutual benefits to be gained from an agreement. For the workers, the benefits are jobs with decent wages and working conditions. For the employer, the benefit is productive labor at a cost that permits a profit. Both sides are aware from the outset that these benefits cannot be obtained without cooperation.

[3]See Sloane and Witney, pp. 18–21.

But in addition to cooperation, there is also an element of conflict in collective bargaining. The conflict comes from the fact that there is always more than one way to divide up the benefits. The element of cooperation makes collective bargaining partly an exchange of information; the element of conflict makes it partly a contest of wills.

In this section we will look at the process of collective bargaining under five headings: (1) the steps in the bargaining process, (2) the issues that are likely to arise, (3) the factors that determine the bargaining power of the two sides, (4) sources of help in settling conflicts, and (5) administration of the contract once it has been agreed upon.

Steps in the Bargaining Process

The bargaining process can be divided into three steps: preparing, presenting, demands and offers, and negotiating.

Preparing. For both sides, preparation begins with the gathering of information. Both sides will want to be well informed on general economic conditions. Management will need to gather data to show the effects of higher wages on the firm's competitive position. Union negotiators will have to be prepared to evaluate those data. Top managers should be sure to involve supervisors at this stage. They often know best which parts of current labor agreements are working well, and which will need to be changed.

Presenting demands and offers. In most cases bargaining opens with the union presenting a set of demands. Many unions begin by asking for things that seem preposterous—handfuls of new holidays, country club facilities, or free transportation to work. Sometimes these demands are favorite ideas of rank-and-file members. Even though union leaders know that these ideas are not realistic, they would rather have them shot down by management than do the job themselves. Other times, demands that seem extreme the first time they are made—such as dental care benefits for workers and their families—gradually become part of the union's serious agenda.

Sometimes managers open with demands of their own. Recently, for example, Eastern Airlines asked its employees to accept a 15 percent wage cut, claiming that it needed the cut to stay in business. In its initial demands and its first response to the union's demands, management, too, may ask for more than it seriously thinks it can get.

Negotiating. After the first round of proposals, the sides are likely to be far apart. Bargaining then starts in earnest in the hope of narrowing the gap.

Sometimes the bargaining takes the form of a series of counterproposals. For example, the union may open with demands that would raise total labor costs by $3.25 an hour. The company may come back with a counterproposal that would raise costs by $1.75 an hour. As this goes on, each side should have a clear idea of the maximum concession it would be willing to make—although it need not reveal it in its first counterproposal.

At other times, bargaining may develop through a series of trading points. In this process each side tries to find which of the other side's demands it is least strongly opposed to. For example, the union may have

Drawing by Stan Hunt; © 1984 *The New Yorker Magazine*, Inc.

"The talks are in a delicate stage."

demanded a 10 percent pay raise, and management may want a change in work rules to allow production workers to do maintenance tasks during slack hours. The union may offer to accept the work rule change if it gets the full 10 percent pay raise.

Whatever the process, good negotiators know that it is wise to stay flexible. Both sides know that there are gains from an agreement and losses from a strike. Neither side should state positions from which it cannot back off without loss of face, unless those really are bottom-line positions.

Issues in Bargaining

The law sets few limits on the issues that can be raised during collective bargaining. Unions and management cannot reach agreements that discriminate on grounds of race or sex. They cannot conspire in criminal acts. But aside from these limits, they can bargain over practically anything. In this section we consider three sets of issues that are often dealt with in collective bargaining: wages and fringe benefits, union security, and management rights.

Wages and fringe benefits. Wages are a key issue in almost every bargaining session. Wages paid by other firms for the same kinds of work are a starting point, but only that. Unions may demand to be paid more if the firm makes more than average profits. Employers may insist on paying less than the average during a start-up period (as Volkswagen of America did when it opened its first U.S. plants) or to get through a crisis (as Chrysler did in the early 1980s). Once an average wage rate has been

Cost-of-living adjustment (COLA): An agreement to increase wages by a set amount for each percentage point increase in the government's consumer price index.

Fringe benefits: Nonwage supplements to a worker's pay, such as paid holidays, vacations, pensions, and health insurance.

Union security agreement: An agreement that requires all workers who benefit from a contract negotiated by a union to join that union.

Closed shop: An agreement under which an employer can hire only workers who are already members of a particular union.

Union shop: An agreement under which workers must join a union within a specified time after starting work.

Right-to-work laws: State laws, permitted under the Taft-Hartley Act, that prohibit union shops.

agreed upon, there are questions of wage rates for different levels of skill, seniority, and so on. Unions also often ask for a **cost-of-living adjustment (COLA)**. This is an agreement to increase wages a set amount for each percentage point increase in the government's consumer price index.

Fringe benefits are all nonwage supplements to a worker's pay. They may include pension plans, health care benefits, life insurance, meals on company time, and so on. Such benefits account for some three eighths of the average firm's labor costs. Unions often prefer fringe benefits over higher pay, since most fringe benefits are not taxed.

Union security. One union problem that was not solved by the Wagner Act is the threat that some workers will act as "free riders." Free riders are workers who benefit from union-negotiated contracts but do not join the union themselves and do not pay dues. To guard against the free-rider problem, many unions negotiate **union security agreements**. These ensure that all workers who benefit from union activities must join the union or at least pay dues.

The strongest kind of security agreement is the **closed shop**. In a closed shop the employer agrees to hire only workers who are members of the union. The Taft-Hartley Act outlawed the closed shop in most cases, so this type of agreement is rare.

Another kind of security agreement is the **union shop**. Under such an agreement workers do not have to belong to the union before they are hired, but they have to join soon after they start work, usually within thirty days. Union shops are legal under the Taft-Hartley Act, but states can prohibit them. Twenty states have passed laws doing so; these are called **right-to-work laws**. Today about 70 percent of all labor contracts in the United States include union shop clauses.

Management rights. A final set of issues in collective bargaining comes under the heading of management rights. In the past the attitude of most managers was "I'm the boss, you're the hoss," meaning that once a wage-and-benefits package has been agreed upon, management should be free to run the show. Running the show, in this sense, refers to all matters of hiring, firing, scheduling, work assignments, investment decisions, and so on.

Unions have responded to this attitude at the bargaining table. One of the top items on their list of demands has been that members with seniority be given preference in such matters as layoffs, pension benefits, and choice of jobs within the plant. Almost all labor agreements include seniority clauses. Unions may also want some control over hiring and firing. For example, when jobs are lost because of automation, they may demand that the work force be reduced only through voluntary quits and retirement.

Production standards and work rules are another subject that often comes up in collective bargaining. One goal of unions has been to keep managers from responding to each wage increase by speeding up the rate of production. A second common aim is to require a certain minimum number of workers to do a given job—five people per freight train, three in the airplane cockpit, and so on. A third aim is work rules that define jobs narrowly and prevent one worker from doing the work of another. For example, when a maintenance worker takes an electric motor out for repair, an electrician might have to be on hand to unhook the wires, even though no special skill is needed for the job. Union work rules pose major problems for productivity-minded managers. We will come back to this subject in the last section of the chapter.

Box 15–2 The Bargaining Range

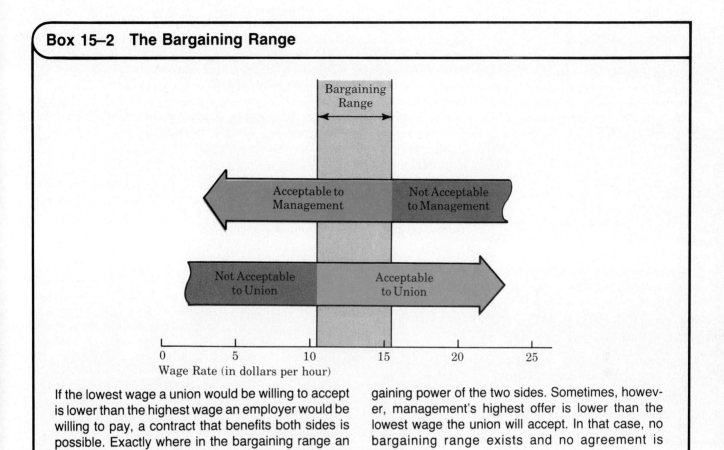

Bargaining
Range

Acceptable to
Management

Not Acceptable
to Management

Not Acceptable
to Union

Acceptable
to Union

0   5   10   15   20   25

Wage Rate (in dollars per hour)

If the lowest wage a union would be willing to accept is lower than the highest wage an employer would be willing to pay, a contract that benefits both sides is possible. Exactly where in the bargaining range an agreement is reached depends on the relative bar-gaining power of the two sides. Sometimes, however, management's highest offer is lower than the lowest wage the union will accept. In that case, no bargaining range exists and no agreement is possible.

Bargaining Power

If an agreement is to be reached, there must be an overlap between the lowest offer that the union is willing to accept and the highest offer that management is willing to make. (See Box 15–2.) This overlap is called the **bargaining range**. Just where in the bargaining range the two sides end up depends on their bargaining power. That, in turn, depends on economic conditions and on the weapons each side can use against the other. Let's look at each of these factors.

Bargaining range: The range between the lowest offer that a union is willing to accept and the highest offer that an employer is willing to make.

Economic conditions. The bargaining power of unions has tended to be strong in good times and weak in recessions. There are three reasons for this. First, during a boom, labor shortages make it hard to replace striking workers. Second, high profits make it easier for a firm to increase wages and fringe benefits. And third, it is more costly to have production inter-rupted by a strike when business is booming than when sales are slow.

In addition to general economic conditions, special conditions must be taken into account. For example, a union that threatens a strike just before a firm is slated to bring out a new product might catch the firm at a weak moment. On the other hand, an employer who knows that a union has been losing members or has just lost a costly strike somewhere else may be able to bargain a little harder than it otherwise could.

Strike: A collective refusal to work by a group of workers.

Strike fund: A fund maintainted by a union to pay striking workers.

Picketing: A demonstration at the site of a labor dispute informing people that a dispute is in progress.

Picketing and boycotts are among the bargaining weapons available to unions.

Union weapons.   The **strike** is far and away the union's strongest bargaining weapon. A strike is a collective refusal to work by a group of workers. Employers fear strikes because of lost sales, production, and profits. Customers lost during strikes may never be regained. But the strike is a two-edged sword. It inflicts pain on workers as well as on employers. To lessen the pain, many unions use dues to build up **strike funds** that can be used to pay striking workers.

Unions often use **picketing** to increase the impact of a strike. Picketing workers stand outside an employer's place of business to inform workers (and others) that a labor dispute is in progress. The ethics of the labor movement decree that union members should never cross picket lines. Often members of unions that are not involved in the dispute (for example, members of other craft unions who work for the same employer) strike in sympathy rather than cross a picket line.

© Paul Conklin, Monkmeyer Press

© Vic Cox, Peter Arnold

Boycott: A campaign aimed at persuading people not to do business with a firm engaged in a labor dispute.

Primary boycott: A boycott aimed at persuading workers not to buy the products of a firm that is engaged in a labor dispute.

Secondary boycott: A boycott aimed at persuading other firms not to do business with a firm that is involved in a labor dispute.

Strikebreaker: A person hired to replace a worker who is on strike.

Boycotts are a third union weapon. A boycott is a campaign aimed at persuading people not to do business with a firm that is engaged in a labor dispute. **Primary boycotts** are aimed at the employer involved in the dispute. For example, union members might be asked not to buy the firm's products. **Secondary boycotts** are strikes that try to prevent other firms from doing business with a firm that is involved in a labor dispute. For example, if aluminum workers strike Alcoa in a wage dispute, aircraft workers at Boeing might go on strike to keep Boeing from buying supplies from Alcoa. The Taft-Hartley Act outlawed secondary boycotts.

Although union leaders discourage it, intimidation is still used by union members in many labor disputes. For example, in a bitter strike against Phelps-Dodge in 1983, state troopers had to be called in to protect nonstriking workers from violent picketers. In the short run such tactics may keep some workers from crossing picket lines, but in the long run they are very costly to unions. A reputation for violence causes loss of public support, and often loss of votes in representation elections.

Management weapons.   Management's most powerful weapon in labor disputes is the use of **strikebreakers**. These are people who are hired to replace workers who are on strike. In recent years more employers have been using this weapon. (See Case 15–1.) High unemployment and changing attitudes have made it easier to hire workers who are willing to cross picket lines. Also, the trend toward automation means that fewer people are needed to keep a plant running.

Management has other weapons as well. To counter a union's stike fund, the firm can build up inventories of finished goods so that it can continue to ship its products during a strike. Management can even use the strike in reverse, in the form of a **lockout**. If an agreement has not been reached when a contract expires, the company shuts down while negotiations continue. Lockouts are used much less often than strikes, however.

Lockout: The closing of a plant by a firm involved in a labor dispute whose workers have not yet gone on strike.

Supporters of one side or the other will argue forever about whether unions or management have an unfair advantage in bargaining power. The real answer is that it all depends. Each side has powerful weapons. The outcome depends on the situation and the specific people involved.

Help in Settling Disputes

What happens if management and the union just cannot reach an agreement? Must they fight to the death, until the union is busted or the company is broke? Not necessarily.

One way to settle stubborn disputes is through **mediation**. Mediation is a process in which the two sides call in a third party to evaluate their positions and help each side see what can and cannot be achieved. Mediators are like marriage counselors—they have no power to impose a solution, but they may help the two sides see their common interests. The government offers help in the form of the Federal Mediation and Conciliation Service.

Mediation: Assistance, in the form of nonbinding suggestions, that is given by a third party to settle a dispute.

A second way of settling disputes is **arbitration**. An arbitrator is a third party whose judgment is binding on both management and the union. In the United States, arbitration is not used in private disputes unless both sides agree to abide by the outcome. For example, baseball owners and players have agreed that certain types of salary disputes will be settled by arbitration. In some states, arbitration is required when the employer is a unit of government. Some countries, including Canada, New Zealand, and Australia, have compulsory arbitration laws for private disputes.

Arbitration: A binding settlement of a dispute by a third party.

The Taft-Hartley Act provides for a sixty-day "cooling-off period" when a strike threatens to cause a national emergency. During that time mediators are supposed to help the parties resolve the dispute. However, if an agreement is not reached in sixty days, the strike may proceed.

Handling Grievances

The signing of a contract does not mean the end of all disputes. Disputes may arise over facts—what did John really say to Joan? Was it sexual harassment or a simple misunderstanding? They may arise over the meaning of loosely worded contract provisions. Or they may arise over personalities—supervisor Frank is a bully; we're going to walk of the job if you don't get rid of him.

Almost all labor contracts include some way of resolving **grievances**, as such disputes are called. In a typical grievance procedure, the first step is for a worker to report a grievance to a **shop steward**, a worker who has been elected by the union to handle such matters. In most cases the shop steward works the matter out with a supervisor on the spot. If the dispute

Grievance: A dispute between management and a worker or union over the interpretation of a contract.

Shop steward: A union official who aids union members in resolving grievances.

cannot be settled right away, the contract usually provides for an appeal to a committee of higher managers and union officials. As a last resort, most contracts provide for arbitration by a neutral party.

A good grievance procedure is a key element in healthy management-labor relations. Its importance goes beyond settling disputes. It also helps build an agenda of issues to be dealt with in the next contract negotiations. And it helps managers pinpoint weak spots in their organization.

MANAGING IN A UNIONIZED ENVIRONMENT

The art of labor relations involves far more than just negotiating contracts and settling grievances. The real test for managers is whether they can get the most out of their work force, unionized or not.

The techniques of managing for productivity and quality that were discussed in Chapter 14 are valid for both union and nonunion firms. But the manager who tries to use them in a unionized environment faces a special set of challenges and opportunities. The challenges come from the need to break the habits learned in decades of union-management conflict. The opportunities come from the power of the union itself, given a chance, to mobilize the full potential of the workers who belong to it. This section will look at ways of meeting the challenges and taking advantage of the opportunities.

© Peter Arnold

Overcoming Theory X Thinking

Theory X, we recall, is a set of assumptions in which people are seen as disliking work, lacking creativity, avoiding responsibility, and being motivated mainly by pay. Unions have evolved in part as a response by workers to theory X thinking by managers. In the process, union leaders have developed a set of attitudes that are, in a sense, the mirror image of theory X. These attitudes include the following.

1. Unions and management are locked in a struggle over a pie of fixed size. Anything management wins is a loss for the union; any costs imposed on management are gains for the union.
2. Wages come out of profits. As long as the firm is making a profit, it can afford to pay more.
3. Because the interests of unions and management are fundamentally opposed, confrontation is the proper approach to all dealings with management. Cooperation is not only useless but dangerous.

Together, theory X thinking by managers and the mirror-image attitudes of union leaders have produced a pattern that is repeated over and over again in collective bargaining sessions. Part of this pattern is a tendency for firms to grant pay and benefit increases in order to preserve what are seen as the sacred rights of managers. Unions have accepted each increase in the pay-and-benefits package as a victory, with little thought for the long-run effects on jobs or the firm's ability to compete. Restrictive work rules are a second aspect of the pattern. Such rules are meant to defend workers against arbitrary acts by theory X managers. Rather than change its methods of supervision, management has tended to view these work rules as an unavoidable evil of dealing with unions. As each side's actions have confirmed the other's assumptions, the pattern has become more and more firmly entrenched.

But theory X is not the only possible basis for union-management relations. In the preceding chapter we saw that managers are gradually shifting from theory X to theory Y. Under the assumptions of theory Y, people are seen as finding satisfaction in their work. Creativity and imagination are seen as common traits. And people are seen as not only willing but eager to take responsibility and to take part in decision making.

At least the beginnings of a new set of union attitudes can also be seen. They are the mirror image of theory Y, just as the old attitudes were the mirror image of theory X.

1. Anything that raises productivity increases the size of the pie to be split between unions and management.
2. A firm's ability to pay wages and benefits is limited by its competitive position. In the long run, an employer with good profits and a strong competitive position can pay more and provide more jobs.
3. There is an element of conflict in negotiating wages and benefits within the range of the firm's ability to pay, but many other aspects of bargaining call for an attitude of cooperation. Only cooperation can tap the full productive power of the work force, which is the real source of the union's bargaining power.

When unions and management come to the bargaining table with theory Y assumptions, a different kind of agreement is possible. Management encourages workers to take part in decision making instead of jealously guarding management rights. Unions balance their wage and benefit demands against members' desire for more jobs and better working conditions. When management gives up theory X attitudes, unions are less fearful of relaxing work rules. The unions still represent their members' interests while management looks after those of shareholders, but they do so in a spirit of cooperation.

There is a big payoff for both unions and management in moving from theory X to theory Y, but the shift will not be an easy one. Each side needs to concede some things that it has won at great cost in the past. Concessions on wages and benefits are not always needed, but where they are needed, they can be painful. Let's turn to this problem next.

Concession Bargaining

Not in all unionized industries, but in some, theory X bargaining has pushed wages to levels that are out of line with competitive reality. The problem is greatest in industries where firms have only recently been exposed to the full impact of competition.

The steel and automobile industries, for example, used to view the U.S. market as their own. They got used to passing higher wages and benefits along to consumers in the form of higher prices. Between 1950 and 1980, auto workers' wages rose from a level about 20 percent above the average for all manufacturing jobs to 50 percent above the average. The wages and benefits of steelworkers rose even higher, to nearly twice the average. Now the protected markets are gone; steel and auto firms must compete in a worldwide market, not only with other high-wage countries such as Germany, Sweden, and Japan but also with low-wage countries such as Korea and Brazil. The airline and trucking industries are also facing new competitive pressures, in this case not from imports but from nonunionized firms started under deregulation.

Unions in these industries must face some unpleasant facts. Between 1980 and 1983, for example, membership in the United Steelworkers Union fell from over 1 million to 700,000. Auto workers, teamsters, and airline unions faced similar drops in membership. In all of these industries there are ways to raise output per worker, but that is not enough. It is impossible for a firm to be competitive in the long run at wage levels that are far out of line with those paid for the same kinds of jobs elsewhere.

Realizing this, the steel, auto, airline, and trucking unions have all made wage concessions. But concession bargaining raises some special problems.

- The need to make concessions causes workers to have less confidence in management. This makes for a poor climate in which to form a new, more cooperative relationship.
- A firm that cannot grant wage increases and must even ask for concessions lacks flexibility in bargaining over work rules. It may not be able, as other firms are, to grant wage increases as a trade-off for work rule changes that boost productivity.
- Industries whose wage levels are out of line with those of competitors need to make permanent cuts in wages. However, workers are likely to demand that wage cuts made during hard times be restored as soon as the company shows a profit again. If investors feel that wage concessions create claims against future profits, the firm's ability to raise capital is damaged.

Negotiators are struggling with these problems in several industries. Solutions may be found. For example, wage cuts are sometimes applied only to newly hired workers. And formal profit-sharing plans may look better to investors than vague union threats to get tough in the next business upturn. Both sides know that if the problems of concession bargaining are not solved, sales and jobs will continue to shift to nonunion and foreign firms.

Lessons to Be Learned from Nonunion Firms

This discussion of concession bargaining might make it appear that low wages are the biggest advantage enjoyed by nonunion firms. But this is not always the case. According to a study by Fred K. Foulkes of such top nonunion firms as Black & Decker, Eli Lilly, Gillette, Grumman, IBM, and Polaroid, managers believe high productivity is the main benefit of not having a union.[4] Higher productivity comes partly from lower employee turnover and less absenteeism. It also comes from greater worker loyalty and increased acceptance of new technology.

What can unionized firms learn from these companies? How exactly do the nonunion firms do it? Foulkes lists the following practices.

[4]Fred K. Foulkes, "How Top Nonunion Companies Manage Employees," *Harvard Business Review*, September-October 1981, pp. 90–96.

- *Equality for workers.* Many of the top nonunion firms work hard to create a sense of equality for all employees. Everyone from the vice-president to the sweeper parks in the same lot, eats in the same cafeteria, and gets the same health care benefits. Executive status symbols like country clubs are avoided.
- *Employment security.* Many of the nonunion firms go to great lengths to avoid layoffs. When possible, slack periods are handled by reducing work schedules or producing for inventory. Peak demand is met with part-time or retired workers, rather than by hiring regular workers who would soon be laid off.
- *Promotion from within.* The top nonunion firms like to promote from within. In order to do so, they offer training and career counseling to workers who want to upgrade their skills. Often they announce job openings in the plant and offer training in needed skills.
- *Competitive pay and benefits.* All of the firms studied by Foulkes pay wages and benefits that match or exceed the standard levels for their community and industry.[*] The nonunion firms also place heavy emphasis on raises based on merit and tend to pay blue-collar workers salaries rather than hourly wages.
- *Managers who listen.* The top nonunion firms are very careful about the way they handle grievances. They survey worker attitudes, encourage workers to talk directly to middle and top managers, and keep office doors open. And of course their managers listen to suggestions as well as complaints.

Should we conclude that firms that do not have unions should do everything they can to keep them out, and that firms that have unions should try to get rid of them? Not necessarily. As Thomas Kochan and Robert McKersie have pointed out, the important thing is not to avoid unions but to avoid bad relations with employees.[5] The policies we have just listed tend to reduce the likelihood that the firm will be unionized. But these policies are the right ones whether the firm is unionized or not. If the workers want a union—and the law gives them the right to have one if they want it—management had better learn to deal with it in a spirit of cooperation. An all-out effort to keep the union out is not the best way to start.

Making the Transition

Suppose we have the worst possible case: years of conflict in a unionized plant, or workers who have just joined a union after a bitterly fought representation election. Starting from this point, suppose that high costs, poor product quality, shrinking market share, and lost jobs have convinced both managers and union leaders that a new start must be made. How can it be done? Drawing on a number of cases—some successes and some failures—Donald N. Scobel offers the following advice.[6]

[*]Exceptions would be found in such industries as steel, airlines, and trucking. Foulkes' study did not include firms in those industries.

[5]Thomas A. Kochan and Robert B. McKersie, "Collective Bargaining—Pressures for Change," *Sloan Management Review*, Summer 1983, pp. 59–65.

[6]Donald N. Scobel, "Business and Labor—From Adversaries to Allies," *Harvard Business Review*, November-December 1982, pp. 129–36.

- *Management should offer the olive branch.* Union leaders may find it hard to make the first move. Scobel thinks a two- to four-day retreat for managers and union leaders, away from the plant site, is a good way to begin.
- *Tackle the easiest issues first.* Under our worst-case assumptions, there will be a huge backlog of touchy issues—rigid work rules, unfair performance standards, and so on. Trying to deal with these issues first may cause each side to feel that the other is trying to outmaneuver it in the name of cooperation.
- *Ask workers for input on new technologies and processes.* We have made the point before that worker suggestions have value in themselves. They are also one of the best ways to build trust.
- *Get rid of policies that show mistrust.* A good first step is to find some annoying policies that are no longer useful and make a show of scrapping them. (One firm had a rule that spouses could not pick workers up at the plant, even when it was raining. The rule had been put in thirty years before because one worker had arranged for his wife to pick him up there as part of a plan to steal a saw.) Where rules are needed, rewrite them in broader terms. (Instead of "No radios in the plant," make it "No radios where they are a safety hazard.")
- *Don't raise unrealistic expectations.* Avoid public relations statements that promise the moon. In the words of the song, "Don't talk of love, show me!"
- *Share information.* We have said this before, and it is important enough to say again. In most cases the gains in trust that can result from sharing information far outweigh the harm that might be caused by leaks to competitors.

The words of a union leader at a plant that made the transition from conflict to cooperation provide a good note on which to end this chapter.

> Improving people's worklives is the guts of unionism. For years, we went after wages, hours, and so on. Now we're moving toward trust and dignity. To me, saying that cooperation can hurt our ability to represent people is a cop-out. All I know is that when we all try to get along, we get fewer employee complaints and we are more in tune with our members.[7]

SUMMARY

1. A *labor union* is an association of workers formed for the purpose of engaging in *collective bargaining* with an employer over the wages and working conditions of its members. Today somewhat less than 20 percent of the American nonfarm labor force belongs to labor unions.

2. The modern labor movement in the United States

began with the founding of the *American Federation of Labor* in 1881. The AFL is composed of *craft unions*, that is, unions of workers who all practice the same trade. Workers in mass-production industries like autos, steel, and rubber are members of *industrial unions.* Such unions include all of a firm's workers, regardless of their skill. In the 1930s the *Congress of*

[7]Quoted in Scobel, p. 135.

Industrial Organizations, a group of industrial unions, split off from the AFL. The two federations merged again in 1955.

3. Until the 1930s courts were hostile to unions. Unions were not illegal, but their activities were restricted. The *Norris–La Guardia Act* of 1932 established basic legal rights for unions. Three years later the *Wagner Act* put government actively on the side of unions. It established the *National Labor Relations Board* to administer the act and oversee union elections. It also outlawed certain unfair labor practices of employers. In 1946 the *Taft-Hartley Act* amended the Wagner Act, swinging the law back toward a neutral stance. The *Landrum-Griffin Act* of 1959 gave the government the power to act against union corruption and established a bill of rights for rank-and-file union members.

4. The desire to improve wages and working conditions is one reason why workers join unions. However, workers with the very lowest wages and worst working conditions have tended not to be very successful in forming unions. Workers also join unions in order to gain security, a sense of belongingness, and self-esteem. Many writers believe that a job in any well-managed firm should provide these things. In this sense, unions can be viewed as a response to management failure.

5. The collective bargaining process is a mixture of cooperation and conflict. It is cooperative in the sense that there are mutual benefits to be gained from an agreement—jobs for workers and profits for the firm. Conflicts arise because there is more than one way to divide up the potential gains. Major issues in collective bargaining include wages and benefits, *union security*, and management rights.

6. The *strike*—a collective refusal to work—is the union's chief weapon in collective bargaining. The strike is reinforced by *picketing* and sometimes by *boycotts*. The main weapon used by management is the threat to keep the plant running during a strike by using *strikebreakers*. Other management weapons include building up inventories of finished goods and shutting the plant down (this is called a *lockout*).

7. If managers and unions cannot resolve collective bargaining issues on their own, they may resort to *mediation* or *arbitration*. Even after a contract has been signed, *grievances* may arise. Most labor contracts state how grievances will be handled.

8. Managers in a unionized environment face some special challenges and opportunities. The challenges come from the need to overcome the habits learned in decades of conflict. The opportunities come from the ability of unions to mobilize the full potential of the workers who belong to them.

KEY TERMS

You should be familiar with the following terms and concepts. Check their meanings by referring to the marginal definitions in the chapter or to the glossary at the end of the book.

Labor union

Collective bargaining

American Federation of Labor (AFL)

Craft union

Business unionism

Injunction

Norris–La Guardia Act

Yellow-dog contract

Wagner Act

National Labor Relations Board (NLRB)

Authorization card

Representation election

Unfair labor practice

Industrial union

Congress of Industrial Organizations (CIO)

Taft-Hartley Act

Cost-of-living adjustment (COLA)

Fringe benefits

Union security agreement	Strike fund	Lockout
Closed shop	Picketing	Mediation
Union shop	Boycott	Arbitration
Right-to-work laws	Primary boycott	Grievance
Bargaining range	Secondary boycott	Shop steward
Strike	Strikebreaker	

QUESTIONS FOR REVIEW AND DISCUSSION

1. Since its early days, the AFL (now the AFL-CIO) has not formed a labor party. Instead, it has worked through the other political parties to reward its friends and punish its enemies. Scan the newspapers or TV news for items on the political activities of the AFL-CIO. What policies is it supporting? What candidates, if any, is it backing? Who is it trying to reward and who is it trying to punish? Do you think it has stayed true to Gompers' principles?

2. The business press—newspapers and magazines like the *Wall Street Journal*, *Business Week*, *Fortune*, and *Forbes*—report labor news on a regular basis. Scan recent issues of these periodicals and try to find an example of each of the following: a campaign to organize a group of workers (or a campaign by workers to decertify a union); a strike; and a case of union-management cooperation. Discuss each in terms of the ideas presented in this chapter.

3. Are you a member of a union? Do you know any union members? If so, why did you, or the union members you know, join the union? Discuss in terms of ideas presented in this chapter. Bonus question: Read some publications put out by your union or those of

question 2. How does the union's viewpoint differ from that of the business press?

4. Do you think Herzberg's two-factor theory of motivation (see page 353) is useful in explaining why workers join unions? What is the role of Herzberg's sources of dissatisfaction? His sources of satisfaction?

5. This chapter suggests that workers at the top of Maslow's hierarchy of needs—that is, workers whose strongest need is for self-actualization—are not likely to join unions. However, the union movement is very strong among performing artists, such as musicians, ballet dancers, and actors. Why, do you think, is this so?

6. Peter Drucker believes that unions put too much emphasis on fringe benefits as opposed to wages.[8] He argues that fringe benefits are not fair to many workers, such as part-time workers or workers whose spouses are already covered by pensions and insurance. Instead, he suggests that unions and management agree on a total cost per labor hour and allow workers to choose how much they want in cash, and how much in benefits. What do you think of this idea?

Case 15–1: Extrusion Technology Weathers a Strike

Extrusion Technology, a Randolph, Massachusetts, manufacturer of aluminum extrusions, says that for a dozen years it caved in to union demands. "When we had our first labor negotiations with the Teamsters twelve years ago, they stood up and stormed out of the room," says

[8]Peter F. Drucker, "Where Union Flexibility's Now a Must," *Wall Street Journal*, September 23, 1983, p. 30.

Steven Smith, the company's president. "We rushed after them to come back in and give us a contract. That set the tempo for a dozen years. We felt a strike would be deadly."

Losses in 1981 and 1982 strengthened the company's resolve. A six-week strike began last April when the company insisted on a wage-scale plan tied to job classifications and the right to assign mandatory overtime. Initially, the company tried to operate its plant with about 20 nonunion office workers. But after about three weeks Smith hired about 15 workers by placing newspaper ads. The plant began running at about 50 percent of capacity.

The 34-year-old Smith drove a company truck through the picket line himself to deliver products and pick up supplies. "I wasn't going to ask my people to do that," he says. After three more weeks, the union settled. Smith says he won on the overtime issue and reached a compromise on the wage scale.

"I wasn't out to break the union; I was out to settle the dispute," he says. "But I wanted to keep my customers while I was resolving it," he adds. "If the union says 'strike' three years from now, they better be prepared to stay out for a long time."

Source: Robert S. Greenberger, "More Firms Get Tough and Keep Operating in Spite of Walkouts," *Wall Street Journal*, October 11, 1983, p. 1. Reprinted by permission of the *Wall Street Journal*. © Dow Jones and Company, Inc. 1983. All Rights Reserved.

Questions:

1. What changed the relative bargaining power of the firm and the union in this case? Do you think such changes are widespread, or is this case not typical?

2. What were the benefits to Extrusion Technology of keeping its plant running during the strike? What were the costs of doing so?

3. How do you think Smith's strikebreaking tactics will affect relations between managers and workers at Extrusion Technology?

Chapter 16

MANAGING HUMAN RESOURCES

When you have completed this chapter, you should be able to

- Discuss the role of planning, organizing, leading, and controlling in human resource management.

- Define *equal employment opportunity*, *affirmative action*, and *reverse discrimination*, and explain how they are related to one another.

- Outline the process of human resource or *personnel* management from recruitment to separations.

- List seven steps in selecting new employees and explain how each is carried out.

- Define *orientation*, *socialization*, *training*, and *development*, and explain the relationships among them.

- Explain how career movement is managed, including *transfers*, *promotions*, and *separations*.

- Discuss the principles on which compensation plans are based and the major laws that apply to compensation.

When employees at Petrie Stores Corporation swap stories, they often talk about the time a Petrie executive broke his wrist while racing into Chairman Milton Petrie's office. Details of the story vary. One version has the executive tripping over some open drawers. Another has him crashing into a locked door.

But by all accounts the flustered manager, dazed and injured in the accident, still made it into Petrie's office in record time with the information requested. Only later did he head for a hospital.

The story may well be true. Petrie employees have always put their hearts and souls into pleasing their fiercely demanding and impatient chairman, who can be as benevolent at some times as he is bad-tempered at others. In fifty-six years, his iron rule has built Petrie from a small hosiery shop in Cleveland to a $600 million empire of women's clothing stores that stretches from Hawaii to the Virgin Islands.

But that same domineering style has kept the eighty-one-year-old Petrie from grooming a successor. "Milton is a brilliant person, but unfortunately he doesn't realize we're all mortal, and he isn't making plans to assure the continuity of Petrie Stores," says Gilbert Harrison, a Philadelphia takeover specialist who has tried to persuade Petrie to merge his company with another retailer.

Relaxing in his lavish, salmon-colored stucco home in Southampton, New York, Petrie acknowledges that without a successor, there is a "weakness in the business." He insists, however, that he is working to correct the problem. "We've got our irons out in a few spots, looking for a president," says Petrie, a thin but imposing man who often puffs a cigar. "It'll come to pass one of these days. We'll find somebody."

Petrie has tried twice since 1980 to recruit outsiders to follow him as chairman, and neither candidate lasted very long. Earlier this year he fired the most recent candidate, thirty-eight-year-old Michael Boyle, only seven weeks after hiring him as president and heir apparent. Boyle, who had been chairman and chief executive of Federated Department Stores' Lazarus division, now is suing Petrie Stores, demanding more than $1.7 million in salary and benefits and charging that he was dismissed without cause. Petrie has countersued, raising questions about expenses incurred by Boyle.

A financial adviser to Petrie, Sandy Lewis, managing partner of the securities firm of S. B. Lewis & Company, suggests that Petrie may bring in a successor who would involve the chairman "in the critical decisions" affecting the business but save him from bothersome details. Petrie would maintain his active relationship with his employees. "They would continue to be able to bring him their problems," Lewis says, "and he would be certain to be consulted in important decisions."

Lewis notes that Petrie is very attached to his company. "It will be very difficult" for him to deal with succession, he says. "But he wants to deal with it and I believe he will."[1]

---

[1]Claudia Ricci, "At Petrie Stores Corp., Key to Future Success May Be the Succession," *Wall Street Journal*, September 16, 1983, p. 1. Reprinted by permission of the *Wall Street Journal*. © Dow Jones & Company, Inc., 1983. All Rights Reserved.

Although we have stressed again and again that people are important, we have not yet said much about the fact that they come and go. As the case of Petrie Stores shows, the boxes of an organization chart aren't filled by plastic figures labeled "worker" and "manager." They are filled by real people, all different, who must be found, trained to do their jobs, encouraged to grow, and someday—gracefully, one hopes—replaced.

This chapter ties together several threads that have run through earlier ones. First, it rounds out Part IV of the book, which has been devoted to the management of production systems, especially the role of people who make these systems work. Second, it continues the theme of planning, organizing, leading, and controlling. Much of this chapter deals with staffing, which we listed in Chapter 5 as a part of leading, but human resource management also involves planning, organizing, and controlling. Box 16–1 links the four functions of management to the job of the human resource manager.

Finally, this chapter complements the material in the sections on careers at the ends of the various parts of book. Those sections look at careers from the bottom up, that is, from the point of view of a person making his or her way up through the ranks of a company. This chapter looks at careers from the top down. It focuses on the manager's job of helping subordinates build their skills and advance in their careers.

Box 16–1 Functions of Human Resource Management

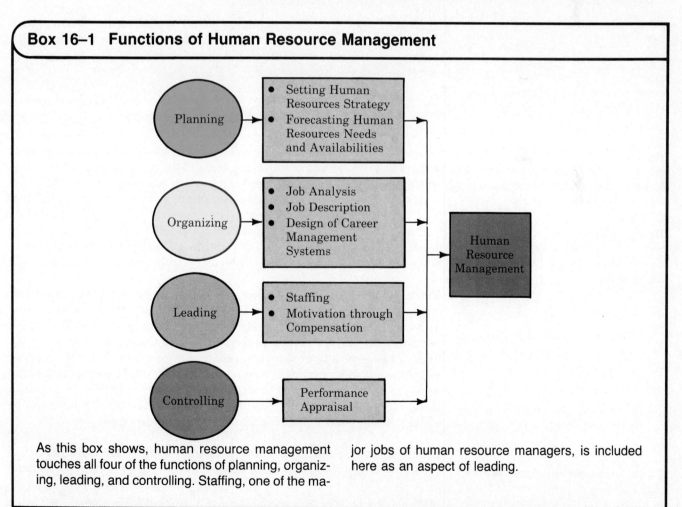

As this box shows, human resource management touches all four of the functions of planning, organizing, leading, and controlling. Staffing, one of the major jobs of human resource managers, is included here as an aspect of leading.

The chapter opens with a section on human resource planning. Next comes a section on the process of human resource management, in which the topics of recruitment, selection, orientation of new employees, training and development, performance appraisal, and managing career movement are discussed. The final section of the chapter covers the subject of compensation—pay and fringe benefits.

HUMAN RESOURCE PLANNING

"A few years ago," writes William E. Bright of Union Oil, "we were building a plant overseas. Planning its financing and construction had consumed months of executive time. Just one element was missing. No one had so much as raised the question of staffing."

"When the issue finally did come up, the executive in charge seemed surprised. 'We've got all the planning done,' he said. 'When the plant is built, we'll think about staffing.' "

"To a human resource planner," says Bright, "that comment sounded disturbingly like 'When the horse has been stolen, we'll lock the barn door.' "[2]

Bright's point is that planning ahead is just as important where human resources are concerned as it is when managers are dealing with marketing strategy, production systems, financial needs, or any other aspect of business management.

The Human Resources Strategy

Human resources strategy: A set of broad policies for the acquisition, retention, and use of human resources to achieve the company's goals.

Human resource planning: The process of forecasting human resource needs and developing procedures for filling them.

In Chapter 5 we defined *strategic planning* as the systematic long-range process used to set and achieve the goals of an organization. Part of this process should be the development of a **human resources strategy**—a set of broad policies for the acquisition, retention, and use of human resources to achieve the organization's goals. The organization's strategy guides its **human resource planning**—the process of forecasting human resource needs and developing procedures for filling them. Two major issues in human resources strategy are job security and equal opportunity.

Planning for job security. Job security, as we have said several times, is important to employees at all levels. It is a key factor in attracting first-rate people. But job security requires a long-term commitment—it cannot be turned on and off. Concern for job security may even affect the lines of business a firm chooses to enter. For example, Hewlett-Packard avoids government contracts when it thinks they would create big ups and downs in workloads. A firm that supplies goods and services to a cyclical industry like housing or autos might want to balance its business by adding other product lines for which the demand is more constant.

Equal employment opportunity (EEO): A policy of not discriminating in hiring, pay, job assignments, and promotion.

Planning for equal opportunity. Title VII of the Civil Rights Act of 1964 makes **equal employment opportunity (EEO)** the law of the land.

[2]William E. Bright, "How One Company Manages Its Human Resources," *Harvard Business Review*, January-February 1976, p. 81.

The Civil Rights Act of 1964 made equal employment opportunity the law of the land. Many help-wanted ads now include the phrase "an equal opportunity employer." © Freda Leinwand

Affirmative action: A policy that involves seeking out, hiring, and promoting members of specific groups, such as minorities, women, older workers, and the handicapped.

Reverse discrimination: Denying a job or promotion to a white or male candidate in favor of a less qualified minority group member or woman.

A strong EEO program also requires a commitment. A series of short-term personnel decisions does not always add up to a good equal-opportunity record, even when each decision is reasonable in itself.

EEO means a policy of not discriminating in hiring, pay, job assignments, and promotion. It is a policy of neutrality or "color blindness" in which personnel decisions are made solely on the basis of each employee's skills and performance. Federal EEO laws originally covered discrimination based on race, sex, religion, color, and national origin. They have been extended to cover older workers and handicapped people. Some state and local laws also forbid discrimination based on sexual preference.

EEO is required of almost all employers. The next step is **affirmative action**, which is required of firms that do business with the federal government. Affirmative action goes beyond neutrality. It involves seeking out, hiring, and promoting members of specific groups such as minorities, women, older workers, and the handicapped. Examples of affirmative action efforts are placing help-wanted ads in publications read by women or minority group members; Spanish-language recruitment campaigns; screening of job specifications to remove any that are not really relevant; checking the validity of tests to see that they do not discriminate against some group; or using a computer to call up the names of possible women and minority candidates for a certain job.

One of the most hotly debated subjects in human resource management is where to draw the line between affirmative action and **reverse discrimination**. Reverse discrimination means denying a job or promotion to a white or male candidate in favor of a less qualified minority group member or woman.

Neither legislation nor court decisions have made clear at what point affirmative action ends and reverse discrimination begins. White males have won a few reverse discrimination suits, but the courts have decided against them in other cases in which the facts seemed just as clear-cut. There is also some doubt about when affirmative action programs can legally use quotas or other kinds of numerical targets. Finally, legal tangles can arise when affirmative action conflicts with union seniority rules. These issues are sure to be argued both in and out of court for years to come.

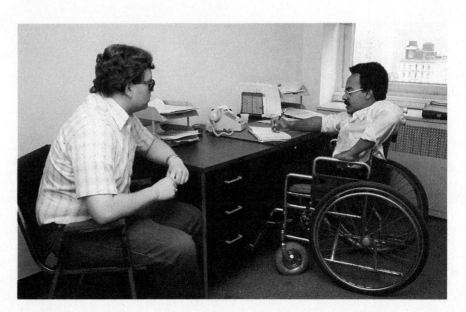

Affirmative action involves seeking out, hiring, and promoting members of specific groups, such as minorities, women, older workers, and the handicapped. © Freda Leinwand

Filling in the Details

When strategic policies have been set, human resource planners need to think about specific jobs. This task can be discussed in terms of three steps: job analysis, job description, and job specification.

Job analysis: An analysis of the tasks to be performed by the person holding a particular job.

The first step, **job analysis**, looks at the job itself. What are the duties and responsibilities of the job? What tasks must be performed by the person holding it? If the job is an existing one, this information can be obtained from the person holding the job. If the job is a newly created one, the job analysis is based on knowledge of the purpose of the job and how it is intended to mesh with others.

Job description: A summary of the duties and responsibilities of a job.

When the job has been analyzed, the results can be summarized as a **job description**. The job description is the basis on which the jobholder builds an understanding of his or her role. Except for newly created jobs, the person currently holding the job should help write the job description.

Job specifications: A set of brief statements of the knowledge, skills, and abilities required of the person who will hold a particular job.

The final step is filling in the details, thus creating a set of **job specifications**. These are brief statements of the knowledge, skills, and abilities required of the person who will hold the job. The specifications should be objective and realistic.

Clear, objective job descriptions and specifications are essential in carrying out an equal-opportunity program. The law states that only factors that are genuinely relevant to a job can be taken into account in hiring and promotion. For example, minimum height and weight standards cannot be used unless a certain height or weight is really needed, because such job specifications tend to discriminate against women. And jobs that must be done by strong people cannot be limited to men, because doing so would discriminate against any women who are strong enough to qualify.

When only factors that are genuinely relevant to a job are taken into account in hiring and promotion, women find opportunities in occupations that formerly were closed to them. Sally Ride, America's first woman astronaut, is a case in point. Courtesy of NASA

The Human Resources Information System

Human resources information system (HRIS): A system for gathering information on human resources, processing it, and making it available to decision makers.

Human resource managers need information to carry out their plans. The system for gathering that information, processing it, and making it available to decision makers can be called a **human resources information system (HRIS)**. It plays much the same role in the work of a human resource manager as a marketing information system plays in that of a marketing manager. (See Chapter 8.)

The HRIS should be designed to answer questions like the following: How many openings will occur at various levels in the next few years? Are there positions for which replacements will be hard to find? Are there others in which good people are going to seed because positions above them are blocked? Some companies use a formal, computer-based HRIS. Others use less formal methods. But whether formal or informal methods are used, the important thing is for human resource managers to be able to answer questions like these.

THE PROCESS OF HUMAN RESOURCE MANAGEMENT

Plans are worth nothing unless they are carried out. In this section we will look at the tasks of bringing people into a firm, guiding their careers within it, and managing their departure.

Whatever their functional area, all managers play a role in training and evaluating the people who work for them. In a small business, all the tasks of human resource management are typically carried out by the proprietor. Larger firms usually have specialists with the title of human resource manager or personnel manager. Let's take a look at some tasks of human resource management that must be done in every firm, whether they are done by line managers or by staff specialists.

Recruitment

Recruitment: The process of attracting a pool of candidates from which jobs can be filled.

Recruitment—the process of attracting a pool of candidates from which jobs can be filled—is the first step in finding the people a firm needs.

All recruiting starts from the job description and specifications. The job description must be attractive enough to interest candidates, but at the same time it must be realistic. Unrealistic job descriptions are a recipe for dissatisfied employees and high turnover. Poorly written job specifications can also cause problems. People will not be happy in jobs for which they are greatly underqualified or overqualified. And as mentioned earlier, firms must make sure their job specifications conform to EEO law.

For reasons we have already discussed, many firms view the question of whether to recruit candidates for promotion from inside or outside as a strategic one. There are several ways in which firms that recruit from the inside can find candidates. Getting recommendations from superiors is one of the most frequently used of these. Posting notices to advertise openings is another common method. It not only finds good candidates but also adds to employee morale. Finally, some companies use a computerized human resource information system to find candidates who are already on the payroll.

A common way of recruiting employees is to post a notice in a prominent place. © Freda Leinwand

Newspaper ads are an important recruiting method, but word of mouth and personal contacts are equally effective. © Freda Leinwand

Even companies that like to promote from within sometimes have to look outside. Entry-level employees always come from the outside. Firms may also recruit from the outside to get candidates with skills that no one in the company has. (For example, Apple Computer, which was founded by a group of technical wizards, felt that it needed some marketing zip to stay in the big time in the mid-1980s. To get the needed boost, it hired a new president, John Sculley, from Pepsico, where he had masterminded the "Pepsi Generation" campaign.) Finally, a firm whose work force is not balanced in terms of race or sex may need to do more outside recruiting than usual in order to meet affirmative action goals.

Word of mouth and personal contacts are a major source of recruits from outside the company as well as from inside it. Placing ads in newspapers and trade publications is another important recruiting method. As Box 16–2 shows, newspaper ads are used for recruiting at all levels, from manual workers to executives. For jobs that require a college education, on-campus recruiting is a major tool. But companies do not always have to take the initiative: most firms fill at least some positions with applicants who come in on their own.

Some mention should also be given to job market intermediaries. All states have employment departments that keep lists of people who are looking for work. There are also private employment agencies that help match candidates with jobs at all levels.

Selection

Once a pool of candidates has been recruited, the next step is to select those to whom the job will be offered. Selection is a two-sided process: while the firm is deciding whether or not to offer the job, the candidate is deciding whether or not to take it if it is offered. The selection process can be broken down into seven steps, as shown in Box 16–3.

The application form. Most firms require applicants to fill out an application form. One use of this form is to make sure the candidate meets the job specifications. Usually such forms also ask for references and work

Box 16–2 Help-Wanted Ads

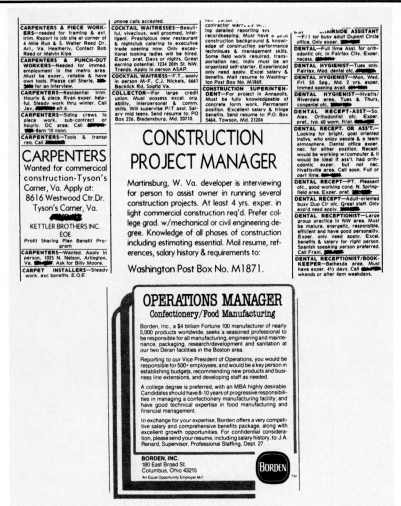

Help-wanted ads are a major recruitment tool. These ads show the wide range of jobs for which such advertising is used. Note that the larger ads include detailed job descriptions and job specifications.

Sources: *Washington Post*, November 5, 1983, p. C–16, and *Wall Street Journal*, November 1, 1983, p. 27.

experience. To comply with EEO law, an application form must ask only for information that is relevant to the job.

The screening interview.   The next step is usually a brief screening interview. Sometimes the candidate goes to the employer's place of business for the interview, but often a college placement office or a hotel room is used instead. The screening interview gives the employer a chance to judge whether the applicant's style and personality are suited to the organization.

Testing.   Many employers follow up the screening interview with some kind of testing. This may range from a typing test for clerical jobs to psychological testing for management positions. Management candidates

Box 16–3   The Selection Process

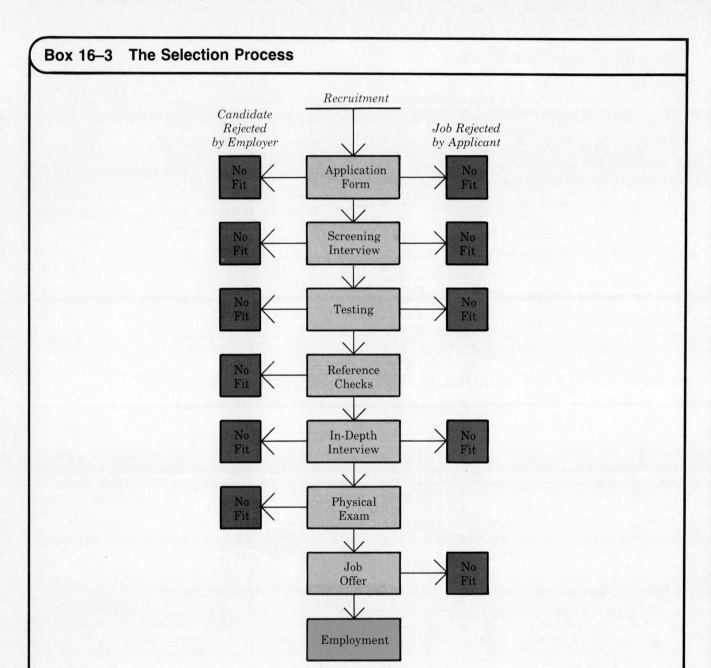

The selection process, which begins after a pool of candidates has been recruited, is shown here as a series of seven steps. Each step is a two-sided process. The firm looks at the candidate, and rejects the candidate if his or her qualifications do not fit the needs of the firm. At the same time, the candidate, at each step, looks at the firm. If the firm does not fit his or her requirements, the candidate rejects the job.

Assessment center: A center where job applicants or candidates for promotion are asked to participate in realistic exercises designed to predict their future performance.

are sometimes tested in **assessment centers**. At such centers, candidates are asked to take part in realistic exercises designed to predict their future performance.

EEO law requires that tests given to job applicants be reliable and valid. They must really measure what they attempt to measure, and the traits they measure must be relevant to the job. Suppose, for example, that a firm is hiring an armed guard. Should it use a lie detector test to check whether the application form has been filled in honestly? Honesty is a valid requirement for the job, but some experts question the reliability of the testing method. Should it use a test of math skills? Probably not; math skills are not important for performance on this job. Tests of vision and skill in using firearms would certainly be appropriate, however.

Reference checks. Reference checks serve two purposes. First, they check the truthfulness of information given on the application form and in the screening interview. Second, they are a way of finding out how other people feel about the candidate. For some kinds of jobs, a more thorough investigation is made. For example, a firm that is hiring a truck driver might want to check for any history of alcohol or drug abuse.

The in-depth interview. For managerial jobs, an in-depth interview is usually the most important part of the selection process. This interview serves several purposes. First, it fills in gaps left in previous steps. Second, it is a realistic test of communication skills. Third, it is a chance to explore such questions as whether the applicant will fit into the employer's corporate culture. And finally, it gives the applicant a chance to ask questions about the job.

In-depth interviews are usually conducted by the person for whom the applicant will work. Because interviews are subjective, many firms have more than one person talk to candidates for important positions.

For managerial jobs, an in-depth interview, usually conducted by the person for whom the applicant will work, is a key part of the selection process. Marc P. Anderson

The physical examination. Many firms require a physical exam for all job applicants. Some jobs, such as those of airline pilots and bus drivers, have physical standards related to public safety. In other cases the exam may be used to screen out people who would be vulnerable to certain hazards in the workplace. Many companies want a checkup simply because the employee will be eligible for company health benefits, or because the employee might file a workers' compensation claim related to an injury or health hazard on the job.

The job offer. If an applicant passes all the hurdles in the selection process, a job offer will be made. If the wage or salary proposed is acceptable, and if the job description is both attractive and realistic, the result will be an employee who is happy to join the firm and will stay with it. An offer that the applicant feels is too low may well be turned down. However, being turned down is not the worst thing that can happen. An employee who insists on an offer far above what other people in the firm are being paid can become a source of discontent. And one who reluctantly accepts a low offer is likely to keep right on looking for something better.

Orientation and Socialization

It is widely agreed that a new employee's first weeks and months on the job are crucial to his or her future performance. As soon as the new person arrives, the processes of orientation and socialization begin.

Orientation: The process by which a new employee learns about the employer and the job.

Orientation is the process by which a new employee learns about the employer and the job. Often it begins with a formal briefing by the personnel department. For example, new employees of the U.S. Department of Justice spend their first day at work in a briefing session in which the agency's structure and mission are explained, a code of conduct is presented, and procedures are outlined for such matters as reporting travel expenses and applying for sick leave. The employee is introduced to people who can answer questions and explain details of the job.

Socialization: The informal process through which new employees absorb the values, language, manners, unwritten rules, and other elements of the firm's culture.

Socialization is the less formal, but no less important, process through which new employees absorb the values, language, manners, unwritten rules, and other elements of the firm's culture. Socialization processes are most intense when an employee first joins the firm. The degree of challenge in the first job assignment has a major effect on socialization. New workers who are given challenging tasks tend to develop high standards of performance. These have a lasting effect on their success within the firm.

Training and Development

Training: An activity aimed at improving a person's ability to do his or her present job.

Development: An activity aimed at upgrading the skills of employees so that they will be able to move up in the company and meet its future needs.

Companies gain when their employees upgrade their skills and abilities. Programs to help them do this go beyond the orientation period. People may take part in them, at least from time to time, throughout their careers. **Training** is aimed at improving a person's ability to do his or her present job. Teaching a secretary how to use a word processor or teaching a manager how to conduct on-campus interviews are examples. **Development** is aimed at upgrading the skills of present employees so that they will be able to move up in the firm and meet its future needs.

Training and development are key parts of the EEO programs of many firms. Since the members of minority groups often have received an inadequate education, training and development programs may be almost the only sources of qualified minority candidates for higher-level positions.

Training and development programs use a variety of techniques. Among them are the following.

1. *Apprenticeship.* An apprentice is a person who is a beginner or learner. An apprentice learns a job by watching experienced people

An apprentice learns a job by watching experienced people and helping them. © Rhoda Sidney, Monkmeyer Press

and helping them. At first the apprentice may do only easier parts of the work, taking on harder tasks one at a time. Apprenticeship has long been used in crafts like printing and metalworking, but it is not limited to them. Management trainees are also apprentices.

2. *Job rotation.* Job rotation is a second way of encouraging learning in the workplace. It improves the morale of production workers and creates a more flexible work force. At higher levels, it is used to develop general managers.

3. *Classroom instruction.* Some kinds of skills are best learned outside the workplace, through classroom instruction. For example, auto dealers send mechanics to factory training schools; churches run seminars on counseling for their ministers; and firms send managers to university classes to learn new skills.

Some kinds of skills are best learned through classroom instruction. © David Strickler, Monkmeyer Press

"Mr. Gottlieb recently read one of those books on Japanese management techniques."

From the *Wall Street Journal*. Reprinted by permission of Cartoon Features Syndicate.

Performance Appraisal

Chapter 14 stressed the need to let people know how they are doing in their jobs. From Blanchard and Johnson's one-minute goals, praisings, and reprimands to the formal system of management by objectives, the theme is much the same: frequent and fair performance appraisal is a key to career growth. Without repeating the whole discussion, let's recall three key points.

1. Performance appraisal should be an ongoing process. It is fine to have a formal performance review every year or six months, but in between, praise and criticism should be given when the situation calls for it. That way, formal reviews, when they do come, will contain no surprises.
2. The standards by which performance is appraised should be clear to everyone. They should also be the same for everyone who does the same kind of job. Participation by the people whose performance is being appraised is one of the best ways to set clear, fair standards.
3. Performance appraisal should use positive reinforcement whenever possible. When reprimands are given, they should be aimed at the unsuitable behavior, not at the person's character. An especially bad technique is to save up many small criticisms and then dump them on a person all at once.

Managing Career Movement

In some cases—college professors are an example—one runs into people who have held the same job for decades without a promotion or transfer. Such careers are rare, however. Even when people stay with one organization throughout their career, they tend to move from job to job within it.

Promotion: A movement to a job involving greater authority and responsibility.

Transfer: A movement to a job involving about the same degree of authority and responsibility in another place or another functional unit of the firm.

The career cone. Edgar Schein has suggested that movement within an organization can be pictured in terms of the cone shown in Box 16–4. The career cone shows three directions of movement. The first is upward. A **promotion** moves a person to a higher-level job that is nearer to the tip of the cone. The second direction is around the outside of the cone. These movements are **transfers** from one job to another in a different place or functional unit. The final direction is inward toward the cone's core. Inward movement is not a formal matter like promotion or transfer. Instead, it represents an increase in respect and authority among one's colleagues. This kind of movement is captured by such expressions as "Talk to her—she's one of the inner circle," or "That guy's really on the inside track."

One of the major tasks of human resource management is that of moving people around within the career cone in a way that both develops their careers and makes the most of their abilities. Consider job rotation. Transfers from one job to another at the same level of the cone are a way of keeping people interested and productive. On the other hand, rotation combined with promotions at each stage is a common method of developing the careers of general managers. In terms of Schein's cone, such a career path is an upward spiral.

Box 16–4   The Career Cone

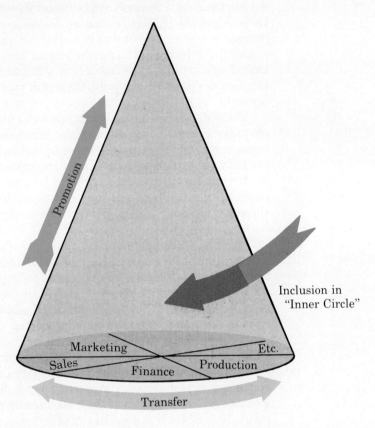

Edgar Schein has suggested that career movement within a firm can be pictured in terms of the cone shown in Box 16–4. The career cone shows three directions of movement. The first is toward the top of the cone, through promotions. The second is around the outside of the cone, through transfers. The third is toward the center of the cone, through acceptance by the "inner circle" of employees at any given level.

Source: Adapted from Edgar H. Schein, "The Individual, the Organization, and the Career: A Conceptual Scheme," *Journal of Applied Behavioral Science* 7 (1971).

If a firm wants to keep the best young people it hires, it should try to draw them into the inner circle even while their rank is low. However, those picked early to be the superstars of tomorrow should have to meet the same performance standards as others at their level. Most people can live with others who outdo them in a fair contest. But favoritism that is not based on performance will be resented.

Equal-opportunity issues.   An EEO employer must, at the very least, not allow race or sex to affect promotion decisions. But, as in the case of recruitment, equal opportunity in promotion is not always enough. Many employers have chosen, or are required by law, to follow a policy of affirmative action in making promotion decisions.

Affirmative action in promotion means pulling women, blacks, and members of other disadvantaged groups up the ladder. It is easy to say that these people will not be promoted unless they are qualified, but saying that does not solve all the problems connected with affirmative action promotions. First, each such promotion leaves behind other qualified people. Some of them may be content to wait their turn, but others may resent the situation. "Why should he get the job just because my grandfather discriminated against his grandfather?" is a frequent complaint. If situations of this sort are handled clumsily, the result may be a reverse discrimination lawsuit.

Second, affirmative action promotions place an added burden on people to perform well in their new jobs. Employers who think they are doing women or minority group members a favor by promoting them before they are fully qualified may be making a mistake. Such people are likely not to be able to pull their weight in the new position, and their colleagues will be the first ones to know. A few such promotions run the risk of casting suspicion, however unfairly, on other recently promoted women or minority group members.

Finally, some firms that do a good job of promoting women and members of minority groups neglect the need for movement toward the core of the career cone. The result is to create *figureheads*—people whose real status and authority does not match their formal rank. Managers cannot promote and forget. They must promote, and then continue to develop the careers of those whom they have promoted.

Despite these problems, many firms remain strongly committed to affirmative action in promotions. Suppose, for example, that in the past a firm has employed few women or minority group members but it is now recruiting many more at the entry level. The new recruits will need mentors and role models of their own sex or race at all levels of management. This is not just a matter of idealism—it is a matter of turning the new recruits into satisfied, productive employees. Under these conditions, a completely color-blind promotion policy just won't get the job done soon enough.

Managing Separations

Separation: The voluntary or involuntary departure of a person from an organization.

Layoff: A temporary involuntary separation of an employee, made with the expectation of recall at a later date.

Termination (firing): A permanent involuntary separation.

A **separation** takes place whenever a person leaves an organization, whether by choice or not. Voluntary separations include quits and retirements. Federal law prohibits mandatory retirement before age seventy. Involuntary separations include **layoffs**, which are temporary and are made with the expectation of recall at a later date, and **terminations** (firings), which are permanent.

Retirements. In the area of retirements, the most obvious task is that of replacing the people who retire. Unless a firm has a program that grooms such replacements, it is likely to end up in a situation like that faced by Petrie Stores, which was described at the beginning of this chapter. Many firms keep replacement charts for all levels of mangement. Procter & Gamble and some other firms will not promote managers until they have trained a replacement.

Some firms use voluntary retirements rather than layoffs in slow periods. For example, people who are nearing retirement age may be offered bonuses or extra pension benefits if they will retire early. Early retirement can also be a way of easing the conflict between affirmative action programs and seniority systems by opening up higher-level jobs for women and minority group members.

Terminations.   In the days of "I'm the boss, you're the hoss," workers could be fired at any time for any reason. But the old doctrine of **employment at will** is crumbling fast. Terminations of union workers are subject to review under grievance procedures. And firings of nonunion workers are open to legal challenges.

Among the steps that firms are taking to cut the risk of lawsuits for wrongful dismissal are the following.[3]

Employment at will: A doctrine under which an employer could terminate any employee at any time for any reason.

- Companies like GE and Control Data have set up formal grievance procedures for their nonunion employees. These include joint worker-management panels to review terminations.
- Other companies are improving their performance appraisal methods. Managers are pressed to be truthful when appraising the performance of the people who work for them. They are also asked to keep records and to use stronger language for each successive slip-up. A former manager of Bissell, Inc., won a $61,354.02 wrongful-dismissal case because his superiors expressed only vague discontent with his performance and did not give him a fair chance to improve it before he was fired.
- Some companies are rewriting their employee handbooks so as to avoid statements that seem to promise job security. For example, they may change the term *permanent position* to *regular position*. Blue Cross goes further, warning its employees that they "can be terminated at any time without reason." But others think such harsh language is harmful to employee relations.

Although many managers are sorry to see the end of employment at will, it may not be such a bad thing to bid this doctrine good-bye. Fair grievance procedures and performance appraisals are worth having for their own sake. The same can be said for honest statements of the degree of job security the company offers its employees.

However, there are also dangers in offering too much job security. Consider the federal government's civil service rules. It is all but impossible to fire a civil servant for poor performance. Managers use various methods to deal with civil servants who do not perform well, none of which is fully satsifactory. Sometimes such employees are promoted, thus passing the burden on to someone else. (In government circles this is known as the "upward failure.") Sometimes they are moved to special units where they can do no harm because no work that anyone really needs is ever assigned to them. (These units are known as "turkey farms.") Most often, though, they are simply left where they are. Other employees work around them, but at a cost to their morale. There is a positive side to this situation, however. A high degree of job security allows the government to attract many kinds of workers at somewhat lower salaries than are paid by private firms. And it is good to know that even in a system where it is almost impossible to be fired, most people work hard at their jobs.

[3]See Joann S. Lublin, "Legal Challenges Force Firms to Revamp Ways They Dismiss Workers," *Wall Street Journal*, September 13, 1983, p. 1.

COMPENSATION

In Chapter 15 we saw how wages and fringe benefits for unionized workers are set through collective bargaining. Now we turn to some of the factors that affect the pay of the other four fifths of the labor force—employees who are not unionized. First we will consider the total level of compensation. Next we will discuss how compensation should be divided between wages and fringe benefits. Finally, we will discuss various legal constraints on compensation.

How Much to Pay?

Compensation: The total cost to a firm of employing a person.

Compensation is the price a firm must pay to get employees. Like other prices, the level of wages, salaries, and fringe benefits is influenced by supply and demand. On the supply side of the market are all the factors that affect people's willingness to work. Supply sets a lower limit to what a firm can pay and still get the employees it needs. On the demand side are all the factors that affect a firm's ability to pay. The demand for its products places an upper limit on what a firm can pay its employees and still make a profit. (For not-for-profit firms and units of government, the upper limit is set by the need to stay within a budget.)

Between the upper and lower limits set by supply and demand there are many decisions that must be made by human resource managers. It is not enough just to pay what it takes to get a body to fill every job. The people who are hired must be the right ones for the job, and once on the job they must be motivated to do their best. Let's look briefly at some of the factors that have to be taken into account in setting the level of pay for each job.

Fairness. If a firm wants satisfied employees and low turnover, it must have a pay policy that is fair by both internal and external standards.

External fairness means paying about the same amount that other firms in the area pay for the same or similar work. Failure to meet this standard makes people feel exploited. Their motivation suffers, and they will always be on the lookout for better jobs elsewhere.

Internal fairness requires two things. First, it requires that people doing similar jobs get about the same pay. (We will return to this subject later in the chapter.) Second, it requires that positions that involve more skill and authority receive more pay than those below them. Some spread in compensation is needed to give people an incentive for training and development. However, too wide a spread may be seen as unfair. As we noted in the last chapter, in the interest of good employee relations many companies avoid such executive "perks" as country clubs, lavish offices, and separate parking lots.

Job evaluation technique: A technique in which points are assigned to each job for such factors as skill, effort, working conditions, and degree of responsibility.

Job evaluation. One approach to setting fair pay is the **job evaluation technique**. This technique assigns points to each job for such factors as skill, effort, working conditions, and degree of responsibility. The points are added up and each job is given a rating on a scale of, say, 1 to 100. The ratings are then used to set levels of compensation.

Job evaluation is attractive from the point of view of fairness. It gives a clear, objective reason for differences in pay. At the same time, it gives everyone an incentive to move up to a job with a higher rating. The technique has one major drawback, however. In focusing on the difficulty of the job and its value to the firm, it ignores conditions in the labor market.

Marc Wallace and Charles Fay give an example of this problem from the experience of Gulf States Petroleum Corporation.[4] Gulf States had a job evaluation system that gave the same rating to entry-level jobs in accounting, law, and petroleum engineering. For each of these jobs, the work was about equally hard, required the same number of years of schooling, and so on. However, Gulf States found that it could get all the accountants and attorneys it needed for $22,000 a year but could not get an engineer for less than $32,000. To get around this problem, the company had to break its job evaluation schedule into two "job families," each with a separate pay scale.

Merit pay and seniority. Job evaluation can be used to set the base pay for each job, but that does not mean that everyone who does the same job will be paid the same amount. For reasons both of fairness and of motivation, most firms modify their pay scales to take seniority, merit, or both into account. Seniority-based systems pay employees more for any given job the longer they have been with the firm. Merit-based systems are sometimes tied directly to productivity (piecework pay and sales commissions are examples) and sometimes tied to performance appraisals. As we noted in the last chapter, unions tend to favor seniority pay, while non-union firms lean more toward merit pay. Governments at all levels rely almost entirely on seniority pay, although some experiments with merit pay (for example, for teachers) are taking place.

Pay versus Fringe Benefits

Once the total level of compensation for each job has been set, the next step is to break it down into a "package" of cash payments and fringe benefits. As Box 16–5 shows, fringe benefits account for about three eighths of the total payroll costs of U.S. firms. How does a firm arrive at the proper mix between cash payments and fringe benefits?

Advantages of fringe benefits. Many kinds of fringe benefits have special tax advantages. Health and life insurance premiums, for example, are deductible as expenses for the employer but are not counted as taxable income for the employee. Pension contributions are not taxed until after retirement, when the benefits are received. With even blue-collar and clerical workers often facing income tax rates of 35 percent or more, these tax advantages make a big difference.

Some fringe benefits have a second advantage: they can be purchased at a lower rate by a group than by individuals. For example, employees get more for their money when their firm puts dollars into group health and

[4]Marc J. Wallace, Jr., and Charles H. Fay, *Compensation Theory and Practice* (Boston: Kent, 1983), pp. 6–9.

Box 16–5   Fringe Benefits of U.S. Workers

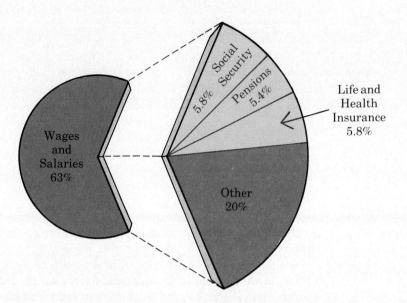

This chart shows the major types of fringe benefits received by U.S. workers as of 1980. Employers' contributions to Social Security, pension plan premiums, and life and health insurance premiums were the largest categories. Benefits added up to 37 percent of total compensation.

Source: U.S. Chamber of Commerce, Survey Research Center, "Employee Benefits, 1980" (Washington, D.C., 1981).

life insurance plans than they would if they put those same dollars into individual plans.

Other fringes have benefits of their own. Discounts on the firm's products boost employees' loyalty and increase their concern with quality. Day care facilities make it possible to attract some women to full-time jobs and may be part of an equal-opportunity program. Finally, some firms feel that fringe benefits are a way of showing social responsibility.

Disadvantages of fringe benefits.   Fringes have the disadvantage that all workers bear their costs even though they do not all benefit equally. For example, older workers tend to like pension benefits, while younger workers often prefer cash. Also, benefits like health care are of no use to a worker whose spouse is already covered by another employer's plan. To get around this problem, a few companies have experimented with **cafeteria-type benefit plans**. These allow employees to tailor a mix of benefits to their needs. For example, a plan started in 1979 by American Can Company provides a core of retirement, vacation, and insurance benefits for all employees. Employees then get credits that can be used to buy other benefits of their choice.[5]

Cafeteria-type benefit plan: A benefit plan that allows each employee to choose a mix of fringe benefits from a selection offered by the employer.

[5]For a description of the American Can plan, see Herbert G. Heneman III et al., *Personnel/ Human Resource Management* (Homewood, Ill.: Irwin, 1980), pp. 423–24.

Compensation and the Law

Federal, state, and local governments have many laws that bear on compensation. To round out this chapter, we will look at the most important of those laws.

Fair Labor Standards Act (FLSA): A federal law governing minimum wages, payment of overtime, equal pay, and certain other matters of compensation policy.

The federal minimum wage. The **Fair Labor Standards Act (FLSA)** sets a federal minimum wage. The act has been amended to broaden its coverage and raise the wage. It now applies to almost all workers, and as of 1983 the minimum was $3.35 per hour.

Overtime standards. The FLSA also requires that most workers who work overtime (more than forty hours per week) be paid at least time and a half for each extra hour worked. Executive and professional employees, outside sales representatives, and a few other groups are exempt from this requirement.

Required fringe benefits. Besides laws governing wages, there are a number of federal laws that require certain fringe benefits. The most important of these is the Old Age, Survivors, Disability, and Health Insurance Program, or Social Security. This program provides retirement benefits, Medicare, and certain other benefits. As of 1984, employers and employees were each required to pay 7 percent of the first $37,800 earned per year into the Social Security program. Unemployment insurance and workers' compensation are other fringe benefit programs to which every employer must contribute. There is no law that requires employers to offer private pension benefits. However, the terms of pension programs, if they are offered, are regulated by the federal government.

Equal pay. The Equal Pay Act of 1963 (an amendment to the FLSA) and the Civil Rights Act of 1964 forbid discrimination in pay. Workers who do the same job must not be paid different wages because of their race, sex, religion, or national origin. Various laws have extended this protection to handicapped people, certain veterans, and other groups. Differences in pay for the same work are allowed only if they are based on merit or seniority.

The equal-pay laws define equal work quite narrowly. If jobs differ in any of several ways—skill, working conditions, effort, or responsibility— workers doing one of those jobs do not have to be paid the same amount as those doing the other. A major issue in compensation policy today has to do with efforts to broaden coverage of the law so that it would require equal pay for jobs that are different in one of the ways just noted but are of *comparable worth.*

Consider this case. In 1978 a group of nurses employed by the city of Denver sued the city because they were paid less than parking meter repairers, sign painters, and tree trimmers. They argued that their work as nurses was worth just as much to society as that of these manual workers, and that they were being paid less only because most nurses are women. The city replied that discrimination had nothing to do with it. The higher wages for the manual workers, most of whom were men, were a result of market conditions. Without those wages, not enough workers could be attracted to fill the jobs. Nurses were paid less because they were in plentiful supply even at the lower wage.

The court decided in favor of the city. It ruled, in effect, that employers could take supply and demand into account in setting wage rates for different jobs. The issue is not dead, however. A recent court action brought by women employees of the state of Washington has been decided in favor of equal pay for comparable work.

The end result could be some sort of legally required job evaluation system for setting wage rates. If sign painters' and nurses' jobs were assigned equal points in terms of skill, working conditions, effort, and responsibility (as they might well be), then they would have to be paid at the same rate. How employers would deal with the problem of attracting the right number of candidates for each job under such a system is not clear.

While courts debate these issues, another change is taking place: more women are training for high-paying jobs that have traditionally been held by men. For example, in 1983 more than half of all pharmacy students were women, up from 28 percent ten years earlier. The same trends can be found in law schools, business schools, and even craft workers' apprentice programs. As a result, it is getting harder to find good women candidates for low-paying jobs. (See Case 16–1.) In the long run, these trends will move the economy toward equal pay for comparable work whatever the courts decide.

SUMMARY

1. Planning is as important when dealing with human resources as it is when dealing with marketing, production, finance, or any other aspect of business. Human resource planning should begin with strategic matters such as job security and equal opportunity. Details can be filled in with *job analyses*, *job descriptions*, and *job specifications*. A good *human resources information system* will improve decision making in this area.

2. *Equal employment opportunity* means a policy of not discriminating in hiring, pay, job assignments, and promotion. *Affirmative action* is a stronger policy that involves seeking out, hiring, and promoting candidates from groups such as minorities, women, and the handicapped. There is a somewhat hazy line between affirmative action and *reverse discrimination*, which means denying a job or promotion to a qualified white or male candidate in favor of a less qualified member of another group.

3. *Recruitment* is the process of attracting a pool of candidates from which jobs can be filled. Once such a pool has been assembled, the next task is to select those to whom the job will be offered. The steps in the selection process are the application form, the screening interview, testing, reference checks, the in-depth interview, the physical examination, and the job offer.

4. *Orientation* is the process by which new employees learn about the employer and the job. *Socialization* is the less formal process through which they absorb the values, language, manners, and unwritten rules of the firm. Orientation takes place in the first few weeks of employment. Socialization processes are also most intense when an employee first joins the firm. In contrast, *training* and *development* may continue throughout an employee's career with a firm.

5. Performance appraisal is one of the key tasks of the personnel manager. Performance appraisal should be an ongoing process. It should be done in terms of clear, fair standards. And it should use positive reinforcement as much as possible.

6. *Promotions* and *transfers* are types of career movement that are useful in developing the careers of the firm's future managers. *Separations* are another kind of career movement. They can be either voluntary (quits and retirements) or involuntary (*terminations* and *layoffs*). Erosion of the *employment at will* doctrine has limited the ability of managers to fire employees without cause.

7. Supply and demand set upper and lower limits to the level of compensation offered for any job. Within these limits, compensation must be set at a level that is fair and maintains motivation. Job evaluations are helpful in setting base pay rates. Those rates can be modified to take into account seniority and merit.

8. The law requires employers to provide workers with certain fringe benefits. Among these are Social Security, unemployment insurance, and workers' compensation. The law also requires equal pay for equal work. Whether equal pay should be required for work that is not equal, but is of comparable value, is a subject of lively debate.

KEY TERMS

You should be familiar with the following terms and concepts. Check their meanings by referring to the marginal definitions in the chapter or to the glossary at the end of the book.

Human resources strategy	Training
Human resource planning	Development
Equal employment opportunity (EEO)	Promotion
Affirmative action	Transfer
Reverse discrimination	Separation
Job analysis	Layoff
Job description	Termination
Job specifications	Employment at will
Human resources information system (HRIS)	Compensation
Recruitment	Job evaluation technique
Assessment center	Cafeteria-type benefit plan
Orientation	Fair Labor Standards Act (FLSA)
Socialization	

QUESTIONS FOR REVIEW AND DISCUSSION

1. Choosing a location for an office or plant is a decision that has long-term strategic importance. In what ways is it important for human resource planning?

2. Classify each of the following policies as an example of equal employment opportunity, affirmative action, or reverse discrimination. Explain your reasoning in each case.

a. Your company has always given a basic math test to applicants for the job of machinist. A high proportion of applicants from mostly black central-city schools have failed the test. You scrap the test and, instead, offer remedial math training to any worker who needs it.

b. The first page of your company's job application

form asks for the applicant's name and address, and has a place for a photo to be attached. You instruct your personnel staff to detach this page and replace it with an identification number before the forms are evaluated.

c. Your company has, for the first time, hired a number of black and Hispanic production workers. Now a recession forces you to make layoffs. Instead of laying off workers on the basis of seniority, you order that one white worker be laid off for each black or Hispanic one until the total number of layoffs required is reached.

3. Have you ever applied for or been offered a job? If so, describe the recruitment and selection processes used by the employer. If you cannot answer this question from your own experience, interview a friend or relative.

4. If you have ever held a job, describe the orientation and socialization processes you went through. Did they include any negative socialization? For example, did you learn from your fellow workers any ways of faking or avoiding work? Did you learn about any rules, or particular managers, that did not really need to be respected? If you cannot answer this question from your own experience, interview a friend or relative.

5. According to the *Wall Street Journal*, Michael Boyle, who was fired as president of Petrie Stores after only a few weeks, did not fit into Petrie's penny-pinching way of doing business. He came to work in a chauffeured limousine, stayed at the Ritz-Carlton instead of the Holiday Inn when he visited Chicago, and ate at the best restaurants (at company expense) instead of going to McDonald's. He also built an expensive conference room, which Petrie thought was a waste because all decisions were made in his own office. What steps could Petrie have taken to protect himself against Boyle's $1.7 million lawsuit for wrongful dismissal?

6. A 1978 law let an employer pay for an employee's education and deduct the cost from its taxable income whether the education was related to the job or not. The law expired in 1983. As the expiration date approached, the U.S. Treasury opposed renewal of the law. It wanted the law changed so that this fringe benefit would be tax deductible only if the education was related to the job. What are the advantages and disadvantages of this fringe benefit? Do you think it should be tax deductible? Why or why not?

7. Do you think it is discriminatory to pay petroleum engineers more than accountants, even though the two jobs require equal amounts of training and skill? Why or why not? Is it discriminatory to pay sign painters more than nurses, even though nurses' jobs require at least as much training and skill, if not more? Why or why not? If the pay of nurses were raised to match that of sign painters, what do you think would happen to the number of nursing jobs offered? To the number of applicants for those jobs? What if the pay of sign painters were lowered to match that of nurses?

Case 16–1: Recruiting Problems at Mary Kay Cosmetics

Mary Kay Cosmetics was founded in 1963 by Mary Kay Ash. The firm sells cosmetics directly to customers, using the "party plan." In this plan, also used by Tupperware and some other firms, potential customers are invited to a "party" at the salesperson's home. At the party the product is demonstrated and orders are taken. Until recently the party plan has been a formula for success. But according to the *Wall Street Journal*, Mary Kay and other direct-sales companies are running into recruiting problems.

"Mary Kay Cosmetics' sales pitch has always been designed to tap the 'old girls network' in neighborhoods," the *Wall Street Journal* reports. "The salespeople, called 'beauty consultants,' are generally persuaded to spend between $500 and $3,000 on their initial inventory—Mary Kay beauty-care kits. The kits cost them $20.75 each and cost their customers $41.50. Their profit is thus 100 percent.

"But for most, the big money is in recruiting a flock of other consultants. Mary Kay gives consultants 8 percent commissions on orders of their recruits if they have eight recruits or more, and they become directors by recruiting 12 other consultants. Directors get even higher commissions of 9 percent to 12 percent of their units' sales, depending on volume (a unit consists of a director and her recruits). They also get prizes, such as the use of a pink Cadillac if a unit's sales exceed $72,000 in a six-month period.

"With that kind of motivation, Mary Kay

salespeople recruited like press gangs, roping in their friends and relatives, then starting on friends and relatives of friends and relatives. The total sales force swelled to 175,000 in 1982, from 40,000 in 1978."

In the second half of 1983, however, recruiting and profits began to fall. Mary Kay's stock price fell from just under $45.00 in April to $15.75 in October. The company began a new recruitment drive, but the *Wall Street Journal* thinks this and other direct-sales companies face some long-term problems.

"A key long-term problem for direct-sales companies is the ever-increasing availability to women of better or steadier jobs in other fields. Debbie Durkee, a Mary Kay consultant in Oklahoma City, says she was dismissed by the company after one year and a $500 loss because she never really got interested. But then it wasn't absolutely

necessary for her to sell—she had a $13,000-a-year job as an interior designer. In another typical incident, a Boulder, Colorado, consultant recently quit to take a job as a real estate manager.

"Diana Beck of Dallas says that many of her prime recruiting candidates are already employed and want the security of a salaried job. 'The sharp people, the ones I'd really like to see in my unit, already have jobs and can't break away,' she says. Others, including Beck's sister, who initially recruited her to Mary Kay, have left the company in search of more stable, full-time work."

Source: Dean Rotbart and Laurie P. Cohen, "The Party at Mary Kay Isn't Quite So Lively, as Recruiting Falls Off," *Wall Street Journal*, October 28, 1983, p. 1. Reprinted by permission of the *Wall Street Journal*. © Dow Jones & Company, Inc., 1983. All Rights Reserved.

Questions:

1. What is typical about Mary Kay's recruiting method? What is not typical about it? Do you think a policy of paying employees a bonus for bringing in new recruits would work for a manufacturing firm? Why or why not?

2. Mary Kay's sales force consists of some 200,000 women and a few hundred men. Do you think this is a sign of reverse discrimination? Do you think Mary Kay should have an affirmative

action program to attract more men? Why or why not?

3. What options are open to women who think their jobs as Mary Kay beauty consultants do not pay as much as other work of comparable worth? Do you think there are grounds to fear (as some do) that the cost advantage of direct sales over in-store retailing will be erased by changes in the labor market? Explain.

Case 16–2: Incentive Pay at Lincoln Electric

Lots of companies these days are huffing and puffing to find some good way to motivate workers. Lincoln Electric Company found the way in 1907 and says it has liked the results ever since.

The company relies on incentives. It pays most of its 2500 employees on a piecework basis. In 1933, it added an annual bonus system. Based on performance, bonuses may exceed regular pay, and they apply far more extensively than in most companies. A secretary's mistakes, for example, can cut her bonus.

The company calls its incentive pay system "the low cost of high wages." Given the weakness of the company's industrial markets, employees now work only 30 hours a week. But even with the reduced workweek, they would average between $30,000 and $35,000 a year, including bonus, says Richard S. Sabo, an official.

In 1981, employees earned an average of about $45,000, including the bonus, Sabo adds.

Lincoln employees don't mind the high pay—or the company's guarantee of at least 30 hours of

Case 16–2: Incentive Pay at Lincoln Electric (continued)

work each week for workers with at least two years of service. But they say there is a price.

"It's physically and mentally tough on you," says one former worker who quit after eight years. "You work so fast."

Lorenzo Hilles, a 42-year-old worker with 17 years of service, says, "There comes a time when you want to slow down." He says he'd like to move out of the piecework factory environment "if something else comes available" elsewhere in the company. But as Lincoln doesn't have any seniority system, he'll have to compete on a merit basis with the newest employees for one of the few jobs that doesn't involve piecework.

In order to guarantee steady work, Lincoln hires cautiously in boom times. This means employees may work 50 hours a week or more for prolonged periods. And they must accept any position in any department, even if it means a pay cut.

Some employees say the system can generate unfriendly competition, too. A certain number of merit points are allotted to each department. An unusually high rating for one person usually means a lower rating for another. "There's a saying around here that you don't have a friend at Lincoln Electric," says a worker with nearly 20 years of service.

But management defends the system. It certainly hasn't hurt the company itself. Volume and profits have risen over the years. Customers praise the company's product quality, too. "I don't ever remember having one problem with quality from Lincoln," says Samuel Flager, purchasing agent for an Ashland Oil Corporation unit that buys $1.8 million of Lincoln welding equipment a year. "We'd expect some problems with this volume of business," he says.

Source: Maryann Mrowca, "Ohio Firm Relies on Incentive-Pay System to Motivate Workers and Maintain Profits," *Wall Street Journal*, August 12, 1983, p. 37. Reprinted by permission of the *Wall Street Journal*. © Dow Jones & Company, Inc., 1983. All Rights Reserved.

Questions:

1. What are the distinctive aspects of Lincoln Electric's human resources strategy?
2. If Lincoln's incentive pay plan has led to high earnings for workers and high profits for the company, why do you think it has not been widely imitated?

3. In what ways is Lincoln's system more fair or less fair than other compensation plans? Comment in terms of both external and internal fairness.
4. Lincoln employees are not unionized. Why, do you think, is this so?

SUGGESTED READINGS, PART IV

Fearon, Harold E., William A. Ruch, Ross R. Reck, Vincent G. Reuter, and C. David Wieters. *Fundamentals of Production/Operations Management*, 2nd ed. St. Paul, Minn.: West, 1983.

Schonberger, Richard J. *Japanese Manufacturing Techniques*. New York: Free Press, 1982.

Dilworth, James B. *Production and Operations Management: Manufacturing and Nonmanufacturing*, 2nd ed. New York: Random House, 1983.

Wheelwright, Steven C. "Japan—Where Operations Really Are Strategic." *Harvard Business Review*, July-August 1981, pp. 67–74.

Garvin, David A. "Quality on the Line." *Harvard Business Review*, September-October 1983, pp. 65–75.

Kanter, Rosabeth Moss. *The Change Masters: Innovations for Productivity in the American Corporation*. New York: Simon and Schuster, 1983.

"Intrapreneurial Now," *The Economist*, April 17, 1982, pp. 67–72.

Steers, Richard M., and Lyman W. Porter. *Motivation and Work Behavior*, 3rd ed. New York: McGraw-Hill, 1983.

Blanchard, Kenneth, and Spencer Johnson. *The One Minute Manager*. New York: Morrow, 1982.

Miles, Raymond E. "Human Relations or Human Resources." *Harvard Business Review*, July-August 1965, pp. 148-63.

French, Wendell L. *The Personnel Management Process*, 5th ed. Boston: Houghton Mifflin, 1982.

Holley, William H., Jr., and Kenneth M. Jennings. *The Labor Relations Process*, 2nd ed. Chicago: Dryden Press, 1984.

Useful periodicals:

Industry Week
Personnel

CAREERS IN PRODUCTION AND HUMAN RESOURCE MANAGEMENT

If there was ever a time when POM and human resource management were overshadowed by marketing and finance as fields in which to make a career, that time has passed. The current drive for productivity and quality, spurred in part by competition from abroad, has brought these areas to center stage. Top managers recognize the importance of POM specialists and human resource workers to the success of their organizations. More and more often, the top managers themselves may have backgrounds in these fields.

Production and operations jobs include those of designers, engineers, and technicians. They emphasize technical skills, but many require those skills in combination with creativity, ability to communicate, and management skills. Jobs in personnel, human resource management, and labor relations are often rewarding ones for those who like to work with people. As it becomes a more and more widely accepted fact that people are the key to productivity, the prestige and influence of human resource managers within the firm is rising.

In addition to the jobs discussed in this section, it should be made clear that any job that involves the hands-on transformation of inputs into outputs can be an entry into a career in production. Such jobs include those of a factory worker, a clerk in an insurance company, a public school teacher, or a government meat inspector. These jobs can be either careers in themselves or the first step toward a technical, supervisory, or management career.

Many of these entry-level production jobs require a high school degree or less, but it is far more common than it once was to find holders of two- and four-year college degrees starting their careers in such jobs. Sometimes they do so in order to learn a business from the ground up, in the hope of one day starting a business of their own. Sometimes they do so because the pay is good. The starting wage in a factory job is often higher than that of, say, a junior computer programmer or a marketing research assistant. And some people take production jobs with the intention of working hard and standing out. As we saw earlier, supervisors, the first level in the management hierarchy, are frequently recruited from among outstanding production workers. In the job descriptions that follow, we will note frequently that practical experience in a production capacity is an asset.

Here, then, is a sampling of jobs in the fields of POM and human resource management. In addition to the jobs discussed here, remember that production line, clerical, and supervisory management positions are also entry-level jobs in these fields.

Job Title: Engineering and Science Technician

Description. Engineering and science technicians work in business, government, and not-for-profit firms. Their duties range from research and design to manufacturing, sales, and customer service. Although their jobs are more limited in scope and more practically oriented than those of engineers or scientists, technicians often have the satisfaction of applying theoretical knowledge to practical situations. Science technicians help scientists set up experiments and calculate results, often with the aid of computers. Engineering technicians help engineers develop new equipment by making models, doing routine phases of design work, and so on. Service technicians assist in installation and maintenance of computers and machinery.

Qualifications. Although a person can qualify for technician jobs through many combinations of work experience and education, most employers prefer applicants who have had some specialized technical training. This may be obtained at technical institutes, junior and community colleges, universities and their extensions, and vocational-technical schools. The armed forces also offer technical training in some fields. An aptitude for mathematics and science and the ability to do detailed work accurately are necessary.

Job outlook. About 885,000 people worked as engineering and science technicians in 1980, four fifths of them in private business. The number of jobs in most technical fields is expected to grow faster than the average for all occupations. Opportunities will be best for graduates of formal training programs.

Earnings. Starting salaries for graduates of two-year training programs were about $11,600 in 1979. Those with five years' experience earned about $14,300. Senior technicians earned $22,300 on the average.

Job Title: Industrial Designer

Description. Industrial designers combine artistic talent with technical knowledge and knowledge of marketing to create products that are attractive, safe, and easy to use. They work as part of a product development team. Industrial designers may also be called upon to design containers, packages, display exhibits, or even trademarks. Some designers work for corporate product development departments. Others work as freelance industrial designers or members of consulting firms.

Qualifications. The usual requirement is a course of study in industrial design at an art school, university, or technical college. A bachelor's degree is required for most jobs. In addition to artistic talent and training, a good understanding of marketing is helpful. Applicants for jobs need to assemble a portfolio of photographs, drawings, and sketches to demonstrate their creative ability.

Job outlook. Industrial design is a relatively small occupation—just 13,000 people worked in this field in 1980. Employment is expected to grow somewhat more slowly than the average for all occupations. However, there will be more job openings in some areas, such as the design of high-technology and medical products.

Earnings. Starting salaries for holders of the bachelor's degree averaged about $15,000 a year in 1980. Those with two years of experience earned about $18,000. Designers with outstanding talent earned much more. Those with the talent and management ability to start their own consulting firms earned more, on the average, than corporate industrial designers.

Job Title: Food Technologist

Description. Food technologists study the chemical, physical, and biological nature of food in order to learn how to process, preserve, package, and store it safely and attractively. Some work in research and development, others in quality assurance departments. Tasks may include conducting chemical or microbiological tests to see that products meet government standards; determining the nutritive content of food; and checking raw ingredients for freshness.

Qualifications. The usual minimum educational requirement is a bachelor's degree with a major in food technology. Some food technologists have degrees in chemistry, biology, engineering, agriculture, or business. Almost half of all food technologists have advanced degrees, which are necessary for many research and management positions.

Job outlook. About 15,000 people worked as food technologists in 1980. Jobs in this field are expected to increase somewhat more slowly than the average throughout the 1980s. Research jobs may increase faster than others in this field.

Earnings. The average salary for food technologists was about $29,500 a year in 1980. Those with 11-15 years' experience and a Ph.D. degree earned $36,500 on the average.

PRODUCTION AND HUMAN RESOURCE MANAGEMENT (CONTINUED)

Job Title: Industrial Engineer

Description. Industrial engineers determine the most effective ways for an organization to use the basic factors of production—people, machines, and materials. Duties include application of computers to production systems; development of management systems for planning, cost analysis, and control; and plant location surveys.

Qualifications. A bachelor's degree in engineering is the usual requirement. Some openings may also be available for college graduates majoring in science or mathematics. Graduates of two-year programs tend to be limited to practical design and production work. Sometimes experienced technicians, with additional education, advance to engineering positions.

Job outlook. About 160,000 people worked as industrial engineers in 1982. The number of jobs in this field is expected to grow faster than the average throughout the 1980s. Opportunities for advancement are good. Many top managers have engineering backgrounds. As businesses place increasing emphasis on productivity and quality, the importance of engineering as an entry into general management is likely to increase.

Earnings. The average starting salary for industrial engineers with a bachelor's degree was $19,860 per year in 1980. Engineers with twenty years of experience earned $34,000 per year on the average. Many engineers in management positions earned much more.

Job Title: Technical Writer

Description. Technical writers put scientific and technical information into readily understandable language. They use their knowledge of a technical area together with their knowledge of language to write reports, sales materials, instruction books, and so on.

Qualifications. There are no set qualifications other than good writing skills and knowledge of a technical area. Many employers look for candidates with a college degree in an area like engineering, computer science, or biochemistry plus a minor in English, journalism, or technical communication. Others prefer a major in English or journalism with a minor or some practical experience in the technical area. People seeking work in this area should prepare a portfolio of writing samples. It is often possible to gain experience and demonstrate ability by doing unpaid writing for local newspapers or student publications. Many technical writers begin their careers as research assistants, editorial assistants, scientists, or engineers instead of entering the field of technical writing straight from college.

Job outlook. About 25,000 people were employed as technical writers and editors in 1980. Growth of employment in this field is expected to be average. Many work for large firms in the electronics, chemical, aircraft, and pharmaceutical industries. A few writers work on a freelance basis.

Earnings. Starting salaries for technical writers averaged $15,200 a year in 1980. Experienced technical writers and editors earned from $21,000 to $31,000.

Job Title: Personnel and Labor Relations Specialist

Description. Attracting the best employees available and matching them to the correct jobs is a crucial task for every firm. Personnel and labor relations specialists provide the link between top management and employees in carrying out this task. They assist management in making the best use of employees' skills, and they help employees find satisfaction in their jobs.

Personnel and labor relations work covers a broad range of specific jobs. A recruiter develops contacts, talks to job applicants, administers preemployment tests, and makes recommendations. EEO representatives and affirmative action coordinators handle the complex and sensitive task of achieving equality in employment opportunities for women and minority employees in large organizations. Job analysts develop job descriptions that explain the duties, training, and skills that each job requires. Compensation managers ensure that pay rates within a firm are fair and equitable, and make sure they meet legal requirements. Training specialists are responsible for a broad range of employee education and training programs. Employee-welfare specialists handle insurance and benefit programs.

Labor relations specialists are employed by unionized firms. They provide background information for managers conducting contract negotiations. Much of their work concerns interpretation and administration of the contract once it has been signed. They handle grievances and matters of seniority rights. Doing this job well requires ongoing liaison with union officials.

Qualifications. A college degree is required for most positions. A wide range of majors are acceptable. Some employers prefer job candidates who

have majored in personnel administration or labor relations. Others prefer those with a general business background. Still others look for liberal arts graduates, often with degrees in psychology, sociology, counseling, or education. An MBA degree can be an advantage for employment in this field.

Job outlook. About 203,000 people worked as personnel and labor relations specialists in 1982. Most of them worked for businesses, but some also worked for consulting firms, government, and not-for-profit firms. Jobs in this field are expected to grow about as fast as the average for all jobs. Opportunities for advancement to positions of personnel supervisor or personnel manager are good, and some personnel specialists advance to general-management positions.

Earnings. Salaries vary widely, depending on specialty, location, and size of firm. To take some examples, in 1982 starting salaries averaged $22,000 for job analysts, $25,500 for EEO representatives, and $25,500 for training specialists. Salaries for personnel directors in private industry ranged from $32,678 to $62,645.

Job Title: Occupational Safety and Health Worker

Description. Occupational safety and health workers strive to control occupational accidents and diseases, property losses from accidents and fires, and injuries from unsafe products. The largest group within this category of workers are safety engineers. They analyze each job in a plant to identify potential hazards and prevent accidents. When accidents occur, they try to determine the cause. This category of workers also includes fire protection engineers, industrial hygienists, loss control consultants, and occupational health consultants. Health and safety workers are employed by industrial firms, service firms, insurance companies, and government agencies. Some also work as independent consultants.

Qualifications. The usual qualification is a bachelor's degree in engineering or one of the physical or biological sciences. Many employers prefer a bachelor's or master's degree in safety engineering, industrial hygiene, or another field directly related to the job. There are some open-

ings as safety and health technicians for graduates of two-year programs.

Job prospects. About 80,000 people were employed as health and safety workers in 1980. The majority were safety engineers and fire protection engineers. The number of jobs in this field is expected to increase at about the average rate for all occupations. Opportunities for advancement vary from one industry to another. In industrial firms, beginning health and safety workers may advance to supervisory positions. In the insurance industry, people with a background in health and safety engineering often make their way into general-management jobs. In some cases, experienced technicians may advance to professional positions.

Earnings. Starting salaries for safety and health workers with bachelor's degrees were between $20,000 and $22,000 per year in 1980. The average salary for all workers in the field was $28,000 per year.

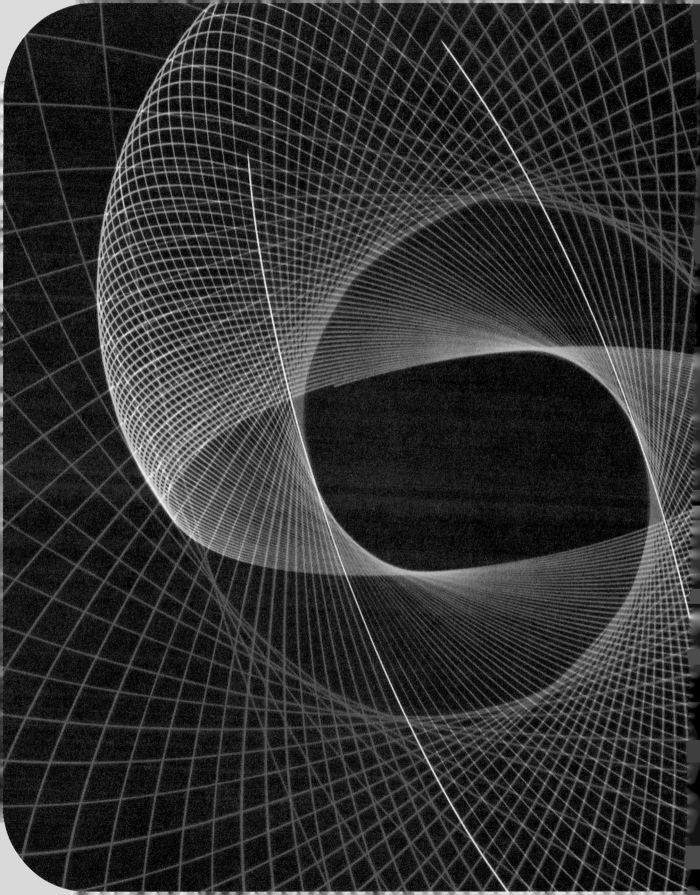

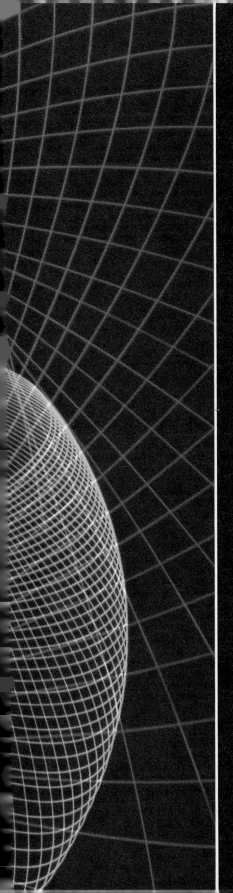

Part V

FINANCE

Finance is the process of getting the funds a firm needs and putting them to use. It is a key task in any organization, whether it is a business, a unit of government, or a not-for-profit firm. All of these organizations need funds to buy equipment, buildings, and other long-term assets. They also have short-term needs, such as meeting payrolls and paying for inventory. Overseeing the use of funds for both long- and short-term uses is the job of financial management.

Chapter 17 gives an overview of the financial manager's job. In it, we will see that the financial manager faces many choices in the sources and uses of funds. Chapter 18 follows with an overview of accounting, which can be thought of as the language of financial management.

The next two chapters turn from the inner workings of the firm to the financial system with which the firm does business. Chapter 19 covers banking. Every firm deals with banks, so it is important to understand how they work. In Chapter 20 we will look at the securities markets, in which stocks, bonds, and other securities are bought and sold. The securities markets, as we will see, are both a source of funds for firms and an investment opportunity for individuals.

Chapter 21 rounds out the discussion of the financial system by looking at risk management and insurance. We will look at the major types of risk to which businesses and households are exposed, and will discuss several ways of dealing with them. We will also explain the workings of insurance companies and look at some of the issues facing the insurance industry.

Chapter 17
FINANCIAL MANAGEMENT

When you have completed this chapter, you should be able to

- Define *finance* and explain the job of the financial manager.

- Show why all firms need both *fixed* and *working capital*.

- Explain the roles of the chief financial officer, the treasurer, and the controller.

- List the main sources and uses of funds for a business firm.

- Distinguish between *current* and *fixed assets*, and discuss how each is managed.

- Discuss the main types of *short-* and *long-term debt*, and list the advantages and disadvantages of each type.

- Explain the concept of *leverage* and its role in striking a balance between debt and equity.

Wedtech Corporation, whose home is a brick building in the Bronx, was proud of its status as one of the few manufacturing firms that could make a profit in an urban ghetto. Its sales had grown from $300,000 in 1976 to more than $20 million in 1982. Then it got its biggest break ever—a $30 million contract to produce six-horsepower engines for the Defense Department. Added to contracts for cooling and suspension systems for the Army's M-113 armored personnel carrier, the new contract filled Wedtech's order books. It also nearly caused the firm to fail.

The trouble was that getting these contracts and starting work on them had cost Wedtech a pile of money. Some of the money had been spent just getting the contracts. More was spent buying parts and getting started. All of these expenses were running ahead of payments for completed work.

By July 1983 the firm was teetering on the brink. There was only $110,000 of cash on hand. If it were used to meet the payroll, there would be no money to buy parts and the workers would stand idle. But if the money were used to buy parts, the workers couldn't be paid. The workers agreed to give up a payday to keep the company open, but this was clearly a stopgap measure. Wedtech needed cash, and fast.

The firm had already borrowed up to the limit from banks, individuals, and the Small Business Administration. It was more than $12 million in debt and had been unable to make payments on any of the loans since March. No one was willing to lend it more.

Wedtech had one thing going for it, though, that most failing firms do not. It was highly profitable, and its new contracts made it seem likely to stay that way if the cash could be found to complete the work. This situation put it in a good position to sell shares to the public. By doing this, in effect, it would raise cash now in exchange for a share of future profits. But arranging a public stock issue takes time. The stock issue became a race against the clock.

With help from securities regulators, who handled last-minute changes in registration documents by telephone, Wedtech just made its deadline. In late August it sold 1.9 million shares of stock at $16 each. Half of this went straight to creditors; the other half became working capital. The future now looks bright.[1]

[1] Adapted from Barbara Ettorre, "Not a Minute Too Soon," *Forbes*, December 5, 1983, p. 162.

Finance: The process of getting the funds a firm needs and putting them to use.

The story of Wedtech's near-collapse brings us to yet another aspect of business: finance. **Finance** is the process of getting the funds a firm needs and putting them to use. In many ways, Wedtech was a well-managed company. It was making a profit. With constantly growing sales, it was a marketing success. Its production system used state-of-the-art lasers and computer-run tools. And its relations with its workers seem to have been sound: it took just fifteen minutes for them to agree to postpone a paycheck in order to give the firm a few more days to raise funds. Wedtech, in short, did not have a marketing, production, or people problem. It had a finance problem.

This chapter and the next four will all be devoted to finance. This chapter will give an overview of financial management, stressing the choices that must be made regarding sources and uses of funds. Chapter 18 will discuss accounting, which is concerned with control of financial flows. Chapters 19 and 20 will talk about the main sources of funds: the banking system and the securities markets. Finally, Chapter 21 will discuss risk management and insurance.

AN OVERVIEW OF FINANCIAL MANAGEMENT

The financial manager's job is to arrange for the firm to get the funds it needs on favorable terms and to make sure they are used effectively. This job must be done not only in businesses but also in not-for-profit firms and units of government. The best way to begin looking at the role of the financial manager is to see why all organizations need capital funds.

The Need for Capital

In Chapter 1 we listed human resources, capital, and natural resources as the three factors of production that all firms need. To get a clearer picture of the role of capital, let's see why Wedtech needed more capital if it was to meet its new $30 million contract.

To begin with, it is likely that Wedtech needed some new equipment. Making the six-horsepower motors may have required, say, some precision tools that were not needed for products that the firm had made before. In addition, the firm's general purpose equipment was probably already being used to capacity, so that more such equipment would be needed for the new contract. And the firm's office staff would need new typewriters and filing cabinets just to keep up with the paperwork required by the Defense Department. Durable production equipment like this is called **fixed capital**. Wedtech could not start making the motors until it had the funds to buy more fixed capital.

Fixed capital: Capital in the form of durable structures, machinery, and equipment.

Durable production equipment like these weaving machines is known as fixed capital. Courtesy of Burlington Industries

Working capital: Funds used to pay for labor and materials between the time when production is begun and the time when finished goods are shipped and paid for.

But funds to buy fixed capital would not have been the only funds Wedtech needed to meet its new contract. It would also need funds to build up inventories. (Inventories, as we saw in Chapter 1, are a form of capital.) First, the firm would have to buy parts and materials to make the motors. As it began production, it would have to pay workers to put the motors together. It would also have to pay electric bills to run the machines. These payments would be reflected in a growing inventory of finished and partly finished goods. The funds a firm needs for all of these uses, from the time the first batch of parts is ordered until the finished goods are shipped and paid for, are known as **working capital**. Wedtech almost came to grief because, although it had the fixed capital it needed, it did not have enough working capital.

All firms, as we will see, need both fixed and working capital just as Wedtech did. The Wedtech story shows what happens when firms do not plan carefully for their financial needs. Let's turn now to the kind of financial planning a firm needs to do.

Financial Planning and Control

Planning for working-capital needs.   The financial manager's duties include planning for the use of both fixed and working capital. The critical factor in planning the use of working capital is the timing of receipts and expenses. The firm must plan to have enough working capital available to cover costs from the time production is begun until the customer pays for the product.

A new contract is only one kind of event that requires planning for working-capital needs. Many firms have seasonal variations in costs and revenues. For example, stores need working capital to build up inventories to get ready for Christmas shoppers. Firms also pay attention to forecasts of booms or recessions in planning their finances.

Planning for fixed-capital needs.   As a firm grows, machines wear out, and technology changes, firms need new buildings, equipment, computers, and other kinds of fixed capital. Many kinds of fixed-capital purchases have long lead times. In may be possible to order a truck or a typewriter and have it delivered in a few days, but building a new plant, constructing a new rail line, or opening a coal mine can take many years. The growing number of government regulations, especially those designed to protect the environment, have made lead times longer than ever.

These long lead times mean that it is crucial to include financial planning in the firm's strategic planning process. If a firm wants to enter new markets or expand output of a product it already makes, it has to think of capital needs at the same time that it makes long-range marketing plans and does basic research on production methods.

Planning sources of funds.   There are many possible sources of funds for a firm, including revenue from sales of its product, investments by its owners, and loans. Later in this chapter, and in Chapters 19 and 20, we will discuss these and several other sources in detail. We simply note here that the financial manager must plan ahead in order to tap the best source of funds for each need at the time when it is needed.

Wedtech's problems illustrate some of the dangers of poor planning. As the company grew, it depended too much on loans, rather than bringing in additional owners by issuing new shares of stock. When it did decide to issue new stock, it did not allow enough time to comply with securities regulations. Fortunately, federal officials were willing to do some last-minute business by telephone, but good financial planning would have allowed more room for error.

Good planning is required not only to have funds when they are needed but also to get them at the lowest cost. Getting funds at the lowest cost is more than a matter of finding the bank that is quoting the lowest rates today. It is partly a matter of fitting the sources of funds to the purposes for which they will be used. It is partly a matter of balancing sources of funds—rarely is it best to rely only on bank loans, only on stock issues, or only on earnings held back from revenues. And it is partly a matter of timing: selling stock when the stock market is booming, not borrowing when interest rates are high, and so on. We will return to the subject of balancing sources of funds later in the chapter.

Controlling finances. Controlling—comparing planned performance with actual performance and fixing things when they go wrong—is a key job of all managers. It is especially important for financial managers. For most firms, profits are very small compared with total sales. In 1982, the average profit as a percentage of sales for the Fortune 500 companies was just 4.6 percent. This means that profits are a small amount that is left over after large flows of costs are subtracted from large flows of revenues. Financial managers must watch costs and revenues closely, since small changes in either can result in large changes in profits.

Budgets are one of the tools of financial control. Budgets break down short- and long-term financial plans into specific items. They show the planned size and timing of flows of funds into and out of each part of the firm. A good system of financial controls constantly compares budgets with actual flows of funds. When they don't match, it is a sign that circumstances have changed in ways that were not foreseen in the plan, or that plans are not being carried out correctly. In either case, managers are alerted to the need for corrective action.

Accounting is another aspect of financial control. The purpose of accounting is to keep track of sources and uses of funds and to give an accurate picture of the firm's financial state at all times. Accounting will be discussed in the next chapter.

Financial Managers

In a small business, the proprietor takes care of finance along with all the other management tasks. A more complex division of labor is found in large corporations. Not all corporations divide up the work of financial management in the same way, but the structure shown in Box 17–1 is typical.

The chief financial officer (CFO) reports to the president and has equal rank with the heads of marketing, operations, and other major departments. The CFO is often given the title of vice-president for finance. The CFO is in charge of all financial activities and acts as liaison with the heads of marketing and operations and any other managers who draw on the corporation's funds.

The CFO has two key subordinates. The first of these is the treasurer. The treasurer's job is to manage the firm's cash, securities, and credit

Box 17–1 Financial Management in the Corporation

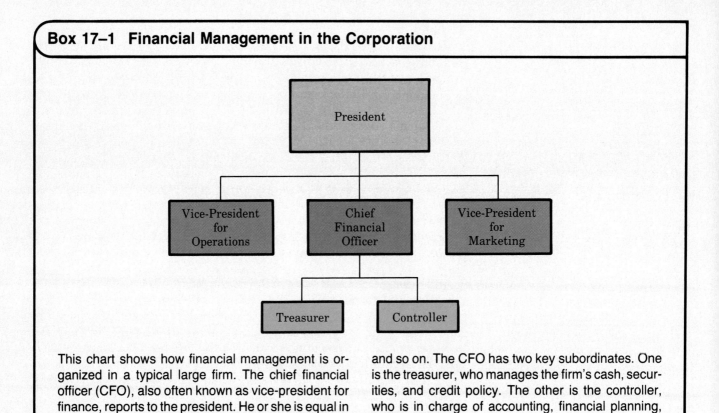

This chart shows how financial management is organized in a typical large firm. The chief financial officer (CFO), also often known as vice-president for finance, reports to the president. He or she is equal in rank to the vice-presidents for marketing, operations, and so on. The CFO has two key subordinates. One is the treasurer, who manages the firm's cash, securities, and credit policy. The other is the controller, who is in charge of accounting, financial planning, and budgeting.

policy. He or she acts as liaison with financial institutions such as banks and securities markets.

The second key officer who reports to the CFO is the controller. The controller is in charge of accounting and, usually, financial planning and budgeting. In contrast to the treasurer, who looks outward toward the financial markets, the controller's focus is on internal concerns.

The CFO, the treasurer, and the controller are specialists who spend all of their time on finance, but they are not the only people in the organization who make financial decisions. In fact, all business decisions have financial implications. A marketing manager's decision to bring out a new brand and to spend money on advertising for it affects flows of funds into and out of the organization. So does a personnel manager's decision to introduce a new system of merit pay. So does a production manager's decision to close a plant. When decisions like these involve large sums, they are made in direct consultation with the CFO. Smaller financial decisions may be made independently by marketing or production managers. In a multi-plant firm, local plant managers may be given authority to make some financial decisions on their own. Among other things, this means that all managers, whatever their specialty, must have some familiarity with principles of finance.

The fact that all business decisions affect the firm's finances also means that financial managers need to learn something about all aspects of the firm's operations. This is one of the reasons that finance is so often a route to the top in the corporate world. According to some reports, nearly a third of all corporate presidents have backgrounds in finance or related fields. The financial disturbances of the 1970s, with their record levels of inflation and interest rates, reinforced this trend. The number of top executives with backgrounds in finance increased at the expense of those with backgrounds in production or engineering. This trend seems to have run its course, however; now marketing, and in some firms, production, are challenging finance as the fast track to the top.

MANAGING ASSETS

As funds come into the firm from sales and other sources, financial managers must decide how to use them. Operating expenses—purchases of raw materials, parts, and supplies; payment of wages and salaries, interest, utility bills, and taxes—are the biggest use of funds for most firms. As Box 17–2 shows, any surplus funds left over after operating expenses have been met can be used in one of three ways.

- *Increasing assets.* As explained in Chapter 4, a firm's *assets* are all the things of value that it owns and that are owed to it. Cash,

Box 17–2 Uses of Funds

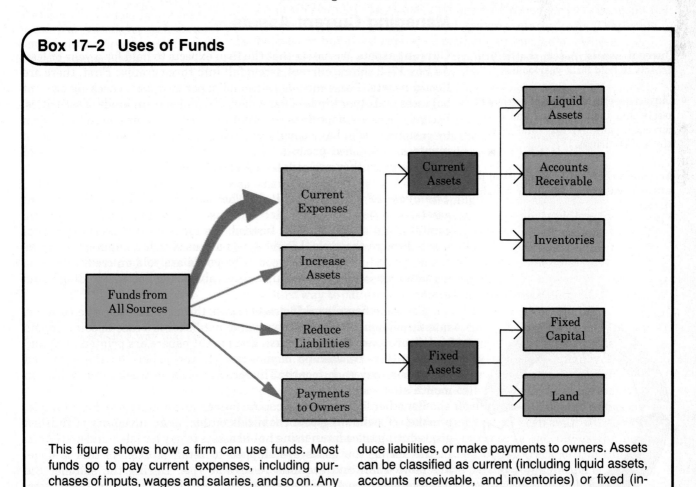

This figure shows how a firm can use funds. Most funds go to pay current expenses, including purchases of inputs, wages and salaries, and so on. Any funds left over can be used to increase assets, re- duce liabilities, or make payments to owners. Assets can be classified as current (including liquid assets, accounts receivable, and inventories) or fixed (including fixed capital and land).

Managing Fixed Assets

Fixed assets: Assets that a firm expects to hold for more than a year, including fixed capital and land.

Fixed assets are those that a firm expects to hold for more than a year. These include fixed capital (buildings and equipment) and natural resources (land, mineral deposits, and so on).

One of the duties of financial managers is to decide when to use available funds to acquire fixed capital instead of adding to current assets, reducing liabilities, or making payments to owners. In making this kind of decision, the financial manager must compare the cost of the new capital with the added revenue or cost savings that it will produce. Will an addition to a restaurant bring in enough new customers to pay for itself? How much will payroll costs be reduced if a $100,000 welding robot is added to the assembly line? How much will productivity increase if the firm buys a word processor? If more than one possible investment looks attractive, which is the most attractive? These are typical problems of fixed-capital management.

In deciding whether to use available funds to acquire fixed capital, the financial manager must ask such questions as, How much will office productivity increase if the firm buys a word processor? Courtesy of Apple Computers

Capital budgeting: The process of deciding what fixed capital to acquire.

The process of deciding what fixed capital to acquire is called **capital budgeting**. Such decisions are complex because the benefits of added fixed assets usually come in over a period of years. Perhaps the restaurant addition will pay for itself in three years, the robot in seven years, and the word processor in ten years. Financial managers must look at these payoff periods in the light of the firm's goals and the cost of raising capital funds before deciding whether any given purchase is worthwhile. They also have to grapple with the problems of imperfect measurement of both the costs and benefits of investments in fixed capital.

The focus on fixed capital should not distract financial managers from the need for effective management of real estate. According to one recent study, real estate accounts for some 25 percent of the assets of American firms. Yet the same study found that 60 percent of firms do not subject their real estate holdings to the same standards they use for working capital or fixed capital. For example, one company had a manufacturing plant on land near the the Los Angeles airport. In its current use, the land was worth about $5 per year per square foot. But if the plant were moved to a more remote site where land was less valuable, the firm could lease the land for $25 to $30 per square foot per year for commercial or office use.[2]

SOURCES OF FUNDS

Choosing among uses of funds is only half of the job of financial management. The other half is choosing among sources of funds. In a small firm this is one of the many tasks of the owner; in a large corporation, it is part of the treasurer's job.

Box 17–3 shows the major sources of funds for a business. The first of these, and the largest for most firms, is revenue from sales of goods and services. In a profitable firm this source is enough to cover all costs, with some left over. Many firms need to draw on other sources as well, however. If the firm is operating at a loss, it will need some source of funds besides sales in order to cover current costs. Even if it is operating at a profit, the surplus of revenues over costs may not be enough for the purchases of assets, reductions of liabilities, and payments to owners that its managers think are worthwhile. If the firm wants to tap sources of funds other than sales revenue, it can turn to one of the following.

Debt: Any process by which a firm gets cash or some other asset in return for a promise to pay an agreed-upon sum plus interest.

- *Debt financing*. The firm can get funds for any use by going into **debt**. The term *debt* refers to any process by which the firm gets cash or some other asset in return for a promise to pay an agreed-

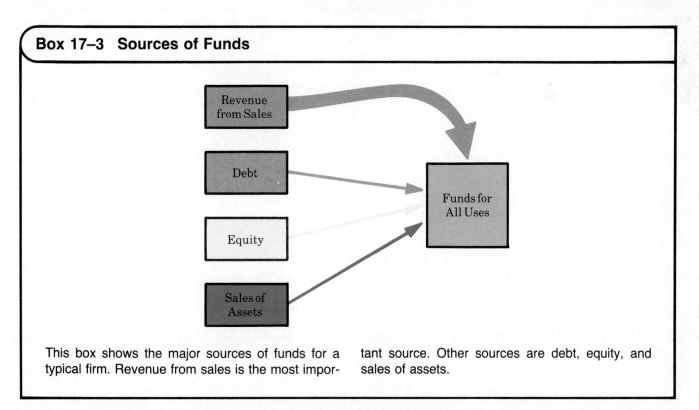

Box 17–3 Sources of Funds

This box shows the major sources of funds for a typical firm. Revenue from sales is the most important source. Other sources are debt, equity, and sales of assets.

---

[2]Christopher B. Leinberger, "Your Greatest Asset May Be Your Own Backyard," *Wall Street Journal*, November 28, 1983, p. 30.

Businesses often borrow from banks, not only to cover current costs but also to purchase assets or reduce liabilities. © Mimi Forsyth, Monkmeyer Press

upon sum plus interest. Borrowing from banks and making purchases on credit are examples of debt finance.

Equity financing: Any process by which a firm raises funds in return for a share in its ownership and management.

- *Equity financing*. If the firm does not want to go into debt, it can raise funds from owners. This is known as **equity financing**. Owners who contribute equity capital are not promised a set return. Instead, they get a share of future profits, if any, and a voice in the management of the firm.
- *Sales of assets*. For completeness, sales of assets should be mentioned as a source of funds. Some firms hold interest-earning liquid assets in addition to working capital. These assets can be sold to raise funds when needed. Buildings, equipment, or real estate that a firm no longer needs can also be sold to raise funds. Sometimes firms sell off whole lines of business in order to invest the funds in other uses. For example, Westinghouse recently sold its lighting division and its heating and cooling divisions in order to move into robotics, cable TV, and defense electronics.

Sources of funds can also be viewed along the following dimensions.

- *Short-term versus long-term*. Short-term sources are those that provide funds for a year or less. Long-term sources provide funds for more than a year.

Secured debt: A debt for which repayment is guaranteed by pledging a certain property to the lender.

Collateral: Property that is pledged as a guarantee for repayment of a debt.

Unsecured debt: Debt that is backed only by the borrower's willingness and ability to repay.

- *Secured versus unsecured*. If the borrower pledges certain property to the lender to guarantee repayment, the debt is said to be **secured**. The property that is pledged is called **collateral**. A mortgage loan is a common form of secured debt; if the borrower fails to repay the loan, the lender takes over the property used as collateral. Debt that is backed only by the borrower's willingness and ability to repay is said to be **unsecured**.
- *Source of funds*. All funds except revenue from current sales come from someone's savings. Sometimes households invest their savings in firms directly, as when the owner of a small business buys new equipment for the firm, or when a person buys stock in a corporation. In other cases, people put their savings into institu-

tions like banks that act as intermediaries between savers and borrowers. Chapters 19 and 20 will discuss the major channels through which funds flow from savers to firms.

Financial managers have to take many factors into account in choosing among sources of funds. In the rest of this section we will look at the pros and cons of some of the most common sources. First we will cover unsecured short-term debt, then secured short-term debt, then long-term debt, and finally equity.

Unsecured Short-Term Debt

Trade credit: The purchase on credit of goods for resale or materials to be used in production.

Trade credit. The most common form of unsecured short-term debt is **trade credit**. Trade credit means purchases on credit of goods for resale or materials to be used in production.

Trade credit is widely used by wholesalers, retailers, and manufacturers. It tends to be more important for small firms than for large ones. The reason is that large firms often have better credit ratings, more bargaining power with banks, and greater access to other sources of funds. In times when credit is hard to get, large firms often extend extra trade credit to smaller customers in order to keep their business.

Trade credit is very convenient. Once the seller has made a credit check on the buyer, credit is extended every time the buyer makes a purchase. But although sellers do not usually charge interest for trade credit, it can still be costly for the buyer. The reason is that sellers often offer discounts for prompt payment. For example, Zeus Plastics might sell $1000 worth of materials to Ace Records on terms of "2/10, net 30." This means that Ace would owe Zeus $1000 (the net amount) if it paid within thirty days, but it would get a 2 percent discount if it paid within ten days. Two percent of $1000 is $20. That is the cost of using the added twenty days of trade credit. There are 18.25 twenty-day periods each year, so 2 percent for each twenty days is equivalent to a 36.5 percent annual interest rate. If Ace buys from Zeus regularly, and if it has any other source of funds (such as bank loans) that it can use at an interest rate below 36.5 percent, it probably should get its working capital from the other source and pay its Zeus bills within ten days.

Unsecured bank loans. Unsecured bank loans are a second major source of short-term funds. Firms usually get unsecured loans from the banks where they keep checking accounts, deposit their daily cash register receipts, and so on. A bank that is familiar with a firm's way of doing business and knows that it is creditworthy need not ask for collateral for each and every loan. The interest rate at which large banks make short-term loans to their most creditworthy customers is known as the **prime rate**.

Prime rate: The interest rate charged by banks for short-term loans to their most creditworthy customers.

Often firms arrange for short-term bank loans in advance. *Lines of credit* and *revolving credit agreements* are two arrangements of this type. Short-term bank loans are often used by firms that have seasonal needs for working capital.

Large firms with very good credit ratings are often able to borrow short-term funds from other nonfinancial firms, insurance companies, and even individuals, as well as from banks. In return for these unsecured

Commercial paper: Unsecured promises to pay that can be used by a highly creditworthy firm to borrow short-term funds.

short-term loans, they give written promises to repay that are known as **commercial paper**. Small firms and those with less than the top credit ratings usually cannot find lenders that are willing to make loans on the basis of commercial paper.

Secured Short-Term Debt

Secured short-term debt, in which current assets are used as collateral for loans, is another common source of funds. One might expect secured short-term loans to be less costly than unsecured loans because they present less risk to the lender, but this is not always the case. For one thing, secured loans require more paperwork than unsecured loans because specific assets must be pledged to the lender. Also, lenders are willing to supply funds to creditworthy firms without collateral, so that in practice, secured loans are used more often by firms that do not have good credit ratings or have used up their unsecured lines of credit.

Inventories are one type of current asset that is often used as collateral for loans. For example, auto dealers commonly use a type of financing called **floor planning**. In floor planning the manufacturer ships cars to the dealer, who raises funds to pay for them by assigning the title to the cars to a bank. The cars remain on the dealer's lot, but the bank owns them. When the dealer finds a buyer for a car, the buyer pays the dealer, the dealer repays the bank loan (with interest), and the bank releases the title to the customer.

Floor planning: A type of financing in which dealer inventories of goods like automobiles are used as collateral for short-term loans.

Floor planning can be used only for goods with a high unit value. Sometimes firms are able to borrow against other kinds of inventories, such as raw materials or finished products. Such loans can hold unpleasant surprises for the lender, however. In a famous scandal that took place in 1963, a swindler named Anthony DeAngelis borrowed $150 million, using as collateral 161 million gallons of salad oil that he claimed were stored in huge tanks in New Jersey. When DeAngelis failed to repay the loans, the lenders found that the tanks contained almost no oil. DeAngelis was able

Auto dealers commonly use a type of financing called floor planning, in which the cars are displayed on the dealer's lot but are owned by a bank until they are purchased. Courtesy of Ford Motor Co.

to achieve this swindle only because honest dealers had been using inventories of goods like salad oil as collateral for years.

Accounts receivable from companies with good credit ratings also make especially good collateral. Pledging accounts receivable as collateral for loans gives a company instant cash. Some firms prefer to use their accounts receivable as collateral for loans instead of selling them to factors.

Long-Term Debt

Firms that need funds for more than a year can use several kinds of long-term debt. The most important of these are bonds and mortages.

Bond: A promise to repay a certain sum on a set maturity date, and, in the meantime, to pay interest at an agreed-upon rate.

Bonds. A **bond** is a promise to repay a certain sum on a set maturity date and, in the meantime, to pay interest at an agreed-upon rate. Bonds are usually issued in units of $1000. Maturity dates are commonly ten to thirty years from the date of issue, but longer and shorter terms are possible. The interest payments are usually made twice a year, and are fixed for the life of the bond. For example, in 1985 Pacific Gas and Electric Company might raise $50 million for a new generating plant by selling thirty-year bonds at an interest rate of 12 percent. This means that the holder of each $1000 bond would receive a payment of $60 twice a year for thirty years and would be repaid the $1000 when the bond matures in 2015.

Bonds may be either secured or unsecured. Secured bonds are backed by pledges of items of fixed capital, such as factory buildings. Unsecured bonds, called **debentures**, are backed only by the firm's ability to repay.

Debenture: An unsecured bond.

Convertible bond: A bond that can be exchanged for a stated number of shares of a firm's common stock at a stated price.

Sometimes firms issue **convertible bonds**. These can be exchanged for shares of the firm's common stock at a stated price, usually higher than the stock's price at the time when the bond is issued. For example, at a time when a firm's stock was trading for $40 a share, it might issue a series of bonds with a $1000 face value and the right to convert each bond to twenty shares of common stock at $50 each. If the price of the stock later rose to, say, $60 a share, the bondholder could trade the $1000 bond for $1200 worth of stock. The right to convert is a "sweetener" that allows convertible bonds to be sold at a lower interest rate than ordinary bonds.

Mortgage: A long-term loan secured by land or buildings.

Mortgages. A **mortgage** is a long-term loan secured by land or buildings. Mortgages are the main way of financing houses, apartments, and commercial developments. Owners of small businesses often raise funds with mortgages on their own homes as well as on their business property. Mortgage lenders may be banks, insurance companies, or other financial firms.

Equity Financing

Equity financing includes all funds that are contributed by owners of the firm.

As we said in Chapter 3, the sources of equity funds for a new firm depend on its form of organization. Proprietorships and partnerships draw on the savings of their owners, who are also the firm's managers. Corporations raise equity funds by selling stock, sometimes (as in the case of

Corporations raise equity capital by selling stock, sometimes to the firm's founders and managers and sometimes to the general public. Marc P. Anderson

closely held firms) to the firm's founders and managers, and sometimes to the public.

As a firm grows, there are three ways in which it can raise more equity funds. First, the owners can contribute more. Proprietors or partners can put more funds into the firm from their personal savings. New shares of stock can be sold to a corporation's present shareholders.

Second, the firm can bring in new owners. A proprietorship can become a partnership or corporation. A partnership can incorporate or bring in new partners. And a corporation can issue new shares of stock, selling them to people who are not among its present shareholders. (When a closely held corporation offers to sell stock to anyone who is willing to buy it, it is said to be "going public.")

Third, the firm can obtain equity funds by keeping some of its profits for reinvestment. As we noted in Chapter 3, profits that are held for reinvestment rather than being paid out to shareholders as dividends are known as retained earnings. Using retained earnings as a source of funds does not increase the number of shares in the corporation. However, because each share represents part ownership of a firm with more total capital than before, retained earnings tend to raise the stock's value.

We will return to the subject of equity financing in Chapter 20. There we will look at securities markets, at the process of issuing stock, and at some of the factors that affect the price of a firm's stock.

Sources of Funds for Nonbusiness Organizations

Not-for-profit firms and units of government, like businesses, need both fixed and working capital. Some sources of funds available to businesses are not available to these other organizations. However, they also have some sources of funds of their own.

One major difference is that neither not-for-profit firms nor units of government can make use of equity capital. Not-for-profit firms, as we saw in Chapter 3, are barred by law from distributing earnings to outside owners. And government cannot issue stock because to do so would be to submit to control by shareholders, rather than to control by voters. Nonbusiness organizations are thus cut off from the largest source of funds used by business firms.

On the other hand, both not-for-profit firms and units of government have sources of funds that are not available to businesses. For not-for-profit firms, the source is voluntary donations. Some not-for-profit firms rely entirely on donations as a source of capital. Others, like many not-for-profit hospitals, bring in revenues that more than cover operating costs. These firms thus have some retained earnings avaliable to acquire capital. But even they may ask for donations to finance special, costly capital projects.

Governments receive some voluntary donations, but these are not a major source of funds. Most of their revenue comes from taxes. As in the case of businesses, however, revenues and costs do not exactly balance each year. When tax revenues fall short of expenditures, they must be supplemented by borrowing. The credit of the federal government is so good that it can borrow both short- and long-term funds without offering any security other than its promise to repay. State and local governments use both secured and unsecured borrowing. Because interest earned on state and local government bonds is exempt from the federal income tax, these units of government are able to borrow at somewhat lower interest rates than are paid by businesses and the federal government.

BALANCING THE FIRM'S FINANCIAL STRUCTURE

Striking the right balance among the many sources of funds is a big part of the financial manager's job. In this section we will discuss the balance between long- and short-term debt and the balance between debt and equity.

Short-Term versus Long-Term Sources

There is no one "best" balance between long- and short-term debt. The proper balance varies from one firm to another and from one time to another. Three factors must be weighed in choosing the right balance: cost, risk, and how the funds are to be used.

Cost. Over a span of many years, the interest cost of short-term funds tends to be lower than that of long-term funds. The reason is that short-term loans give the lender more flexibility. They do not require the lender to commit funds at a fixed rate into a future that can be only dimly foreseen. However, as Box 17–4 shows, short-term interest rates are much more volatile than long-term rates. During periods when all rates are high, short-term rates rise above long-term rates.

Risk. Although short-term debt is often cheaper than long-term debt, there is a risk in relying on it too much. The risk is that the short-term debt may come due when interest rates are very high. For example, Box 17–4 shows that in 1978 a firm could have gotten short-term loans at a prime rate of 7.99 percent, which was lower than the 8.73 percent rate on corporate bonds in that year. But a year later the prime rate had risen above the long-term bond rate. The prime rate stayed above the bond rate

Box 17–4 The Cost of Short- and Long-Term Debt

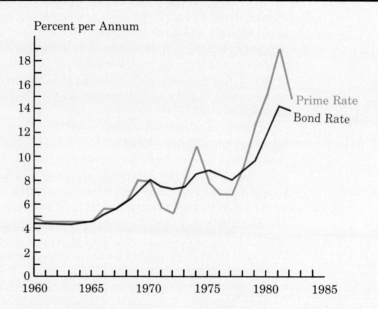

Percent per Annum

This chart shows the average interest rates that major firms have had to pay for short- and long-term debt each year since 1960. The short-term rate is the prime rate that banks charge for loans to their most creditworthy customers. The long-term rate is the interest rate on bonds rated Aaa by Moody's Investors Service. Firms with lower credit ratings have to pay more for both long- and short-term debt.

Source: President's Council of Economic Advisers, *Economic Report of the President*, (Washington, D.C.: Government Printing Office, 1983), Table B-67.

for three years. Many firms that had to renew short-term loans in those years—housing contractors and car dealers, for example—were forced into bankruptcy because they simply could not pay the high short-term rates.

Uses of funds. Finally, in deciding whether to borrow for a short or a long term, one should take into account how the funds are to be used. Seasonal needs for working capital, such as those of farmers or retailers, are often financed by short-term loans. But it is risky to use short-term loans to buy fixed assets.

Debt versus Equity

Striking the right balance between debt and equity is another big part of the financial manager's job. Again, use of funds, cost, and risk must be weighed.

Use of funds. Just as short-term debt is used to finance short-term uses of funds, long-term debt and equity are used to buy fixed assets. Long-term debt can be tailored to the life of the assets being bought. Equity funds have no set term; a share of ownership, once sold, continues for the life of the firm.

Cost. The cost of long-term debt is fixed by the terms of the loan. The cost of equity is the share of profits paid to the shareholders or other contributors of equity capital. The cost of equity thus depends on investors' opinion of the firm. Shares of stock in a firm with very good growth prospects and earning potential can be sold at a high price, so that fewer shares have to be sold to raise any given quantity of funds. Firms that are not well known or have poor prospects would have to sell many more shares at a lower price to raise the same amount.

Leverage: A firm's ratio of total debt to total equity.

Risk. A firm with a large ratio of debt to equity is said to have a high degree of **leverage**. A firm's degree of leverage strongly affects the amount of risk faced by its shareholders. An example will show why.

Box 17–5 shows income statements for two firms, Hi-Lev Company and Lo-Lev Company. Both have total capital of $1 million. Hi-Lev raised $500,000 of this sum by selling long-term bonds at 10 percent interest. It thus has fixed interest costs of $50,000 per year. The rest of its funds came

---

Box 17–5 Effects of Leverage on Risk and Earnings of Two Firms

	Hi Lev Co. (50,000 shares)	Lo Lev Co. (90,000 shares)
Year 1		
Earnings	$200,000	$200,000
Interest Paid	$50,000	$10,000
Income to Shareholders	$150,000	$190,000
Income per Share	$3.00	$2.11
Year 2		
Earnings	$50,000	$50,000
Interest Paid	$50,000	$10,000
Income to Shareholders	$0	$40,000
Income per Share	$0	$0.44

This table presents financial data for two firms. Hi-Lev Company has raised half of its capital by issuing $500,000 of long-term bonds and the other half by selling 50,000 shares of stock at $10 per share. Lo-Lev Company has borrowed $100,000 in the bond market and has sold 90,000 shares of stock at $10 per share. In year 1, when each firm earns $200,000 after paying all costs except interest, Hi-Lev's stockholders get more per share than Lo-Lev's. In year 2, when each firm earns only $50,000, Hi-Lev can barely pay its bondholders, and its stockholders get nothing. In general, greater leverage increases the potential return to stockholders, but it also increases their risk.

from selling 50,000 shares of stock at $10 per share. Lo-Lev, on the other hand, sold $100,000 worth of bonds at 10 percent and 90,000 shares of stock at $10 per share.

Results for each of two years are shown for each firm. In year 1 each firm earns $200,000 after paying current expenses and before paying any interest or dividends. Hi-Lev pays $50,000 of this to its bondholders, leaving $150,000, or $3.00 per share, for its stockholders. Lo-Lev pays $10,000 to its bondholders, leaving $190,000 for its stockholders. However, since Lo-Lev has more stock outstanding than Hi-Lev, its stockholders get just $2.11 per share. The lesson is that in a good year leverage increases the return on a firm's common stock.

In a poor year, however, the situation is reversed. In year 2 each firm earns only $50,000 after current costs are paid. For Hi-Lev this is barely enough to pay its bondholders; its stockholders get nothing. Lo-Lev is able to pay its bondholders and still have $40,000, or $0.44 per share, left for its stockholders. In a poor year, then, stockholders in the highly leveraged firm are worse off.

In an even worse year Hi-Lev's stockholders would be in still deeper trouble. Unless the firm has at least $50,000 income after current expenses, it cannot pay all the interest due on its bonds. Unless it can raise new equity funds quickly (which would be hard to do when the firm is having a bad year), it will fail. Lo-Lev, on the other hand, could survive on as little as $10,000. We see, then, that leverage increases a firm's risk of failure.

Financial Balance and Strategy

There are no simple formulas for finding the best financial structure for a firm. Well-managed companies do not all strike the same balance between long- and short-term debt or between debt and equity. At Wang Laboratories, for example, debt has at times accounted for as much as 57 percent of total capital. In contrast, Hewlett-Packard avoids long-term debt altogether. For each firm, the chosen financial structure seems to work.

The one thing well-managed firms have in common is that their financial structure is tailored to serve their overall strategy. In such firms, the job of the financial manager is to maintain a flow of funds so that no worthwhile project will be rejected for financial reasons alone. But the same cannot be said for all companies. At some, the financial tail wags the corporate dog.

Some critics see a connection between the weakness of many American firms in marketing, production, and management of human resources and the fact that a high proportion of top managers have backgrounds in finance. Financial indicators like bond ratings and debt/equity ratios, they say, should be treated as means to an end—not as ends in themselves. A firm exists for the purpose of selling products, not bonds. But, writes Richard R. Ellsworth in the *Harvard Business Review*, "in many large American companies, the most innovative competitive strategies are restricted and blocked by the financial policies necessary to fund them."[3] The top managers at such firms view themselves as guardians of financial purity; production and marketing managers who come up with too many ideas for spending capital funds are their enemies. These managers see a

Despite its high level of debt, Wang Laboratories is a very successful company. Courtesy of Wang Laboratories

[3]Richard R. Ellsworth, "Subordinate Financial Policy to Corporate Strategy," *Harvard Business Review*, November-December 1983, p. 170.

Drawing by Mulligan; © 1983 *The New Yorker Magazine, Inc.*

"That's for the lucky few who did manage to take it with them."

good bond rating as the basis for a good night's sleep; the future benefits of investment and innovation are only sources of worry.

Ellsworth calls for closer ties between financial, marketing, and production managers. Financial managers should have production experience whenever possible. Production managers should be brought into financial decision making at an early stage, when capital budgets are still flexible. The country's productivity crisis will not be solved, Ellsworth argues, as long as arbitrary financial policies divert the flow of funds from their most productive uses.

SUMMARY

1. *Finance* is the process of getting the funds a firm needs and putting them to use. Firms need funds for two purposes. First, they need funds to buy durable production equipment, or *fixed capital*. Second, they need funds to cover expenses between the time production starts and the time the finished product is paid for. Funds used for this second purpose are known as *working capital*.

2. In small firms, the proprietor is in charge of finance as well as all the other management functions. Large firms have a more extensive division of labor. The chief financial officer (CFO) of a corporation has two key subordinates. The first is the treasurer, who manages the firm's cash, securities, and credit policy. The second is the controller, who is in charge of all the accounting, planning, and budgeting functions performed within the firm.

3. Operating expenses—parts and supplies, wages and salaries, interest and taxes—are the biggest use of funds for most firms. Any funds that are not used to cover those expenses can be used to increase *assets*, reduce *liabilities*, or make payments to owners.

4. A firm's assets are all the things of value that it owns and that are owed to it. *Current assets* are those that the firm expects to hold for a year or less. They fall into three groups. First, there are *liquid assets*, which include currency, bank deposits, and certain kinds of securities. Second, there are *accounts receivable*, which are sums owed to the firm by customers who have bought on credit. Third, there are inventories. *Fixed assets* are those that a firm expects to hold for more than a year. These include fixed capital and land.

5. Revenues from sales are the biggest source of funds for most firms. From time to time, however, most firms draw on other sources as well. Those sources are *debt financing*, *equity financing*, and *sales of assets*.

6. Debt financing means obtaining funds in return for a promise to repay the amount borrowed plus interest. *Trade credit*, or purchases on credit of goods for resale or materials to be used in production, is a common form of short-term *unsecured* debt. Unsecured bank loans and *commercial paper* are others. Short-term debt can also be *secured* by pledging inventories, accounts receivable, or other short-term assets as *collateral*. The two most common forms of long-term debt are *bonds* and *mortgages*.

7. Equity financing includes funds that are contributed by owners of the firm. A firm can raise new equity funds by issuing new shares of stock or by reinvesting profits. Profits that are reinvested in the firm are called retained earnings.

8. The greater a firm's reliance on debt, rather than equity, as a source of funds, the greater its *leverage*. Leverage increases the potential rate of return to stockholders if the firm does well, but it also increases risk. Striking the correct balance between debt and equity is one of the main tasks of the company's financial manager.

KEY TERMS

You should be familiar with the following terms and concepts. Check their meanings by referring to the marginal definitions in the chapter or to the glossary at the end of the book.

Finance	Factor	Secured debt	Floor planning
Fixed capital	Cash management	Collateral	Bond
Working capital	Fixed asset	Unsecured debt	Debenture
Current asset	Capital budgeting	Trade credit	Convertable bond
Liquid asset	Debt	Prime rate	Mortgage
Accounts receivable	Equity financing	Commercial paper	Leverage

QUESTIONS FOR REVIEW AND DISCUSSION

1. In the light of what you have learned in this chapter, why do you think Wedtech chose to obtain working capital through a sale of stock instead of going to some other source of funds? In what ways did the sale of stock help the firm achieve a better balance between debt and equity?

2. Describe the fixed capital and working capital of your college. List some fixed assets that it owns. List some current assets.

3. What were your own sources of funds during the past year? Earnings from employment? Contributions from parents or others? Sales of assets (including withdrawals from savings)? Loans? Any others? How did you use these funds? To meet current expenses? To buy assets? To reduce liabilities? Any other uses? Make a chart showing these sources and uses of funds.

4. Using the latest issue of the *Economic Report of the President* or the *Federal Reserve Bulletin* as a guide, update the chart shown in Box 17–4. Which interest rate is higher, the rate on long-term Aaa-rated bonds or the short-term prime rate?

5. Ron opens a record store. Using $20,000 that he has saved, he rents a small shop and buys an inventory of records. This and the revenue from sales are his only sources of funds. His friend Rita starts a refrigerated delivery service at the same time. She buys a $20,000 truck, using $2000 of her own savings and borrowing the rest from a bank. The truck is used as collateral for the loan. Which firm has the greater leverage? What are the risks and possible benefits of the high-leverage strategy? Under what conditions will the low-leverage strategy prove the better of the two?

Case 17–1: The Rise and Fall of Osborne Computer

In 1981 columnist Adam Osborne, an outspoken critic of the computer industry, surprised many people by announcing that he would start a computer company of his own. With many firms already in the field, the venture seemed like a long shot, but Osborne thought he had the ideas that would make it work. First, his machine would be the first truly portable computer. Second, he would sell a complete package of software and hardware, saving the user the trouble of having to shop for the central processor, monitor and disk drives, and the programs needed to run them. And by packaging everything as a unit he would be able to sell it for a third less than competitors' prices.

Like anyone who starts a new business, Osborne needed capital. He raised part of the needed funds by selling a technical-manual company that he had started earlier. He raised more—some $20 million—by selling stock to venture capital specialists. Finally, to complete the financing package, he arranged with software suppliers like Microsoft and MicroPro to get their programs at low prices in return for more Osborne stock.

The firm's first product, the Osborne I, was a wild success. By the end of 1982 the company was selling 10,000 machines a month and bringing in revenue at a $100 million annual rate. But competitors were copying Osborne's formula for success. Kaypro, for example, brought out, at about the same price, a somewhat more compact machine that gained rapidly on the Osborne I. To produce new models, Osborne needed still more financing. In January of 1983, the firm announced that it was going public. In a strong market for high-tech stocks, the planned offering of stock was expected to be a smash hit.

Then things began to fall apart. The first blow came in April. Word leaked out that the firm

had a new model ready for the market, the Osborne Executive. Not wanting to be caught with large inventories of the older model, dealers by the dozen canceled orders for the Osborne I. Last-minute production snags delayed delivery of the Executive until May. For a month the flow of funds into Osborne Computer virtually dried up.

Then came a second unpleasant surprise. In January Osborne had hired a new president, Robert Jaunich II. Jaunich found Osborne's financial structure in chaos. "They didn't know how much inventory they had. They didn't know how much they were spending," a former manager said. When the mess was untangled, Jaunich discovered that the firm had been operating at a loss, not at a profit as everyone had thought.

Jaunich clamped down on spending, but it was too late. The Executive did not do well. In designing it, Osborne had failed to realize how important it would be for any new computer, even a portable model, to use programs written for the IBM personal computer. A new model, the Executive II, was on the drawing boards, but it couldn't be brought out on time. Starved for cash and unable to find new investors, Osborne filed for bankruptcy in September 1983. The company's dramatic rise and fall spanned just two years.

Sources: Based on Richard A. Shaffer, "Riding the Success of Hot Product, Osborne Computer Is Going Public," *Wall Street Journal*, January 19, 1983, p. 33; Erik Larson, "Snags in Introducing New Computer Sidetrack Osborne's Stock Offering," *Wall Street Journal*, July 13, 1983, p. 33; Erik Larson and Ken Wells, "Shaken Osborne Computer Seeking Suitor in the Face of Possible Failure," *Wall Street Journal*, September 12, 1983, p. 35; "Osborne Goes into Chapter 11," *Business Week*, September 26, 1983, p. 50.

Questions:

1. What sources of funds did Osborne rely on at first? Leaving aside the marketing and production problems that arose later, do you think it was reasonable for Osborne to plan to go public in January 1983?
2. To what extent was Osborne's failure a result of poor financial management? To what extent was it caused by marketing and production mis-

takes? How did the various kinds of problems interact to cause the firm's downfall?
3. What similarities do you see between Osborne's problems in the spring of 1983 and Wedtech's problems in the summer of the same year? What differences allowed Wedtech to survive while Osborne failed?

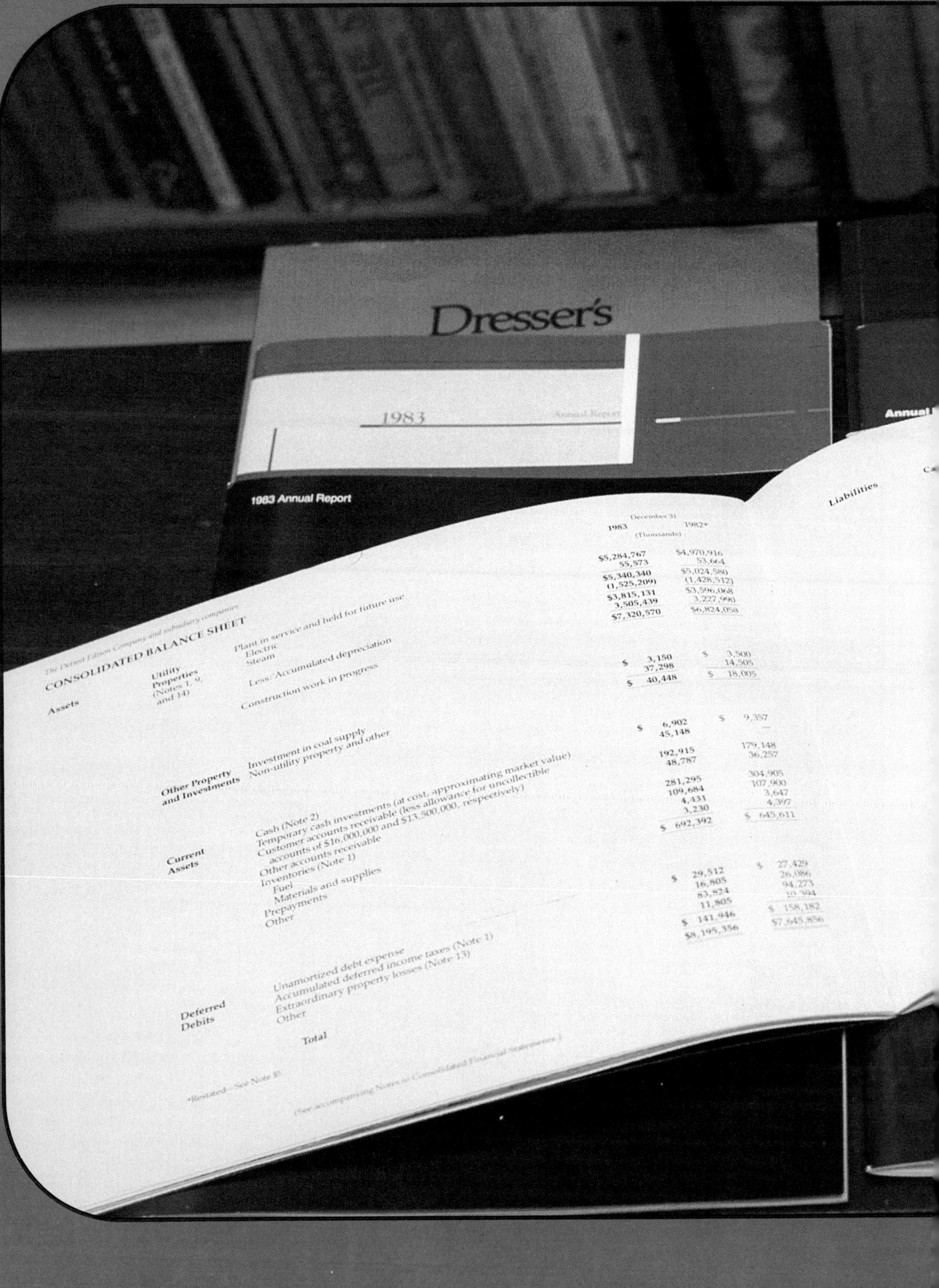

Dresser's

1983   Annual Report

1983 Annual Report

Annual

Liabilities   Ca

The Detroit Edison Company and subsidiary companies

CONSOLIDATED BALANCE SHEET

			December 31	
			1983	1982*
			(Thousands)	

Assets	Utility Properties (Notes 1, 9, and 14)	Plant in service and held for future use		
		Electric	$5,284,767	$4,970,916
		Steam	55,573	53,664
			$5,340,340	$5,024,580
		Less: Accumulated depreciation	(1,525,209)	(1,428,512)
			$3,815,131	$3,596,068
		Construction work in progress	3,505,439	3,227,990
			$7,320,570	$6,824,058

	Other Property and Investments	Investment in coal supply	$ 3,150	$ 3,500
		Non-utility property and other	37,298	14,505
			$ 40,448	$ 18,005

	Current Assets	Cash (Note 2)	$ 6,902	$ 9,357
		Temporary cash investments (at cost, approximating market value)	45,148	—
		Customer accounts receivable (less allowance for uncollectible accounts of $16,000,000 and $13,500,000, respectively)	192,915	179,148
		Other accounts receivable	48,787	36,257
		Inventories (Note 1)		
		Fuel	281,295	304,905
		Materials and supplies	109,684	107,900
		Prepayments	4,431	3,647
		Other	3,230	4,397
			$ 692,392	$ 645,611

	Deferred Debits	Unamortized debt expense	$ 29,512	$ 27,429
		Accumulated deferred income taxes (Note 1)	16,805	26,086
		Extraordinary property losses (Note 13)	83,824	94,273
		Other	11,805	10,394
			$ 141,946	$ 158,182
		Total	$8,195,356	$7,645,856

*Restated—See Note 10.

†See accompanying Notes to Consolidated Financial Statements.

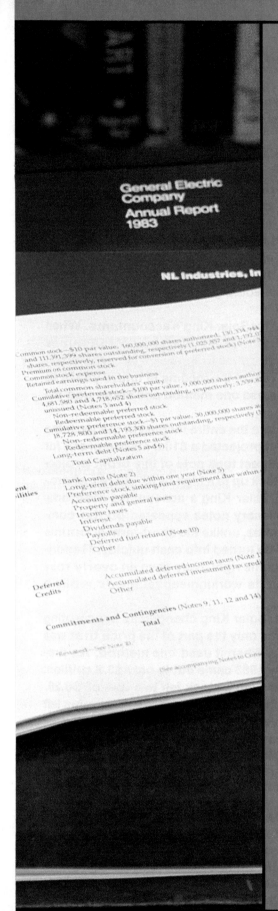

Chapter 18

ACCOUNTING, THE LANGUAGE OF FINANCE

When you have completed this chapter, you should be able to

- Define *accounting* and explain how it is related to data processing.

- Distinguish among *bookkeeping*, *financial accounting*, and *managerial accounting*.

- Describe the work of *public accountants*, *private accountants*, and accountants who work for units of government and not-for-profit firms.

- Interpret a *balance sheet* and explain *double-entry bookkeeping*.

- Interpret an *income statement* and describe the methods used to draw up such a statement.

- Explain how financial comparisons and ratios are used in interpreting financial statements.

- Discuss the limitations of accounting.

Things the Numbers Don't Tell

First, users of financial information should keep in mind that accounting is a backward-looking process. It is not always possible, on the basis of financial statements alone, to tell whether a firm has been well managed or has been poorly managed but lucky. Investors who want to know how well a firm will do in the future need other information as well. Is competition likely to increase? How will the firm be affected by trends in the economy? Is it committed to serving customer needs? Does it produce a quality product? How well does it manage its human resources? The answers to questions like these often say more about future performance than financial ratios.

Fool's Gold on the Bottom Line

Both investors and managers need to watch out for policies that boost net income in the short run but hurt the firm's long-run prospects. As a case in point, think about research and development. Funds spent for research do not always pay off in the short run, but they appear as costs on this year's income statement. If a firm's sales slip a little, its managers may be tempted to slash research spending in order to avoid reporting a drop in net income. But that may not be in the firm's long-run strategic interest.

Investments in quality assurance, funds spent to keep workers on the job during a recession, and advertising to build up brand loyalty are other examples of spending that goes on the books as current costs but pays off only in the long run. Managers who try to pump up the bottom line by cutting such expenses are going after fool's gold.

In some cases the problem may lie in bonus plans that are tied to short-run net income. Some observers have blamed the problem on too many top managers with financial and legal backgrounds.[4] Whatever the cause, too strong a focus on short-run financial results is one of the most common criticisms of American management.

The Dangers of Historical-Cost Accounting

We saw earlier that historical-cost accounting often yields higher reported profits than inflation-adjusted accounting. The illusion of high profits becomes a real danger when it causes a firm to pay out, as dividends and taxes, funds that it ought to retain.

To stay in business without shrinking, a firm needs to retain enough funds from sales to replace inventories as they are used up and fixed capital as it wears out. Income statement A in Box 18–5 illustrates this point. Alpha Corporation has sales of $1 million. Its payroll costs are $500,000. It will cost $150,000 to replace inventories used up during the year, and it will cost $200,000 to cover depreciation, that is, to replace the portion of fixed capital that is worn out during the year. This gives Alpha a net income of $150,000. That is the most that it can afford to pay out as taxes and dividends.

The replacement costs shown in statement A are adjusted for the effects of inflation. In contrast, look at statement B, which is based on

Managers should avoid the temptation to cut spending on research and development for the sake of higher net income in the short run. Courtesy of AT&T Bell Laboratories

[4]See, for example, Robert H. Hayes and William J. Abernathy, "Managing Our Way to Economic Decline," *Harvard Business Review*, July-August 1980, pp. 67–77.

Box 18–5   Dangers of Historical-Cost Accounting

Statement A: Net income at replacement cost	
Sales	$1,000,000
Payroll costs	500,000
Cost of replacing materials used from inventory	150,000
Depreciation (cost of replacing fixed capital worn out during the year)	200,000
Income before taxes (inflation-adjusted)	$ 150,000

Statement B: Net income at historical cost	
Sales	$1,000,000
Payroll costs	500,000
Original cost of materials used from inventory	100,000
Depreciation based on historical cost	150,000
Income before taxes (historical-cost)	$ 250,000

This box shows two income statements for Alpha Corporation, an imaginary company. Statement A is drawn up in terms of replacement costs. It shows costs of $150,000 to replace inventories used up and $200,000 to replace fixed capital worn out during the year. The inflation-adjusted net income of $150,000 is the most Alpha can pay out in taxes and dividends and still operate at current levels. Statement B is drawn up in terms of historical cost. It shows lower costs of inventories used up and depreciation, and, hence, a higher net income—$250,000. However, if Alpha pays out the entire $250,000 in taxes and dividends, it will not be able to replace inventories and worn-out fixed capital at their current inflated costs.

historical costs. The historical cost of inventory used is only $100,000, and depreciation based on the historical cost of fixed capital is only $150,000. Statement B thus shows a net income before taxes of $250,000. But what will happen to Alpha if it pays out that $250,000—say, if the government takes $125,000 in taxes and the firm pays out the remaining $125,000 in dividends? Where will it get the $350,000 it needs to replace inventories and fixed capital? Either it will have to look for outside sources of funds, which are likely to cost more than retained earnings, or it will have to cut back its operations year by year until it shrinks to nothing.

Some observers think that one of the greatest burdens inflation places on the economy is this tendency to drain capital from private firms. Two remedies have been suggested. First, firms should use inflation-adjusted accounts as a basis for dividend decisions. Second, the government should permit firms to use inflation-adjusted accounting for tax purposes. Some steps have been taken in this direction. As of 1981, nearly half of all large

U.S. firms were using some sort of inflation-adjusted accounting.[5] And Congress has permitted firms to adjust their depreciation costs in a way that takes inflation at least partly into account. But much still remains to be done.

SUMMARY

1. Accounting is the process of capturing, processing, and communicating financial information. *Bookkeeping* is the data capture phase. *Managerial accounting* is concerned with providing information to be used within the firm. *Financial accounting* is concerned with reporting information to outside users.
2. The accounting profession consists of *public accountants*, *private accountants*, and accountants who work for government units and not-for-profit firms. Public accountants are independent professionals who provide auditing, tax preparation, and other services for a fee. Private accountants are employees of business firms.
3. According to the *accounting equation*, a firm's assets are equal to its liabilities plus owner's equity. This equation is the basis of the *balance sheet*, a financial statement that lists a firm's assets, liabilities, and net worth at a given point in time. According to the principle of *double-entry bookkeeping*, each transaction must be recorded as two separate entries on the balance sheet so that the accounting equation always holds.
4. An *income statement* shows a firm's sales, costs, and *net income* (profit) for a given period. A number of choices need to be made in drawing up an income statement. For example, income and costs can be re-

ported on either an *accrual* or a *cash basis*. Inventories can be valued according to either the first in, first out (FIFO) or the last in, first out (LIFO) principle. Finally, accounts can be kept in terms of either *historical costs*, or costs adjusted for inflation.
5. Comparisons with other years, other firms, or other items are useful in interpreting a firm's financial statements. Often these comparisons are made by looking at financial ratios. Some ratios measure solvency, for example, the ratio of current assets to current liabilities, known as the *current ratio*. Others indicate efficiency, such as the ratio of sales to inventory, known as the inventory turnover ratio. Still others indicate profitability, for example, the ratio of net income to owners' equity, known as *return on equity*.
6. Useful though accounting is, it has its limitations. For one thing, accounting always looks backward; other information is needed to judge a firm's future prospects. Second, managers may be tempted to take actions that will make their financial statements look good in the short run but may not be in the firm's best interests in the long run. Finally, tax and dividend policies based on historical-cost accounting may drain capital from the firm during periods of inflation.

KEY TERMS

You should be familiar with the following terms and concepts. Check their meanings by referring to the marginal definitions in the chapter or to the glossary at the end of the book.

Accounting	Financial accounting	Auditing
Bookkeeping	Public accountant	Private accountant
Managerial accounting	Certified public accountant (CPA)	Certified management accountant (CMA)

[5]See Cornelius J. Casey and Michael J. Sandretto, "Internal Uses of Accounting for Inflation," *Harvard Business Review*, November-December 1981, pp. 149–56.

Balance sheet	Cost of goods sold	Last in, first out (LIFO)
Accounting equation	Depreciation	Historical cost
Liquidation	Gross profit	Solvency
Owner's equity	Operating income	Current ratio
Net worth	Income before tax	Debt-to-equity ratio
Double-entry bookkeeping	Net income	Inventory turnover ratio
Income statement	Accrual basis	Return on equity (ROE)
Net sales	Cash basis	Return on assets (ROA)
	First in, first out (FIFO)	

QUESTIONS FOR REVIEW AND DISCUSSION

1. Look under "Accountants" in the yellow pages of your local telephone directory or the directory of a nearby city. How many accounting firms are listed? How many of them call themselves CPAs? Do any of the Big Eight have offices in your area? Do any firms have display ads listing the services they offer? If so, what are the most fequently offered services?

2. Look under *accountants* in the help-wanted ads of your local newspaper or a newspaper from a nearby city. What kinds of jobs are being offered? Do any of the ads mention salary? Which of the jobs are for public accountants? Which are for private accountants?

3. Turn to the last of the balance sheets given for Carl's Cookie Cart (page 467). Beginning from that point, show how each of these transactions would be recorded on the balance sheet.

  a. Carl decides that his used pushcart isn't good enough anymore. He finds a new one that costs $2000. The dealer gives him a trade-in of $800 on the old cart. Carl raises the other $1200 with a short-term unsecured bank loan. What does his balance sheet look like now?

  b. One day Carl bakes 500 cookies, as usual, at a cost of $100. He hits the street with his inventory, but before he has sold a single cookie a violent thunderstorm strikes. The storm blows away the umbrella from his cart, and all the cookies are ruined by the rain. What effect does this have on each side of the balance sheet?

4. We have not yet seen an income statement for Carl's Cookie Cart. Suppose that Carl is able to sell cookies on 100 days during the year. He sells an aver-

age of 500 cookies a day. Ingredients cost 20¢ per cookie, and the cookies are sold for 30¢ each. Carl puts down $200 of depreciation on his cart as a general expense. Interest on his loan for the year is $150. Carl is not incorporated, so he figures taxes at his personal income tax rate, which is 35 percent. Arrange this information in the form of an income statement for the 100-day period, using 3M's income statement (page 468) as a guide. (Note that in Carl's case depreciation is considered a general expense rather than a cost of goods sold.) What is Carl's gross profit? Operating income? Income before taxes? Net income?

5. The income statement for 3M (page 468) was drawn up using the FIFO method of inventory valuation. Assuming that the prices of goods carried in inventory were rising throughout the early 1980s, how would 3M's income statement have differed if LIFO had been used? (You won't be able to figure exact numbers—just note the direction of change and which items would have been affected.)

6. An oil company buys heating oil at various times during the year, stores it in tanks, and sells it during the winter. In 1982 and 1983, heating oil prices, both wholesale and retail, fell slowly but steadily. Which accounting method, FIFO or LIFO, would cause a higher net income to be reported on the firm's 1983 income statement? Why?

7. Using the income statement from question 4, calculate the following financial ratios for Carl's Cookie Cart: current ratio, debt-to-equity ratio, inventory turnover ratio, return on assets, and return on equity. You will need to update Carl's balance sheet in order to calculate some of these ratios. Begin with the balance sheet in your answer to question 3b. Add a cash asset equal to the net income shown on the income statement from question 4; add the same amount to owner's equity. Assume that Carl has paid only interest on the loan and that the balance is still $1200 at the end of the year.

Case 18–1: Debt with Mirrors

In 1980 Avis Rent-A-Car, a subsidiary of Norton Simon Inc., needed to buy some new cars. Cars are good collateral for loans, so Avis might well have been expected to borrow the funds it needed. Borrow it did, but not in the usual way. It first set up a separate corporation that it called a trust. The trust borrowed the money, bought the cars, and leased them to Avis. As a result, Norton Simon kept $400 million in debt off its balance sheet (the debt appeared only on the balance sheet of the trust, which was not combined with that of the parent firm in its annual report). Without the trust, Norton Simon's debt-to-equity ratio would have been 1.40 to 1. With it, the ratio was 0.56 to 1.

The *Wall Street Journal* cites this ploy as an example of a growing trend. "Reacting to inflationary distortions, accounting loopholes, and heavy debt burdens," says the *Journal*, "corporations have concocted so many ways to hide or disguise borrowings that deciphering their true liabilities is often impossible. Sometimes debt isn't acknowledged anywhere; at other times, it's there, but finding it would take a financial wizard with hours of free time and a computer."

"It's all done with mirrors," Loyd Heath of the University of Washington told a *Wall Street Journal* reporter. "Under current accounting rules, companies apparently can call debt whatever they like."

"Calling it something doesn't merely face-lift a company's balance sheet," the *Journal* points out. "It undercuts the usefulness of balance sheets, which list assets and liabilities and provide major clues to corporate cash flow—and does so at a time when balance sheets have increasingly replaced profit-and-loss statements as thermometers of corporate health.

"But most investors, bankers, and economists aren't sophisticated enough to see through many off-balance-sheet borrowing tactics. So investors may make ill-informed decisions. Banks often don't know that a company seeking a loan already is deep in hock. And economists misjudge how highly leveraged American business really is.

"That could be dangerous. If, for instance, companies are borrowing more than they otherwise could, they may be stretching their resources too thin, and they, and their banks, will become more vulnerable in economic downturns. If the economy sours and banks start calling in loans, some companies will be hard pressed to repay their debts."

Questions:

1. Why would a financial accountant see an advantage in hiding debt in financial statements put out for the general public? Would a managerial accountant see an advantage in hiding debt in financial statements used within the firm? Discuss the points of view of the two types of accountants.

2. The *Wall Street Journal* refers to "inflationary distortions" as one reason that firms want to hide debt. In part, what they are referring to is the fact that fixed assets are often really worth more than the historical-cost values that appear on the balance sheet. If a firm felt that this caused its assets to be undervalued by $100 million, would it be misleading investors and lenders if it hid $100 million in debt? Why or why not?

3. The *Wall Street Journal* reports that the Financial Accounting Standards Board plans to investigate a number of hidden-debt tactics. Do you think it should insist on fuller public disclosure of off-balance-sheet borrowing? Explain your answer.

Case 18-2: Financial Statements of Convergent Technologies, Inc.

Convergent Technologies is a California-based computer manufacturer that was founded in 1979. Its 1982 annual report gave the following information (all figures in thousands of dollars).

Accounts receivable	$25,366
Accounts payable	6475
Net sales	96,462
Inventories	30,077
Fixed assets	6735
Cost of goods sold	61,758
Selling, general, and administrative expenses	16,497
Net interest income	3397
Income taxes	9689
Liquid assets	37,305
Current capital lease obligations[a]	241
Long-term capital lease obligations[b]	895
Other current assets	1289
Other assets	96
Other current liabilities	13,586
Other liabilities	67

[a]Equivalent to short-term debt.
[b]Equivalent to long-term debt.
Source: Based on Convergent Technologies, Inc., Annual Report, 1982, pp. 17-18.

Questions:

1. Which of the items listed belong on Convergent's balance sheet? Arrange them into a balance sheet, using 3M's (page 465) as a model. What is the firm's total owners' equity?

2. Which of the items listed belong on Convergent's income statement? Arrange them into an income statement, using 3M's (page 468) as a model. Be sure to include entries for gross profit, operating income, income before taxes, and net income. Note that depreciation is not stated separately.

Note also that Convergent earned more interest than it paid in 1982. As a result, its income before taxes was higher than its operating income.

3. Calculate the following ratios for Convergent: current ratio, inventory turnover ratio, return on equity, and return on assets.

4. Compare Convergent's financial statements with 3M's. What major differences do you see? How do the ratios that you have calculated help you spot differences?

Chapter 19

BANKING AND THE FINANCIAL SYSTEM

When you have completed this chapter, you should be able to

- Explain the difference between *direct* and *indirect financing*, and the role of *financial intermediaries* in the U.S. financial system.

- Define *money* and list the assets used as money in the United States.

- Use a balance sheet for a simple bank to show how banks earn profits, how they act as financial intermediaries, and how they create money.

- Describe the structure of the Federal Reserve System and explain how it provides services to banks, stabilizes the banking system, and shares in economic policy making.

- List the major changes brought about by the deregulation of banking since 1980, and explain how banks are responding to the challenges posed by deregulation.

There is almost nothing out of the ordinary about Dee Tiffany's weekly trip to the Dahl's Supermarket on Fleur Drive in Des Moines. The thirty-year-old Mary Kay Cosmetics sales director strolls the aisles, making sure not to forget the Prairie Farms milk or the Colonial bread. At a checkout counter in Iowa, like everywhere else, the food bill seems to have one digit too many. Nothing unusual, until it comes time to pay.

Then Tiffany takes her green Norwest Bank debit card and slides it through a $400 tan-and-black NCR magnetic stripe reader no bigger than a notebook. She punches an identification number into a keyboard, and in less than ten seconds has paid for her groceries. No messy checks, no filthy lucre. It's all done electronically.

Des Moines, Iowa, is probably the last place in the world you would expect to find the banking of tomorrow. Nevertheless, Dahl's nine electronic funds transfer point-of-sale checkout terminals, along with fifteen more at the Hy-Vee supermarket on Thirty-fifth Street in West Des Moines, are the first two such operating systems in the United States. A small start, but they look like prototypes for the entire country, if not for the world.

Since the systems were installed, Barclay's Bank, Security Pacific, and Kroger Company executives, to name but a few, have dropped in for a look-see, as have bankers from Germany, Japan, France, Australia, and South America. "Barnett Banks has been here three times," counts Dale Dooley, president of ITS Inc., which operates the computer "switch" that makes electronic funds transfers possible for some 205 participating Iowa banks, savings and loan associations, and credit unions. "Bank of America has been here five times." Visitor traffic became so heavy that ITS now charges $500 for a two-hour consultation and $1000 if a guest wants to go to the supermarket too.

Of course, this type of electronic checkout won't spread overnight. Dooley estimates it could be at least the late 1980s before such systems gain wide acceptance, considering that NCR is the only show in town today and considering the cost and lead times involved. But Dahl's Supermarkets president Robert Hand is more optimistic: "One day this is just going to explode."[1]

[1]Jeff Blyskal, "Iowa, the Debit Card State," *Forbes*, August 29, 1983, pp. 45–46.

In the last two chapters we have often mentioned banks as sources of funds for business firms. In this chapter we will take a broader look at the services that banks provide, both traditional ones like checking accounts and new ones like point-of-sale electronic payment systems.

We will begin with an overview of the U.S. financial system, in which banks occupy a central place. Next we will look at the role of banks in providing firms and consumers with money. After that we will look at how banks function as businesses, turning inputs into outputs and earning profits as they do so. We will then take a closer look at the Federal Reserve System, first mentioned in Chapter 2, which regulates banking. Finally, we will look at some of the challenges that banking faces in the 1980s.

THE U.S. FINANCIAL SYSTEM

Financial system: The network of institutions through which firms, households, and units of government get the funds they need and put surplus funds to work.

In Chapter 17, we defined *finance* as the process of getting and putting to use the funds that a firm needs to do its business. The **financial system** is the network of institutions through which firms, households, and units of government get the funds they need and put surplus funds to work.

The Structure of the Financial System

Box 19–1 outlines the financial system of the United States. Investment funds are shown flowing from savers, who act as sources of funds, to borrowers, who use them. Any financial unit is considered to be a saver if it earns more than it spends, and a borrower if it spends more than it earns. Some households are savers and some are borrowers, but on the whole,

---

Box 19–1 The Financial System of the United States

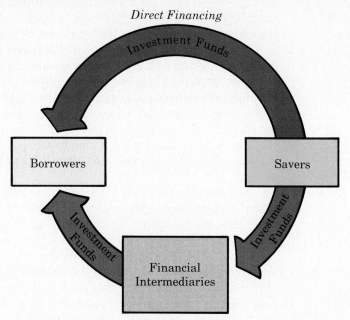

The financial system is the network of institutions through which firms, households, and units of government get the funds they need and put surplus funds to work. Households are the chief savers, serving as a source of funds. Businesses and units of government, on the whole, are borrowers who use the funds.

Two pathways connect savers and borrowers. In direct financing, users of funds sell stocks, bonds, and other securities directly to savers. In indirect financing, users get funds from financial intermediaries, which, in turn, get them from savers. The financial intermediaries include banks, thrift institutions, insurance companies, pension funds, mutual funds, and finance companies.

households earn more than they spend. Thus, they serve as a source of funds in the financial system. Likewise, some firms and some units of government are savers while others are borrowers, but on the whole, the business and government sectors spend more than they save. They are thus users of funds.

Savers and borrowers are linked by two sets of arrows in Box 19–1. The upper set represents **direct financing**, or any process in which a user of funds gets them directly from savers. Corporations use direct financing when they sell stocks and bonds to the public. Units of government use direct financing when they sell bonds and other securities.

The lower set of arrows in Box 19–1 represents **indirect financing**, or any process in which a user of funds gets them from an intermediary, such as a bank, which in turn gets them from savers. Banks and other institutions that aid in this process are known as **financial intermediaries**.

Direct financing has its strong points. It is suitable for savers who want the risks and potential rewards of ownership. It is also suitable for savers who have large amounts of funds to lend. For them, the fact that bonds come in denominations of $1000 or more is no problem. From the saver's point of view, direct financing is a bit like buying goods directly from the factory.

For many savers, though, indirect financing is a better way to put funds to work. The role of financial intermediaries in the financial system is a bit like that of wholesalers and retailers in the distribution of goods: they provide services that their customers believe are worth paying for.

One service that banks and other financial intermediaries provide is matching the size and terms of borrowers' needs with those of savers. For example, suppose a borrower needs a twenty-year $100,000 loan to buy a building. It would not be easy to find one saver who was willing to commit such a large block of funds for such a long time. But there are always many savers looking for a chance to put small amounts of funds to work for short periods. A bank can gather a steady stream of short-term deposits from such savers and use them to make large, long-term loans to suit borrowers' needs.

A second service that financial intermediaries provide is reducing the risk to savers. In any business loan there is some risk that the borrower will not be able to repay. If a household were to place all of its savings in a loan to a single firm, failure of that firm would be a disaster for the household. But a bank makes loans to many firms using funds gathered from many depositors. A few of the loans will not be repaid. But the bank can absorb these losses by charging borrowers a slightly higher interest rate than the rate it pays to depositors. Depositors are happy to accept the lower interest rate in return for avoiding the risk that all their savings will be wiped out by a single business failure.

The Financial Intermediaries

Financial intermediaries come in many sizes and kinds. They fall into three broad groups: the banking group, the insurance group, and the investment group. Let's look at each of these in turn.

The banking group. The banking group is made up of all financial intermediaries that accept deposits from the public. The most important members of this group are **commercial banks**. Commercial banks accept

---

Direct financing: Any process in which a user of funds gets them directly from savers.

Indirect financing: Any process in which a user of funds gets them from an intermediary, such as a bank, that in turn gets them from savers.

Financial intermediary: A bank or other institution that gathers funds from savers and supplies them to borrowers.

Commercial bank: A financial intermediary that accepts checking and other deposits from firms and households and makes many kinds of loans, including long- and short-term loans to business firms.

a wide variety of deposits, offer a full range of services, and make many kinds of loans to households and firms.

Next come **savings and loan associations** (often called simply "savings and loans"). These serve household depositors and specialize in home mortgage loans. **Mutual savings banks** are a smaller group of institutions, mainly in the Northeast, that are much like savings and loan associations. The last members of the banking group are **credit unions**. These are small-scale intermediaries that typically are sponsored by a company or union. They accept deposits from their members and make loans to them for such uses as buying appliances or taking vacations. Savings and loans, mutual savings banks, and credit unions are referred to as **thrift institutions** or **thrifts**.

In the past, a maze of federal regulations limited competition between banks and thrifts. For example, until the 1970s only commercial banks were allowed to offer checking accounts. Savings and loans and mutual savings banks were largely restricted to home mortgage loans. Credit unions were limited to small loans to consumers. In recent years, though, these regulations have been relaxed. Both banks and thrifts can now offer checking accounts, and they can make more kinds of loans than before. These institutions are becoming more alike as competition among them increases. Because of these changes, almost everything that we say about banks in the rest of this chapter applies to thrift institutions as well.

The insurance group. The insurance group includes two related kinds of firms. The first are **insurance companies**. These collect charges, called premiums, from firms and households. In return they offer financial protection against certain risks. *Life insurance* pays benefits to a policyholder's dependents in the event of his or her death. *Fire insurance* pays for damage caused by fire. *Casualty insurance* covers theft, accident, illness, and other risks. The insurance group also includes **pension funds**. These collect payments from working people and pay them an income after they retire.

Insurance companies and pension funds are sources of funds for investment because people make payments to them before—often long before—they receive benefits from them. As funds come in, they are put to work earning interest. Members of the insurance group buy corporate bonds and stocks. They also buy government securities and make mortgage loans. The greater the interest earned from these investments, the greater the benefits that can be paid out. Profit-making insurance companies use some of their investment income to pay dividends to their shareholders. However, some insurance companies and pension funds are run on a not-for-profit basis. All of their income, after allowing for administrative costs, is paid out in benefits. Insurance companies will be discussed in detail in Chapter 21.

The investment group. The most important members of the investment group are **mutual funds**. These sell shares to individuals and use the proceeds to buy stocks, bonds, and government securities. Earnings from these investments are passed along to the shareholders after a small service fee has been deducted. There are mutual funds tailored to the needs of every investor. Some buy risky stocks with high growth prospects. Others buy the stocks of firms that are known for paying consistent dividends over time. Some buy corporate bonds, others government bonds. All of them offer investors a chance to own a share of a large, professionally

---

Savings and loan association (savings and loan): A financial intermediary that accepts checking and savings deposits from households and makes home mortgage loans.

Mutual savings bank: A depositor-owned financial intermediary that resembles a savings and loan association.

Credit union: A small-scale financial intermediary, often sponsored by a company or union, that accepts deposits from members and makes consumer loans to them.

Thrift institution (thrift): A general term for savings and loan associations, mutual savings banks, and credit unions.

Insurance company: A financial intermediary that collects charges, called premiums, from firms and households and, in return, offers financial protection against certain risks.

Pension fund: A financial intermediary that collects payments from working people and pays them an income after they retire.

Mutual fund: A financial intermediary that sells shares to individuals; uses the proceeds to buy stocks, bonds, and other securities; and passes the income from those securities along to its shareholders after deducting a small service fee.

Money market fund: A type of mutual fund that buys short-term government securities and may offer checking services to its shareholders.

chosen pool of securities. The investor does not have to choose the securities and can make payments and withdrawals in fairly small amounts.

A fast-growing group of mutual funds are the so-called **money market funds**. These buy short-term government securities that are almost risk-free. Many investors think shares in money market funds are as safe as bank deposits. Most such funds even offer checking services.

Finance companies, which use funds supplied by investors to make consumer loans for cars, appliances, and other uses, are also part of the investment group of financial intermediaries. Some finance companies make business loans, but their share of the loan business is declining.

Finance companies like Beneficial use funds supplied by investors to make consumer loans. Courtesy of Beneficial Corporation

Sources of funds compared. Box 19–2 compares all the sources of funds in the U.S. financial system in 1983. About one third of all funds were raised by direct financing. Individuals contributed about half of all direct-financing funds, followed by units of government, foreign investors, and nonfinancial businesses, in that order.

The other two thirds of all funds were raised indirectly, through financial intermediaries. Half of all indirect financing came from the banking group, with commercial banks supplying $2 for every $1 supplied by thrifts. The insurance group was next in importance, supplying nearly a quarter of all funds raised. Mutual funds supplied 9 percent of all funds raised, and others, chiefly finance companies, supplied the rest.

MONEY AND THE BANKING SYSTEM

Banks, as we have seen, play a key role as financial intermediaries. As such, they channel funds from savers to firms that need them to finance inventories, buy fixed capital, and so on. In this section we will look at a second key role that banks play, that of supplying money.

What Is Money?

Money: An asset that serves as a means of payment, a store of value, and a unit of account.

Money is an asset that serves as a means of payment, a store of value, and a unit of account. Money was invented a long time ago. Gold and silver

Box 19–2 Sources of Investment Funds in the United States, 1983

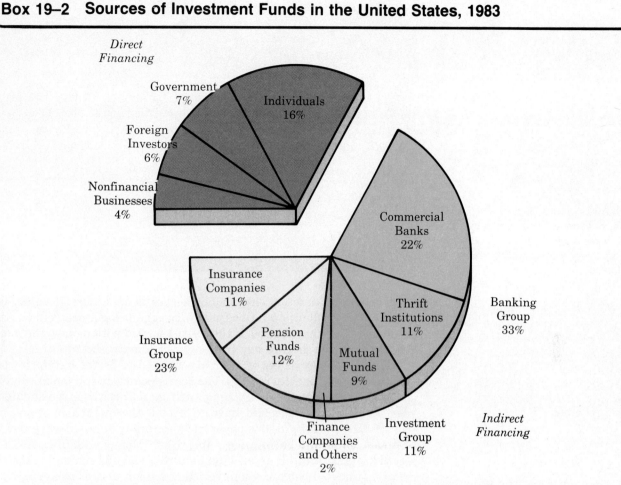

Direct Financing

Government 7%

Foreign Investors 6%

Nonfinancial Businesses 4%

Individuals 16%

Commercial Banks 22%

Insurance Companies 11%

Pension Funds 12%

Mutual Funds 9%

Thrift Institutions 11%

Banking Group 33%

Insurance Group 23%

Finance Companies and Others 2%

Investment Group 11%

Indirect Financing

About one third of all investment funds are raised through direct financing. Individuals supply about half of all direct financing. Government, foreign investors, and nonfinancial businesses supply the rest. The remaining two thirds of all investment funds are raised through indirect financing. The banking group supplies about half of these funds. Insurance companies, pension funds, and mutual funds account for most of the rest.

coins stamped with the likenesses of rulers are a form of money that dates back to the earliest city-states. Societies lacking gold and silver have used other things as money, including shells, beads, and beaver pelts. Anything can serve as money that is easily recognized, widely accepted, and not easily copied.

Whatever its form, money serves three functions. First, it serves as a means of payment. People accept money in payment for goods and services because they know that others will accept it in turn. Exchanges using money are much more convenient than **barter**, or the exchange of one good or service for another. In a barter system, each party to an exchange must have something that the other party needs. A dentist with a plugged drain must find a plumber with a toothache; an electrician with a toothache or a plumber with a stomachache won't do. With money, needs are matched more easily. The electrician can pay the dentist to fill a tooth; the dentist can use the money to hire the plumber to fix a drain; the plumber can pay a doctor to cure a stomachache, and so on.

Barter: The exchange of one good or service for another without the use of money as a means of payment.

Exchanges using money are much more convenient than barter; as a result, some form of money is used in almost every known society. Marc P. Anderson

The second function that money serves is as a store of value. In a barter system, a dentist who was paid with eggs or tomatoes would have to eat them before they spoiled. If the dentist is paid with money, the money can be saved and used to buy fresh eggs or tomatoes at any time.

Finally, money serves as a unit of account. In a barter system, it would be hard to keep financial records. The dentist's income statement would be a list of all the eggs, tomatoes, and plumbing services received during the year. A new-car loan would have to list all the quantities of goods or services that could be used to pay it back—so many hundred watermelons, so many hours of legal services, and so on. Money simplifies financial record keeping. Income, assets, and liabilities can all be stated in terms of dollars, ounces of gold, or whatever the common unit of money is.

Money in the United States

Currency: Coins and paper money issued by the federal government.

Checking deposit: Any deposit at a bank or thrift institution from which the depositor may withdraw funds, or transfer funds to another party, by writing a check.

Gold, shells, and beaver pelts are no longer used as money in the United States, although all of these things have served as money in the past. Today two kinds of financial assets serve as money: **currency** (coins and bills) and **checking deposits** at banks and thrift institutions.

Coins make up about 3 percent of the total money supply, as shown in Box 19–3. Paper currency accounts for another 22 percent. The rest of the money supply consists of checking deposits. These are supplied not by the government but by banks and thrifts. Checking deposits serve all three of the functions of money, just as currency does. They are a means of payment: by writing a check, you can transfer part of the balance in your checking account to the seller. They are a store of value: you deposit your paycheck in your checking account and spend the money when you need to. And the dollars in your checking account serve as a unit of account just as dollars of currency do.*

---

*Money as we use the term here—currency plus checking deposits at banks and thrifts—is often called *M1*. Some writers prefer a broader concept of money that includes balances in money market funds, savings deposits in banks and thrifts, and certain other liquid assets. This broader concept is called *M2*. The terms *M1* and *M2* are often used in financial columns in newspapers and other writings on monetary matters.

Box 19–3 Money in the U.S. Economy

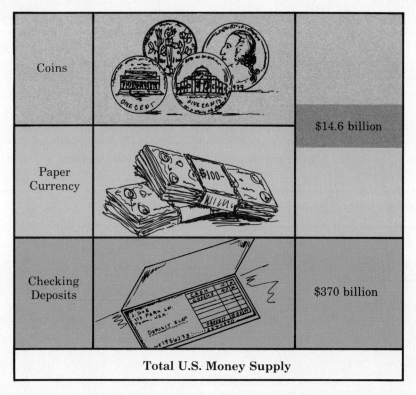

Coins		
		$14.6 billion
Paper Currency		
Checking Deposits		$370 billion

Total U.S. Money Supply

Money is an asset that serves as a means of payment, a store of value, and a unit of account. Two types of assets are used as money in the United States. Currency, which includes coins and the paper bills in $1, $5, and other denominations, accounts for about a quarter of the total money supply. The rest consists of deposits in checking accounts at banks and thrift institutions.

Source: Economic Report of President, 1984, Table B-62.

Plastic Money

We have mentioned coins, paper currency, and checking deposits, but we have not yet said anything about "plastic money"—the handy VISA cards, MasterCards, and other all-purpose charge cards that so many people carry these days. "Plastic money" comes in two forms—credit cards and debit cards. They look much alike and, from the consumer's point of view, are used in much the same way, but they serve different functions.

Credit card: A plastic card that allows a customer to obtain a bank loan and, at the same time, arrange for the bank to send the amount of the loan to a merchant from whom goods or services are purchased.

Credit cards, which are the more common of the two, are a quick way of getting a bank loan. Suppose you go into a gas station to buy $20 worth of gas and pay for it with your VISA card. By signing the credit card slip, you do two things. First, you ask your bank for a loan of $20. Second, you ask your bank to send the amount of the loan to the gas station. Later, your bank will send you a bill and you will repay the loan. The transaction is then complete.

Debit card: A plastic card used by a customer in place of a check to instruct a bank to transfer funds from the customer's checking account to that of a merchant from whom goods or services are purchased.

Debit cards work differently. A debit card is a way of using the balance in your checking account without writing a check. When you use a debit card to pay for $20 worth of groceries in a supermarket like Dahl's in Des Moines, you ask your bank to transfer $20 from your bank account to Dahl's, much as if you had written an ordinary paper check. Debit cards are not yet as common as credit cards or paper checks, but they are quicker and cheaper to use than either. For this reason, their use is expected to grow rapidly in coming years.

Box 19–4 compares credit cards and debit cards. The box makes it clear that these cards are not new forms of money. Instead, they are convenient ways of using checking account money. Credit cards do so indirectly by initiating a loan, which the customer later repays by writing a check. Debit cards use checking account money directly by moving it from one account to another without using a paper check.

Box 19–4 How "Plastic Money" Works

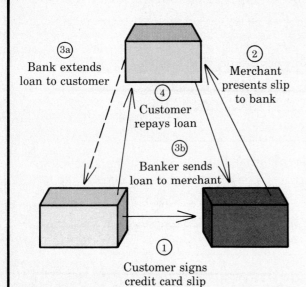 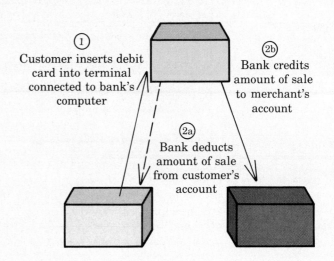

So-called plastic money, such as VISA cards and MasterCards, is not really a new form of money. Instead, it is a way of using checking account money. Plastic money comes in two varieties. The use of a *credit card* causes the customer's bank to extend a loan to the customer, and pay the amount of the loan to the merchant. The customer later writes a check to repay the loan. The use of a *debit card* at a point-of-sale terminal linked to the bank's computer causes the bank to move funds from the customer's account to the merchant's account. Debit cards can also be used where there is no point-of-sale terminal. In this case (not shown) the transfer of funds does not take place until the merchant sends the debit card slip to the bank.

BANKING AS A BUSINESS

Mutual savings banks and some other thrift institutions are not-for-profit firms. In the world of banking, however, they are exceptions; most banks are in business to make a profit. In this section we will look at banking as a

A popular form of "plastic money" is the bank credit card. © Freda Leinwand

business. First we will work through the balance sheet of a simplified bank. This will show us how a bank earns a profit. Then we will use balance sheets to give a more detailed picture of the way banks fill their role as financial intermediaries, and to explain how they create checking account money.

The Balance Sheet of a Simple Bank

The financial position of a bank, like that of any other firm, can be shown by means of a balance sheet. As usual, assets are listed on the left-hand side of the balance sheet and liabilities and owner's equity on the right-hand side. Following the accounting equation, assets are equal to liabilities plus owner's equity.

Setting up a bank. Let's begin by looking at a bank that has just been started. As a model, we will use the Wolf Creek Bank, located in the town of Wolf Creek, Idaho. Bill Winchester starts the bank with $10,000 of his own savings. The $10,000 buys a used mobile home, which Bill sets up as the bank's office. The day the bank opens for business, its balance sheet looks like this:

Assets		*Liabilities and Owner's Equity*	
Fixed assets	$10,000	Liabilities	$ 0
		Owner's equity	10,000
Total assets	$10,000	Liabilities plus owner's equity	$10,000

Accepting a deposit. The first customer to walk into Bill's bank is Edith Bender. She brings in $1000 in currency that she has been keeping in her cookie jar because there was no bank in town. She deposits the $1000 in an account that will allow her to write checks and will yield interest at a 6 percent annual rate. At that point Bob's balance sheet looks like this:

Assets		*Liabilities and Owner's Equity*	
Cash	$ 1,000	Liabilities:	
		Checking deposits	$ 1,000
Fixed assets	10,000	Owner's equity	10,000
Total assets	$11,000	Liabilities plus owner's equity	$10,000

Following the principle of double-entry bookkeeping, Edith's deposit has created two entries on Bill's balance sheet. First, the bank has a new asset in the form of $1000 of cash. Second, it has a matching liability in the form of Edith's deposit. Deposits appear on a bank's balance sheet as liabilities because the bank must pay the money out on demand, either to the depositor or to any person who presents a check that Edith writes against the money in her account.

Making a loan. Bill does not yet have a source of income. The next customer to come into the bank solves this problem. Roger Kahn, the

Banking is a business whose chief goal is to make a profit. In the course of doing so, banks serve as financial intermediaries and creators of money. © Freda Leinwand

Fractional-reserve banking: A system in which a bank accepts deposits, keeps a fraction of each deposit as reserves, and lends out the rest to earn income.

owner of Roger's Grocery, comes in to ask for a loan. Bill looks at his books to decide how much he can lend to Roger. The bank has $1000 in cash, but it would not be safe to lend out the whole amount. Edith might write a check on her account at any time, and Bill will need cash in reserve to pay the check. On the other hand, it seems unlikely that Edith will withdraw the whole $1000 any time soon. Bill decides that it will be safe to lend $800 to Roger and keep $200 in reserve. Roger agrees to pay 12 percent interest on the loan and walks out of the bank with the $800. Now Bill's balance sheet looks like this.

Assets		Liabilities and Owner's Equity	
Reserves (cash)	$ 200	Liabilities:	
Loans	800	Checking deposits	$ 1,000
Fixed assets	10,000	Owner's equity	10,000
Total assets	$11,000	Liabilities plus owner's equity	$11,000

Making the loan has not changed Bill's total assets, liabilities, or net worth. It has, however, traded a nonearning asset for one that pays 12 percent interest. In the coming year Bill will receive $96 in interest on the $800 loan to Roger and will pay $60 to Edith as interest on her account. The $36 difference is income to the bank. Of course, the bank will also have costs—heat for the trailer, the clerical costs of processing checks and loan payments, and so on. But if Bill gets enough deposits, makes enough loans, and controls his costs, he will be able to make a profit.

This example says most of what needs to be said about how banks earn profits. What makes it possible for them to earn profits is the fact that they keep as reserves only a fraction of what they take in from depositors. The rest is lent back out at an interest rate higher than the rate paid on deposits. The difference between the rate paid on deposits and the rate received on loans covers the bank's costs and, if the bank is properly managed, leaves enough for its owners to make a profit. This way of doing business is called **fractional-reserve banking**.

Banks as Financial Intermediaries: Another Look

Box 19–1 showed in general terms how banks act as financial intermediaries. Now we can use balance sheets to give a more detailed picture. This is done in Box 19–5, which shows balance sheets for Bill's bank, Roger's Grocery, and Edith Bender. The three are linked in a chain with the bank in the middle.

Edith's personal balance sheet shows assets of $35,000, including a car, a house, and her checking account balance. We assume that she doesn't owe anyone any money, so her liabilities are zero and her net worth is equal to her total assets. (The term *net worth* is used instead of *owner's equity* on a personal balance sheet.) The checking account links the two balance sheets. It is an asset on Edith's balance sheet and a liability on the bank's.

The bank's balance sheet is also linked to that of Roger's Grocery. Here the link is the loan, which is an asset on Bill's balance sheet and a liability on Roger's.

Box 19–5 Banks as Financial Intermediaries

Edith Bender's Balance Sheet

Assets		Liabilities and Owner's Equity	
Checking account	$ 1,000	Liabilities	$ 0
Car	4,000		
House	30,000	Net worth	35,000
Total	$35,000	Total	$35,000

Balance Sheet of Bill's Bank

Assets		Liabilities and Owner's Equity	
Reserves (cash)	$ 200	Liabilities:	
Loans	800	Checking deposits	$ 1,000
Fixed assets	10,000	Owner's equity	10,000
Total assets	$11,000	Total	$11,000

Balance Sheet of Roger's Grocery

Assets		Liabilities and Owner's Equity	
Inventory	$ 5,000	Short-term debt	$ 800
Fixed assets	10,000	Owner's equity	14,200
Total	$15,000	Total	$15,000

Balance sheets can be used to show how banks act as financial intermediaries. In this box, Bill's bank serves as an intermediary between Edith Bender, a source of funds, and Roger's Grocery, a user of funds. Edith is linked to the bank by a deposit, which appears as an asset on her balance sheet and a liability on the bank's. The bank is linked to Roger's Grocery by a loan, which appears as an asset on the bank's balance sheet and a liability on the grocery's.

What is true of Bill's Wolf Creek Bank is true of all financial intermediaries—insurance companies, pension funds, mutual funds, and the rest. As they pass funds from savers to borrowers, their balance sheets gain both liabilities (claims of the savers against the intermediary) and assets (claims of the intermediary against the borrowers).

How Banks Create Money

As we have seen, the main forms of money in the United States are currency, which is issued by the government, and checking deposits, which are created by banks. The balance sheets in our example can be used to show just how banks create money.

Let's suppose that before Bill's bank opened, currency was the only form of money used in Wolf Creek. The total currency in the town was, say, $100,000. This included the $1000 in Edith Bender's cookie jar.

When Edith deposited her $1000 in the bank, a new form of money was created. Instead of the $1000 in currency that she had before, she now had a checking account balance of $1000. As long as the $1000 in currency stayed in the bank's vault, however, the total amount of money in the town did not increase because only currency outside of banks is counted as part of the nation's money supply.

But the $1000 did not stay in the bank for long. Very soon $800 of it was lent to Roger. When Roger walked out of the bank with his $800 (which we assume he took in cash), Wolf Creek's money supply increased. There was now $99,800 in currency in the town plus Edith Bender's $1000 checking account balance, for a total money supply of $100,800. In this way, by accepting deposits and using them to make loans, banks create money.

As more people make deposits at Bill's bank, the total amount of money continues to grow. There is a limit to how much it can grow, however, because the bank can never lend out the full amount that it receives in deposits. It always has to keep some reserves.

THE FEDERAL RESERVE SYSTEM

Let's turn now from the simple banking system of Wolf Creek to the more complex system of the United States. We will begin with a look at the history of that system.

In the nineteenth century the U.S. banking system lacked strong central control. Some banks were chartered by the federal government, but many were chartered by the states. There was a constant tug-of-war over monetary policy. Westerners and farmers tended to favor "easy money." Easy money at that time meant silver coinage and policies that made it easy for banks to make loans. Easterners, especially eastern bankers, tended to favor "hard money." This meant gold coinage and strict controls over the loans made by banks. Meanwhile, the banking system went through cycles of rapid growth followed by depression and widespread bank failures. No one was happy with the system.

In 1907 a short but sharp recession brought several big New York banks close to failure. In response Congress appointed a commission to look into setting up a central bank. Five years later, in 1913, the Federal Reserve System was established as the nation's central bank.

The Structure of the Federal Reserve System

The Federal Reserve System—or "Fed," as it is known in financial circles—is an independent agency of Congress. The system consists of twelve

The Federal Reserve System consists of twelve district banks located in cities like New York and San Francisco, and a Board of Governors located in Washington, D.C. © Freda Leinwand

district banks and a board of governors. The locations of the district banks are shown in Box 19–6. The board of governors has its headquarters in Washington, D.C.

Members of the Fed's board of governors are appointed by the president of the United States and confirmed by the Senate. However, the Fed

Box 19–6   The Federal Reserve System

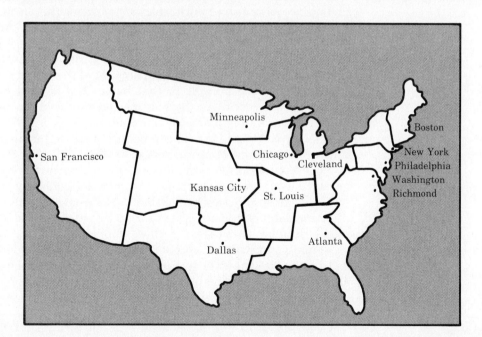

The Federal Reserve System, founded in 1913, provides services to banks, stabilizes the banking system, and helps make economic policy. The system consists of the twelve district banks shown on this map and a board of governors located in Washington, D.C.

Source: Board of Governors of the Federal Reserve System.

maintains a degree of independence from both Congress and the executive branch. This is due in part to the governors' long terms of office—fourteen years. The chairman of the board of governors is chosen by the president from among the seven board members and serves as chairman for four years.

The Fed serves three major functions. It provides services to the banking system and the federal government; it stabilizes the banking system; and it controls the quantity of money in circulation. Each of these deserves some comment.

Services

The most important service of the Fed is making sure that checks written on one bank can be accepted at any other bank in the country. The process of moving funds between banks when a check written on one is deposited in another is known as **check clearing**.

Check clearing: The process of moving funds between banks when a check written on one is deposited in another.

When a check written on an account in one bank is deposited at another bank in the same city, the clearing process is fairly simple. Bank A may send the check to bank B and ask for payment. Often all the banks in a city form a *clearinghouse* at which officials of each bank meet to exchange checks. When a check is deposited in a bank in a distant city, however, it is usually cleared through the Federal Reserve.

Box 19–7 outlines the process. The sequence of events begins when Amy Armand of Anchorage receives a $10 check from her uncle, Bill Bonkowski, written on the Liberty National Bank of Buffalo. Armand deposits the check in the National Bank of Alaska, which credits her savings account with $10. This bank then sends the check to the nearest Federal Reserve district bank, that in San Francisco. The Anchorage bank has an account at the San Francisco Fed, to which the Fed credits the $10. The check is then sent to the Federal Reserve Bank of New York. The New York Fed deducts the $10 from the account of the Liberty National Bank and sends the check itself to that bank. The bank deducts $10 from Bonkowski's account. As the last step in the clearing process, Liberty sends the check to Bonkowski, who then has a record of the fact that his niece received the money. This process is repeated more than 12 billion times a year by the Federal Reserve System.

The Fed performs a number of other services for banks and thrift institutions. It provides currency to banks and collects worn currency for credit. It transfers funds between banks electronically when asked to do so. (Electronic funds transfer is faster than clearing a check.) It also provides safekeeping for securities.

Finally, the Fed performs banking services for the federal government and foreign governments. It maintains U.S. Treasury accounts from which all federal government payments are made. In addition, it assists in international transfers of funds by private firms, governments, and international agencies.

Stabilizing the Banking System

Services like check clearing are just a small part of the Fed's duties. A second function of the Federal Reserve is stabilizing the banking system.

Box 19–7   How the Federal Reserve Clears a Check

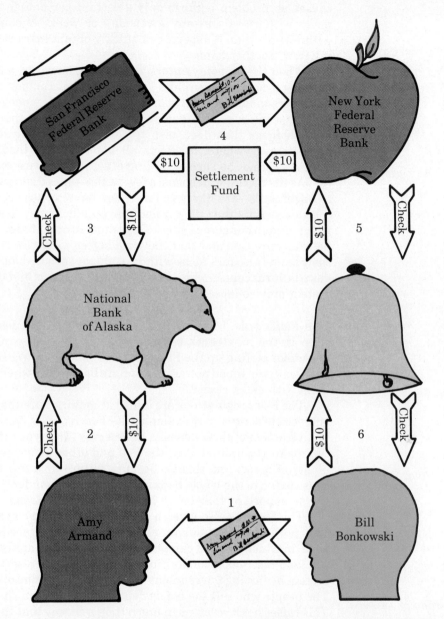

This figure diagrams how the Federal Reserve clears a check that Bill Bonkowski of Buffalo has sent to Amy Armand of Anchorage. Armand gives the check to her local bank, receiving $10 in return. The bank sends it to its district Federal Reserve bank in San Francisco and receives credit for it. The San Francisco Fed sends the check along to the Federal Reserve district bank nearest the issuing bank—the New York Federal Reserve Bank. At this time the San Francis-co Fed receives credit from an interbank settlement fund maintained by the Federal Reserve System. When the New York Fed gets the check, it pays $10 into the settlement fund. It then sends the check along to Bonkowski's bank, Liberty National, collect-ing $10 from that bank. Liberty finally deducts the $10 from Bonkowski's balance and sends the check to him for his records.

The concept of fractional-reserve banking contains a built-in source of instability. In order to make a profit, the bank can afford to hold reserves equal to only a fraction of the deposits it takes in. In normal times this causes no problem because only a certain percentage of depositors will make withdrawals in any given day or week. A bank that has more withdrawals than it expects can quickly obtain extra reserves by borrowing from another bank.

When the economy enters a recession, however, a fractional-reserve banking system can run into trouble. As the economy slows down, more depositors than usual will want to withdraw their money from banks. They may be people who are unemployed and need to use their savings, or they may be firms that need cash to cover accounts payable. Because this happens everywhere, it affects all banks. Those that first run low on reserves cannot be sure of finding others with spare reserves to lend.

As the recession deepens, a few banks—ones that may have been weak to begin with—are likely to fail. They have to close their doors and tell their depositors that they cannot have their money. News of these bank failures has a dangerous effect. Depositors in other banks begin to fear that no banks are safe and that they had better withdraw their money before their banks also fail. More withdrawals cause more bank failures; news of more failures causes more panic among depositors; and the whole banking system may collapse.

The Fed's role. Banking panics of the type just described took place often in the nineteenth century. Preventing such panics was the main reason for setting up the Federal Reserve System. With this in mind, the Fed was given broad powers to regulate banks and, when needed, to supply them with extra reserves.

The Fed's regulations are aimed at making sure that banks use sound business practices. For example, the Fed requires banks to hold a minimum fraction of their deposits as reserves. The types of loans that banks can make are limited. And the Fed and other agencies conduct frequent audits of banks and thrifts. Because failure by a few weak banks could cause panic in the whole banking system, the founders of the Fed thought it was important to keep all banks financially strong.

The Fed was also given a second line of defense against bank panics. This is the power to supply extra reserves when needed. There are two ways in which the Fed can put reserves into the banking system. First, it can lend reserves to banks. Second, it can supply reserves to the banking system by buying government bonds from the public on the open market. The people who sell the bonds deposit the money in their bank accounts. This raises bank reserves in much the same way that the reserves of Bill's bank rose when Edith Bender deposited the money she had previously been keeping in her cookie jar; the difference is that the Fed's cookie jar is bottomless. An injection of reserves into the banking system through the purchase of bonds from the public is known as an **open-market operation**.

Open-market operation: A process in which the Federal Reserve System injects added reserves into the banking system by buying government securities from the public, or withdraws reserves from the banking system by selling government securities.

Federal deposit insurance. Despite its powers, the Fed failed to stabilize the banking system after the stock market crash of 1929. In the first years of the Great Depression, a great many banks failed. As a result, a new agency, the Federal Deposit Insurance Corporation (FDIC), was set up in 1934 to give the system further stability. The FDIC promises to pay depositors the full amount of their deposits, up to a limit, in the event that

The FDIC promises to pay depositors the full amount of their deposit in the event that their bank fails. Courtesy of National Bank of Alaska

their bank fails. At present the limit is $100,000 for any one person's deposits at any one bank.

Deposit insurance does more than just compensate the victims of bank failures—it prevents most failures from happening. With deposit insurance, there is no reason for people to panic at the news of a bank failure. They do not need to run to be first in line to withdraw their money. Thus, deposit insurance breaks the domino effect that caused the failure of a few weak banks to bring many healthy banks down with them.

Since the FDIC was established, there have continued to be bank failures, including some big ones. But there has never again been a runaway banking panic in which the whole system was threatened with collapse.

The Fed as Economic Policymaker

Today the Fed continues to regulate and stabilize the banking system, but it has taken on another role as well—one that was not clearly foreseen in 1913. This is the role of partner, with Congress and the executive branch, in the making of economic policy. The Fed's power as an economic policymaker comes from its ability to control bank reserves and, hence, to control the total amount of checking account money in circulation.

The Fed and inflation. The Fed's control over the money supply has a major effect on the rate of inflation. Suppose, for example, that the Fed pursues an easy money policy, using open-market operations to increase bank reserves.* Such a policy allows banks to increase the volume of loans they make and allows the amount of money in circulation to rise. More

---

*Open-market operations are the most frequently used means of adjusting bank reserves to ease or tighten monetary policy. The Fed can also lower the *discount rate*—the rate at which it lends reserves—to make it easier for banks to borrow reserves, or it can raise the rate to make it more expensive to borrow reserves. And it can ease monetary policy by lowering the percentage of deposits that banks are required to hold as reserves, or tighten monetary policy by raising that percentage.

money and easy access to loans make it possible for businesses and consumers to increase their purchases of goods and services of all kinds. Following the law of supply and demand, the surge of buying tends to push prices up. The result is inflation.

The Fed can fight inflation by pursuing a tight money policy. By slowing the growth of bank reserves, it limits the funds banks have on hand for making loans. A tight money policy forces businesses and consumers to cut back on their spending plans. Demand for goods and services drops. As demand falls, there is less upward pressure on prices. As a result, the rate of inflation falls. The dramatic drop in the rate of inflation from a rate of 13.5 percent in 1980 to 3.2 percent in 1983 is widely credited to the Fed's tight money policy during those years.

The Fed's control over inflation is not complete. Outside events like oil crises or bad harvests can make it hard to keep prices stable. Controlling inflation with a tight money policy is not painless, either. The same spending cutbacks that are needed to reduce upward pressure on prices also cause lower sales by businesses and throw many people out of work. Still, the Fed has more control over the rate of inflation than any other government agency.

The Fed and interest rates. The Fed's power to inject reserves into the banking system allows it to influence interest rates as well as the rate of inflation. An easy money policy lets reserves grow fast and gives banks plenty of money to lend. In the short run, competition among banks to offer the best loan terms puts downward pressure on interest rates. On the other hand, a tight money policy slows the growth of reserves. With less money to lend, banks can charge higher interest rates and still attract borrowers.

But a policy of trying to keep interest rates low with an easy money policy can backfire in the long run. As we saw earlier, if bank reserves and the money supply are allowed to grow too fast over a long period, the rate of inflation will increase. During a period of inflation, lenders must charge higher interest rates than they otherwise would in order to offset the fact that a dollar will have less purchasing power when the loan is repaid than when it was made.[*] This tendency of inflation to push up interest rates greatly limits the Fed's ability to control interest rates.

CHALLENGES TO THE FINANCIAL SYSTEM

The U.S. financial system has changed rapidly since 1980, and the pace of change shows no sign of slowing. In the past, banks and thrifts were sheltered from competition. Now the barriers to competition are falling. As a result managers of financial institutions face many new challenges.

---

[*]Suppose, for example, that you lend me $5000 to buy a car, charging 10 percent interest for one year. I will owe you $5500 at the end of the year. If there has been no inflation, you can take the loan payment, buy a car for yourself, and pocket a $500 profit. Suppose, though, that inflation has driven the price of the car up to, say, $5600 in the meantime. (This would be an inflation rate of 12 percent per year.) In that case, the $5500 loan payment wouldn't give you enough to buy a car, let alone give you a profit. I would have to pay you $6100 at the end of the year (a 22 percent interest rate) to preserve your $500 profit during a period of 12 percent inflation. Using this reasoning, during periods of inflation lenders often add an "inflation premium" to the interest rates that they would otherwise charge.

Falling Barriers to Competition

In the past, banks and thrift institutions were limited in terms of the services they could offer, the areas in which they could operate, and the interest rates they could pay on deposits. These restrictions protected them from competition with one another and with other financial intermediaries. Now regulations in all of these areas are changing.

From the *Wall Street Journal.* Reprinted by permission of Cartoon Features Syndicate.

- *Product competition.* In the past only commercial banks could offer checking accounts. Then, in 1980, the Depository Institutions Deregulation and Monetary Control Act (the Monetary Control Act, for short) gave thrifts the right to compete with banks by offering checking accounts of their own. (Thrifts in New England had won this right a few years before.) At the same time, the act put banks and thrifts in more direct competition for loans. Savings and loans and mutual savings banks were allowed to make more consumer and business loans, and credit unions were allowed to make some mortgage loans.
- *Interest competition.* Before 1980, regulations limited the rates that could be paid on deposits. Checking accounts at commercial banks paid no interest at all. Savings accounts and certificates of deposit paid interest at rates that were low, but slightly higher for thrifts than for banks. The Monetary Control Act phased out the old interest rate ceilings and allowed banks and thrifts to compete for depositors on an equal footing.
- *Geographic competition.* Banks and thrifts have long been protected against interstate competition. With few exceptions, banks cannot set up out-of-state branches that accept deposits. In some states banks are not allowed to have branches at all. The Monetary Control Act did not remove these limits on interstate banking, but they are crumbling nonetheless. Some banks have been allowed to take over banks or thrifts outside their home states when a takeover seemed to be the only way to prevent a failure and a suitable in-state buyer could not be found. Banks have also set up offices outside their home states that make loans, conduct international business, and do almost everything except accept deposits. Finally, many banks have used the mails to solicit deposits and credit card business outside their own states. Thus, banks now face competition from outside their home states, and some observers predict that full interstate banking is not far in the future.

Surviving in the New Competitive World

Surviving in the new competitive business of banking is a big challenge. Bank managers will have to change old points of view and old ways of doing business. Writing in the *Harvard Business Review*, George G. C. Parker offers the following advice:[2]

- *Innovation.* The banks that survive will be those that learn how to innovate. Innovations that make full use of computers and telecom-

---

[2]George G. C. Parker, "Now Management Will Make or Break the Bank," *Harvard Business Review*, November-December 1981, pp. 140–48.

Increased competition in the banking industry has put pressure on banks to offer innovative new services. © Freda Leinwand

munications will be among the most important. The Des Moines banks' use of debit cards and supermarket point-of-sale terminals is an example.

- *Managing interest rate risks.* Banks will make more use of loans that have variable interest rates to avoid the danger that a rise in interest rates will leave them with low-yielding loans at a time when they are forced to pay higher rates on deposits.
- *People management.* Banking has not always attracted the most ambitious, hard-hitting managers. The new high-risk, high-reward world of banking will place a premium on managers with energy, creativity, and vision.
- *Marketing.* Banks will have to use such strategies as market segmentation and product differentiation to attract more customers. (See Case 11–2, page 287.)
- *Strategic planning.* Few banks will be able to do everything well. Bank managers should do some careful strategic planning to decide just what type of banking their firm can do best.

In short, Parker concludes, banking is entering a new era. The old protections against competition are gone. Like other newly deregulated industries, banking must go through a learning period in which there will be a new batch of winners and losers. The winners in the new world of banking, as in other fields of business, will be those who best learn the art of management.

SUMMARY

1. The *financial system* is the network of institutions through which firms, households, and units of government get the funds they need and put surplus funds to work. On the whole, households earn more than they spend; they therefore serve as sources of funds. Businesses and units of government, on the average, spend more than they earn, so they are users of funds.

2. There are two ways in which savers and borrowers are linked. *Direct financing* is any process in which a user of funds gets them directly from savers. *Indirect financing* is any process in which a user of funds gets them from a *financial intermediary* that in turns gets them from savers. Financial intermediaries include *commercial banks, thrift institutions, insurance com-*

panies, pension funds, mutual funds, and a few others.

3. *Money* is an asset that serves as a means of payment, a store of value, and a unit of account. In the U.S. economy two types of assets serve as money: *currency* (coins and bills) and *checking deposits* at banks and thrift institutions.

4. Deposits appear as liabilities on a bank's balance sheet. Under a system of *fractional-reserve banking* like that of the United States, banks keep as reserves a fraction of the deposits they take in and lend out the rest. Banks earn a profit by charging a higher interest rate on loans than the rate they pay on deposits. In the process of accepting deposits and making loans, banks create money. About three quarters of the U.S. money supply is in the form of checking deposits at banks and thrift institutions.

5. The Federal Reserve System, or Fed, was formed in 1913. It provides services like check clearing, but the main reason for setting up the Fed was to stabilize the banking system. The Fed does this by making sure that banks follow sound business practices and by supplying them with extra reserves when needed. In 1934 federal deposit insurance was introduced to give the banking system further stability.

6. Today the Fed serves as a partner, with Congress and the executive branch, in the making of economic policy. The Fed can pursue an easy money policy by injecting reserves into the banking system, thereby making loans more available and causing the money supply to grow. However, this tends to cause inflation. The Fed can fight inflation with a tight money policy, which is achieved by slowing the growth of bank reserves. Federal Reserve policy also has a major effect on the level of interest rates.

7. The U.S. financial system is going through a period of change. The Monetary Control Act of 1980 relaxed many of the restrictions that formerly protected banks and thrifts from competition. In order to survive in the new competitive world of banking, bank managers will have to pay more attention to innovation, marketing, and strategic planning.

KEY TERMS

You should be familiar with the following terms and concepts. Check their meanings by referring to the marginal definitions in the chapter or to the glossary at the end of the book.

Financial system	Credit union	Currency
Direct financing	Thrift institution (thrift)	Checking deposit
Indirect financing	Insurance company	Credit card
Financial intermediary	Pension fund	Debit card
Commercial bank	Mutual fund	Fractional-reserve banking
Savings and loan association (savings and loan)	Money market fund	Check clearing
	Money	Open-market operation
Mutual savings bank	Barter	

QUESTIONS FOR REVIEW AND DISCUSSION

1. Look in the yellow pages of your local telephone directory or the directory of a city near you. See how many different kinds of financial intermediaries you can find. What services are offered by each kind? How many kinds of intermediaries have you done business with at one time or another?

2. In the world of finance, money has the precise meaning given in the text. In everyday life, we use the word *money* more loosely. For example, we might say, "Look at that lady in the fur coat—she must have a lot of money." In fact, the woman in question has a house worth $500,000, a car worth $50,000, a fur coat worth $10,000, stocks and bonds worth $1 million, a $5000 balance in her checking account, and $310.37 in currency in her purse. What is her total wealth (*wealth* refers to the total value of a person's assets)? How much money does she have? What is the difference between money and wealth?

3. In everyday life we often say "money" when we should say "income." For example, you might say, "I want to study accounting so that I can make a lot of money after I graduate." But only the government and counterfeiters "make" money. How should you rephrase the statement about why you want to study accounting? What is the difference between money and income?

4. Do you have a bank credit card such as a VISA card or MasterCard? Do you have a debit card? If you have either type of card, what was the most recent purchase you made with it? Describe the sequence of events that resulted from your use of the card.

5. Turn to the last balance sheet for Bill's Wolf Creek Bank (page 492). Starting at that point, enter the following transactions on the bank's balance sheet.

a. Carl Cramer deposits $5000 in a savings account. List the savings account separately from checking accounts under the heading of liabilities. Make the matching change on the left-hand side of the balance sheet.

b. Bill keeps $1000 of Carl's deposit as reserves. No one applies for a loan right away. In order to put the remaining $4000 of Carl's deposit to work earning interest, Bill buys $4000 worth of government bonds. Update the balance sheet.

c. Edith Bender comes into the bank and withdraws $50 from her account. Update the balance sheet.

6. It is 1893 and you are living in Toledo, Ohio. Your neighbor stops you on the street and says, "Did you hear? The Merchant's Commercial Bank of Cleveland has closed its doors. It can't pay its depositors!" What will you do about your account at the First Toledo Bank? Why?

7. Go to your library and browse through all the issues of the *Wall Street Journal* for a recent week. Look through both sections of the paper for articles that discuss money, interest rates, inflation, and the actions of the Federal Reserve. How are the Fed's actions expected to affect inflation and/or interest rates?

Case 19–1: The Balance Sheet of the Palmer National Bank

Here are some items from the balance sheet of the Palmer National Bank (amounts, in millions of dollars):

Cash and other reserves	4.1
Checking deposits	2.5
Savings and other deposits	11.4
Government bonds and other securities owned	3.5
Loans	7.9
Fixed assets	0.5
Other assets	1.5
Other liabilities	2.2

Questions:

1. Arrange these items in the form of a balance sheet. What is the owner's equity in the bank? What are total assets? Total liabilities?

2. Which items are income-producing assets? Which result in interest expenses for the bank?

Chapter 20
THE SECURITIES MARKETS

When you have completed this chapter, you should be able to

- Explain the difference between *investment income* and *speculative income*.

- Discuss the connection between the riskiness of securities and their rates of return, and explain how risk can be reduced through *diversification*.

- Distinguish between *primary* and *secondary* securities markets and explain the roles of intermediaries in those markets, including *investment bankers*, *stockbrokers*, and *dealers*.

- Explain how stocks and bonds are traded on *stock exchanges* and in the *over-the-counter market*.

- Describe the main federal and state regulations that govern securities markets.

- Contrast three theories of investment: *fundamental analysis*, *technical analysis*, and the *efficient-market hypothesis*.

Blue-sky law: Any of a number of state laws that attempt to combat fraud in securities markets.

Securities and Exchange Commission (SEC): The federal agency that regulates securities markets.

The Securities and Exchange Commission, headquartered in Washington, D.C., is charged with regulating the securities markets. Courtesy of Securities & Exchange Commission

Insider trading: Purchase or sale of a firm's stock by its officers or other people with access to information that is not yet known to the public.

They have come to be known as **blue-sky laws** because fraudulent stocks and bonds were said to have no more value than pieces of blue sky. The blue-sky laws require companies that issue securities to provide investors with basic financial information and to meet certain standards of financial soundness. They also require securities firms and brokers to be licensed.

Besides the state laws, a series of federal laws regulate securities markets. The Security Act of 1933 set up the **Securities and Exchange Commission (SEC)**. All firms that issue securities are required to register them with the SEC. In doing so they must disclose certain information to investors in the form of a document called a *prospectus*.

Since 1933 the Security Act has been supplemented by other federal laws. A 1934 law extended its coverage from new issues to all securities. In 1940 it was extended again to cover shares in mutual funds.

Firms with listed securities must file an annual statement, known as a 10-K report, with the SEC. The 10-K report contains financial information like the balance sheets and income statements discussed in Chapter 18.

Self-Regulation

The securities industry also regulates itself. The stock exchanges require their members to know their field of work and to follow a code of ethics. They prohibit specialists and other members from unfairly profiting at the expense of clients. Over-the-counter markets are regulated by the National Association of Securities Dealers.

The Securities Investor Protection Corporation

In the 1960s some major brokerage firms went bankrupt. Some of their clients lost large sums. To reduce this risk and build confidence in securities markets, Congress formed the Securities Investor Protection Corporation (SIPC) in 1970. The SIPC insures investors against losses up to $500,000 that result from failures of brokerage firms. Of course, this does not protect investors against losses caused by changes in the prices of securities or by failure of the firms that issue them.

Insider Trading Regulations

Among the most controversial of the SEC's regulations are its bans on **insider trading**. Insider trading means sales or purchases of a stock by a firm's officers or other people with access to information that is not yet known to the public. For example, a manager of a drug company learns that its researchers have made a breakthrough in finding a cure for the common cold. Knowing that the new drug would be worth billions, the manager could make a huge profit by buying the firm's stock before the breakthrough is announced. But SEC rules prohibit the purchase. They also outlaw sales of the stock based on bad news that has not yet been announced. Violators are subject to criminal penalties and are also required to pay back any gains they have made as a result of insider trading.

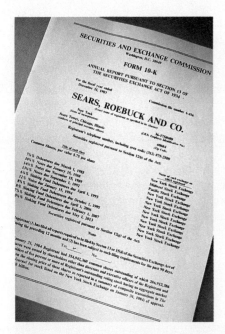

Firms with listed securities must file a 10-K report with the Securities and Exchange Commission. Marc P. Anderson

In recent years the SEC has stepped up enforcement of its ban on insider trading.

Investors and regulators tend to see the ban on insider trading as a key part of the SEC's job of maintaining a fair playing field. But many students of the market believe the rules do little good and may even be harmful.

One problem is that most inside information does not come in the form of sudden news of a research breakthrough or product disaster. Instead, it comes in the form of knowledge that something *might* happen. Everyone knows a certain drug firm is working on a cure for the common cold. The public might give it a 10 percent chance of succeeding. As lab reports come in, it may seem to insiders on some days that the chance has risen to 12 percent, or fallen to 8 percent. Trading on this kind of information cannot be prevented unless ownership of a firm's stock by its managers is outlawed altogether. And given the role of stock ownership as a management incentive, no one would want to do that.

The upshot is that a lot of insider trading goes on that the SEC is powerless to stop. Studies have shown time and again that good and bad news tends to be reflected in a stock's price before formal announcements are made. The handful of cases in which insider trading takes a form that the SEC can prosecute are only the tip of the iceberg.

Critics of the SEC also point out that insider trading is itself a way of disclosing information to the public. This disclosure takes the form of movements in stock prices that result from inside trading. To continue our example, suppose that the drug company discovers its cold remedy on March 1 and plans to announce it on March 15. Without insider trading, the market price will stay low until the 15th and will then jump. With insider trading, the price will start rising soon after the first of the month as a result of active buying by insiders. If John Public had planned to buy the firm's stock on, say, March 14, he will be harmed by the insider trading, because he will have to pay more for the stock than he otherwise would. But what if John had planned to sell the stock on the 14th? In that case insider trading will make him better off because the price will already have risen by that date. In short, insider trading may hurt some outsiders, but it helps others. There is no reason, say the critics, to think that more people are hurt than are helped.[2]

It should be kept in mind that those who think insider trading should be legal are, for the most part, economists and professors of business. Those who think it should be outlawed are running the SEC and have the power to prosecute.

PLAYING THE MARKETS

Up to this point we have looked at securities markets as part of the financial system. We have seen how both primary and secondary markets are needed to supply firms with a steady flow of investment funds. We have

---

[2]The leading critic of the SEC's ban on insider trading is lawyer-economist Henry Manne. His 1966 book *Insider Trading and the Stock Market* is the most thorough statement of the case. For a summary of the debate, see Daniel Seligman, "An Economic Defense of Insider Trading," *Fortune*, September 5, 1983, pp. 47–48.

looked at some of the mechanics of stock and bond trading. And we have seen how markets are regulated. In this last section we will look at the same markets from a different point of view: the point of view of the individual investor.

Not all investors come to the market with the same goals. Some come as speculators, taking big risks in the hope of making big gains. Some buy for investment income with well-defined goals, such as providing for their retirement or paying for their children's education. Just as investors' goals differ, theories about how to achieve those goals differ too. Here we will look at three theories of investment. Each has its supporters who are sure that their theory is right and the others are nonsense. This clash of views is one of the things that makes the study of securities markets so fascinating. And as we will see, the followers of each theory, in their own way, contribute to the strength of the securities markets.

Fundamental Analysis

Fundamental analysis: An approach to stock market trading based on the study of trends in the economy and analysis of the strengths and weaknesses of individual firms and industries.

The first theory of investment says that the best way to play the market is to study every detail of firms, industries, and economic trends before choosing a portfolio. An ideal portfolio, in this view, contains securities whose potential returns are highest relative to their current market prices. This approach is known as **fundamental analysis**.

Fundamental analysis begins with an evaluation of factors that affect the market as a whole. For example, the NYSE composite average began 1984 at a level of 95. The first question that an analyst of fundamentals would ask is whether this level is too high or too low in relation to the outlook for business in general. Profit forecasts for 1984 were very favorable, but one can assume that other investors already knew this in bidding the average up to 95 from its level of 81 a year earlier. The analyst would want to go over the economic forecasts line by line, maybe adding some judgments on the outcome of the 1984 elections. If the market average of 95 was thought to be too optimistic, the investor would switch some of his or her portfolio out of stocks and into less risky bonds. If it was judged to be not optimistic enough, the portfolio would be loaded up with stocks.

The next step is to look at stocks on an industry-by-industry basis. Will a big federal budget deficit push interest rates up? If so, industries that need to borrow heavily might be at a disadvantage. Are high profits likely to make unions aggressive in 1984? If so, highly unionized industries like steel and autos might be hurt. In each case the industry's prospects are compared with the current prices of stocks of the firms in that industry. It may be that buying into a sluggish industry whose shares have been scorned by other investors will be smarter than following the pack into a high-flying sector whose prices have already been bid up above their true value.

Finally, the analyst looks at individual firms. Every shred of data that bears on a firm's prospects is studied. How strong is the firm's balance sheet? Every accounting assumption gets a critical look. How do the firm's customers view its products? A serious analyst might do some market research. To find out about the firm's labor relations, the analyst might visit a plant and chat with some of the workers. Information that everyone in the market knows will not help, because it will already be reflected in the market price of the firm's stock. Instead, the analyst is searching for

Drawing by Saxon; © 1983 *The New Yorker Magazine*, Inc.

"Mrs. Liscombe? We are from the S.E.C. As you undoubtedly know, the stock market dropped 21.5 points last Thursday because of a rumor that interest rates are going up. We have traced that rumor to you, Mrs. Liscombe, and we are here to request that you keep your perceptions to yourself."

some extra information or an added insight that offers a clue that other investors have undervalued or overvalued the firm's stock.

Fundamental analysis is the most respected approach to investment among Wall Street professionals. Thousands of men and women, highly trained in finance, accounting, statistics, economics, and production technology, spend their full time following the activities of listed and OTC firms. Some of these analysts work for brokerage firms and give advice to the firms' clients. Others work for pension funds, mutual funds, or other institutional investors. Some write newsletters or columns in financial newspapers. Some are speculators who use what they learn to buy and sell on their own account. Untold millions of shares of stock are traded on the basis of fundamental analysis.

Technical Analysis

Technical analysis: An approach to stock market trading that attempts to pick winners by studying the behavior of other investors as revealed in past stock price movements.

The second approach to playing the stock market is **technical analysis**. Technical analysts believe that winners can be picked not by looking at the companies that issue the stocks but, instead, by studying the behavior of other investors.

For technical analysts, clues to the future behavior of investors can be found by studying their past behavior as reflected in past stock price movements. As an example, look at the "head-and-shoulders" approach outlined in Box 20–7. A user of this approach searches through the price charts for many stocks, looking for a certain pattern. The pattern shows a tentative peak in the price, followed by a modest decline. This is the "left shoulder." Next a stronger peak appears (the "head"), followed by another

Box 20–7 The Head-and-Shoulders Formation

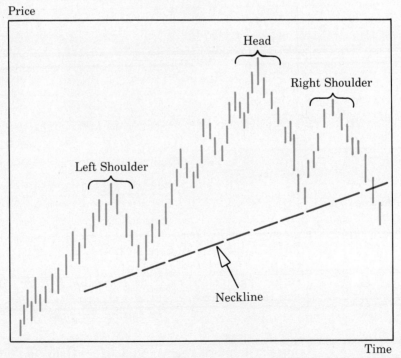

Technical analysts try to predict movements in stock prices by looking for patterns in past movements. One of the classic patterns is the so-called head-and-shoulders formation shown here. First the stock price rises to a low peak, called the left shoulder; then it falls. Next it rises to a stronger peak, the head, and then to a third peak, the right shoulder. The analyst then watches to see if the price will fall through the "neckline"—a line connecting the previous lows. A fall through the neckline is viewed as a signal to sell. If the price rises again without breaking through the neckline, the stock should be held for a while.

decline. Before it reaches its previous low, however, the price climbs to a third peak at the right shoulder. Now the analyst draws a "neckline" connecting the previous lows for the stock. If the price drops past the right shoulder and keeps heading down, the theory goes, it is in for a long decline. As soon as the price breaks through the neckline, it should be sold.

Technical analysts claim to see hundreds of patterns, many of which are much more subtle than the head-and-shoulders pattern. Fundamental analysts view the technicians' charts as little more than black magic. Even so, technical analysis has a lot of suppport on Wall Street. The claim that the charts can pick stock market winners and losers does not hold up well in statistical studies, but a good living can still be made selling advice based on them.

The Efficient-Market Hypothesis

The third approach to playing the market is very different from either fundamental or technical analysis. Both of those approaches are attempts to practice informed speculation. They look for winning stocks and for the best times to buy and sell. The third approach says that attempts at informed speculation are doomed to failure because all available information is already reflected in the price of every security. Because this approach assumes that markets are efficient processors of information, it is known as the **efficient-market hypothesis (EMH)**.

Efficient-market hypothesis (EMH): The belief that securities prices reflect all the information available at any given time.

Believers in the EMH offer this advice to investors: First, decide on the general types of securities that your portfolio should contain, taking into account your feelings about risk, your need for cash, and your tax situation. (For example, to reduce risk you might buy relatively more bonds and relatively less stock.) Second, choose a diversified portfolio so that the risks of some securities will be offset by the risks of others. Don't worry much about which firms to choose within each category of risk or tax treatment. And third, once you have assembled a portfolio, hold onto it. Active trading in the hope of speculative gains will only enrich your broker through the commissions you will have to pay each time stocks are bought and sold.

The EMH is far and away the dominant view among economists and others who have studied the securities markets. There is very strong evidence that portfolios chosen by technical or fundamental analysis do not, except by chance, earn better returns than equally diversified portfolios chosen at random. For example, mutual funds that are based on fundamental or technical analysis do not, on the average, earn higher than normal returns even though they hire the most talented managers they can find.

There is a paradox in the EMH, however. Although it says that the average investor should not spend money on analysts' advice and should not speculate, the EMH does assign a role to analysts and speculators. Trading by analysts and speculators is the thing that makes the market efficient in the first place. The EMH says that all new information that becomes available is soon reflected in the prices of securities, but how does that happen? It happens because as soon as a good guess can be made about an event that will favorably affect the outlook for a firm, speculators begin buying its stock, thereby driving up the price. Likewise, at the first glimpse of bad news those same traders sell, driving the price down. But because there are so many analysts, all of whom are so good at their jobs, no one of them can hope to be the first to trade on new information very often. At best, their efforts give them a very slight edge, just enough to repay the energy they put into their analysis and the commissions they pay their brokers. Luckily, this is enough to get them to stick to their jobs of analyzing and speculating, thereby making the market efficient for the rest of us.

SUMMARY

1. Both *individual investors* (households) and *institutional investors* (pension funds, mutual funds, and so on) buy stocks, bonds, and other securities as a source of income. The income comes in two forms. *Investment income* is the expected return from holding a stock or bond that is bought at a fair price. *Speculative income* is the return from holding a stock or bond whose price increases more than expected. The line between investment and speculation is not a sharp one, however. There are risks in all securities, and riskier ones tend to yield higher returns than less risky ones. The riskiness of a *portfolio* of securities can be reduced through *diversification*.

2. The *primary securities market* is the set of institutions through which newly issued securities are sold to investors. Some firms market their own securities, but many use intermediaries known as *investment bankers*. Investment bankers sometimes act as agents, arranging sales of securities and charging a commission. More often they act as *underwriters*. As such, they buy securities at a discount from the firm that issues them, and sell them to investors at a price high enough to yield a profit.

3. *Secondary securities markets* are those in which owners of previously issued securities buy and sell them. The best known of these markets are the *stock exchanges*. These have trading floors where *stockbrokers* meet to make trades for their clients. The New York Stock Exchange is by far the largest.

4. Securities that are not listed on one of the stock exchanges are traded in the so-called *over-the-counter (OTC) market*. The OTC market has no trading floor. It is a network of hundreds of *dealers* who keep in touch by telephone and computer. OTC dealers, unlike brokers on the stock exchanges, buy and sell securities on their own accounts. They make a profit by offering to buy at a *bid* price that is slightly lower than the *asked* price at which they offer to sell. Stocks of smaller firms, many government securities, and most short-term securities are traded over the counter.

5. Securities markets, like other financial institutions, are regulated by state and federal governments. The chief federal regulatory agency is the *Securities and Exchange Commission*. Regulations set standards of conduct for dealers and brokers, require firms that issue securities to give accurate information to investors, and try to keep trading fair.

6. There are three major schools of thought about how to go about investing in securities. *Fundamental analysis* holds that the best way to assemble a portfolio is to study economic forecasts, industry trends, and data on specific firms. The *technical analysis* school believes that winners can be picked by watching the behavior of other investors as revealed by past movements of stock prices. The third school, based on the *efficient-market hypothesis* (EMH), believes that all the available information about a firm is already reflected in the price of its stock. Supporters of this approach advise buying a diversified portfolio and holding it for investment income.

KEY TERMS

You should be familiar with the following terms and concepts. Check their meanings by referring to the marginal definitions in the chapter or to the glossary at the end of the book.

Securities	Institutional investor	Speculative income
Individual investor	Investment income	Diversification

Portfolio

Primary securities market

Secondary securities markets

Private placement

Investment banker

Underwriting

Stock exchange

Stockbroker

Commission broker

Specialist

Stock option

Over-the-counter (OTC) market

Dealer

Bid price

Asked price

Discount broker

Blue-sky law

Securities and Exchange
    Commission (SEC)

Insider trading

Fundamental analysis

Technical analysis

Efficient-market hypothesis
    (EMH)

QUESTIONS FOR REVIEW AND DISCUSSION

1. Comment on the Super Bowl–stock market relationship from the point of view of fundamental analysis, technical analysis, and the efficient-market hypothesis. Which of these, if any, would see the Super Bowl as a valid indicator of stock price movements?

2. Do you own any stocks? If so, in what firms? If not, why not? Don't say it's because you can't afford it! Even the New York Stock Exchange lists many stocks priced at less than $5 a share. But would there be any point in buying one or a few shares in such a firm? Why or why not?

3. Go to your library and find some old copies of the *Wall Street Journal*, the *New York Times*, or some other newspaper with a financial section that carries daily stock market reports. Pick one or a few stocks and "buy" 100 shares of each on a date that you choose. You can pick your stocks at random, but to make the game more interesting you may want to read some articles in the paper and find a company that looks promising. Next check the prices of your stocks six months or a year later. Has the value of your portfolio increased? Do you think the increase, if any, is speculative or investment income? What would you need to know to tell which kind of income it is?

4. Compare what you have learned about intermediaries in financial markets with what you learned about wholesalers and retailers in Chapter 10. Include both the securities intermediaries discussed in this chapter and the financial intermediaries discussed in Chapter 19. Which ones perform retail-type functions? Which ones are more like wholesalers? Which take title to the goods they deal in and then resell them, as merchant wholesalers do? Which ones arrange trades without taking title, as agent wholesalers do? What differences set the investment bankers, brokers, and dealers discussed in this chapter apart from the banking, insurance, and investment groups discussed in Chapter 19?

5. In January 1984, Kmart stock is selling at a market price of $32.50 a share. You feel sure that it will fall to $25 or less in the next three months. What are three ways in which you could profit from your hunch?

6. Suppose that legislation modeled after federal deposit insurance is introduced in Congress to protect investors against losses caused by declines in stock prices. For example, if you bought 100 shares of United Airlines at $37 and later sold them at $20, the government would pay you $1700 ($17 per share). The limit might be set at, say, $10,000 per investor per year. Would you favor such legislation? Do you think it would strengthen the securities market the way federal deposit insurance seems to have strengthened the banking system? Why or why not? Write a short letter to your member of Congress saying why you favor or oppose the proposed law.

7. Go to your library and browse through some financial magazines, such as *Business Week*, *Fortune*, or *Forbes*. Look for articles suggesting that certain firms or industries are good or bad ones to invest in. Which approach to investing do the articles seem to follow—fundamental analysis, technical analysis, or the efficient-market hypothesis? Explain how the articles fit one or another of these schools of thought.

Case 20–1: An Improving Environment for Waste Control Stocks

Disposing of toxic wastes is a dirty, smelly, and potentially deadly undertaking. But with public opinion, growing government regulation, and an expanding economy all pointing to increased demand for hazardous-waste disposal services, the outlook has never been rosier for the handful of public companies in this business. Scared off earlier this year by adverse publicity surrounding Waste Management Inc., investors are just beginning to recognize the improved fundamentals for this much-maligned industry.

After lagging behind the market throughout 1983, the "pollution control" group of Standard & Poor's 500-stock index perked up in late August. The group rose 4.7 percent during the final week, more than double the market's gain. The biggest advance was posted by Waste Management, the country's largest waste-disposal company, rising to about $48.50 from $43 in only seven trading days. Even so, since January 1 the pollution control group has dipped by 2.1 percent, while the Standard & Poor 500 has risen 16.9 percent.

Most of the good news for the hazardous-waste disposal industry is emanating from Washington. The Environmental Protection Agency recently raised its estimate of the amount of hazardous waste generated yearly in the country from 40 million to 150 million metric tons, suggesting that the potential market for hazardous waste processors is much larger than previously thought. To get at some of the worst messes, the EPA is just beginning to parcel out some $1.6 billion in cleanup funds set aside by Congress in 1980.

Moreover, Congress in October is expected to enact laws so extensive that even such small-scale toxic waste producers as neighborhood dry cleaners and service stations will come under the regulators' scrutiny. "Almost all the new people pulled under the regulatory umbrella will be without their own means to get rid of the waste," says Henry L. Jicha, Jr., an analyst for Prudential-Bache Securities Inc. The legislation could enlarge the toxic-waste disposal market by 30 percent, predicts Jack Lurcott, a vice-president of Browning-Ferris Industries Inc., the No. 2 waste disposer.

The law, by requiring incineration, is also expected to push the industry away from the relatively cheap but environmentally suspect method of dumping wastes in landfills. Browning-Ferris and Waste Management rely on landfills, but have been expanding their incineration capacity. Although the stocks of SCA Services Inc. and Rollins Environmental Services Inc. have lagged, these companies are expected to profit through heavy investments in incineration.

Rollins is the only major company that is a "pure play" in hazardous wastes. The others primarily collect, process, and dispose of residential, commercial, and industrial garbage. But Rollins' stock already sells at a hefty 32 times last year's earnings. Because of its high price-earnings ratio, Wall Street analysts are not pushing it and are lining up instead behind Waste Management (with a price-earnings ratio of 20) and Browning-Ferris (price-earnings ratio of 17). Anchored by their garbage businesses, both companies are expected to rack up annual earnings growth of 20 to 30 percent over the next five years.

Unlike some growth businesses, hazardous waste processors get a boost from a turn in the economy because they feed off the highly cyclical chemical industry. On the other hand, these stocks are continually haunted by the threat of a toxic-waste equivalent of Three Mile Island. The sudden fall of Waste Management demonstrated the group's extreme vulnerability to the vagaries of public opinion. Following published reports of alleged mismanagement and illegal disposal of toxic substances last March, the stock dropped 34 percent in just a few weeks.

"Those articles were just a rehash," contends Kay Hahn, an analyst with A. G. Becker Paribas Inc. Waste Management denied the allegations but nonetheless instituted new management controls at its dump sites. Had they been in place earlier, they "would have prevented what was alleged to have happened," concedes Harold Gershowitz, a senior vice-president at Waste.

Yet not everyone on Wall Street is a cheerleader for Waste Management. E. F. Hutton Group Inc.'s Douglas R. Augenthaler is bullish on the industry but wary of the company; cleaning up a Colorado landfill site under pressure from the state could cost Waste $10 million. Although this would amount to only 10 cents a share on earnings of $2.70 per share likely this year, Augenthaler argues that the problem refutes Waste's "supposed infallibility."

Source: "An Improving Environment for Waste Disposal Stocks," *Business Week*, September 19, 1983, p. 102.

Questions:

1. Which theory of investment underlies this case—fundamental analysis, technical analysis, or the efficient-market hypothesis? Explain.

2. Fundamental analysis looks at investment prospects on three levels: prospects for the economy, for the industry, and for individual firms. Give examples from this case of all three levels of analysis.

3. "You might as well pick stocks by throwing darts as by reading articles like this one. Even if the writer is correct about the future profits of the firms discussed, you can be sure that a lot of people will already have used the information as a basis for buying and selling stocks before the magazine reaches subscribers. The prices of the firms with good growth prospects will thus already be bid up to a level that leaves no room for speculative profits by readers." Do you think this argument is valid? Why or why not?

4. You are a supervisor at a facility belonging to Waste Disposal, Inc. You find out that the site's manager, hoping to look good on his annual performance review, has been cutting corners on safety procedures in order to keep costs down. Taking advantage of what you know, you call your broker and ask that certain securities transactions be made that will put you in a position to profit if the price of Waste Disposal's stock falls. You then make an anonymous phone call to the local TV station and reveal that the company is violating safety standards.

What transactions would you have asked your broker to carry out? Would your actions be legal? Why or why not? Who would have been harmed by your actions? Who would have been helped?

Chapter 21

INSURANCE AND RISK MANAGEMENT

When you have completed this chapter, you should be able to

- Define *risk* and distinguish between *speculative* and *pure* risk.

- List four methods of *risk management* and explain the uses of each.

- Outline the six steps in the process of risk management.

- Compare stockholder-owned companies, mutual companies, *Lloyd's associations*, and government agencies as ways of providing insurance.

- Define *insurable risk*, *insurable interest*, *moral* and *morale hazard*, and *adverse selection*, and explain the role of each in determining the kinds of coverage that private insurance companies can provide.

- Discuss the regulation of insurance.

- Discuss current issues facing the insurance industry in the areas of life and health insurance, and sex discrimination in insurance.

James H. Smith and his wife, intending to panel their bathroom, bought two 1-gallon cans of Wal-lite, a solvent-based adhesive. The directions on the can were as follows:

DANGER
EXTREMELY FLAMMABLE
VAPORS MAY CAUSE FLASH FIRE
VAPORS HARMFUL
See Cautions on back panel

The back label carried the following admonitions:

CONTAINS HEXANE. Vapors may ignite explosively. Prevent buildup of vapors—open windows and doors—use only with cross ventilation. Do not smoke, extinguish all flames and pilot lights; turn off stoves, heaters, electric motors, and other sources of ignition during use and until all vapors are gone. Do not take internally. Avoid prolonged contact with skin and breathing of vapor. Keep away from heat, sparks, and open flame. Close container after each use.

Mr. Smith turned off the hot water heater and the pilot light on the kitchen stove and opened the front and back doors. He opened a can of Wal-lite and started to apply the adhesive over the bathroom window, which was closed and sealed shut. Mrs. Smith turned on a fan across the hall from the bathroom. As she reentered the bathroom, a blue flame erupted under Mr. Smith's trowel and an explosion occurred, injuring him seriously. Smith sued the manufacturer, U.S. Gypsum Company, and the distributor, Chicago Mastic Company, for product liability. A jury trial was held and Smith won a judgment for $600,000 in damages.

U.S. Gypsum filed an appeal, holding that its product was not unreasonably dangerous. It argued that Smith had ignored the warning that Wal-lite should be used only in a room with cross-ventilation.

In deciding the appeal, the judge noted that "unreasonably dangerous" is defined as "dangerous to an extent beyond that which would be contemplated by the ordinary consumer who purchases it." "A manufacturer must anticipate all foreseeable uses of his product," the judge said. U.S. Gypsum "should have known that some users would install paneling in a room without a window." He noted that far from ignoring the warnings on the can, the Smiths had read them and had complied in the best way they thought possible. They saw the open door and the fan as added precautions that were needed because the room did not have a window that could be opened. They could not reasonably have foreseen that a spark from the fan's motor, across the hall, could set off an explosion, and in fact it was not proved that the fan had caused the explosion. The judge upheld the judgment against U.S. Gypsum.[1]

[1] *Smith* v. *United States Gypsum Co.*, 612 P.2nd 251 (Okla. 1980). This account of the case is based on a summary in Ralph C. Hoeber et al., *Contemporary Business Law*, 2nd ed. (New York: McGraw-Hill, 1982), pp. 115–17.

The story of Wal-lite is one of risk—risk of injury to the Smiths and risk of business loss to U.S. Gypsum. The case is not unusual. A firm makes a product that is hazardous to use and prints a warning on it. A consumer buys it, reads the warning, and takes care, but an accident happens anyway. The case illustrates the central point of this chapter: risk is a fact of life that will not go away. The challenge is how best to manage it.

We will begin the chapter by discussing the meaning of risk and the process of risk management. Next we will look at the role of insurance companies in managing risk. In the final section we will look at a number of issues facing the insurance industry in the 1980s.

RISK AND RISK MANAGEMENT

Risk: Uncertainty about a possible loss.

Risk means uncertainty about a possible loss. We face risks every day. Some, like the risk of being struck by a meteor, are trivial. Some, like that of being injured in an auto accident, must be taken seriously. Some are risks that we get ourselves into—when we buy a lottery ticket, we accept a high risk of losing the price of the ticket in exchange for a small chance of winning a lot of money. Some are unavoidable—we are uncertain about the length of our lives, but we know we will not live forever. Some risks, like that of a broken leg, involve physical pain. Some, like the risk of a fall in the price of a stock, hurt only our wallets. Some, like the risk of being turned down when asking for a date, threaten our egos. The factor of uncertainty is common to all these risks.

Types of Risks

There are several ways to classify risks. It is common, for example, to distinguish *speculative risk* from *pure risk*. A **speculative risk** is one that involves the chance of a gain as well as the chance of a loss. Buying a lottery ticket or a share of stock is a speculative risk. A **pure risk**, on the other hand, involves only the chance of a loss. The chance of an airplane crash is a pure risk. If the plane lands safely, the passengers don't feel that they have won anything, but if it does not, they have certainly lost.

Speculative risk: A risk that involves the chance of a gain as well as the chance of a loss.

Pure risk: A risk that involves only the chance of a loss.

Both pure and speculative risks can be managed. In earlier chapters we discussed the management of speculative risks at some length. Chapter 17 showed how the proper balance of long- and short-term financing and the proper degree of leverage can control the risks of raising funds for a firm. In Chapter 19 we discussed the risks of the banking business and explained the steps that the government has taken to limit them. And Chapter 20 showed how diversification can be used to manage the risks of buying stocks and bonds. In this chapter, we turn to the management of pure risk.

Personal risk: The risk of a direct loss to a person, such as a risk to life or health.

Property risk: The risk of destruction, theft, or loss of the use of property.

Pure risks can be grouped by type of loss. A **personal risk** is one that causes direct loss to a person—risks to life and health and the risk of the loss of one's job are examples. A **property risk** is one that affects people indirectly through destruction, theft, or loss of the use of property. Finally, a **liability risk** is the risk of financial loss when a firm's or a person's actions cause personal or property loss to someone else. The $600,000 loss

Liability risk: The risk of financial loss when a firm's or a person's actions cause personal or property loss to someone else.

suffered by U.S. Gypsum when its adhesive exploded and injured Mr. Smith was a personal risk for Smith and a liability risk for the company.

As the chapter continues, we will find still other useful ways to classify risk.

Methods of Risk Management

Risk management: The task of reducing the costs connected with risk.

Risk management is the task of reducing the costs connected with risk. This means more than just keeping losses to a minimum. Losses are costly, but taking steps to keep them from happening is costly too. A good risk manager balances these two kinds of costs in planning how best to deal with a risky world. This means choosing among four methods of managing risk: avoidance, loss prevention and control, insurance, and absorption.

Avoidance. The first method of risk management is to avoid the risk. For a person, this might mean not smoking or not flying. For a firm, it might mean taking a product like Wal-lite adhesive off the market, even though it does the job well when used safely.

Risk avoidance is an effective way to cut losses. The problem is that in avoiding the risks of some activities one also avoids the benefits. People who choose not to fly miss many chances to see faraway friends and places. Firms that avoid new products because they might be risky cut themselves off from markets that might be profitable. Risk avoidance thus is not the whole answer to risk management.

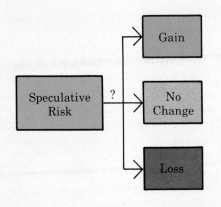

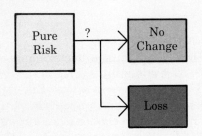

Loss prevention and control. Losses caused by risky activities that one chooses not to avoid can often be either prevented or controlled. To prevent a loss means to keep it from happening; to control it means to limit the damage if a loss does occur. A good rule of loss prevention for a person is not to drive after drinking. But since some accidents happen even when one is sober, it is also a good idea to wear a seat belt to limit injuries. A gas station owner might try to prevent loss from robbery by keeping the office well lit after dark. But since there is a chance that even a well-lit station will be robbed, losses can be controlled by limiting the amount of cash kept in the office.

To prevent a loss means to keep it from happening. Many firms attempt to prevent losses by warning employees about hazards in the workplace. © Freda Leinwand

Insurance: A process in which a group of people who are exposed to the same kinds of risks place funds in a common pool from which members who suffer losses are compensated.

Insurance. Even when all cost-effective steps are taken to avoid, prevent, and control losses, some will occur. A balanced risk management program therefore almost always includes **insurance**. Insurance is a process in which a group of people who are exposed to the same kinds of risks place funds in a pool from which members who suffer losses are compensated.

Look at fire insurance. The chance that any one house in a town of 1000 houses will burn down in a given year is, say, 1 in 200. For the few whose houses burn down, the loss will be severe; the average house might cost $80,000 to rebuild. Instead of accepting a 1-in-200 chance of an $80,000 loss, the homeowners could agree that each would put $400 a year into an insurance fund. (This sum is equal to the $80,000 value of the average house divided by the 1-in-200 chance of fire.) In return, the fund would pay for rebuilding the five houses that burn down in an average year.

This example is simplified, of course. Later sections of the chapter will fill in the details of how insurance works. But the example captures the main idea of insurance, that of spreading losses among a group of people who are exposed to the same kind of risk.

Absorption. The final method of risk management is to absorb the risk, that is, to accept the risk of loss without spreading it by means of insurance. A person or firm may decide to absorb risks for two reasons.

First, there are cases in which other methods of risk management are not worth the cost. This is often the case with risks that have only a small chance of taking place. For example, most people absorb the risk of being hit by a meteor rather than, for example, living near the North or South Pole, where fewer meteors strike. Absorption is also the best way to handle risks that involve small losses. For example, many people who drive old clunkers don't find it worthwhile to buy collision insurance.

Self-insurance: A process in which an organization that is exposed to many risks of the same kind sets aside funds from which to cover any losses that result.

Large firms may have a second reason to absorb risks. They may be able to practice **self-insurance**, a process in which an organization that is exposed to many risks of the same kind sets aside funds from which to cover any losses that result. For example, the owner of a single taxi would probably buy collision insurance to pay for the cost of repairing the cab in case of an accident. But the owner of a big fleet of taxis could predict a certain number of accidents a year and set aside a fund for making the repairs. This would save some of the costs of dealing with an insurance company. The federal government self-insures for most risks. Some large

Some automobile owners prefer to absorb the risk of damage rather than buy collision insurance. © Charles Anderson

firms form "captive" insurance companies that provide insurance only for the parent firm.

The Process of Risk Management

Many large firms employ full-time risk managers. These managers plan the firm's risk management strategy, buy insurance, and direct the firm's efforts to control losses. In small firms, risk management is one of the many jobs of the proprietor. Risk management is also a major part of managing a household.

Small-business managers and households often depend on insurance agents for risk management planning and advice. A good agent does much more than sell insurance. He or she also gives advice on how to save on insurance premiums by choosing which losses to avoid, prevent, control, or absorb.

Whoever is in charge of risk management, the process can be broken down into six steps: setting goals, identifying risks, evaluating the risks, choosing methods of managing the risks, carrying out these methods, and reviewing the results.

Setting goals. The first step is to set goals. For a household, those goals might include access to good health care; maintenance of the family's standard of living in case of the death or disability of an income earner; and protection of major assets like cars and a house. For a business, the chief goal is often to ensure the survival of the firm in case of losses caused by such events as fires or liability suits.

Identifying risks. The next step is to identify the risks to which a household or firm is exposed. An agent can supply a checklist of risks that can be covered by insurance. Box 21–1 lists the types of insurance that are commonly bought by households and business firms. Risk managers should use their eyes and ears. Management by walking around can be useful in finding ways of preventing or controlling losses. Both large and

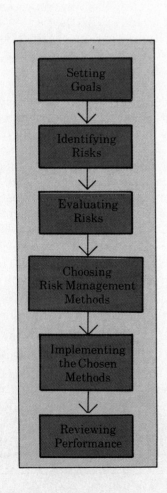

Setting
Goals

Identifying
Risks

Evaluating
Risks

Choosing
Risk Management
Methods

Implementing
the Chosen
Methods

Reviewing
Performance

Box 21–1 Major Types of Insurance

For Households

Life insurance. Pays a benefit to survivors upon the death of the insured person, usually a principal earner of income.

Health insurance. Pays costs of hospital and doctor services for all members of a household.

Auto insurance. Depending on the coverage, pays for medical care, repairs, liability for injuries to others, and sometimes other losses caused by automobile accidents.

Homeowners' insurance. A package policy covering losses due to fire, theft, liability for injuries to others, and sometimes other losses. Renters' policies are also sold; these cover theft and liability.

Disability insurance. Compensates a household for loss of income due to the disability of a principal earner. Often provided by employers as a fringe benefit for their employees.

For Businesses

Fire insurance. Covers losses due to fire.

Marine insurance. Covers loss of or damage to goods shipped by sea (ocean marine insurance) or other modes of transportation, such as truck or rail (inland marine insurance).

Liability insurance. Covers losses resulting from injuries to others caused by defective products, carelessness by employees, and the like.

Workers' compensation. Covers work-related injuries and illnesses of employees.

Fidelity and surety bonds. Compensates for losses due to dishonesty of an employee or failure of another party to live up to the terms of a contract.

Loss-of-earnings insurance. Compensates for losses that result when a fire or other disaster causes a firm to shut down temporarily; for the costs of operating in temporary quarters; and for other losses caused by the interruption of business.

Life insurance. Used to compensate firms for losses resulting from the death of key employees.

---

small firms should consult legal advisers about ways to avoid or control liability losses.

Evaluating the risks.   After risks have been identified, the next step is to find out how serious they are. For a household, the illness or death of an income earner is the most serious risk. A business might sort risks into three groups: those that would bankrupt the firm; those that would require major borrowing for it to stay in operation; and those that can be absorbed from the firm's current assets.

Choosing methods of managing the risks.   The four risk management methods—avoidance, loss prevention and control, insurance, and absorption—have already been discussed. After risks have been identified and evaluated, the firm or household should know enough to choose one of these methods, or a mix of them, to deal with each risk.

Carrying out the chosen method.   If the chosen method of risk management is insurance, the next step is to buy it. It usually pays to compare the policies offered by different companies. They may differ in terms of both price and coverage. The amount of coverage chosen depends on the firm's or household's goals and its ability to absorb some losses from its own assets.

Besides insurance, every firm's risk management strategy should include a program to prevent and control losses. In some firms, running this program is a full-time job. Every aspect of management—planning, organizing, leading, and controlling—comes into play. Managing for loss prevention and control is in many ways like managing for productivity and quality. It calls for leadership in the form of actions, not just words. It calls for a theory Y approach in which employees are given trust and responsibility. And it calls for working closely with unions. Because worker safety is a prime concern of unions, this is often a good starting point for building cooperative labor relations.

Reviewing the results. The final step in risk management is reviewing the results. A strong information system is needed to keep track of losses and take action when it is needed. Changes in a household's financial state or a firm's strategy may call for changes in its approach to the management of risk.

THE INSURANCE BUSINESS

We turn now from the process of risk management to the business of providing insurance. The insurance industry in the United States is a big one. It provides some 2 million jobs. In 1982 the assets under its control totaled $820 billion. By some counts there are more than 5000 insurance companies in the United States, although almost all of the business is handled by about 900 of them.[2]

In Chapter 17 we looked at insurance companies in their role as financial intermediaries. As we have seen, these companies collect premiums from many firms and households that are exposed to the same kinds of risks. They pool the premiums to form a fund from which policyholders are compensated in the event of a loss. Funds that have been paid in as premiums but not yet paid out to cover losses are invested in stocks, bonds, commercial mortgages, and other assets. The financial role of insurance companies is not our focus here, however. Instead, we will look at the role they play in the process of risk management.

Structure

Claim: A payment made by an insurance company to a policyholder who suffers a loss.

All insurance companies have two sources of income: premiums paid in by the policyholders whose risks the company insures, and investment income earned on the pool of funds that have been paid in as premiums but not yet paid out to cover losses. They also have two types of costs: the cost of **claims** paid to policyholders who suffer losses, and other expenses, including the costs of administration and marketing.

[2]Insurance Information Institute, *Insurance Facts* (New York, 1983), p. 5.

Insurance companies have two types of costs: claims paid to policyholders who suffer losses, and other expenses, including administrative costs like the costs of running this claims department. Photo courtesy of Metropolitan Life Insurance Company, N.Y.

Mutual insurance company: An insurance company that is owned and controlled by its policyholders.

Lloyd's association: A network of insurers who accept risks through a central exchange.

Stockholder-owned companies. Many insurance companies are ordinary corporations. They issue stock and are owned and controlled by the stockholders. The goal of such firms is to earn a profit for their owners. This can be done only if premiums plus investment income amount to more than total claims plus operating costs. If costs exceed income, claims must still be paid, and the stockholders suffer a loss. Stockholder-owned firms are the main type of property and liability insurance company.

Mutual insurance companies. Like mutual savings banks, **mutual insurance companies** are a type of cooperative. They are owned and controlled by their policyholders. Like stockholder-owned companies, they must have enough income to cover their costs in order to remain solvent, but their profits and losses are handled in different ways. The most common method is to set premiums high enough to cover claims and expenses, with a generous margin for error. At the end of each year, the surplus is refunded to policyholders as a dividend. Less often, mutual companies charge a premium that is just high enough to cover normal claims and expenses. If claims are higher than expected, the company has the right to charge policyholders an extra amount to make up the difference. Mutual insurance companies are the main type of life insurance company.

Lloyd's associations. A **Lloyd's association** is a third way of offering insurance. It is a network of insurers who accept risks through a central exchange.

The best known of these associations is Lloyd's of London. Lloyd's of London is not an insurance company in the ordinary sense. Instead, it is much like a stock exchange. A person who wants to be insured by Lloyd's of London contacts a broker, who in turn seeks to place the insurance with some of the 1800 members of Lloyd's. To handle large risks, the members form syndicates of as many as 200 or 300 members. For example, a shipowner might get $10 million worth of coverage for a round trip by an oil tanker from a syndicate of 200 members, each of which receives half of one percent of the premium and must pay $50,000 of the claim in the event of a total loss. Lloyd's of London has strict rules to make sure that its members are able to cover the risks they take on.

Lloyd's of London maintains a central exchange through which a network of insurers accept risks of all kinds. © Adam Woolfitt, Woodfin Camp

Insurable risk: A risk with certain traits that make it feasible for a private insurance company to offer coverage for that risk.

Law of large numbers: The principle that the frequency of a certain type of loss can be predicted with a high degree of accuracy when many similar units are exposed to the loss

There are a few Lloyd's associations in the United States. None of them has the prestige or financial strength of Lloyd's of London, however.

Government insurance agencies. Many government agencies also provide insurance. The Federal Deposit Insurance Corporation insures savers against the risk of bank failure. Federal agencies provide crop and flood insurance. States provide many types of insurance—life insurance in Wisconsin, crop insurance in Montana, and auto insurance in Maryland, to name just a few. All states provide unemployment insurance.

Some government agencies offer true insurance. They collect premiums, pool the funds, and pay claims out of the pool. Other government programs are insurance in name only. Social Security (old-age, survivors, disability, and health insurance) is a case in point. Social Security benefits, unlike claims against a true insurance company, are not paid out of a pool of funds that have been paid in by the beneficiaries. Instead, benefits to people who are retired or disabled are paid out of taxes that have been paid in by people who are currently working.

The Concept of Insurable Risk

Insurance companies take on many kinds of risks—fire, shipwreck, sudden death, illness, theft, and many more. They do not take on risks of all kinds, however. With few exceptions, they do not insure speculative risks. Even among pure risks, some are insurable and some are not. Ideally, an **insurable risk** has six traits: (1) many similar units are exposed to the risk; (2) the loss is accidental; (3) the loss can be measured; (4) the loss is not catastrophic; (5) the chance of loss can be calculated; and (6) the premium must not be excessively high. Let's look at each of these traits in turn.

Many similar units. An insurable risk should be one that many similar units are exposed to. Risks of fire, illness, burglary, and so on all fit this requirement. When many similar units are exposed to a risk, the insurance company can use the **law of large numbers** to predict losses with

An insurable risk has six traits: many similar units are exposed to the risk; the loss is accidental; the loss can be measured; the loss is not catastrophic; the chance of loss can be calculated; and the premium is not excessive. © Erik Anderson, Stock, Boston

great accuracy. For example, given a group of 10,000 fifty-five-year-old men, no one can be sure which ones will die in a given year. However, using the law of large numbers, an insurance company can predict with a high degree of accuracy that about 105 of them will die. It can adjust its premiums to fit this expected death rate, leaving a margin for error and expenses, and be sure that it will be able to pay all claims.

Unique events, by contrast, usually are not insurable. For example, the builder of a titanium-hulled, wind-powered oil tanker might find it hard to insure the ship against sinking because insurers lack a large number of cases on which to base an estimate of the chance of loss.

Accidental loss. Normally only accidental losses can be insured. Suppose a firm offered insurance against house fires set by owners. Only people who intended to burn down their houses would buy such insurance, so the concept of pooling risks would not apply. There are, however, a few exceptions to the rule that only accidental losses are insurable. For example, many life insurance policies cover the risk of suicide if the policy has been in force for a year or more.

Measurable loss. Insurable losses must be measurable, meaning that it must be possible to determine whether a loss has actually occurred and, if so, how great the loss is. Events like fire, death, robbery, and most illnesses meet this requirement. Mental illness is a borderline case. Some health insurance policies cover treatment of mental illness, but they often include safeguards against frivolous use of such treatments. For example, they may pay only half the cost of mental health services. In the case of life insurance, no attempt is made to measure how great the loss is. Instead, the amount to be paid is agreed upon when the policy is bought.

No catastrophic loss. A catastrophic loss is one that affects a large number of policyholders at the same time. Such losses cannot be insured because they do not follow the rule that the few who suffer the loss are paid out of the pool of funds paid in by the many who do not suffer the loss. Thus, insurance policies routinely exclude coverage for the risk of nuclear war. Government programs sometimes insure catastrophic losses like floods or crop failure that private firms will not insure.

Calculable chance of loss. For a risk to be insurable, it should be possible to calculate the chance of a loss. As explained earlier, this calculation is made easier if many similar people or firms are exposed to the same risk. That is not the only requirement, however. Some events are so rare that it is hard to calculate the chance of their occurring, even though many people are exposed to the risk. For example, it is impossible to calculate the chance that a volcano will erupt. This fact (as well as the catastrophic nature of an eruption) makes volcanic action an uninsurable risk. Most of the billions of dollars' worth of losses caused by the eruption of Mount Saint Helens in 1980 were not covered by insurance.

Reasonable premium. The final trait of an insurable risk is that the premium is reasonable. If the premium required is almost as great as the loss, or even exceeds it, no one will buy the insurance. For example, the law of large numbers suggests that 66 out of every 100 ninety-eight-year-old men will die within one year. A company that was asked to write $100,000 of life insurance on such a man would have to charge a premium of $66,000 for the first year just to break even on the probable cost of claims. By the

Since it is impossible to calculate the chance that a volcano will erupt, the risk of an eruption is not insurable. Most of the losses caused by the eruption of Mount Saint Helens in 1980 were not covered by insurance. © Roger Werth, Woodfin Camp

time the firm's expenses were added in, the premium would be close to the face value of the policy. To take another example, private firms do not like to sell auto insurance to people with very bad driving records.

Insuring the uninsurable. The concept of insurable risk is not absolute. In some cases it is possible to buy insurance when one of the six factors that we have listed is not present. Lloyd's of London is famous for insuring unique risks. In one case it insured NBC television against the risk that the United States would pull out of the 1980 Moscow Olympics. When the United States did pull out, Lloyd's paid NBC nearly $80 million. Lloyd's is able to insure such risks because it spreads them among syndicates with many members. The members offset losses with profits on policies for other unique risks where no loss takes place.

Many of the government agencies mentioned earlier exist to cover risks that are uninsurable by private firms. They insure against catastrophes like floods and crop loss. They offer auto insurance to drivers with bad records, although the premiums are high. And they insure people against unemployment, a risk that private insurers would view as both catastrophic and, in some cases, not accidental.

Other Factors That Affect Insurability

The six traits that we have listed define an insurable risk. If any one of them is missing, risk management through private insurance becomes difficult if not impossible. Other factors also can make private insurance difficult or impossible.

Insurable interest: A state of affairs in which a policyholder will suffer if a loss takes place.

Insurable interest. For one thing, the buyer of an insurance policy is expected to have an **insurable interest** in the risk. This means that the policyholder must suffer if the loss takes place. Thus, a family can buy fire insurance on its own house, and so can a bank that holds a mortgage on the house. A person can buy life insurance on his or her own life, or on the life of a relative, and a firm can insure the lives of its key managers. But a person cannot buy insurance on a neighbor's house or on the life of a movie star in the hope of collecting if a loss occurs.

Moral hazard: The danger that a policyholder will fake a loss in order to collect a claim.

Moral hazard. As we have seen, to be insurable a risk must be accidental. However, there is a chance that a policyholder will fake a loss in order to collect a claim. The owner of an apartment building that cannot be rented at a profit might burn down the building to collect insurance, or a worker might fake an injury to collect disability payments. This possibility is known as **moral hazard**. Insurance companies must allow for moral hazard when setting premiums. All policyholders are forced to pay more in order to cover losses caused by the dishonest few. In some cases moral hazard may drive the premium so high that the risk becomes uninsurable. Fire insurance on buildings in run-down urban areas is hard to buy for just this reason.

Morale hazard: The danger that a policyholder will allow a loss to take place through carelessness, knowing that insurance will pay for the loss.

Morale hazard. Moral hazard is a matter of dishonesty. But insurance companies also face the risk that policyholders will become careless or take extra chances because they know they are insured. This is known as **morale hazard**. Would you ski on less dangerous slopes if you were not insured against the risk of a broken leg? Would you be more careful about locking your car if you were not insured against the risk of theft? Insurance companies say that the answer to such questions is yes, at least for many people. When big policies are involved—such as fire insurance for an office building—the company may insist on certain loss control measures in order to reduce morale hazard.

Adverse selection: The fact that people who are more likely to suffer a loss also are more likely to buy insurance.

Adverse selection. A final problem is **adverse selection**. This refers to the fact that people who are more likely than average to suffer a loss also are more likely to buy insurance. Suppose that an insurance company finds that one gas station out of one hundred is robbed in an average year, and it sets its premium on this basis. Owners of gas stations in bad parts of town will think the premium is a bargain. Fewer owners of gas stations in safe parts of town will sign up. As a result, actual losses will be more than 1 in 100. If the company responds by raising its premium, station owners will drop their policies until only the most crime-prone stations are left in the program. If adverse selection cannot be limited, the risk may become uninsurable.

Underwriting: In insurance, classifying potential policyholders into groups on the basis of risk.

Underwriting. The insurance industry's chief weapon against adverse selection is **underwriting**. In the insurance world, this means classifying potential policyholders into groups according to risk, setting premiums for the groups based on the degree of risk, and rejecting applications that exceed certain levels of risk. In the case of robbery insurance for gas stations, an underwriter for one company might decide to base its premium on a 1-in-100 chance of loss. He or she would check each application and reject those from stations that were judged to be above-average risks. A second company might set a higher premium and would thus be willing to sell policies to stations with greater exposure to robbery.

Selective underwriting can be found in every area of insurance. For example, life insurance companies classify applicants by age in setting premiums. They often charge lower premiums to nonsmokers than to smokers of a given age, and they often try to avoid high-risk cases by requiring applicants to pass a physical exam.

Regulation of the Insurance Industry

The insurance industry, like other parts of the financial system, is closely regulated. Unlike the regulation of banking and securities, however, most regulation of insurance takes place at the state level. Insurance regulation has four main goals: to make sure that insurance companies stay solvent, to prevent fraud, to guard against excessive charges, and to make insurance available to anyone who needs it. Let's look at each of these in turn.

Solvency. Insurance premiums are paid in advance; claims are made later. This fact leaves policyholders open to loss if the company fails between the time they pay premiums and the time they make claims. Regulators take a number of steps to guard against this risk. They screen firms that want to enter the insurance business for honesty and financial strength. They insist that insurance companies hold enough liquid assets to pay claims. They control the accounting methods used by insurance companies. And they limit the kinds of investments that insurance companies can make. High-risk investments like common stocks are limited, while low-risk investments like bonds and mortgages are favored.

Preventing fraud. Insurance policies are complex legal documents. A dishonest company can easily write a document so loaded with exceptions and exclusions that it is worthless, yet so hard to understand that it may seem reasonable to the average buyer. Misleading contracts combined with verbal misleading of buyers by agents have led many people into financial traps.

One welcome trend in regulation is to require insurance companies to write policies, or at least policy summaries, in plain English. (See Box 21–2.) If policies are written in language that is easy to understand, and if agents do not mislead buyers, most people are able to judge whether or not a given policy is worth buying.

Despite all regulations, some kinds of insurance are sold that, experts think, are poor buys for the average consumer. Policies like cancer insurance that cover only a narrow class of risks are a case in point. Cancer is a frightening disease, but in financial terms many cancer insurance policies are a bad bargain compared with policies that cover a broad range of health risks.

Box 21–2 Plain and Not-So-Plain English in Insurance

Plain English

Continuation of Coverage. You may renew this policy if premiums are paid when due or within the one-month grace period, provided we haven't given at least 31 days' notice of our decision not to renew all similar policies then in force in your state or jurisdiction (you cannot be singled out for a nonrenewal of your policy); even then, coverage will still continue until your policy's annual anniversary date.

Source: A brochure describing a major-medical policy sold by Washington National Insurance Company.

Not-So-Plain English

When the company elects not to renew this policy, it shall mail notice not less than forty-five (45) days prior to the expiration date of its intention not to renew to the named insured and to any mortgagee or loss payee named in the Declarations, provided that the number of days notice shall not be less than that required by law; but even though the company has not given notice of its intention not to renew, this policy shall terminate automatically on the expiration date stated in the Declarations if the insured has failed to discharge when due any of his obligations in connection with the payment of premium for this policy or any installment thereof whether payable directly to the company or its agent or indirectly under any premium finance plan or extension of credit.

Source: A personal comprehensive protection policy issued by the Continental Insurance Companies.

Rate regulation. All states except Illinois regulate rates (that is, premiums) charged by insurance companies. The amount of regulation varies widely, however. At one extreme, some states set rates by law. Most commonly, companies set their own rates but must have them approved before they can be put in force. In the most liberal forms of regulation, companies simply keep regulators informed of the rates they charge.

Evidence on the effects of rate regulation is mixed. A study by the General Accounting Office found that there was not much difference in the cost of insurance between states with strict rate regulation and those with more liberal regulation.[3] This suggests that competition is the main force that keeps rates down. On the other hand, some companies complain that regulators are slow to allow needed rate increases to go into effect. Some companies even refuse to operate in certain states because they think the allowed rates do not cover their costs.

Availability.   A final goal of regulation in some states is to make sure that insurance is available to anyone who needs it. For example, as we have mentioned, some states insist that insurance be made available even to drivers with poor records. Other states are concerned about the fact that companies sometimes refuse to insure property in low-income, high-crime neighborhoods. In recent years regulators have also become concerned about discrimination by age and sex in insurance. We will come back to the issue of discrimination in the next section.

ISSUES IN INSURANCE

Any business as big as insurance is sure to have its share of issues. We will close this chapter by looking at three of these. They involve life insurance, health insurance, and the problem of discrimination.

Life Insurance: What Needs Should It Serve?

The main purpose of life insurance is to provide financial security for survivors in the event of the death of the insured person. Consider the case of Ray and Abby Schmidt, a husband and wife, both twenty-five years old, with two children. Their earnings are high enough to allow them to own a house and to put away a little money each year toward the children's college education. If all goes well, the family will be financially secure. But what if one parent dies? The other may earn enough to live on, but not enough to pay the mortgage and send the kids to college. The family needs life insurance.

The couple decide that if one of them dies, they would need $100,000 to pay off the mortgage and set up a college fund. They call their insurance agent, Karen White, to ask how much they will have to pay for the kind of protection they need. White explains that one alternative is for Ray and Abby to buy **term insurance** policies like those illustrated in Box 21–3.

The buyer of term insurance pays a yearly premium and, in return, is covered for an agreed-upon amount (here, $100,000) for one year. The annual premium that must be paid to keep the coverage in force rises year by year, as shown in the box. The increase in the premium reflects the increasing chance that a person will die in a given year as he or she gets older. Notice that Abby's premium is somewhat lower than Ray's each year. This reflects the fact that death rates are lower for women than for men at any given age.

Term insurance: A form of life insurance in which coverage is granted for a fixed term in return for payment of a premium based on the chance of death during that term.

[3]General Accounting Office, *Issues and Needed Improvements in State Regulation of the Insurance Business* (Washington, D.C., 1979).

Term insurance is the cheapest way for young people to get a high level of protection. As a person ages, however, the premium rises sharply. For example, Box 21–3 shows that for Ray Schmidt, the premium for $100,000 of coverage rises from $167 at age twenty-five to $2470 at age sixty-five. At still older ages, the premium would become too high to afford. If Ray and Abby want insurance protection that lasts throughout their life, they need a different kind of policy, called **whole life insurance**. The premium on whole life insurance is much higher at the outset, but it does not increase with age. And because the higher premiums are invested by the company for the benefit of the policyholder, a whole life policy builds up a cash value that can be used in later years.

Box 21–4 shows a typical whole life policy for Ray Schmidt with the same $100,000 death benefit in the first year as the term insurance policy shown in Box 21–3. The annual premium on the whole life policy is

Whole life insurance: A form of life insurance in which coverage is granted for a person's whole life in return for payment of a fixed annual premium.

Box 21–3 Term Insurance Premiums

Age	Premium for Ray Schmidt	Premium for Abby Schmidt
25	$ 167	$ 163
26	173	168
27	178	174
28	184	178
29	189	185
30	195	190
31	201	197
32	207	203
33	213	208
34	220	216
35	228	223
36	244	225
37	261	227
38	282	231
39	302	247
40	328	264
41	353	285
42	384	305
43	415	330
44	454	355
60	1,547	1,106
62	1,907	1,263
65	2,470	1,675
69	3,243	2,393

This table shows premium schedules for $100,000 of term insurance for Ray and Abby Schmidt, both twenty-five-year-old nonsmokers. The premium for a given amount of term insurance rises each year, because the chance of death increases as a person becomes older. Note that premiums are higher for the man's policy each year than for the woman's. This is because a woman's chance of dying in a given year is lower than a man's at any given age. The illustration is based on the premium schedules of a major mutal life insurance company.

Box 21–4 Premiums, Cash Values, and Benefits for a Whole Life Policy

Age	Premium	Cash Value	Death Benefit
25	$1,046		$ 100,000
26	$1,046	$ 180	100,000
27	$1,046	1,129	101,017
28	$1,046	2,254	102,334
29	$1,046	3,574	103,967
30	$1,046	4,995	105,960
31	$1,046	6,637	108,310
32	$1,046	8,297	111,033
33	$1,046	10,211	114,142
34	$1,046	12,402	117,668
35	$1,046	14,742	121,631
36	$1,046	17,288	125,993
37	$1,046	20,175	130,786
38	$1,046	23,271	136,044
39	$1,046	26,666	141,811
40	$1,046	30,455	148,117
41	$1,046	34,567	154,994
42	$1,046	39,596	162,478
43	$1,046	44,876	171,105
44	$1,046	50,598	180,167
62	$1,046	291,089	502,843
65	$1,046	386,969	615,251
75	$1,046	961,906	1,235,446

This table shows premiums, cash values, and death benefits for a whole life insurance policy for Ray Schmidt, a twenty-five-year-old nonsmoker. The premium of $1046 per year is higher initially than the premium for the term insurance policy shown in Box 21–3, but it does not increase as the policyholder grows older. This policy combines pure insurance with savings. Each year the cash value of the policy grows, providing the policyholder with a sum of money that can be used as retirement income. Also, the death benefit paid by this policy increases each year. The figures given here are based on a typical whole life policy offered by a major mutual life insurance company.

$1046—much higher than the premium in the early years of the term policy. However, the death benefit and the cash value of the whole life policy increase year by year. By the time Ray is sixty-five, the policy will have a death benefit of $615,251 and a cash value of $386,969. At that point the cash value could be converted to a monthly income of $3692 payable for the rest of Ray's life.

Which type of policy should the Schmidts buy? This question has been much debated. Whole life insurance was once thought to be one of the soundest savings plans a family could enter into. In 1981 Americans owned well over $1 trillion worth of whole life insurance. But many experts challenge the idea of whole life insurance. They claim that other investments available to the family could yield a higher rate of return. For example, Ray Schmidt could could buy the term life insurance policy and invest the difference between the term insurance premium and the whole life premium in an individual retirement account (IRA) at his bank. Taking into account the tax advantages of the IRA, and using reasonable assumptions about the interest rate the bank would pay, he could easily have far more at age sixty-five than the $386,969 cash value of the whole life insurance policy.

A 1979 report by the Federal Trade Commission attacked whole life insurance in strong terms. It said, in effect, that many people were being bilked by their insurance companies. Even the best whole life plans sold at that time offered only moderate returns. For this or other reasons, more and more people have been buying term insurance. In 1981 term insurance accounted for 59 percent of all life insurance bought, up from 41 percent in 1971.[4]

In order to keep premiums coming in, the insurance companies have done a lot to make whole life insurance more attractive. Many plans that are sold today offer much better rates of return than those that were being sold when the FTC study was made. And the simple kind of whole life plan shown in Box 21–4 is by no means the only one available. Their agent could tailor a policy to fit the Schmidts' financial needs that would combine some of the best features of both term and whole life insurance.

Health Insurance: Can Costs Be Controlled?

An item of good news in the 1980s is that Americans are healthier and living longer than ever before. Life expectancy at birth has reached almost seventy-five years, up from forty-seven at the turn of the century. Age-adjusted death rates from heart disease, cancer (except lung cancer), and infectious diseases are at new lows. The bad news is that Americans are paying record amounts for health care. As Box 21–5 shows, the cost of health care has risen much faster than other kinds of costs in recent years. Total spending on health care ballooned from 6 percent of gross national product in 1965 to 10.5 percent in 1983.

Some critics blame insurance for soaring health care costs, at least in part. Nine out of ten Americans are covered by some form of health insurance. Many of these have "first-dollar coverage," which means that the insurance company pays the entire cost of even small, routine medical bills. This system does not give either patients or doctors much of a reason to hold costs down. Patients seek care for minor ills, and they may choose hospital care when cheaper out-patient care would be possible. Doctors can order extra tests, extra medication, and extra days in the hospital knowing that these will not put a financial burden on the patient. Surgeons can pick up big fees for coronary bypass operations and Caesarean childbirths when the medical need for them could be questioned. This happens partly because insurance short-circuits the law of supply and demand in the medical marketplace.

How can doctors and patients be encouraged to cut down on unneccessary use of health care? Banning health insurance would do the job, but no one suggests such a drastic step. Without health insurance, most people could not afford the kind of care that serious illnesses require. In fact, in recent years the trend has been to extend health insurance to more people, partly through government programs like Medicare and Medicaid, and

---

[4]American Council of Life Insurance, *Life Insurance Fact Book* (Washington, D.C., 1983), p. 12.

Box 21–5 The Rising Cost of Health Care and Other Items

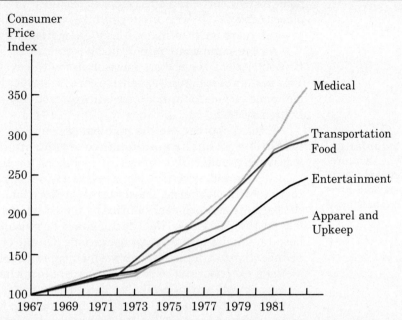

This chart shows the rates at which the prices of health care, food, transportation, clothing, and entertainment rose between 1967 and 1983. An index value of 100 for 1967 is used as a basis for comparison. The price of medical care more than tripled in the period, rising faster than any of the other items shown.

Source: Council of Economic Advisers, *Economic Report of the President* (Washington, D.C.: Government Printing Office, 1984), Table B-52.

Deductible clause: A clause in an insurance policy under which claims can be made only after expenses reach a certain level.

Coinsurance clause: A clause in an insurance policy under which the policyholder agrees to pay a certain percentage of all costs up to some fixed amount.

partly through union- and employer-sponsored plans. Let's look at three ideas for dealing with the problem while still maintaining wide access to health care.

The first and most moderate suggestion is to make greater use of deductible and coinsurance clauses in health insurance programs. A **deductible clause** is one under which claims can be made only after expenses reach a certain level. For example, a person might have to pay the first $100 of medical costs each year before the insurance company would pay anything. A **coinsurance clause** is one under which the policyholder must pay a percentage of all costs up to some maximum amount. For example, the policyholder might pay 20 percent and the insurance company 80 percent of all costs up to $5000, after which the company would pay 100 percent of any further costs. Deductible and coinsurance clauses are an attempt to discourage overuse of doctor and hospital services for trivial ills, while still protecting people against the crushing costs of major medical problems. Many, but by no means all, insurance plans now include such clauses.

A second suggestion is a public health care system like the British National Health Service (NHS). In that system, hospitals are owned by the government, and doctors are salaried employees of the government. The NHS provides care free of charge, and yet it keeps total health care costs down to a much smaller share of GNP than in the United States. However,

Health maintenance organization (HMO): An organization that provides a broad range of prepaid health care services to members and pays doctors and other professionals fixed salaries.

many of the cost savings come through rationing, which is done through long waiting lists for many kinds of care. For example, infants with hole-in-the-heart problems, elderly people who need to have a hip replaced, and people with kidney failure who need dialysis often must wait several years for treatment. Many die while on the waiting list.

At the same time, minor medical treatment is free and easy to get. British citizens see doctors more often, on the average, than Americans. This system of rationing expensive care for serious illnesses and providing generous service for minor ones is not attractive to American critics of the British system.[5]

A third approach to the problem of health care costs discards insurance in favor of **health maintenance organizations (HMOs)**. An HMO is a private prepaid plan in which members (or their employers) pay a monthly fee and, in return, get access to a wide range of doctor and hospital services without charge. The doctors who work for an HMO are not paid by the patient; they are paid salaries by the HMO. Because they are not paid fees for their services, HMO doctors have no reason to prescribe unneeded hospital admissions, tests, or operations. On the other hand, HMOs have an incentive to practice preventive medicine—regular checkups, advice on diet and exercise, and so on. Many private firms have turned to HMOs as an economical way of providing health benefits for their employees.

It is not clear in what direction the American health care system will move in coming years. But the rise in the cost of care under first-dollar insurance programs makes it certain that debate and experimentation will go on.

Sex and Insurance: Discrimination or Fair Play?

Insurance companies discriminate on the basis of sex. Sex discrimination is, in fact, one of the basic features of underwriting. Women's premiums average 60 percent of men's for auto insurance, 72 percent for term life insurance, 144 percent for disability insurance, and 148 percent for major-medical insurance. Insurance companies also discriminate in selling **annuities**. An annuity is a contract under which an insurance company or pension plan agrees, in exchange for a fixed payment, to pay a person a certain number of dollars per year as long as he or she lives. Women pay about 9 percent more than men for the same kinds of annuities. Under many pension plans, a woman must either make larger payments during her working years or accept smaller payments after retirement than a man who works for the same number of years at the same salary.

Annuity: A contract under which an insurance company or pension plan agrees, in exchange for a fixed payment, to pay a person a fixed amount per year as long as he or she lives.

To see why men and women are treated differently, turn to Box 21–6. As the table shows, a woman's life expectancy is higher than a man's at every age. Using the law of large numbers, an insurance company knows that it will pay more claims in a given year on men's life insurance policies than on women's in any given age group. With this in mind, it charges women smaller premiums. In the case of annuities, the tables are turned. Again using the law of large numbers, the underwriter sees that payments will have to be made for more years to the average woman than to the average man.

[5]For a critical discussion of the NHS, see John C. Goodman, *National Health Care in Britain* (Dallas: Fisher Institute, 1980).

Because women live longer, on the average, than men, they pay less for life insurance and more for annuities.
© Freda Leinwand

Underwriters of health and auto insurance work from other tables that show differences in men's and women's exposure to risk. Young unmarried men have more than twice as many auto accidents as unmarried women of the same age. Women, on the other hand, run up a third more major-medical bills. Thus, women pay less for auto insurance but more for health insurance.

Many women's groups, including the American Association of University Women, the National Women's Political Caucus, and the Coalition of Labor Union Women, claim that these practices are unfair.[6] Bills to outlaw sex bias in insurance have been introduced in both the U.S. Senate and the House of Representatives. Even if the tables used by insurance companies are accurate, the women's rights groups say that it is offensive to use them as a basis for pricing insurance. They believe that men and women should be treated equally, even though women will have to pay more for many kinds of insurance if the bills they back become law.

Do insurance companies really need to take sex into account in setting rates? Can't other data, such as a person's occupation, health record, driving record, and so on, be used instead? Insurance companies answer that those data are already used and that the use of sex in addition allows them to calculate risks more accurately.

The debate over sex discrimination, like that about the cost of health insurance or the best form of life insurance, is not likely to be resolved soon. And these are only some of the issues faced by the insurance industry. In the field of auto insurance, there is a debate over the value of "no-fault" insurance. Property insurance raises the issue of "redlining"— alleged discrimination against owners of property in low-income areas. Product liability insurance and medical malpractice insurance raise the question of whether courts are too generous in the awards they give to injured parties. The list goes on. Insurance, like other areas of American business, has its share of challenges to meet in the 1980s.

[6]See Daniel Seligman, "Insurance and the Price of Sex," *Fortune*, February 21, 1983, pp. 84–85.

Box 21–6 Life Expectancy of Men and Women at Various Ages

Commissioners 1980 Standard
Ordinary (1970—1975)

	Male		Female			Male		Female	
Age	Deaths per 1000	Expectation of Life (Years)	Deaths per 1000	Expectation of Life (Years)	Age	Deaths per 1000	Expectation of Life (Years)	Deaths per 1000	Expectation of Life (Years)
0	4.18	70.83	2.89	75.83	50	6.71	25.36	4.96	29.53
1	1.07	70.13	.87	75.04	51	7.30	24.52	5.31	28.67
2	.99	69.20	.81	74.11	52	7.96	23.70	5.70	27.82
3	.98	68.27	.79	73.17	53	8.71	22.89	6.15	26.98
4	.95	67.34	.77	72.23	54	9.56	22.08	6.61	26.14
5	.90	66.40	.76	71.28	55	10.47	21.29	7.09	25.31
6	.86	65.46	.73	70.34	56	11.46	20.51	7.57	24.49
7	.80	64.52	.72	69.39	57	12.49	19.74	8.03	23.67
8	.76	63.57	.70	68.44	58	13.59	18.99	8.47	22.86
9	.74	62.62	.69	67.48	59	14.77	18.24	8.94	22.05
10	.73	61.66	.68	66.53	60	16.08	17.51	9.47	21.25
11	.77	60.71	.69	65.58	61	17.54	16.79	10.13	20.44
12	.85	59.75	.72	64.62	62	19.19	16.08	10.96	19.65
13	.99	58.80	.75	63.67	63	21.06	15.38	12.02	18.86
14	1.15	57.86	.80	62.71	64	23.14	14.70	13.25	18.08
15	1.33	56.93	.85	61.76	65	25.42	14.04	14.59	17.32
16	1.51	56.00	.90	60.82	66	27.85	13.39	16.00	16.57
17	1.67	55.09	.95	59.87	67	30.44	12.76	17.43	15.83
18	1.78	54.18	.98	58.93	68	33.19	12.14	18.84	15.10
19	1.86	53.27	1.02	57.98	69	36.17	11.54	20.36	14.38
20	1.90	52.37	1.05	57.04	70	39.51	10.96	22.11	13.67
21	1.91	51.47	1.07	56.10	71	43.30	10.39	24.23	12.97
22	1.89	50.57	1.09	55.16	72	47.65	9.84	26.87	12.28
23	1.86	49.66	1.11	54.22	73	52.64	9.30	30.11	11.60
24	1.82	48.75	1.14	53.28	74	58.19	8.79	33.93	10.95
25	1.77	47.84	1.16	52.34	75	64.19	8.31	38.24	10.32
26	1.73	46.93	1.19	51.40	76	70.53	7.84	42.97	9.71
27	1.71	46.01	1.22	50.46	77	77.12	7.40	48.04	9.12
28	1.70	45.09	1.26	49.52	78	83.90	6.97	53.45	8.55
29	1.71	44.16	1.30	48.59	79	91.05	6.57	59.35	8.01
30	1.73	43.24	1.35	47.65	80	98.84	6.18	65.99	7.48
31	1.78	42.31	1.40	46.71	81	107.48	5.80	73.60	6.98
32	1.83	41.38	1.45	45.78	82	117.25	5.44	82.40	6.49
33	1.91	40.46	1.50	44.84	83	128.26	5.09	92.53	6.03
34	2.00	39.54	1.58	43.91	84	140.25	4.77	103.81	5.59
35	2.11	38.61	1.65	42.98	85	152.95	4.46	116.10	5.18
36	2.24	37.69	1.76	42.05	86	166.09	4.18	129.29	4.80
37	2.40	36.78	1.89	41.12	87	179.55	3.91	143.32	4.43
38	2.58	35.87	2.04	40.20	88	193.27	3.66	158.18	4.09
39	2.79	34.96	2.22	39.28	89	207.29	3.41	173.94	3.77
40	3.02	34.05	2.42	38.36	90	221.77	3.18	190.75	3.45
41	3.29	33.16	2.64	37.46	91	236.98	2.94	208.87	3.15
42	3.56	32.26	2.87	36.55	92	253.45	2.70	228.81	2.85
43	3.87	31.38	3.09	35.66	93	272.11	2.44	251.51	2.55
44	4.19	30.50	3.32	34.77	94	295.90	2.17	279.31	2.24
45	4.55	29.62	3.56	33.88	95	329.96	1.87	317.32	1.91
46	4.92	28.76	3.80	33.00	96	384.55	1.54	375.74	1.56
47	5.32	27.90	4.05	32.12	97	480.20	1.20	474.97	1.21
48	5.74	27.04	4.33	31.25	98	657.98	.84	655.85	.84
49	6.21	26.20	4.63	30.39					

This table shows the expected life span of men and women in the United States at various ages. Insurance companies use tables similar to these to set premiums for life insurance policies and annuities. At any given age, women have a longer expected life span than men. For this reason, insurance companies usually charge men more than women for life insurance, and charge women more than men for annuity contracts.

Source: American Council of Life Insurance, *Life Insurance Fact Book* (Washington, D.C., 1983), pp. 108–09.

SUMMARY

1. *Risk* means uncertainty about a possible loss. A *speculative risk* involves the chance of a gain as well as the chance of a loss. A *pure risk* involves only the chance of a loss.

2. *Risk management* is the task of reducing the costs connected with risk. A risk manager balances the costs of losses against the costs of preventing losses. The four methods of risk management are avoidance, loss prevention and control, insurance, and absorption. The six steps in the process of risk management are setting goals, identifying risks, evaluating the risks, choosing methods of managing the risks, carrying out those methods, and reviewing the results.

3. Insurance companies receive income from investments and from premiums paid by *policyholders*. Their costs include the costs of *claims* and the costs of administration and marketing. Stockholder-owned companies, *mutual* companies, and *Lloyd's associations* are three kinds of private firms that provide insurance. Also, governments provide insurance coverage for floods, crop loss, unemployment, and many other kinds of risks.

4. For a risk to be *insurable*, it should have six traits: many similar units are exposed to the risk; the loss is accidental; the loss can be measured; the loss is not catastrophic; the chance of loss can be calculated; and the premium is not excessive. Companies also require a policyholder to have an *insurable interest* in the risk. *Moral hazard, morale hazard,* and *adverse selection* make some kinds of insurance costly or even impossible.

5. Insurance is a closely regulated industry, with most regulation taking place at the state level. The main goals of regulation are to keep insurance companies solvent, to prevent fraud, to guard against excessive charges, and to make insurance available to anyone who needs it.

6. Critics of the insurance industry have raised many issues. They have charged that some types of life insurance are poor buys for consumers; that current forms of health insurance add to the high cost of health care; and that the industry practices unfair sex discrimination. These issues and others are likely to be subjects of debate for years to come.

KEY TERMS

You should be familiar with the following terms and concepts. Check their meanings by referring to the marginal definitions in the chapter or to the glossary at the end of the book.

Risk	Claim	Underwriting
Speculative risk	Mutual insurance company	Term insurance
Pure risk	Lloyd's association	Whole life insurance
Personal risk	Insurable risk	Deductible clause
Property risk	Law of large numbers	Coinsurance clause
Liability risk	Insurable interest	Health Maintenance Organization (HMO)
Risk management	Moral hazard	
Insurance	Morale hazard	Annuity
Self-insurance	Adverse selection	

QUESTIONS FOR REVIEW AND DISCUSSION

1. Insurance is sometimes compared with gambling. "If I pay a premium of $200 to insure my house and it doesn't burn down," some people say, "I have lost a bet. If it does burn down and I collect a claim of $50,000, I have won." What, if anything, makes this "bet" different from buying a lottery ticket? In what sense is it a bigger gamble not to buy insurance? Discuss.

2. Fatal botulism poisoning is very rare in the United States. The toxin produced by botulism bacteria is destroyed by heat, so poisoning can occur only in the case of foods that are served cold or not fully cooked. Suppose you own a restaurant. What methods of managing risk could you use to guard against liability loss caused by botulism poisoning of a customer?

3. You are thinking about visiting a large city to see some plays and concerts, but you have heard that street crime is a serious problem in the theater district. What methods might you use to deal with this risk? What are some methods of managing risk that would probably work but would not be worth using in this case?

4. Review the section on product safety in Chapter 9 (pages 228–229). Do you think the Smiths' problem with Wal-lite adhesive was one of product design or product use? If people like the Smiths are able to sue the maker of the product and collect damages, the firm must carry insurance against such suits, and it will raise the price of the product to cover the cost of the insurance. If such suits were not allowed, consumers would not have to pay as much for the adhesive, but they would have to carry more insurance to cover medical costs in case of an accident. Are consumers better off, on balance, with or without the right to sue? Does it make much difference? Discuss.

5. What are your own risk management goals? Make a list of the risks you face. Which ones are most serious? What methods do you use to manage those risks?

6. Most people insure their cars against the risk of damage in a collision but do not have insurance to cover the costs of mechanical failures like worn-out bearings and broken transmissions. This is so even though the costs of such failures can be as great as those of collisions. Do you think the risk of mechanical failure is less insurable than the risk of collision? If so, why? Recently it has become common for automakers to offer new-car buyers the chance to buy an extended warranty contract that will protect them against certain mechanical failures for, say, five years or 50,000 miles. Are such contracts a form of insurance?

7. At age twenty-five, Ray Schmidt, a white man, can expect to live to age seventy-three. His neighbor Ron Sloane, a black man of the same age, can expect to live only to age sixty-seven, according to statistics based on the U.S. population. Years ago, underwriters took differences between black and white life expectations into account in setting premiums for life insurance policies; they charged black men more than white men of the same age for the same kinds of policies. Do you think this was fair? Why or why not? Now consider pensions. Today black men and white men make equal payments to pension plans and get equal benefits each year after retirement, but because, on the average, black men die sooner, they collect fewer total benefits. Do you think this is fair? Or should black men not have to pay as much into the pension plan? Discuss this issue, and compare it with the issue of sex discrimination in insurance.

Case 21–1: Insurance in Orbit

In February 1984, an American space shuttle attempted to launch two large communications satellites. One of them belonged to Western Union Corporation, the other to the government of Indonesia. Both launch attempts failed, resulting in total loss of the satellites. Washington Post *writer James L. Rowe, Jr., had this to say about the implications of the mishaps for the insurance industry.*

Both Western Union and Indonesia were insured—Western Union for $105 million to cover the cost of the satellite and potential revenue, while Indonesia insured the $75 million cost of building and launching the payload.

Robert J. Tirone, vice-president of the large insurance broker Alexander & Alexander, said underwriters are likely to hold off issuing any new policies until they find out what went wrong with the two satellites.

"Something went wrong, and it went wrong twice," Tirone said.

A spokesman for McDonnell Douglas said the company is puzzled by the apparent failure of the rockets that were supposed to lift both satellites into stationary orbits about 22,300 miles from the earth. The space shuttle orbit is between 115 and 690 miles from the earth.

The rockets, called payload assist modules, had been used successfully in 16 previous commercial satellite launches—5 of them from the space shuttle and 11 by missiles. Two payload assist modules also performed according to plan on an Air Force satellite launch last summer, a McDonnell Douglas spokesman said. The failed modules cost about $5 million each.

Joseph Grochmal, an analyst with Conning & Company, a Hartford-based brokerage firm that specializes in insurance stocks, said that while the overall insurance payout is large, no one company or insurance syndicate had a big enough piece of the coverage to be seriously hurt. About half of the insurance was placed in the United States and the rest in London and Europe.

Although satellite insurance has been used since 1964, Alexander & Alexander's Tirone said,

the industry has not made a profit on it yet. At the end of last year, the industry had collected $205 million in premiums and paid off $210 million in claims.

As a result of the two failures, claims will rise to about $420 million. Even if every premium anticipated this year were paid, Tirone said, total revenue on the insurance would be about $340 million. But he said some scheduled launches will be postponed until the cause of the failures is determined, reducing the 1984 premiums.

This was the year the underwriters expected to make some profits, Tirone said. His company, Alexander & Alexander, was the broker for Western Union. Brokers are paid a commission to find underwriters, but generally do not assume any risk themselves.

Another insurance broker, who asked not to be identified, said that he expected premiums to quadruple as a result of the loss of the two satellites.

Typically, the cost of satellite insurance has been about 6 cents on the dollar.

Source: James L. Rowe, Jr., "Claims for Lost Satellites Will Top $200 Million," *Washington Post*, February 8, 1984, p. D2.

Questions:

1. How well does the launching of a satellite fit each of the six traits of an insurable risk? Did Western Union and Indonesia have insurable interests in the satellites? Does the article indicate any problem of moral hazard, morale hazard, or adverse selection?

2. The risk of loss of the satellites was not insured with a single company. Instead, an insurance broker—an intermediary who served, in effect, as an insurance wholesaler—found several different companies each of which was willing to accept a part of the risk. This process of splitting the risk among several companies is known as *reinsurance*. Why do you think reinsurance was used in this case?

3. Why would the cost of satellite insurance go up as a result of the loss of these two satellites? Is there any evidence in the article that, even before these losses, premiums may have been set too low?

4. If, as one broker predicts, satellite insurance quadruples in price as a result of this loss, some satellite owners may want to consider other methods of risk management. What other methods could be used? What would be their advantages and disadvantages compared with insurance?

SUGGESTED READINGS, PART V

Weston, J. Fred, and Eugene F. Brigham. *Managerial Finance*, 8th ed. Chicago: Dryden Press, 1984.

Van Horne, James C. *Fundamentals of Financial Management*, 5th ed. Englewood Cliffs, N.J.: Prentice-Hall, 1983.

Meigs, Walter B., and Robert F. Meigs. *Accounting: The Basis for Business Decisions*, 6th ed. New York: McGraw-Hill, 1984.

Stevens, Mark. *The Big Eight*. New York: Macmillan, 1981.

Ritter, Lawrence S., and William L. Silber. *Principles of Money, Banking, and Financial Markets*. New York: Basic Books, 1983.

Mayer, Thomas, James S. Duesenberry, and Robert Z. Aliber. *Money, Banking, and the Economy*, 2nd ed. New York: W. W. Norton, 1984.

Radcliffe, Robert C. *Investment: Concepts, Analysis, and Strategy*. Glenview, Ill.: Scott, Foresman, 1982.

Vaughan, Emmett J. *Fundamentals of Risk and Insurance*, 3rd ed. New York: Wiley, 1982.

Insurance Information Institute. *Insurance Facts*. New York, annual.

Useful periodicals:

Financial Week
Barrons
Banking
Institutional Investor

CAREERS IN FINANCE AND ACCOUNTING

There are many jobs in finance and accounting, for the simple reason that all types of organizations have financial needs. Training in finance or accounting can open the door to a career in a church, a trade association, a university, or a congressional committee staff as easily as it can lead to a career in private business. In addition, there are careers in the financial system itself—loan officer at a bank, broker in a securities firm, or underwriter in an insurance company. And in all of these organizations, as we have pointed out, experience in finance can lead to jobs in general management.

Not only does training in finance or accounting result in a broad choice of employers; it also leads to a wide variety of jobs. In some of these jobs, people work alone much of the time. In others, they work in constant contact with customers and clients. Some of the jobs require skill with numbers; others, skill in working with people. Some financial jobs relate closely to general management, others to marketing, and still others to production and operations. This section covers only a small sample of the many jobs that are available.

Job Title: Bookkeeper and Accounting Clerk

Description. Bookkeepers and accounting clerks maintain systematic and up-to-date records of business transactions. They may keep these records by hand in ledgers or, more and more frequently, use computers to do the job. They prepare periodic statements showing money received and paid out. Bookkeepers often prepare payrolls and bills to customers.

Qualifications. The minimum requirement for many jobs is a high school diploma with courses in business arithmetic and bookkeeping. However, many employers prefer applicants who have completed courses in accounting and business at a community college, junior college, or business school. Knowledge of computers and the use of other business machines is quite helpful. Ability to work with numbers and concentrate on details is essential.

Job outlook. About 1,713,000 people were employed as bookkeepers and accounting clerks in 1982. About one in three of these worked for a wholesaler or retailer. The other jobs were scattered throughout the economy. Newly hired bookkeepers usually work at recording routine transactions, and are promoted to more responsible jobs as they gain experience. With some additional college courses, experienced bookkeepers may advance to jobs as accountants.

Earnings. Beginning accounting clerks in private firms earned an average of $11,190 per year in 1983. More experienced clerks and bookkeepers earned from $13,000 to $19,000 per year.

Job Title: Accountant and Auditor

Description. Accountants and auditors prepare and analyze financial reports that contain the information managers need to make business decisions. Managerial accountants work within an organization, responding to the needs of its management. Public accountants work by themselves or in accounting firms to serve the needs of clients. Many public accountants specialize in auditing, the process of checking a client's financial records and reports for conformity with generally accepted standards.

Qualifications. Some jobs are available for graduates of two-year schools and business schools, but most employers prefer a bachelor's or master's degree in accounting. Certification as a CPA or CMA is essential for many jobs. Knowledge of computers is increasingly important.

Job outlook. About 856,000 people worked as accountants and auditors in 1982, including about 200,000 CPAs. Employment in this field is expected to grow faster than the average for all

CAREERS IN FINANCE AND ACCOUNTING (CONTINUED)

occupations. Opportunities will be better for college graduates than for others, and better still for those who have qualified as CPAs. Opportunities for advancement are good for people with backgrounds in accounting. Management accountants often become controllers, treasurers, financial vice-presidents, or corporate presidents. Beginning accountants in public accounting firms have an opportunity, after they have gained experience, to become partners in the firm.

Earnings. In 1982, graduates of bachelor's degree programs in accounting received average starting salary offers of $18,400 per year. Graduates of master's degree programs started at about $21,600 a year. Experienced accountants and auditors earned $23,300 to $51,800. Accountants in managerial positions and partners in public accounting firms often earned much more.

Job Title: Credit Manager

Description. Credit managers decide whether to accept or reject credit applications in firms where credit is an established way of doing business. They work for retailers, such as sellers of furniture, appliances, and cars, and also for wholesalers and sellers of industrial goods. In deciding whether to extend credit, credit managers look at financial statements submitted by applicants, review credit agency reports, and often conduct interviews.

Qualifications. Some jobs are available for holders of associate degrees, but a bachelor's degree is increasingly important. Business administration is the most common major for this job, but many employers also hire applicants with liberal-arts majors.

Job Outlook. Some 55,000 people were employed as credit managers in 1980. About half of these worked in wholesale and retail trade. The others worked for manufacturing and financial firms. Growth of employment in this field is expected to be somewhat slower than average. The work of credit managers allows them to become familiar with all phases of their firm's business, thus opening the way for advancement to general-management positions.

Earnings. In 1980, a credit manager trainee with a college degree earned $12,000 to $14,000 per year. Experienced credit managers earned from $22,000 to $25,000 per year.

Job Title: Economist

Description. Economists study the relationships among household, business, and government decisions regarding the use of scarce resources. They analyze trends in inflation, unemployment, and economic growth and the impact of these trends on businesses and other organizations. Many economists work for private financial and nonfinancial businesses, where they advise managers on trends in the economic environment. Others work for government, where they help formulate policies in areas ranging from government spending and taxation to energy and transportation. About a third of all economists hold

teaching and research positions at colleges and universities.

Qualifications. Many entry-level positions are available for holders of a bachelor's degree with a major in economics. Advancement to more responsible positions usually requires a graduate degree. University jobs and research jobs in business firms usually require a Ph.D. in economics. A strong background in statistics is important in almost all areas of economics.

Job outlook. About 30,000 people worked as

economists in 1982. Employment in this area is expected to grow faster than the average for all occupations. There will be an increasing demand for economists to advise lawyers, health service administrators, accountants, urban and regional planners, and so on. The job outlook for economists in universities and government agencies will not be as strong as in other areas.

Earnings. Starting salaries for economists in government positions ranged from about $13,000 for those with bachelor's degrees to about $23,800 for those with a Ph.D. University economists with a Ph.D. degree earned from $19,100 for an assistant professor to $34,100 for a full professor. The median salary for all business economists was $43,000 in 1982.

Job Title: Bank Teller

Description. Bank tellers cash checks and process withdrawals and deposits for customers. Small banks usually employ one or two general-purpose tellers. In larger banks, tellers may specialize in such functions as accepting utility bill payments, selling foreign currencies, or handling consumer loan payments. Tellers count cash, examine checks and deposit slips for accuracy, and verify that customers have enough money in their accounts to cover checks.

Qualifications. In selecting tellers, banks look for clerical skills, friendliness, and attentiveness to detail. A high school education is the usual minimum educational requirement. Prospects for

promotion to supervisory and managerial positions are better for those with a two- or four-year college education.

Job outlook. Banks employed about 539,000 tellers in 1982, including many part-time workers. Growth of employment in this field is expected to be better than the average for all occupations through the 1980s. Automated equipment will eliminate some routine duties, but it is not expected to affect total employment.

Earnings. Tellers earned from $7,900 to $16,800 per year in 1982.

Job Title: Bank Officer and Manager

Description. Banks employ many kinds of managers and officers. Loan officers handle consumer and commercial loans. They analyze financial statements submitted by applicants for loans, make credit checks, and conduct interviews. Trust officers manage investment funds for customers of the bank. They help their clients plan for such financial needs as college education and retirement. Operations officers are responsible for the administrative workings of the bank. They plan, coordinate, and control workflow, update data processing systems, and so on. Some banks also have officers who specialize in relations with other banks and in international transactions.

Qualifications. A bachelor's degree with a major in business administration or finance is the most common background for management trainees hired by banks. Some banks prefer an

MBA degree. Some banks hire officers with backgrounds in such specialties as petroleum engineering or forestry to meet the needs of industries with which they do business. Outstanding tellers are promoted to management positions by some banks.

Job outlook. Banks employed over 424,000 officers and managers in 1982. Employment in this field is expected to grow faster than the average for all occupations. However, the pool of qualified applicants for these jobs is also expected to grow, so competition will be keen.

Earnings. Trainees with bachelor's degrees received annual salaries of $13,200 to $21,600 in 1982. Those with MBA degrees started at salaries of $21,600 to $36,800 per year. Senior officers often earned several times these starting salaries.

CAREERS IN FINANCE AND ACCOUNTING (CONTINUED)

Job Title: Securities Sales Worker

Description. Securities sales workers put the machinery of securities markets to work for investors who want to buy or sell stocks and bonds. These workers are often called brokers, registered representatives, or account executives. They are expected to offer advice to clients in selecting securities to fit their investment goals. Much of the time of beginning securities sales workers may be spent prospecting for new customers for their firm.

Qualifications. A college education is increasingly important as a qualification for this field of work. Courses in business administration, economics, and finance are helpful. As in the case of other sales jobs, personality is as important as specific training. Maturity, ability to work independently, and ability to get along with people are essential. Sales experience in other areas, including part-time and summer work, can be helpful. Most securities firms offer training for new sales workers to help them meet licensing and registration requirements.

Job outlook. About 78,000 people worked as securities sales workers in 1982. Jobs in this field are expected to increase faster than average through the 1980s. Opportunities for advancement take the form of changes in the size and number of accounts handled. Beginners usually service individual accounts. Senior sales workers handle accounts of banks, pension funds, and so on.

Earnings. Commissions are the main source of earnings for securities sales workers. Those who service individual investors earned an average of $60,000 per year in 1980. Those who serviced institutional investors averaged $150,000 per year. Trainees are often paid a salary of $10,000 to $12,000 a year until they have attracted enough customers to assure them of regular commission earnings.

Job Title: Insurance Agent and Broker

Description. Insurance agents and brokers sell insurance to households and firms. They help their clients evaluate the risks they face and select insurance policies that meet their needs. They also help policyholders settle claims for losses. Agents are employees of insurance companies; brokers are independent businesspeople who sell many companies' insurance. Aside from this distinction, they do much the same sort of work.

Qualifications. Some companies prefer college graduates, but there are also openings for high school graduates and graduates of two-year programs. College courses in insurance and business administration are useful, as are courses in psychology and sociology. As in all sales jobs, personality and motivation count for as much as education. All agents and most brokers must pass an examinination and obtain a state license.

Job outlook. More than 361,000 people worked as insurance agents and brokers in 1982, including many part-time workers. Jobs in this field are expected to increase about as fast as the average for all jobs. Experienced agents with outstanding ability may become sales managers. However, those who have built up a good base of customers often can earn more by remaining agents or starting their own brokerage firms.

Earnings. Beginners often receive a modest salary of $1,200 a month or so during a six-month training period. After that their earnings come from commissions. As in other sales jobs, earnings vary widely. For example, the median income of life insurance agents in 1982 was $36,000 per year, but thousands earned $50,000 or more. The earnings of casualty insurance agents tend to be higher than those of life insurance agents.

Job Title: Actuary

Description. Actuaries design insurance and pension plans in ways that make them attractive to clients and, at the same time, keep them financially sound. They assemble and analyze statistics to calculate the likelihood of death, sickness, injury, disability, property loss, and so on. They then set premiums in keeping with the risk of loss. Actuaries must be familiar not only with statistics and the insurance business but also with broad economic, social, and legal trends that might affect the frequency of losses.

Qualifications. The basic qualification for a starting job is a bachelor's degree with a major in mathematics or statistics or, in schools where it is offered, actuarial science. Courses in accounting, computer science, and economics are also useful.

Beginning actuaries often rotate among jobs to learn various aspects of actuarial operations. Advancement depends on experience and scores on a series of professional examinations that all workers in this field are encouraged to take.

Job outlook. About 8,000 people were employed as actuaries in 1982. Most of them worked for insurance companies, but there are also some jobs in government and private consulting firms. The number of jobs in the field is expected to grow faster than average. In 1982, beginners in the field who had not yet passed any of the professional examinations earned about $16,000 per year. Those who had completed the examinations and had several years of experience earned from $35,000 to $50,000 a year.

Job Title: Underwriter

Description. Underwriters appraise and select the risks that an insurance company will insure. They analyze applications from clients, reports from loss control experts, and reports from actuaries. If they turn down too many risks, their companies may loose good business to competitors; if they accept too many risks, their companies will have to pay out too much in claims. Underwriters usually specialize in one type of insurance—life, health, fire, or whatever.

Qualifications. Most large insurance companies seek college graduates with a degree in business administration or liberal arts. Trainees begin by evaluating routine applications under

the supervision of an experienced underwriter. As they develop judgment, they are given more complex assignments. Many companies encourage their junior underwriters to take additional courses once they are on the job.

Job outlook. Some 76,000 people worked as underwriters in 1982. Employment in this field is expected to grow at about the average rate.

Earnings. The median yearly salary for underwriters was $18,500 in 1982. Trainees earned somewhat less, while experienced underwriters earned more than $24,000.

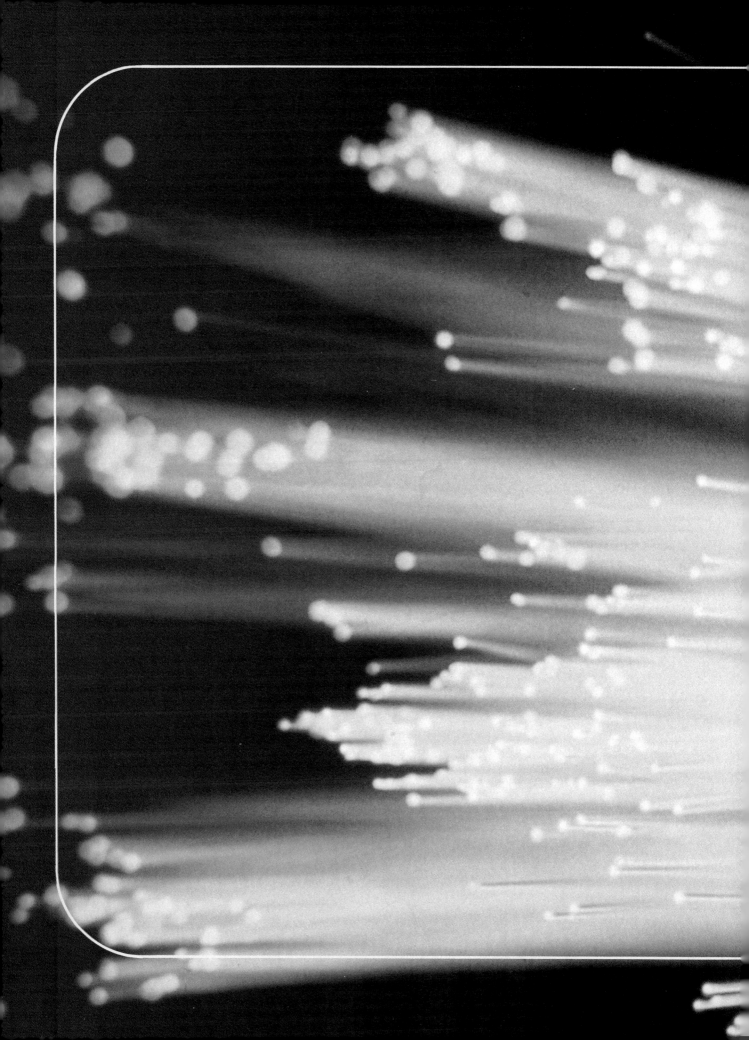

Part VI

BUSINESS AND THE WORLD

This book began with an overview of business and its role in the economy. The next four parts looked separately at four aspects of running a business: management, marketing, production and operations, and finance. This last section will put the pieces back together again and look at business in its social context.

Chapter 22 begins this process by looking at business and government, law, and ethics. These are all topics that have come up repeatedly but need to be drawn together. As we have done elsewhere in the book, we will explore the conditions under which a business can prosper by being a good citizen—those under which, that is, it can do well by doing good.

Chapter 23 turns from the role of business in the national economy to its role in the world economy. In it, we will look at several ways in which a firm can take part in the world economy—by importing, by exporting, and by carrying on operations abroad. The chapter will explain the basic concepts of balance of payments and international finance, and will discuss the issue of free trade versus protectionism.

Finally, Chapter 24 will look at the future of business. The future is hard to predict. Thirty years ago, people were mistakenly predicting an airplane in every garage by 1985, but they largely missed the possibility of a computer in every home. Despite the difficulties of forecasting the future, however, looking ahead remains a basic part of planning. As an aid to planning, we will examine a number of trends in economics, population growth, and other aspects of social change that will affect business in years to come.

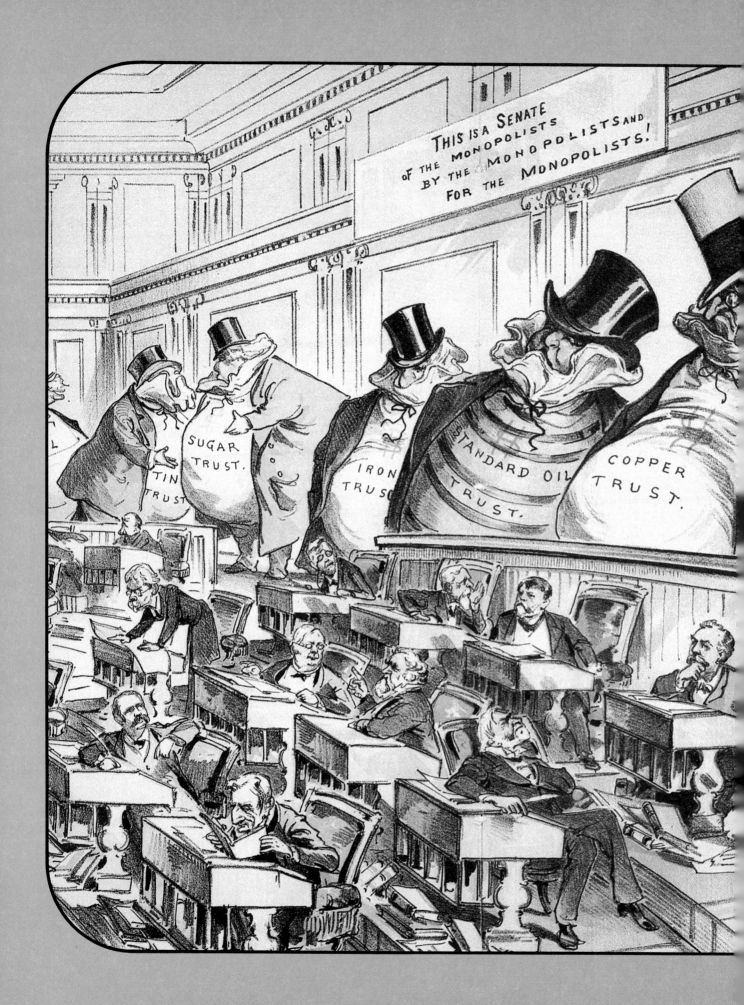

Chapter 22

BUSINESS AND GOVERNMENT, LAW, AND ETHICS

When you have completed this chapter, you should be able to

- Discuss how government regulates, taxes, and supports business, and how business influences government.

- Define *industrial policy* and explain the strengths and weaknesses of this concept.

- List the major types of law that affect business.

- Explain the requirements for a valid *contract* and describe three kinds of remedies for breach of contract.

- Discuss the law of *property*, *agency*, and *torts* as applied to business.

- List three kinds of bankruptcy proceedings, and explain the uses of each.

- Discuss the main issues in *business ethics*, and explain how managers can promote ethical conduct.

On November 12, 1976, a Piper Cheyenne took off from Shannon International Airport in Ireland. Moments later it crashed, killing all of its occupants: four executives of Digital Equipment Corporation and their pilot. Families of the victims filed a federal court suit charging that the crash was caused by defects in the airplane that Piper knew about but concealed from federal regulators.

The Cheyenne was approved for service by the Federal Aviation Administration (FAA) in 1974. At that time Piper had financial problems. The firm needed to add a prop jet like the Cheyenne to its product line if it was to survive. However, the FAA was reluctant to approve the plane. It gave its OK only after two years of testing, modification, and retesting.

The Cheyenne, it seems, had serious stability problems. Under certain conditions it would pitch nose down as if, said one test pilot, "the tail had come off." To get FAA approval of the plane, Piper engineers added a spring to the control stick that gave the pilot a greater feeling of stability. The spring, however, did not satisfy everyone.

David Lister, formerly a flight test engineer at Piper, told the *Wall Street Journal* that the spring "was a half-assed system. It really didn't make the airplane any more stable than it was, but it gave you a feeling of stability."

Jim Wrisley, also a former Piper flight test engineer, calls the spring a "Band-Aid." The Cheyenne, he says, "was a poor design to begin with." The spring made the plane "widely divergent at low speeds in the climb configuration."

A few months after the Cheyenne was approved by the FAA, a team of test pilots from the British Civil Aviation Authority (CAA) arrived to test the plane. The British test routine was tougher than the FAA's. After

A crash of the Piper Cheyenne led to a major lawsuit against the manufacturer, and charges that its managers had acted unethically in pushing the FAA to approve the plane. Courtesy of Piper Aircraft Corporation

taking the Cheyenne through some maneuvers that the FAA had not tried, the CAA pilots were appalled. They said that the plane's instability was "so extreme that we just did not believe that it could possibly be true."

The CAA pilots met with top Piper executives to express their concern. At that meeting, the CAA pilots told the court in the Shannon crash case, "Piper . . . asked quite specifically that the results of our tests be treated with as much confidence as possible and in particular that we do not discuss them with the FAA." The FAA and the CAA have a written agreement to exchange information on all aircraft tests. Later the CAA did send a report to the FAA, but in watered-down language that did not express the strength of the pilots' feeling about the Cheyenne.

Piper officials who were at the meeting deny that the British pilots were asked to conceal the results of the test.

In April 1984 the judge in the Shannon crash case ruled that Piper had intentionally destroyed large amounts of evidence pertaining to the Cheyenne's safety. Piper, he said, had submitted "blatantly" false statements under oath, and had misleadingly substituted documents. Calling Piper's conduct "shocking" and "willful," he ruled that the company had forfeited its right to defend itself against the lawsuit. A date was set for a separate trial to determine the damages to be awarded the families of the victims.[1]

[1]Jonathan Kwitny, "Did Piper Aircraft Try to Keep FAA in Dark on Air Safety Problem?" *Wall Street Journal*, December 15, 1983, p. 1, and "Piper Deliberately Destroyed Evidence of Aircraft Defect, Federal Judge Rules," *Wall Street Journal*, April 2, 1984, p. 4.

The story of the Cheyenne raises many questions. If we accept the judge's ruling that Piper officials broke the law, what pressures led them to do so? What can managers do to keep their subordinates from giving in to such pressures? When do business ethics require more than just staying within the law? What is the proper role of agencies like the FAA in regulating business? Questions like these, which involve law, ethics, and relations between business and government, are the subject of this chapter.

The chapter will open with a review of business-government relations, a subject that we have touched upon at many earlier points in the book. Next we will look at the legal system within which American business operates. In the last section of the chapter we will look at business ethics and at how mangement can promote ethical behavior.

GOVERNMENT AND BUSINESS

In Chapter 2 we called the American economy a *free enterprise* economy, meaning one in which firms can choose whom to buy from and sell to, and whom to compete with. Government plays a big role in the American free enterprise system, however. Federal, state, and local governments tax and regulate business, but they often play a supportive role as well. And the relationship between business and government is not a one-way street. While government affects what business does, business affects the actions of government.

Regulation and Deregulation

We have discussed many forms of regulation in previous chapters. The major regulatory agencies, most of which have been mentioned before, are listed in Box 22–1. They fall into six groups: safety, health, and environmental regulation; regulation of transportation and communications; trade regulation; regulation of labor relations; financial regulation; and energy regulation. As the list shows, there is no area of management that is unaffected by regulation.

Box 22–1 Major Regulatory Agencies

Safety, Health, and Environment

Environmental Protection Agency (EPA): air pollution, water pollution, and solid-waste disposal.

Occupational Safety and Health Administration (OSHA): health and safety hazards in the workplace.

Consumer Product Safety Commission (CPSC): safety of consumer goods.

Food and Drug Administration (FDA): prescription and nonprescription drugs and food additives.

National Highway Traffic Safety Administration (NHTSA): automobile safety.

Transportation and Communications

Interstate Commerce Commission (ICC): truck, rail, and bus regulation.

Civil Aeronautics Board (CAB): regulation of air fares and schedules.

Federal Aviation Administration (FAA): air traffic control and air safety.

Federal Maritime Commission (FMC): ocean shipping.

Federal Communications Commission (FCC): telephone, radio, and television.

Trade Regulation

Federal Trade Commission (FTC): advertising and antitrust.

Antitrust division of the U.S. Department of Justice: enforcement of antitrust laws.

Labor Relations

National Labor Relations Board (NLRB): union-management relations.

Equal Employment Opportunity Commission (EEOC): equal employment opportunity and affirmative-action programs.

Financial

Securities and Exchange Commission (SEC): securities markets.

Federal Reserve System (Fed): banks and thrift institutions.

State insurance commissioners: all aspects of insurance.

Energy

Federal Energy Regulatory Commission (FERC): interstate pipelines, natural-gas pricing, interstate transmission of electric power.

Nuclear Regulatory Commission: construction and operation of nuclear-power plants.

State utility commissions: electric and other utilities.

This box lists some regulatory agencies and their functions. Many of them have been discussed in previous chapters. The list is not intended to be complete. State agencies are mentioned only when the main source of regulation is at the state level. Most states also have agencies, such as state environmental agencies, that parallel the federal regulators listed here.

Some industries—nuclear power, for instance—are regulated more closely today than ever before. In others the trend has been toward *dereg*ulation. Transportation, communications, and finance have been strongly affected by this trend.

Airlines were the first major industry to be deregulated. The Civil Aeronautics Board, which has controlled airline fares and routes since the 1930s, is scheduled to go out of business. (The FAA will continue to police airline safety.) As we noted in Chapter 10, trucking and railroads have also been deregulated. In communications, the most dramatic step has been the breakup of the AT&T telephone monopoly. The Federal Communications Commission has relaxed its regulation of radio and television broadcasting in some ways, too.

Turning to the financial sector, as we noted in Chapter 19, the banking sector has also been partially deregulated. Interest rates on most deposits have been freed from government control, and banks and thrift institutions now compete more directly than before. The Securities and Exchange Commission has taken some steps toward deregulation too. Greater freedom in pricing brokerage services and shelf registration of corporate securities are examples.

Wherever deregulation has been tried, certain effects have resulted. Chief among these are the following.

1. *More competition.* Some of the increase in competition comes from new firms. More than 10,000 small firms have entered the trucking industry since 1980. Several long-distance telephone services now compete with AT&T. In other cases the new competition is between firms that were kept apart by regulation in the past. Railroad

piggyback service is taking traffic away from long-haul trucking. Banks and thrifts now compete more directly with one another as well as with money market mutual funds.

2. *Pressure to cut costs.* Competition is forcing deregulated firms to cut costs. Unions like the Teamsters and the Airline Pilots Association have been forced to accept wage cuts as new, nonunionized firms have entered their industries. Banks are setting up automatic teller machines in order to save on payroll costs. Firms that have not been able to control costs have been driven out of business. In other cases, firms are merging in order to become more efficient.

3. *Greater choice for consumers.* Regulated industries tend to offer consumers a few standardized products. Deregulation has resulted in much wider choice. Air travelers can now choose anything from no-frills PEOPLExpress to all-first-class Air One. Savers and borrowers can deal with a small "boutique" bank like the Palmer National Bank, or with a financial supermarket like Sears, where banking, brokerage, real estate, and insurance are all available. And consumers can now choose among hundreds of kinds of telephones instead of the handful offered by AT&T in its monopoly days.

4. *Lower prices, but not for everyone.* In all the deregulated industries, competition, innovation, and cost cutting have resulted in a lower average level of prices. But that has not meant lower prices for everyone. Under regulation, some services were overpriced and the profits were used to offer others at prices that were below costs. Prices of those services tend to go up after deregulation. Thus, rates for local phone service, which used to be priced below cost, are going up, while rates for long-distance service, which used to be overpriced, are going down.

The move toward deregulation has not affected all of the agencies listed in Box 22–1. The Federal Trade Commission and the antitrust division of the U.S. Department of Justice have changed some of their rules

Government regulation of business has become tighter in some areas, while in others the trend is toward deregulation. Controls on oil prices were lifted in 1981. An Exxon Photo

in ways that they think will promote competition, but they have increased their enforcement of other rules, such as those against price fixing. In the area of energy, controls on oil prices have been lifted since 1981, but controls on natural-gas prices have remained in place. In general, regulations in the areas of health, safety, and the environment have become tighter. Some economists believe that regulation should be reformed in these areas too. They think that changes can make health, safety, and environmental regulations more effective while at the same time making them less burdensome on industry. But at present the deregulation movement seems to be in a resting phase.

Taxation

Businesses are subject to many forms of taxes. Corporate profits are subject to a federal income tax at rates up to 46 percent. Taxes on business property are a major source of revenue for state and local governments. And there are special taxes on goods like liquor and tobacco.

Voters dislike high taxes, but at the same time they demand improved public services. To many politicians, taxing business seems like an easy way to satisfy voters. Economists have long pointed out, however, that the true burden of all taxes, including taxes on business, falls on people. The people who bear the burden of business taxes are either the firms' owners or their customers. If the taxes are passed along to customers in the form of higher prices, they cause inflation. If the burden falls on owners, there are fewer profits to be reinvested, and therefore less growth, less innovation, and fewer jobs. Either way, taxes on business are not a free lunch for the public.

Business taxes not only give government a source of revenue; they also are a way of getting business to do certain things that the government wants done. In Chapter 18, for example, we mentioned that firms that invest in new equipment may defer part of their corporate income taxes. This policy is meant to spur investment and job creation. And in Chapter

People like these California voters dislike high income and property taxes, so politicians often try to satisfy them by taxing business. But business taxes may be passed along to consumers in the form of higher prices. © Jeff Lowenthal, Woodfin Camp

13 we pointed out that states offer tax breaks to induce firms to locate new plants within their borders. One of the jobs of managerial accountants is to advise firms on how to benefit from such incentives in making their investment, location, and production decisions.

Support of Business by Government

Traditional forms of support. Regulation and taxation place burdens on business, but other government policies support business. In the past that support has taken three main forms.

One of the ways in which government supports business is by supplying information and advice. This agricultural extension agent consults with farmers. Courtesy of the Department of Agriculture

- *Information and advice.* The Small Business Administration, discussed in Chapter 4, was formed to support business. The Department of Agriculture gives information and advice to farmers. Many other agencies collect statistics that are useful in planning marketing strategy, plant location, and so on.
- *Loans and loan guarantees.* In 1983 the federal government provided $70 billion in grants, loans, and *loan guarantees* to business. (In a guaranteed loan, a business borrows from a bank or other private source and the government promises to repay the loan if the borrower cannot do so.) Federal loan guarantees are important in the farming and housing industries, and sometimes in others as well. For example, in 1979 and 1980 Congress gave Chrysler Corporation $1.9 billion in loan guarantees to help it get through a crisis. State and local governments often raise funds by selling tax-free bonds and then lend the funds to local businesses at low interest rates, in order to promote growth and jobs.
- *Direct services.* Governments at all levels supply firms with services like roads and sewers. Defense contractors benefit from government-sponsored research, and may be given the free use of government-owned plant and equipment. Perhaps most important of all,

the nation's system of public schools and universities provides business with a steady supply of trained workers.

Industrial policy: A systematic program of government support for business growth and innovation.

Industrial policy. In the 1980s some people have begun to think that these forms of support for business are not enough. If American business is to innovate, grow, and maintain its place in the world economy, they say, the government should provide more and better-coordinated support. What America needs, they say, is an **industrial policy**—a systematic program of government support for business growth and innovation.

Everyone who talks about industrial policy agrees that it means support for growth and innovation, but there is little agreement on the details. To some, industrial policy means "picking winners." They would have the government identify high-growth industries, such as computers and genetic engineering, and support them with research aid and capital funds. To others, industrial policy means "helping losers." They want the government to help troubled industries like steel slim down, modernize, and retrain laid-off workers. Still others see industrial policy as venture capitalism on a grand scale. They would channel billions of tax dollars into a National Industrial Development Bank. This bank, in turn, would make low-cost loans both to help winners grow and to help losers adjust.

Critics of industrial policy agree with the objectives of innovation and growth, but they point out that other countries that have tried industrial policy have had mixed success. For example, Britain and France thought they had a winner in the supersonic Concorde airliner, but they got a flying white elephant instead. In the case of troubled industries, foreign governments have often caved in to pressures to preserve jobs with massive subsidies, rather than helping them to slim down, innovate, and adjust.

At bottom, the debate is over who can best plan, organize, lead, and control in a changing and uncertain world. Advocates of industrial policy think private firms need government help. Its opponents say that government has no better ways of anticipating the future than private managers have. Adding layers of bureaucrats to second-guess winners and bail out losers would do more harm than good.

The Concorde airliner was developed by Britain and France within the framework of a joint industrial policy. Courtesy of Air France

The Chamber of Commerce of the United States, headquartered in Washington, D.C., is among the strongest business lobbies. Courtesy of the Chamber of Commerce of the U.S.

Lobbying: A systematic effort by an interest group to inform and persuade government decision makers in the hope of having an influence on policy.

Trade association: An association of firms in the same line of business formed to pursue their shared interests.

Political-action committee (PAC): A committee that accepts donations for a political cause and uses the funds to make contributions to candidates or for other political activities.

The Political Influence of Business

Because government has such a strong impact on business, many firms do all they can to influence government policies. In part, their aim is to promote an economic climate that is favorable to business—growth, low inflation, and low interest rates. In part, their aim is to counterbalance the influence of unions. And in part, their aim is to get special help for certain firms and industries. Lobbying and campaign contributions are their chief tools.

Lobbying is a systematic effort by an interest group to inform and persuade government decision makers in the hope of having an influence on public policy. The National Association of Manufacturers, the Chamber of Commerce of the United States, and the Business Roundtable are three of the strongest business lobbies. They are dominated by big firms. The National Federation of Independent Businesses represents the point of view of small firms.

In addition to these "umbrella" groups, almost every industry has a **trade association**—an association of firms in the same line of business formed to pursue their shared interests. Competing firms that would be barred by law from joining together to fix prices or divide up markets can join together to influence public policy. Box 22–2 gives a partial list of trade associations. Those that have their headquarters in Washington, D.C., or its suburbs are highlighted. More than half of them are within a five-minute walk of one another in a neighborhood that sprouts trade associations the way Iowa soil sprouts corn.

Besides lobbying, business makes its influence felt through donations to political campaign funds. It is illegal for firms to give money directly to candidates or officeholders. However, the 1974 campaign law permits corporations to form **political-action committees (PACs)**. A PAC is a committee that accepts donations for a political cause and uses the funds to make contributions to candidates or for other political activities. PACs are a major source of campaign contributions for members of the U.S. Senate and House of Representatives. Few members of Congress would sell a vote in return for a PAC contribution. But the funds that PACs give to their campaigns buy something very valuable: it is a rare member of Congress who will not make time in a busy schedule to sit down with a lobbyist whose PAC helped him or her win the last election.

Is the political influence of business a good or a bad thing for American democracy? Don't expect agreement on that question! It is probably safe to say that in a system where consumers, unions, religious groups, and so on, are free to lobby, letting business do so too provides a healthy balance. But not all business lobbyists are concerned with the good of the free enterprise system as a whole. Many aim for narrow benefits at the expense of consumers, workers, taxpayers, and competitors. Case 22–1 gives one example of a kind of lobbying that is routine in Washington.

BUSINESS AND THE LEGAL SYSTEM

Law: A body of principles, standards, and rules used to settle disputes in an orderly way.

Law is a body of principles, standards, and rules used to settle disputes in an orderly way. As an alternative to war, private gangs of thugs, and the simple punch in the nose, it is one of the great human inventions. People engaged in business are subject to the law just as everyone else is, and

Box 22–2   Trade Associations

Industrial Heating Equipment Assn 9101 N Moore St	Arlington VA 22209
Information Industry Assn 316 Pennsylvania Ave SE	Washington DC 20003
Intl Airforwarder & Agents Assn 8212A Old Court House Rd	Vienna VA 22180
Intl Council of Shopping Centers 665 Fifth Ave	New York NY 10022
Intl Entrepreneurs Assn 2311 Pontius Ave	Los Angeles CA 90064
Intl Franchise Assn 1026 Connecticut Ave NW	Washington DC 20036
Lead Industries Assn 292 Madison Ave	New York NY 10017
Luggage & Leather Goods Mfrs of America	
350 Fifth Ave	New York NY 10001
Marble Institute of America 33506 State	Farmington MI 48024
Menswear Retailers of America 2011 Eye St NW	Washington DC 20006
Mica Industry Assn 233 Broadway	New York NY 10007
Millinery Institute of America 200 Madison Ave	New York NY 10016
Motor & Equipment Mfrs Assn 222 Cedar Lane	Teaneck NJ 07666
Motor Vehicle Mfrs Assn of the US 300 New Center Bldg	Detroit MI 48202
Motorcycle Industry Council 2400 Michelson Dr	Irvine CA 92715
Natl Agricultural Chemicals Assn 1155 15th St NW	Washington DC 20006
Natl Air Transportation Assn 1010 Wisconsin Ave NW	Washington DC 20007
Natl Alliance of Business 1015 15th St NW	Washington DC 20006
Natl Assn of Chemical Distributors	
300 Arcade Sq Box 1288	Dayton OH 45402
Natl Assn of Diemakers & Diecutters 3255 South US 1	Fort Pierce FL 33450
Natl Assn of Furniture Mfrs 5515 Security Lane	Rockville MD 20652
Natl Assn of Greeting Card Publishers	
600 Pennsylvania Ave SE	Washington DC 20003
Natl Assn of Home Builders of the US	
15th & M Sts NW	Washington DC 20005
Natl Assn of Mfrs 1776 F St NW	Washington DC 20006
Natl Assn of Music Merchants 500 N Michigan Ave	Chicago IL 60611
Natl Assn of Plumbing-Heating-Cooling Contractors	
1016 20th St NW	Washington DC 20036
Natl Assn of Printers & Lithographers 780 Palisade Ave	Teaneck NJ 07666
Natl Assn of Printing Ink Mfrs 550 Mamaroneck Ave	Harrison NY 10528
Natl Assn of Recycling Industries 330 Madison Ave	New York NY 10017
Natl Assn of Retail Grocers of the US	
1100 Sunrise Valley Dr	Reston VA 22091
Natl Assn of Wholesaler-Distributors 1725 K St NW	Washington DC 20006
Natl Assn of Women Business Owners	
500 S Michigan Ave	Chicago IL 60611
Natl Automobile Dealers Assn 8400 Westpark Dr	McLean VA 22102
Natl Beauty Culturists League 25 Logan Circle NW	Washington DC 20005
Natl Business Aircraft Assn One Farragut Sq	Washington DC 20006
Natl Coal Assn 1130 17th St NW	Washington DC 20036

Trade associations are associations of firms in the same industry. This box presents a partial list of trade associations taken from a national directory. Lobbying is one of the main activities of trade associations, as suggested by the high proportion of them that have their headquarters in Washington, D.C., or its suburbs.

Source: *The National Directory of Addresses and Telephone Numbers* (New York: Concord Reference Books, 1984), p. 35.

businesses as organizations are subject to some special laws of their own. In this section we will look at the most important of these laws.

Kinds of Law

There are many branches of law, many ways in which laws can be classified. One of the basic distinctions is between public and private law. *Public law* deals with the organization of government and the relationships between people and their government. *Private law* deals with relationships among private people and organizations. Our concern here is with the branches of private law that affect business, such as the law of contracts and property.

A second distinction is between criminal and civil law. *Criminal law* deals with offenses against society. When a person commits an armed robbery, a rape, or a murder, he or she is considered to have injured not just the victim but society as a whole. The criminal is brought to court and punished by the government. *Civil law* deals with disputes that are not offenses against society. Failure to live up to a contract and damage done to another person's property are matters of civil law. Civil law cases take the form of a suit by one private party against another.

A third distinction is between common and statutory law. *Common law* is based on earlier decisions of judges in similar cases. The English common law, which can be traced back a thousand years, was brought to America by the English colonists. It underlies much of our civil law. *Statutory law* is based on the acts of legislatures at the federal, state, and local levels. Over time, much of English common law has been made a part of statutory law, so the distinction between them is not as sharp as it was in the past.

Laws of all kinds are enforced by a system of courts. The court system of the United States is outlined in Box 22–3. As the box shows, both state governments and the federal government have court systems. Some of these, such as tax courts, hear only certain kinds of disputes. Others deal with a broader range of issues. Also, as the box shows, some kinds of

Laws of all kinds are enforced by the courts, but not all business disputes are settled in this way. © Rhoda Sidney, Monkmeyer Press Photo Service

10

Box 22–3 The Structure of the Court System

THE FEDERAL COURT SYSTEM

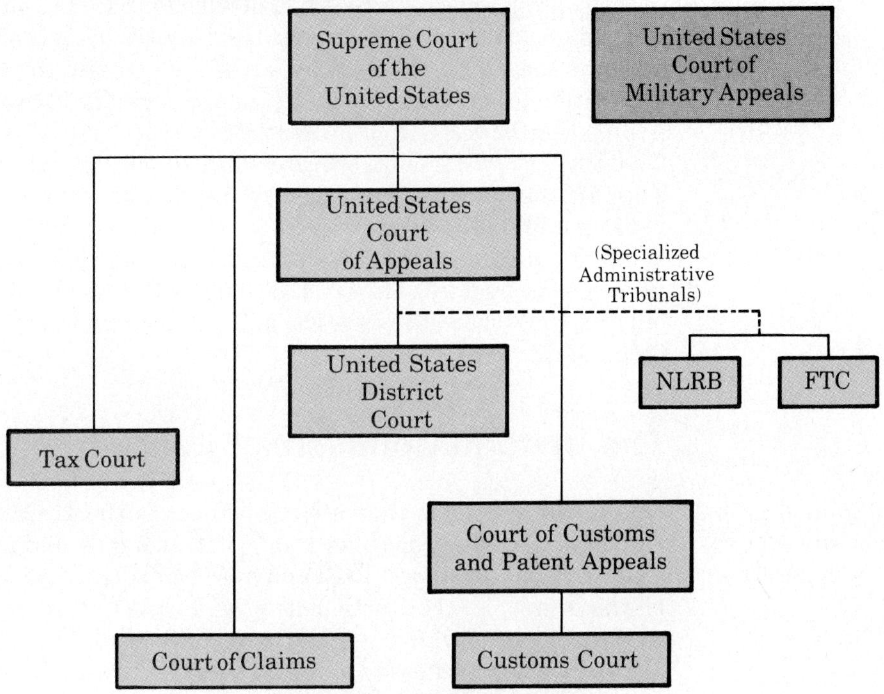

Supreme Court of the United States

United States Court of Military Appeals

United States Court of Appeals

(Specialized Administrative Tribunals)

United States District Court

NLRB   FTC

Tax Court

Court of Customs and Patent Appeals

Court of Claims   Customs Court

A TYPICAL STATE COURT SYSTEM

State Supreme Court

State Appellate Court

State Trial Court of General Jurisdiction

(Special Inferior Courts)

Probate   Criminal   Family   County

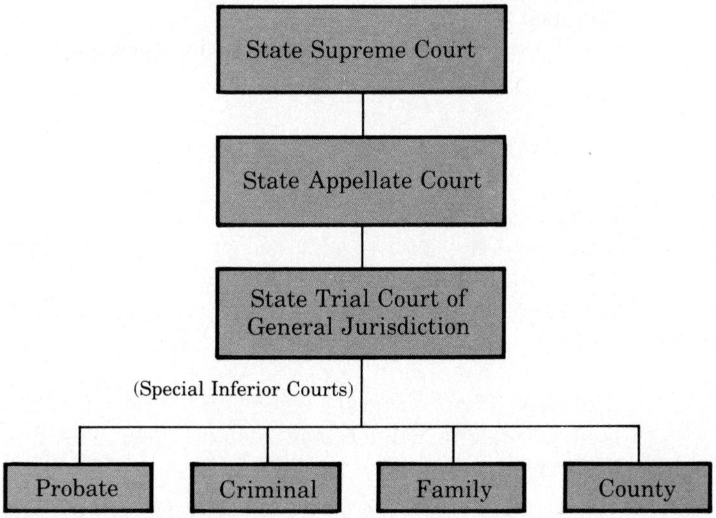

This figure shows the structure of the federal court system and that of a typical state court system. Lower courts in both systems are specialized by subject matter. Some types of cases are heard by administrative law judges at such agencies as the National Labor Relations Board and the Federal Trade Commission. Decisions of all the lower courts can be appealed to higher courts and, ultimately, to the Supreme Court of the United States.

Source: Joseph L. Frascona, *Business Law* (Dubuque, Iowa: William C. Brown, 1981), p. 29. From Frascona, Joseph L., et al, BUSINESS LAW: TEXT AND CASES, 2nd ed. © 1981, 1984 Wm. C. Brown Publishers, Dubuque, Iowa. All Rights Reserved. Reprinted by permission.

disputes are settled by administrative agencies. Rulings by all courts—state, federal, and administrative—can be appealed to the Supreme Court of the United States.

It is worth mentioning that not all business disputes need to be settled in the courts. For one thing, the knowledge that the courts are there as a last resort makes it easier to resolve disputes by agreement. Even when disputes cannot be resolved by agreement, many firms turn to private arbitration to avoid the cost and hassle of lawsuits. Firms like Washington Arbitration Services Inc. of Seattle, Judicate Inc. of Philadelphia, and Civicourt Inc. of Phoenix operate what amount to private court systems. They often employ retired judges with years of experience. Some firms go further and avoid even private courts. Instead, they hold "minitrials" before a panel of executives chosen by the two sides. Because the executives see the business issues that underlie the dispute instead of thinking only in legal terms, they may be able to reach a compromise faster than a judge could.

The Uniform Commercial Code

Uniform Commercial Code (UCC): A body of law that deals with sale of, transfer of, and payment for goods.

One of the key laws that affect business is the **Uniform Commercial Code (UCC)**, which deals with sale of, transfer of, and payment for goods. The UCC was drafted in 1952 and has been adopted, at least in part, in all of the states. It sets forth rules for a valid sales agreement and the conditions under which a seller can reclaim goods that were sold on credit. It also lays down rules for warranties. If the buyer and seller want to, they can reach an agreement that differs from the standard form. Unless there is some other agreement, however, the terms of the UCC apply. For example, if a good is sold without a written warranty, the UCC provides an implied warranty. (See Chapter 9, page 228.)

Contracts

Contract: An agreement that can be enforced in court.

Contracts are one of the central concepts of business law. A contract is an agreement that can be enforced in court. The subject of a contract can be almost anything—selling a car, building a house, acting in a movie, providing insurance. The people or organizations that enter into the agreement are known as the *parties* to the contract.

Validity of contracts. Over time, a set of common law rules evolved that determine when a contract is valid. The following six rules have entered into statutory law as well.

1. *There must be an offer.* An offer expresses the willingness of one party to enter into an agreement on certain terms. "I will do this if you will do that" is an offer. An invitation to negotiate does not count as an offer. Most advertisements are treated as invitations, not offers. However, if the ad is specific enough—"One slightly damaged Zenith TV, $250, first come, first served"—it can be viewed as an offer.
2. *The offer must be accepted voluntarily.* Both the offer and its acceptance by the other party must be voluntary. There must be no threat

of force and no fraud. A mistake or a failure to ask the right question does not always make a contract invalid, however. If a used-car dealer cuts fake treads in a car's bald tires, you can get your money back if you discover the fraud. But if the tires are worn and you forget to look at them, you may be stuck with the deal.

3. *Both parties must be competent.* Minors and people who are mentally ill cannot, in most cases, make valid contracts.

4. *There must be a consideration.* In contract law, a **consideration** is whatever one party gives in exchange for the promises made by the other. Most often, the consideration takes the form of money, as when I sell you a poppyseed bagel and you give me fifty cents. The consideration can also be a promise to trade one good for another or to do some service. Normally a promise to make a gift is not a legal contract because it is not backed by a consideration.

5. *The contract must have a lawful purpose.* Courts will not enforce contracts to perform illegal acts. For example, a contract between competing firms to fix prices could not be enforced because it would violate antitrust law. If the law changes, a contract that was once valid may become invalid. For example, in the past houses were often sold subject to an agreement that they be resold only to white people. Such contracts can no longer be enforced.

6. *The contract must be in the proper form.* Under common law, oral contracts are valid. However, by statute certain kinds of contracts are valid only if they are made in writing. Contracts for the sale of land or buildings must be in writing. And the UCC requires contracts for the sale of goods to be in writing if the price is $500 or more. Even when it is not strictly required by law, it is a good idea to put all important contracts in writing.

Consideration: Whatever one party to a contract gives in exchange for the promise made by the other.

Breach of contract.   When one party fails to carry out the terms of a contract, a **breach of contract** is said to occur. The other party is then entitled to some sort of remedy.

The simplest remedy is to declare the contract ended or *discharged.* For example, I might make a contract to cut your lawn each week. If I don't show up as I promised, you can declare the contract discharged. I have no further duty to cut your lawn, and you are free to look for someone else to do the job.

A second remedy is payment of a sum of money as *damages.* The purpose of paying damages is to compensate the injured party for losses suffered as a result of the breach. If the breach does not cause a loss, payment of damages is not required. For example, I might contract to perform emergency plumbing service for some apartments that you own. During cold weather the pipes freeze, but I fail to respond to a call. Leaking water does $5000 worth of damage to the apartment. You can sue me for damages.

As a third remedy, much less common, a court may require *specific performance* of the contract. This means that the party who breaches the contract must carry out the promise as it was made. This remedy is most often used when the subject of the contract is unique, so that a payment of money is not adequate compensation. For example, if I make a contract with you to buy your house and you try to back out, I can ask a court to force the sale, because each house is unique. But in the cases given earlier you could not force me to mow your lawn or fix your plumbing, since someone else could be found to do the job.

Breach of contract: Failure of one party to carry out the terms contained in a contract.

Property

Property: A set of legal rights to use a thing, to keep others from using it, and to sell it.

Real property: Rights to land or buildings.

Personal property: Any property other than real property.

A large part of business law is concerned with **property**. In law, property means a set of legal rights to use a thing, to keep others from using it, and to sell it.

The law recognizes many kinds of property. **Real property** or **real estate** refers to rights to land or buildings. All other kinds of property are known as **personal property**. Personal property includes not only things like cars and clothing that one owns for personal use, but also things like equipment and inventories that a firm uses in its business. Personal property includes both things that can be touched, like a typewriter or a shirt, and abstract forms of property, such as bonds or checking account balances.

Patent: A guarantee to an inventor of the right to seventeen years' exclusive use of the invention.

Copyright: A guarantee to a writer or artist of the right to exclusive use of a book, article, photograph, or other creation.

Among the types of intangible personal property that are recognized in business law are trademarks, patents, and copyrights. A trademark, as explained in Chapter 9, is a symbol or brand name that is legally protected. A **patent** is a guarantee to an inventor of the right to seventeen years' exclusive use of the invention. A patent is awarded by the U.S. Patent Office after the invention has been proved to be truly original. A **copyright** is a similar guarantee to a writer or artist of the right to exclusive use of a book, article, photograph, or other creation. Copyrights run for the author's lifetime plus fifty years.

Agency

Agency: A legal relationship in which one person (called the agent) agrees to act as a representative of another (called the principal).

Principal: The person in an agency relationship who wants to get something done.

Agent: The person in an agency relationship who represents the principal.

Agency is a legal relationship in which one person agrees to act as a representative of another. The person who wants to get something done is called the **principal**; the person who acts for the principal is known as the **agent**. Agent wholesalers, advertising agents, stockbrokers, and financial underwriters are examples of agents that we have discussed in previous chapters. The managers of a firm are agents of its owners.

Both the principal and the agent have certain duties under common law. The principal is responsible for all acts of the agent as long as the agent acts within his or her authority. If a purchasing agent makes a contract to buy office supplies for a bank, the bank cannot get out of the contract just because the deal is not a good one. Principals are responsible for accidents caused by agents, and even for criminal acts of agents while on duty. If the driver of a bread truck runs a red light and smashes into your car, you can sue the bakery.

Agents have a duty to act in the interest of the principal and to act only within their authority. A purchasing agent who accepts gifts or favors from a supplier in return for buying certain goods, knowing that better quality or a better price could be obtained elsewhere, could be sued by his or her employer for violation of the agency relationship. An agent also owes loyalty to the principal. For example, a sales representative should not gossip with a representative from another company about plans for a new product.

Torts

Tort: A civil wrong, other than a breach of contract, for which a court can award damages.

A **tort** is a civil wrong, other than a breach of contract, for which a court can award damages. A tort differs from a crime in that the injured party, rather than the state, has the right to bring legal action. Some actions, such as assault, count as both crimes and torts. If you punch me in the nose, the police can charge you with a crime and I can also sue you for damages.

Assault is an intentional tort, but many torts are unintentional. Injuries caused by **negligence** are a kind of tort that is of special concern to businesses. Negligence means failure to exercise due care when there is a foreseeable risk of harm to others. Businesses are liable for negligent acts of their agents, as in the example of the speeding bread truck.

Negligence: Failure to exercise due care when there is a foreseeable risk of harm to others.

Bankruptcy

Every year many businesses fail. Through bad management or conditions beyond their control, they reach a point at which their liabilities exceed their assets. They can no longer pay their bills as they come due. In Chapter 4 we defined *bankruptcy* as the legal recognition of business failure. Individuals, too, can declare bankruptcy when they cannot pay their debts.

Bankruptcy serves two aims. First, it permits evenhanded treatment of creditors. And second, it gives debtors a chance to make a fresh start. Before the development of bankruptcy law, neither of these results was guaranteed. The most powerful creditors might get all their claims paid while weaker but equally deserving ones, such as the employees of a bankrupt firm, might get nothing. And the debtor did not always get a fresh start. Debtors could be thrown into jail until someone paid their debts. Even if they were not jailed, they could be hounded by creditors for the rest of their lives. By setting a limit to how much a person can suffer for financial mistakes, bankruptcy law serves the useful function of encouraging people to put funds into risky business ventures.

Types of bankruptcy. A bankruptcy proceeding begins when a petition is filed with a federal court declaring that the firm or household is unable to pay its debts. If the debtor files the petition, the bankruptcy is said to be voluntary. If creditors (those to whom the debts are owed) do so, the bankruptcy is said to be involuntary. In either case, the bankruptcy can be resolved in one of three ways.

Chapter 7 bankruptcy: A type of bankruptcy in which the debtor's assets are liquidated and the proceeds are used to pay creditors.

In a **Chapter 7 bankruptcy** the debtor's assets are liquidated, that is, sold for cash. The proceeds of the sale are used to pay creditors at least part of what they are owed. When an asset has been pledged as security for a loan, the proceeds of its sale go straight to the creditor that made the loan. For example, a bank that holds a mortgage on a house would be paid from the proceeds of sale of the house. Proceeds from the sale of other assets go into a common pool from which unsecured creditors are paid. Chapter 7 bankruptcy is available both to firms and to individuals. Individuals who file for bankruptcy are allowed to keep certain personal assets, as shown in Box 22–4.

Chapter 11 bankruptcy: A type of bankruptcy in which a firm continues to operate under court supervision while arranging to settle its debts.

The second type of bankruptcy, which can be used only by businesses, is **Chapter 11 bankruptcy**. In a Chapter 11 bankruptcy the firm continues to operate under the supervision of a court. This type of bankruptcy tends to be used when a firm is able to earn some operating profits, but not enough to make payments in full on its long-term debt. In such a case the firm's creditors will get more by allowing it to stay in business than if they were to insist on liquidation under Chapter 7. Eventually the firm is **reorganized** in a way that makes it solvent once again. This may require some creditors to accept partial payment of what they are owed, or to accept payment in the form of common stock in the reorganized company.

Reorganization: The outcome of a Chapter 11 bankruptcy, in which the firm becomes solvent once again and court supervision ends.

Box 22–4 Debtor's Exemptions Under the Federal Bankruptcy Code

$7500 of equity in a residence; if not applicable, $7500 of any assets, including cash, may be substituted

$1200 equity in one motor vehicle
$200 in household furnishings
$500 in personal jewelry
$400 in any other property
$750 in tools of one's trade
Unmatured life insurance policies
Health care aids
Rights to receive Social Security, pensions, alimony, child support payments, unemployment compensation, and certain other benefits

Because the purpose of bankruptcy law is, in part, to give the debtor a chance to make a fresh start, individual debtors are allowed to keep certain assets when they declare bankruptcy. The exemptions listed here are set by federal bankruptcy law. Some states have higher or lower limits. Married couples filing jointly are allowed to double the amounts shown here.

Firms have been known to file for Chapter 11 bankruptcy when they are not insolvent in order to escape long-term threats to their financial health. For example, in 1982 Manville Corporation, a maker of asbestos products, filed for bankruptcy at a time when it had a net worth of $1.1 billion. It did so because it faced a flood of lawsuits from people who claimed that their health had been injured by Manville asbestos products. The firm was afraid that the damages awarded in those cases would exceed its net worth. In other cases, firms have filed for Chapter 11 bankruptcy in order to free themselves from certain union contracts they thought were unreasonably burdensome. (See question 6, page 592.) Such uses of the bankruptcy laws by solvent firms are controversial.

Chapter 13 bankruptcy: A type of bankruptcy in which an individual debtor with a steady income agrees to pay creditors a fraction of what is owed to them, or to repay the whole debt over an extended period.

The third type of bankruptcy is **Chapter 13 bankruptcy**. It is available only to individuals. Under Chapter 13, a debtor with a regular income agrees to pay creditors a fraction of what is owed to them, or to repay the whole debt over an extended period. Creditors must get at least as much as they would get in a Chapter 7 liquidation. Debtors benefit from the exemptions listed in Box 22–4, just as they would under Chapter 7.

BUSINESS ETHICS

Starting in the first chapter of this book and at many points throughout, we have discussed what a business should do to be a good citizen in a democratic society. One aspect of good citizenship is paying attention to

Business ethics: Concern with truthfulness, honesty, and fairness in business dealings.

social responsibilities toward the environment, employees, and consumers. We turn now to another aspect: that of **business ethics**. Business ethics is concerned with truthfulness, honesty, and fairness in business dealings. It is related to business law in that many kinds of untruthful and dishonest conduct are illegal. But ethics is a broader concept than law. An ethical person is truthful, honest, and fair even when the law does not require it. Such a person also respects the law even when illegal acts are unlikely to be discovered and punished.

"Of course, honesty is one of the better policies."

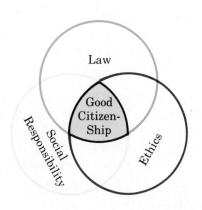

The case at the beginning of this chapter shows how closely law, ethics, and social responsibility are linked. The firm was charged with using a "Band-Aid" to get a product that it knew to be unsafe approved by the FAA, and with having pressured the British pilots not to reveal their concerns. A federal judge found Piper in violation of the law. And if Piper did act as the judge believed it to have done, the firm not only broke the law but also ignored its social responsibility toward its customers and acted unethically in covering the matter up.

Problem Areas in Business Ethics

Almost any ethical problem can arise in a business context. Some of those problems are unique to business life. The following is not a complete list of problems of business ethics, but it is a good sample.

Disclosure. One problem concerns how far a business must go in telling the truth. In the Piper example, top executives did not pass along to the FAA all of its test pilots' concerns about the safety of the Cheyenne. This was telling less than the whole truth, whether actual lies were told or not.

In sales situations there is often a temptation to tell less than the whole truth, especially if the customer does not know the right questions to ask.

Conflict of interest. A conflict of interest arises when a person's own interests conflict with those of an organization to which he or she is expected to be loyal. The best way to take care of conflicts of interest is to avoid them. For example, a person should not serve as a director of two competing firms, and a law firm should not represent parties on both sides of the same dispute.

Political activities. Corporations can form PACs to which their employees may contribute, but they cannot put corporate funds into a PAC. Violation of this rule is a common breach of business ethics. There are also ethical questions about the purpose of political activities by businesses. Is it ethical to lobby for special tax favors for your firm? To lobby for subsidies that enrich your stockholders at the expense of taxpayers? To lobby to get your bid for a government contract accepted when you know that a competitor can do the job more cheaply? Washington is full of people from both large and small firms who do these things every day.

Foreign bribery. Paying bribes to government officials in the United States is clearly unethical. Paying bribes to officials in other countries is more controversial. The Foreign Corrupt Practices Act of 1977 forbids U.S. firms to pay bribes to government officials anywhere. But some firms complain that the rule does not make sense in some Third World countries, where bribery is a way of life. Not paying bribes only means giving the job or order to a firm in a country that does not forbid the practice—and few other countries do. However, some firms say the law gives them a helpful excuse to resist extortion.

Human relationships. The need to relate to people both as employees and as human beings can lead to ethical dilemmas for managers. Suppose a drop in sales requires you to lay off 10 percent of your staff. Should you do this solely on the basis of the last performance review? Or should you keep a mediocre worker who must support two children and a handicapped spouse? Is keeping the mediocre worker fair to the better worker who gets laid off? No one has ever discovered easy answers to questions like these.

Cheating the company. No one condones theft from an employer, but where should the line be drawn? Is it OK to make a personal phone call on company time? To copy some tax forms on the office copier? To take home a pencil? A box of pencils? As Box 22–5 shows, business executives tend to take a more critical view of such actions than members of the public.

Pressures That Lead to Unethical Behavior

There may be people who have no sense of right and wrong, but most people will lie or act dishonestly or unfairly only under pressure. W. L. LaCroix lists three sources of pressure to act in these ways.[2]

[2]Wilfred L. LaCroix, *Principles for Ethics in Business* (Washington, D.C.: University Press of America, 1979), cited in William A. Evans, *Management Ethics* (Boston: Martinus Nijhoff, 1981), pp. 28–29.

Box 22–5 Executive and Public Perceptions of Office Ethics

Action	Percentage Thinking the Action Is Wrong	
	Executives	Public
Charging an employer for a $5 cab ride when you really walked	76%	52%
Acceptance by a purchasing agent of a case of liquor offered as a Christmas gift by a supplier	75	29
Taking an ashtray from a neighbor's house	99	84
Taking an ashtray from an office	90	62
Ordering the most expensive item on the menu when employer is paying for dinner	23	29
Personal use of office photocopier	20	25

A poll conducted for the *Wall Street Journal* by the Gallup Organization asked executives and members of the public whether certain actions are ethical. The actions listed here are minor abuses of the sort that are common in any office or workplace. For the most part, executives took a stricter view than members of the public.

Source: Roger Ricklefs, "On Many Ethical Issues, Executives Apply Stiffer Standard Than Public," *Wall Street Journal*, November 1, 1983, p. 33.

Pressures from superiors. Middle managers often feel pressure from superiors to act unethically. This pressure takes various forms. Sometimes it is said or implied that ethical concerns cannot serve as an excuse for poor performance. Sometimes a subordinate is invited to act in a less than ethical way. For example, suppose that you have written a report that expresses concern about the safety of a new hair spray being developed by your company. Your boss reviews the report and suggests that you tone it down a bit; he is counting on the new product to boost the division's sales next year. What would you do?

Family pressures.   Loyalty to one's family is another source of pressure. Suppose you know that your firm is turning off pollution control equipment except on days when inspectors are scheduled to visit. You complain to your superior, who tells you to mind your own business or you will be fired. Should you blow the whistle by calling the local newspaper? Can you risk being an out-of-work hero?

Pressure from peers.   Some of the strongest pressures to act unethically come from peers. On the shop floor, this may take the form of pressure on people who make slackers look bad by working too hard. At the middle-management level, it may take the form of pressure to steal other people's ideas or run down their work in order to get ahead. In a situation where "everyone does it," it can be very hard to resist this kind of pressure.

The Granger Collection

Managing for Ethical Conduct

Responsibility for business ethics starts at the top of any firm. As principals of the firm, top managers are legally responsible for the acts of employees, who are agents of the firm. They are also responsible for the ethical conduct of their employees. Managing for ethical conduct does not require one to be like Christ or Socrates. It just means putting planning, organization, leadership, and control to work in one more area of business.

Archie Carroll, in his book *Business and Society*, lists the following steps that managers can take to promote ethical behavior.[3]

- *Provide leadership.* As always, what you do must match what you say.
- *Set realistic goals.* If you ask for 25 percent growth in sales when you know that only 15 percent is realistic, you put pressure on subordinates to cut ethical corners.
- *Establish a code of ethics.* Some codes of ethics are pompous and long-winded. Cummins Engine Company has one that could be called the one-minute code of ethics. (See Box 22–6.)
- *Punish violators of ethics codes.* There is no better way to get people to see that you mean what you say about ethics. If you let people off the hook as long as their sales or output figures look good, you might as well toss your ethics code out the window.
- *Provide a whistle-blowing mechanism.* Employees who "blow the whistle" by telling government or the media about wrongdoing often try to raise the issue with a supervisor first, only to be given a

---

Box 22–6 Code of Ethics of the Cummins Engine Company

1. Obey the law.
2. Be honest—present the facts fairly and accurately.
3. Be fair—give everyone appropriate consideration.
4. Be concerned—care about how Cummins' actions affect others and try to make those effects as beneficial as possible.
5. Be courageous—treat others with respect even when it means losing business. (It seldom does. Over the long haul, people trust and respect this kind of behavior and wish more of our institutions embodied it.)

Source: Quoted in Oliver F. Williams, "Business Ethics: A Trojan Horse?" *California Management Review*, Summer 1982, p. 20.

---

[3]Archie B. Carroll, *Business and Society* (Boston: Little, Brown, 1981), pp. 77–87.

brush-off. Potential whistle blowers should be invited to bring their concerns straight to the top.

- *Provide training in ethics*. Many firms provide formal training in business ethics.
- *Support industry codes of ethics*. Most industries have a code of ethics. It is easier to act ethically if your competitors do so too.

There is one last way to promote ethical behavior among employees: hire the right people to begin with. Irwin Miller, then chairman of Cummins Engine, gave this advice.

> *We must aim at recruiting persons of stable character, who are able to commit themselves to a common undertaking, and who want to do good work. We must aim at secure persons, who are not afraid to speak up and who do not think only of themselves. . . . So what are we looking for in our recruiting? Character and maturity before specific skills—every time; intelligence and the capacity to identify responsibility with our common objectives.*[4]

SUMMARY

1. Government plays a big role in the American economy. Taxes and regulation place burdens on business. In recent years regulation has been eased in transportation, communications, and finance, but it has been tightened in other areas. At the same time, government supports business in many ways. It provides information and advice, loans and loan guarantees, and direct services. Some people believe that these forms of support are not enough. They think that government should have an *industrial policy*—a systematic program of government support for business growth and innovation. *Lobbying* and campaign contributions are methods that businesses use to influence government.

2. *Law* is a body of principles, standards, and rules used to settle disputes in an orderly way. The main areas of business law are the *Uniform Commercial Code* and the law of *contract, agency, property, torts,* and *bankruptcy*. Laws are enforced by a system of state and federal courts. Many firms prefer to settle disputes privately when possible.

3. In order for a contract to be valid, a number of conditions must be met: one party must make an offer; both the offer and the acceptance must be voluntary; both parties must be competent; there must be a *con-*

sideration; the contract must have a lawful purpose; and the contract must be in the proper form. Remedies for *breach of contract* include discharge of the contract, payment of damages, and requiring specific performance of the contract.

4. Bankruptcy is the legal recognition of business failure. The purposes of bankruptcy are to permit evenhanded treatment of creditors and to give the debtor a chance to make a fresh start. There are three kinds of bankruptcy. In *Chapter 7 bankruptcy*, the debtor's assets are liquidated and the proceeds used to pay creditors. In *Chapter 11 bankruptcy*, which is used only by businesses, the bankrupt firm continues to operate under court supervision and is reorganized after its creditors have been satisfied. In *Chapter 13 bankruptcy*, which is available only to individuals, a person with a steady income arranges to pay creditors part of what they are owed, or to pay them over an extended period.

5. *Business ethics* is concerned with truthfulness, honesty, and fairness in business dealings. Problem areas in business ethics include disclosure, conflict of interest, political activities, foreign bribery, human relationships, and cheating the company.

---

[4]Quoted by Oliver F. Williams, "Business Ethics: A Trojan Horse?" *California Management Review*, Summer 1982, p. 22.

6. Managing for ethical conduct means putting planning, organizing, leading, and controlling to work in one more area of business. Important steps in managing for ethical conduct include providing leadership from the top, setting realistic goals, establishing a code of ethics, punishing those who violate the code, providing a whistle-blowing mechanism, providing training in ethics, and supporting industry codes of ethics.

KEY TERMS

You should be familiar with the following terms and concepts. Check their meanings by referring to the marginal definitions in the chapter or to the glossary at the end of the book.

Industrial policy	Breach of contract	Principal
Lobbying	Property	Agent
Trade association	Real property	Tort
Political-action committee (PAC)	Real estate	Chapter 7 bankruptcy
Law	Personal property	Chapter 11 bankruptcy
Uniform Commercial Code (UCC)	Patent	Reorganization
Contract	Copyright	Chapter 13 bankruptcy
Consideration	Agency	Business ethics

QUESTIONS FOR REVIEW AND DISCUSSION

1. Advocates of industrial policy believe that government aid to business can speed growth and innovation. Do you think a government agency like the proposed National Industrial Development Bank would have more reason to pursue these goals than private firms do? Why or why not? Do you think it would have better sources of information as to which investments are worthwhile than private investors do? If so, what sources? If not, why not?

2. Describe a written or unwritten contract that you have entered into. Who were the parties? Were all six of the requirements for a valid contract met? How? Does the contract state what remedy will be used in the event of a breach? If the contract does not state the remedy, what kind of remedy do you think would apply?

3. Scan the news for a report of a business bankruptcy. What was the cause of the bankruptcy? Was it voluntary or involuntary? Who were the main creditors? Did the firm continue to operate? What chapter of bankruptcy law was used? Does it seem likely that the bankrupt firm will be able to reorganize on a profitable basis?

4. The federal government has special tax incentives to attract firms to Puerto Rico in order to provide jobs and raise incomes there. Your firm has built a plant there that makes mining equipment. To keep the plant open, you need to close a big order from the government of Zawalla. In Zawalla, bribery is common in even the most routine business transactions. You are told that you will have to pay a $1000 bribe to get an import license. If you don't pay the bribe, a European competitor will be happy to do so and take the order. What would you do? How do law, social responsibility, and business ethics enter into your decision?

5. What pressures might have led Piper officials to act illegally in getting FAA certification for the Cheyenne? What pressures might have kept Piper test pilots from taking their concerns about the plane directly to the FAA?

6. In 1983 Continental Airlines voluntarily filed for Chapter 11 bankruptcy. At the time, the company was solvent and had a positive net worth. Its purpose in declaring bankruptcy was to void high-wage contracts with its labor unions that threatened its long-run financial health. (Efforts had been made to negotiate

with the unions, and some, but not all, had agreed to givebacks.) After entering bankruptcy, Continental resumed operations, using nonunion employees and some union employees who crossed picket lines. A court found Continental's actions to be legal. Do you think they were socially responsible? Do you think they were ethical? Discuss.

7. Have you ever been pressured by fellow workers to work less hard in order not to make them look bad? Do you consider such pressure unethical? Is it unethical to give in to it? Discuss.

Case 22–1: Lobbying for a Lemon of a Program

Under a 1935 law, growers of certain fruit and nut crops can apply to the Department of Agriculture for "marketing orders." A marketing order is an agreement among farmers to limit the quantity of a crop that is taken to market; the effect is to raise its price. By act of Congress, marketing orders are exempt from the antitrust laws.

One of the biggest marketing orders applies to lemons. It is run by the Lemon Administrative Committee (LEA), a group of growers dominated by the giant Sunkist cooperative. The LEA limits the number of fresh lemons sold. Up to three fourths of the lemons grown in California and Arizona are thrown out or wasted in order to keep the price of lemons high. Farmers who do not comply can be punished by law and even jailed.

When the Reagan administration came to office, a task force on regulatory relief proposed ending the use of marketing orders. In mid-1983

Secretary of Agriculture John Block decided not to extend the lemon marketing order.

Sunkist lobbyists reacted furiously to Block's decision. They went straight to the White House, and after a late-night meeting President Reagan reversed Block's decision. The lobbyists marched on Congress too. They persuaded Congress to cut off all funds for the study of marketing orders. Even consumer advocates in Congress voted for the cutoff. For example, Representative Leon Panetta of California, a democrat who had expressed "grave concern" that the administration was doing too little to fight hunger, apparently saw no problem in destroying mountains of lemons.

Source: Based on Doug Bandow, "White House Hasn't Soured on Marketing Orders," *Wall Street Journal*, January 10, 1984, p. 32.

Questions:

1. Who benefits from the lemon marketing order? Who loses? Do you think this type of regulation is socially useful?

2. Suppose it were found that a PAC sponsored by Sunkist had contributed to the campaigns of President Reagan and Representative Panetta. (The *Wall Street Journal* does not say whether such contributions were made.) Would Reagan

and Panetta then be guilty of conflict of interest in intervening in the lemon case? Do you think public officials should be allowed to take part in decisions affecting businesses that contribute to their campaigns? Why or why not?

3. Do you think Sunkist's actions were ethical? Do you think the Sunkist group was socially responsible? Discuss.

Case 22–2: The Ethics of Frequent-Flier Coupons

Only about one million people in the United States fly more than 12,000 miles a year on commercial airlines, but they account for some 65 percent of all air travel. Most of them are employees of corporations and are flying at the company's expense.

In 1981 American Airlines introduced a new marketing program to attract the business of frequent flyers. It invited them to join a bonus club. Each time they flew American, they would earn points toward valuable prizes. For example, the prize for flying 75,000 miles was two round-trip tickets to almost anywhere, plus car and hotel discounts. Points could also be earned by renting Hertz cars or staying in Hyatt hotels.

American was soon joined in the frequent-flyer game by Continental, Delta, Eastern, and several other airlines. The programs were a great success, especially for airlines with extensive route systems. In order to pile up points as fast as possible, business travelers try to do as much of their traveling as possible on one airline. With such big prizes at stake, it is often worthwhile to wait an hour or two for a flight on the right airline, or even to take an indirect route.

Not all the frequent flyers' employers are happy about the programs, however. Most business travelers make their own travel arrangements and are trusted to do so with the company's interests in mind. The frequent-flier programs clearly put a strain on that trust. Employers don't like the prospect of high-paid executives passing extra hours in an airport lounge or choosing costlier flights than necessary. A few companies have asked travelers to turn in their prizes, but such rules are hard to enforce. Airlines make it easy to evade them by sending mail related to frequent-flier programs to travelers' homes.

Source: Stratford P. Sherman, "The Airlines' Flying Jackpots," *FORTUNE*, November 29, 1982, pp. 103–8. Reprinted with permission from FORTUNE © 1982, Time, Inc. All rights reserved.

Questions:

1. Suppose that you are a frequent flier and a member of American's bonus club. Would you have any doubts about choosing American over United for a business trip if the fares and schedules were about the same? If choosing American gave you slightly less time to make a sales call? If flying American Airlines added $100 to the fare?
2. Suppose that you are a paint maker. You read about American's program and it gives you a great idea. You start a "frequent-buyer" program under which you give points to purchasing agents for each gallon of paint they buy from you. The prize is a trip for two to Hawaii. You raise the price of your paint to cover the cost of the program, and you are careful to use home addresses and phone numbers when corresponding with buyers about the plan. Is the frequent-buyer program ethical? Is it different in any significant way from the frequent-flier program? Discuss.
3. Suppose that you are a manager for a large firm with a big travel budget. What steps would you take to limit abuse of frequent-flier programs?

Chapter 23

INTERNATIONAL BUSINESS

When you have completed this chapter, you should be able to

- Describe the benefits of international trade, and list some of the factors that may limit those benefits.

- Explain the difference between foreign direct and foreign indirect investment, and list the benefits and drawbacks of operating abroad.

- Define *multinational enterprise* (MNE) and discuss the impact of MNEs on the world economy.

- Define *balance of trade* and *balance of payments*.

- Discuss *international capital flows* and their connection to the balance of payments.

- List the major policies and institutions that promote international trade and investment.

- Review the ongoing debate over free trade versus *protectionism*.

There are tests and there are tests. To measure resistance against flying objects, engineers recently fired chicken carcasses at 300 miles per hour at the windshield of the new Saab-Fairchild twin-engine turbo-prop airplane. "The windshield held," recalls Tom Turner, president of the joint venture, but "mud, blood, and feathers were everywhere."

Turner could just as well be describing the dogfight among aircraft manufacturers to supply corporations and commuter airlines with a modern thirty-to-forty seat aircraft. The competition includes Brazil, Canada, a French-Italian combine, and the Swedish-American venture of Saab-Fairchild, among others. The winners will deliver planes through the 1990s; the losers will have to swallow millions in development costs.

Saab-Fairchild appears to be ahead. With one hundred firm orders, the company plans to deliver its first SF340, a thirty-five-seat, $5.75 million aircraft, to Switzerland's Crossair in April—six to twelve months ahead of the competition. Other buyers include Philip Morris, Comair, and Pittsburgh's Mellon Bank.

The battle is not over. De Havilland Aircraft of Canada Ltd. in Toronto will deliver its first thirty-six-seat Dash 8 plane this fall and has fifty-four orders. The Canadian government helped by allocating $48.6 million last summer.

The Franco-Italian joint venture between Aerospatiale and Aeritalia says it has forty-six orders for its new forty-two-to-fifty seater. "The direct operating costs of the ATR42 are going to be 15 percent less than the Saab because we carry more passengers," claims Henri-Paul Puel, commercial director of the turboprop project. But Erik W. Methven, director of sales support for the British-based Saab-Fairchild marketing team, retorts: "It only works if you've got forty-six butts to put on the seats. Economy of scale comes only if the market supplies you with the passengers."

Brazil's Embraer has a thirty-passenger model called the Brasilia that costs just $4.5 million, with cheap 8.5 percent financing. Still, some prospective buyers are shying away. "The price is low," says one, "but does Brazil have the dollars to buy components and provide spares?"

Until recently, no manufacturer was building a commuter plane for high-frequency use in hops of less than 600 miles. But the market has taken off: commuter traffic in the United States grew from 6 million passengers in 1973 to 18.5 million in 1983 and could grow by 20 percent annually to the end of the century. "The market could exceed twelve hundred airplanes by 1990," says Turner.

Since Fairchild Industries Inc. and Saab-Scania joined up in 1979 to share the risk of developing a new plane, the two have spent $128.5 million on the project, which is based in Linköping, Sweden.

Although both sides insist the SF340 project has proceeded smoothly, some insiders say that management conflicts were a problem. But the slow Swedish pace that initially frustrated U.S. management turned out well, says Edward G. Uhl, Fairchild's chairman. "In reality, the quality control was so good that the parts all fit perfectly the first time."

In fact, to counter the cheap financing offered by government-backed competitors, the joint venture is guaranteeing operating and fuel

efficiency with a pledge to pay for any extra expenses. Says Comair President David R. Mueller, "If Saab-Fairchild is confident enough to do that, we are confident enough to believe them."[1]

[1]"How Saab-Fairchild Is Winning a Commuter Plane Dogfight," *Business Week*, February 13, 1984, p. 54.

As the commuter-plane competition shows, we live in an age of world markets. The firms and their customers in this case sound like a United Nations committee. Newly industrialized countries like Brazil have become major players. Governments don't just stand on the sidelines and cheer—many pitch in with grants and subsidies. And the competition is not just between nations. Businesses like the joint venture of American Fairchild and Swedish Saab, or that of French Aerospatiale and Italian Aeritalia, are truly international.

American business is in the thick of this international economy. Look at Box 23–1, which lists the world's fifty largest industrial corporations. Twenty-one of the top fifty, including eight of the top ten, are American. Most of those twenty-one firms are not stay-at-homes; fourteen of them brought in 20 percent or more of their revenues from foreign operations. For that matter, most of the twenty-nine foreign firms on the top-fifty list

Box 23–1 The World's Largest Industrial Corporations

Rank	Company	Percent of Sales from Foreign Operations	Headquarters	Sales (000)
1	Exxon	71	New York	97,172,523
2	Royal Dutch/Shell Group	na	The Hague/London	83,759,375
3	General Motors	24	Detroit	60,025,600
4	Mobil	62	New York	59,946,000
5	British Petroleum	na	London	51,322,452
6	Texaco	66	Harrison, N.Y.	46,986,000
7	Ford Motor	45	Dearborn, Mich.	37,067,200
8	International Business Machines	45	Armonk, N.Y.	34,364,000
9	Standard Oil of California	49	San Francisco	34,362,000
10	E. I. du Pont de Nemours	33	Wilmington, Del.	33,331,000
11	Gulf Oil	40	Pittsburgh	28,427,000
12	Standard Oil (Ind.)	17	Chicago	28,073,000
13	ENI	na	Rome	27,505,858
14	General Electric	20	Fairfield, Conn.	26,500,000
15	Atlantic Richfield	9	Los Angeles	26,462,150
16	IRI	na	Rome	24,815,296
17	Unilever	na	London/Rotterdam	23,120,471
18	Shell Oil	na	Houston	20,062,000
19	Française des Petroles	na	Paris	20,029,197
20	Petrobrás (Petróleo Brasileiro)	na	Rio de Janeiro	19,004,999

International Trade

Even a firm that makes no special effort to enter world markets may be approached by buyers from other countries. This kind of casual exporting often leads to a planned export effort—sending salespeople abroad, opening foreign branches, or changing the design of products to fit the needs of foreign buyers. Sometimes firms export know-how rather than goods. In some cases this is done by licensing foreign firms to use patents or production techniques. In other cases complete factories are built in a foreign country, to be owned and run by local firms.

Sometimes firms export technology rather than goods. An example is this AT&T Technologies microwave project in Saudi Arabia. Courtesy of AT&T Technologies

Foreign sourcing: A planned effort to seek foreign sources of supply.

In much the same way, a firm can be either casually or intensely involved in importing. If a firm is offered goods made abroad and the price and quality are right, it may buy them without thinking much about the matter. For example, Canadian firms export many tons of nails to the United States, but most carpenters probably don't even notice where their nails come from. Other firms make a planned effort to seek foreign sources of supply. Such efforts are called **foreign sourcing**. Foreign sourcing means shopping abroad, often arranging for goods to be made by a foreign firm or sometimes a foreign subsidiary of one's own firm. For example, a U.S. furniture maker might have a mill in the Philippines produce a certain type of plywood to be used in making bedroom suites. U.S. firms also buy equipment from foreign sources.

The examples just given involve industrial goods, but of course consumer goods are imported too. Wholesalers and retailers engage in both casual importing and foreign sourcing. Even services can be imported, as, for example, when a U.S. firm gets insurance from Lloyd's of London, or when a Peruvian travels to Dallas, Texas, for heart surgery.

Benefits of international trade. The benefits of international trade are much the same as those of trade within a country: by expanding the market, trade makes possible more specialization, lower costs, and greater variety.

What determines which products a country specializes in? This is one of the oldest questions of international trade. Economists answer that a country chooses to import and export certain goods on the basis of **comparative advantage**.

A country is said to have a comparative advantage in goods that it can make relatively cheaply compared with its trading partners. Suppose that

Comparative advantage: The ability to produce a good or service relatively cheaply compared with one's trading partners.

By expanding markets, international trade makes possible more specialization, lower costs, and greater variety. © Harvey Lloyd, Peter Arnold

in Mexico it costs the same amount to produce 200 barrels of oil as to produce one personal computer. In the United States, the cost of making a computer is the same as that of producing 100 barrels of oil. Compared with the cost of oil, computers can be made more cheaply in the United States. Compared with the cost of computers, oil can be produced more cheaply in Mexico. It follows that Mexico can get computers more cheaply by importing them than by making them at home. Likewise, the United States can get oil more cheaply by importing it than by producing it at home.

Trade based on comparative advantage leads to specialization. Oil is a good export opportunity for Mexico. That fact attracts capital to oil exploration, provides jobs for workers in the oil industry, and so on. A Mexican computer maker, on the other hand, would face stiff competition from American firms. By letting the United States specialize in computers, Mexican oil companies (and other Mexican buyers) can get better computers at a lower price.

Drawbacks of international trade. If the principle of comparative advantage were taken literally, there would be total specialization. Each product would be made in only one country—the one with the greatest comparative advantage in that product. In fact, this does not happen. Specialization is only partial because trade has drawbacks as well as benefits. The following are among the factors that offset the benefits of comparative advantage.

- *Transportation costs.* For some goods that are bulky or perishable, transportation costs can offset the advantage of buying from the lowest-cost producer. Thus, every country makes its own bricks.
- *Communication.* Distance, language problems, and cultural barriers can make it hard to communicate with foreign suppliers. To be sure of getting just what is wanted, it may be easier to buy at home.
- *Consumer preferences.* Consumers like variety. Goods sold on the basis of taste and style tend to be made in many countries, not just those with the lowest costs. Many Americans like French wine and cheese, even though good wine and cheese are made at home. In return, French consumers think American sheets and towels are the height of fashion.
- *Uncertainty.* Buying and selling in world markets adds new uncertainties to those that are always present in business. Political instability and labor unrest are problems in some countries. Export licenses may not be granted. And, as we will see later in the chapter, there are special financial uncertainties in foreign trade.
- *Learning by doing.* Sometimes a firm or a country that imports from the cheapest source may pass up a chance to learn how to produce just as cheaply at home. For example, U.S. steel makers are at a disadvantage because they were slow to adopt the continuous-casting process widely used in Europe and Japan. They could give up in the face of low-cost imports, but instead many are trying to learn how to use the new technology in an effort to get their own costs down.

Some products are made in almost every country. © Hugh Rogers, Monkmeyer Press Photo Service

"I'm sorry to report that after the first, I'll be moving operations to Taiwan."

From the Wall Street Journal; by permission of Cartoon Features Syndicate.

Foreign direct investment: The process of setting up a foreign operation through a joint venture, establishment of a foreign branch, or the purchase or formation of a foreign subsidiary.

Foreign indirect investment: The process of supplying capital to a foreign institution, through a loan or purchase of stock, without sharing in the institution's management.

• *National security*. Governments may decide to keep some high-cost domestic producers in business for reasons of national security. American shipyards are supported for this reason even though ships—even warships—could be made more cheaply in foreign yards.

In short, although trade based on comparative advantage helps make the world economy more efficient, it has its limits. Despite the benefits of specialization, most goods are made in more than one country and some are made in almost every country.

International Operations

Importing, exporting, and licensing are not the only ways to go international. Many firms also operate outside their home country. A joint venture like the Fairchild-Saab commuter plane project is one way to set up a foreign operating base. A foreign branch is another. As we saw in Chapter 3, a foreign branch is an operating division of the company located in another country. The large banks of New York, London, and other cities maintain many foreign branches. Finally, a firm can set up a foreign subsidiary. Unlike a branch, a subsidiary is incorporated in the country where it operates. The parent company owns a controlling share of the stock of the subsidiary and determines its strategies.

Setting up a foreign operation is known as **foreign direct investment**. The firm that does this is an exporter of capital and management skills. Foreign direct investment is not the same as **foreign indirect investment**, in which an individual or firm supplies capital to a foreign firm without sharing in its management. A purchase of stock in a German firm by an American investor or a loan by a New York bank to a British filmmaker would be examples of foreign indirect investment.

Reasons for foreign direct investment. There are a number of reasons to set up operations in another country. Some are the same as those that lead to building a new plant or starting a joint venture at home. Others are unique to the international scene. The following are among the key reasons.

• *Advantages of location*. In Chapter 13 we discussed the location decision for new facilities. Such factors as transportation costs, availability of inputs, and the wages and skills of the labor force clearly count just as much in choosing a country in which to locate. U.S. firms have set up plants in low-wage countries to make products that require unskilled hand labor. On the other hand, foreign firms often invest directly in the United States in order to be close to customers in U.S. markets. (See Case 23–1.)
• *Combining strengths*. Often no one country offers the perfect set of conditions for making a product. In such cases joint ventures can be used to combine strengths. For example, the Fairchild-Saab venture combines American capital and engineering with Swedish production skills to make a winning product.
• *Vertical integration*. Many U.S. firms follow the principle of comparative advantage and import raw materials or semifinished parts. Some firms prefer to set up their own foreign subsidiaries as

sources of supply. Doing so retains the benefits of comparative advantage while improving communication and control.
- *Overcoming trade barriers.* Often a key reason for setting up foreign operations is to overcome barriers to trade. As we will see in the last section of this chapter, many countries limit imports in one way or another. Foreign operations may be the only way to gain access to some markets. For example, Mexico bans imports of cars. To gain access to the large Mexican market, Ford, Chrysler, Volkswagen, and other firms have built plants in Mexico.

Problems with foreign direct investment. Foreign direct investment has its drawbacks as well as benefits. It is not a route to growth that all firms should take. The problems include the following.

- *Sticking to what one knows best.* One of the basic rules of good management is to stick to what one knows best. An overseas venture can violate that rule. Being able to run a plant in St. Paul does not mean that one has the skills to run a plant in Egypt. The business environment of every country is unique.
- *Financial risk.* Operating overseas means increased financial risk. Changes in the values of foreign currencies can wipe out profits. Sky-high inflation and interest rates make doing business in many countries more difficult than it is at home.
- *Political risks.* There is always an element of political risk in operating abroad. In a few cases, such as the fall of the Shah in Iran, American business can be wiped out by a new anti-American government. In less extreme cases, American firms abroad face many forms of discrimination. Even in friendly countries like France or Britain, a change from a conservative to a socialist government can cause a big change in the business climate.

Sometimes the most prudent thing for a firm to do is to stay at home. More and more firms are finding, though, that the risks of direct foreign investment are worth taking and can be managed with proper planning. Let's take a closer look at firms that operate in more than one country.

The Multinational Enterprise[2]

Trade among communities is older than civilization. At Stone Age campsites jewelry and tools have been found that were made of materials brought from hundreds of miles away, perhaps by traders. In the sixteenth and seventeenth centuries, Dutch, English and Italian trading companies spanned the globe. Those companies were concerned mostly with trade, not with foreign investment, but in the nineteenth century foreign investment became more important. The canals and then the railroads of North and South America were built largely with European capital. Most of this capital was invested indirectly. Bonds and stocks were sold in Europe, but the companies were under local management.

By the end of the nineteenth century, overseas operations were becoming more common. Sewing machines and farm machinery were made in

---

[2]The brief history of multinational enterprise given in this section draws on Neil H. Jacoby, "The Multinational Corporation," *The Center Magazine*, May 1970, pp. 37–55.

England by American companies in large enough numbers to inspire the publication of a book called *The American Invasion* in 1902. But oil and mining firms, not manufacturers, were the leaders in large-scale foreign direct investment. British Petroleum, Standard Oil, and Anaconda Copper were among the pioneers. After World War I, tire makers, automakers, and firms in other fast-growing industries started foreign operations, but the depression of the 1930s put an end to that expansion.

Foreign operations on the modern scale began after World War II. Oil and mining were still important, but manufacturing was the most active sector. Firms from many countries grew into **multinational enterprises (MNEs)**, a term that is now used to describe a firm that has operations in several countries. Many MNEs are based in the United States, but not all of them. Among the largest MNEs today are Mitsubishi and Toyota (Japan), Unilever and Philips (Netherlands), Daimler-Benz and Bayer (Germany), Nestlé (Switzerland), Fiat (Italy), and Imperial Chemicals (United Kingdom).

Multinational enterprise (MNE): A firm that has operations in several countries.

A multinational enterprise has operations in several countries. This AT&T Technologies plant is located in Korea. Courtesy of AT&T Technologies.

Multinationals in the Third World. MNEs carry on operations in countries at all levels of economic development. For the most part, the developed countries welcome one another's MNEs. In the less developed countries of the Third World, however, MNEs have not always been so welcome.

Some of the Third World's opposition to MNEs is political rather than economic. Radicals in many less developed countries dislike capitalism in any form. They condemn American MNEs without much caring whether they do harm or good to their country's economy. Opponents of MNEs also remember the days of colonialism, when industrial countries used military force to promote the interests of their firms in foreign countries. The United States had fewer outright colonies than the European powers or Japan, but in countries like Cuba, Honduras, and Nicaragua it used "gunboat diplomacy" freely. This fact has not been forgotten.

Not all objections to MNEs are political. Their operations also raise economic issues. MNEs like to point out that they bring growth and jobs to Third World countries, and that is true enough. But critics say that the growth they bring is often one-sided. They charge that the MNEs want nothing from the Third World except natural resources. Oil or mining operations create a small modern sector with a few high-paid jobs for local citizens, but, the critics say, they bring no real benefits to most of the population.

In the 1980s managers of MNEs that operate in the Third World are starting to realize that they must think of their impact on the host countries in more than dollar terms. If they are not to be forced out by coups or revolutions, MNEs must make every effort to be good citizens of the host countries. Their actions must conform to local cultural values. And they have to try to involve citizens of the host country as decision makers, not just as laborers. Many MNEs are setting good examples. (See Box 23–3.) Doing well by doing good should be the slogan for operations in the Third World just as it is at home.

Box 23–3 Gulf + Western's Social-Development Program

In 1967 Gulf + Western Industries (G+W) bought the operations of the South Puerto Rico Sugar Company in the Dominican Republic. Along with the company's assets—a sugar mill and 275,000 acres—G+W acquired a legacy of neglect, including weak operations, poor housing for workers, few health care services, and few schools for the children of workers. Critics charged the company with perpetuating colonialism in the Dominican Republic.

Since that time, G+W has worked hard to turn its image around. Since 1980 it has spent some $24 million on programs to improve the health, housing, nutrition, and agricultural skills of its Dominican workers. This was done as part of a ten-year "social-development program." By 1983 the firm had built 3,000 houses for its rural workers, mostly poor black Haitians who came to the Dominican Republic to work as cutters. It has helped more than 800 of its urban employees buy homes. In 1982 it finished the first of seven new rural medical clinics. And it has

given more than 70,000 acres of company land, including 20,000 acres of prime farm land, to the government's Agrarian Reform Institute to be used in forming small farms and ranch cooperatives.

In 1978 G+W began a program of "Dominicanization"—replacing of top foreign-born officers with native Dominicans. It appointed Dominican-born Carlos Morales Troncoso as president. Morales has helped improve the firm's relations with unions, the government, and church groups.

When world sugar prices plunged in the 1980s, G+W's profits from the Dominican operations fell despite record output. But, says Morales, G+W intends to "remain loyal" to its social commitments. "We create reserves in the good times so that, when there's a drop in commodity prices, it won't affect our social-development program in a traumatic way."

Source: Joani Nelson-Horchler, "U.S. Multinationals: Benefactors," *Industry Week*, April 18, 1983, pp. 35–39.

Meanwhile, Third World countries are sprouting multinationals of their own. The Birla group of India, United Laboratories from the Philippines, Autlan of Mexico, and Caloi of Brazil are among them. Some of these firms thrive on the basis of skills that MNEs from advanced countries have forgotten or never learned. For example, Packages Ltd. of Pakistan specializes in small-scale plants that make paper from cheap local materials. But some of the Third World MNEs have competed successfully in steel and chemicals as well.[3]

[3]See Louis T. Wells, Jr., "Guess Who's Creating the World's Newest Multinationals," *Wall Street Journal*, December 12, 1983, p. 26.

INTERNATIONAL FINANCE

Firms that operate in several countries need to pay for what they buy and collect payments for what they sell, and they need to borrow and lend just as firms that operate in a single country do. In this section we will look briefly at three aspects of the international financial system. First we will look at payments made to pay for imports and exports, then at international flows of capital, and finally at the process of exchanging one country's currency for another's.

Payments for Imports and Exports

The balance of trade. When a country's firms and consumers buy abroad, they must somehow pay for what they import. Most imports are paid for by exporting things in return—manufactured goods, farm goods, and so on. The total of goods imported does not typically match the total of goods exported exactly, however. The difference between a country's total imports of goods and its total exports of goods is commonly known as its **balance of trade**. (The technical term is the *merchandise trade balance*.) If a country exports more than it imports, it is said to have a balance-of-trade surplus. If it imports more than it exports, it is said to have a balance-of-trade deficit.

Balance of trade: The difference between a country's imports of goods and its exports of goods.

In most recent years the United States has experienced a balance-of-trade deficit. The United States exports more manufactured goods than it imports. (This fact surprises some people, who picture American industry as buried under an avalanche of Toyotas and video recorders.) Farm goods are another important source of export earnings for the United States. But exports of manufactured goods and farm goods are more than offset by imports of raw materials, especially oil.

Patterns of trade differ greatly from one country to another, as Box 23–4 shows. Compared with the United States, Europe and Japan have far larger deficits in food, fuels, and raw materials. In order to pay for these, they depend on large surpluses in exports of manufactured goods. A typical Third World country exports oil or other raw materials and imports manufactured goods.

Box 23–4 also suggests why payments between any pair of countries do not always balance. For example, the United States exports less to Japan than it imports from that country. This is part of a three-cornered pattern of trade. Japan imports oil from the Middle East and other raw materials from the Third World. Those countries import food, capital goods, and services from the United States. The United States then buys goods from Japan, which allows the Japanese to pay for their oil imports and keep the cycle going.

The balance of payments. International trade in goods is only part of the picture. A country can also earn income from the export of services. Payments by foreign firms and consumers for the services of U.S. banks, insurance companies, hospitals, universities, and so on, provide income that helps offset the U.S balance-of-trade deficit. Income earned from

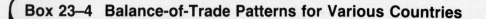

Box 23–4 Balance-of-Trade Patterns for Various Countries

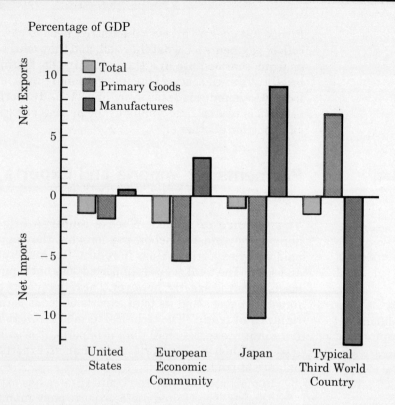

The charts in this box show how patterns of the balance of trade differ from one country to another. Compared with the United States, Europe and Japan have far larger imports for food, fuel, and raw materials. In order to pay for these imports, they must have a large surplus of exports of manufactured goods. A typical Third World country, on the other hand, exports raw materials and imports manufactured goods.

Source: Organization for Economic Cooperation and Development.

Balance of payments: The difference between a country's total imports and its total exports, including both goods and services.

foreign direct investments of U.S. firms is also counted as export of services—management and capital services, in this case.

When trade in both goods and services is taken into account, the difference between a country's total exports and its exports is known as its **balance of payments.*** As Box 23–5 shows, the balance of payments for the United States shows a surplus in years when service earnings more than offset the balance-of-trade deficit. In other years, the balance of payments shows a deficit.

International Capital Flows

As we have seen, even when trade in both goods and services is taken into account, export earnings in a given year are not always enough to pay for

---

*The technical term is *current account balance*. In addition to trade in goods and services, the current account balance also includes private international giving (for example, wages sent home by people working outside their home country) and certain government transactions.

Box 23–5 Trends in the U.S. Balance of Payments

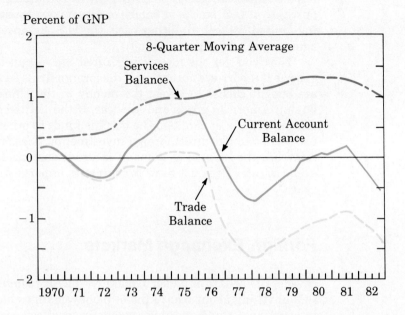

Percent of GNP

8-Quarter Moving Average

Services Balance

Current Account Balance

Trade Balance

1970 71 72 73 74 75 76 77 78 79 80 81 82

Note: — Based on seasonally adjusted data.
Source: Department of Commerce.

This chart shows trends in the U.S. balance of trade and balance of payments since 1970. The trade balance, which takes only goods into account, has dropped far into deficit since the mid-1970s. This has happened because large imports of raw materials, including high-priced oil, have more than offset surpluses in manufactured goods and farm goods. On the other hand, the United States has had a large export surplus in services. In some years this has more than offset the trade deficit, creating an overall balance-of-payments surplus. In other years, the balance of payments has been in deficit despite the surplus in services.

Source: President's Council of Economic Advisers, *Economic Report of the President* (Washington, D.C.: Government Printing Office, 1984), p. 44.

International capital flow: An act of international investing or lending.

imports. When a country has a balance-of-payments deficit, how does it pay for its imports? And when it has a balance-of-payments surplus, what does it do with the surplus? The answer to these questions lies in **international capital flows**, that is, international investing and lending.

International capital flows can best be explained by means of an example. Suppose a U.S. importer buys a shipload of BMW cars from Germany for $5 million. Let's look at three ways in which this transaction could be financed.

First, the importer could pay cash for the cars. The Germans could turn around and spend the $5 million to buy goods or services in the United States. In that case there would be no balance-of-payments surplus or deficit.

Second, the importer could buy the cars on credit. The cars would come to the United States, and the German company (or its bank) would get an IOU for $5 million. In this case, with no exports to offset the imports, the U.S. balance of payments would show a $5 million deficit.

Third, the importer could pay cash, and the Germans could decide to use the $5 million to make an investment in the United States instead of buying American goods. The investment could be either indirect (say, a purchase of U.S. stocks or bonds) or direct (say, construction of a plant in the United States). In either case, the U.S. balance of payments would again show a $5 million deficit.

Now you get the idea. The United States can import more than it exports if it borrows abroad, or if the foreign firms from whom the imports are bought choose to invest the money in the United States instead of buying American goods and services. If the United States exports more than it imports, it can lend the surplus funds to other countries, or it can use them to make direct foreign investments. These international capital flows are the balancing items of international trade. Because of them, every country does not have to match its imports with its exports every year.

Foreign Exchange Markets

One detail needs to be added to make the picture complete. We have not yet said anything about what kind of money changes hands in the course of international trade and investment. In most cases exporters want to be paid in their own currency. For example, when BMW exports a shipload of cars, it doesn't want dollars; it wants German marks that can be used to meet the payroll, pay local suppliers, and so on. Foreign investments also must be paid for in the currency of the country where they are made. For example, a German firm that wants to buy stocks listed on the New York Stock Exchange needs dollars to pay for them.

Foreign exchange market: A network of institutions, including large banks with international operations, through which one currency can be exchanged for another.

There is a special set of markets to meet the needs of international traders and investors. In these **foreign exchange markets**, as they are called, one currency can be exchanged for another. The price paid for each currency is determined by supply and demand. For example, on February 8, 1984, a buyer in the New York foreign exchange market would have paid about $1.42 for a British pound, $0.12 for a French franc, and $0.36 for a West German mark. The price of one currency stated in terms of another is known as the **foreign exchange rate**. Box 23–6 gives a table of foreign exchange rates from a daily newspaper.

Foreign exchange rate: The price of one currency stated in terms of another.

As the box shows, exchange rates change from day to day as market conditions change. Patterns of trade are one factor that affects the supply and demand for foreign exchange, and hence the value of one currency relative to another. International capital flows also affect currency values. Differences in inflation and interest rates from one country to another, political events, and wars are still other factors that affect supply and demand in foreign exchange markets, and the value of one currency in terms of another.

Changes in exchange rates can have a big impact on business. An exchange rate that swings from high to low and back again causes problems first for one set of firms and then for another.

Here is an example. In the late 1970s the dollar fell to a low value on the exchange markets. This hurt firms that depended on imports of raw materials, since they had to pay more dollars to get them. Costs of imported consumer goods rose, putting a squeeze on household budgets. On the other hand, the low value of the dollar was great for U.S. exporters. Made-in-U.S.A. goods became bargains for foreign buyers. Farm exports boomed.

Box 23–6 How to Read Foreign Exchange Tables

Foreign exchange rates change from day to day as supply and demand conditions change.

Price of each currency given both in dollars per unit of foreign currency, and units of foreign currency per dollar.

Important currencies are traded for immediate delivery, and also for delivery 30, 60, or 90 days in the future.

Country	U.S. $ equiv. Thurs.	U.S. $ equiv. Tues.	Currency per U.S. $ Thurs.	Currency per U.S. $ Tues.
Argentina (Peso)	.01956	.01950	51.13	51.27
Australia (Dollar)	.8460	.8576	1.1820	1.1660
Austria (Schilling)	.05038	.05061	19.850	19.76
Belgium (Franc)				
.Commercial rate	.01739	.01746	57.520	57.29
Financial rate	.01718	.01723	58.200	58.050
Brazil (Cruzeiro)	.0005814	.0005787	1719.95	1728.00
Britain (Pound)	1.3185	1.3380	.7584	.7474
30-Day Forward	1.3214	1.3413	.7568	.7455
90-Day Forward	1.3274	1.3473	.7534	.7422
180-Day Forward	1.3355	1.3571	.7488	.7369
Canada (Dollar)	.7592	.7574	1.3171	1.3203
30-Day Forward	.7591	.7574	1.3173	1.3203
90-Day Forward	.7588	.7572	1.3179	1.3207
180-Day Forward	.7582	.7569	1.3190	1.3212
Chile (Official rate)	.01095	.01095	91.30	91.30
China (Yuan)	.4426	.4461	2.2596	2.2417
Colombia (Peso)	.01034	.01015	96.68	98.57
Denmark (Krone)	.09646	.09676	10.3675	10.3350
Ecuador (Sucre)				
Official rate	.01576	.01582	63.46	63.23
Floating rate	.01122	.01069	89.16	93.46
Finland (Markka)	.1675	.1681	5.9700	5.9500
France (Franc)	.1157	.1156	8.6770	8.6525
30-Day Forward	.1153	.1156	8.6745	8.6505
90-Day Forward	.1153	.1156	8.6695	8.6525
180-Day Forward	.1153	.1157	8.6710	8.6425
Greece (Drachma)	.009017	.009038	110.90	110.65
Hong Kong (Dollar)	.1279	.1279	7.8195	7.8180
India (Rupee)	.08905	.08913	11.23	11.22
Indonesia (Rupiah)	.0009878	.0009881	1012.36	1012.00
Ireland (Punt)	1.0825	1.0860	.9238	.9208
Israel (Shekel)	.004222	.004222	236.85	236.85
Italy (Lira)	.0005752	.0005784	1738.50	1729.
Japan (Yen)	.004163	.004174	240.20	239.60
30-Day Forward	.004185	.004196	238.97	238.33
90-Day Forward	.004227	.004239	236.56	235.93
180-Day Forward	.004296	.004293	232.75	232.01
Lebanon (Pound)	.1675	.1653	5.9697	6.05
Malaysia (Ringgit)	.4304	.4302	2.3235	2.3245
Mexico (Peso)				
Floating rate	.005102	.005051	196.	198.
Netherlands (Guilder)	.3133	.3146	3.1920	3.1785
New Zealand (Dollar)	.6245	.6300	1.6013	1.5873
Norway (Krone)	.1229	.1239	8.1380	8.0710
Pakistan (Rupee)	.07194	.07194	13.90	13.90
Peru (Sol)	.0003045	.0003163	3284.49	3161.85
Philippines (Peso)	.05761	.05583	17.3575	17.912
Portugal (Escudo)	.006768	.006791	147.75	147.25
Saudi Arabia (Riyal)	.2848	.2848	3.5115	3.5110
Singapore (Dollar)	.4666	.4673	2.1430	2.1400
South Africa (Rand)	.6945	.7060	1.4399	1.4164
South Korea (Won)	.001239	.001251	807.27	799.20
Spain (Peseta)	.006236	.006264	160.35	159.65
Sweden (Krona)	.1211	.1215	8.2600	8.2275
Switzerland (Franc)	.4214	.4227	2.3730	2.3660
30-Day Forward	.4241	.4255	2.3577	2.3504
90-Day Forward	.4298	.4310	2.3268	2.3202
180-Day Forward	.4385	.4401	2.2803	2.2720
Taiwan (Dollar)	.02525	.02527	39.60	39.57
Thailand (Baht)	.04392	.04344	22.7693	23.02
Uruguay (New Peso)				
Financial	.01867	.01909	53.55	52.38
Venezuela (Bolivar)				
Official rate	.1339	.1333	7.47	7.50
Floating rate	.07138	.07052	14.01	14.18
W. Germany (Mark)	.3536	.3556	2.8280	2.8119
30-Day Forward	.3555	.3576	2.8129	2.7961
90-Day Forward	.3594	.3595	2.7828	2.7814
180-Day Forward	.3652	.3675	2.7385	2.7212

This box shows a table of foreign exchange rates from a daily newspaper. The prices of foreign currencies are quoted in two ways: first, the number of dollars that must be paid for one unit of the foreign currency, and second, the number of units of the foreign currency that must be paid for one dollar. (For example, on Wednesday, February 8, the price of a French franc in dollars was $0.1157 and the price of a dollar in French currency was 8.677 francs.) Prices are given for the most recent day of trading and for the day before. As the table shows, foreign exchange rates change from day to day as supply and demand conditions change.

Major currencies like those of Japan and West Germany are traded on a "futures" basis as well as for immediate sale. In a futures trade, one party agrees to deliver a certain amount of the foreign currency at a date thirty, sixty, or ninety days in the future at an agreed-upon price, and the other party agrees to accept it at that time and price.

Source: *Washington Post,* February 9, 1984, p. B7.

Exporters of computers, construction equipment, drugs, and chemicals did well too.

By 1983 the foreign exchange markets had turned around. The dollar would buy, for example, eight French francs, compared with barely four in the late 1970s. Winners and losers traded places. The costs of imported raw materials and consumer goods fell. Exporters were hit hard, however, as the high value of the dollar made American goods too costly for many foreign buyers. American firms that had to compete with imports were squeezed too. Foreign producers of steel, autos, and other goods found it easy to penetrate U.S. markets.

In short, the ups and downs of exchange rates have become a major uncertainty for American business. In the 1950s and 1960s only a few firms were deeply enough involved in trade to care what happened to the dollar. Now almost everyone feels the effects. But firms in other countries have always lived with such risks. No doubt American firms can learn to live with them too.

FOREIGN TRADE AND PUBLIC POLICY

We began this chapter by stressing the gains that can come from international trade. Trade allows firms to specialize, so that goods and services are produced at less cost. Trade increases competition, breaking the power of local monopolies. It forces all firms to stay lean, efficient, and up to date. Trade brings consumers lower prices, greater choice, and higher living standards. For all these reasons, the governments of major trading nations actively encourage international trade.

But there is another side to international trade. Trade brings increased competition, and competition means losers as well as winners.

Look at the American steel industry, for example. After World War II, it enjoyed a boom. Steel makers invested in huge blast furnaces and rolling mills. They rewarded their workers with the highest average wages of any major industry. But in the rest of the world changes were taking place for which U.S. firms did not prepare.

First, there were big changes in technology. When the Japanese and European steel industries rebuilt after the war, they didn't put in the same blast furnaces and rolling mills that U.S. firms were installing. Instead, they installed more efficient basic-oxygen furnaces and continuous-casting equipment. Second, there were changes in the cast of characters. A number of countries—Korea, Brazil, and Taiwan among them—took giant strides on the road to development. One of the first skills they learned was that of making steel. They, too, installed the latest technology, and their wage scales were far below those in the more advanced countries.

The American steel industry was slow to see these changes, but it sees them now. The United States has lost the comparative advantage it once enjoyed in steel. There has been a wave of layoffs, plant closings, and mergers. Change frequently hurts, and changes put off too long hurt twice as much.

When imports start to hurt, the affected industry cries out for help. Union and management lobbyists march arm in arm to Washington. Then government is tempted to drop its pro-trade stance and take action to block imports.

The conflicting pressures on government result in a trade policy that is full of contradictions. On the one hand, there is strong support for trade in principle. On the other hand, there are countless exceptions in the form of protection for certain industries. We will conclude this chapter with a look at both sides of public policy on international trade.

Policies That Support International Trade and Investment

International trade and investment are supported by many national policies and international organizations. Almost all of the world's noncommunist nations and some of the communist ones support these efforts. They have led to a world economic system that is far more open to trade than was the case before World War II.

Policies to support exports. Exports give a country the earning power that allows it to import. To increase this earning power, most governments have policies that promote exports. The following policies of the U.S. government are typical.

- *Aid in marketing*. Through the Department of Commerce and the State Department, the government aids exporters with marketing research. It also maintains offices abroad to promote the sale of U.S. goods.
- *Financing*. The government's Export-Import Bank offers short- and long-term credit to foreign buyers of U.S. goods. Credit insurance for private loans to foreign buyers is also available.
- *Tax exemptions and subsidies*. In some cases exporters are freed from certain taxes or given subsidies. The United States uses this form of aid less than many of its trading partners.
- *Antitrust exemption*. Under the Webb-Pomerene Act, U.S. firms that want to cooperate to promote exports are exempt from some requirements of the antitrust laws.

Policies to promote investment. Many countries, especially in the Third World, make efforts to attract foreign investment. Foreign firms that invest in a country may, for example, be exempted from local taxes and foreign exchange regulations. Often even countries that denounce U.S. foreign policy and spout anticapitalist slogans quietly welcome investment by U.S. firms.

International organizations. Besides the national policies just described, there are a number of international organizations that support trade and investment. Chief among these are the following.

- *The International Monetary Fund*. The International Monetary Fund (IMF) was set up in 1944 to promote a stable international financial system. It sets rules for orderly foreign exchange markets. It also serves as a lender to countries with temporary foreign payments problems. As a condition for loans to such countries, it insists that they adopt responsible economic policies.
- *The World Bank*. The World Bank (officially, the International Bank for Reconstruction and Development) is a means of channel-

World Bank Photo by Sennett

World Bank Photo

The World Bank makes loans to less developed countries for a variety of long-term projects.

World Bank Photo by J. Pickerell

ing capital from developed countries to those that are less developed. The World Bank makes loans at market interest rates for long-term development projects such as dams or road systems. "Soft" loans with long repayment schedules and below-market interest rates are made to needy countries.

- *GATT.* The **General Agreement on Tariffs and Trade (GATT)** was formed after World War II to prevent the reappearance of the antitrade policies that were common in the 1930s. It sets guidelines for trade policies and provides a framework for negotiations between and among nations on matters of trade and tariffs.

General Agreement on Tariffs and Trade (GATT): An international agreement, to which most major trading nations subscribe, that sets guidelines for trade policies and provides a framework for negotiations on matters of trade and tariffs.

Throughout the post–World War II period, the United States has been a strong supporter of these pro-trade institutions. Contributions to the capital of the IMF and the World Bank are made in proportion to the size of each member's economy, so the United States is the biggest contributor. U.S. diplomats have also played a key role in negotiations conducted within the framework of GATT. Even so, as we will see, the U.S. record on trade policy is not entirely consistent.

Policies That Restrain Trade

Protectionism: A national policy of restraining international trade.

National policies that restrain international trade are known as **protectionism**. The term stems from the fact that such policies protect domestic firms from foreign competition. Protectionist policies include tariffs, quotas, and other nontariff barriers. Let's look at each of these in turn.

Tariff: A tax on goods that enter a country.

Tariffs. A **tariff** is a tax on goods that enter a country. The tariff may be stated either as a percentage or in terms of a certain number of dollars per ton, barrel, or other unit. Tariffs protect firms in the home country by making foreign goods more expensive for domestic buyers.

Reducing tariffs has been the foremost goal of GATT. The main tool for tariff reduction has been a series of negotiations in which each country agrees to lower its tariffs if others will do so to. Under GATT, a country must apply the same tariff rates to all nations that subscribe to the agreement. This is known as the **most favored nation** principle. At present, 130 countries follow GATT rules. The Soviet Union is the largest nonmember nation, but some eastern European countries have been granted most favored nation treatment. Four decades of effort have resulted in much lower average tariff rates among GATT members.

Most favored nation: A nation that, under GATT rules, is given the same treatment with respect to tariffs and quotas as all other nations that subscribe to GATT.

Import quota: A limit on the amount of a good that is allowed to enter a country.

Quotas. An **import quota** is a limit on the amount of a good that is allowed into a country. The limit may apply to one country, a few, or all. GATT rules discourage the use of quotas, but there are many loopholes in these rules. One such loophole permits so-called voluntary quotas, in which trading partners agree to limit the quantities of certain goods allowed into a country. Beginning in 1981, for example, Japan agreed to limit the number of cars it would export to the United States. Despite the name, there is nothing voluntary about such agreements. They are negotiated under the threat of tariffs or even stronger restraints on trade.

Quotas, like tariffs, limit foreign competition and raise the prices paid by consumers. They differ somewhat in their effects, however. If the United States places a tariff on Japanese cars, the price paid by consumers goes up and the U.S. Treasury gets the increase in the form of tariff revenue. If a quota is used, the price still goes up, but the increase goes to Japanese automakers in the form of higher profits.

Other nontariff barriers. GATT's success in lowering tariffs and its rules limiting quotas have led to the use of many other kinds of barriers to trade. Health standards that only domestic firms can meet are one such barrier; the United States limits imports of fresh meat in this way. Technical standards are another; thus, foreign automakers claim that U.S. safety and pollution rules discriminate in favor of American-made cars. Finally, government procurement policies often favor goods made in the home country. For years the Japanese government-owned telephone company would not let American firms bid for a share of its $3 billion annual equipment purchases.

The Ongoing Debate over Free Trade

The debate over free trade versus protectionism is one of the longest-running shows in politics and economics. In the United States of the 1980s, the debate is in full swing. Almost every industry that faces foreign competition—steel, autos, textiles, wine, you name it—lobbies for protection. Ranged against them are consumer groups, importers, exporters and their workers, and firms that use imports as inputs. A full account of the debate would require a chapter in itself, but two issues seem to stand out. These are the issues of jobs and of free trade versus fair trade.

Trade and jobs. By far the most common argument for protection is that it saves jobs. Cars built in Detroit mean jobs for Americans; cars built in Japan mean jobs for Japanese. Consumers are asked to give up a little variety and a few hundred dollars a car for the sake of their fellow Americans. Since many of them don't really want to buy American cars, tariffs and quotas are used to make them do so.

Advocates of free trade concede that protection can save certain jobs, such as those of auto workers. They point out some problems with this argument, though.

One problem is that saving the jobs of some workers is not the same as raising the number of jobs in the economy as a whole. While protection saves some jobs, it threatens others. First, all actions that limit imports also injure exports. After all, selling goods to us is the main way foreign buyers get the money to buy our exports. Second, protection threatens jobs in industries that use imported goods as inputs. For example, tariffs on steel raise the price of steel, and hence raise costs in every steel-using industry. Jobs saved in the steel industry are thus offset by job losses in industries like cars and farm equipment that become less competitive when the price of steel goes up. Third, because protection raises the prices of goods, it cuts consumer purchasing power. For example, although quotas force more people to buy American cars, they must pay more for those cars, and thus, they have less to spend on houses, vacations, and so on. That means that jobs are lost in the construction industry, the hotel industry, and others.

If protection threatens some jobs in the process of saving others, why is there so much support for it in Congress? One reason seems to be that the jobs saved by protection are often located in one or a few Congressional districts, whereas those that are lost are scattered here and there. Given the way the American political system works, this fact tilts the scale in favor of protection.

A second problem with using protection to save jobs, even leaving aside jobs lost elsewhere, is the cost. Jobs saved by protection often have a high price tag. For example, according to a Federal Trade Commission study, limits on textile imports increased jobs in the U.S. textile industry by 8 percent. However, the cost to consumers was $1.4 billion per year, or $13,200 per job saved. This was almost double the average wage in the industry. It would have cost only half as much to pay the workers to do nothing as it cost to keep them on the job. And textiles are by no means an extreme case. The same study put the cost of each job saved through tariffs on CB radios at $80,000.[4]

Why pay these huge sums? If workers in industries that are affected by changes in the world economy deserve special consideration, the free-traders say, give them help in adjusting to the changes. The United States does have some programs that provide training or other benefits to workers whose jobs are lost because of imports. These programs are costly too, but they are often less costly than trade restrictions.

Free trade versus fair trade.   Many businesspeople feel uncomfortable about going to Washington to ask for protection against competition. After all, competition is what business is all about. Asking for protection sounds too much like admitting failure. To avoid embarrassment, they take another line. "Free trade is fine," they say. "We're all for competition. But the competition must be fair as well as free."

What exactly are the unfair trade practices that businesses complain of? First, it is viewed as unfair for a country to seek access to American markets while not letting American goods into its own. Japan is a favorite target of this criticism, and with some justification. The strong buy-Japanese policies of the Japanese government have already been mentioned. In addition, Japan has placed high barriers in the way of imports of meat, citrus fruits, and tobacco, which are major exports of the United States. The Japanese are by no means the only offenders, however.

A second trade practice that is widely seen as unfair is *dumping*. Dumping, as explained in Chapter 12, means selling goods in export markets for less than their price in home markets. GATT rules are supposed to prevent dumping, but the practice is hard to police. Dumping has been a frequent complaint of the steel industry. European steel makers have been hit just as hard as those in the United States by competition from the newly industrialized countries. They have been charged with dumping steel in the American market in order to keep their own mills running.

Export subsidies are a third trade practice that is claimed to be unfair. These are subsidies paid to exporters by their own governments, thereby allowing them to undercut competitors in world markets. The commuter-plane case at the beginning of this chapter gave two examples of export subsidies—Canada's aid to de Havilland and the 8.5 percent financing arranged for buyers of the Brazilian plane.

What, if anything, should the U.S. government do about unfair trade practices? Should it counter the protectionist policies of other countries with more protection of its own? Free-traders say no. If two people with guns are stuck in a lifeboat and one shoots a hole in the bottom of the boat, the other would be stupid to retaliate by shooting a second hole. If the boat of international trade sinks, say the free-traders, we will all go down with it.

Free-traders also question the wisdom of actions against dumping and export subsidies. Under GATT rules, a country can impose extra tariffs to offset dumping or subsidies. But, the free-traders say, why should we

[4]See Morris E. Morkre and David G. Tarr, *Effects of Restrictions on United States Imports: A Staff Report of the Bureau of Economics to the Federal Trade Commission* (Washington, D.C.: Government Printing Office, 1980).

Courtesy of Kentucky Fried Chicken

object if foreign producers want to sell us goods for less than they cost? When we give goods to developing countries or sell them below cost, we call it foreign aid. Why should we object if the Europeans want to give us a little foreign aid?

Even the most adamant free-traders admit, however, that a world in which all nations open their markets is better than one in which just some do so. Free-traders and protectionists agree that mutual reductions in tariffs are beneficial. Sometimes threats of retaliation may be needed to get negotiations moving. But a world in which negotiations stopped and the threats were carried out would be a less prosperous one for everyone.

SUMMARY

1. International trade benefits firms and their customers by expanding markets, increasing specialization, lowering costs, and increasing variety. Which goods and services a country imports and which ones it exports is determined by the principle of *comparative advantage*. According to this principle, a country exports goods and services that it can produce relatively cheaply compared with its trading partners, and it imports those that its trading partners can produce relatively cheaply. However, comparative advantage does not, in practice, lead to complete specialization. Most goods are made in more than one country.

2. Importing and exporting are not the only ways to go international. Firms can also operate outside their home country. Foreign operations can take the form of joint ventures, branches, or subsidiaries. The process of setting up a foreign operation is known as *foreign direct investment*. Firms that operate in many countries are known as *multinational enterprises* (MNEs).

3. The difference between a country's imports of goods and its exports of goods is known as the *balance of trade*. If imports exceed exports, a country is said to have a balance-of-trade deficit; if exports exceed imports, it has a balance-of-trade surplus. The *balance of payments* surplus or deficit includes trade in services as well as trade in goods.

4. Borrowing and lending across national boundaries result in *international capital flows*. Countries that have balance-of-payments deficits offset them by borrowing from countries that have balance-of-payments surpluses.

5. *Foreign exchange markets* are markets in which one currency can be exchanged for another. The price of one currency in terms of another is known as the *foreign exchange rate*. Foreign exhange rates vary from day to day as supply and demand conditions change.

6. The governments of the United States and other developed countries support international trade and investment. In part, they do so through such policies as marketing assistance, financing, and tax exemptions for exporters. In part, they do so through support of institutions like the International Monetary Fund (IMF), the World Bank, and the General Agreement on Tariffs and Trade (GATT).

7. Changing patterns of foreign trade are painful for firms that become less competitive as a result. Governments often practice *protectionism* in order to shield firms from foreign competition. *Tariffs* (taxes on imports), *quotas* (limits on imports), and other barriers to trade are used by the United States and many other countries. Protectionism is the subject of a lively ongoing debate.

KEY TERMS

You should be familiar with the following terms and concepts. Check their meanings by referring to the marginal definitions in the chapter or to the glossary at the end of the book.

Foreign sourcing

Comparative advantage

Foreign direct investment

Foreign indirect investment

Multinational enterprise (MNE)

Balance of trade

Balance of payments

International capital flow

Foreign exchange market

Foreign exchange rate

General Agreement on Tariffs and Trade (GATT)

Protectionism

Tariff

Most favored nation

Import quota

QUESTIONS FOR REVIEW AND DISCUSSION

1. Make a list of imported items that you have bought recently—food, clothing, durable goods, or whatever. In which cases could you also have bought an American-made brand of the same item? Why, in those cases, did you choose the import? In which cases were only imports available? Why do you think there are no domestic brands of those items?

2. What makes a firm a multinational enterprise? Search the *Wall Street Journal*, *Business Week*, *Fortune*, *Forbes*, or other business publications for an article about a U.S. firm operating abroad or a foreign firm operating in the United States. What possible benefits led the firm to set up the foreign operation? Have there been any problems? If so, what were they?

3. Watch the business press for news about the balance of trade and balance of payments, or look up the latest data in a government source such as the *Economic Report of the President*. Is the United States currently running a surplus or deficit in these balances? What reasons, if any, are given for the current state of the balances?

4. Suppose Singapore Airlines buys three Boeing 747s. What are three ways in which it can pay for them?

5. Look for a table of foreign exchange rates in a daily newspaper. Which currencies, if any, have a higher value relative to the dollar than those listed in Box 23–6? Which currencies, if any, have a lower value? Other things being equal, do you think changes in exchange rates have made life easier or harder for U.S. exporters, compared with the situation prevailing in early 1984?

6. In 1983 and 1984, California wine makers claimed that they were being injured by imports of French and Italian wines. They began lobbying for higher tariffs on imported wines. They argued that without import restrictions they would have to lay off many of their workers. Also, they claimed that the French and the Italians were not observing the rules of fair trade, in that their health standards for imported wines tended to discriminate against wines made in California. Outline a conversation between a wine industry lobbyist and a member of Congress (not from a wine-producing state) who supports free trade.

Case 23–1: Foreign Truck Makers Invade the United States

Foreign motor vehicle makers have invaded the U.S. market for medium- and heavy-duty trucks, long dominated by American firms like Ford, GM, Freightliner, Mack, White, and PACCAR Inc., maker of Kenworth and Peterbilt trucks. The invasion began from a beachhead in Hampton, Virginia, where 115 workers, using parts from Brazil, began assembling Mercedes-Benz trucks in 1981.

Daimler-Benz, the parent company, now also owns Freightliner of Portland, Oregon, which makes some of the biggest trucks on American highways. Sweden's Volvo has bought White Motor. The French automaker Renault, which has bought a 45 percent interest in Mack Trucks Inc., is a third entry.

The newcomers are pushing computerized transmissions and electronic engine controls designed to save fuel and other costs. They are also challenging one of the symbols of automotive Americana—the rig with special paint, pinstripes, racehorse engine, and wall-to-wall chrome. As the Europeans see it, a car is a fine vehicle for self-expression but a truck is a business investment.

Larry Strawhorn of the American Trucking Association comments that the European approach was "180 degrees away from what American buyers wanted." Independent truckers, whose trucks often serve as home and office as well as transportation, have not gone for the utilitarian approach. But cost-conscious fleet operators are being won over.

Strawhorn gives the foreign-owned firms credit for saving companies like Mack and White, and for increasing competition in other ways. "You take their philosophy on warranties," he says. One of the foreigners "might have a 200,000 mile warranty, but will raise it to 300,000 if it finds out that that's what some other manufacturer is doing. The customer benefits from that kind of thing."

Peter E. Rupp of Daimler-Benz explains that his firm planned its purchase of Freightliner carefully. It especially liked the Portland firm's strong distribution network. Without the Freightliner purchase, he says, Mercedes would not have entered the U.S. market. Exports were out of the question, he says, because of the way American heavy-duty trucks are sold. Buyers don't just order a truck—they pick the engine, the transmission, even the rear axle, and have the truck built to order. Add to that the complex American truck regulations, which vary from state to state, and it would be impossible to compete with a truck built abroad.

Source: Warren Brown, "Mercedes Leads Foreign Attack on Nation's Big-Truck Makers," *Washington Business*, January 30, 1984, p. 31.

Questions:

1. Why have Daimler-Benz, Volvo, and Renault chosen to enter the U.S. market via direct foreign investment rather than via exports? What strengths do they bring to the American automotive industry? What weaknesses?

2. What do American consumers gain from the entry of foreign firms into this market? What do American workers gain? What Americans, if any, are hurt by these investments? If this case is typical, do you think the U.S. government should encourage investment here by foreign firms, discourage it, or stay neutral?

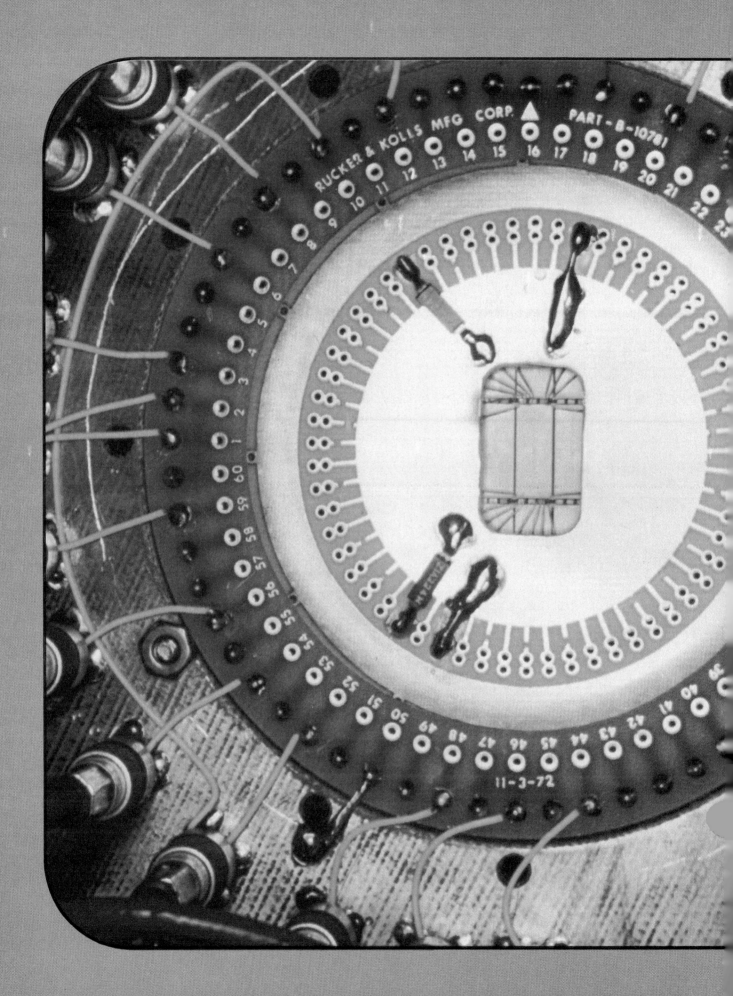

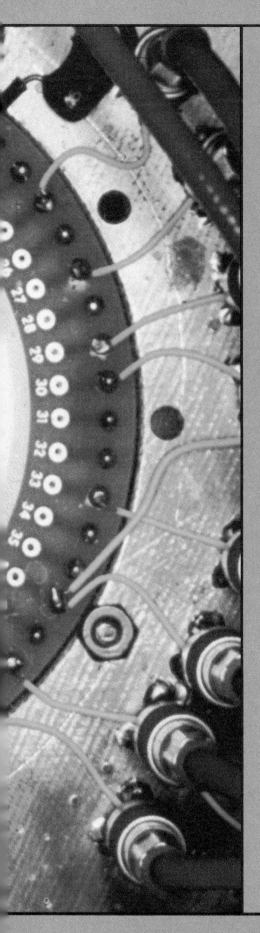

Chapter 24

THE FUTURE OF BUSINESS

When you have completed this chapter, you should be able to

- Describe several broad trends that seem likely to affect business in the next ten years.

- List the major changes in the business environment that firms will have to react to in coming years.

- Discuss the impact of these trends and changes on the management of marketing, production, human resources, and finance.

- Discuss the likely effects of these trends and changes on careers in business.

Once the Wright brothers took off, the prophets knew that everyone would soon have a helicopter or some other flying machine parked in the backyard. A ten-minute commute to downtown. A quick getaway to the lake. At last, a set of wings for everyone.

Naturally, it would be as easy to fly these machines as it is to drive the family car. In fact, in many cases the machine would *be* the family car—with a few accessories that never made it to Detroit. Like detachable wings and tails or wings that fold back. Whether it was called an autoplane or a giro-car or an aerocar, the sales pitch was basically the same: It's a great little car. It's a sturdy little plane. It takes you an easy twenty minutes to make the plane a car or the car a plane. Fly over those traffic jams to the city limits. Minutes later you'll be zipping about town.

Photograph by Richard Lakin

UPI

Several autoplane prototypes were built. They were pretty impressive and certainly more "convertible" than a canvas-topped T-bird. And before long they would surely be equipped to land on water as well, like a magic carpet. As UPI said in its caption to a 1961 photo of this machine, "Tomorrow's magic carpet may be a compact flying platform that operates on cheap, low-octane fuel, requires neither drive shaft nor gears, and whose structure, mechanisms, and controls are extremely simple to operate, according to the January issue of *Mechanix Illustrated*. This artist's sketch shows the vertical-takeoff-and-landing aircraft in flight. Small enough to fit into the average two-car garage, it could take off from any lawn or driveway and fly in any direction—forward, backward, or sideways—and land on any clear patch of ground, water, marsh, or snow."[1]

[1] John Tierney, "If This Is the Future . . .," *Science 84*, January-February 1984, pp. 34–43.

The future is an endless source of fun and fantasy. What we think about the future does not always turn out to be correct, of course. Did the people who dreamed up those autoplanes and magic carpets give any thought to safety, pollution control, or fuel efficiency? These and other factors have kept most people crawling along the highways much as they have since the days of the Model T. And take a look at the old-fashioned tent in the picture of the magic carpet. The 1980s are here, and we still don't have personal flying machines, but tents have changed wonderfully. Twenty-five years ago, who would have predicted a four-person tent that is small and light enough to slip into the corner of a backpack, with no inside poles to get in the way and, best of all, truly waterproof?

Thinking about the future is more than just a game. It is a key part of planning, one of the four functions of management. Some people, like Alvin Toffler, author of *Future Shock*, John Naisbitt, author of *Megatrends*, and the late Herman Kahn of the Hudson Institute, have made a profession of thinking about the future. These futurists, as they are called, face a task that seems to be getting more difficult because the pace of change is increasing. New technologies appear more often, and are outdated sooner. The notion that the future will be an extension of the past becomes less and less valid as time goes by.

Certainly planning would be easier if predictions about the future were always correct, but the fact that predictions do not always work out does not mean we shouldn't try to predict the future at all. In fact, it means we must try harder: we must make plans to deal with the future as we think it will be, and at the same time we must be prepared to react to the unexpected. This may require making a set of forecasts of possible futures and being prepared for each of them. It also requires that forecasts be revised from time to time, and bad ones thrown out, in the light of what actually happens.

In this chapter we will look at a number of trends that seem likely to affect business in the future. We will also note the implications of these trends for careers in business and other organizations. There is no guarantee that these trends will develop as we describe them, but they are certainly worth thinking about.

MEGATRENDS

John Naisbitt coined the word *megatrend* to refer to a broad change in attitudes that is expected to continue for at least a decade. Courtesy of Warner Books

In 1982 John Naisbitt coined a new word, *megatrends*, in a book by that name.[2] A megatrend is a broad, general change in attitudes and behavior that is expected to continue for a decade or more. After studying more than 6000 local newspapers for clues about what people are thinking, Naisbitt listed ten such trends. (See Box 24–1.) For the purposes of this book, a shorter list will do. Each of the following four trends has been noted more than once in previous chapters. Each of them seems likely to affect business for the rest of the twentieth century.

The Growing Role of Information

Information has always been important, even in sectors of the economy that may be in decline. Managers have always needed information about prices, markets, sources of supply, and production techniques. Information has always made the difference between good decisions and bad ones.

[2]John Naisbitt, *Megatrends* (New York: Warner Books, 1982).

Box 24–1 Megatrends: Ten New Directions Transforming Our Lives

1. Although we continue to think we live in an industrial society, we have in fact changed to an economy based on the creation and distribution of information.

2. We are moving in the dual direction of high tech/high touch. This means that to be successful, new technologies must allow people to relate easily to them.

3. No longer do we have the luxury of operating within an isolated, self-sustaining, national economic system; we now must acknowledge that we are part of a global economy.

4. We are restructuring from a society run by short-term considerations and rewards in favor of dealing with things in much longer-term time frames.

5. In cities and states, in small organizations and subdivisions, we have rediscovered the ability to act innovatively and to achieve results—from the bottom up.

6. We are shifting from institutional help to more self-reliance in all aspects of our lives.

7. We are discovering that the framework of representative democracy has become obsolete in an era of instantaneously shared information. The new trend is toward participatory democracy.

8. We are giving up our dependence on hierarchical structures in favor of informal networks.

9. More Americans are living in the South and West, leaving behind the old industrial cities of the North.

10. From a narrow either/or society with a limited range of personal choices, we are exploding into a freewheeling multiple-option society.

Source: John Naisbitt, *Megatrends* (New York: Warner Books, 1982), pp. 1–2.

There was never an age in which uninformed people could succeed in business.

Still, there seems to be some truth in Naisbitt's idea that information is becoming more important than ever before. For one thing, look at the spreading use of computers. These machines, as we saw in Chapter 7, allow data to be collected and processed in greater volume than ever before. Firms that learn to use these machines effectively have an advantage over competitors that do not do so. We have seen many ways of using computers in business: management information systems, marketing information

Computers are being used in more ways than ever as people continue to think of new applications for these amazing tools. © John Zoiner, Peter Arnold

systems, computer-assisted design/computer-assisted manufacturing, human resources information systems, managerial accounting systems, and electronic funds transfer systems, among others. Making these systems work requires a growing number of people with information-processing skills.

There is another sense in which we are moving from an industrial age to an information age. For many years manufacturing's share of the economy has been decreasing while that of service industries has been growing. Many of the fastest-growing service industries are largely or wholly concerned with transmitting or keeping track of information. This is clearly true of communications, financial services, and education. Other services also are concerned with information in a broader sense, including medicine and even entertainment.

The Return to a Long-Run Outlook

Naisbitt sees a change of focus from the short run to the long-run as another megatrend. Some people might prefer to see this as a return to a long-run outlook. The nation's founders appear to have thought in long-run terms too. They built to last, both in the abstract sense of building a system of laws and in the physical sense of building houses and bridges that are still in use today. In more recent years it became popular to portray American business as shortsighted. Detroit's failure to make small cars soon enough and the steel industry's failure to modernize are favorite examples. But now shortsightedness is out of fashion.

We have stressed the need for long-run thinking in every area of management that we have discussed. In Part II we stressed strategic planning as one of the key functions of management. In Part III we discussed the total-marketing orientation. In this approach the firm begins with a long-run commitment to finding out and meeting the needs of customers, rather than making whatever it wants to make and then worrying about how to sell it. In Part IV we discussed the need for a long-run human resources strategy in such areas as career development, affirmative action, and job security. And Part V warned of the dangers of placing too much emphasis on short-run profits at the expense of long-run financial strength.

Growing attention to environmental values is another example of the trend toward long-run thinking. In the past, resources were used and wastes dumped without much thought about the long-run effects. Today such shortsighted treatment of the environment is seen as irresponsible— and it is illegal as well.

The Trend Toward a World Economy

Much of Chapter 23 was devoted to the trend toward a world economy. Three aspects of this trend were discussed: the growth of imports and exports as a share of GNP, the growth of multinational enterprises, and the growing impact of foreign exchange markets. This trend interacts with the two that we have just mentioned. To succeed in the world economy, a firm needs more information than ever before. And to meet foreign competition it must plan a sound long-run strategy.

Changing Attitudes Toward Organizations

Several of the ten megatrends that Naisbitt lists have to do with changing attitudes toward organizations. People are becoming impatient with organizations that are big and inflexible. Peters and Waterman, often cited in this book, stress that excellently managed firms are flexible and allow room for entrepreneurship.

As a part of this pattern, Naisbitt thinks, new technologies will be able to survive only when they are made easy to use—only when "high touch" is added to "high tech," in his phrase. He sees more vitality in local political units than in the federal government, and a greater role for participatory democracy than for traditional representative democracy. Naisbitt's trends toward self-help and informal networks also fit this pattern.

Finally, this trend is seen in the growing respect for small business. Small businesses, rather than the Fortune 500, have been the main source of growth in jobs and output in recent years, and will probably continue to be so. Even large firms have often found it worthwhile to assign special projects to small teams that are given a lot of independence.

Going together with this new respect for small firms is a growing sense that an organization of any size is only as strong as the people who work in it. Theory X management, which viewed workers as interchangeable parts in a system, is out. Theory Y management, which sees people as eager to take responsibility and work creatively even on routine tasks, is in.

CHANGES IN THE BUSINESS ENVIRONMENT

Besides the "megatrends" that we have discussed, there will be other changes in the business environment to which firms must adjust. Some of these—such as demographic changes—can be predicted fairly accurately. Others, such as changes in politics and economics, are almost impossible to predict. Let's take a look at three of the most likely areas of change.

Demographics

The American population is going to change in a number of ways in coming decades. First, people will live in different places. (See Box 24–2.) The shift, as noted by Naisbitt, is mainly from North to South and from East to West. Tiny New Hampshire is the only major holdout against this trend.

Second, the U.S. population will get older. This will happen partly because the average life expectancy will continue to rise, and partly because of the aging of the "baby boom" generation born just after World War II. Over the next half-century, the portion of the population aged sixty-five or over, now about 12 percent, is expected to double.

Third, the population will become more diverse in terms of race and culture. The black, Hispanic, and Asian-American sectors will grow faster than average. Also, immigration will continue to add to the ethnic diversity of the U.S. population.

The population as a whole will grow only slowly, however. By some estimates, the growth of the total population will come to a halt early in

Box 24–2 Where Population Growth Will Be Fastest and Slowest, 1980–2000

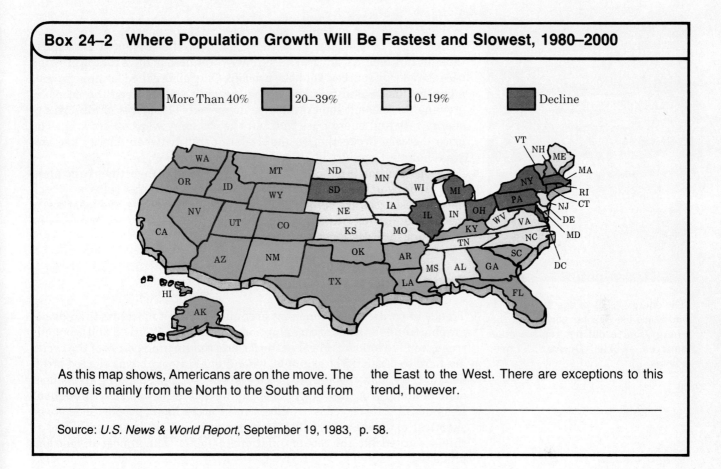

More Than 40% 20–39% 0–19% Decline

As this map shows, Americans are on the move. The move is mainly from the North to the South and from the East to the West. There are exceptions to this trend, however.

Source: *U.S. News & World Report*, September 19, 1983, p. 58.

the twenty-first century as the percentage of women of childbearing age declines.

Natural Resources and Technology

During the 1970s people became very concerned about the prospect of running out of energy sources, minerals, clean air, clean water, food, and almost everything else. This concern set off a debate between two camps. On the one hand, pessimists foresaw a day, not far off, when we would start running out of one vital resource after another. The economy would then go into a tailspin. On the other hand, optimists thought we would surely be rescued by something called technology. Superplastics would be invented in time to replace metals; fusion energy would arrive just as we ran out of oil; and so on. Both camps were partly right, but both were also partly wrong. Managers who must guide their firms through the coming decades will need a more balanced understanding of the link between natural resources and technology.

The environmentalists of the last decade tended to ignore the fact that the process of running out of any resource gives rise to self-correcting forces. As resources become scarcer, competition drives their market prices upward. Higher prices are an incentive to conserve the scarce resources and search for substitutes. Projections of past trends that do not take such price changes into account are always wrong.

The energy crisis of the 1970s led to increased use of solar power, but this energy source did not replace other sources. © Alec Duncan, Taurus Photos

For years, for example, the consumption of energy in the United States grew in lockstep with the growth of the economy. Pessimists thought this meant that the U.S. economy would soon have to stop growing because energy sources would be used up. Optimists called for huge investments in fusion and solar power as the only way to keep the economy growing. In the end something else happened. The prices of all forms of energy rose and energy use fell, but the economy went on growing. The price increase broke the lockstep relationship between energy use and gross national product.

Conservation is not costless, though. It requires investment and planning. It is worthwhile to look ahead and measure the rates at which natural resources are being used up. With good planning, the least costly means of adjusting to scarcity can be used. Firms that do not plan may be forced to use costly emergency measures.

Economics and Politics

Trends in politics and economics are much harder to forecast than demographic trends or rates of consumption of resources. Political and economic trends tend to follow cyclical patterns, and the turning points of the cycles are hard to predict. For example, when Ronald Reagan was elected president in 1980, many people predicted that government spending and budget deficits would drop. Instead, both spending and the deficit rose throughout Reagan's first three years in office. On the other hand, people tended to be skeptical of Reagan's promise to bring inflation under control. Yet as things worked out, the rate of inflation fell faster than almost anyone had predicted.

Even when broad trends can be identified, it is hard to guess the exact form they will take. For example, there seems to be a trend toward more cooperation between government and business. When a trend like this affects both of the major political parties, it is more likely to persist than if it affects only one of them. However, this trend could take more than one form. It could take the form of continued loosening of regulations on

Drawing by Modell; © 1983 *The New Yorker Magazine, Inc.*

THE FUTURE OF BUSINESS / 631

business, with government taking more and more of a hands-off attitude.
But the trend toward cooperation could also take the form of an industrial
policy that would give government a bigger say in business decisions than
ever before. Finally, as mentioned in Chapter 23, cooperation might take
the form of protecting American firms against foreign competition. In that
case, business and government would be cooperating at the expense of
consumers.

IMPACTS ON MANAGEMENT

One thing we can be sure of is that the future will hold many changes. The
businesses and other organizations that succeed will be those that adapt to
those changes most effectively. This, of course, has always been true, but
the need to adapt quickly and effectively seems to be increasing, for three
reasons.

First, the business environment is becoming more competitive. Large
firms that used to have to worry about only a handful of large rivals now
have at least two other sources of competition to worry about. One is
foreign firms. The other is small businesses. Together, these keep the
giants on their toes.

Second, there seems to be a speed-up in the pace of change. New
technologies appear at a faster rate. New competitors spring up more
quickly. Major price changes take place in world markets, such as the rise
in oil prices during the 1970s or the rise in the value of the dollar in foreign
exchange markets at the beginning of the 1980s. These changes call for
fast reactions.

Finally, in the 1980s many firms have less "fat" or "slack" to carry
them through changing times than they once did. The inflation of the
1970s and the back-to-back recessions of the early 1980s led to heroic
cost-control measures at many firms. The lack of room to maneuver shows
up partly in staffing levels—both middle management and production
staff have been slimmed down. The lean, trim look of the 1980s also shows
up on balance sheets.

Keeping in mind the need to adapt quickly, let's look again at the
trends discussed earlier in the chapter.

Marketing

"Most businessmen don't realize it yet, but the middle class—the principal
market for much of what they make—is gradually being pulled apart."[3] So
wrote Bruce Steinberg in a 1983 *Fortune* article on trends in marketing.
Steinberg, and others who have reached the same conclusion, cite data like
those given in Box 24–3. As the chart shows, the upper and lower ends of
the family income distribution are growing while the middle-income class
is shrinking.

The pulling apart of the mass market is due partly to the growth of the
service and information sector of the economy. Manufacturing provides
many high-paid blue-collar jobs that make possible a middle-class life-

[3]Bruce Steinberg, "The Mass Market Is Splitting Apart," *Fortune*, November 28, 1983, p. 76.

Box 24–3   The Shrinking Middle Class

Family Incomes (in constant 1982 dollars)

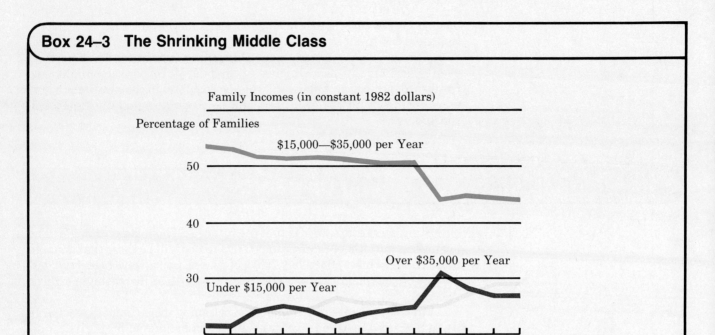

The percentage of families in the "middle class," here defined as those with incomes of $15,000 to $35,000 in constant 1982 dollars, dropped sharply in the past ten years. Families at the extremes increased as a proportion of the total, especially after 1978.

Source: *Fortune*, November 28, 1983, p. 78.

style for millions of Americans. Services provide some such jobs, but not as many. Instead, they provide very highly paid jobs for managers, lawyers, engineers, and computer specialists, and low-paid jobs for clerks, waiters, hospital workers, and so on. The mass market is changing in other ways, too. Growing numbers of older people have money to spend, but they do not spend it in the same ways as the younger households that were the targets of marketers in the past.

The result of all this is a trend toward greater diversity in marketing. We have seen this in several areas. In retail trade, for example, both off-price stores and upscale boutiques are growing. Traditional mass marketers like department stores and supermarkets are on the defensive. Makers of foods, cigarettes, cosmetics, and even cars are putting out more and more brands, each one geared to the needs of a specific group based on age, cultural background, or income. To succeed in this new environment, a firm must have a better idea than ever of just who its customers are and what they want.

Managing Production Systems and Human Resources

Growing competition, both at home and abroad, will make efficient production a key to survival. This is true for both manufacturing firms and service firms. The status of production and human resource managers within the firm is likely to go on rising.

One of the biggest challenges will be that of putting more and more robots and computers to work in production systems. This is more than a technical challenge. The key is getting people to accept and work well with the new tools. As Box 24–4 shows, many people are fearful of these new

Box 24–4 Poll Finds Widespread Fear of Automation

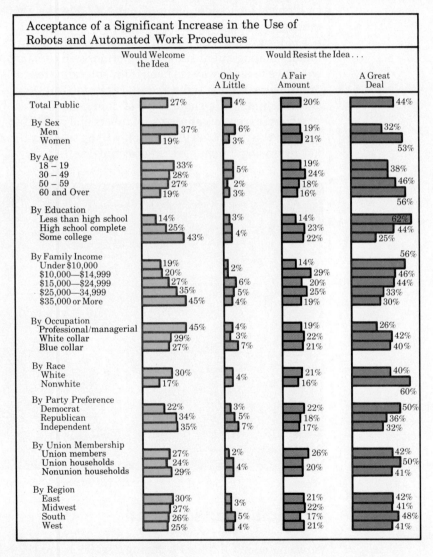

In 1983 Opinion Research Corporation of Princeton, New Jersey, conducted a telephone poll of 1005 people to find out how they felt about automation. The question asked was whether people would welcome a significant increase in the use of robots and automated work procedures, or would resist the idea. Note that women expressed more resistance than men, older workers more than younger workers, and members of minority groups more than whites.

Source: *Iron Age*, February 25, 1983, p. 52. Reprinted by permission of Iron Age.

machines, and will resist them unless their introduction is handled very carefully.

Resistance to new technologies is lessened when their users are given a voice in decision making. Whether the technology is office automation or robots on the production line, the people who will use the new machines must be involved in decision making from the earliest stages. When the work force is unionized, a cooperative relationship with union leaders is needed. Retraining programs for displaced workers can reduce threats to job security.

Not all of the challenges to human resource managers will be found on the shop floor. The changing age structure of the population will create challenges for middle and top managers. In the 1960s and 1970s, middle managers could expect fast promotion in most firms because there were few older workers ahead of them. As the baby boom generation enters the middle-management ranks, promotions will come more slowly. Managers will have to learn ways to keep their subordinates satisfied and challenged despite less frequent advances in rank. Job rotation, job enlargement, and job enrichment are some ways of doing so.

Despite the spreading use of robots and computers, the most successful firms in the future, as in the past, will be those that recognize that people, not technology alone, are what count.

Putting robots to work in production systems is more than a technical challenge. It also involves getting people to accept and work with the new tools. © Richard Kalvar, Magnum Photos

Financial Management

As we noted in Chapter 17, during the 1960s and 1970s finance became the fast track to the top levels of management. There are signs that this pattern has changed, and that managers with marketing and production backgrounds are getting equal play at the top. Financial management will remain important in the future, but like other areas of management, it will have to change with the times.

One change corresponds to the "megatrend" shift from a short-run to a long-run outlook. One of the things that has given finance a bad name in some circles is a narrow short-run focus on the "bottom line." For example, as we saw in Chapter 18, a firm's short-run net income can be boosted by cutting back on investments in research and development, advertising, and job security for employees. However, in terms of long-run profitability these investments are just as important as investments in plant and equipment.

A second trend that affects financial management is the fast pace of technological change. The computer has already changed the way financial functions are carried out within a firm. Tasks like inventory control, cash management, and accounting are computerized even in very small firms. The next step will be linking the financial systems of individual firms to form a national network for electronic funds transfer. In the long run even households will be hooked into this system through point-of-sale debit card terminals and other devices.

Finally, financial managers, like other managers, will have to adopt an international outlook. They will have to get used to dealing with the uncertainties caused by changes in foreign exchange markets. And they will have to shop abroad for sources of funds and for financial services like insurance. The biggest multinational enterprises have been doing these things for years. In the future, managers of small- and medium-sized businesses will have to do them too.

IMPLICATIONS FOR CAREERS IN BUSINESS

All of the trends and changes that we have discussed will affect careers in business. Tomorrow's careers will be found in different places than today's. (See Box 24–2.) They will also be found in different industries. (See Box 24–5.) However, while some people will find careers in exotic new fields like robot repair, continuity is as important as change in thinking about future careers.

By and large, the skills that were most useful in the past—being able to communicate well and deal with people—will continue to be keys to success in the future. Another key asset in tomorrow's job market, as in the past, will be flexibility. If the futurists are right in thinking that the pace of change is getting faster, flexibility will be even more important.

Formal education will still be a major part of preparing for a career, but perhaps in a different way than in the past. There was a time when a college or graduate degree was seen as a sure ticket to a good, perhaps even excellent job. Formal qualifications meant quite a bit when relatively few people had them. At that time a college degree might have been a sufficient basis for a career.

Now, when so many people have college and graduate degrees, the situation is changing. A degree may be viewed as necessary if one is to be considered for a position, but it is not a guarantee that a good position will be offered. As a result, the importance of what one actually learns at college has gone up compared with the importance of simply having a college degree.

One big question in preparing for a career is how much to specialize. To get started in a career, most of us need to specialize to some extent. For some people, this specialization will continue throughout life. The career sections at the end of each part of this book can give you an idea of some promising areas in which to specialize.

Box 24–5 Where Jobs Were Gained and Lost, 1977–82

(Thousands)

Telecommunications	184.9
Food, beverage	184.5
Electronics	101.9
Office equipment	88.2
Chemicals	52.8
Aerospace	36.7
Instruments	25.7
Personal/home care	14.7
Fuel	14.5
Drugs	11.4
Leisure toys	5.6
Misc. mfg.	3.8
Appliances	(0.6)
Farm-const. equip.	(22.8)
Containers	(44.5)
Electrical	(49.5)
Auto-parts	(50.1)
Machine tools	(67.8)
Paper	(78.3)
Steel	(148.8)
Bldg. materials	(168.0)
Auto-vehicles	(188.1)
Tire and rubber	(199.3)

This box lists major industries in terms of the numbers of jobs gained or lost between 1977 and 1982. Telecommunications, a high-tech industry, leads the list of gainers, but it is followed closely by the low-tech food and beverage industry. Figures in parentheses indicate job losses.

Source: *Business Week's Guide to Careers* (New York: McGraw-Hill, 1984), p. 37.

For many people, though, changes in the business environment will make narrow specialization risky. For one thing, specialized jobs may be eliminated by changes in technology. The jobs of people who operated newspaper typesetting machines are an example. For another, a person who is too specialized may be passed over for promotion because he or she is needed in one narrow position. Finally, people who are too specialized may simply become bored.

All in all, the person who is best equipped for a career in the future world of business will be the one who views a college education as a platform on which to build a habit of lifelong learning. The business environment is getting better at supporting such learning. New technologies, attitudes, and techniques stress training and development on the job. Not all lifelong learning is a formal process, however. As was true in the past, the people who are most successful will be those who can learn from their bosses and colleagues as well as from formal programs.

The futurist Marvin Cetron believes that career changes will be more common in the future. He even foresees a day when many people will retrain themselves for a new career every ten years. The flexibility needed for such a pattern will be helped, he thinks, by the larger number of dual-career families.

Perhaps the most important thing to remember is that a career in business, like any other career, is a journey rather than a destination. To be successful on the journey, and to enjoy it, you must think often about what you want to do, what you are good at, and where it can be done. We have been glad to have you with us for a course that is an early stage in your career journey. We wish you well as you continue it.

SUMMARY

1. A megatrend is a broad, general change in attitudes and behavior that is expected to continue for a decade or more. The following trends fit this definition: the growing role of information, the return to a long-run outlook, the trend toward a world economy, and changing attitudes toward organizations.

2. Besides the megatrends, there will be other changes in the business environment to which firms will have to adjust. Demographic changes can be predicted fairly accurately. Changes in technology and supplies of natural resources are less easy to predict. Hardest of all to predict are economic and political trends.

3. All of these trends and changes will be important for management. In marketing, the old mass market—the middle class—seems to be splitting apart. In the future successful marketing will require more spe-

cialization and careful product positioning. Production and human resources management will face the major tasks of introducing new technologies in a way that makes the best use of people, the most important asset of any firm. Financial managers will have to cope with new technologies like electronic funds transfers. They will also have to develop a long-run outlook and adjust to changes in the world economy.

4. In the future, careers will be found in different places and different industries than in the past. Yet the skills of communicating and dealing with people will continue to be keys to success. Flexibility will be an even greater factor in career success. A key part of flexibility will consist of treating a college education as a platform on which to build a habit of lifelong learning.

QUESTIONS FOR REVIEW AND DISCUSSION

1. Which of Naisbitt's megatrends do you think will affect your career plans during the coming decade? How will they affect those plans?

2. Housing construction is one of the largest industries in the United States. How would you expect it to

be affected by the changes described in this chapter?

3. Not-for-profit organizations like your college will be affected by trends and changes in the business environment. Explain how those trends and changes are likely to affect your college during the coming decade.

Case 24–1: Bridge to the Twenty-first Century

"As I see it, the future looks mostly good," wrote Herman Kahn in a 1982 article. While others were worried about what the future might bring, Kahn called attention to ten trends in the United States that he thought would bring about economic revitalization by the end of the twentieth century. The trends are as follows.

- The recession and the high value of the U.S. dollar have resulted in cost cutting, technical improvements, and better utilization of labor and equipment. American business is becoming leaner, tougher, hungrier, and more competitive.
- The business environment has become less

Case 24–1: Bridge to the Twenty-first Century (continued)

hostile and chaotic. We are seeing the end of almost two decades of widespread concern over discrepancies between our traditional ideals and our actual practices.

- Relatively inexperienced entrants to the labor force in the 1960s and 1970s (including the baby boom generation, women, and minority groups) now have much more useful experience and thus greater productivity.
- Many productivity-raising capital investments, deferred because of bad economic times, will soon be made as industry begins to use more of its existing capacity.
- Reaganomics should help create a supportive and stimulating business environment for such investment; in particular, increased savings and cash flow should help make the needed financial resources available.
- Enormous increases in the productivity of both goods and service industries should result directly from new computer, communications, and sensor technologies. This trend also encourages capital investment.

- Many creative developments will occur in biotechnologies, new materials, and other high-tech industries, and there will be heavy capital investments in traditional technologies that are now becoming more cost-effective. We should see these developments especially in the areas of environmental protection, better transportation, and more efficient use of energy.
- The emerging synthesis of new and traditional values and greater concern about economic growth and competitiveness have resulted in positive changes in the attitudes, values, and skills of labor, management, government, and the general public with regard to investment and productivity.
- Greater general confidence and more inspiring visions of the future should lead to the restoration of what John Maynard Keynes called the "animal spirits" of businessmen and entrepreneurs.
- Finally, we may use some gimmicks (e.g., indexing of the principal of loans) to deal better with both existing inflation and fear of future inflation.

Source: Herman Kahn, "The Economic Bridge to the Twenty-first Century," *Institutional Investor*, December 1982, p. 68. Written with the assistance of Carol Kahn.

Questions:

1. Compare Kahn's list of trends to Naisbitt's list of megatrends (Box 24–1). How are they similar? How are they different? Do they contradict each other in any way?
2. Do you think Kahn's optimism is justified? Do you think he is too optimistic about any of the trends?

3. Whatever your own point of view, play the role of devil's advocate and make a list of the most negative trends you can think of that point to a worse future for business. Set your list against Kahn's optimistic one and discuss how each might affect the future.

SUGGESTED READINGS, PART VI

Anderson, Ronald A., Juan Fox, and David P. Twomey. *Business Law*. Cincinnati: South-Western, 1984.

Hysom, John L., and William J. Bolce. *Business and Its Environment*. St. Paul, Minn.: West, 1983.

Carroll, Archie B. *Business and Society: Managing Corporate Social Performance*. Boston: Little, Brown, 1981.

Hoffman, W. Michael, and Jennifer Mills Moore. *Business Ethics: Readings and Cases in Corporate Morality*. New York: McGraw-Hill, 1984.

Walters, Kenneth D. "Your Employees' Right to Blow the Whistle." *Harvard Business Review*, July-August 1975, pp. 26–28.

Robinson, Richard D. *Internationalization of Business: An Introduction*. Chicago: Dryden Press, 1984.

Robock, Stefan H., and Kenneth Simmonds. *International Business and Multinational Enterprise*, 3rd ed. Homewood, Ill.: Irwin, 1983.

"Deregulating America," *Business Week*, November 28, 1984, pp. 80–83.

Magaziner, Ira C., and Robert B. Reich. *Minding America's Business*. New York: Vintage Books, 1983.

Naisbitt, John. *Megatrends*. New York: Warner Books, 1982.

Useful periodicals:

The Economist
Columbia Journal of World Business

Appendix A
GETTING STARTED IN YOUR BUSINESS CAREER

At the end of Part I, we defined a career as a sequence of work-related experiences that form a work history and reflect a chosen work-related life theme. This definition stresses the fact that a career is more than simply a job. But, just as a long journey must begin with a single step, a career must begin with a first job.

Getting Your First Job

Whether your first job is that of a blue-collar supervisor, a computer programmer, a sales worker, an insurance adjuster, or any of the others we have profiled in this book, the process of entering the job market is much the same. In this section, we focus on six steps: (1) self-exploration, (2) exploring the job market, (3) obtaining interviews, (4) interviewing, (5) following up after the interview, and (6) accepting a job offer. This information will be valuable whether you are looking for your first full-time position, entering the job market after a prolonged absence, or looking for a job in a different field. If you already have a full-time position in your chosen field, some of this material will be familiar to you—but you may still find it helpful if you are planning to change jobs.

Step 1: Self-exploration.   The first step toward a successful career is self-exploration. But self-exploration is not something you do only once. You do it again and again over time as you grow and change. Each time you change jobs or reach a major turning point in your career it is a good idea first to review where you are, where you want to go, and how you can get there. The period in which you are looking for a job is a particularly good time for self-exploration, for several reasons. First, you are likely to be highly motivated. Second, self-assessment is useful in helping you decide what to look for and what to avoid. And third, feedback tends to come fairly quickly both from the market (in the form of interviews and offers, or the lack of them) and from your own feelings and reactions. The suggested readings at the end of this chapter include *What Color Is Your Parachute?*, by R. N. Bolles, a popular book about self-exploration that provides step-by-step guidelines.

Step 2: Exploring the Job Market.   When you start exploring the job market, you will probably do so in two stages. In the first stage you will decide what industry or sector you want to enter and what general types of jobs would interest you. In the second stage you will begin to focus on particular companies and a more restricted set of job possibilities. These stages often overlap, but there is an obvious advantage to making broad decisions early in the process and specific ones later.

This course and others can provide guidance in deciding what kinds of jobs might interest you and what general field you might enter. (Refer back to the career sections at the ends of earlier parts of this book for specific information.) At this early stage, the possible choices are practically endless. For example, you might want to pursue a career in finance but be quite flexible when it comes to the specific industry or sector in which that career could start. Or you might want to find a position in the computer industry but be willing to start out in marketing, sales, production, or some other area.

When you have a clear idea of the kind of work you would like to do and are ready to look for a specific job, you might start with the placement center at your college or university. These centers frequently can provide information on types of jobs and careers, as well as various industries and companies. In addition, they may have specific information on employers and job openings in the local community.

Another important source of information is friends and associates who already have full-time positions in the field or sector that you have chosen. They can tell you what it's like to be an accountant, a salesperson, or whatever, and what it's like to work for company X in industry Y. They are also a useful source of information about specific job openings. (Incidentally, if you have a job and are planning to switch to a similar positon somewhere else, your most important leads will come from the people you work with now.) You should keep in mind, however, that the information you get from friends is "filtered" by their personalities and experiences; Joe may describe an accounting job or a computer company quite differently than Jean describes it, since he hates his job and she loves hers.

In addition to your college placement office and your friends and acquaintances, there are several published sources of job information. Newspapers and newsmagazines often carry stories about particular industries or businesses, as well as advertisements of job openings. From publications like *Time, Newsweek,* the *New York Times,* and the *Wall Street Journal* you can get both general descriptions and specific information such as the names of people and organizations and recent developments in industries you're interested in. You should also look at trade publications like *ComputerWorld* and *Advertising Age.* Other valuable sources are the *Encyclopedia of Associations,* which lists over 1200 associations in practically every field, and *Standard Rate & Data,* which lists thousands of trade publications, by topic.

When you reach the point at which you want to find out about specific companies, you can get information about them from the following sources, many of which are available at the library.

- The company's annual report
- the *Value Line Investment Survey*
- the *Dun & Bradstreet Reference Book*
- *Standard & Poor's Stock Reports*
- *Standard & Poor's Register of Corporations, Directors, and Executives*
- Moody's Manuals
- Fitch Corporations Manuals
- The *F&S Index of Corporations and Industries*

You might also look at Better Business Bureau reports and Chamber of Commerce publications.

Step 3: Obtaining Interviews. The next step is to obtain an interview at the company or companies you would like to work for. To do this, you must first make contact with someone in the company, preferably the person who might be interested in hiring you. In many cases this initial contact is "cold"—you are responding to an ad in a newspaper or writing to the company's personnel office—and the chances of obtaining an interview are not very high. But even in a "cold" situation your chances can be improved by a good *cover letter*, that is, the letter you enclose with your resume.

Your cover letter should be neatly typed and *accurate*—if you misspell your potential employer's name, your chances of getting a job there are practically nil! The letter should be fairly short—just long enough to present the following information.

1. The job you are applying for and how you found out about it.
2. Your reasons for believing you would be a good person for the job or company (be brief).
3. When and how you will follow up (for example, early next week, by telephone).
4. The fact that you are enclosing your resume, which indicates where you can be reached.

Two sample cover letters are shown in Box A–1.

Note that a cover letter is intended to be read by only one person. (A resume, on the other hand, is meant to be read by several potential employers.) You may send out 15 or 20 cover letters, but each one will be written for a particular company and addressed by name to a specific individual. The letter should focus on how your skills relate to your potential employer's needs (which you are aware of as a result of the research you did in step 2). The more specific you can be about this, the better. And if you write on printed personal letterhead you will make an even better impression.

Just as important as the cover letter, if not more so, is the *resume*. Your resume (the word is French for "summary") not only sums up your experience and education but also advertises you to potential employers. Its purpose is to arouse an employer's interest in you and thereby to gain an interview. Later in the hiring process the resume is circulated among the various people involved in the decision.

If you view your resume as an advertisement for a unique product—yourself—you will understand how important it is for the resume to be good looking and accurate. It should be well organized, carefully edited and proofread, typed on a top-quality typewriter, and professionally copied. Above all, it should reflect care and thought.

Before writing your resume, ask yourself what an employer would want to know about you—what tasks you could perform, what kind of experience you have had, what skills you can offer. Make a list of all these items and then weed out the ones that seem least significant (a resume shouldn't be too long—two pages at the most, one is better). Next decide on the approach or format that will work best in your particular situation.

There are two basic approaches to writing a resume: chronological (or historical) and functional. (The suggested readings at the end of the chap-

Box A-1 Sample Cover Letters

351 Palm Frond Road
Coral Gables, FL 33134

January 4, 1985

Mr. Robert Hernandez
President
Hernandez Hardware
19411 Westway
North Miami, FL 33161

Dear Mr. Hernandez,

My four years of sales management experience and nine years in the hardware business have given me a background that would seem ideal for the position opening of sales manager in your firm.

I have succeeded in increasing sales to hotels and institutions by more than half in the past year alone at Causeway Supply.

I am sure that I will be similarly successful in your company. A personal meeting would give us both the opportunity to explore this further. I look forward to hearing from you soon.

Sincerely,

William R. Lee

14 Cherry Street
Saginaw, MI 48606
517-369-1223

January 3, 1985

Mr. Anthony E. Hammond
Marketing Research Department
Perkins Coatings Corp.
Flint, MI 48502

Dear Mr. Hammond,

I read about your firm's new product development program in yesterday's *Detroit Free Press*. Your department's role in this plan is something that interests me and to which I am sure my experience in marketing research at Saginaw Plastics would make a direct and immediate contribution. Details are in the enclosed resume. I would like the opportunity to discuss this with you sometime next week if possible.

Sincerely,

Anna Quinn

ter include a guide to resume writing.) The *chronological* format (see Box A–2) is most familiar to employers and is easier to write. It presents information in inverse chronological order, that is, beginning with the most recent item and moving back through time. The resume begins with your name and address, followed by your job objective. Then it lists your employment and educational experiences, including months and years. (It's customary to present employment and education in two separate sections.)

Box A-2 A Chronological Resume

Anna Quinn
14 Cherry Street
Saginaw, MI 48606
517-738-5996

Job Objective: Marketing Researcher

Work Experience:

1981–1985, Marketing Researcher,
Saginaw Plastics Co., Saginaw, Michigan

—Developed and administered surveys to consumers and distributors of firm's products

—Collected and interpreted data from salespeople

1979–1981, Sales Department Assistant,
Polonia Chemicals, Inc., Clare, Michigan

—Prepared scheduling of product promotions

—Represented firm at trade shows and conventions

—Monitored advertising, pricing and promotions of competitors

1977–1979, Billing Clerk,
Polonia Chemicals, Inc., Clare, Michigan

—handled billing and other correspondence with customers

Education:

B.S., Central Michigan University, 1981
Mathematics major, Dean's List of Honor Students

A.A.S., Delta College, 1977
Marketing major

A *functional* resume is organized by skill or ability; it emphasizes your qualifications for a specific job. (See Box A–3.) Dates are not given, or at least are not featured. In this format you put your most important experience first (for example, the job with the most significant functions and responsibilities), followed by less important items. Again, your educational background should be presented in a separate section. You can also add a brief chronological listing of the jobs you have held in the past, since employers are likely to ask for this information if they do not see it.

There are some things that should *not* be included in a resume. Among these are your sex, age, race, religion, marital status, number of children, and references (except in the form "References available on request").

Box A-3 A Functional Resume

William R. Lee
351 Palm Frond Road
Coral Gables, FL 33134
305–761–0957

Offering a comprehensive background in industrial hardware sales and merchandising.

Sales Management:
Responsible for planning and directing sales for hardware supply firms. Made key strategic decisions in sales area. Successfully increased sales by 55% in one year at one firm.

Outside sales:
Worked closely with purchasing agents of major customers including construction firms, hotels, and hospitals in servicing their hardware needs.

Inside sales:
Worked as a sales clerk in store. Developed detailed knowledge of hardware items.

Causeway Supply Company   1980–1985
343 East 163rd St.
Miami, FL 33125

Started as inside sales clerk and worked way up to sales manager in 1981.

Williamson & Bros., Inc.   1977–1980
14471 Collins Avenue
Dania, FL 33004

Retail Sales Clerk in plumbing and janitorial supplies store.

Education:
A.A.S., Retailing, Miami-Dade Junior College, 1977.

Step 4: Interviewing. Assuming that your resume and cover letter have had the desired effect and you have been invited to the company for an interview, the next step is to prepare for the interview. In addition to the research you did in step 2 to learn about the company, you should find out as much as you can about the interviewer (for example, his or her place of birth, education, current position, areas of expertise). This kind of information is usually available only if you know someone in the company or if your interview has been arranged by an agency.

Being well prepared contributes a great deal to the impression you make during the interview. But you should also keep in mind the importance of first impressions. Numerous research studies have shown that interviewers frequently reach a decision *within 60 seconds of the beginning of the interview!* Therefore, it is important to dress suitably, presentably, and neatly, and to arrive on time or a few minutes early. Don't smoke unless you are invited to (and even then it's a good idea not to), don't fidget, and DON'T CHEW GUM.

In your resume you are advertising yourself in writing. In an interview you are selling yourself in person. Your goal is to present yourself as honest, intelligent, competent, and likable. There is no sure-fire formula for accomplishing this, but there are a few simple rules that can help. Among these are looking the interviewer in the eye, making sure you get his or her name right, and letting him or her set the pace of the interview and decide when to end it. Some things to avoid are an excessive show of respect, overuse of the interviewer's name, mumbling, telling jokes, and criticizing present or past employers. (Other rules of this type are presented in the book by H. Anthony Medley listed in the suggested readings.) Above all, *listen*. And if you have doubts about yourself or the job, keep them to yourself.

The following advice on interviewing is distributed by the Columbia business school to its MBA candidates:

> *In general, show familiarity with current events as they affect the industry and firm. . . . However, avoid discussion of sensitive issues unless the recruiter mentions them first. Your intimate knowledge of the problems a firm is experiencing may not favorably impress a recruiter. Be tactful and accentuate the positive. Don't ask trivial questions just to ask questions. Don't be verbose. Do be genuinely interested in knowing the answers to the questions you ask and listen patiently and attentively as they are given. Expand upon the answer to the question if you feel it is appropriate. Questions about salary, benefits, and vacation are more appropriate to ask in a second or third interview after it is determined that there is a substantial level of interest in you as a candidate for the position.*

Box A–4 lists some questions that are frequently asked by interviewers.

If the interview is an initial screening on campus, your primary goal is to be invited to the company for a series of hiring interviews. In a hiring interview, the goal is to obtain a job offer. In both cases a secondary goal is to learn more about the company—information that will prove useful in deciding whether or not to accept the job if it is offered to you. Keep in mind, though, that information gathering is not the main purpose of the interview. Your earlier research has probably eliminated most companies for which you don't want to work, and the person who is interviewing you

Box A-4 Questions Frequently Asked by Job Interviewers

1. What are your long-range career goals?
2. What do you see yourself doing five years from now?
3. How do you plan to achieve your career goals?
4. What do you expect to be earning in five years?
5. What are your greatest strengths and weaknesses?
6. How would you describe yourself?
7. Why should I hire you?
8. What qualities do you have that make you think you will be successful in your career?
9. What do you think it takes to succeed in a company like ours?
10. In what ways do you think you can contribute to our company?
11. Which of your accomplishments have given you the most satisfaction? Why?
12. If you were hiring someone for this position, what qualities would you look for?
13. In what kind of work environment are you most comfortable?
14. How do you work under pressure?
15. How would you describe the ideal job for you?
16. Why did you decide to seek a position with this company?
17. What do you know about the company?
18. What things are most important to you in your job?
19. Are you willing to travel?
20. Are you willing to spend at least six months as a trainee?

Source: Based on *The Endicott Report* (Northwestern University, 1975).

may not have all the information you need. Since you will not be expected to accept a job offer the moment it is made, you will have time to do further research after you have received the offer.

Step 5: Following Up.   It is important to follow up after the interview. Send a card or letter saying that you appreciate the time the interviewer spent with you and look forward to hearing from him or her soon. (See Box A–5.) If you receive a rejection, call or write to ask why the employer does not consider you to be the right person for the job. This information could be valuable in future job applicatons and interviews. (In following up after a rejection, *do not* give any sign of anger or hostility. It will do you no good and could do a great deal of harm.)

Step 6: Accepting a Job Offer.   One fine day you will be offered a job—maybe two or three. When you accept a job offer, you again have a chance to make a good impression on your employer. Write a letter in which you formally accept the offer, confirm the date on which you will start work, and express pleasure and enthusiasm about joining the organization. In addition, in some cases it is a good idea to write informal notes to the people who interviewed you, expressing the same sentiments and thanking them again for their interest in you. If you receive more than one offer, each one that you reject should be handled in the same positive manner: express appreciation for the offer and politely decline it. Usually it is not necessary to give a reason for rejecting a job offer. However, if you accept an offer while you are still being considered for other jobs, write to the companies involved and inform them of your decision.

That's all there is to it It really isn't hard to find a job if you follow the six steps just outlined. Knowledge is power, and if you know yourself and

Box A-5 A Follow-Up Letter

> Anna Quinn
> 14 Cherry Street
> Saginaw, MI 48606
>
> January 31, 1985
>
> Mr. Anthony E. Hammond
> Marketing Research Department
> Perkins Coatings Corp.
> Flint, MI 48502
>
> Dear Mr. Hammond,
>
> Thank you for the time that you spent Wednesday January 29th reviewing my qualifications for the position of Marketing Researcher. I was especially impressed with the comprehensiveness of the inhouse training program and the growth record of your firm.
>
> My four years of experience as a marketing researcher at the Saginaw Plastics Company and my A.A.S. degree in Marketing and my B.S. degree in Mathematics have prepared me with a strong background for the marketing research position we discussed.
>
> I am at your convenience for additional discussion concerning employment with Perkins and look forward to your reply.
>
> Sincerely,
>
> Anna Quinn

are familiar with the industry you want to enter, and know something about the companies you would like to work for, you are in a position of strength. The rest of the process consists mainly of presenting as good a picture of yourself as you can—in your resume, cover letters, interviews, and follow-up letters and calls.

Managing Your Career

Getting the first job is the beginning of your career, but it isn't the end of it. As you career proceeds, you will need to manage it. We will round out this appendix by discussing three aspects of managing your career: entering an organization, maintaining mobility within the organization, and deciding whether to leave or stay.

Entering an organization.   Once you have accepted a job, you enter an organization. There you are confronted with certain predictable events.

One of these is *reality shock*. This is the clash between your previous, probably rose-colored, view of your chosen career and your first actual on-the-job experiences. You may have been wooed like a bride at your job interview, only to arrive at work and find yourself treated as nothing special. The challenges may not be as great as you had hoped; besides, someone has to do the routine work, and the newcomer often gets the job.

Once on the job, you will also encounter your first supervisor. Interviews with managers have shown that one's first supervisor has a strong influence on one's career. Unfortunately, your superior may not be the most sensitive person in the world, and may even be threatened by your gleaming new educational credentials.

In addition, you will have to adjust to the organizational culture of your employer. You may find yourself wearing a white shirt and tie or a business suit for the first time in your life. You may find yourself in a part of the country far from your home, with different attitudes and ways of doing business. Adjustment to cultural diversity is part of what career success is all about. If you can't stand the culture of your first employer, you can eventually move—but right now you have just gotten the job.

Confronted with events like these, it is easy to become preoccupied with the impression the organization is making on you. But you are also making your first impression on the organization, and first impressions count for a lot. While you are adjusting, you should also be doing all you can to become recognized as an excellent performer—even if your first assignment is dull, confusing, or badly supervised.

Maintaining mobility within the organization. Once you have entered an organization, you will begin to move within it. In Chapter 16 we used Edgar Schein's career cone to distinguish among three types of movement. (See Box 16–4, page 413.) One type of movement is vertical, by promotion toward the top of the firm's hierarchy. A second type of movement is lateral, by transfer from one department to another. A third type is toward the center of the organization—a matter of being informally accepted by the "inner circle" rather than a matter of formal promotion or transfer.

Douglas T. Hall offers some useful tips for maintaining mobility in all three directions.[1] First, he says, keep many options open by not being overspecialized. Second, don't be blocked by a superior who is immobile. If there is no way up within your department, seek a transfer. Third, if your superior is on an upward track, become a "crucial subordinate" and be pulled along. And finally, always seek visibility. Don't wait for others to nominate you for challenging tasks—put your own name forward.

Staying or leaving. A few people stay with one organization throughout their careers, but most do not. If you are like most people, it is likely that you will move to another organization at least once during your career. Hall views mobility among organizations as an extension of mobility within them. Here is some advice he gives on the subject.

1. Leave at your own convenience. If problems develop, don't wait for a confrontation. A timely departure makes it easier to leave friends, rather than enemies, behind.

[1]Douglas T. Hall, *Careers in Organizations* (Pacific Palisades, Calif.: Goodyear, 1976), pp. 186–87.

2. Rehearse before quitting. Don't leave in a state of high emotion. Talk it over with your family or take a vacation. But don't spend years rehearsing. Make up your mind and go, or stay and adjust.

3. Be flexible enough to put down new roots elsewhere. Two or three strong job skills are both an aid to mobility and a guard against obsolescence.

4. Be willing to seek help. Professional placement services are often worth using, and some schools maintain ongoing placement services for their graduates.

5. Develop contingency plans. If you understand your career and are constantly reassessing it, you will recognize favorable opportunities when they arise.

SALLY FORTH by Greg Howard © 1984 Field Enterprises, Inc. Courtesy of News America Syndicate.

SALLY FORTH   by Greg Howard

SUGGESTED READINGS

Azibo, Moni, and Therese Unumb. *The Mature Woman's Back to Work Book*. Chicago: Contemporary Books, 1980. Useful advice and guidance for women reentering the job market after a prolonged absence.

Bolles, R. N. *What Color Is Your Parachute*? Berkeley, Calif.: Ten Speed Press, 1978. The all-time best seller among career-planning books; step-by-step guidelines for self-exploration and finding a job.

Business Week's Guide to Careers. New York: McGraw-Hill, published four times per year. Articles on career opportunities, the job market, and other subjects. Articles are particularly suitable for recent college graduates and current college students.

Crystal, John C., and Richard N. Bolles. *Where Do I Go from Here with My Life*? Berkeley, Calif.: Ten Speed Press, 1974. A systematic life and work planning manual for individuals at any stage in their life and career.

Jackson, Tom. *Guerrilla Tactics in the Job Market*. New York: Bantam Books, 1981. Techniques for finding and securing a job.

Jackson, Tom, and Davidyne Mayleas. *The Hidden Job Market of the 1980s*. New York: Times Books, 1981. Guidelines for self-exploration, finding unique job opportunities, and finding the right job for you.

Lewis, Adele. *How to Write Better Resumes*. Woodbury, N.Y.: Barron's Educational Series, 1977. Detailed guidelines for writing a resume.

Medley, H. Anthony. *Sweaty Palms: The Neglected Art of Being Interviewed*. Belmont, Calif.: Lifetime Learning Publications, 1978. Guidelines for preparing for and achieving success in interviews.

Souerwine, Andrew H. *Career Strategies: Planning for Personal Achievement*. New York: Amacom, 1978. Good guidelines for managing one's own career.

Stanat, Kirby W., and Patrick Reardon. *Job Hunting Secrets and Tactics*. Milwaukee: Westwind Press, 1977.

Appendix B

PREPARING BUSINESS REPORTS AND USING STATISTICS

At many points in this book we have noted that managers use information presented in numerical form in making decisions. The science of collecting, analyzing, interpreting, and presenting numerical information is known as *statistics*. (The word *statistic* is sometimes used to mean a single item of data or information in the form of a number. *Statistics* can mean a collection of numerical data as well as the science of working with such data.)

In some cases top managers have direct access to statistics through a management information system (MIS). Less often, they may have a computerized decision support system (DSS) that allows them to analyze and interpret statistical data without anyone's help. (The concepts of an MIS and a DSS were presented in Chapter 7.) Most commonly, though, data collection and statistical analysis are carried out by middle managers and staff specialists, and presented to key decision makers in the form of *business reports*. These are documents that present the information relevant to a decision, analyze the data, and present tentative recommendations and alternatives. A flow of concise, well-drafted, unbiased business reports is essential to effective decision making in any large organization. In small businesses, where the top manager is more likely to have direct knowledge of all the firm's activities, formal reports are used less often, but they may still be appropriate on occasion.

If you enter any organization in a staff or mangement position, chances are you will sooner or later be called upon to write reports and act on the basis of reports written by others. This appendix outlines the concept of a business report and some fundamentals of statistics that are useful in preparing them.

Preparing Business Reports

Before getting into the statistical content of business reports, we would like to make some general comments on their form. We will explain how business reports differ from other forms of writing, and give some guidelines for preparing them.

Purpose. The first thing to understand about business reports is that they are written for people whose time is valuable. The report writer therefore must present complete and accurate information in as clear and concise a form as possible. In particular, report readers want to know the conclusions right away. This makes reports different from many college term papers, and even more different from most essays and fiction. A murder mystery is worthless if it reveals "who done it" as soon as it has gotten the reader's attention; a business report is likely to be worthless if it does not do so.

A second essential point is that business reports should be objective. Report writers are often called upon to recommend a course of action for higher-level managers, but they should not argue one-sidedly in favor of the recommendations they make. Evidence or circumstances that would support another course of action should be noted. In short, just as a business report is not a murder mystery, neither is it a lawyer's brief for the defense or the prosecution.

The executive summary. To help the reader understand the major points, reports longer than a page or two commonly begin with an *executive summary*. This is a brief overview—one or, at most, two pages—setting forth the report's purpose, scope, and conclusions.

The opening paragraph of the executive summary explains the report's purpose. Usually the purpose is to provide the information needed to make a certain decision. The summary should say which decisions and decision makers the report is addressed to.

Next the executive summary explains the scope of the report. How does it attempt to address the questions it raises? What kinds of data were available to the report writer? How were the data analyzed? What data were not looked at, and what kinds of analysis were not performed?

Finally, the summary sets forth conclusions or recommendations. If the conclusions are well-founded, the decision makers to whom the report is addressed will act on them. If the decision makers still have doubts, the report will help them understand what additional information they need before they can take action.

Box B–1 gives an example of an executive summary of a business report.

The body of the report. The body of the report gives a more extensive discussion of the points covered in the executive summary. Details of the sources of information and methods of analysis should be given. If any data sources or methods were considered and rejected, an explanation should be given.

In the body of the report, findings should be given in detail. As we will see shortly, charts and graphs are often useful in presenting findings. The findings should be interpreted. Where more than one interpretation is possible, the various alternatives should be presented. If one interpretation seems most sensible, the writer should explain why. Conclusions and recommendations should be explained more fully than in the executive summary. The report may include ideas for putting the recommendations into practice.

Appendixes. In some cases, it is a good idea to attach one or more appendixes to the report. The purpose of the appendixes is to present information that is too technical or detailed to be of interest to all readers. Consider the report of frozen-dinner sales (Box B–1). The body of the report might use line and pie charts to show sales trends by region and the market share for various kinds of menus. An appendix might present the detailed data used to prepare the charts. As another example, the research department of a chemical company might prepare a report on a new-product proposal for the firm's board of directors. Because only a few of the directors have a background in chemical engineering, technical details of

Box B–1 Executive Summary of a Typical Business Report

FROM: Andy Willis, Director of Marketing Research
TO: Hanna Trask, Vice-President for Marketing
SUBJECT: Report on frozen dinner sales in Region 10

EXECUTIVE SUMMARY

Purpose of the study. During the first half of 1984, sales of our line of frozen dinners continued to drop in Region 10, while they rose in all other parts of the country. We undertook this study to find out the cause of this trend and identify possible steps to reverse it.

Scope of study. Our approach was to look in detail at sales trends for each menu within the frozen dinner line, and to interpret these trends against the background of data on the population of Region 10. Interviews with customers and supermarket managers would probably give a more complete picture, but we did not have time to make use of those sources of information.

Our investigation produced two significant findings.

First, we found that sales of traditional menus (roast beef and gravy, turkey and dumplings, etc.) were just as strong in Region 10 as in other parts of the country. However, sales of menus designed for the Hispanic submarket, which have accounted for much of recent sales growth nationally, were very weak in Region 10. We believe this can be explained by the fact that the population in Region 10 is older than the national average, is less concentrated in urban areas, and contains fewer people of Hispanic origin.

Second, we found that sales of dinners packed for microwave cooking were increasing in this region (as elsewhere in the country), while sales of those packed in aluminum trays, not suitable for microwave cooking, were falling rapidly.

Recommendations. We recommend that local advertising in Region 10 emphasize our traditional selections. Our sales force should also encourage supermarkets to give more shelf space to these selections. In addition, we recommend a speedup of our program for converting all frozen dinners to microwave-type packaging.

the process for making the new product would be best presented in an appendix.

Gathering Data

The first step in writing a report is to gather the data on which it will be based. It is important to have a clear idea of the purpose of the report before you begin to gather data—otherwise you will waste time on data that are not really relevant. Usually the purpose will be defined for you by the person who assigned the report, but it will often be your job, as the report writer, to state the purpose precisely.

Once the problem is clearly stated, you need to find data for the report. Data sources can be classified as *primary* and *secondary*. Primary sources refer to data gathered specifically for the report in question. Data from secondary sources have been gathered for other purposes but are relevant to the report.

Secondary sources. There are many kinds of secondary sources of useful data. Statistical handbooks, almanacs, and government documents present statistical data on business activity and the economic environment. Books, newspapers, magazines, and professional journals report the results of similar studies done at other times and places. Encyclopedias give background information. The usual place to begin a search for secondary sources is a good library. Indexes, such as the *Business Periodicals Index* and the *Wall Street Journal* index, can be very helpful. Increasingly, the search for secondary sources can be speeded by using computer services that will locate articles on any chosen subject.

Experimentation. Primary sources include all means of gathering original data that bear on the problem at hand. *Experimentation* is one such source. In an experiment, the researcher tests the effects of changing one factor while holding all other conditions constant. An experiment in microbiology, for example, might test the effect of a change in temperature on the growth rate of a strain of bacteria, while holding other conditions constant.

In business it is not always as easy to hold other conditions constant as it is in a laboratory. Still, experiments can be conducted. Test marketing is one example. A new product can be introduced in two or more different markets at different prices, or in different packages, or with different brand names. To hold other conditions constant, the test markets are carefully matched for population, average income of consumers, and so on.

Observation. *Observation* means making a record of events as they take place. For example, the ratings of television programs are based on observation of the number of people who have their sets tuned to a given program at a given time. Observation also includes the use of company records. For example, a person writing a report on the effects of temperature on electricity consumption in a certain city would want to look at records of past consumption and compare them with records of the weather.

Surveys. A *survey* is a way of gathering data that consists of asking and recording the answers given by a number of people to a set of questions. For example, people might be asked how often they use seatbelts when driving, how often they eat chicken, or whether they prefer sample X or sample Y of peanut butter. Surveys can be conducted by telephone, by means of mailed questionnaires, or by interviews. Surveys have the advantage of making it possible to ask people *why* they do certain things. By comparison, experiments and observations only record *what* people do.

Sampling. Observations and surveys can rarely be exhaustive. The viewing habits of only a few thousand out of millions of households are used in rating television programs. Marketing researchers for a peanut butter maker might ask only a few hundred people which of two varieties they prefer. The process of collecting data from only a few of all possible cases is known as *sampling*. The science of statistics devotes careful attention to the process of sampling. Two principles of sampling are especially important.

The first principle concerns the size of the sample. Too small a sample may lead, by chance, to incorrect conclusions. For example, it would be risky to introduce a new peanut butter formula nationwide on the basis of a single survey in one supermarket in Norman, Oklahoma. On the other hand, taking too large a sample may inflate the cost of research without improving the answer very much. For example, a survey that tested a new peanut butter formula in one store in each state might yield results that were nearly as accurate as a survey that tested the formula in a hundred stores in each state.

The second principle of sampling concerns the problem of *bias*. A sample is said to be biased if the people or cases included in the sample are not typical of the whole population. A famous case of sampling bias occurred in the 1936 presidential election. A telephone survey predicted that the Republican candidate, Alfred E. Landon, would win over the Democrat, Franklin D. Roosevelt, by a wide margin. But in 1936 many lower- and middle-income households did not have telephones. The telephone survey therefore was biased toward upper-income households that were more likely to vote Republican. Roosevelt's victory in the election made political pollsters rethink their sampling methods.

Analyzing Data

As we explained in Chapter 7, data are not the same as information. To generate information that is useful for making decisions, data have to be processed, analyzed, and summarized in a form that can be interpreted more easily than a mass of raw numbers. A great part of the science of statistics is devoted to methods of data analysis. Here we will simply list a few of the most common techniques.

Averages. We very often use the phrase "on the average" in making generalizations based on data that we have collected. In speaking of an average, we intend to represent some typical case from among all the various cases that we have observed. In statistical work, three kinds of averages are often used.

The most commonly used average is the *mean*. The mean is the sum of all the items in a group divided by the number of items. Consider the data on family size and family income shown in Box B–2. The nine families on which data have been gathered have a total of 21 children and a total income of $153,671 per year. The mean number of children per family thus is 2.33 and the mean income is $17,075.

The mean is not always a perfect indication of what we mean by "typical," however. The main problem with the mean is that it can be strongly influenced by a single atypical case. For example, family 3 has 11 children, far higher than the mean, and family 4 has an income of $75,200, also far higher than the mean. Two other "averages" are often used to eliminate the undue influence of a few outlying cases.

When the data tend to fall into a small number of categories, as in the case of the number of children per family, the *mode* can give a better idea of

Box B–2 Averages

Family	Number of Children	Annual Income
1	0	$ 10,110
2	2	4,206
3	11	8,500
4	2	75,200
5	3	9,500
6	0	6,300
7	1	14,718
8	2	8,220
9	0	16,917
Total	21	$153,671
Mean	2.33	$ 17,075
Mode	2	—
Median	2	$ 9,500

Three kinds of averages are commonly used in business reports. These are illustrated here for a set of data on the number of children and annual income of nine families. The *mean* is the sum of the items in a set of data divided by the number of items. In this case, the mean number of children per family is 2.33 and the mean income per family is $17,075 per year. The *mode* is the most frequent number in a set of data. It is most useful when the observations fall into a small number of categories. Here the mode for the number of children per family is 2. The *median* is the case that divides the items in half, with equal numbers of items falling above and below it. In this case, the median income is $9,500 per year. Both the mode and the median have the advantage of being less strongly influenced by a single unusual case.

the typical case than the mean. The mode is the number that occurs most often in a set of observations. In Box B–2, the modal number of children per family is 2. It makes better sense to think of the typical family as having 2 children than to think of it as having 2.33 children.

When few, if any, items of data are exactly the same, the mode is not very useful. In such cases, the *median* is used to eliminate the influence of a few atypical cases. The median is the midpoint of the set of observations, that is, the point above which half of the observations lie and below which the other half of them lie. In Box B–2, the median income is $9,500 per year. Four of the families earn more than this, and four earn less. The mean of $17,075 is less typical than the median in this case, because only one family earns more than the mean.

The average that best represents the typical case depends on circumstances. In writing a report, it is a good idea to begin with the mean as a way of summarizing a set of observations. Then, if the mean appears to be unduly influenced by a few atypical cases, you should also report the mode or median to give a more complete picture. The word "average" used without further explanation normally indicates the mean.

Index numbers.   When data are presented in a report, it is often important to emphasize how much they have changed relative to some base period. One way to do this is to use *index numbers*. An index number is an item of data reported in the form of a percentage of a given base period. For example, the Bureau of Labor Statistics reports trends in consumer prices in the form of the consumer price index. This gives the average level of prices of consumer goods in a given year as a percentage of the average price level in 1967. In December of 1983, the consumer price index stood at 303.5, indicating that prices in that month were, on the average, 303.5 percent of their 1967 level.

In a business report, index numbers might be used to compare the performance of different plants of a manufacturing firm. Saying that plant A had an average cost per unit of $4.56 in 1984 while plant B had an average cost per unit of $6.67 might, by itself, be taken to mean that plant A's manager was doing a better job of cost control than plant B's manager. However, suppose plant A's costs had been $4.00 per unit in 1980, while plant B's had been $7.00 per unit in that year. A comparison of cost indexes would give a better indication of how well mangement had done. Plant A's 1984 costs were 114 percent of its 1980 costs, while plant B's costs were 95 percent of its 1980 costs. Comparison of the indexes shows that, starting from a higher cost base, plant B's manager has done a better job of cost control than plant A's.

Time series analysis.   Report writers are frequently faced with the task of analyzing the performance of some number over time. How have sales of frozen dinners in region 10 behaved over the past two years? How much have costs increased in the Adams plant? How are total sales this summer compared to the previous three summers? The area of statistics devoted to studying changes in a quantity over time is known as *time series analysis*.

One important goal of time series analysis is the identification of trends. For example, sales of frozen dinners might be increasing over time, but in some months they might temporarily drop. Box B–3 shows a typical example. In this case, the upward trend of sales can be estimated fairly accurately by sketching a line passing through the monthly sales data. There are mathematical methods to calculate the trend exactly when more precision is needed.

A second use of time series analysis is to eliminate seasonal effects from business data. For example, sales of retail stores typically increase in December as Christmas approaches. Suppose that a store owner looks at December sales for 1983 and finds that they were 35 percent above the monthly average for the rest of the year. Is this good or bad? A statistical analysis of sales in previous years might show that December sales were, on the average, 40 percent above those for the rest of the year. By adjusting the December 1983 data to take normal seasonal variations into account, the store owner would see that Christmas sales that year were less than they ought to have been.

Correlation.   Still another important statistical technique is *correlation*. Correlation means examining the relationship between two variables based on a set of observations. For example, a maker of children's clothing might collect data on the height and weight of a sample of children. The data would indicate a *positive correlation* between height and weight; that

Box B–3 Time Series Analysis

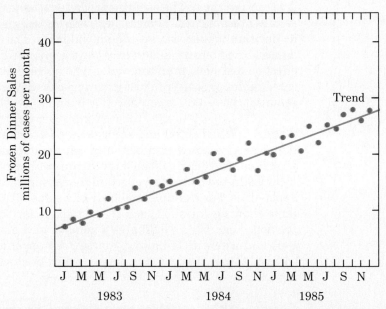

Time series analysis is used to summarize and interpret data that relate to changes in some quantity over time. In this case, the data refer to nationwide sales of frozen dinners by a large firm. Sales vary from month to month, sometimes rising and sometimes falling. The trend, however, is clearly upward, as indicated by the line drawn through the points representing month-by-month data. In a simple case like this, a freehand line shows the trend clearly enough. When more precision is needed, mathematical methods can be used to find the line that best represents the trend.

is, they would show that taller children tend to be heavier than shorter children. Although there would be exceptions—Johnny might be both shorter and heavier than Dick—knowledge of the correlation would clearly be useful in producing the right mix of clothing sizes. A *negative correlation*, on the other hand, shows that as one variable increases, the other tends to decrease. For example, a study of schools might show that larger class sizes tend, on the average, to be associated with poorer student performance on standardized tests.

Correlations are one of the most useful statistical techniques, but they are also one of the easiest to misuse. The most common mistake is to confuse a correlation between two sets of numbers with a cause-and-effect relationship. Sometimes a correlation *does* indicate cause and effect. The negative correlation between class size and student performance could be an example. But other correlations indicate nothing of the kind. For example, the states with the greatest number of hospital beds also tend to have the highest death rates from cancer. Does this mean that hospital beds cause cancer? Hardly. It means that something else—perhaps differences in the age structure of the population—causes cancer deaths to vary from state to state. In turn, more beds are needed to take care of the greater number of patients in states with high cancer rates.

Presenting Data

When data have been collected and analyzed, the report writer's final task is to present them. The usefulness of a report often depends on the writer's skill in presentation. Remember, business reports are intended to be used by decision makers whose time is valuable. The writer who can present data in vivid, easily understood ways is more likely to have a favorable effect on decisions than the writer who buries key information in complicated tables or long, rambling paragraphs. Several methods of data presentation have won acceptance for business reports.

Tables.   When detail and accuracy are needed, nothing beats a table. A table can give exact numbers and can include as many numbers as the writer wants. Clearly labeled tables are not hard to read and can often be included in the body of a report. More detailed tables can be presented in appendixes. For example, the body of a sales report might include a brief table showing sales for each of ten regions for the current year and the previous year. This would give a general idea of where the firm is doing well and where it is having trouble. An appendix might include more detailed tables breaking the data down by product or by state, or comparing sales over a longer period.

Charts.   Although tables are fine when precision is needed, business reports are often improved by the use of charts. Charts give a quick, visual impression of trends and percentages. Often they are understood more quickly and remembered more easily than numerical data. When precision is needed, a chart in the body of a report can be followed by a table in an appendix.

Box B–4 shows three common kinds of business charts. *Line charts* are especially useful for showing trends over time. The example given, taken from Box 1–4, shows the trend in the unemployment rate for workers from 1960 to the present. *Pie charts* are good for showing the percentage that each of a number of items contribute to a total. The example, from Box 11–4, shows various categories of marketing costs as percentages of total consumer spending. *Bar charts* are a way of presenting data to make the largest or most important cases stand out. The example, from Box 4–1, shows that small businesses are especially important in agriculture, construction, and wholesale and retail trade, but less important in manufacturing, mining, and transportation.

In recent years, computer programs have become available to produce line charts, pie charts, and bar charts quickly and easily. Report writers should learn how to use these programs if they are available. Thousands of years ago, Chinese report writers knew that a picture can be worth a thousand words. This principle is no less true in the age of computers. If anything, the ability of computers to spew out huge tables of data, too large for any human brain to comprehend, makes the use of charts even more important.

This appendix has only scratched the surface of the subject of report writing and use of statistics. Our earlier sections on careers in business have noted that communication skills, including skill in written communication, are important for almost every job in business. Further information about this important subject can be found in the suggested readings that follow.

Box B–4 Common Types of Business Charts

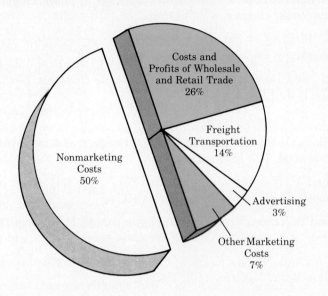

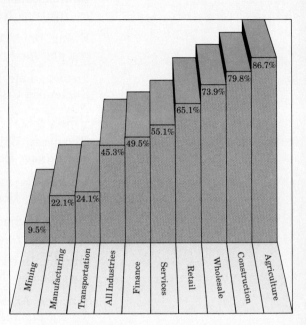

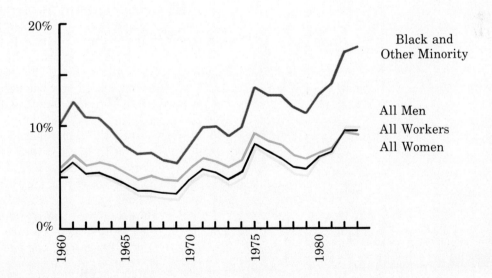

In business reports, as elsewhere, a picture can be worth a thousand words. These examples illustrate the three most common types of business charts. Line charts are useful for showing trends over time.

Pie charts are good for presenting percentage information. Bar charts make the most important and least important cases stand out clearly.

SUGGESTED READINGS

Bowman, Joel P., and Bernadine P. Branchaw. *Successful Communication in Business*. New York: Harper & Row, 1980.

Ewing, David W. *Writing for Results in Business, Government, the Sciences, and the Professions*, 2nd ed. New York: Wiley, 1979.

Fielden, John S., and Ronald E. Dulek. *Bottom Line Business Writing*. Englewood Cliffs, N.J.: Prentice-Hall, 1984.

Haggblade, Berle. *Business Communication*. St. Paul, Minn.: West, 1982.

Himstreet, William C., and Wayne M. Baty. *A Guide to Business Communication*. Homewood, Ill.: Irwin, 1981.

Lesikar, Raymond V. *How to Write a Report Your Boss Will Read and Remember*. Homewood, Ill.: Dow Jones-Irwin, 1974.

Lesikar, Raymond V. *Report Writing for Business*, 6th ed. Homewood, Ill.: Irwin, 1981.

Murphy, Herta A., and Charles E. Peck, *Effective Business Communications*, 2nd ed. New York: McGraw-Hill, 1976.

Scheider, Arnold E., William C. Donaghy, and Pamela Jane Newman. *Organizational Communication*. New York: McGraw-Hill, 1975.

Glossary

Accountability: Being required to answer for the results of one's actions. (p. 145)

Accounting: The process of capturing, processing, and communicating financial information. (p. 459)

Accounting equation: An equation stating that a firm's assets must equal its liabilities plus its owners' equity. (p. 464)

Accounts receivable: Sums owed to a firm by customers who have bought on credit. (p. 440)

Accrual basis: An accounting principle according to which the revenues and costs associated with a sale are recorded in the year in which the sale is made, whether or not payment is received in that year. (p. 469)

Adverse selection: The fact that people who are more likely to suffer a loss also are more likely to buy insurance. (p. 545)

Advertising: The delivery of a paid promotional message to a large number of potential customers through a public communications medium such as television, magazines, or billboards. (p. 266)

Advertising agency: A firm that can be hired to create advertising messages and buy media services. (p. 275)

Advertising medium (plural **media**): Any means of bringing an advertising message to the public. (p. 272)

Affirmative action: A policy that involves seeking out, hiring, and promoting members of specific groups, such as minorities, women, older workers, and the handicapped. (p. 403)

Agency: A legal relationship in which one person (the agent) agrees to act as a representative of another (the principal). (p. 582)

Agent: (1) An intermediary that brings buyers and sellers together without taking title to the good or service. (p. 238) (2) The person in an agency relationship who represents the principal. (p. 582)

American Federation of Labor (AFL): An association of independent craft unions, founded in 1881. (p. 378)

Analytic process: A production process in which output is produced by separating a whole into its component parts. (p. 324)

Annuity: A contract under which an insurance company or pension plan agrees, in exchange for a fixed payment, to pay a person a fixed amount per year as long as he or she lives. (p. 552)

Antitrust laws: A set of laws that prohibit attempts to achieve a monopoly through mergers of competing firms or by other means. (p. 63)

Arbitration: A binding settlement of a dispute by a third party. (p. 389)

Asked price: The price at which a dealer in an over-the-counter securities market offers to sell a given security. (p. 520)

Assessment center: A center where job applicants or candidates for promotion are asked to participate in realistic excercises designed to predict their future performance. (p. 408)

Asset: Anything of value that a firm owns. (p. 84)

Auditing: A process in which an independent accountant examines a firm's records and financial statements and offers an opinion on their accuracy and reliability. (p. 462)

Authority: The power to take the actions necessary to make a decision or solve a problem. (p. 145)

Authorization card: A card signed by a worker showing that he or she is willing to accept a union as a bargaining agent. (p. 380)

Autonomy: The authority to make decisions and act independently. (p. 146)

Bait-and-switch: A sales tactic in which customers are drawn into a store by ads for a cheap model of a product and then pressured into buying a more expensive model. (p. 283)

Balance of payments: The difference between a country's total imports and its total exports, including both goods and services. (p. 608)

Balance of trade: The difference between a country's imports of goods and its exports of goods. (p. 607)

Balance sheet: A financial statement that lists a firm's assets, liabilities, and owners' equity at a particular point in time. (p. 464)

Bankruptcy: Legal recognition of a business failure through the filing of a petition with a federal bankruptcy court. (p. 80)

Bargaining range: The range between the lowest offer that a union is willing to accept and the highest offer that an employer is willing to make. (p. 387)

Barter: The exchange of one good or service for another without the use of money as a means of payment. (p. 487)

Batch process: A production process in which inputs are assembled and processed separately for each unit of output. (p. 324)

Bid price: The price at which a dealer in an over-the-counter securities market offers to buy a given security. (p. 521)

Blue-sky law: Any of a number of state laws that attempt to combat fraud in securities markets. (p. 522)

Bookkeeping: The process of capturing and recording financial information. (p. 459)

Bond: A promise to repay a certain sum on a set maturity date, and, in the meantime, to pay interest at an agreed-upon rate. (p. 447)

Boycott: A campaign aimed at persuading people not to do business with a firm that is engaged in a labor dispute. (p. 388)

Brand name: The part of a brand that can be spoken—a name or a combination of letters and numbers. (p. 223)

Branding: The use of a design, symbol, name, or some mix of these things to identify a product. (p. 223)

Breach of contract: Failure of one party to carry out the terms of a contract. (p. 581)

Break-even analysis: A method of pricing that involves comparing fixed and variable costs with estimated revenues at several possible prices and levels of output. (p. 298)

Broker: See *agent*.

Business: A competitive, profit-seeking organization that produces and sells goods or services. (p. 5)

Business cycle: A cycle in which periods of economic expansion, often accompanied by rising prices, alternate with periods of falling output, accompanied by high unemployment. (p. 33)

Business ethics: Concern with truthfulness, honesty, and fairness in business dealings. (p. 585)

Business failure: A firm that goes out of business without paying all its debts. (p. 80)

Business format franchising: A form of franchising in which the franchisor supplies the franchisee with a complete business plan and the help needed to put it into operation. (p. 88)

Business unionism: A union policy of focusing on issues of wages and working conditions rather than on political or social issues. (p. 379)

Buyer behavior: The decision process that buyers go through in deciding what products to buy and from what sources. (p. 199)

Cafeteria-type benefit plan: A benefit plan that allows each employee to choose a mix of fringe benefits from a selection offered by the employer. (p. 418)

Capital: Durable productive inputs that are made by people, such as machines, structures, and office equipment. (p. 7)

Capital budgeting: The process of deciding what fixed capital to acquire. (p. 442)

Capital gain: The profit made when a share of stock or any other asset is sold for a price higher than the amount paid for it. (p. 62)

Capital goods: Industrial goods that are durable additions to the buyer's plant or equipment. (p. 215)

Capitalism: An economic system in which production decisions are controlled by those who invest capital in private businesses. (p. 29)

Carrying costs: The costs of keeping goods in stock, including interest expenses, inventory taxes, and storage costs. (p. 251)

Cash basis: An accounting principle according to which the revenues and costs associated with a sale are recorded in the year in which payment is received. (p. 469)

Cash management: The task of managing liquid assets in a way that produces the maximum possible income. (p. 441)

Central processing unit (CPU): The part of a computer in which arithmetic, comparison, and other operations are performed. (p. 161)

Centralization: A situation in which all authority is retained by top management. (p. 146)

Certified management accountant (CMA): A title

equivalent to that of certified public accountant, awarded by the Institute of Management Accounting. (p. 463)

Certified public accountant (CPA): A title and license to practice public accounting awarded to people who meet educational and experience requirements and can pass a state examination. (p. 462)

Chain of command: The set of authority relationships, or who reports to whom, in an organization. (p. 131)

Channel captain: A channel member that controls a distribution channel as a result of its size or economic power. (p. 240)

Chapter 7 bankruptcy: A type of bankruptcy in which the debtor's assets are liquidated and the proceeds are used to pay creditors. (p. 583)

Chapter 11 bankruptcy: A type of bankruptcy in which a firm continues to operate under court supervision while arranging to settle its debts. (p. 583)

Chapter 13 bankruptcy: A type of bankruptcy in which an individual debtor with a steady income agrees to pay creditors a fraction of what is owed to them, or to repay the whole debt over an extended period. (p. 584)

Check clearing: The process of moving funds between banks when a check written on one bank is deposited in another. (p. 496)

Checking deposit: Any deposit at a bank or thrift institution from which the depositor may withdraw funds, or transfer funds to another party, by writing a check. (p. 488)

Claim: A payment made by an insurance company to a policyholder who suffers a loss. (p. 540)

Clayton Act: A 1914 antitrust law that prohibits certain techniques of control of distribution channels when the effect is to limit competition. (p. 255)

Closed shop: An agreement under which an employer can hire only workers who are already members of a particular union. (p. 386)

Closely held corporation: A corporation in which one stockholder or a close-knit group, such as a family, controls the firm by electing themselves or their allies to the board of directors. (p. 61)

Coinsurance clause: A clause in an insurance policy under which the policyholder agrees to pay a certain percentage of all costs up to some fixed amount. (p. 551)

Cold canvassing: A sales technique in which potential customers are approached without any previous prospecting. (p. 276)

Collateral: Property that is pledged as a guarantee for repayment of a debt. (p. 444)

Collective bargaining: The process by which a union negotiates wages and working conditions for its members. (p. 377)

Commercial bank: A financial intermediary that accepts checking and other deposits from firms and households, and makes many kinds of loans, including long- and short-term loans to business firms. (p. 484)

Commercial paper: Unsecured promises to pay that can be used by a highly creditworthy firm to borrow short-term funds. (p. 446)

Commercial puffery: Claims made in advertising that cannot be proved but do not really mislead the consumer. (p. 282)

Commission broker: A partner in a brokerage firm who carries out trades for the firm's clients. (p. 515)

Committee: A permanent working or advisory group that is made up of people drawn from various parts of an organization. (p. 144)

Common stock: Stock in a corporation that entitles the owner to a vote in the election of management and to a share of the firm's profits when they are paid out as dividends. (p. 61)

Communism: A type of socialism in which key economic decisions are made by a central government acting in the name of the workers. (p. 30)

Comparative advantage: The ability to produce a good or service relatively cheaply compared with one's trading partners. (p. 601)

Comparative advertising: Advertising that mentions competing brands by name. (p. 271)

Compensation: The total cost to a firm of employing a person. (p. 416)

Computer: An electronic machine that processes, stores, and communicates information. (p. 153)

Computer assisted design/computer assisted manufacturing (CAD/CAM): A technique in which parts are designed on a computer and instructions for producing them are transmitted directly to computer controlled machine tools. (p. 341)

Concentrated marketing: An approach to marketing in which the firm chooses a single market segment as its target and tries to offer the ideal marketing mix for that segment. (p. 203)

Conglomerate merger: A merger between firms in unrelated lines of business. (p. 63)

Congress of Industrial Organizations (CIO): An organization of industrial unions that broke away from the AFL in 1936 and rejoined it in 1955. (p. 380)

Consideration: Whatever one party to a contract gives in exchange for the promise made by the other. (p. 581)

Consumer price index (CPI): A weighted average of the prices of goods and services bought by a typical household. (p. 34)

Containerization: A form of intermodal transportation in which goods are packed in truck-body-sized containers, which are hauled by road to ports, where they are loaded onto oceangoing ships. (p. 253)

Continuous process: A production process in which inputs enter the production system and outputs leave it in a steady flow. (p. 324)

Contract: An agreement that can be enforced in court. (p. 580)

Controlling: Checking to see that an organization is progressing toward its goals, and taking corrective action if it is not. (p. 112)

Convenience goods: Goods that are bought often, routinely, and with little comparison shopping. (p. 214)

Convertible bond: A bond that can be exchanged for a stated number of shares of a firm's common stock at a stated price. (p. 447)

Cooperative: A business that is owned and controlled by its members, usually its customers or suppliers but sometimes its employees. (p. 59)

Copyright: A guarantee to a writer or artist of the right to exclusive use of a book, article, photograph, or other creation. (p. 582)

Corrective advertising: Advertising that corrects false or misleading claims made in previous ads. (p. 282)

Corporate culture: A system of shared values, memories, priorities, and unwritten rules about how things are done in a corporation. (p. 369)

Corporation: A firm that exists as an independent legal entity, with ownership divided into shares. (p. 51)

Cost of goods sold: All costs that can be assigned to specific products, including parts, materials, labor, and so on. (p. 467)

Cost-of-living adjustment (COLA): An agreement to increase wages by a set amount for each percentage point increase in the government's consumer price index. (p. 386)

CPM: The cost of an advertisement per thousand people reached. (p. 273)

Craft union: A labor union whose members are skilled workers who all practice the same trade or craft. (p. 379)

Credit card: A plastic card that allows a customer to obtain a bank loan and, at the same time, arrange for the bank to send the amount of the loan to a merchant from whom goods or services are purchased. (p. 489)

Credit union: A small-scale financial intermediary, often sponsored by a company or union, that accepts deposits from members and makes consumer loans to them. (p. 485)

Critical path method (CPM): A scheduling method that uses a PERT chart to identify a critical sequence of activities that limits the speed with which a project can be carried out. (p. 335)

Currency: Coins and paper money issued by the federal government. (p. 488)

Current assets: Assets that a firm expects to hold for a year or less. (p. 440)

Current ratio: The ratio of total current assets to current liabilities. (p. 472)

Cyclical unemployment: The extra unemployment, in excess of the normal level, that occurs during a recession. (p. 36)

Data: Unorganized facts such as numbers, names, and quantities. (p. 153)

Data-processing system (DPS): A system that captures data, processes them, and communicates the information it produces. (p. 155)

Dealer: An intermediary in an over-the-counter securities market who makes a market in certain stocks by offering to buy and sell them at announced prices. (p. 520)

Dealer selection: A situation in which a producer selects its customers and will not sell to some intermediaries. (p. 256)

Debenture: An unsecured bond. (p. 447)

Debit card: A plastic card used by a customer in place of a check to instruct a bank to transfer funds from the customer's checking account to that of a merchant from whom goods or services are purchased. (p. 490)

Debt: Any process by which a firm gets cash or some other asset in return for a promise to pay an agreed-upon sum plus interest. (p. 443)

Debt-to-equity ratio: The ratio of total debt (short- and long-term) to owners' equity. (p. 472)

Decision support system (DSS): A system that puts high-quality information at the fingertips of managers and aids them in the analysis of complex problems. (p. 158)

Deductible clause: A clause in an insurance policy under which claims can be made only after expenses reach a certain level. (p. 551)

Delegation: Assigning part of one's work to a subordinate. (p. 145)

Demand: The amount of a product that customers are willing and able to buy at a given price. (p. 293)

Demand curve: A graph that shows the relationship between the demand for a product and its price. (p. 294)

Department store: A store that carries a broad range of product lines and offers a variety of services. (p. 246)

Departmentalization: Grouping people who do related work into logical units or departments. (p. 129)

Depreciation: The cost of the gradual wearing out or obsolescence of fixed assets. (p. 467)

Derived demand: Demand for a good that is derived from its usefulness in making consumer goods. (p. 215)

Development: An activity aimed at upgrading the skills of employees so that they will be able to move up in the company and meet its future needs. (p. 410)

Differentiated marketing: An approach to marketing in which the firm produces a range of related products or brands, each one tailored to the needs of a specific market segment. (p. 203)

Direct-action advertising: Advertising that aims to close a sale. (p. 271)

Direct financing: Any process in which a user of funds gets them directly from savers. (p. 484)

Discount broker: A brokerage firm that charges low commissions and offers a bare-bones trading service. (p. 521)

Discount store: A store that carries complete product lines at low prices, which are made possible by aggressive cost cutting. (p. 248)

Distribution channel: A series of firms that take part in buying or selling a good as it moves from the producer to the user. (p. 238)

Diversification: Reducing risk by holding a variety of securities so that the risks of some will offset the risks of others. (p. 512)

Double-entry bookkeeping: A principle that states that each transaction must be recorded on the balance sheet as two separate entries so that the accounting equation will hold at all times. (p. 466)

Dumping: Selling a product in a foreign country at a price less than that at which it is sold in the home market. (p. 303)

Durable goods: Goods that last a year or more, such as furniture, appliances, and cars. (p. 214)

Economies of scale: A situation in which the average cost per unit of output falls as the rate of output rises. (p. 78)

Effectiveness: The ability to choose the right goals on which to focus the energies of the organization. (p. 107)

Efficiency: Acting with a minimum of expense, waste, or effort. (p. 107)

Efficient-market hypothesis (EMH): The belief that securities prices reflect all the information available at any given time. (p. 527)

Employment at will: A doctrine under which an employer could terminate any employee at any time for any reason. (p. 415)

Entrepreneurship: The ability to compete successfully by developing new products, finding new ways to reduce costs, and thinking of new ways to make products attractive to consumers. (p. 13)

Environmental-impact statement: A document that explains in detail how a new plant or project will affect the environment. (p. 333)

Equal employment opportunity (EEO): A policy of not discriminating in hiring, pay, job assignments, and promotion. (p. 402)

Equity financing: Any process by which a firm raises funds in return for a share in its ownership and management. (p. 444)

Exclusive dealing: A situation in which a producer does not allow intermediaries to carry its competitors' products. (p. 255)

Exclusive territories: A situation in which a producer requires intermediaries to sell only to customers in certain territories. (p. 255)

Expense goods: Goods that are used up in the course of producing the buyer's output, such as raw materials, component parts, and maintenance supplies. (p. 215)

External costs: Costs of production that a firm imposes on other firms or on the public at large. (p. 18)

Factor: A firm that buys accounts receivable from other firms for less than their full face value and takes on the costs of collecting the account. (p. 441)

Factors of production: The basic inputs used in all production processes: labor, capital, and natural resources. (p. 7)

Fair labor standards act (FSLA): A federal law governing minimum wages, payment of overtime, equal pay, and certain other matters of compensation policy. (p. 419)

Federal budget deficit: The difference between what the federal government spends and what it takes in as taxes. (p. 42)

Federal Reserve System (Fed): The federal government agency that is charged with the conduct of monetary policy and regulation of the banking system. (p. 42)

Feudalism: An economic system in which production decisions are controlled by landowners. (p. 30)

Finance: The process of getting the funds a firm needs and putting them to use. (p. 434)

Financial accounting: The branch of accounting that is concerned with reporting financial information to parties outside the firm. (p. 461)

Financial intermediary: Banks and other institutions that gather funds from savers and supply them to borrowers. (p. 484)

Financial system: The network of institutions through which firms, households, and units of government get the funds they need and put surplus funds to work. (p. 483)

First in, first out (FIFO): An accounting method according to which the first items of inventory bought are assumed to be the first that are used. (p. 470)

First-line managers: See *supervisory managers*.

Fiscal policy: The branch of economic policy that is concerned with taxes and government spending. (p. 41)

Fixed assets: Assets that a firm expects to hold for more than a year, including fixed capital and land. (p. 442)

Fixed capital: Capital in the form of durable structures, machinery, and equipment. (p. 435)

Fixed costs: Costs that are the same regardless of the quantity of a good or service produced. (p. 298)

Fixed-position layout: A plant layout in which workers and equipment are brought to the product as work progresses. (p. 333)

Flexible manufacturing system (FMS): The use of robots and computer-controlled tools that can be programmed to perform a variety of tasks. (p. 343)

Flexitime: A system in which members of an organization set their own hours of work, usually with the requirement that they all be present during certain core hours. (p. 366)

Floor planning: A type of financing in which dealer inventories of goods like automobiles are used as collateral for short-term loans. (p. 446)

Flowchart: A diagram that shows the main features of a program in a form that is easy for a human to read and understand. (p. 165)

Foreign direct investment: The process of setting up a foreign operation through a joint venture, establishment of a foreign branch, or the purchase or formation of a foreign subsidiary. (p. 603)

Foreign exchange market: A network of institutions, including large banks with international operations, through which one currency can be exchanged for another. (p. 610)

Foreign exchange rate: The price of one currency stated in terms of another. (p. 610)

Foreign indirect investment: The process of supplying capital to a foreign institution, through a loan or purchase of stock, without sharing in the institution's management. (p. 603)

Foreign sourcing: A planned effort to seek foreign sources of supply. (p. 600)

Fractional-reserve banking: A system in which a bank accepts deposits, keeps a fraction of each deposit as reserves, and lends out the rest to earn income. (p. 492)

Franchise: An arrangement in which the owner of a trademark, trade name, or copyright (the franchisor) allows another firm (the franchisee) to use it subject to certain agreed-upon conditions. (p. 57)

Fraud: Knowingly selling a good or service that is not suitable for the purpose for which the seller claims it is suitable. (p. 15)

Free enterprise: An economic system in which businesses are free to choose whom to buy from and sell to and on what terms, and free to choose whom to compete with. (p. 30)

Frictional unemployment: The part of total unemployment accounted for by people who are out of work for short periods, either between jobs or looking for their first job. (p. 36)

Fringe benefits: Nonwage supplements to a worker's pay, such as paid holidays, vacations, pensions, and health insurance. (p. 386)

Fundamental analysis: An approach to stock market trading based on the study of trends in the economy and analysis of the strengths and weaknesses of individual firms and industries. (p. 524)

General agreement on tariffs and trade (GATT): An international agreement, to which most major trading nations subscribe, that sets guidelines for trade policies and provides a framework for negotiations on matters of trade and tariffs. (p. 614)

Generic product: A product whose label identifies it only by the type of product. (p. 225)

GIGO principle ("garbage in—garbage out"): Computer jargon for the principle that useful information cannot be derived from inaccurate data. (p. 160)

Grievance: A dispute between management and a worker or union over the interpretation of a contract. (p. 389)

Gross national product (GNP): The economy's total output of goods and services. (p. 33)

Gross profit: Net sales minus cost of goods sold. (p. 468)

Hard automation: The use of equipment that is specially designed to make a certain product. (p. 342)

Hardware: In a computer system, the physical equipment that performs input, output, processing, and storage functions. (p. 160)

Hawthorne effect: The tendency of people to do a better job when they are made to feel useful and important. (p. 357)

Health maintenance organization (HMO): An organization that provides a broad range of prepaid health care services to members, and pays doctors and other professonals fixed salaries. (p. 552)

Hierarchy of needs: A ranking of five levels of needs originated by Abraham Maslow in which a need at any level becomes an important motivator only after lower-level needs have been satisfied. (p. 353)

Historical cost: The price at which an item of inventory or fixed asset was actually bought. (p. 470)

Horizontal coordination: A technique of coordination that depends on direct communication among departments on the same level of the organization. (p. 142)

Horizontal merger: A merger between firms that compete in the same market. (p. 63)

House brand: A brand given by a large retail chain to a line of products sold only in its own stores. (p. 225)

Human relations approach: An approach to managing for productivity and quality that is based on the assumptions that people want to feel useful, are motivated by social rewards in the workplace, and are willing to take responsibility for routine matters. (p. 357)

Human resources approach: An approach to managing for productivity and quality that is based on the assumptions that people find satisfaction in their work, are creative, and are eager to participate in the whole range of management functions. (p. 359)

Human resources information system (HRIS): A system for gathering information on human resources, processing it, and making it available to decision makers. (p. 405)

Human resources planning: The process of forecasting human resource needs and developing procedures for filling them. (p. 402)

Human resources strategy: A set of broad policies for the acquisition, retention, and use of human resources to achieve the organization's goals. (p. 402)

Import quota: A limit on the amount of a good that is allowed to enter a country. (p. 615)

Income before tax: Operating income minus net interest expense (or plus net interest income). (p. 469)

Income statement: A statement that shows a firm's sales, costs, and profits for a given period. (p. 467)

Indirect financing: Any process in which a user of funds gets them from an intermediary, such as a bank, that in turn gets them from savers. (p. 484)

Individual contributors: The people who do the actual work of an organization and do not supervise other workers. (p. 105)

Individual investor: A person or household that owns securities. (p. 509)

Industrial policy: A systematic program of government support for business growth and innovation. (p. 575)

Industrial union: A union that includes all the employees of a firm or industry regardless of their skill or craft. (p. 380)

Inflation: A sustained increase in the average price of all goods and services. (p. 33)

Information: Data that have been processed so that they can be used in making decisions. (p. 153)

Injunction: A court order that prohibits some activity, such as picketing or a strike. (p. 379)

Input device: Any device, such as a keyboard, through which data and instructions can be fed into a computer. (p. 161)

Insider trading: Purchase or sale of a firm's stock by its officers or other people with access to information that is not yet known to the public. (p. 522)

Institutional advertising: Advertising that promotes the virtues of a firm rather than any of its products. (p. 271)

Institutional investor: A financial intermediary that owns securities. (p. 509)

Insurable interest: A state of affairs in which a policyholder will suffer if a loss takes place. (p. 544)

Insurable risk: A risk with certain traits that make it feasible for a private insurance company to offer coverage for that risk. (p. 542)

Insurance: A process in which a group of people who are exposed to the same kinds of risks place funds in a common pool from which members who suffer losses are compensated. (p. 537)

Insurance company: A financial intermediary that collects charges, called premiums, from firms and households and, in return, offers financial protection against certain risks. (p. 485)

Intermediary: A firm that provides distribution services for firms that choose not to deal directly with users of their products. (p. 237)

Intermodal transportation: The use of more than one mode of transportation to move goods from one point to another. (p. 253)

Internal accounting system: As part of a marketing information system, a set of procedures for keeping track of income, costs, and other financial information. (p. 195)

Internal costs: Costs of production that are borne by the producing firm itself. (p. 18)

International capital flow: An act of international investing or lending. (p. 609)

Intrusiveness: The degree to which consumers cannot avoid seeing or hearing an advertisement. (p. 272)

Inventory: A stock of finished goods on hand and ready for shipment. (p. 250)

Inventory turnover ratio: The ratio of sales to inventory. (p. 473)

Investment banker: An intermediary that specializes in the marketing of new issues of securities. (p. 514)

Investment income: The return from holding a stock or bond that is bought at a fair price. (p. 509)

Job analysis: An analysis of the tasks to be performed by the person holding a particular job. (p. 404)

Job description: A summary of the duties and responsibilities of a job. (p. 404)

Job enlargement: Making a job more interesting by giving the worker a broader range of tasks. (p. 135)

Job enrichment: Making a job more interesting by giving the worker more decision-making power and more control over his or her work. (p. 135)

Job evaluation technique: A technique in which points are assigned to each job for such factors as skill, effort, working conditions, and degree of responsibility. (p. 416)

Job specifications: A set of brief statements of the knowledge, skills, and abilities required of the person who will hold a particular job. (p. 404)

Joint venture: An association of two or more firms for a specific, limited purpose. (p. 59)

Just-in-time production: An approach to production scheduling that cuts inventories to a minimum by arranging for them to be delivered to the assembly line just in time to be used. (p. 336)

Labor: The direct contributions to production made by people working with their minds and their hands. (p. 7)

Labor union: An association of workers formed for the purpose of negotiating with an employer over the wages and working conditions of its members. (p. 377)

Landrum-Griffin Act: A 1947 law that gave the government the power to act against union corruption and established a bill of rights for rank-and-file union members. (p. 381)

Last in, first out (LIFO): An accounting method according to which the last items of inventory bought are assumed to be the first that are used. (p. 470)

Law: A body of principles, standards, and rules used to settle disputes in an orderly way. (p. 576)

Law of large numbers: The principle that the frequency of a certain type of loss can be predicted with a high degree of accuracy when many similar units are exposed to the loss. (p. 542)

Law of supply and demand: The principle that prices tend to rise when there is a shortage, and to fall when there is a surplus. (p. 32)

Layoff: A temporary involuntary separation of an employee, made with the expectation of recall at a later date. (p. 414)

Leading: Getting people to work together willingly to achieve the organization's goals. (p. 111)

Leverage: A firm's ratio of total debt to total equity. (p. 451)

Liability: Anything a firm owes to anyone. (p. 84)

Liability risk: The risk of financial loss when a firm's or a person's actions cause personal or property loss to someone else. (p. 535)

Limited liability: A legal arrangement under which part-owners who contribute capital to a business are responsible for the liabilities of the business only to the extent of the capital they contributed. (p. 55)

Limited partnership: A partnership that includes one or more general partners who bear full liability and run the business, plus one or more limited partners who bear limited liability and do not have a voice in the firm's day-to-day management. (p. 59)

Line organization: An organizational structure in which all units are linked to those above and below them by a clear chain of command. (p. 138)

Line and staff organization: An organization that includes both line and staff positions. (p. 139)

Liquidation: A process in which a firm sells all of its assets, uses the proceeds to pay off all of its liabilities, and distributes the remainder (if any) to its owners. (p. 464)

Liquid assets: Members of a group of assets that includes coins and paper currency, bank deposits, and certain kinds of securities. (p. 440)

Lloyd's association: A network of insurers who accept risks through a central exchange. (p. 541)

Lobbying: A systematic effort by an interest group to inform and persuade government decision makers in the hope of having an influence on policy. (p. 576)

Lockout: The closing of a plant by a firm involved in a labor dispute whose workers have not yet gone on strike. (p. 389)

Loss: Revenues minus costs in cases in which costs exceed revenues. (p. 9)

Macromarketing: See *marketing*.

Mainframe: A large, powerful computer that permits a full range of applications. (p. 163)

Management: The art of getting things done through people. (p. 104)

Management by objectives (MBO): A formal system in which each manager, in cooperation with his or her superior, sets specific medium-term goals and is periodically reviewed for success in achieving them. (p. 365)

Management hierarchy: A ranking of members of an organization according to authority and, usually, status. (p. 105)

Management information system (MIS): A data processing system designed to supply all levels of management with the internal and external information needed to make decisions. (p. 157)

Managerial accounting: The branch of accounting that is concerned with providing information to be used within the firm. (p. 461)

Market: Any set of arrangements through which buyers and sellers make contact and do business. (p. 31)

Market economy: An economic system in which coordination is achieved by means of markets. (p. 31)

Market segmentation: The process of dividing a market into submarkets, each made up of groups of customers who are alike in some key way. (p. 202)

Marketing: (1) Micromarketing: The process of finding out the needs of customers or clients and channeling a flow of goods or services to meet those needs. (p. 187) (2) Macromarketing: The process by which the productive potential of the economy is used to satisfy individual and social needs of all kinds. (p. 191)

Marketing decision support system: A decision support system that has been set up to serve the needs of marketing decision makers. (p. 196)

Marketing information system (MKIS): A set of procedures for collecting, processing, and presenting information on which marketing decisions can be based. (p. 195)

Marketing intelligence system: A set of procedures for collecting information about consumers and competitors in the market where the firm sells its product. (p. 196)

Marketing mix: The mix of product, distribution system, promotion, and price that a firm uses to serve customers in a target market. (p. 202)

Marketing research: A systematic, objective way of getting information needed to solve specific marketing problems. (p. 196)

Marketing strategy: The choice of a target market and a marketing mix to serve that market. (p. 202)

Markup percentage: The amount by which the price of a product is raised above its cost, expressed either as a percentage of cost or as a percentage of the selling price. (p. 296)

Markup pricing: Any method of pricing a product that begins by adding a certain percentage to its cost. (p. 296)

Materials requirements planning (MRP): A method for scheduling purchases of inputs in such a way as to do away with excess inventories. (p. 336)

Matrix organization: An organizational form in which projects are assigned to task forces composed of people drawn from various functional departments. The task force members report to a task force leader and also to their supervisors. (p. 143)

Mediation: Assistance, in the form of nonbinding suggestions, that is given by a third party to help settle a dispute. (p. 389)

Mentor: A supervisor or experienced worker to whom a new employee looks for advice and support. (p. 112)

Merchant: An intermediary that takes title to a good and then resells it. (p. 238)

Microcomputer: A small, inexpensive computer designed for home use or limited business uses. (p. 163)

Micromarketing: See *marketing*.

Middleman: An intermediary. (p. 237)

Middle managers: Managers in intermediate positions who spend at least some of their time directing the work of other managers. (p. 106)

Minicomputer: A computer that is somewhat larger and more expensive than a microcomputer and is designed for home use by professionals or small businesses. (p. 163)

Minority enterprise small business investment corporation (MESBIC): A company sponsored by the Small Business Administration that provides venture capital for small businesses owned by members of minority groups. (p. 87)

Mixed economy: An economic system in which private businesses exist side by side with industries owned and run by the government. (p. 30)

Monetary policy: The branch of economic policy that is concerned with controlling the supply of money and credit. (p. 42)

Money: An asset that serves as a means of payment, a store of value, and a unit of account. (p. 486)

Money market fund: A type of mutual fund that buys short-term government securities, and may offer checking services to its shareholders. (p. 486)

Monopoly: A firm that has no competitors in the market where it sells its output. (p. 12)

Moral hazard: The danger that a policyholder will fake a loss in order to collect a claim. (p. 544)

Morale hazard: The danger that a policyholder will allow a loss to take place through carelessness, knowing that insurance will pay for the loss. (p. 544)

Mortgage: A long-term loan secured by land or buildings. (p. 447)

Most favored nation: A nation that, under GATT rules, is given the same treatment with respect to tariffs and quotas as all other nations that subscribe to GATT. (p. 615)

Motivation: A psychological drive that gives a person's actions purpose and direction. (p. 351)

Multinational enterprise (MNE): A firm that has operations in several countries. (p. 605)

Mutual fund: A financial intermediary that sells shares to individuals; uses the proceeds to buy stocks, bonds, and other securities; and passes the income from those securities along to its shareholders after deducting a small service fee. (p. 485)

Mutual insurance company: An insurance company that is owned and controlled by its policyholders. (p. 541)

Mutual savings bank: A depositor-owned financial intermediary that resembles a savings and loan association. (p. 485)

National Labor Relations Board (NLRB): A federal agency set up to administer the Wagner Act. (p. 380)

Natural resources: Things that are useful as productive inputs in their natural state, such as farm land, mineral deposits, and the like. (p. 8)

Negligence: Failure to exercise due care when there is a foreseeable risk of harm to others. (p. 583)

Net income: Income minus taxes, also known as profit. (p. 469)

Net sales: The total value of the products sold by the firm minus any items that were returned for credit. (p. 467)

Net worth: See *owners' equity*.

Nondurable goods: Goods that last less than a year, such as food, medicines, and fuel. (p. 214)

Norris-La Guardia Act: A law passed by Congress in 1932 that established the right of unions to exist, and prohibited courts from issuing injunctions against peaceful union activities. (p. 379)

Not-for-profit firm: A private organization that is barred by its charter from distributing any earnings to outside ownership interests. (p. 64)

Objective product: A good or service described in terms of its physical properties. (p. 213)

Off-price retailer: A store that can offer even lower prices than discount stores because it carries incomplete product lines bought below normal wholesale prices, such as factory overruns and imperfect items. (p. 248)

Open-market operation: A process in which the Federal Reserve System injects added reserves into the banking system by buying government securities from the public, or withdraws reserves from the banking system by selling government securities. (p. 498)

Operating income: Gross profit minus costs that cannot be assigned to specific products (selling, general, and administrative expenses). (p. 468)

Operations: See *production*.

Opportunity cost: The value of the best alternative way of using the time and capital put into a firm by its owner or owners. (p. 84)

Organization chart: A chart showing the division of work, the chain of command, and the departmentalization of an organization. (p. 130)

Organizing: Dividing work among individuals and groups and coordinating their actions. (p. 111)

Orientation: The process by which a new employee learns about the employer and the new job. (p. 410)

Output device: Any device, such as a printer, by means of which a computer supplies information to users. (p. 161)

Over-the-counter (OTC) market: A secondary securities market that consists of a network of traders who keep in touch by telephone and computer. (p. 520)

Owners' equity: A firm's assets minus its liabilities, also known as net worth. (p. 464)

Partnership: A voluntary legal association of two or more people for the purpose of running a business. (p. 51)

Patent: A guarantee to an inventor of the right to 17 years' exclusive use of the invention. (p. 582)

Penetration: A strategy in which a new product is brought out at a low price in order to build up a large market share quickly. (p. 302)

Pension fund: A financial intermediary that collects payments from working people and pays them an income after they retire. (p. 485)

Personal property: Any property other than real property. (p. 582)

Personal risk: The risk of a direct loss to a person, such as a risk to life or health. (p. 535)

Personal selling: A promotion presentation made directly to a potential customer, usually in a face-to-face meeting. (p. 267)

Physical distribution: All the functions required to move goods from the producer to the consumer. (p. 237)

Picketing: A demonstration at the site of a labor dispute informing people that a dispute is in progress. (p. 388)

Planning: Setting goals and deciding how to achieve them. (p. 108)

Political-action committee (PAC): A committee that accepts donations for a political cause and uses the funds to make contributions to candidates or for other political activities. (p. 576)

Portfolio: The set of securities that an investor owns. (p. 512)

Positioning: The process of fitting a product's image to the needs of its target market. (p. 222)

Positive reinforcement: Rewards given for desirable behavior. (p. 363)

Predatory pricing: Selling a product at a price below cost in order to drive competitors out of the market. (p. 303)

Preferred stock: Nonvoting stock in a corporation that puts its holders first in line for dividends, ahead of holders of common stock. (p. 61)

Price: The amount of money a customer must pay for a product. (p. 291)

Price discrimination: Selling a product at different prices to different buyers. (p. 303)

Price fixing: An agreement among competing firms to hold prices above some minimum level. (p. 255)

Price leader: A firm whose price changes are followed by other firms in the same industry. (p. 292)

Primary advertising: Advertising, usually by a trade association, that promotes a certain type of product rather than a specific brand. (p. 271)

Primary boycott: A boycott aimed at persuading workers not to buy the products of a firm that is engaged in a labor dispute. (p. 388)

Primary securities market: The set of institutions through which newly issued securities are sold to investors. (p. 514)

Primary storage: Storage space contained within a computer's central processing unit, used to store instructions and data that are currently in use. (p. 161)

Prime rate: The interest rate charged by banks for short-term loans to their most creditworthy customers. (p. 445)

Principal: The person in an agency relationship who wants to get something done. (p. 582)

Private accountant: An accountant employed by a business firm. (p. 463)

Private placement: The sale of a whole new issue of securities to one or a few buyers. (p. 514)

Process layout: A plant layout in which equipment is grouped by the function it performs. (p. 333)

Product: Anything that can be supplied to a market in order to satisfy customer needs. (p. 213)

Product layout: A plant layout in which equipment is set up so that the product can move directly from one work station to the next. (p. 332)

Product line: A group of products that are closely related in how they are used. (p. 216)

Product mix: The complete list of products offered by a firm, including all of its product lines. (p. 216)

Product-specific advertising: Advertising that tells buyers about the virtues of a specific brand or product. (p. 269)

Production: The function of transforming inputs into outputs. (p. 323)

Production and operations management (POM): The task of managing the transformation of inputs into outputs. (p. 323)

Production orientation: An orientation toward marketing that focuses on producing a good-quality product at low cost. (p. 192)

Productivity: The quantity of output produced per worker. (p. 36)

Profit: Revenues minus costs. (p. 8)

Program: A detailed set of instructions that tells a computer to perform some useful task. (p. 163)

Programming language: A set of rules for writing the instructions that are fed into a computer. (p. 165)

Project evaluation and review technique (PERT): A method of production scheduling that breaks a process down into individual activities and analyzes the relationships among them. (p. 334)

Promotion: (1) The process of telling consumers about a product and getting them to buy it. (p. 265). (2) A movement to a job involving greater authority and responsibility. (p. 412)

Promotional mix: The mix of advertising, personal selling, sales promotions, and public relations used to promote a product. (p. 267)

Promotional strategy: A plan that states what the content of a promotional message will be, how it will be delivered, and whom it will be delivered to. (p. 265)

Property: A set of legal rights to use a thing, to keep others from using it, and to sell it. (p. 582)

Property risk: The risk of destruction, theft, or loss of the use of property. (p. 535)

Prospecting: The process of locating potential customers. (p. 276)

Protectionism: A national policy of restraining international trade. (p. 615)

Proxy: A device by which stockholders can pledge the votes of their shares to a slate of candidates for the board of directors in a corporate election; in a proxy contest, backers of opposing slates try to collect pledges that represent a majority of the voting shares. (p. 61)

Public accountant: An independent professional accountant who performs services for a fee. (p. 462)

Public relations: A planned effort to create a good image of a product or firm by some means other than paid advertising. (p. 267)

Public-service advertising: Advertising that aims to change consumer behavior in a beneficial way, for example, by promoting the use of auto seatbelts. (p. 271)

Publicity: Any nonpaid public mention of a company or its product. (p. 281)

Pull: Any promotion effort aimed at consumers. (p. 267)

Pure risk: A risk that involves only the chance of a loss. (p. 535)

Push: Any promotional effort aimed at wholesalers or retailers in the distribution channel. (p. 267)

Quality assurance: The process of planning, leading, organizing, and controlling production in order to achieve a desired standard of quality. (p. 337)

Quality circle: A group in which workers and managers meet on a regular basis to discuss ways of improving quality. (p. 368)

Rate of turnover: The average number of times per year that goods in stock are sold and replaced. (p. 296)

Real property: Rights to land or buildings. (p. 582)

Real estate: See *real property*.

Recession: A period of six months or more during which the total output of the economy declines. (p. 33)

Recruitment: The process of attracting a pool of candidates from which jobs can be filled. (p. 405)

Reliability engineering: A set of techniques, including statistical analysis of failure rates of individual components, used for designing reliable products. (p. 327)

Reorganization: The outcome of a Chapter 11 bank-

ruptcy, in which the firm becomes solvent once again and court supervision ends. (p. 583)

Representation election: A vote by secret ballot, supervised by the NLRB, in which workers may indicate whether or not they want to be represented by a particular union. (p. 380)

Responsibility: The duty to make a certain decision or solve a certain problem. (p. 145)

Retailing: Selling directly to consumers. (p. 237)

Retained earnings: After-tax profits that are held by a corporation for reinvestment rather than being paid out as dividends. (p. 62)

Return on assets (ROA): Net income plus interest expense expressed as a percentage of total assets. (p. 473)

Return on equity (ROE): Net income expressed as a percentage of owners' equity. (p. 473)

Reverse discrimination: Denying a job or promotion to a white or male candidate in favor of a less qualified minority group member or woman. (p. 403)

Right-to-work laws: State laws, permitted under the Taft-Hartley Act, that prohibit union shops. (p. 386)

Risk: Uncertainty about a possible loss. (p. 535)

Risk management: The task of reducing the costs connected with risk. (p. 536)

Robinson-Patman Act: A 1936 law, also known as the "chain store act," that outlaws certain forms of price discrimination. (p. 255)

Sales branch: A branch of a producer, separate from the manufacturing plant, that maintains a sales force and stocks inventories of the product. (p. 241)

Sales office: A branch of a producer, separate from the manufacturing plant, that maintains a sales force but does not stock inventories of the product. (p. 241)

Sales orientation: An orientation toward marketing that stresses persuasive selling efforts. (p. 193)

Sales promotion: The use of short-term incentives, such as store displays, special discounts, or coupons, to boost sales of a product. (p. 267)

Savings and loan association (savings and loan): A financial intermediary that accepts checking and savings deposits from households and makes home mortgage loans. (p. 485)

Scanlon plan: A plan for rewarding useful suggestions in which bonuses are shared by the worker who makes the suggestion and his or her work group. (p. 368)

Scientific management: An approach to production management developed in the early twentieth century that stresses improved supervision and scientific analysis of the jobs of individual workers. (p. 339)

Secondary boycott: A boycott aimed at persuading other firms not to do business with a firm that is involved in a labor dispute. (p. 388)

Secondary securities markets: Institutions through which investors can buy and sell previously issued securities. (p. 514)

Secondary storage: A storage device outside a computer's central processing unit, such as magnetic tapes or disks, used to store information that is not currently in use. (p. 161)

Secured debt: A debt for which repayment is guaranteed by pledging a certain property to the lender. (p. 444)

Securities: A general term for corporate stocks and bonds, government bonds and short-term notes, commercial paper, and the like. (p. 509)

Securities and Exchange Commission (SEC): The federal agency that regulates securities markets. (p. 522)

Self-insurance: A process in which an organization that is exposed to many risks of the same kind sets aside funds from which to cover any losses that result. (p. 537)

Separation: The voluntary or involuntary departure of a person from an organization. (p. 414)

Services: Actions performed directly for the benefit of the consumer, such as haircuts, concerts, and tax preparation. (p. 214)

Sherman Act: An antitrust law passed in 1890 that outlaws price fixing and certain other monopolistic practices. (p. 256)

Shop steward: A union official who aids union members in resolving grievances. (p. 389)

Shopping goods: Goods that are bought only after an effort to gather information on the price, quality, and other features of competing brands. (p. 214)

Skimming: A strategy in which a new product is brought out at a high price, which is then reduced a step at a time. (p. 302)

Small business: A business that is independently owned and operated and is not dominant in its field. (p. 72)

Small business investment corporation (SBIC): A company sponsored by the Small Business Administration that makes loans to small businesses. (p. 86)

Socialism: An economic system in which production decisions are made by workers or their representatives. (p. 30)

Socialization: The informal process through which new employees absorb the values, language, manners, unwritten rules, and other elements of the firm's culture. (p. 410)

Software: A collective name for programs and computer languages. (p. 163)

Sole proprietorship: A business that is owned, and often run, by one person, who receives all the profits and bears all the liabilities of the business. (p. 51)

Solvency: The ability of a firm to meet its short-term liabilities as they come due. (p. 472)

Span of management: The number of subordinates reporting to each manager. (p. 140)

Specialist: A broker who is assigned to a specific stock or bond and assists commission brokers in trading that stock or bond. (p. 515)

Specialty goods: Goods that are bought without much comparison shopping because they are thought to offer unique features or brand images. (p. 214)

Speculative income: The return from holding a stock or bond whose price increases more than expected. (p. 512)

Speculative risk: A risk that involves the chance of a gain as well as the chance of a loss. (p. 535)

Staff positions: Positions that lie outside the chain of command and offer advice or support services to line managers. (p. 139)

Staffing: The choice of specific people to fill positions in an organization. (p. 112)

Stock exchange: A place where brokers who represent buyers and sellers of securities meet to arrange trades for their clients. (p. 515)

Stock option: A contract between two investors, one of whom receives the right to buy a stock from the other (or sell it to the other) at an agreed-upon price at any time during an agreed-upon period. (p. 518)

Stockbroker: A person who arranges trades between buyers and sellers of securities without taking title to the securities. (p. 515)

Stockholder (shareholder): The owner of one or more shares of common stock in a corporation. (p. 51)

Strategic planning: The systematic long-range planning process used to define and achieve an organization's goals. (p. 108)

Strike: A collective refusal to work by a group of workers. (p. 388)

Strike fund: A fund maintained by a union to pay striking workers. (p. 388)

Strikebreaker: A person hired to replace a worker who is on strike. (p. 388)

Structural unemployment: The part of total unemployment that results from a mismatch between the skills of workers and the types of jobs available. (p. 36)

Subchapter S corporation: A corporation that meets certain standards, such as a limit on the number of stockholders, and chooses to be taxed as a proprietorship or partnership. (p. 57)

Subjective product: A good or service described in terms of the needs it will satisfy. (p. 213)

Subsidiary: A corporation that is controlled by a parent corporation that owns enough stock to enable it to appoint the subsidiary's top managers. (p. 62)

Supercomputer: A term reserved for the largest, most powerful class of computers. (p. 163)

Supervisory managers: Managers who direct the work of individual contributors but not that of other managers. (p. 106)

Syndicate: An association of two or more people or firms for a limited purpose, usually more limited than a joint venture. (p. 59)

Synthetic process: A production process in which parts or materials are assembled into a whole. (p. 325)

Taft-Hartley Act: A 1947 law amending the Wagner Act in ways that limit union powers. (p. 381)

Target market: The particular group of customers whose needs a firm aims to satisfy. (p. 202)

Target pricing: A method of setting prices that is intended to yield a desired rate of return on the capital invested. (p. 297)

Tariff: A tax on goods that enter a country. (p. 615)

Task force: A formal working group made up of people drawn from various parts of an organization and formed to carry out a specific project. (p. 142)

Technical analysis: An approach to stock market trading that attempts to pick winners by studying the behavior of other investors as revealed in past stock price movements. (p. 526)

Tender offer: An offer to buy shares of a target corporation from its stockholders. (p. 61)

Termination (firing): A permanent involuntary separation. (p. 414)

Term insurance: A form of life insurance in which coverage is granted for a fixed term in return for payment of premium based on the chance of death during that term. (p. 547)

Theory X: A set of assumptions about people, including the assumptions that they dislike work, lack creativity, and are motivated mainly by pay. (p. 356)

Theory Y: A set of assumptions about people, including the assumptions that people find satisfaction in their work, are creative, and are eager to participate in the whole range of management functions. (p. 359)

Thrift institution (thrift): A general term for savings and loan associations, mutual savings banks, and credit unions. (p. 485)

Top managers: Managers who are responsible for defining broad goals and strategies and directing the work of middle managers. (p. 106)

Tort: A civil wrong, other than a breach of contract, for which a court can award damages. (p. 582)

Total marketing orientation: An approach to marketing in which the firm plans all of its operations around customer needs and uses a balanced mix of marketing activities. (p. 193)

Trade association: An association of firms in the same line of business formed to pursue their shared interests. (p. 576)

Trade credit: The purchase on credit of goods for resale or materials to be used in production. (p. 445)

Trademark: A symbol or brand name that is legally protected. (p. 223)

Training: An activity aimed at improving a person's ability to do his or her present job. (p. 410)

Transfer: A movement to a job involving about the same degree of authority and responsibility in another place or another functional unit of the firm. (p. 412)

Tying contract: A situation in which a producer sells one product on the condition that the customer also buy another product from the same producer. (p. 255)

Underwriting: (1) In finance, a process in which an investment banker or syndicate buys a whole new issue of securities from a firm and sells them to the public. (p. 514) (2) In insurance, classifying potential policyholders into groups on the basis of risk. (p. 545)

Undifferentiated marketing: An approach to marketing in which the firm offers a single product to all consumers. (p. 204)

Unemployment rate: The percentage of the labor force who cannot find jobs. (p. 35)

Unfair labor practice: Any of a number of antiunion practices of employers that were made illegal by the Wagner Act; also certain union practices that were made illegal by the Taft-Hartley amendments to the Wagner Act. (p. 380)

Uniform Commercial Code (UCC): A body of law that deals with sale of, transfer of, and payment for goods. (p. 580)

Union security agreement: An agreement that requires all workers who benefit from a contract negotiated by a union to join that union. (p. 386)

Union shop: An agreement under which workers must join a union within a specified time after starting work. (p. 386)

Unity of command: The principle that each employee should have only one boss. (p. 144)

Unsecured debt: Debt that is backed only by the borrower's willingness and ability to repay. (p. 444)

Variable costs: Costs that change along with the quantity of a good or service produced. (p. 298)

Venture capital market: A market in which specialists put entrepreneurs in touch with people who are willing to take risks by buying stock in new firms. (p. 54)

Vertical coordination: A technique of coordinating the work of departments that depends on instructions passed along the chain of command. (p. 140)

Vertical merger: A merger between firms with a seller-customer relationship. (p. 63)

Vertical price fixing: An agreement between a producer and retailers of its products to hold prices above some minimum level. (p. 256)

Vertically integrated marketing channel (VIMC): A distribution channel in which a producer and one or more intermediaries are bound together by ownership or contract. (p. 240)

Wagner Act: A law passed in 1935, officially known as the National Labor Relations Act, that provided an orderly process for unions to gain recognition and limited antiunion activities of employers. (p. 379)

Warranty: A statement of what the seller will do if a product is defective or fails to work the way it should within a specified period after the sale. (p. 228)

Whole life insurance: A form of life insurance in which coverage is granted for a person's whole life in return for payment of a fixed annual premium. (p. 548)

Wholesaling: Selling to retailers, industrial customers, or other wholesalers. (p. 237)

Word processor: A specialized computer used to prepare written material such as letters and reports. (p. 154)

Working capital: Funds used to pay for labor and materials between the time when production is begun and the time when finished goods are shipped and paid for. (p. 436)

Yellow-dog contract: A contract in which a worker agrees, as a condition of employment, not to join a union. (p. 379)

Subject Index

Name and Title Index

Companies Index

Credits for Part and Chapter Openers

Title page: Marc P. Anderson

Part Openers
I   © Reginald Wickham
II   Courtesy of AT&T Technologies
III © Reginald Wickham
IV   © Bruce Davidson, Magnum
V   © Reginald Wickham
VI   Courtesy of AT&T Technologies

Chapter Openers
1   Courtesy of General Motors
2   © Charles Anderson
3   Courtesy of Agway, Inc.
4   © Freda Leinwand
5   © Michael Melford, Peter Arnold
6   Courtesy of General Electric Company
7   Courtesy of International Business Machines Corporation

8   Courtesy of BMW of North America
9   Courtesy of International Paper Company
10   Courtesy of Sears, Roebuck and Company
11   "Coke is it!" is a registered trademark of the Coca-Cola Company
12   Marc. P. Anderson
13   Courtesy of General Electric
14   © Stephanie Maze, Woodfin Camp
15   © Freda Leinwand
16   Courtesy of AT&T, Bell Laboratories
17   © Freda Leinwand
18   © Freda Leinwand
19   Courtesy of International Business Machines Corporation
20   Marc P. Anderson
21   © Freda Leinwand
22   The Granger Collection
23   Courtesy of General Electric
24   Courtesy of AT&T Technologies

The Top 25 U.S. Industrial Corporations,

1909

1. United States Steel Corp.
2. Standard Oil Co. (New Jersey)
3. American Tobacco Co.
4. International Mercantile Marine Co.
5. Anaconda Co.
6. International Harvester Co.
7. Central Leather Co.
8. Pullman Co.
9. Armour & Co.
10. American Sugar Co.
11. United States Rubber Co.
12. American Smelting & Refining Co.
13. Singer Manufacturing Co.
14. Swift and Co.
15. Pittsburgh Consolidation Coal Co.
16. General Electric Co.
17. A.C.F. Industries, Inc.
18. Colorado Fuel and Iron Corp.
19. Corn Products Co.
20. New England Navigation Co.
21. American Can Co.
22. American Woolen Co.
23. Lackawanna Steel Co.
24. Jones & Laughlin Steel Corp.
25. Westinghouse Electric Corp.

1929

1. United States Steel Corp.
2. Standard Oil Co. (New Jersey)
3. General Motors Corp.
4. Standard Oil Co. (Indiana)
5. Bethlehem Steel Corp.
6. Ford Motor Co.
7. Socony Mobil Oil Co., Inc.
8. Anaconda Co.
9. Texaco Inc.
10. Standard Oil Co. of California
11. General Electric Co.
12. E.I. duPont de Nemours & Co.
13. Shell Oil Co.
14. Armour & Co.
15. Gulf Oil Corp.
16. Sinclair Oil Corp.
17. International Harvester Co.
18. General Theatres Equipment, Inc.
19. Swift and Co.
20. Kennecott Copper Corp.
21. Republic Steel Corp.
22. Pullman Co.
23. Western Electric Co., Inc.
24. United States Rubber Co.
25. Union Carbide Corp.

1919

1. United States Steel Corp.
2. Standard Oil Co. (New Jersey)
3. Armour & Co.
4. Swift and Co.
5. General Motors Corp.
6. Bethlehem Steel Corp.
7. Ford Motor Co.
8. United States Rubber Co.
9. Socony Mobil Oil Co., Inc.
10. Midvale Steel and Ordnance
11. General Electric Co.
12. International Mercantile Marine Co.
13. International Harvester Co.
14. Anaconda Co.
15. Sinclair Oil Corp.
16. Texaco Inc.
17. American Smelting & Refining Co.
18. E.I. duPont de Nemours & Co.
19. American Tobacco Co.
20. Union Carbide Corp.
21. Phelps Dodge Corp.
22. Magnolia Petroleum Co.
23. B.F. Goodrich Co.
24. Standard Oil Co. of California
25. Jones & Laughlin Steel Corp.

1935

1. Standard Oil Co. (New Jersey)
2. United States Steel Corp.
3. General Motors Corp.
4. Socony Mobil Oil Co., Inc.
5. Standard Oil Co. (Indiana)
6. Ford Motor Co.
7. Bethlehem Steel Corp.
8. Anaconda Co.
9. E.I. duPont de Nemours & Co.
10. Standard Oil Co. of California
11. Texaco Inc.
12. Gulf Oil Corp.
13. General Electric Co.
14. International Harvester Co.
15. Shell Oil Co.
16. Sinclair Oil Corp.
17. Koppers Co.
18. Kennecott Copper Corp.
19. Swift and Co.
20. Armour & Co.
21. Republic Steel Corp.
22. Union Carbide Corp.
23. American Tobacco Co.
24. Pullman Co.
25. Allied Chemical & Dye Corp.